# What's on the CD-ROM

## Test Engine

The CD-ROM supplied with this book contains a Java program written by Simon Roberts, a key player in the development of the Java Certification Program, that allows you to test yourself. The program simulates the actual Java Certification Exam, and allows you to test your knowledge of Java and to make a reasonable estimate of whether you are sufficiently prepared for the exam. The tester uses some of the questions from each chapter, you can impose a time limit and control the number of questions and the categories of the questions. When you are done, the program will explain the correct answer.

## Java 2 SDK, Standard Edition, Version 1.2

The CD-ROM also contains the Java 2 SDK, Standard Edition, Version 1.2, the full development package from Sun Microsystems, Inc., for creating Java applications and applets. Versions are released periodically and can be downloaded from http://www.java.sun.com/products/jdk/1.2

---

*The CD-ROM will run on Windows 95, Windows 98, Windows NT Workstation 4, and Unix.

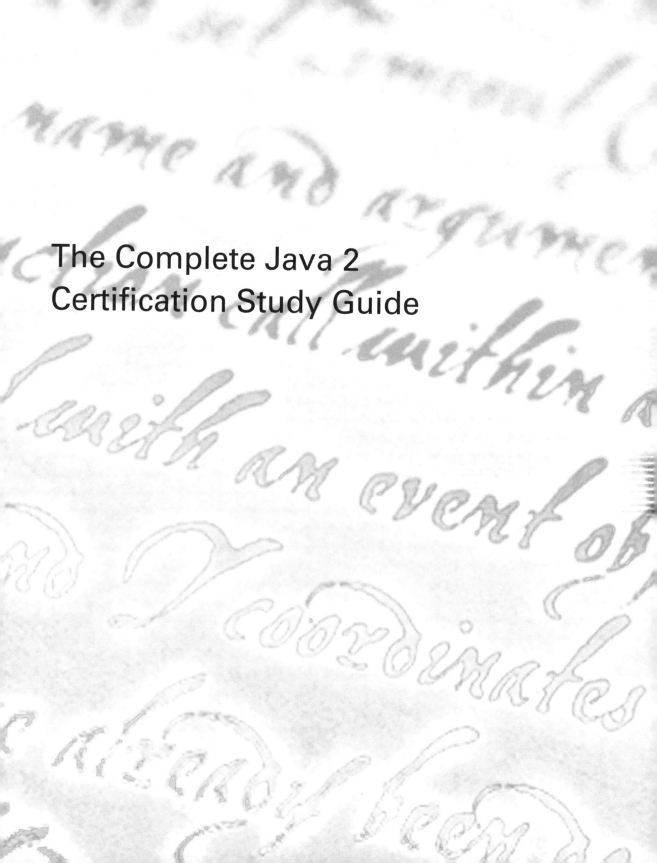

# The Complete Java 2
# Certification Study Guide

# Complete Java™ 2
# Certification Study Guide

Simon Roberts
Philip Heller
Michael Ernest

San Francisco • Paris • Düsseldorf • Soest • London

SYBEX

Associate Publisher: Gary Masters
Contracts and Licensing Manager: Kristine O'Callaghan
Acquisitions & Developmental Editor: Denise Santoro
Editor: Ed Copony
Technical Editors: Simon Roberts, Philip Heller, Michael Ernest
Book Designer: Bill Gibson
Graphic Illustrators: Tony Jonick, Jerry Williams
Electronic Publishing Specialist: Maureen Forys, Happenstance Type-O-Rama
Project Team Leader: Teresa Trego
Proofreader: Susan Berge
Indexer: Ted Laux
Companion CD: Ginger Warner
Cover Designer: Design Site
Cover Illustrator: Design Site, Jack D. Myers

Library of Congress Card Number: 99-61816
ISBN: 0-7821-2463-1

Manufactured in the United States of America

10 9 8 7 6 5 4 3 2 1

# Acknowledgments

I would like to thank Annie Colvin, Mike Bridwell, Ray Moore, Gary Taylor, and Brian Couling—all of Sun Microsystems—who made it possible for me to work on the certification project.

—Simon Roberts

I would like to thank Josh Krasnegor, Cindy Lewis, Suzanne Rotondo, Laura Arendal, James Casaletto, and everybody at Pastis.

—Philip Heller

My contribution to this book would not have been possible without the encouragement and support of John Varel, CEO of Synergistic Computer Solutions. John provided company time and moral support through both a hectic sales quarter and a frustrating string of illnesses, and I'm grateful for his energy and faith. My wife Heather listened as I recited text to ensure it sounded intelligible; more importantly, she put up with an absentee husband. Pete Royce had to get by without a full-time engineer, and yet remained positive about the whole thing.

—Michael Ernest

The authors would also like to thank the people at Sybex: Gary Masters, Denise Santoro, Ed Copony, Maureen Forys, Tony Jonick, Jerry Williams, Teresa Trego, Susan Berge, Ted Laux, and Ginger Warner.

# Contents at a Glance

# Table of Contents

# Introduction

**H**ello! Come in, sit down, and make yourself at home. Please get comfortable; there are a lot of topics to cover in this book.

You have come here because you are ready. Ready to *get* ready, at least, which is practically the same thing. Now all that's left to do is the work.

And there is a lot of work to be done. Probably you heard that the 1.1 version of the exam was difficult. That was true; the Java 2 version is harder still, since it covers a few more topics. Not everybody passes—even on repeated attempts. We want to change these statistics. It wouldn't hurt to get a little help—and we're the ones to help.

Since this is, after all, the Introduction, allow us to introduce ourselves: Simon, Mike, and Phil. We are Java instructors by day, and by night we write.

What we teach (by day) are Sun Microsystems' Java courses. When the 1.1 edition of this book was published, we wrote that among us we had taught Java to more than 1,000 people. By now the number is well into the thousands. And the Java courses that we teach are Sun's own courses. We have been through our own certification process for instructors, and Sun trusts us to teach people the Java facts that Sun considers important. Recently, Simon has been developing new course material. We want you to know all this because we want to be the ones to help you pass the certification exam.

What we write (by night) are Java books. (Phil keeps talking about a novel; we will just have to wait and see.) We wrote the *Java 1.1 Developer's Handbook* (Sybex, 1997) and we contributed to *Mastering Java 1.1* (Sybex, 1997). Then we wrote the *Java 1.1 Certification Study Guide*. After that we revised the *Developer's Handbook* to reflect new Java 2 material. And now here we are, presenting the Java 2 version of the *Certification Study Guide*.

We thought we were the best team to write this book. Simon led the team that wrote all of the questions for the exam. Phil was a consultant for developing the exam and is one of the graders for the developer's exam, so he also has the inside view of things. And Mike, who wrote the chapters about the developer's exam, has been on the front lines of Java instruction for years.

Simon's unique position at Sun places a few restrictions on us. We can't give away any answers to the questions on the exam. (We wouldn't want to do that anyway; we want you to pass because you're good at Java, not because we slipped you a crib.) We had to make sure that the sample questions did not accidentally match any of the real test questions. It took a bit more work, but we think the benefit to you is tremendous: Everything in this book is here for a very good reason. If it's here, then it's here because we know you need to know about it. We understand that buying a book like this costs you money, reading it costs you time, and absorbing it costs you effort. We appreciate your investment and we believe it will pay off.

If you read this book, absorb it, solve the practice questions at the end of each chapter, and work through the practice exam on the CD-ROM, you will be in the best possible position when you walk through the doors of your local testing center.

Let's just take care of a few standard formalities and then we can really get started.

## What's New in This Edition

The original edition of this book covered the 1.1 version of the programmer's exam. When Sun released Java 2, they also released new versions of both the programmer's exam and the developer's exam, along with corresponding lists of study objectives.

There were more than 90 objectives for the 1.1 programmer's exam; that number has been reduced for Java 2 to about 30. The huge reduction doesn't mean that the exam is simpler; it just means that redundant objectives have been combined or eliminated. We have stayed with the format that we introduced in the original edition of this book: a chapter begins with a list of the objectives covered in the chapter. All of the objectives appear at least once, so if you master each chapter, you will have mastered all of the objectives.

So, our first change was to introduce the new Java 2 material. We also thought it would be appropriate to upgrade the test engine. The sample questions at the end of each chapter are for the most part unchanged, because we originally designed those questions to teach you as much as possible. The original questions were very well accepted, so we stayed with them, but we made two additions. First, of course, we added questions to cover the new Java material as reflected in the new objectives. Second, we added many new questions to the test engine on the CD-ROM that accompanies this book. Please refer to Appendix B for information on how to use the test engine.

If you are intrigued by the idea of sample questions, here is a sample of the samples:

**3.** Which of the following statements is true?

   **A.** An abstract class may not have any final methods.

   **B.** A final class may not have any abstract methods.

Here is a typical code-related question:

**3.** Will the following code compile?

```
1. byte b = 2;
2. byte b1 = 3;
3. b = b * b1;
```

Feel free to look up the answers in Appendix A. The first question is #3 from Chapter 3; the second question is #3 from Chapter 4.

The other big change was to include an extensive new section on the Java Developer's Exam. We received a lot of feedback from readers who said that they were interested in complete certification, not just programmer certification. So Mike was brought in to write about developer certification. We can't tell you what your developer's assignment will be (any more than we can tell you about questions on the programmer's exam); but we have given you a similar problem, one that can serve as a metaphor and that requires you to master the same skills that you will need for the real exam.

We hope that the Java 2 edition of this book will be all you need to catapult you into both programmer and developer certification.

## Taking the Exam

You can take the Java Certification Exam whenever you like, by making an appointment with Sylvan Prometric or Sun Educational Services. Sylvan Prometric administers the exam on Sun's behalf; they have test centers throughout the world, so hopefully you won't have to travel far. The cost of taking the exam is $150.

The telephone number for Sylvan Prometric is 800-795-EXAM; their URL is www.sylvanprometric.com. The number for Sun Educational Services is 800-422-8020; their URL is www.sun.com/sunservice/suned/certif_programs.html. For people outside the United States, information on registration in any of the eighty-eight countries that Sylvan services is available at this site: www.hibbertco.com/sun/suncontacts/contacts.html.

You can make an appointment any time during regular business hours. You will be given two hours and fifteen minutes and you will probably need every minute. You will not be allowed to bring food or personal belongings into the test area. One piece of scratch paper is permitted; you will not be allowed to keep it after you have finished the exam. (See the end of Chapter 9, "Layout Managers," for a suggestion about how to use the scratch paper.) Most sites have security cameras.

You will be escorted to a cubicle containing a PC. The exam program will present you with randomly selected questions. Navigation buttons take you to the next question or to previous questions for review and checking. When you have finished the test, the program will immediately present you with your score and a pass/fail indication. You will also be given feedback that indicates how well you performed in each of the dozen or so categories of the objectives. You will not be told which particular questions you got right or wrong.

## Formalities of the Exam

There are no trick questions on the exam, but every question requires careful thought. The wording of the questions is highly precise; the exam has been reviewed not just by Java experts, but also by language experts whose task was to eliminate any possible ambiguity. All you have to worry about is knowing Java; your score will not depend on your ability to second-guess the examiners.

It is not a good idea to try to second-guess the question layout. For example, do not be biased toward answer C simply because C has not come up recently. The questions are taken from a pool and presented to you in a random order, so it is entirely possible to get a run of a particular option; it is also possible to get the answers neatly spread out.

Most of the questions are multiple choice. Of these, some have a single answer while others require you to select all the appropriate responses. The Graphical User Interface of the test system indicates which kind of answer you should supply. If a question only has one correct answer, you will be presented with radio buttons, so that selecting a second answer cancels the selection of a previous answer. With this kind of question, you have to select the most appropriate answer. If, on the other hand, you are presented with check boxes, then you may need to make more than one selection, so every possible answer has to be considered on its own merits—not weighed against the others.

You should be aware that where multiple answers are possible, you are being asked to make a decision about each answer, rather as though the question were five individual true/false questions. This requires more effort and understanding from you, but does not actually mean that more than one answer is correct. Think carefully, and always base your answer on your knowledge of Java.

The short-answer, type-in questions often cause undue concern. How are they marked? What happens if you omit a semicolon? These worries can stem from the knowledge that the questions are marked electronically and the belief that an answer might be marked wrong simply because the machine didn't have the sense to recognize a good variation of what it was programmed to accept.

As with all exam questions, you should be careful to answer precisely what is asked. However, you should also be aware that the system does accept a variety of different answers; it has been set up with all the variations that the examination panel considered to be reasonable.

Some of the type-in questions provide specific instructions concerning the format of the answer. Take this guidance seriously. If, for example, a question says, "Answer in the form `methodname()`," then your answer should be

```
method()
```

and not any of these answers

```
object.method()
method();
method(a, b)
method
```

Some of the other answers might well be accepted, but programming is a precision job and you should be accustomed to following precise directions.

The test is taken using a windowed interface that can be driven almost entirely with the mouse. Many of the screens require scrolling; the scroll bar is on the right-hand side of the screen. Always check the scroll bar so you can be sure you have read a question in its entirety. It would be a shame to get a question wrong because you didn't realize you needed to scroll down a few lines.

The exam contains about 60 questions. On average, this gives you a little more than two minutes per question. Some of the questions are easier than others, and undoubtedly there will be some that you can answer faster than others. However, you really do need to answer all the questions, if you possibly can. The test system allows you to review your work after you reach the end. The system will explicitly direct your attention toward any multiple-choice questions that have no items selected. So if you find a particular question difficult, consider moving on and coming back to it later.

If you pass, you will be given a temporary certificate. A few weeks later you will receive by mail a permanent certificate, along with an artwork sheet. The artwork shows the "Sun Certified Java Programmer" logo at various magnifications. By passing the exam, you have earned the right to display the logo. Printers know how to reproduce the artwork onto business cards, stationery, and so on. The lettering is legible (just barely, by people who eat carrots) down to a reduction of about 5/8" wide by 3/8" high.

## Conventions Used in This Book

This book uses a number of conventions to present information in as readable a manner as possible. Tips, Notes, and Warnings, shown below, appear from time to time in the text, in order to call attention to specific highlights.

This is a Tip. Tips contain specific programming information.

This is a Note. Notes contain important side discussions.

This is a Warning. Warnings call attention to bugs, design omissions, and other trouble spots.

This book takes advantage of several font styles. **Bold font** in text indicates something that the user types. A `monospaced font` is used for code, output, URLs, and file and directory names.

These style conventions are intended to facilitate your learning experience with this book—in other words, to increase your chances of passing the exam.

Let's begin.

# PART

# I

## The Programmer's Exam

# CHAPTER

# 1

## Language Fundamentals

**T**his chapter covers aspects of the following Java Certification Exam objectives:

- Identify correctly constructed source files, package declarations, import statements, class declarations (of all forms including inner classes), interface declarations and implementations (for `java.lang.Runnable` or other interface described in the test), method declarations (including the main method that is used to start execution of a class), variable declarations, and identifiers.

- Identify all Java programming language keywords and correctly constructed identifiers.

- State the range of all primitive data types and declare literal values for `String` and all primitive types using all permitted formats, bases, and representations.

- Write code that declares, constructs, and initializes arrays of any base type using any of the permitted forms both for declaration and for initialization.

- State the effect of using a variable or array element of any kind when no explicit assignment has been made to it.

- State the correspondence between index values in the argument array passed to a main method and command line arguments.

- Determine the effect upon objects and primitive values of passing variables into methods and performing assignments or other modifying operations in that method.

- State the behavior that is guaranteed by the garbage collection system and write code that explicitly makes objects eligible for collection.

This book is not an introduction to Java. Since you are preparing for certification, you are obviously already familiar with the fundamentals. The purpose of this chapter is to make sure you are 100 percent clear on those fundamentals covered by the Certification Exam objectives.

# Source Files

**A**ll Java source files must end with the .java extension. A source should generally contain at most one top-level public class definition; if a public class is present, the class name should match the unextended filename. For example, if a source file contains a public class called RayTraceApplet, then the file must be called RayTraceApplet.java. A source file may contain an unlimited number of non-public class definitions.

This is not actually a language requirement, but is an implementation requirement of the many compilers including the reference compilers from Sun. It is therefore unwise to ignore this convention since doing so limits the portability of your source files (but not, of course, your object files).

There are three *top-level* elements that may appear in a file. None of these elements is required. If they are present, then they must appear in the following order:

1. package declaration

2. import statements

3. class definitions

The format of the package declaration is quite simple. The keyword package occurs first, and is followed by the package name. The package name is a series of elements separated by periods. When class files are created they are placed in a directory hierarchy that reflects their package names. You must therefore be careful that each component of your package name hierarchy is a legitimate directory name on all platforms. Therefore, you must not use characters such as the space, forward slash, backslash, or other symbols.

Import statements have a similar form, but you may import either an individual class from a package or the entire package. To import an individual class, simply place the fully qualified class name after the import keyword and finish the statement with a semicolon to import an entire package simply as an asterisk at the end of the package name.

Whitespace and comments may appear before or after any of these elements. For example, a file called `Test.java` might look like this:

```
1. // Package declaration
2. package exam.prepguide;
3.
4. // Imports
5. import java.awt.Button; // imports a specific class
6. import java.util.*;     // imports an entire package
7.
8. // Class definition
9. public class Test {...}
```

# Keywords and Identifiers

The Java language specifies 49 keywords and other reserved words, which are listed in Table 1.1.

**T A B L E 1.1:** Java Keywords

| abstract | const | implements | import | package | synchronized | while |
|----------|----------|------------|------------|-----------|--------------|-------|
| boolean | false | final | instanceof | private | this | |
| break | continue | finally | int | protected | throw | |
| byte | default | float | interface | public | throws | |
| case | do | for | long | return | true | |

**T A B L E  1.1:**  Java Keywords *(Continued)*

| catch | double  | goto | native | transient | try      |
|-------|---------|------|--------|-----------|----------|
| char  | else    | if   | short  | static    | void     |
| class | extends | new  | null   | super     | volatile |

The words `goto` and `const` are reserved: Although they have no meaning in Java, programmers may not use them as identifiers.

An *identifier* is a word used by a programmer to name a variable, method, class, or label. Keywords and reserved words may not be used as identifiers. An identifier must begin with a letter, a dollar sign ($), or an underscore (_); subsequent characters may be letters, dollar signs, underscores, or digits. Some examples are

```
1. foobar               // legal
2. BIGinterface         // legal: embedded keywords are OK.
3. $incomeAfterExpenses // legal
4. 3_node5              // illegal: starts with a digit
5. !theCase            // illegal: must start with letter,
                            $ or _
```

Identifiers are case-sensitive. For example, `radius` and `Radius` are two distinct identifiers.

# Primitive Data Types

**J**ava's primitive data types are

- boolean
- char
- byte
- short
- int
- long

- float
- double

The sizes of these types are defined in the Java language specification and are listed in Table 1.2.

| **T A B L E 1.2** Primitive Data Types and Their Sizes | Type | Representation Size (bits) | Type | Representation Size (bits) |
|---|---|---|---|---|
| | boolean | 8 | char | 16 |
| | byte | 8 | short | 16 |
| | int | 32 | long | 64 |
| | float | 32 | double | 64 |

Variables of type boolean may only take the values true and false. The four signed integral data types are

- byte
- short
- int
- long

Variables of these types are two's-complement numbers. Their ranges are given in Table 1.3. Notice that for each type, the exponent of 2 in the minimum and maximum is one less than the size of the type.

| **T A B L E 1.3** Ranges of the Integral Primitive Types | Type | Size | Minimum | Maximum |
|---|---|---|---|---|
| | byte | 8 bits | $-2^7$ | $2^7-1$ |
| | short | 16 bits | $-2^{15}$ | $2^{15}-1$ |
| | int | 32 bits | $-2^{31}$ | $2^{31}-1$ |
| | long | 64 bits | $-2^{63}$ | $2^{63}-1$ |

The char type is integral but unsigned. The range of a variable of type char is from 0 through $2^{16}-1$. Java characters are in Unicode, which is a 16-bit encoding. If the most significant nine bits of a char are all 0, then the encoding is the same as seven-bit ASCII.

The two floating-point types are

- `float`
- `double`

These types conform to the IEEE 754 specification. Many mathematical operations can yield results that have no expression in numbers (infinity, for example). To describe such non-numerical situations, both doubles and floats can take on values that are bit patterns that do not represent numbers. Rather, these patterns represent non-numerical values. The patterns are defined in the `Float` and `Double` classes and may be referenced as

- `Float.NaN`
- `Float.NEGATIVE_INFINITY`
- `Float.POSITIVE_INFINITY`
- `Double.NaN`
- `Double.NEGATIVE_INFINITY`
- `Double.POSITIVE_INFINITY`

(*NaN* stands for *Not a Number*.)

The code fragment below shows the use of these constants:

```
1. double d = -10.0 / 0.0;
2.    if (d == Double.NEGATIVE_INFINITY) {
3.       System.out.println("d just exploded: " + d);
4.    }
```

In this code fragment, the test on line 2 passes, so line 3 is executed.

All the numerical primitive types (that is, all except `boolean` and `char`) are signed.

# Literals

**A** *literal* is a value that may be assigned to a primitive or string variable or passed as an argument to a method call.

## *boolean* Literals

The only valid literals of `boolean` type are `true` and `false`. For example

```
1. boolean isBig = true;
2. boolean isLittle = false;
```

## *char* Literals

A char literal can be expressed by enclosing the desired character in single quotes, as shown here:

```
char c = 'w';
```

Of course, this technique only works if the desired character is available on the keyboard at hand. Another way to express a character literal is as four Unicode hexadecimal digits, preceded by \u, with the entire expression in quotes. For example

```
char c1 = '\u4567';
```

Java supports a few escape sequences for denoting special characters:

- `'\n'` for Newline
- `'\r'` for Return
- `'\t'` for Tab
- `'\b'` for Backspace
- `'\f'` for Formfeed
- `'\''` for Single Quote
- `'\"'` for Double Quote
- `'\?'` for Question Mark

## Integral Literals

Integral literals may be expressed in decimal, octal, or hexadecimal. The default is decimal. To indicate octal, prefix the literal with 0 (zero). To indicate hexadecimal, prefix the literal with 0x or 0X; the hex digits may be upper- or lowercase. The value *twenty-eight* may thus be expressed six ways:

- 28
- 034
- 0x1c
- 0x1C
- 0X1c
- 0X1C

By default, an integral literal is a 32-bit value. To indicate a long (64-bit) literal, append the suffix L to the literal expression. (The suffix can be lowercase, but then it looks so much like a 1 that your readers are bound to be confused.)

## Floating-Point Literals

A *floating-point literal* expresses a floating-point numerical value. In order to be interpreted as a floating-point literal, a numerical expression must contain one of the following:

- A decimal point: 1.414
- The letter E or e, indicating scientific notation: 4.23E+21
- The suffix F or f, indicating a 32-bit float literal: 1.828f
- The suffix D or d, indicating a 64-bit double literal: 1234d

A floating-point literal with no F or D suffix defaults to a 64-bit double literal.

## String Literals

A *string literal* is a run of text enclosed in double quotes. For example

```
String s = "Characters in strings are 16-bit Unicode.";
```

Java provides many advanced facilities for specifying non-literal string values, including a concatenation operator and some sophisticated constructors for the String class. These facilities are discussed in detail in Chapter 8, "The java.lang Package."

# Arrays

A Java *array* is an ordered collection of primitives, object references, or other arrays. Java arrays are homogeneous: Except as allowed by polymorphism, all elements of an array must be of the same type. That is, when you create an array you specify the element type, and the resulting array can contain only elements that are instances of that class or sub-classes of that class.

To create and use an array, you must follow three steps:

**1.** Declaration

**2.** Construction

**3.** Initialization

Declaration tells the compiler what the array's name is and what the type of its elements will be. For example

```
1. int ints[];
2. double dubs[];
3. Dimension dims[];
4. float twoDee[][];
```

Lines 1 and 2 declare arrays of primitive types. Line 3 declares an array of object references (Dimension is a class in the java.awt package). Line 4 declares a two-dimensional array: that is, an array of arrays of floats.

The square brackets can come before or after the array name. This is also true, and perhaps more useful, in method declarations. A method that takes an array of doubles could be declared as myMethod(double dubs[]) or as myMethod(double[] dubs), and a method that returns an array of doubles may be declared as either double [] anotherMethod() or as double another-Method() [] in this last case, the first form is probably more readable.

Notice that the declaration does *not* specify the size of an array. Size is specified at runtime, when the array is allocated via the new keyword. For example

```
1. int ints[];          // Declaration to the compiler
2. ints = new int[25];  // Run time construction
```

Since array size is not used until runtime, it is legal to specify size with a variable rather than a literal:

```
1. int size = 1152 * 900;
2. int raster[];
3. raster = new int[size];
```

Declaration and construction may be performed in a single line:

```
1. int ints[] = new int[25];
```

When an array is constructed, its elements are automatically initialized exactly as for object member variables. Numerical elements are initialized to zero; non-numerical elements are initialized to values similar to zero, as shown in Table 1.4.

| **T A B L E   1.4**<br>Array Element<br>Initialization Values | Element Type | Initial Value | Element Type | Initial Value |
|---|---|---|---|---|
| | byte | 0 | short | 0 |
| | int | 0 | long | 0L |
| | float | 0.0f | double | 0.0d |
| | char | '\u0000' | boolean | false |
| | object reference | null | | |

If you want to initialize an array to values other than those shown in Table 1.4, you can combine declaration, construction, and initialization into a single step. The line of code below creates a custom-initialized array of five floats:

```
1. float diameters[] = {1.1f, 2.2f, 3.3f, 4.4f, 5.5f};
```

The array size is inferred from the number of elements within the curly braces.

Of course, an array can also be initialized by explicitly assigning a value to each element:

```
1. long squares[];
2. squares = new long[6000];
3. for (int i=0; i<6000; i++)
4.    squares[i] = i * i;
```

When the array is created at line 2, it is full of default values (0L); the defaults are immediately replaced. The code in the example works but can be improved. If the array size changes (in line 2), the loop counter will have to change (in line 3), and the program could be damaged if line 3 is not taken care of. The safest way to refer to the size of an array is to apply .length to the array name. Thus our example becomes

```
1. long squares[];
2. squares = new long[6000];
3. for (int i=0; i<squares.length; i++)
4.    squares[i] = i * i;
```

Java's array indexes always start at 0.

# Class Fundamentals

Java is all about classes, and a review of the Certification objectives will show that you need to be intimately familiar with them. Classes are discussed in detail in Chapter 6; for now there are a few fundamentals to examine.

# The *main()* method

The main() method is the normal entry point for Java applications. To create an application, you write a class definition that includes a main() method. To execute an application, you type **java** at the command line, followed by the name of the class whose main() method is to be executed.

The signature for main() is

```
public static void main(String args[ ])
```

The main() method is declared public by convention. However, it is a requirement that it be static so that it may be executed without the necessity of constructing an instance of the corresponding class.

The args array contains any arguments that the user might have entered on the command line. For example, consider the following command line:

```
% java Mapper France Belgium
```

With this command line, the args[] array has two elements: "France" in args[0], and "Belgium" in args[1]. Note that neither the class name ("Mapper") nor the command name ("java") appears in the array. Of course, the name args is purely arbitrary: Any legal identifier may be used, provided the array is a single dimensional array of String objects.

# Variables and Initialization

Java supports variables of two different lifetimes:

- A *member variable* of a class is created when the instance is created, and is accessible from any method in the class.

- An *automatic variable* of a method is created on entry to the method, exists only during execution of the method, and is only accessible within the method.

All member variables that are not explicitly assigned a value upon declaration are automatically assigned an initial value. The initialization value for member variables depends on the member variable's type. Values are listed in Table 1.5.

The values in Table 1.5 are the same as those in Table 1.4; member variable initialization values are the same as array element initialization values.

| T A B L E   1.5 | Element Type | Initial Value | Element Type | Initial Value |
|---|---|---|---|---|
| Initialization Values for Member Variables | byte | 0 | short | 0 |
| | int | 0 | long | 0L |
| | float | 0.0f | double | 0.0d |
| | char | '\u0000' | boolean | false |
| | object reference | null | | |

A member value may be initialized in its own declaration line:

```
1. class HasVariables {
2.    int x = 20;
3.    static int y = 30;
```

When this technique is used, non-static instance variables are initialized just before the class constructor is executed; here x would be set to 20 just before invocation of any HasVariables constructor. Static variables are initialized at class load time; here y would be set to 30 when the HasVariables class is loaded.

Automatic variables (also known as *local variables*) are not initialized by the system; every automatic variable must be explicitly initialized before being used. For example, this method will not compile:

```
1. public int wrong() {
2.    int i;
3.    return i+5;
4. }
```

The compiler error at line 3 is, "Variable i may not have been initialized." This error often appears when initialization of an automatic variable occurs at a lower level of curly braces than the use of that variable. For example, the method below returns the fourth root of a positive number:

```
1. public double fourthRoot(double d) {
2.    double result;
```

```
3.      if (d >= 0) {
4.         result = Math.sqrt(Math.sqrt(d));
5.      }
6.      return result;
7. }
```

Here the result is initialized on line 4, but the initialization takes place within the curly braces of lines 3 and 5. The compiler will flag line 6, complaining that "Variable result may not have been initialized." The solution is to initialize `result` to some reasonable default as soon as it is declared:

```
1. public double fourthRoot(double d) {
2.    double result = 0.0;  // Initialize
3.      if (d >= 0) {
4.         result = Math.sqrt(Math.sqrt(d));
5.      }
6.      return result;
7. }
```

Now `result` is satisfactorily initialized. Line 2 demonstrates that an automatic variable may be initialized in its declaration line. Initialization on a separate line is also possible.

# Argument Passing

**W**hen Java passes an argument into a method call, it is actually a copy of the argument that gets passed. Consider the following code fragment:

```
1. double radians = 1.2345;
2. System.out.println("Sine of " + radians + " = " + _
   Math.sin(radians));
```

The variable `radians` contains a pattern of 64 bits that represents the number 1.2345. On line 2, a copy of this bit pattern is passed into the Java Virtual Machine's method-calling apparatus.

When an argument is passed into a method, changes to the argument value by the method do not affect the original data is untouched. Consider the following method:

```
1. public void bumper(int bumpMe) {
2.    bumpMe += 15;
3. }
```

Line 2 modifies a copy of the parameter passed by the caller. For example

```
1. int xx = 12345;
2. bumper(xx);
3. System.out.println("Now xx is " + xx);
```

On line 2, the caller's xx variable is copied; the copy is passed into the bumper() method and incremented by 15. Since the original xx is untouched, line 3 will report that xx is still 12345.

This is still true when the argument to be passed is an object rather than a primitive. However, it is crucial for you to understand that the effect is very different. In order to understand the process, you have to understand the concept of the *object reference*.

Java programs do not deal directly with objects. When an object is constructed, the constructor returns a value—a bit pattern—that uniquely identifies the object. This value is known as a *reference* to the object. For example, consider the following code:

```
1. Button btn;
2. btn = new Button("Ok");
```

In line 2, the Button constructor returns a reference to the just-constructed button—not the actual button object or a copy of the button object. This reference is stored in the variable btn. In many implementations of the JVM, a reference is simply the 32-bit address of the object; however, the JVM specification gives wide latitude as to how references are to be implemented. You can think of a reference as simply a pattern of bits that uniquely identifies an individual object. When Java code appears to store objects in variables or pass objects into method calls, it is actually object *references* that get stored or passed.

Consider this code fragment:

```
1. Button btn;
2. btn = new Button("Good");
3. replacer(btn);
4. System.out.println(btn.getLabel());
5.
6. public void replacer(Button replaceMe) {
7.   replaceMe = new Button("Evil");
8. }
```

Line 2 constructs a button and stores a reference to that button in btn. In line 3, a copy of the reference is passed into the replacer() method. Before execution of line 7, the value in replaceMe is a reference to the Good button. Then line 7 constructs a second button and stores a reference to the second button in replaceMe, thus overwriting the reference to the Good button. However, the caller's copy of the reference is not affected, so on line 4 the call to btn.getLabel() calls the original button; the string printed out is "Good".

You have seen that called methods cannot affect the original value of their arguments, that is, the values stored by the caller. However, when the called method operates on an object via the reference value that is passed to it, there are important consequences. If the method modifies the object via the reference, as distinguished from modifying the method argument—the reference—then the changes will be visible to the caller. For example

```
1. TextField tf;
2. tf = new TextField("Yin");
3. changer(tf);
4. System.out.println(tf.getLabel());
5.
6. public void changer(TextField changeMe) {
7.   changeMe.setText("Yang");
8. }
```

In this example there is a single-text field. The caller refers to it as tf; the changer() method refers to it as changeMe. The text field originally contains the string "Yin;" the call to changer() changes the contents to "Yang." Thus line 4 prints out "Yang," not "Yin."

Arrays are objects, meaning that programs deal with references to arrays, not with arrays themselves. What gets passed into a method is a copy of a reference to an array. It is therefore possible for a called method to modify the contents of a caller's array.

---

### How To Create a Reference to a Primitive

This is a useful technique if you need to create the effect of passing primitive values by reference. Simply pass an array of one primitive element over the method call, and the called method can now change the value seen by the caller. Like this:

```
1. public class PrimitiveReference {
2.   public static void main(String args[]) {
3.     int [] myValue = { 1 };
4.     method(myValue);
5.     System.out.println("myValue contains " + _
       myValue[0]);
6.   }
7.   public static void modifyIt(int [] value) {
8.     value[0]++;
9.   }
}
```

---

# Garbage Collection

**M**ost modern languages permit you to allocate data storage during a program run. In Java, this is done when you create an object with the new operation. The point of this type of storage allocation is that the storage can remain allocated longer than the lifetime of any one method call. This increased lifetime raises the question of when the storage can be released. Some languages require that you, the programmer, explicitly release the storage when you have finished with it. This approach has proven seriously error-prone, since you might easily release the storage too soon (causing corrupted data) or forget to release it altogether (causing a memory shortage).

In Java, you never explicitly free memory that you have allocated; instead, Java provides automatic garbage collection. The runtime system keeps track of the memory that is allocated and is able to determine whether that memory is still useable. This work is usually done in the background by a low-priority thread that is referred to as the *garbage collector*. When the garbage collector finds memory that is no longer accessible from any live thread, it takes steps to release it back into the heap for re-use.

Garbage collection can be done in a number of different ways; each has advantages and disadvantages, depending upon the type of program that is running. A real-time control system, for example, needs to know that nothing will prevent it from responding quickly to interrupts; this requires a garbage collector that can work in small chunks or that can be interrupted easily. On the other hand, a memory-intensive program might work better with a garbage collector that stops the program from time to time but recovers memory more urgently as a result. At present, garbage collection is hardwired into the Java runtime system; most garbage collection algorithms use an approach that gives a reasonable compromise between speed of memory recovery and responsiveness. In the future, you will probably be able to plug in different garbage-collection algorithms or buy different JVMs with appropriate collection algorithms, according to your particular needs.

This all leaves one crucial question unanswered: When is storage recovered? The best you can answer is that storage is not recovered unless it is definitely no longer in use. That's it. Even though you are not using an object any longer, you cannot say if it will be collected in 1 millisecond, in 100 milliseconds—or even if it will be collected at all. There are methods, `System.gc()` and `Runtime.gc()`, that look as if they "run the garbage collector." Even these cannot be relied upon in general, since some other thread might prevent the garbage collection thread from running. In fact, the documentation for the `gc()` methods states:

> "Calling this method *suggests* that the Java Virtual Machine expend effort toward recycling unused objects." (Author's italics.)

---

### How To Cause Leaks in a Garbage Collection System

There is an important consequence of the nature of automatic garbage collection. You can still get memory leaks. If you allow live, accessible references to unneeded objects to persist in your programs, then those objects cannot be garbage collected. Therefore it may be a good idea to explicitly assign null into a variable when you have finished with it. This is particularly noticeable if you are implementing a collection of some kind. In this example, assume the array "storage" is being used to maintain the storage of a stack. This pop() method is inappropriate:

```
1. public Object pop() {
2.    return storage[index--];
3. }
```

If the caller of this pop() method abandons the popped value, it will not be eligible for garbage collection until the array element containing a reference to it is overwritten. This might take a long time. You can speed up the process like this:

```
1. public Object pop() {
2.    Object returnValue = storage[index];
3.    storage[index--] = null;
4.    return returnValue;
5. }
```

---

# Chapter Summary

**A** source file's elements must appear in this order:

1. package declaration

2. import statements

3. Class definitions

There may be at most one public class definition per source file; the filename must match the name of the public class.

An identifier must begin with a letter, a dollar sign, or an underscore; subsequent characters may be letters, dollar signs, underscores, or digits.

Java's four signed integral primitive data types are `byte`, `short`, `int`, and `long`; all four types use two's-complement notation. The two floating-point primitive data types are `float` and `double`. The `char` type is unsigned and represents Unicode characters. The `boolean` type may only take on the values `true` and `false`.

Arrays must be (in order)

1. Declared

2. Allocated

3. Initialized

Default initialization is applied to both member variables and array elements, but not automatic variables. The default values are zero for numerical types, the null reference for object references, the null character for `char`, and `false` for `boolean`. Applying `.length` to an array returns the number of elements in the array.

A class with a `main()` method can be invoked from the command line as a Java application. The signature for `main()` is `public static void main(String args[])`. The `args[]` array contains all command-line arguments that appeared after the name of the application class.

Method arguments are copies, not originals. For arguments of primitive data type, this means that modifications to an argument within a method are not visible to the caller of the method. For arguments of object or array reference type, modifications to an argument within a method are still not visible to the caller of the method; however, modifications to the object or array referenced by the argument do appear to the caller.

Java's garbage collection mechanism recovers unused memory. It is not possible to force garbage collection reliably. It is not possible to predict when a piece of unused memory will be collected, only when it becomes eligible for collection.

# Test Yourself

1. A signed data type has an equal number of non-zero positive and negative values available.

   A. True

   B. False

2. Choose the valid identifiers from those listed below.

   A. `BigOlLongStringWithMeaninglessName`

   B. `$int`

   C. bytes

   D. `$1`

   E. finalist

3. Which of the following signatures are valid for the `main()` method entry point of an application?

   A. `public static void main()`

   B. `public static void main(String arg[])`

   C. `public void main(String [] arg)`

   D. `public static void main(String[] args)`

   E. `public static int main(String [] arg)`

4. If all three top-level elements occur in a source file, they must appear in which order?

   A. Imports, package declaration, classes.

   B. Classes, imports, package declarations.

   C. Package declaration must come first; order for imports and class definitions is not significant.

   D. Package declaration, imports, classes.

   E. Imports must come first; order for package declaration and class definitions is not significant.

**5.** Consider the following line of code:

```
int x[] = new int[25];
```

After execution, which statement or statements are true?

**A.** x[24] is 0.

**B.** x[24] is undefined.

**C.** x[25] is 0.

**D.** x[0] is null.

**E.** x.length is 25.

**6.** Consider the following application:

```
1. class Q6 {
2.    public static void main(String args[]) {
3.       Holder h = new Holder();
4.       h.held = 100;
5.       h.bump(h);
6.       System.out.println(h.held);
7.    }
8. }
9.
10. class Holder {
11.    public int held;
12.    public void bump(Holder theHolder) { theHolder.held++; }
13. }
```

What value is printed out at line 6?

**A.** 0

**B.** 1

**C.** 100

**D.** 101

**7.** Consider the following application:

```
1. class Q7 {
2.    public static void main(String args[]) {
3.       double d = 12.3;
4.       Decrementer dec = new Decrementer();
5.       dec.decrement(d);
6.       System.out.println(d);
7.    }
8. }
9.
10. class Decrementer {
11.    public void decrement(double decMe) { _
       decMe = decMe - 1.0; }
12. }
```

What value is printed out at line 6?

**A.** 0.0

**B.** −1.0

**C.** 12.3

**D.** 11.3

**8.** How can you force garbage collection of an object?

**A.** Garbage collection cannot be forced.

**B.** Call System.gc().

**C.** Call System.gc(), passing in a reference to the object to be garbage-collected.

**D.** Call Runtime.gc().

**E.** Set all references to the object to new values (null, for example).

**9.** What is the range of values that can be assigned to a variable of type short?

   **A.** It depends on the underlying hardware.

   **B.** 0 through $2^{16}-1$

   **C.** 0 through $2^{32}-1$

   **D.** $-2^{15}$ through $2^{15}-1$

   **E.** $2^{31}$ through $2^{31}-1$

**10.** What is the range of values that can be assigned to a variable of type byte?

   **A.** It depends on the underlying hardware.

   **B.** 0 through $2^{8}-1$

   **C.** 0 through $2^{16}-1$

   **D.** $-2^{7}$ through $2^{7}-1$

   **E.** $2^{15}$ through $2^{15}-1$

# CHAPTER

# 2

## Operators and Assignments

**T**his chapter covers aspects of the following Java Certification Exam objectives:

- Determine the result of applying any operator, including assignment operators and `instanceof`, to operands of any type, class, scope, or accessibility, or any combination of these.

- Determine the result of applying the `boolean equals(Object)` method to objects of any combination of the classes `java.lang.String`, `java.lang.Boolean`, and `java.lang.Object`.

- In an expression involving the operators &, |, &&, | |, and variables of known values, state which operands are evaluated and the value of the expression.

Java provides a fully featured set of operators, most of which are taken fairly directly from C and C++. However, Java's operators differ in some important aspects from their counterparts in these other languages, and you need to understand clearly how Java's operators behave. This chapter describes all the operators: Some are described briefly, while others receive significantly more attention. Operators that sometimes cause confusion are described in detail. You will also learn about the behavior of expressions under conditions of arithmetic overflow.

Java's operators are shown in Table 2.1. They are listed in precedence order, with the highest precedence at the top of the table. Each group has been given a name for reference purposes. That name is shown in the left column of the table.

| **T A B L E  2.1** | Unary | ++  --  +  -  !  ~  () |
|---|---|---|
| Operators in Java | Arithmetic | *  /  % |
| | | +  - |
| | Shift | <<  >>  >>> |
| | Comparison | <  <=  >  >=  instanceof |
| | | ==  != |
| | Bitwise | &  ^  \| |
| | Short-circuit | &&  \|\| |
| | Ternary | ?: |
| | Assignment | =  "op=" |

The rest of this chapter examines each of these operators, but before we start, let's consider the general issue of evaluation order.

# Evaluation Order

In Java, unlike many other languages, the apparent order of evaluation of operands in an expression is fixed. Specifically, all operands are evaluated left to right, even if the order of execution of the operations is something different. This is most noticeable in the case of assignments. Consider this code fragment:

```
1. int [] a = { 4, 4 };
2. int b = 1;
3. a[b] = b = 0;
```

In this case, it might be unclear which element of the array is modified: What is the value of b used to select the array element, 0 or 1? An evaluation from left to right requires that the leftmost expression, a[b], be evaluated first, so it is a reference to the element a[1]. Next, b is evaluated, which is simply a reference to the variable called b. The constant expression 0 is evaluated next, which clearly does not involve any work. Now that the operands have been evaluated, the operations take place. This is done in the order specified by precedence and associativity. For assignments, associativity is right-to-left, so the value 0 is first assigned to the variable called b and then the value 0 is assigned into the last element of the array a.

The following sections examine each of these operators in turn.

Although Table 2.1 shows the precedence order, the degree of detail in this precedence ordering is rather high. It is generally better style to keep expressions simple and to use redundant bracketing to make it clear how any particular expression should be evaluated. This approach reduces the chance that less experienced programmers will find it difficult trying to read or maintain your code. Bear in mind that the code generated by the compiler will be the same despite redundant brackets.

# The Unary Operators

The first group of operators in Table 2.1 consists of the *unary operators*. Most operators take two operands. When you multiply, for example, you work with two numbers. Unary operators, on the other hand, take only a single operand and work just on that. Java provides seven unary operators:

- The increment and decrement operators: ++  --
- The unary plus and minus operators: +  -
- The bitwise inversion operator: ~
- The boolean complement operator: !
- The cast: ()

Strictly speaking, the cast is not an operator. However, we discuss it as if it were for simplicity, because it fits well with the rest of our discussion.

These operators are discussed in the following sections.

## The Increment and Decrement Operators ++ and −−

These operators modify the value of an expression by adding or subtracting 1. So, for example, if an int variable x contains 10, then ++x results in 11. Similarly −−x, again applied when x contains 10, gives a value of 9. Since, in this case, the expression −−x itself describes storage (the value of the variable x) the resulting value is stored in x.

The preceding examples show the operators positioned before the expression. They can, however, be placed after the expression instead. To understand how the position of these operators affects their operation, you must appreciate the difference between the value stored by these operators and the result value they give. Both x++ and ++x cause the same result in x. However, the apparent value of the expression itself is different. For example, you could say y = x++; then the value assigned to y is the original value of x. If you say y = ++x; then the value assigned to y is 1 more than the original value of x. In both cases, the value of x is incremented by 1.

Let us look more closely at how the position of the increment and decrement operators affects their behavior. If one of these operators is to the left of an expression, then the value of the expression is modified *before* it takes part in the rest of the calculation. This is called pre-increment or pre-decrement, according to which operator is used. Conversely, if the operator is positioned to the right of an expression, then the value that is used in the rest of the calculation is the *original* value of that expression, and the increment or decrement only occurs after the expression has been calculated.

Table 2.2 shows the values of x and y, before and after particular assignments, using these operators.

| **T A B L E  2.2** | **Initial value of** x | **Expression** | **Final value of** y | **Final value of** x |
|---|---|---|---|---|
| Examples of Pre-Modify and Post-Modify with the Increment and Decrement Operators | 5 | y = x++ | 5 | 6 |
| | 5 | y = ++x | 6 | 6 |
| | 5 | y = x-- | 5 | 4 |
| | 5 | y = --x | 4 | 4 |

## The Unary + and – Operators

The unary + and – operators are distinct from the more common binary + and – operators, which are usually just referred to as + and – (add and sub-tract). Both the programmer and the compiler are able to determine which meaning these symbols should have in a given context.

Unary + has no effect beyond emphasizing the positive nature of a numeric literal. Unary – negates an expression. So, you might make a block of assignments like this:

```
1. x = -3;
2. y = +3;
3. z = -(y + 6);
```

In such an example, the only reasons for using the unary + operator are to make it explicit that y is assigned a positive value and perhaps to keep the code aligned more pleasingly. At line 3, notice that these operators are not restricted to literal values but can be applied to expressions equally well, so the value of z is initialized to –9.

## The Bitwise Inversion Operator: ~

The ~ operator performs *bitwise inversion* on integral types.

For each primitive type, Java uses a virtual machine representation that is platform-independent. This means that the bit pattern used to represent a particular value in a particular variable type is always the same. This feature makes bit manipulation operators even more useful, since they do not intro-duce platform dependencies. The ~ operator works by converting all the 1 bits in a binary value to 0s and all the 0 bits to 1s.

For example, applying this operator to a byte containing 00001111 would result in the value 11110000. The same simple logic applies, no matter how many bits there are in the value being operated on.

# The *Boolean* Complement Operator: !

The ! operator inverts the value of a boolean expression. So !true gives false and !false gives true.

This operator is often used in the test part of an if() statement. The effect is to change the value of the affected expression. In this way, for example, the body of the if() and else parts can be swapped. Consider these two equivalent code fragments:

```
1. public Object myMethod(Object x) {
2.   if (x instanceof String) {
3.     // do nothing
4.   }
5.   else {
6.     x = x.toString();
7.   }
8.   return x;
9. }
```

and

```
1. public Object myMethod(Object x) {
2.   if (!(x instanceof String)) {
3.     x = x.toString();
4.   }
5.   return x;
6. }
```

In the first fragment a test is made at line 2, but the conversion and assignment, at line 6, occurs only if the test failed. This is achieved by the somewhat cumbersome technique of using only the else part of an if/else construction. The second fragment uses the complement operator so that the overall test performed at line 2 is reversed—it may be read as, "If it is false that x is an instance of a string" or more likely, "If x is not a string." Because of this change to the test, the conversion can be performed at line 3 in the situation that the test has succeeded; no else part is required, and the resulting code is cleaner and shorter.

This is a simple example, but such usage is common, and this level of understanding will leave you well armed for the certification exam.

## The Cast Operator: *(type)*

Casting is used for explicit conversion of the type of an expression. This is only possible for plausible target types. The compiler and the runtime system check for conformance with typing rules, which are described below.

Casts can be applied to change the type of primitive values, for example forcing a double value into an int variable like this:

```
int circum = (int)(Math.PI * diameter);
```

If the cast, which is represented by the (int) part, were not present, the compiler would reject the assignment. This is because a double value, such as is returned by the arithmetic here, cannot be represented accurately by an int variable. The cast is the programmer's way to say to the compiler, "I know this is risky, but trust me—I'm a programmer." Of course, if the result loses value or precision to the extent that the program does not work properly, then you are on your own.

Casts can also be applied to object references. This often happens when you use containers, such as the Vector object. If you put, for example, String objects into a Vector, then when you extract them, the return type of the elementAt() method is simply Object. To use the recovered value as a String reference, a cast is needed, like this:

```
1. Vector v = new Vector();
2. v.addElement("Hello");
3. String s = (String)v.elementAt(0);
```

The cast here occurs at line 3, in the form (String). Although the compiler allows this cast, checks occur at runtime to determine if the object extracted from the Vector really is a String. Casting, the rules governing which casts are legal and which are not, and the nature of the runtime checks that are performed, are covered in Chapter 4.

Now that we have considered the unary operators, which have the highest precedence, we will discuss the five arithmetic operators.

# The Arithmetic Operators

Next highest in precedence, after the unary operators, are the *arithmetic operators*. This group includes, but is not limited to, the four most familiar operators, which perform addition, subtraction, multiplication, and division. Arithmetic operators are split into two further subgroupings, as shown in Table 2.1. In the first group, you will see *, /, and %. In the second group, at lower precedence, are + and –. The following sections discuss these operators and also what happens when arithmetic goes wrong.

## The Multiplication and Division Operators: * and /

The operators * and / perform multiplication and division on all primitive numeric types and char. Integer division can generate an ArithmeticException from a division by zero.

You probably understand multiplication and division quite well from years of rote learning at school. In programming there are, of course, some limitations imposed by the representation of numbers in a computer. These limitations apply to all number formats, from byte to double, but are most noticeable in integer arithmetic.

If you multiply or divide two integers, the result will be calculated using integer arithmetic in either int or long representation. If the numbers are large enough, the result will be bigger than the maximum number that can be represented, and the final value will be meaningless. For example, byte values can represent a range of –128 to +127, so if two particular bytes have the values 64 and 4 respectively, then multiplying them should, arithmetically, give a value of 256. Actually, when you store the result in a byte variable you will get a value of 0, since only the low-order eight bits of the result can be represented.

On the other hand, when you divide with integer arithmetic, the result is forced into an integer, and typically, a lot of information that would have formed a fractional part of the answer is lost. For example, 7 / 4 should give 1.75, but integer arithmetic will result in a value of 1. You therefore have a choice in many expressions: Multiply first and then divide, which risks overflow, or divide first and then multiply, which almost definitely loses precision. Conventional wisdom says that you should multiply first and then divide, because this at least might work perfectly, whereas dividing first almost definitely loses precision. Consider this example:

```
1. int a = 12345, b = 234567, c, d;
2. long e, f;
3.
4. c = a * b / b;
5. d = a / b * b;
6. System.out.println("a is " + a +
7.    "\nb is " + b +
8.    "\nc is " + c +
9.    "\nd is " + d);
10.
11. e = (long)a * b / b;
12. f = (long)a / b * b;
13. System.out.println(
14.    "\ne is " + e +
15.    "\nf is " + f);
```

The output from this code is

```
a is 12345
b is 234567
c is -5965
d is 0

e is 12345
f is 0
```

Do not worry about the exact numbers in this example. The important feature is that in the case where multiplication is performed first, the calculation overflows when performed with int values, resulting in a nonsense answer. However, the result is correct if the representation is wide enough—as when using the long variables. In both cases, dividing first has a catastrophic effect on the result, regardless of the width of the representation.

Although multiplication and division are generally familiar operations, the *modulo operator* is perhaps less well known. The next section discusses this operator.

# The Modulo Operator: %

The modulo operator gives a value which is related to the remainder of a division. It is generally applied to two integers, although it can be applied to floating point numbers, too. So, in school, we would learn that 7 divided by 4 gives 1 remainder 3. In Java, we say x = 7 % 4;, and expect that x will have the value 3.

The previous paragraph describes the essential behavior of the modulo operator, but additional concerns appear if you use negative or floating point operands. In such cases, follow this procedure: Reduce the *magnitude* of the left-hand operand by the *magnitude* of the right-hand one. Repeat this until the magnitude of the result is less than the magnitude of the right-hand operand. This result is the result of the modulo operator. Figure 2.1 shows some examples of this process.

**FIGURE 2.1**

Calculating the result of the modulo operator for a variety of conditions

$17 \% 5$

$17 - 5 \rightarrow 12$
$12 - 5 \rightarrow 7$
$7 - 5 \rightarrow 2$
$2 < 5$ so $17 \% 5 = \underline{\underline{2}}$

$21 \% 7$

$21 - 7 = 14$
$14 - 7 = 7$
$7 - 7 = 0$
$0 < 7$ so $21 \% 7 = \underline{\underline{0}}$

$7.6 \% 2.9$

$7.6 - 2.9 = 4.7$
$4.7 - 2.9 = 1.8$
$1.8 < 2.9$ so $7.6 \% 2.9 = \underline{\underline{1.8}}$

$-5 \% 2$

Here, to reduce absolute value by 2, we must <u>add</u>

$-5 + 2 = -3$
$-3 + 2 = -1$
Absolute value of $-1$ is 1 and $1 < 2$
so $-5 \% 2 = \underline{\underline{-1}}$

$-5 \% -2$

Again, we must reduce absolute value of $-5$ by the absolute value of $-2$ which is 2

$-5 - (-2) = -3$
$-3 - (-2) = -1$
so again, $-5 \% -2 = \underline{\underline{-1}}$

Note that the sign of the result is entirely determined by the sign of the left-hand operand. When the modulo operator is applied to floating point types, the effect is to perform an integral number of subtractions, leaving a floating point result that might well have a fractional part.

A useful rule of thumb for dealing with modulo calculations that involve negative numbers is this: Simply drop any negative signs from either operand and calculate the result. Then, if the original left-hand operand was negative, negate the result. The sign of the right-hand operand is irrelevant.

The modulo operation involves division during execution. Because of this, it can throw an `ArithmeticException` if applied to integral types and the second operand is zero.

Although you might not have learned about the modulo operator in school, you will certainly recognize the + and – operators. Although basically familiar, the + operator has some capabilities beyond simple addition.

# The Addition and Subtraction Operators: + and –

The operators + and – perform addition and subtraction. They apply to operands of any numeric type but, uniquely, + is also permitted where either operand is a `String` object. In that case, the other operand is used to create a `String` object, whatever its original type. Creating a `String` object in this way is always possible, but the resulting text might be somewhat cryptic and perhaps only useful for debugging.

## The + Operator in Detail

Java does not allow the programmer to perform operator overloading, but the + operator is overloaded by the language. This is not surprising, because in most languages that support multiple arithmetic types the arithmetic operators (+, –, *, /, and so forth) are overloaded to handle these different types. Java, however, also overloads the + operator to support clear and concise *concatenation*—that is joining together—of `String` objects. The use of + with `String` arguments also performs conversions, and these can be succinct and expressive if you understand them. First we will consider the use of the + operator in its conventional role of numeric addition.

*Overloading* is the term given when the same name is used for more than one piece of code, and the code that is to be used is selected by the argument or operand types provided. For example the `println()` method can be given a `String` argument or an `int`. These two uses actually refer to entirely different methods; only the name is re-used. Similarly, the + symbol is used to indicate addition of `int` values, but the exact same symbol is also used to indicate the addition of `float` values. These two forms of addition require entirely different code to execute; again, the operand types are used to decide which code is to be run. Where an operator can take different operand types, we refer to *operator overloading*. Some languages, but not Java, allow the programmer to use operator overloading to define multiple uses of operators for their own types. Overloading is described in detail in Chapter 6.

Where the + operator is applied to purely numeric operands, its meaning is simple and familiar. The operands are added together to produce a result. Of course, some promotions might take place, according to the normal rules, and the result might overflow. Generally, however, numerical addition behaves as you would expect.

If overflow or underflow occurs during numeric addition or subtraction, then meaning is lost but no exception occurs. A more detailed description of behavior in arithmetic error conditions appears in the next section, "Arithmetic Error Conditions." Most of the new understanding to be gained about the + operator relates to its role in concatenating text.

Where either of the operands of a + expression is a String object, the meaning of the operator is changed from numeric addition to concatenation of text. In order to achieve this, both operands must be handled as text. If both operands are in fact String objects, this is simple. If, however, one of the operands is not a String object, then the non-string operand is converted to a String object before the concatenation takes place.

## How Operands Are Converted to String Objects

Although a review of the certification objectives will show that the certification exam does not require it, it is useful in practice to know a little about how + converts operands to String objects. For object types, conversion to a String object is performed simply by invoking the toString() method of that object. The toString() method is defined in java.lang.Object, which is the root of the class hierarchy, and therefore all objects have a toString() method. Sometimes, the effect of the toString() method is to produce rather cryptic text that is only suitable for debugging output, but it definitely exists and may legally be called.

Conversion of an operand of primitive type to a String is typically achieved by using, indirectly, the conversion utility methods in the wrapper classes. So, for example, an int value is converted by the static method Integer.toString().

The toString() method in the java.lang.Object class produces a String that contains the name of the object's class and some identifying value—typically its reference value, separated by the at symbol (@). For example, this might look like java.lang.Object@1cc6dd. This behavior is inherited by subclasses unless they deliberately override it. It is a good idea to define a helpful toString() method in all your classes, even if you do not require it as part of the class behavior. Code the toString() method so that it represents the state of the object in a fashion that can assist in debugging, for example, output the names and values of the main instance variables.

To prepare for the certification exam questions, and to use the + operator effectively in your own programs, you should understand the following points.

For a + expression with two operands of primitive numeric type, the result

- Is of a primitive numeric type.

- Is at least `int`, because of normal promotions.

- Is of a type at least as wide as the wider type of the two operands.

- Has a value calculated by promoting the operands to the result type, then performing the addition calculation using that type. This might result in overflow or loss of precision.

For a + expression with any operand that is not of primitive numeric type

- One operand must be a `String` object, otherwise the expression is illegal.

- If both operands are not `String` objects, the non-`String` operand is converted to a `String`, and the result of the expression is the concatenation of the two.

To convert an operand of some object type to a `String`, the conversion is performed by invoking the `toString()` method of that object.

To convert an operand of a primitive type to a `String`, the conversion is performed by a static method in a container class, such as `Integer.toString()`.

**NOTE** If you want to control the formatting of the converted result, you should use the facilities in the `java.text` package.

Now that you understand arithmetic operators and the concatenation of text using the + operator, you should realize that sometimes arithmetic does not work as intended—it could result in an error of some kind. The next section discusses what happens under such error conditions.

# Arithmetic Error Conditions

We expect arithmetic to produce "sensible" results that reflect the mathematical meaning of the expression being evaluated. However, since the computation is performed on a machine with specific limits on its ability to represent numbers, calculations can sometimes result in errors. You saw, in the section on the multiplication and division operators, that overflow can easily occur if the operands are too large. In overflow, and other exceptional conditions, the following rules apply:

- Integer division by zero, including a modulo (%) operation, results in an `ArithmeticException`.

- No other arithmetic causes any exception. Instead, the operation proceeds to a result, even though that result might be arithmetically incorrect.

- Floating-point calculations represent out-of-range values using the IEEE 754 infinity, minus infinity, and Not a Number (NaN) values. Named constants representing these are declared in both the `Float` and `Double` classes.

- Integer calculations, other than division by zero, that cause overflow or similar error, simply leave the final, typically truncated, bit pattern in the result. This bit pattern is derived from the operation and the number representation and might even be of the wrong sign. Because the operations and number representations are platform-independent, so are the result values under error conditions.

These rules describe the effect of error conditions, but there is some additional significance associated with the NaN values. NaN values are used to indicate that a calculation has no result in ordinary arithmetic, such as some calculations involving infinity or the square root of a negative number.

## Comparisons with Not a Number

Some floating-point calculations can return a NaN. This occurs, for example, as a result of calculating the square root of a negative number. Two NaN values are defined in the `java.lang` package (`Float.NaN` and `Double.NaN`) and are considered non-ordinal for comparisons. This means that for any value of x, including NaN itself, all of the following comparisons will return `false`:

- x < Float.NaN
- x <= Float.NaN
- x == Float.NaN
- x > Float.NaN
- x >= Float.NaN

In fact, the test

`Float.Nan != Float.NaN`

and the equivalent with `Double.NaN` return `true`, as you might deduce from the item above indicating that x == Float.NaN gives false even if x contains Float.NaN.

The most appropriate way to test for a NaN result from a calculation is to use the `Float.isNaN(float)` or `Double.isNaN(double)` static methods provided in the `java.lang` package.

The next section discusses a concept often used for manipulating bit patterns read from I/O ports: the shift operators <<, >>, and >>>.

# The Shift Operators: <<, >>, and >>>

**J**ava provides three *shift operators*. Two of these, << and >>, are taken directly from C/C++ but the third, >>>, is new.

Shifting is common in control systems where it can align bits that are read from, or to be written to, I/O ports. It can also provide efficient integer multiplication or division by powers of two. In Java, because the bit-level representation of all types is defined and platform-independent, you can use shifting with confidence.

## Fundamentals of Shifting

Shifting is, on the face of it, a simple operation. It involves taking the binary representation of a number and moving the bit pattern left or right. However, the unsigned right-shift operator >>> is a common source of confusion, probably because it does not exist in C and C++.

The shift operators may be applied to arguments of integral types only. In fact, they should generally be applied only to operands of either int or long type. (See "Arithmetic Promotions of Operands" later in this chapter.) Figure 2.2 illustrates the basic mechanism of shifting.

The diagram in Figure 2.2 shows the fundamental idea of shifting, which involves moving the bits that represent a number to positions either to the left or right of their starting points. This is similar to people standing in line at a store checkout. As one moves forward, the person behind takes their place and so on to the end of the line. This raises two questions:

- What happens to the bits that "fall off" the end? The type of the result will have the same number of bits as the original value, but the result of a shift looks as if it might have more bits than that original.

- What defines the value of the bits that are shifted in? These are the bits that are marked by question marks in Figure 2.2.

**FIGURE 2.2**

The basic mechanisms of shifting

| | | | | | |
|---|---|---|---|---|---|
| Original data | | | 192 | | |
| in binary | | 00000000 | 00000000 | 00000000 | 11000000 |
| Shifted left 1 bit | 0 | 00000000 | 00000000 | 00000001 | 1000000? |
| Shifted right 1 bit | | ?0000000 | 00000000 | 00000000 | 01100000 | 0 |
| Shifted left 4 bits | 0000 | 00000000 | 00000000 | 00001100 | 0000???? |
| | | | | | |
| Original data | | | −192 | | |
| in binary | | 11111111 | 11111111 | 11111111 | 01000000 |
| Shifted left 1 bit | 1 | 11111111 | 11111111 | 11111110 | 1000000? |
| Shifted right 1 bit | | ?1111111 | 11111111 | 11111111 | 00100000 | 0 |

The first question has a simple answer. Bits that move off the end of a representation are discarded.

## Shifting Negative Numbers

The second question, regarding the value of the bits that are shifted in, requires more attention. In the case of the left-shift << and the unsigned right-shift >>> operators, the new bits are set to zero. However, in the case of the signed right-shift >> operator, the new bits take the value of the most significant bit before the shift. Figure 2.3 shows this. Notice that where a 1 bit is in the most significant position before the shift (indicating a negative number), 1 bits are introduced to fill the spaces introduced by shifting. Conversely, when a 0 bit is in the most significant position before the shift, 0 bits are introduced during the shift.

**FIGURE 2.3**

Signed right shift of positive and negative numbers

| | | 192 | | |
|---|---|---|---|---|
| Original data in binary | 00000000 | 00000000 | 00000000 | 11000000 |
| Shifted right 1 bit | 00000000 | 00000000 | 00000000 | 01100000 |
| Shifted right 7 bits | 00000000 | 00000000 | 00000000 | 00000001 |

| | | −192 | | |
|---|---|---|---|---|
| Original data in binary | 11111111 | 11111111 | 11111111 | 01000000 |
| Shifted right 1 bit | 11111111 | 11111111 | 11111111 | 10100000 |
| Shifted right 7 bits | 11111111 | 11111111 | 11111111 | 11111110 |

It might seem like an arbitrary and unduly complex rule that governs the bits that are shifted in during a signed right-shift operation, but there is a good reason for the rule. If a binary number is shifted left one position (and provided that none of the bits that move off the ends of a left-shift operation are lost), the effect of the shift is to double the original number. Shifts by more than one bit effectively double and double again, so the result is as if the number had been multiplied by 2, 4, 8, 16, and so on.

If shifting the bit pattern of a number left by one position doubles that number, then you might reasonably expect that shifting the pattern right, which apparently puts the bits back where they came from, would halve the number, returning it to its original value. If the right shift results in zero bits being added at the most significant bit positions, then for positive numbers, this division does result. However, if the original number was negative, then the assumption is false.

Notice that with the negative number in two's-complement representation, the most significant bits are ones. In order to preserve the significance of a right shift as a division by two when dealing with negative numbers, we must bring in bits set to one, rather than zero. This is how the behavior of the arithmetic right shift is determined. If a number is positive, its most significant bit is zero and when shifting right, more zero bits are brought in. However, if the number is negative, its most significant bit is one, and more one bits must be propagated in when the shift occurs. This is illustrated in the examples in Figure 2.4.

| | | | | | |
|---|---|---|---|---|---|
| **FIGURE 2.4** | Original data | | | 192 | |
| Shifting positive and negative numbers right | in binary | 00000000 | 00000000 | 00000000 | 11000000 |
| | Shifted right 1 bit<br>= 96<br>= 192 / 2 | 00000000 | 00000000 | 00000000 | 01100000 |
| | Shifted right 4 bits<br>= 12<br>= 192 / 16<br>= 192 / $2^4$ | 00000000 | 00000000 | 00000000 | 00001100 |
| | Original data | | | −192 | |
| | in binary | 11111111 | 11111111 | 11111111 | 01000000 |
| | Shifted right 1 bit<br>= −96<br>= −192 / 2 | 11111111 | 11111111 | 11111111 | 10100000 |
| | Shifted right 4 bits<br>= −12<br>= −192 / 16<br>= −192 / $2^4$ | 11111111 | 11111111 | 11111111 | 11110100 |

There is a feature of the arithmetic right shift that differs from simple division by two. If you divide –1 by 2, the result will be 0. However, the result of arithmetic shift right of –1 right is –1. You can think of this as the shift operation rounding down, while the division rounds toward 0.

We now have two right-shift operators: one that treats the left-hand integer argument as a bit pattern with no special arithmetic significance and another that attempts to ensure that the arithmetic equivalence of shifting right with division by powers of two is maintained.

Why does Java need a special operator for unsigned shift right, when neither C nor C++ required this? The answer is simple: Both C and C++ provide for unsigned numeric types, but Java does not. If you shift an unsigned value right in either C or C++, you get the behavior associated with the >>> operator in Java. However, this does not work in Java simply because the numeric types (other than char) are signed.

## Reduction of the Right-Hand Operand

The right-hand argument of the shift operators is taken to be the number of bits by which the shift should move. However, for shifting to behave properly, this value should be smaller than the number of bits in the result. That is, if the shift is being done as an int type, then the right-hand operand should be less than 32. If the shift is being done as long, then the right-hand operand should be less than 64.

In fact, the shift operators do not reject values that exceed these limits. Instead, they calculate a new value by reducing the supplied value modulo the number of bits. This means that if you attempt to shift an int value by 33 bits, you will actually shift by 33 % 32—that is, by only one bit. This produces an anomalous result. You would expect that shifting a 32-bit number by 33 bits would produce zero as a result (or possibly –1 in the signed right-shift case). However, because of the reduction of the right-hand operand, this is not the case.

**Why Java Reduces the Right-Hand Operand of Shift Operators, or "The Sad Story of the Sleepy Processor"**

The first reason for reducing the number of bits to shift modulo the number of bits in the left-hand operand is that many CPUs implement the shift operations in this way. Why should CPUs do this?

Some years ago, there was a powerful and imaginatively designed CPU that provided both shift and rotate operations and could shift by any number of bits specified by any of its registers. Since the registers were wide, this was a very large number, and as each bit position shifted took a finite time to complete, the effect was that you could code an instruction that would take minutes to complete.

One of the intended target applications of this particular CPU was in control systems, and one of the most important features of real-time control systems is the worst-case time to respond to an external event, known as the *interrupt latency*. Unfortunately, since a single instruction on this CPU was indivisible—so that interrupts could not be serviced until it was complete—execution of a large shift instruction effectively crippled the CPU. The next version of that CPU changed the implementation of shift and rotate so that the number of bits by which to shift or rotate were treated as being limited to the size of the target data item. This restored a sensible interrupt latency. Since then, many other CPUs have adopted reduction of the right-hand operand.

## Arithmetic Promotion of Operands

Arithmetic promotion of operands takes place before any binary operator is applied so that all numeric operands are at least int type. This has an important consequence for the unsigned right-shift operator when applied to values that are narrower than int.

The diagram in Figure 2.5 shows the process by which a byte is shifted right. First the byte is promoted to an int, which is done treating the byte as a signed quantity. Next, the shift occurs, and zero bits are indeed propagated into the top bits of the result—but these bits are not part of the original byte. When the result is cast down to a byte again, the high-order bits of that

**FIGURE 2.5**

Unsigned right shift
of a byte

Calculation for –64 >>> 2.

| | |
|---|---|
| Original data (–64 decimal) | 11000000 |

| | | | | |
|---|---|---|---|---|
| Promote to `int` gives: | 11111111 | 11111111 | 11111111 | 11000000 |
| Shift right unsigned 2 bits gives: | 00001111 | 11111111 | 11111111 | 11111100 |
| Truncate to byte gives: | | | | 11111100 |
| Expected result was: | | | | 00001100 |

`byte` appear to have been created by a signed shift right, rather than an unsigned one. This is why you should generally not use the logical right-shift operator with operands smaller than an `int`: It is unlikely to produce the result you expected.

There are still a few more operators to cover before we leave this behind. Let's move on to the comparison operators: <, <=, >, >=, ==, and !=. They are commonly used to form conditions, such as in `if()` statements or in loop control.

# The Comparison Operators

**C**omparison operators all return a `boolean` result; either the relationship as written is `true` or it is `false`. There are three types of comparison: ordinal, object type, and equality. *Ordinal* comparisons test the relative value of numeric operands. *Object-type* comparisons determine if the runtime type of an object is of a particular type or a subclass of that particular type. *Equality* comparisons test if two values are the same and may be applied to values of non-numeric types.

## Ordinal Comparisons with <, <=, >, and >=

The ordinal comparison operators are

- Less than: <

- Less than or equal to: <=

- Greater than: >

- Greater than or equal to: >=

These are applicable to all numeric types and to char and produce a boolean result.

So, for example, given these declarations

```
int p = 9;
int q = 65;
int r = -12;
float f = 9.0F;
char c = 'A';
```

the following tests all return true:

```
p < q
f < q
f <= c
c > r
c >= q
```

Notice that arithmetic promotions are applied when these operators are used. This is entirely according to the normal rules discussed in Chapter 4. For example, although it would be an error to attempt to assign, say, the float value 9.0F to the char variable c, it is perfectly in order to compare the two. To achieve the result, Java promotes the smaller type to the larger type, hence the char value 'A' (represented by the Unicode value 65) is promoted to a float 65.0F. The comparison is then performed on the resulting float values.

Although the ordinal comparisons operate satisfactorily on dissimilar numeric types, including char, they are not applicable to any non-numeric types. They cannot take boolean or any class-type operands.

## The *instanceof* Operator

The instanceof operator tests the class of an object at runtime. The left-hand argument can be any object reference expression, usually a variable or an array element, while the right-hand operand must be a class, interface, or array type. You cannot use a java.lang.Class object or its string name as the right-hand operand.

This code fragment shows an example of how instanceof may be used. Assume that a class hierarchy exists with Person as a base class and Parent as a subclass.

```
1. public class Classroom {
2.    private Hashtable inTheRoom = new Hashtable();
3.    public void enterRoom(Person p) {
4.       inTheRoom.put(p.getName(), p);
5.    }
6.    public Person getParent(String name) {
7.       Object p = inTheRoom.get(name);
8.       if (p instanceof Parent) {
9.          return (Parent)p;
10.      }
11.      else {
12.         return null;
13.      }
14.   }
15. }
```

The method getParent() at lines 6–14 checks to see if the Hashtable contains a parent with the specified name. This is done by first searching the Hashtable for an entry with the given name and then testing to see if the entry that is returned is actually a Parent or not. The instanceof operator returns true if the class of the left-hand argument is the same as, or is some subclass of, the class specified by the right-hand operand.

The right-hand operand may equally well be an interface. In such a case, the test determines if the object at the left-hand argument implements the specified interface.

You can also use the instanceof operator to test if a reference refers to an array. Since arrays are themselves objects in Java, this is natural enough, but the test that is performed actually checks two things: First it will check if the object is an array and then it checks if the element type of that array is some subclass of the element type of the right-hand argument. This is a logical extension of the behavior that is shown for simple types and reflects the idea that an array of, say, Button objects is an array of Component objects, because a Button is a Component. A test for an array type looks like this:

```
if (x instanceof Component[])
```

Note, however, that you cannot simply test for "any array of any element type," as the syntax. This line is not legal:

```
if (x instanceof [])
```

If the left-hand argument is a `null` value, the `instanceof` test simply returns `false`—it does not cause an exception.

Although it is not required by the certification exam, you might find it useful to know that you can determine if an object is in fact an array, without regard to the base type. You can do this using the `isArray()` method of the `Class` class. For example, this test returns true if the variable `myObject` refers to an array: `myObject.getClass().isArray()`.

## The Equality Comparison Operators: == and !=

The operators == and != test for equality and inequality, respectively, returning a `boolean` value. For primitive types, the concept of equality is quite straightforward and is subject to promotion rules so that, for example, a `float` value 10.0 is considered equal to a `byte` value of 10. For variables of object type, the "value" is taken as the reference to the object; typically this is the memory address. You should not use these operators to compare the contents of objects, such as strings, because they will return `true` if two references refer to the same object, rather than if the two objects have an equivalent meaning.

To achieve a content or semantic comparison, for example, so that two different `String` objects containing the text "Hello" are considered equal, you must use the `equals()` method rather than the == or != operators.

To operate appropriately, the `equals()` method must have been defined for the class of the objects you are comparing. To determine whether it has, check the documentation supplied with the JDK or, for third-party classes, produced by javadoc. This should report that an `equals()` method is defined for the class and overrides `equals()` in some superclass. If this is not indicated, then you should assume that the `equals()` method will not produce a useful content comparison. You also need to know that `equals()` is defined as accepting an `Object` argument, but the actual argument must be of the same type as the object upon which the method is invoked—that is for `x.equals(y)` the test y `instanceof` x must be true. If this is not the case, then `equals()` must return `false`.

The information in this warning is not required for the certification exam, but is generally of value when writing real programs. If you define an equals() method in your own classes, you should be careful to observe two rules. If you overlook either of these, your classes might behave incorrectly in some specific circumstances. First, the argument to the equals() method is an Object. You must avoid the temptation to make the argument to equals() specific to the class you are defining. If you do this, you have overloaded the equals() method, not overridden it. This means that functionality in other parts of the Java APIs that depends upon the equals() method will fail. Most significantly, perhaps, lookup methods in containers, such as containsKey() and get() in the HashMap, will fail. The second rule you must observe is that if you define an equals() method, you should also define a hashCode() method. This method should return the same value for objects that compare equal using the equals() method. Again, this behavior is needed to support the containers, and other classes.

# The Bitwise Operators: &, ^, and |

The bitwise operators &, ^, and | provide bitwise AND, Exclusive-OR (XOR), and OR operations, respectively. They are applicable to integral types. Collections of bits are sometimes used to save storage space where several boolean values are needed or to represent the states of a collection of binary inputs from physical devices.

The bitwise operations calculate each bit of their results by comparing the corresponding bits of the two operands on the basis of these three rules:

- For AND operations, 1 AND 1 produces 1. Any other combination produces 0.

- For XOR operations, 1 XOR 0 produces 1, as does 0 XOR 1. (The operation is commutative). Any other combination produces 0.

- For OR operations 0 OR 0 produces 0. Any other combination produces 1.

The names AND, XOR, and OR are intended to be mnemonic for these operations. You get a 1 result from an AND operation if both the first operand and the second operand are 1. An XOR gives a 1 result if one or the other operand, but not both (the exclusivity part), is 1. In the OR operation, you get a 1 result if either the first operand or the second operand (or both) is 1. These rules are represented in Table 2.3 through Table 2.5.

| **T A B L E  2.3** The AND Operation | **Op1** | **Op2** | **Op1 AND Op2** |
|---|---|---|---|
| | 0 | 0 | 0 |
| | 0 | 1 | 0 |
| | 1 | 0 | 0 |
| | 1 | 1 | 1 |

| **T A B L E  2.4** The XOR Operation | **Op1** | **Op2** | **Op1 XOR Op2** |
|---|---|---|---|
| | 0 | 0 | 0 |
| | 0 | 1 | 1 |
| | 1 | 0 | 1 |
| | 1 | 1 | 0 |

| **T A B L E  2.5** The OR Operation | **Op1** | **Op2** | **Op1 OR OP2** |
|---|---|---|---|
| | 0 | 0 | 0 |
| | 0 | 1 | 1 |
| | 1 | 0 | 1 |
| | 1 | 1 | 1 |

Compare the rows of each table with the corresponding rule for the operations listed in the bullets above. You will see that for the AND operation, the only situation that leads to a 1 bit as the result is when both operands are 1 bits. For XOR, 1 bits result when one or other but not both of the operands are 1 bits. Finally for the OR operation, the result is generally a 1 bit, except where both operands are 0 bits. Now let's see how this works when applied to whole binary numbers, rather than just single bits. The approach can be applied to any size of integer, but we will look at bytes because they serve to illustrate the idea without putting so many digits on the page as to cause confusion. Consider this example:

```
        00110011
        11110000
AND     --------
        00110000
```

Observe that each bit in the result above is calculated solely on the basis of the two bits appearing directly above it in the calculation. The next calculation looks at the least significant bit:

```
        0011001|1|
        1111000|0|
AND     -------|-|
        0011000|0|
```

This result bit is calculated as 1 and 0, which gives 0.

For the fourth bit from the left, as shown in the following calculation

```
        00|1|10011
        11|1|10000
AND     --|-|----
        00|1|10000
```

This result bit is calculated as 1 AND 1, which gives 1. All the other bits in the result are calculated in the same fashion, using the two corresponding bits and the rules stated above.

Exclusive-or operations are done by a comparable approach, using the appropriate rules for calculating the individual bits, as the following calculations show:

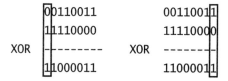

```
        00110011            0011001 1
        11110000            1111000 0
XOR    --------     XOR    ------ --
        11000011            1100001 1
```

All the highlighted bits are calculated as either 1 XOR 0 or as 0 XOR 1, producing 1 in either case.

```
        001 1 0011
        111 1 0000
XOR    -- -- ---
        110 0 0011
```

In the previous calculation, the result bits are 0 because both operand bits were 1.

```
        00110 0 11
        11110 0 00
XOR    ---- --
        11000 0 11
```

And above, the 0 operand bits also result in 0 result bits.

The OR operation again takes a similar approach, but with its own rules for calculating the result bits. Consider this example:

```
        0011001 1
        1111000 0
OR     ------ -
        1111001 1
```

Here, the two operand bits are 1 and 0, so the result is 1.

```
        0011 0 011
        1111 0 000
OR     --- ---
        1111 0 011
```

While in the calculation above, both operand bits are 0, which is the condition that produces a 0 result bit for the OR operation.

Although programmers usually apply these operators to the bits in integer variables, it is also permitted to apply them to `boolean` operands.

# Boolean Operations

The &, ^, and | operators behave in fundamentally the same way when applied to arguments of `boolean`, rather than integral, types. However, instead of calculating the result on a bit-by-bit basis, the `boolean` values are treated as single bits, with `true` corresponding to a 1 bit, and `false` to a 0 bit. The general rules discussed in the previous section may be modified like this when applied to `boolean` values:

- For AND operations, `true` AND `true` produces `true`. Any other combination produces `false`.

- For XOR operations, `true` XOR `false` produces `true`, `false` XOR `true` produces `true`. Other combinations produce `false`.

- For OR operations `false` OR `false` produces `false`. Any other combination produces `true`.

These rules are represented in Table 2.6 through Table 2.8.

| **T A B L E  2.6** The AND Operation on Boolean Values | Op1 | Op2 | Op1 AND OP2 |
|---|---|---|---|
| | false | false | false |
| | false | true | false |
| | true | false | false |
| | true | true | true |

| **T A B L E  2.7** The XOR Operation on Boolean Values | Op1 | Op2 | Op1 XOR OP2 |
|---|---|---|---|
| | false | false | false |
| | false | true | true |
| | true | false | true |
| | true | true | false |

| | Op1 | Op2 | Op1 OR OP2 |
|---|---|---|---|
| **T A B L E  2.8**<br>The OR Operation on<br>Boolean Values | false | false | false |
| | false | true | true |
| | true | false | true |
| | true | true | true |

Again, compare these tables with the rules stated in the bulleted list. Also compare them with Tables 2.3 through 2.5, which describe the same operations on bits. You will see that 1 bits are replaced by true, while 0 bits are replaced by false.

As with all operations, the two operands must be of compatible types. So, if either operand is of boolean type, both must be. Java does not permit you to cast any type to boolean, instead you must use comparisons or methods that return boolean values.

The next section covers the short-circuit logical operators. These operators perform logical AND and OR operations, but are slightly different in implementation from the operators just discussed.

# The Short-Circuit Logical Operators

The short-circuit logical operators && and || provide logical AND and OR operations on boolean types. Note that there is no XOR operation provided. Superficially, this is similar to the & and | operators with the limitation of only being applicable to boolean values and not integral types. However, the && and || operations have a valuable additional feature: the ability to "short circuit" a calculation if the result is definitely known. This feature makes these operators central to a popular null-reference-handling idiom in Java programming. They can also improve efficiency.

The main difference between the **&** and **&&** and between the **|** and **||** operators is that the right-hand operand might not be evaluated. We will look at how this happens in the rest of this section. This behavior is based on two mathematical rules that define conditions under which the result of a boolean AND or OR operation is entirely determined by one operand without regard for the value of the other:

- For an AND operation, if one operand is false, the result is false, without regard to the other operand.

- For an OR operation, if one operand is true, the result is true, without regard to the other operand.

To put it another way, for any boolean value X:

- false AND X = false

- true OR X = true

Given these rules, if the left-hand operand of a boolean AND operation is false, then the result is definitely false whatever the right-hand operand. It is therefore unnecessary to evaluate the right-hand operand. Similarly, if the left-hand operand of a boolean OR operation is true, the result is definitely true and the right-hand operand need not be evaluated.

Note that although these short cuts do not affect the result of the operation, side effects might well be changed. If the evaluation of the right-hand operand involves a side effect, then omitting the evaluation will change the overall meaning of the expression in some way. This behavior distinguishes these operators from the bitwise operators applied to boolean types. Consider a fragment of code intended to print out a string if that string exists and is longer than 20 characters:

```
1. if (s != null) {
2.   if (s.length() > 20) {
3.     System.out.println(s);
4.   }
5. }
```

However, the same operation can be coded very succinctly like this:

```
1. if ((s != null) && (s.length() > 20)) {
2.   System.out.println(s);
3. }
```

If the `String` reference s is `null`, then calling the `s.length()` method would raise a `NullPointerException`. In both of these examples, however, the situation never arises. In the second example, avoiding execution of the `s.length()` method is a direct consequence of the short-circuit behavior of the **&&** operator. If the test (s != `null`) returns `false` (if s is in fact `null`), then the whole test expression is guaranteed to be `false`. Where the first operand is `false`, the **&&** operator does not evaluate the second operand, so in this case the sub-expression (`s.length()` > 20) is not evaluated.

So, the essential points about the **&&** and **||** operators are

- They accept `boolean` operands.

- They only evaluate the right-hand operand if the outcome is not certain based solely on the left-hand operand. This is determined using the identities

  - `false` AND X = `false`

  - `true` OR X = `true`

The next section discusses the ternary, or conditional operator. Like the short-circuit logical operators, this operator may be less familiar than others, especially to programmers without a background in C or C++.

# The Ternary Operator: *?:*

The *ternary* (or *conditional*) operator ?: provides a way to code simple conditions (`if`/`else`) into a single expression. The (`boolean`) expression left of the ? is evaluated. If `true`, the result of the whole expression is the value of the sub-expression to the left of the colon; otherwise it is the value of the sub-expression to the right of the colon. The sub-expressions on either side of the colon must have the same type.

For example, if a, b, and c are `int` variables, and x is a `boolean`, then the statement a = x ? b : c; is directly equivalent to the textually longer version:

```
1. if (x) {
2.     a = b;
3. }
```

```
4. else {
5.   a = c;
6. }
```

Of course x, a, b, and c can all be complex expressions if you desire.

**NOTE**  Many people do not like the ternary operator, and in some companies its use is prohibited by the local style guide. This operator does keep source code more concise, but in many cases an optimizing compiler will generate equally compact and efficient code from the longer, and arguably more readable, if/else approach. One particularly effective way to abuse the ternary operator is to nest it, producing expressions of the form a = b ? c ? d : e ? f : g : h ? i : j ? k : l; . Whatever your feelings, or corporate mandate, you should at least be able to read this operator, as you will find it used by other programmers.

The points you should review for handling operators in an exam question, or to use it properly in a program, are listed below.

In an expression of the form a = x ? b : c;

- The types of the expressions b and c should be compatible and are made identical through conversion.

- The type of the expression x should be boolean.

- The type of the expressions b and c should be assignment compatible with the type of a.

- The value assigned to a will be b if x is true or will be c if x is false.

Now that we have discussed the ternary operator, only one group of operators remains: the assignment operators.

# The Assignment Operators

**A**ssignment operators set the value of a variable or expression to a new value. Assignments are supported by a battery of operators. Simple assignment uses =. Besides simple assignment, compound "calculate and assign" is provided by operators such as += and *=. These operators take a general form op= where op can be any of the binary non-boolean operators already discussed. In general, for any compatible expressions x and y, the expression x op= y is a shorthand for x = x op y. However, be aware that side effects in the expression x are evaluated exactly once, not twice as the expanded view might suggest. Assignment of object references copies the reference value, not the object body.

The statement x += 2; involves typing two fewer characters, but is otherwise no more effective than the longer version x = x + 2; and is neither more nor less readable. However, if x is a complex expression, such as target[temp.calculateOffset(1.9F) + depth++].item, it is definitely more readable to express incrementing this value by 2 using the += 2 form. This is because these operators define that the exact same thing will be read on the right-hand side as is written to on the left-hand side. So the maintainer does not have to struggle to decide whether the two complex expressions are actually the same, and the original programmer avoids some of the risk of mistyping a copy of the expression.

## An Assignment Has Value

All the operators discussed to this point have produced a value as a result of the operation. The expression 1 + 2, for example, results in a value 3, which can then be used in some further way, perhaps assignment to a variable. The assignment operators in Java are considered to be operators because they have a resulting value. So, given three int variables a, b, and c, the statement a = b = c = 0; is entirely legal. It is executed from right to left, so that first 0 is assigned into the variable c. After it has been executed, the expression c = 0 takes the value that was assigned to the left-hand side—that is zero. Next, the assignment of b takes place, using the value of the expression to the right of the equals sign. This is again zero. Similarly that expression takes the value that was assigned, so finally the variable a is also set to zero.

Although execution order is determined by precedence and associativity, evaluation order of the arguments is not. Be sure you understand the points made in the section "Evaluation Order" at the start of this chapter and, as a general rule, avoid writing expressions that are complex enough for these issues to matter. A sequence of simply constructed expressions will be much easier to read, and is less likely to cause confusion or other errors, than complex ones. Importantly, you are also likely to find that the compiler will make just as good a job of optimizing multiple simple expressions as it would a single, very complex, one.

# Chapter Summary

We have covered a lot of material in this chapter, so let's recap the key points.

## The Unary Operators

The seven unary operators are ++, −−, +, −, !, ~, and (). Their key points are

- The ++ and −− operators increment and decrement expressions. The position of the operator (either prefix or suffix) is significant.

- The + operator has no effect on an expression other than to make it clear that a literal constant is positive. The − operator negates an expression's value.

- The ! operator inverts the value of a `boolean` expression.

- The ~ operator inverts the bit pattern of an integral expression.

- The (`type`) operator is used to persuade the compiler to permit certain assignments that the programmer believes are appropriate, but which break the normal, rigorous rules of the language. Its use is subject to extensive checks at compile time and runtime.

# The Arithmetic Operators

There are five arithmetic operators, which are

- Multiplication: *

- Division: /

- Modulo: %

- Addition and `String` concatenation: +

- Subtraction: –

The arithmetic operators can be applied to any numeric type. Additionally, the + operator performs text concatenation if either of its operands is a `String` object. Under the conditions where one operand in a + expression is a `String` object, the other is forced to be a `String` object, too. Conversions are performed as necessary. They might result in cryptic text but they are definitely legal.

Under conditions of arithmetic overflow or similar errors, accuracy is generally lost silently. Only integer division by zero can throw an exception. Floating-point calculations can produce NaN—indicating Not a Number, that is, the expression has no meaning in normal arithmetic—or an infinity as their result under error conditions.

# The Shift Operators

These are the key points about the shift operators:

- The <<, >>, and >>> operators perform bit shifts of the binary representation of the left operand.

- The operands should be an integral type, either `int` or `long`.

- The right-hand operand is reduced modulo x where x depends upon the type of the result of the operation. That type is either `int` or `long`, smaller operands being subjected to promotion. If the left-hand operand is assignment compatible with `int`, then x is 32. If the left-hand operand is a `long`, then x is 64.

- The << operator shifts left. Zero bits are introduced at the least significant bit position.

- The >> operator performs a signed, or arithmetic, right shift. The result has 0 bits at the most significant positions if the original left-hand operand was positive, and has 1 bits at the most significant positions if the original left-hand operand was negative. The result approximates dividing the left-hand operand by two raised to the power of the right-hand operand.

- The >>> operator performs an unsigned, or logical, right shift. The result has 0 bits at the most significant positions and might not represent a division of the original left operand.

## The Bitwise Operators

There are three bitwise operators: &, ^, and |. They are usually named AND, Exclusive-OR (XOR), and OR, respectively. For each operator the following points apply:

- In bitwise operations, each result bit is calculated on the basis of the two bits from the same, corresponding position in the operands.

- For the AND operation, a 1 bit results if the first operand bit and the second operand bit are both 1.

- For the XOR operation, a 1 bit results only if exactly one operand bit is 1.

- For the OR operation, a 1 bit results if either the first operand bit or the second operand bit is 1.

For boolean operations, the arguments and results are treated as single bit values with true represented by 1 and false by 0.

## The Assignment Operators

The key points about the assignment operators are

- Simple assignment, using =, assigns the value of the right-hand operand to the left-hand operand.

- The value of an object is its reference, not its contents.

- The right-hand operand must be a type that is assignment compatible with the left-hand operand. Assignment compatibility and conversions are discussed in detail in Chapter 4.

- The assignment operators all return a value, so that they can be used within larger expressions. The value returned is the value that was assigned to the left-hand operand.

- The compound assignment operators, of the form op=, when applied in an expression like a op= b; appear to behave like a = a op b; except that the expression a, and any of its side effects, is evaluated only once.

Compound assignment operators exist for all binary non-boolean operators: *=, /=, %=, +=, -=, <<=, >>=, >>>=, &=, ^=, and |=. We have now discussed all the operators that are provided by Java and all that remains are the test questions. Good luck!

# Test Yourself

1. After execution of the code fragment below, what are the values of the variables x, a, and b?

   ```
   1. int x, a = 6, b = 7;
   2. x = a++ + b++;
   ```

   **A.** x = 15, a = 7, b = 8

   **B.** x = 15, a = 6, b = 7

   **C.** x = 13, a = 7, b = 8

   **D.** x = 13, a = 6, b = 7

2. Which of the following expressions are legal? (Choose one or more.)

   **A.** `int x = 6; x = !x;`

   **B.** `int x = 6; if (!(x > 3)) {}`

   **C.** `int x = 6; x = ~x;`

3. Which of the following expressions results in a positive value in x? (Choose one.)

   A. `int x = -1; x = x >>> 5;`

   B. `int x = -1; x = x >>> 32;`

   C. `byte x = -1; x = x >>> 5;`

   D. `int x = -1; x = x >> 5;`

4. Which of the following expressions are legal? (Choose one or more.)

   A. `String x = "Hello"; int y = 9; x += y;`

   B. `String x = "Hello"; int y = 9; if (x == y) {}`

   C. `String x = "Hello"; int y = 9; x = x + y;`

   D. `String x = "Hello"; int y = 9; y = y + x;`

   E. `String x = null;int y = (x != null) && (x.length() > 0)`
      `? x.length() : 0;`

5. Which of the following code fragments would compile successfully and print "Equal" when run? (Choose one or more.)

   A. `int x = 100; float y = 100.0F;if (x == y){`
      `System.out.println("Equal");}`

   B. `int x = 100; Integer y = new Integer(100);if (x == y) {`
      `System.out.println("Equal");}`

   C. `Integer x = new Integer(100);Integer y = new`
      `Integer(100);if (x == y) { System.out.println("Equal");}`

   D. `String x = new String("100");String y = new`
      `String("100");if (x == y) {`
      `System.out.println("Equal");}`

   E. `String x = "100";String y = "100";if (x == y) {`
      `System.out.println("Equal");}`

**6.** What results from running the following code?

```
1. public class Short {
2.    public static void main(String args[]) {
3.       StringBuffer s = new StringBuffer("Hello");
4.       if ((s.length() > 5) &&
5.         (s.append(" there").equals("False")))
6.          ; // do nothing
7.       System.out.println("value is " + s);
8.    }
9. }
```

   **A.** The output: value is Hello

   **B.** The output: value is Hello there

   **C.** A compiler error at line 4 or 5

   **D.** No output

   **E.** A NullPointerException

**7.** What results from running the following code?

```
1. public class Xor {
2.    public static void main(String args[]) {
3.       byte b = 10; // 00001010 binary
4.       byte c = 15; // 00001111 binary
5.       b = (byte)(b ^ c);
6.       System.out.println("b contains " + b);
7.    }
8. }
```

   **A.** The output: b contains 10

   **B.** The output: b contains 5

   **C.** The output: b contains 250

   **D.** The output: b contains 245

**8.** What results from attempting to compile and run the following code?

```
1. public class Ternary {
2.    public static void main(String args[]) {
3.       int x = 4;
4.       System.out.println("value is " +
5.          ((x > 4) ? 99.99 : 9));
6.    }
7. }
```

**A.** The output: `value is 99.99`

**B.** The output: `value is 9`

**C.** The output: `value is 9.0`

**D.** A compiler error at line 5

**9.** What is the output of this code fragment?

```
1. int x = 3; int y = 10;
2. System.out.println(y % x);
```

**A.** 0

**B.** 1

**C.** 2

**D.** 3

**10.** What results from the following fragment of code?

```
1. int x = 1;
2. String [] names = { "Fred", "Jim", "Sheila" };
3. names[--x] += ".";
4. for (int i = 0; i < names.length; i++) {
5.    System.out.println(names[i]);
6. }
```

**A.** The output includes `Fred.` with a trailing period.

**B.** The output includes `Jim.` with a trailing period.

**C.** The output includes `Sheila.` with a trailing period.

**D.** None of the outputs shows a trailing period.

**E.** An `ArrayIndexOutOfBoundsException` is thrown.

# CHAPTER

# 3

## Modifiers

T his chapter covers aspects of the following Java Certification Exam objectives:

- Declare classes, inner classes, methods, instance variables, static variables, and automatic (method local) variables making appropriate use of all permitted modifiers (such as public, final, static, abstract, and so forth). State the significance of each of these modifiers both singly and in combination, and state the effect of package relationships on declared items qualified by these modifiers.

- Identify correctly constructed source files, package declarations, import statements, class declarations (of all forms including inner classes), interface declarations and implementations (for `java.lang.Runnable` or other interface described in the test), method declarations (including the main method that is used to start execution of a class), variable declarations, and identifiers.

*Modifiers* are Java keywords that give the compiler information about the nature of code, data, or classes. Modifiers specify, for example, that a particular feature is static, or final, or transient. (A *feature* is a class, a method, or a variable.) A group of modifiers, called *access modifiers*, dictate which classes are allowed to use a feature. Other modifiers can be used in combination to describe the attributes of a feature.

In this chapter you will learn about all of Java's modifiers as they apply to top-level classes. Inner classes are not discussed here, but are covered in Chapter 6.

# Modifier Overview

The most common modifiers are the access modifiers: public, protected, and private. The access modifiers are covered in the next section. The remaining modifiers do not fall into clear categories. They are

- final
- abstract
- static
- native
- transient
- synchronized
- volatile

Each of these modifiers is discussed in its own section.

# The Access Modifiers

Access modifiers control which classes may use a feature. A class' features are

- The class itself
- Its class variables
- Its methods and constructors

Note that, with rare exceptions, the only variables that may be controlled by access modifiers are class-level variables. The variables that you declare and use within a class' methods may not have access modifiers. This makes sense; a method variable can only be used within its method.

The access modifiers are

- public
- protected
- private

The only access modifier permitted to non-inner classes is `public`; there is no such thing as a protected or private top-level class.

A feature may have at most one access modifier. If a feature has no access modifier, its access defaults to `friendly`. Be aware that `friendly` is not a Java keyword; it is just the colloquial name that we humans use for the type of access a feature gets if no modifier is specified.

The following declarations are all legal (provided they appear in an appropriate context):

```
class Parser { ... }
public class EightDimensionalComplex  { ... }
private int i;
Graphics offScreenGC;
protected double getChiSquared(){ ... }
private class Horse { ... }
```

The following declarations are illegal:

```
public protected int x;          // At most 1 access _
modifier allowed
friendly Button getBtn(){ ... }  // "friendly" is not a _
modifier
```

# public

The most generous access modifier is `public`. A public class, variable, or method may be used in any Java program without restriction. An applet (that is, a custom subclass of class `java.applet.Applet`) is declared as a public class so that it may be instantiated by browsers. An application declares its `main()` method to be public so that `main()` may be invoked from any Java runtime environment.

# private

The least generous access modifier is `private`. Top level classes may not be declared private. A private variable or method may only be used by an instance of the class that declares the variable or method. As an example of private access, consider the following code:

```
1. class Complex {
2.    private double real, imaginary;
3.
```

```
 4.    public Complex(double r, double i)  { real = r; _
       imaginary = i; }
 5.
 6.    public Complex add(Complex c) {
 7.       return new Complex(real + c.real, imaginary + _
          c.imaginary);
 8.    }
 9. }
10.
11.
12. class Client {
13.    void useThem() {
14.      Complex c1 = new Complex(1, 2);
15.      Complex c2 = new Complex(3, 4);
16.      Complex c3 = c1.add(c2);
17.      double d = c3.real; // Illegal!
18.    }
19. }
```

On line 16, a call is made to `c1.add(c2)`. Object c1 will execute the method, using object c2 as a parameter. In line 7, c1 accesses its own private variables as well as those of c2. There is nothing wrong with this. Declaring real and imaginary to be private means that they may only be accessed by instances of the Complex class, but they may be accessed by any instance of Complex. Thus c1 may access its own real and imaginary variables, as well as the real and imaginary of any other instance of Complex. Access modifiers dictate which classes, not which instances, may access features.

Line 17 is illegal and will cause a compiler error. The error message says, "Variable real in class Complex not accessible from class Client." The private variable real may only be accessed by an instance of Complex.

Private data can be hidden from the very object that owns the data. If class Complex has a subclass called SubComplex, then every instance of SubComplex will inherit its own real and imaginary variables. Nevertheless, no instance of SubComplex can ever access those variables. Once again, the private features of Complex may only be accessed by an instance of Complex; an instance of a subclass is denied access. Thus, for example, the following code will not compile:

```
1. class Complex {
2.    private double real, imaginary;
3. }
```

```
 4.
 5.
 6. class SubComplex extends Complex {
 7.   SubComplex(double r, double i) {
 8.     real = r;              // Trouble!
 9.   }
10. }
```

In the constructor for class SubComplex (on line 8), the variable real is accessed. This line causes a compiler error, with a message that is very similar to the message of the previous example: "Variable real in class Complex not accessible from class SubComplex." The private nature of variable real prevents an instance of SubComplex from accessing one of its own variables!

# Friendly

*Friendly* is the name of the default access of classes, variables, and methods, if you don't specify an access modifier. A class' data and methods may be friendly, as well as the class itself. A class' friendly features are accessible to any class in the same package as the class in question.

*Friendly* is not a Java keyword; it is simply a name that is given to the access level that results from not specifying an access modifier.

It would seem that friendly access is only of interest to people who are in the business of making packages. This is technically true, but actually everybody is always making packages, even if they aren't aware of it. The result of this behind-the-scenes package making is a degree of convenience for programmers that deserves investigation.

When you write an application that involves developing several different classes, you probably put all your .java sources and all your .class class files in a single working directory. When you execute your code, you do so from that directory. The Java runtime environment considers that all class files in its current working directory constitute a package.

Imagine what happens when you develop several classes in this way and don't bother to provide access modifiers for your classes, data, or methods. These features are neither public, nor private, nor protected. They default to friendly access, which means they are accessible to any other classes in the package. Since Java considers that all the classes in the directory actually make up a package, all your classes get to access one another's features. This makes it easy to develop code quickly without worrying too much about access.

Now imagine what happens if you are deliberately developing your own package. A little extra work is required: You have to put a `package` statement in your source code and you have to compile with the -d option. Any features of the package's classes that you do not explicitly mark with an access modifier will be accessible to all the members of the package, which is probably what you want. Fellow package members have a special relationship, and it stands to reason that they should get access not granted to classes outside the package. Classes outside the package may not access the friendly features, because the features are friendly, not public. Classes outside the package may subclass the classes in the package (you do something like this, for example, when you write an applet); however, even the subclasses may not access the friendly features, because the features are friendly, not protected or public. Figure 3.1 illustrates friendly access both within and outside a package.

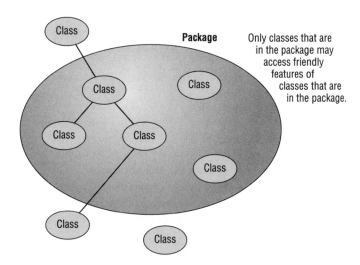

**FIGURE 3.1**

Friendly access

## *protected*

The name *protected* is a bit misleading. From the sound of it, you might guess that protected access is extremely restrictive—perhaps the next closest thing to private access. In fact, protected features are even more accessible than friendly features.

Only variables, methods, and inner classes and methods may be declared protected. A protected feature of a class is available to all classes in the same package, just like a friendly feature. Moreover, a protected feature of a class is available to all subclasses of the class that owns the protected feature. This access is provided even to subclasses that reside in a different package from the class that owns the protected feature.

As an example of protected access, consider the following source module:

```
1. package sportinggoods;
2. class Ski {
3.   void applyWax() { . . . }
4. }
```

The applyWax() method defaults to friendly access. Now consider the following subclass:

```
1. package sportinggoods;
2. class DownhillSki extends Ski {
3.   void tuneup() {
4.     applyWax();
5.     // other tuneup functionality here
6.   }
7. }
```

The subclass calls the inherited method applyWax(). This is not a problem as long as both the Ski and DownhillSki classes reside in the same package. However, if either class were to be moved to a different package, DownhillSki would no longer have access to the inherited applyWax() method, and compilation would fail. The problem would be fixed by making applyWax() protected on line 3:

```
1. package adifferentpackage;   // Class Ski now in a _
   different package
2. class Ski {
3.   protected void applyWax() { . . . }
4. }
```

## Subclasses and Method Privacy

Java specifies that methods may not be overridden to be more private. For example, most applets provide an init() method, which overrides the donothing version inherited from the java.applet.Applet superclass. The inherited version is declared public, so declaring the subclass version to be private, protected, or friendly would result in a compiler error. The error message says, "Methods can't be overridden to be more private."

Figure 3.2 shows the legal access types for subclasses. A method with some particular access type may be overridden by a method with a different access type, provided there is a path in the figure from the original type to the new type.

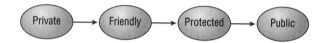

The rules for overriding can be summarized as follows:

- A private method may be overridden by a private, friendly, protected, or public method.

- A friendly method may be overridden by a friendly, protected, or public method.

- A protected method may be overridden by a protected or public method.

- A public method may only be overridden by a public method.

Figure 3.3 shows the illegal access types for subclasses. A method with some particular access type may not be overridden by a method with a different access type, if there is a path in the figure from the original type to the new type.

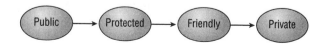

The illegal overriding combinations can be summarized as follows:

- A friendly method may not be overridden by a private method.

- A protected method may not be overridden by a friendly or private method.

- A public method may not be overridden by a protected, friendly, or private method.

## Summary of Access Modes

To summarize, Java's access modes are

- `public`: A public feature may be accessed by any class at all.

- `protected`: A protected feature may only be accessed by a subclass of the class that owns the feature or by a member of the same package as the class that owns the feature.

- friendly: A friendly feature may only be accessed by a class from the same package as the class that owns the feature.

- `private`: A private feature may only be accessed by the class that owns the feature.

# Other Modifiers

The rest of this chapter covers Java's other modifiers: `final`, `abstract`, `static`, `native`, `transient`, `synchronized`, and `volatile`. (Transient and volatile are not mentioned in the Certification Exam objectives, so they are just touched on briefly in this chapter.)

Java does not care about order of appearance of modifiers. Declaring a class to be `public final` is no different from declaring it `final public`. Declaring a method to be `protected static` has the same effect as declaring it `static protected`.

Not every modifier can be applied to every kind of feature. Table 3.1, at the end of this chapter, summarizes which modifiers apply to which features.

## *final*

The final modifier applies to classes, methods, and variables. The meaning of final varies from context to context, but the essential idea is the same: Final features may not be changed.

A final class may not be subclassed. For example, the code below will not compile, because the java.lang.Math class is final:

```
class SubMath extends java.lang.Math { }
```

The compiler error says, "Can't subclass final classes."

A final variable may not be modified once it has been assigned a value. In Java, final variables play the same role as consts in C++ and #define'd constants in C. For example, the java.lang.Math class has a final variable, of type double, called PI. Obviously, pi is not the sort of value that should be changed during the execution of a program.

If a final variable is a reference to an object, it is the reference that must stay the same, not the object. This is shown in the code below:

```
1.  class Walrus {
2.     int weight;
3.     Walrus(int w) { weight = w; }
4.  }
5.
6.  class Tester {
7.     final Walrus w1 = new Walrus(1500);
8.     void test() {
9.        w1 = new Walrus(1400);      // Illegal
10.       w1.weight = 1800;           // Legal
11.    }
12. }
```

Here the final variable is w1, declared on line 7. Since it is final, w1 may not receive a new value; line 9 is illegal. However, the data inside w1 is not final, and line 10 is perfectly legal. In other words

- You *may not* change a final object reference variable.

- You *may* change data owned by an object that is referred to by a final object reference variable.

A final method may not be overridden. For example, the following code will not compile:

```
1. class Mammal {
2.   final void getAround() { }
3. }
4.
5. class Dolphin extends Mammal {
6.   void getAround() { }
7. }
```

Dolphins get around in a very different way from most mammals, so it makes sense to try to override the inherited version of getAround(). However, getAround() is final, so the only result is a compiler error at line 6 that says, "Final methods can't be overridden."

## *abstract*

The abstract modifier can be applied to classes and methods. A class that is abstract may not be instantiated (that is, you may not call its constructor).

Abstract classes provide a way to defer implementation to subclasses. Consider the class hierarchy shown in Figure 3.4.

The designer of class Animal has decided that every subclass should have a travel() method. Each subclass has its own unique way of traveling, so it is not possible to provide travel() in the superclass and have each subclass inherit the same parental version. Instead, the Animal superclass declares travel() to be abstract. The declaration looks like this:

```
abstract void travel();
```

At the end of the line is a semicolon where you would expect to find curly braces containing the body of the method. The method body—its implementation—is deferred to the subclasses. The superclass only provides the method name and signature. Any subclass of Animal must provide an implementation of travel() or declare itself to be abstract. In the latter case, implementation of travel() is deferred yet again, to a subclass of the subclass.

If a class contains one or more abstract methods, the compiler insists that the class must be declared abstract. This is a great convenience to people who

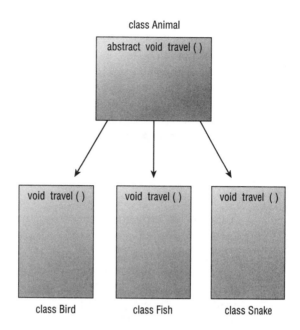

will be using the class: They only need to look in one place (the class declaration) to find out if they are allowed to instantiate the class directly or if they have to build a subclass.

In fact, the compiler insists that a class must be declared abstract if any of the following conditions is true:

- The class has one or more abstract methods.

- The class inherits one or more abstract methods (from an abstract parent) for which it does not provide implementations.

- The class declares that it implements an interface but does not provide implementations for every method of that interface.

These three conditions are very similar to one another. In each case, there is a class that is in some sense incomplete. Some part of the class' functionality is missing and must be provided by a subclass.

In a way, abstract is the opposite of final. A final class, for example, may not be subclassed; an abstract class *must* be subclassed.

## *static*

The static modifier can be applied to variables, methods, and even a strange kind of code that is not part of a method. You can think of static features as belonging to a class, rather than being associated with an individual instance of the class.

The following example shows a simple class with a single static variable:

```
1. class Ecstatic {
2.    static int x = 0;
3.    Ecstatic() { x++; }
4. }
```

Variable x is static; this means that there is only one x, no matter many how many instances of class Ecstatic might exist at any particular moment. There might be one Ecstatic, or many, or even none; there is always precisely one x. The four bytes of memory occupied by x are allocated when class Ecstatic is loaded. The initialization to zero (line 2) also happens at class-load time. The static variable is incremented every time the constructor is called, so it is possible to know how many instances have been created.

There are two ways to reference a static variable:

- Via a reference to any instance of the class

- Via the class name

The first method works, but it can result in confusing code and is considered bad form. The following example shows why:

```
1. Ecstatic e1 = new Ecstatic();
2. Ecstatic e2 = new Ecstatic();
3. e1.x = 100;
4. e2.x = 200;
5. reallyImportantVariable = e1.x;
```

If you didn't know that x is static, you might think that reallyImportant-Variable gets set to 100 in line 5. In fact, it gets set to 200, because e1.x and e2.x refer to the same (static) variable.

A better way to refer to a static variable is via the class name. The following code is identical to the code above:

```
1. Ecstatic e1 = new Ecstatic();
2. Ecstatic e2 = new Ecstatic();
```

```
3. Ecstatic.x = 100;    // Why did I do this?
4. Ecstatic.x = 200;
5. reallyImportantVariable = Ecstatic.x;
```

Now it is clear that line 3 is useless, and the value of `reallyImportantVariable` gets set to 200 in line 5. Referring to static features via the class name rather than an instance results in source code that more clearly describes what will happen at runtime.

Methods, as well as data, can be declared static. Static methods are not allowed to use the non-static features of their class (although they are free to access the class' static data and call its other static methods). Thus static methods are not concerned with individual instances of a class. They may be invoked before even a single instance of the class is constructed. Every Java application is an example, because every application has a `main()` method that is static:

```
1. class SomeClass {
2.    static int i = 48;
3.    int j = 1;
4.
5.    public static void main(String args[]) {
6.      i += 100;
7.      // j *= 5;    Lucky for us this line is commented _
         out!
8.    }
9. }
```

When this application is started (that is, when somebody types `java SomeClass` on a command line), no instance of class `SomeClass` exists. At line 6, the `i` that gets incremented is static, so it exists even though there are no instances. Line 7 would result in a compiler error if it were not commented out, because `j` is non-static.

Non-static methods have an implicit variable named `this`, which is a reference to the object executing the method. In non-static code, you can refer to a variable or method without specifying which object's variable or method you mean. The compiler assumes you mean `this`. For example, consider the code below:

```
1. class Xyzzy {
2.    int w;
3.
```

```
4.  void bumpW() {
5.    w++;
6.  }
7. }
```

On line 5, the programmer has not specified which object's w is to be incremented. The compiler assumes that line 5 is an abbreviation for

```
this.w++;
```

With static methods, there is no this. If you try to access it, you will get an error message that says, "Undefined variable: this." The concept of "the instance that is executing the current method" does not mean anything, because there is no such instance. Like static variables, static methods are not associated with any individual instance of their class.

If a static method needs to access a non-static variable or call a non-static method, it must specify which instance of its class owns the variable or executes the method. This situation is familiar to anyone who has ever written an application with a GUI:

```
1.  import java.awt.*;
2.
3.  public class MyFrame extends Frame {
4.    MyFrame() {
5.      setSize(300, 300);
6.    }
7.
8.    public static void main(String args[]) {
9.      MyFrame theFrame = new MyFrame();
10.     theFrame.setVisible(true);
11.   }
12. }
```

In line 9, the static method main() constructs an instance of class MyFrame. In the next line, that instance is told to execute the (non-static) method setVisible(). This technique bridges the gap from static to non-static, and it is frequently seen in applications.

A static method may not be overridden to be non-static. The code below, for example, will not compile:

```
1. class Cattle {
2.   static void foo() {}
3. }
4.
5. class Sheep extends Cattle {
6. void foo() {}
7.
```

The compiler flags line 6 with the message, "Static methods can't be overridden." If line 6 were changed to "static void foo() { }", then compilation would succeed.

To summarize static methods:

- A static method may only access the static data of its class; it may not access non-static data.

- A static method may only call the static methods of its class; it may not call non-static methods.

- A static method has no this.

- A static method may not be overridden to be non-static.

## Static Initializers

It is legal for a class to contain static code that does not exist within a method body. A class may have a block of initializer code that is simply surrounded by curly braces and labeled static. For example

```
1.   public class StaticDemo {
2.     static int i=5;
3.
4.     static {
5.       System.out.println("Static code: i = " + i++);
6.     }
7.
8.     public static void main(String args[]) {
```

```
 9.        System.out.println("main: i = " + i++);
10.    }
11.  }
```

Something seems to be missing from line 4. You might expect to see a complete method declaration there: `static void printAndBump()`, for example, instead of just `static`. In fact, line 4 is perfectly valid; it is known as `static initializer` code. The code inside the curlies is executed exactly once, at the time the class is loaded. At class-load time, all static initialization (such as line 2) and all free-floating static code (such as lines 4–6) are executed in order of appearance within the class definition.

Free-floating initializer code should be used with caution, as it can easily lead to obfuscated code. The compiler supports multiple initializer blocks within a class, but there is never a good reason for having more than one such block.

## *native*

The `native` modifier can refer only to methods. Like the `abstract` keyword, `native` indicates that the body of a method is to be found elsewhere. In the case of abstract methods, the body is in a subclass; with native methods, the body lies entirely outside the Java Virtual Machine, in a library.

Native code is written in a non-Java language, typically C or C++, and compiled for a single target machine type. (Thus Java's platform independence is violated.) People who port Java to new platforms implement extensive native code to support GUI components, network communication, and a broad range of other platform-specific functionality. However, it is rare for application and applet programmers to need to write native code.

One technique, however, is of interest in light of the last section's discussion of static code. When a native method is invoked, the library that contains the native code ought to be loaded and available to the Java Virtual Machine; if it is not loaded, there will be a delay. The library is loaded by calling `System.loadLibrary ("library_name")`, and to avoid a delay, it is desirable to make this call as early as possible. Often programmers will use the technique shown in the code sample below, which assumes the library name is `MyNativeLib`:

```
1. class NativeExample {
2.   native void doSomethingLocal(int i);
```

```
3.
4.    static {
5.       System.loadLibrary("MyNativeLib");
6.    }
7. }
```

Notice the native declaration on line 2, which declares that the code that implements doSomethingLocal() resides in a local library. Lines 4–6 are static initializer code, so they are executed at the time that class NativeEx-ample is loaded; this ensures that the library will be available by the time somebody needs it.

Callers of native methods do not have to know that the method is native. The call is made in exactly the same way as if it were non-native:

```
1. NativeExample natex;
2. natex = new NativeExample();
3. ne.doSomethingLocal(5);
```

Many common methods are native, including all the number-crunching methods of the Math class and the clone(), and notify() methods of the Object class.

## transient

The transient modifier applies only to variables. A transient variable is not stored as part of its object's persistent state.

Many objects (specifically, those that implement either the Serializable or Externalizable interfaces) can have their state serialized and written to some destination outside the Java Virtual Machine. This is done by passing the object to the writeObject() method of the ObjectOutputStream class. If the stream is chained to a File Output Stream, then the object's state is written to a file. If the stream is chained to a socket's Output Stream, then the object's state is written to the network. In both cases, the object can be recon-stituted by reading it from an Object Input Stream.

There will be times when an object will contain extemely sensitive infor-mation. Consider the following class:

```
1. class WealthyCustomer extends Customer implements _
      Serializable {
2.    private float $wealth;
```

```
3.    private String accessCode;
4. }
```

Once an object is written to a destination outside the JVM, none of Java's elaborate security mechanisms is in effect. If an instance of this class were to be written to a file or to the Internet, somebody could snoop the access code. Line 3 should be marked with the `transient` keyword:

```
1. class WealthyCustomer extends Customer implements _
      Serializable {
2.    private float $wealth;
3.    private transient String accessCode;
4. }
```

Now the value of `accessCode` will not be written out during serialization.

**NOTE** Transient variables may not be final or static.

## *synchronized*

The `synchronized` modifier is used to control access to critical code in multithreaded programs. Multithreading is an extensive topic in its own right and is covered in Chapter 7.

## *volatile*

The last modifier is `volatile`. It is mentioned here only to make our list complete, as it is not mentioned in the exam objectives and is not yet in common use. Only variables may be `volatile`; declaring them so indicates that such variables might be modified asynchronously, so the compiler takes special precautions. Volatile variables are of interest in multiprocessor environments.

# Modifiers and Features

Not all modifiers can be applied to all features. Top-level classes may not be protected. Methods may not be transient. Static is so general that you can apply it to free-floating blocks of code.

Table 3.1 shows all the possible combinations of features and modifiers. Note that classes here are strictly top-level (that is, not inner) classes. (Inner classes are covered in Chapter 6.)

| **T A B L E  3.1**  All Possible Combinations of Features and Modifiers | Modifier | Class | Variable | Method/Constructor | Free-Floating Block |
|---|---|---|---|---|---|
| | public | yes | yes | yes | no |
| | protected | no | yes | yes | no |
| | (friendly)* | yes | yes | yes | no |
| | private | no | yes | yes | no |
| | final | yes | yes | yes | no |
| | abstract | yes | yes | yes | no |
| | static | yes | yes | yes | yes |
| | native | no | no | yes | no |
| | transient | no | yes | no | no |
| | synchronized | no | no | yes | no |

*friendly is not a modifier; it is just the name of the default if no modifier is specified.

# Chapter Summary

**J**ava's access modifiers are

- public
- protected
- private

If a feature does not have an access modifier, its access defaults to "friendly."

Java's other modifiers are

- `final`
- `abstract`
- `static`
- `native`
- `transient`
- `synchronized`
- `volatile`

# Test Yourself

**1.** Which of the following declarations are illegal? (Choose one or more.)

   **A.** `friendly String s;`

   **B.** `transient int i = 41;`

   **C.** `public final static native int w();`

   **D.** `abstract double d;`

   **E.** `abstract final double hyperbolicCosine();`

**2.** Which one of the following statements is true?

   **A.** An abstract class may not have any final methods.

   **B.** A final class may not have any abstract methods.

**3.** What is the minimal modification that will make the code below compile correctly?

```
1. final class Aaa
2. {
3.     int xxx;
4.     void yyy() { xxx = 1; }
5. }
6.
```

```
7.
8. class Bbb extends Aaa
9. {
10.     final Aaa finalref = new Aaa();
11.
12.     final void yyy()
13.     {
14.         System.out.println("In method yyy()");
15.         finalref.xxx = 12345;
16.     }
17. }
```

**A.** On line 1, remove the `final` modifier.

**B.** On line 10, remove the `final` modifier.

**C.** Remove line 15.

**D.** On lines 1 and 10, remove the `final` modifier.

**E.** The code will compile as is. No modification is needed.

**4.** Which one of the following statements is true?

**A.** Transient methods may not be overridden.

**B.** Transient methods must be overridden.

**C.** Transient classes may not be serialized.

**D.** Transient variables must be static.

**E.** Transient variables are not serialized.

**5.** Which one statement is true about the application below?

```
1. class StaticStuff
2  {
3.     static int x = 10;
4.
5.     static { x += 5; }
6.
```

```
7.      public static void main(String args[])
8.      {
9.          System.out.println("x = " + x);
10.     }
11.
12.     static {x /= 5; }
13. }
```

**A.** Lines 5 and 12 will not compile, because the method names and return types are missing.

**B.** Line 12 will not compile, because you can only have one static initializer.

**C.** The code compiles, and execution produces the output x = 10.

**D.** The code compiles, and execution produces the output x = 15.

**E.** The code compiles, and execution produces the output x = 3.

**6.** Which one statement is true about the code below?

```
1. class HasStatic
2. {
3.     private static int x = 100;
4.
5.     public static void main(String args[])
6.     {
7.         HasStatic hs1 = new HasStatic();
8.         hs1.x++;
9.         HasStatic hs2 = new HasStatic();
10.        hs2.x++;
11.        hs1 = new HasStatic();
12.        hs1.x++;
13.        HasStatic.x++;
14.        System.out.println("x = " + x);
15.     }
16. }
```

**A.** Line 8 will not compile, because it is a static reference to a private variable.

**B.** Line 13 will not compile, because it is a static reference to a private variable.

**C.** The program compiles, and the output is x = 102.

**D.** The program compiles, and the output is x = 103.

**E.** The program compiles, and the output is x = 104.

**7.** Given the code below, and making no other changes, which access modifiers (`public`, `protected`, or `private`) can legally be placed before aMethod() on line 3? If line 3 is left as it is, which keywords can legally be placed before aMethod() on line 8?

```
1. class SuperDuper
2. {
3.     void aMethod() { }
4. }
5.
6. class Sub extends SuperDuper
7. {
8.     void aMethod() { }
9. }
```

**8.** Which modifier or modifiers should be used to denote a variable that should not be written out as part of its class' persistent state? (Choose the shortest possible answer.)

**A.** private

**B.** protected

**C.** private protected

**D.** transient

**E.** private transient

The next two questions concern the following class definition:

```
1. package abcde;
2.
3. public class Bird {
4.    protected static int referenceCount = 0;
5.    public Bird() { referenceCount++; }
6.    protected void fly() { /* Flap wings, etc. */ }
7.    static int getRefCount() { return referenceCount; }
8. }
```

**9.** Which one statement is true about class Bird above and class Parrot below?

```
1. package abcde;
2.
3. class Parrot extends abcde.Bird {
4.    public void fly() { /* Parrot specific flight code. */ }
5.    public int getRefCount() { return referenceCount; }
6. }
```

**A.** Compilation of Parrot.java fails at line 4, because method fly() is protected in the superclass and classes Bird and Parrot are in the same package.

**B.** Compilation of Parrot.java fails at line 4, because method fly() is protected in the superclass and public in the subclass and methods may not be overridden to be more public.

**C.** Compilation of Parrot.java fails at line 5, because method getRefCount() is static in the superclass and static methods may not be overridden to be non-static.

**D.** Compilation of Parrot.java succeeds, but a runtime exception is thrown if method fly() is ever called on an instance of class Parrot.

**E.** Compilation of Parrot.java succeeds, but a runtime exception is thrown if method getRefCount() is ever called on an instance of class Parrot.

**10.** Which one statement is true about class Bird above and class Nightingale below?

```
1. package singers;
2.
3. class Nightingale extends abcde.Bird {
4.   Nightingale() { referenceCount++; }
5.
6.   public static void main(String args[]) {
7.     System.out.print("BEFORE: " + referenceCount);
8.     Nightingale florence = new Nightingale();
9.     System.out.println("  AFTER: " + referenceCount);
10.     florence.fly();
11.   }
12. }
```

**A.** The program will compile and execute. The output will be

Before: 0  After: 2.

**B.** The program will compile and execute. The output will be

Before: 0  After: 1.

**C.** Compilation of Nightingale will fail at line 4, because static members cannot be overridden.

**D.** Compilation of Nightingale will fail at line 10, because method fly() is protected in the superclass.

**E.** Compilation of Nightingale will succeed, but an exception will be thrown at line 10, because method fly()is protected in the superclass.

# CHAPTER 4

Converting and Casting

**T**his chapter covers the following Java Certification Exam objective:

- Determine the effect upon objects and primitive values of passing variables into methods and performing assignments or other modifying operations in that method.

Every Java variable has a type. Primitive data types include `int`, `long`, `double`, and so on. Object reference data types may be classes (such as `Vector` or `Graphics`) or interfaces (such as `LayoutManager` or `Runnable`). There can also be arrays of primitives, objects, or arrays.

This chapter discusses the ways that a data value can change its type. Values can change type either explicitly or implicitly; that is, either they change at your request or at the system's initiative. Java places a lot of importance on type, and successful Java programming requires that you be aware of type changes.

# Explicit and Implicit Type Changes

**Y**ou can *explicitly* change the type of a value by *casting*. To cast an expression to a new type, just prefix the expression with the new type name in parentheses. For example, the following line of code retrieves an element from a vector, casts that element to type `Button`, and assigns the result to a variable called btn:

```
Button btn = (Button) (myVector.elementAt(5));
```

Of course, the fifth element of the vector must be capable of being treated as a Button. There are compile-time rules and runtime rules that must be observed. This chapter will familiarize you with those rules.

There are situations in which the system *implicitly* changes the type of an expression without your explicitly performing a cast. For example, suppose you have a variable called myColor that refers to an instance of Color, and you want to store myColor in a vector. You would probably do the following:

```
myVector.addElement(myColor);
```

There is more to this code than meets the eye. The addElement() method of class Vector is declared with a parameter of type Object, not of type Color. As the argument is passed to the method, it undergoes an implicit type change. Such automatic, non-explicit type changing is known as *conversion*. Conversion, like casting, is governed by a number of rules. Unlike the casting rules, all conversion rules are enforced at compile time.

The number of casting and conversion rules is rather large, due to the large number of cases to be considered. (For example, can you cast a char to a double? Can you convert an interface to a final class?) The good news is that most of the rules accord with common sense, and most of the combinations can be generalized into rules of thumb. By the end of this chapter, you will know when you can explicitly cast, and when the system will implicitly convert on your behalf.

# Primitives and Conversion

The two broad categories of Java data types are primitives and objects. *Primitive* data types are ints, floats, booleans, and so on. (There are eight primitive data types in all; see Chapter 1 for a complete explanation of Java's primitives.) *Object* data types (or more properly, *object reference* data types) are all the hundreds of classes and interfaces of the JDK, plus the infinitude of classes and interfaces to be invented by Java programmers.

Both primitive values and object references can be converted and cast, so there are four general cases to consider:

- Conversion of primitives
- Casting of primitives

- Conversion of object references

- Casting of object references

The simplest topic is implicit conversion of primitives (that is, `ints`, `longs`, `chars`, `booleans`, and so on). All conversion of primitive data types takes place at compile time; this is because all the information needed to determine whether or not the conversion is legal is available at compile time. (This is not the case for object data, as you will see later in this chapter.)

There are three contexts or situations in which conversion of a primitive might occur:

- Assignment

- Method call

- Arithmetic promotion

The following sections deal with each of these contexts in turn.

## Primitive Conversion: Assignment

*Assignment conversion* happens when you assign a value to a variable of a different type from the original value. For example:

```
1. int i;
2. double d;
3. i = 10;
4. d = i;     // Assign an int value to a double variable
```

Obviously, d cannot hold an integer value. At the moment that the fourth line of code is executed, the integer 10 that is stored in variable i gets converted to the double-precision value 10.0000000000000 (remaining zeros omitted for brevity).

The code above is perfectly legal. Some assignments, on the other hand, are illegal. For example, the following code will not compile:

```
1. double d;
2. short s;
3. d = 1.2345;
4. s = d;     // Assign a double value to a short variable
```

This code will not compile. (The error message says "Incompatible type for =.") The compiler recognizes that trying to cram a double value into a short variable is like trying to pour a quart of coffee into an eight-ounce teacup, as shown in Figure 4.1. It can be done (that is, the value assignment can be done; the coffee thing is impossible), but you have to use an explicit cast, which will be explained in the following section.

**FIGURE 4.1**

Illegal conversion of a quart to a cup, with loss of data

The general rules for primitive assignment conversion can be stated as follows:

- A boolean may not be converted to any other type.

- A non-boolean may be converted to another non-boolean type, provided the conversion is a *widening conversion.*

- A non-boolean may not be converted to another non-boolean type, if the conversion would be a *narrowing conversion.*

Widening conversions change a value to a type that accommodates a wider range of values than the original type can accommodate. In most cases, the new type has more bits than the original and can be visualized as being "wider" than the original, as shown in Figure 4.2.

**FIGURE 4.2**

Widening conversion

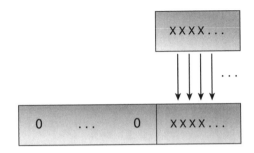

Widening conversions do not lose information about the magnitude of a value. In the first example in this section, an int value was assigned to a double variable. This was legal, because doubles are, so to speak, "wider" than ints, so there is room in a double to accommodate the information in an int. Java's widening conversions are

- From a byte to a short, an int, a long, a float, or a double

- From a short to an int, a long, a float, or a double

- From a char to an int, a long, a float, or a double

- From an int to a long, a float, or a double

- From a long to a float or a double

- From a float to a double

Figure 4.3 illustrates all the widening conversions. The arrows can be taken to mean "can be widened to." To determine whether it is legal to convert from one type to another, find the first type in the figure and see if you can reach the second type by following the arrows.

**FIGURE 4.3**

Widening conversions

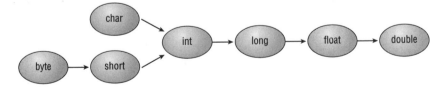

The figure shows, for example, that it is perfectly legal to assign a byte value to a float variable, because you can trace a path from byte to float by following the arrows (byte to short to int to long to float). You cannot, on the other hand, trace a path from long to short, so it is not legal to assign a long value to a short variable.

Figure 4.3 is easy to memorize. The figure consists mostly of the numeric data types in order of size. The only extra piece of information is char, but that goes in the only place it could go: a 16-bit char "fits inside" a 32-bit int. (Note that you can't convert a byte to a char or a char to a short, even though it seems reasonable to do so.)

Any conversion between primitive types that is not represented by a path of arrows in Figure 4.3 is a *narrowing conversion*. These conversions lose information about the magnitude of the value being converted, and are not allowed in assignments. It is geometrically impossible to portray the narrowing conversions in a graph like Figure 4.3, but they can be summarized as follows:

- From a byte to a char
- From a short to a byte or a char
- From a char to a byte or a short
- From an int to a byte, a short, or a char
- From a long to a byte, a short, a char, or an int
- From a float to a byte, a short, a char, an int, or a long
- From a double to a byte, a short, a char, an int, a long, or a float

You do not really need to memorize this list. It simply represents all the conversions not shown in Figure 4.3, which is easier to memorize.

## Primitive Conversion: Method Call

Another kind of conversion is *method-call conversion*. A method-call conversion happens when you pass a value of one type as an argument to a method that expects a different type. For example, the cos() method of the Math class expects a single argument of type double. Consider the following code:

```
1. float frads;
2. double d;
```

```
3. frads = 2.34567f;
4. d = Math.cos(frads);   // Pass float to method that _
   expects double
```

The float value in frads is automatically converted to a double value before it is handed to the cos() method. Just as with assignment conversions, there are strict rules that govern which conversions are allowed and which conversions will be rejected by the compiler. The code below quite reasonably generates a compiler error (assuming there is a vector called myVector):

```
1. double d = 12.0;
2. Object ob = myVector.elementAt(d);
```

The compiler error message says, "Incompatible type for method. Explicit cast needed to convert double to int." This means that the compiler can't convert the double argument to a type that is supported by a version of the elementAt() method. It turns out that the only version of elementAt() is the version that takes an integer argument. Thus a value may only be passed to elementAt() if that value is an int or can be converted to an int.

Fortunately, the rule that governs which method-call conversions are permitted is the same rule that governs assignment conversions. Widening conversions (as shown in Figure 4.3) are permitted; narrowing conversions are forbidden.

## Primitive Conversion: Arithmetic Promotion

The last kind of primitive conversion to consider is *arithmetic promotion*. Arithmetic-promotion conversions happen within arithmetic statements, while the compiler is trying to make sense out of many different possible kinds of operand.

Consider the following fragment:

```
1. short s = 9;
2. int i = 10;
3. float f = 11.1f;
4. double d = 12.2;
5. if (++s * i  >=  f / d)
6.    System.out.println(">>>>");
7. else
8.    System.out.println("<<<<");
```

The code on line 5 multiplies an incremented short by an int; then it divides a float by a double; finally it compares the two results. Behind the scenes, the system is doing extensive type conversion to ensure that the operands can be meaningfully incremented, multiplied, divided, and compared. These conversions are all widening conversions. Thus they are known as *arithmetic-promotion conversions*, because values are "promoted" to wider types.

The rules that govern arithmetic promotion distinguish between unary and binary operators. *Unary* operators operate on a single value. *Binary* operators operate on two values. Figure 4.4 shows Java's unary and binary arithmetic operators.

**FIGURE 4.4**

Unary and binary arithmetic operators

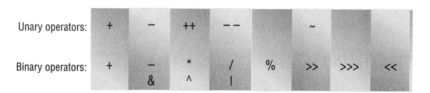

For unary operators, two rules apply, depending on the type of the single operand:

- If the operand is a byte, a short, or a char, it is converted to an int.

- Else if the operand is of any other type, it is not converted.

For binary operators, there are four rules, depending on the types of the two operands:

- If one of the operands is a double, the other operand is converted to a double.

- Else if one of the operands is a float, the other operand is converted to a float.

- Else if one of the operands is a long, the other operand is converted to a long.

- Else both operands are converted to ints.

With these rules in mind, it is possible to determine what really happens in the code example given at the beginning of this section:

1. The short s is promoted to an int and then incremented.

2. The result of step 1 (an int) is multiplied by the int i. Since both operands are of the same type, and that type is not narrower than an int, no conversion is necessary. The result of the multiplication is an int.

3. Before dividing float f by double d, f is widened to a double. The division generates a double-precision result.

4. The result of step 2 (an int) is to be compared to the result of step 3 (a double). The int is converted to a double, and the two operands are compared. The result of a comparison is always of type boolean.

# Primitives and Casting

So far this chapter has shown that Java is perfectly willing to perform widening conversions on primitives. These conversions are implicit and behind the scenes; you don't need to write any explicit code to make them happen.

*Casting* means explicitly telling Java to make a conversion. A casting operation may widen or narrow its argument. To cast, just precede a value with the parenthesized name of the desired type. For example, the following lines of code cast an int to a double:

```
1. int i = 5;
2. double d = (double)i;
```

Of course, the cast is not necessary. The following code, in which the cast has been omitted, would do an assignment conversion on i, with the same result as the example above:

```
1. int i = 5;
2. double d = i;
```

Casts are required when you want to perform a narrowing conversion. Such conversion will never be performed implicitly; you have to program an explicit cast to convince the compiler that what you really want is a narrowing conversion. Narrowing runs the risk of losing information; the cast tells the compiler that you accept the risk.

For example, the following code generates a compiler error:

```
1. short s = 259;
2. byte b = s;    // Compiler error
3. System.out.println("s = " + s + ", b = " + b);
```

The compiler error message for the second line will say (among other things), "Explicit cast needed to convert short to byte." Adding an explicit cast is easy:

```
1. short s = 259;
2. byte b = (byte)s;      // Explicit cast
3. System.out.println("b = " + b);
```

When this code is executed, the number 259 (binary 100000011) must be squeezed into a single byte. This is accomplished by preserving the low-order byte of the value and discarding the rest. The code prints out the (perhaps surprising) message:

```
b = 3
```

The 1 bit in bit position 8 gets discarded, leaving only 3, as shown in Figure 4.5. Narrowing conversions can result in radical value changes; this is why the compiler requires you to cast explicitly. The cast tells the compiler, "Yes, I really want to do it."

**FIGURE 4.5**

Casting a short to a byte

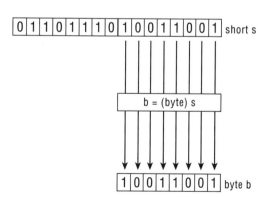

Casting a value to a wider value (as shown in Figure 4.3) is always permitted but never required; if you omit the cast, an implicit conversion will be performed on your behalf. However, explicitly casting can make your code a bit more readable. For example

```
 1. int i = 2;
 2. double radians;
    .       // Hundreds of
    .       // lines of
    .       // code
600. radians = (double)i;
```

The cast in the last line is not required, but it serves as a good reminder to any readers (including yourself) who might have forgotten the type of radians.

There are two simple rules that govern casting of primitive types:

- You can cast any non-boolean type to any other non-boolean type.

- You cannot cast a boolean to any other type; you cannot cast any other type to a boolean.

Note that while casting is ordinarily used when narrowing, it is perfectly legal to cast when widening. The cast is unnecessary, but provides a bit of clarity.

# Object Reference Conversion

**O**bject reference values, like primitive values, participate in assignment conversion, method-call conversion, and casting. (There is no arithmetic promotion of object references, since references cannot be arithmetic operands.) Object reference conversion is more complicated than primitive conversion, because there are more possible combinations of old and new types—and more combinations mean more rules.

Reference conversion, like primitive conversion, takes place at compile time, because the compiler has all the information it needs to determine whether the conversion is legal. Later you will see that this is not the case for object casting.

The following sections examine object reference assignment, method-call, and casting conversions.

# Object Reference Assignment Conversion

Object reference assignment conversion happens when you assign an object reference value to a variable of a different type. There are three general kinds of object reference type:

- A class type, such as `Button` or `FileWriter`
- An interface type, such as `Cloneable` or `LayoutManager`
- An array type, such as `int[][]` or `TextArea[]`

Generally speaking, assignment conversion of a reference looks like this:

```
1. OldType x = new OldType();
2. NewType y = x;    // reference assignment conversion
```

This is the general format of an assignment conversion from an `OldType` to a `NewType`. Unfortunately, `OldType` can be a class, an interface, or an array; `NewType` can also be a class, an interface, or an array. Thus there are nine (= 3×3) possible combinations to consider. Figure 4.6 shows the rules for all nine cases.

**FIGURE 4.6**

The rules for object reference assignment conversion

**Converting Oldtype to Newtype:**

| | Oldtype is a class | Oldtype is an interface | Oldtype is an array |
|---|---|---|---|
| Newtype is a class | Oldtype must be a subclass of Newtype | Newtype must be Object | Newtype must be Object |
| Newtype is an interface | Oldtype must implement interface Newtype | Oldtype must a subinterface of Newtype | Newtype must be Cloneable |
| Newtype is an array | Compiler error | Compiler error | Oldtype must be an array of some object reference type that can be converted to whatever Newtype is an array of |

It would be difficult to memorize the nine rules shown in Figure 4.6. Fortunately, there is a rule of thumb.

Recall that with primitives, conversions were permitted, provided they were widening conversions. The notion of widening does not really apply to references, but there is a similar principle at work. In general, object reference conversion is permitted when the direction of the conversion is "up" the inheritance hierarchy; that is, the old type should inherit from the new type. This rule of thumb does not cover all nine cases, but it is a helpful way to look at things.

The rules for object reference conversion can be stated as follows:

- An interface type may only be converted to an interface type or to Object. If the new type is an interface, it must be a superinterface of the old type.

- A class type may be converted to a class type or to an interface type. If converting to a class type, the new type must be a superclass of the old type. If converting to an interface type, the old class must implement the interface.

- An array may be converted to the class Object, to the interface Cloneable, or to an array. Only an array of object reference types may be converted to an array, and the old element type must be convertible to the new element type.

To illustrate these rules, consider the inheritance hierarchy shown in Figure 4.7 (assume there is an interface called Squeezable).

As a first example, consider the following code:

```
1. Tangelo tange = new Tangelo();
2. Citrus cit = tange;
```

This code is fine. A Tangelo is being converted to a Citrus. The new type is a superclass of the old type, so the conversion is allowed. Converting in the other direction ("down" the hierarchy tree) is not allowed:

```
1. Citrus cit = new Citrus();
2. Tangelo tange = cit;
```

This code will result in a compiler error.

What happens when one of the types is an interface?

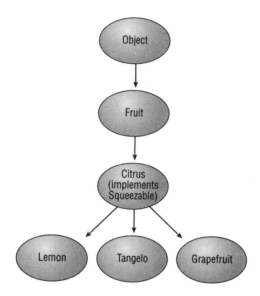

```
1. Grapefruit g = new Grapefruit();
2. Squeezable squee = g;   // No problem
3. Grapefruit g2 = squee;  // Error
```

The second line ("No problem") changes a class type (Grapefruit) to an interface type. This is correct, provided Grapefruit really implements Squeezable. A glance at Figure 4.7 shows that this is indeed the case, because Grapefruit inherits from Citrus, which implements Squeezable. The third line is an error, because an interface can never be implicitly converted to any reference type other than Object.

Finally, consider an example with arrays:

```
1. Fruit fruits[];
2. Lemon lemons[];
3. Citrus citruses[] = new Citrus[10];
4. for (int i=0; i<10; i++) {
5.   citruses[i] = new Citrus();
6. }
7. fruits = citruses;   // No problem
8. lemons = citruses;   // Error
```

Line 7 converts an array of Citrus to an array of Fruit. This is fine, because Fruit is a superclass of Citrus. Line 8 converts in the other direction and fails, because Lemon is not a superclass of Citrus.

# Object Method-Call Conversion

Fortunately, the rules for method-call conversion of object reference values are the same as the rules described above for assignment conversion of objects. The general rule of thumb is that converting to a superclass is permitted and converting to a subclass is not permitted. The specific, formal rules were given in a bulleted list in the previous section and are shown again here:

- An interface type may only be converted to an interface type or to Object. If the new type is an interface, it must be a superinterface of the old type.

- A class type may be converted to a class type or to an interface type. If converting to a class, the new type must be a superclass of the old type. If converting an interface type, the old class must implement the interface.

- An array may be converted to the class Object, to the interface Cloneable, or to an array. Only an array of object reference types may be converted to an array, and the old element type must be convertible to the new element type.

To see how the rules make sense in the context of method calls, consider the extremely useful Vector class. You can store anything you like in a Vector (anything non-primitive, that is) by calling the method addElement(Object ob). For example, the code below stores a Tangelo in a vector:

```
1. Vector myVec = new Vector();
2. Tangelo tange = new Tangelo();
3. myVec.addElement(myTange);
```

The myTange argument will automatically be converted to type Object. The automatic conversion means that the people who wrote the Vector class didn't have to write a separate method for every possible type of object that anyone might conceivably want to store in a vector. This is fortunate: The Tangelo class was developed two years after the invention of the Vector, so the developer of the Vector class could not possibly have written specific Tangelo-handling code. An object of any class (and even an array of any type) can be passed into the single addElement (Object ob) method.

# Object Reference Casting

**O**bject reference casting is like primitive casting: By using a cast, you convince the compiler to let you do a conversion that otherwise might not be allowed.

Any kind of conversion that is allowed for assignments or method calls is allowed for explicit casting. For example, the following code is legal:

```
1. Lemon lem = new Lemon();
2. Citrus cit = (Citrus)lem;
```

The cast is legal, but not needed; if you leave it out, the compiler will do an implicit assignment conversion. The power of casting appears when you explicitly cast to a type that is not allowed by the rules of implicit conversion.

To understand how object casting works, it is important to understand the difference between objects and object reference variables. Every object (well, nearly every object because there are some obscure cases) is constructed via the new operator. The argument to new determines for all time the true class of the object. For example, if an object is constructed by calling new Color(222, 0, 255), then throughout that object's lifetime its class will be Color.

Java programs do not deal directly with objects. They deal with refer-ences to objects. For example, consider the following code:

```
Color purple = new Color(222, 0, 255);
```

The variable purple is not an object; it is a reference to an object. The object itself lives in memory somewhere in the Java Virtual Machine. The variable purple contains something similar to the address of the object. This address is known as a reference to the object. The difference between a reference and an object is illustrated in Figure 4.8. References are stored in variables, and variables have types that are specified by the programmer at compile time. Object reference variable types can be classes (such as Graphics or FileWriter), interfaces (such as Runnable or LayoutManager), or arrays (such as int[][] or Vector[]).

While an object's class is unchanging, it may be referenced by variables of many different types. For example, consider a stack. It is constructed by calling new Stack(), so its class really is Stack. Yet at various moments during the lifetime of this object, it may be referenced by variables of type Stack (of course), or of type Vector (because Stack inherits from Vector), or

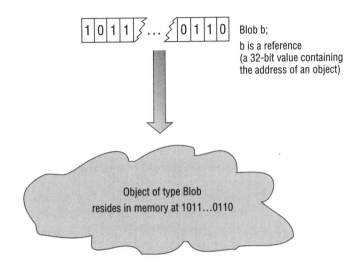

of type Object (because everything inherits from Object). It may even be referenced by variables of type Serializable, which is an interface, because the Stack class implements the Serializable interface. This situation is shown in Figure 4.9.

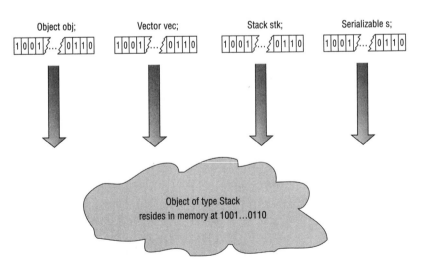

The type of a reference variable is obvious at compile time. However, the class of an object referenced by such a variable cannot be known until runtime. This lack of knowledge is not a shortcoming of Java technology; it results from a fundamental principle of computer science. The distinction between compile-time knowledge and runtime knowledge was not relevant to our discussion of conversions; however, the difference becomes important with reference value casting. The rules for casting are a bit broader than those for conversion. Some of these rules concern reference type and can be enforced by the compiler at compile time; other rules concern object class and can only be enforced during execution.

There is no escaping the fact that there are quite a few rules governing object casting. The good news is that most of the rules cover obscure cases. You might as well start by seeing the big picture in all its complicated glory, but after this glimpse you will be presented with a few simple ideas that will see you through most common situations.

For object reference casting, there are not three but *four* possibilities for both the old type and the new type. Each type can be a non-final class, a final class, an interface, or an array. The first round of rule enforcement happens at compile time. The compile-time rules are summarized in the imposing Figure 4.10.

**F I G U R E  4.10**

Compile-time rules for object reference casting

| | `Oldtype` is a non-final class | `Oldtype` is a final class | `Oldtype` is an interface | `Oldtype` is an array |
|---|---|---|---|---|
| `Newtype` is a non-final class | `Oldtype` must extend `Newtype`, or vice versa | `Oldtype` must extend `Newtype` | Always OK | `Oldtype` must be `Object` |
| `Newtype` is a final class | `Newtype` must extend `Oldtype` | `Oldtype` and `Newtype` must be the same class | `Newtype` must implement interface `Oldtype` | Compiler error |
| `Newtype` is an interface | Always OK | `Oldtype` must implement interface `Newtype` | Always OK | Compiler error |
| `Newtype` is an array | `Newtype` must be `Object` | Compiler error | Compiler error | `Oldtype` must be an array of some type that can be cast to whatever `Newtype` is an array of. |

`Newtype nt; Oldtype ot; nt = (newtype)ot;`

Assuming that a desired cast survives compilation, a second check must occur at runtime. The second check determines whether the class of the object being cast is compatible with the new type. Here *compatible* means that the class can be converted according to the conversion rules discussed in the previous two sections.

What a baffling collection of rules! For sanity's sake, bear in mind that only a few of the situations covered by these rules are commonly encountered in real life. (For instance, final classes are relatively rare.) A few rules of thumb and some examples should help to clarify things.

First, to simplify dealing with the compile-time rules, bear in mind the following facts about casting from Oldtype to Newtype:

- When both Oldtype and Newtype are classes, one class must be a subclass of the other.

- When both Oldtype and Newtype are arrays, both arrays must contain reference types (not primitives), and it must be legal to cast an element of Oldtype to an element of Newtype.

- You can always cast between an interface and a non-final object.

As for the runtime rule, remember that the conversion to Newtype must actually be possible. The following rules of thumb cover the most common cases:

- If Newtype is a class, the class of the expression being converted must be Newtype or must inherit from Newtype.

- If Newtype is an interface, the class of the expression being converted must implement Newtype.

It is definitely time for some examples! Look once again at the Fruit/Citrus hierarchy that you saw earlier in this chapter.

First, consider the following code:

```
1. Grapefruit g, g1;
2. Citrus c;
3. Tangelo t;
4. g = new Grapefruit();  // Class is Grapefruit
5. c = g;                 // Legal assignment conversion, _
                          //   no cast needed
6. g1 = (Grapefruit)c;    // Legal cast
7. t = (Tangelo)c;        // Illegal cast (throws an exception)
```

**F I G U R E   4.11**

Fruit hierarchy
(reprise)

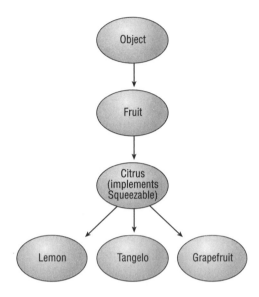

This code has four references but only one object. The object's class is Grapefruit, because it is Grapefruit's constructor that gets called on line 4. The assignment c = g on line 5 is a perfectly legal assignment conversion ("up" the inheritance hierarchy), so no explicit cast is required. In lines 6 and 7, the Citrus is cast to a Grapefruit and to a Tangelo. Recall that for casting between class types, one of the two classes (it doesn't matter which one) must be a subclass of the other. The first cast is from a Citrus to its subclass Grapefruit; the second cast is from a Citrus to its subclass Tangelo. Thus both casts are legal—at compile time. The compiler cannot determine the class of the object referenced by c, so it accepts both casts and lets fate determine the outcome at runtime.

When the code is executed, eventually the Java Virtual Machine attempts to execute line 6: g1 = (Grapefruit)c; The class of c is determined to be Grapefruit, and there is no objection to converting a Grapefruit to a Grapefruit.

Line 7 attempts (at runtime) to cast c to type Tangelo. The class of c is still Grapefruit, and a Grapefruit cannot be cast to a Tangelo. In order for the cast to be legal, the class of c would have to be Tangelo itself or some subclass of Tangelo. Since this is not the case, a runtime exception (java.lang.ClassCast-Exception) is thrown.

Now take an example where an object is cast to an interface type. Begin by considering the following code fragment:

```
1. Grapefruit g, g1;
2. Squeezable s;
3. g = new Grapefruit();
4. s = g;          // Convert Grapefruit to Squeezable (Ok)
5. g1 = s;         // Convert Squeezable to Grapefruit _
                      (Compile error)
```

This code will not compile. Line 5 attempts to convert an interface (Squeezable) to a class (Grapefruit). It doesn't matter that Grapefruit implements Squeezable. Implicitly converting an interface to a class is never allowed; it is one of those cases where you have to use an explicit cast to tell the compiler that you really know what you're doing. With the cast, line 5 becomes

```
5. g1 = (Grapefruit)s;
```

Adding the cast makes the compiler happy. At runtime, the Java Virtual Machine checks whether the class of s (which is Grapefruit) can be converted to Citrus. It can be, so the cast is allowed.

For a final example, involving arrays, look at the code below:

```
1. Grapefruit g[];
2. Squeezable s[];
3. Citrus c[];
4. g = new Grapefruit[500];
5. s = g;              // Convert Grapefruit array to _
                          Squeezable array (Ok)
6. c = (Citrus[])s;   // Cast Squeezable array to Citrus _
                          array (Ok)
```

Line 6 casts an array of Squeezables (s) to an array of Citruses (c). An array cast is legal if casting the array element types is legal (and if the element types are references, not primitives). In this example, the question is whether a Squeezable (the element type of array s) can be cast to a Citrus (the element type of the cast array). The previous example showed that this is a legal cast.

# Chapter Summary

**P**rimitive values and object references are very different kinds of data. Both can be converted (implicitly) or cast (explicitly). Primitive type changes are caused by

- Assignment conversion
- Method-call conversion
- Arithmetic-promotion conversion
- Explicit casting

Primitives may only be converted if the conversion widens the data. Primitives may be narrowed by casting, as long as neither the old nor the new type is boolean.

Object references may be converted or cast; the rules that govern these activities are extensive, as there are many combinations of cases to be covered. In general, going "up" the inheritance tree may be accomplished implicitly through conversion; going "down" the tree requires explicit casting. Object reference type changes are caused by

- Assignment conversion
- Method-call conversion
- Explicit casting

# Test Yourself

**1.** Which of the following statements is correct? (Choose one.)

   **A.** Only primitives are converted automatically; to change the type of an object reference, you have to do a cast.

   **B.** Only object references are converted automatically; to change the type of a primitive, you have to do a cast.

   **C.** Arithmetic promotion of object references requires explicit casting.

   **D.** Both primitives and object references can be both converted and cast.

   **E.** Casting of numeric types may require a runtime check.

**2.** Which one line in the following code will not compile?

```
1. byte b = 5;
2. char c = '5';
3. short s = 55;
4. int i = 555;
5. float f = 555.5f;
6. b = s;
7. i = c;
8. if (f > b)
9.    f = i;
```

**3.** Will the following code compile?

```
1. byte b = 2;
2. byte b1 = 3;
3. b = b * b1;
```

**4.** In the code below, what are the possible types for variable `result`? (Choose the most complete true answer.)

```
1. byte b = 11;
2. short s = 13;
3. result = b * ++s;
```

**A.** byte, short, int, long, float, double

**B.** boolean, byte, short, char, int, long, float, double

**C.** byte, short, char, int, long, float, double

**D.** byte, short, char

**E.** int, long, float, double

**5.** Consider the following class:

```
1.  class Cruncher {
2.     void crunch(int i)    {System.out.println("int _
       version");}
3.     void crunch(String s) {System.out.println("String _
       version");}
4.
5.     public static void main(String args[]) {
```

```
 6.        Cruncher crun = new Cruncher();
 7.        char ch = 'p';
 8.        crun.crunch(ch);
 9.        }
10.   }
```

Which of the statements below is true? (Choose one.)

**A.** Line 3 will not compile, because void methods cannot be overridden.

**B.** Line 8 will not compile, because there is no version of `crunch()` that takes a char argument.

**C.** The code will compile but will throw an exception at line 8.

**D.** The code will compile and produce the following output:

`int version`

**E.** The code will compile and produce the following output:

`String version`

**6.** Which of the statements below is true? (Choose one.)

**A.** Object references can be converted in assignments but not in method calls.

**B.** Object references can be converted in method calls but not in assignments.

**C.** Object references can be converted in both method calls and assignments, but the rules governing these conversions are very different.

**D.** Object references can be converted in both method calls and assignments, and the rules governing these conversions are identical.

**E.** Object references can never be converted.

**7.** Consider the following code:

```
1. Object ob = new Object();
2. String stringarr[] = new String[50];
3. Float floater = new Float(3.14f);
4.
5. ob = stringarr;
6. ob = stringarr[5];
7. floater = ob;
8. ob = floater;
```

Which line above will not compile?

Questions 8–10 refer to the class hierarchy shown in Figure 4.12.

**FIGURE 4.12**

Class hierarchy for
questions 8, 9, and 10

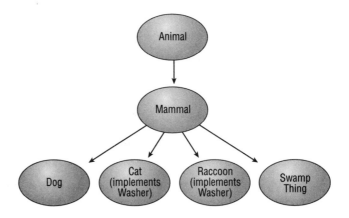

**8.** Consider the following code:

```
1. Dog      rover, fido;
2. Animal   anim;
3.
4. rover = new Dog();
5. anim = rover;
6. fido = (Dog)anim;
```

Which of the statements below is true? (Choose one.)

**A.** Line 5 will not compile.

**B.** Line 6 will not compile.

**C.** The code will compile but will throw an exception at line 6.

**D.** The code will compile and run.

**E.** The code will compile and run, but the cast in line 6 is not required and can be eliminated.

**9.** Consider the following code:

```
1. Cat sunflower;
2. Washer wawa;
3. SwampThing pogo;
4.
5. sunflower = new Cat();
6. wawa = sunflower;
7. pogo = (SwampThing)wawa;
```

Which of the statements below is true? (Choose one.)

**A.** Line 6 will not compile; an explicit cast is required to convert a Cat to a Washer.

**B.** Line 7 will not compile, because you cannot cast an interface to a class.

**C.** The code will compile and run, but the cast in line 7 is not required and can be eliminated.

**D.** The code will compile but will throw an exception at line 7, because runtime conversion from an interface to a class is not permitted.

**E.** The code will compile but will throw an exception at line 7, because the runtime class of wawa cannot be converted to type SwampThing.

**10.** Consider the following code:

```
1. Raccoon rocky;
2. SwampThing pogo;
3. Washer w;
4.
5. rocky = new Raccoon();
6. w = rocky;
7. pogo = w;
```

Which of the following statements is true? (Choose one.)

A. Line 6 will not compile; an explicit cast is required to convert a Raccoon to a Washer.

B. Line 7 will not compile; an explicit cast is required to convert a Washer to a SwampThing.

C. The code will compile and run.

D. The code will compile but will throw an exception at line 7, because runtime conversion from an interface to a class is not permitted.

E. The code will compile but will throw an exception at line 7, because the runtime class of w cannot be converted to type SwampThing.

# C H A P T E R

# 5

## Flow Control and Exceptions

This chapter covers aspects of the following Java Certification Exam objectives:

- Write code using if and switch statements and identify legal argument types for these statements.

- Write code using all forms of loops including labeled and unlabeled use of break and continue and state the values taken by loop control variables during and after loop execution.

- Write code that makes proper use of exceptions and exception handling clauses (try, catch, finally) and declares methods and overriding methods that throw exceptions.

Flow control is a fundamental facility of almost any programming language. Sequence, iteration, and selection are the major elements of flow control, and Java provides these in forms that are familiar to C and C++ programmers. Additionally, Java provides for exception handling.

Sequence control is provided simply by the specification that within a single block of code, execution starts at the top and proceeds toward the bottom. Iteration is catered for by three styles of loop: These are the for(), while(), and do constructions. Selection occurs when either the if()/else() or switch() construct is used.

Java omits one common element of flow control. This is this idea of a goto statement. When Java was being designed, the team responsible did some analysis of a large body of existing code and determined that there were two situations where the use of goto was appropriate in new code. These occasions were breaking out of nested loops and handling of exception conditions or errors. So, the designers left out goto and, in its place, provided alternative constructions to handle these particular conditions. The break and continue statements that control the execution of loops were extended to handle nested loops, and formalized exception handling was introduced, using ideas similar to those of C++.

This chapter discusses the flow-control facilities of Java. We will look closely at the exception mechanism, since this is an area that commonly causes some confusion. But first, we will discuss the loop mechanisms.

# The Loop Constructs

**J**ava provides three loop constructions. Taken from C and C++, these are the while(), do, and for() constructs. Each provides the facility for repeating the execution of a block of code until some condition occurs. We will discuss the while() loop, which is perhaps the simplest, first.

## The *while()* Loop

The general form of the while() loop is

```
1. while (boolean_condition)
2.    repeated_statement
```

In such a construct, the element boolean_condition can be any expression that returns a boolean result. Notice that this differs from C and C++, where a variety of types may be used: In Java you can *only* use a boolean expression. Typically, you might use a comparison of some kind, such as x > 5.

The repeated_statement will be executed again and again until the boolean _condition becomes false. If the condition never becomes false, then the loop will repeat forever. In practice, this really means that the loop will repeat until the program is stopped or the machine is turned off.

You will often need a loop that executes not just a single statement as its body, but a sequence of statements. In fact a block, surrounded by braces, is treated as a single statement, so you will commonly see a while() loop of this form:

```
1. while (boolean_condition) {
2.    do_something..
3.    do_some_more..
4. }
```

Notice the pairing of the curly braces ( { and } ). These make the statements within them appear to be a single statement from the loop's point of view.

The exact position of the opening curly brace that marks a block of code is a matter of near-religious contention. Some programmers put it at the end of a line, as in the examples in this book. Others put it on a line by itself. Provided it is otherwise placed in the correct sequence, it does not matter how many space, tab, and newline characters are placed before or after the opening curly brace. In other words, this positioning is not relevant to syntactic correctness. You should be aware, however, that the style used in presenting the exam questions, as well as that used for the code in the developer-level exam, is the style shown here, where the opening brace is placed at the end of the line.

A second point of style relates to the redundant use of braces. If only one statement is subordinate to a while() condition or other construction, then you can omit the braces. However, it is often a good idea to use these braces anyway, because doing so can avoid the introduction of bugs if you subsequently add statements intended to be subordinate to the loop.

Observe that if the boolean_condition is already false when the loop is first encountered, then the body of the loop will never be executed. This relates to the main distinguishing feature of the do loop, which we will discuss next.

## The *do* Loop

The general form of the do loop is

```
1. do
2.    repeated_statement
3. while (boolean_condition);
```

This is similar to the `while()` loop just discussed, and as before, it is common to have a loop body consisting of multiple statements. Under such conditions, you can use a block:

```
1. do {
2.    do_something
3.    do_more
4. } while (boolean_condition);
```

Again, repetition of the loop is terminated when the `boolean_condition` becomes `false`. The significant difference is that this loop always executes the body of the loop at least once, since the test is performed at the end of the body.

In general, the `do` loop is probably less frequently used than the `while()` loop, but the third loop format is perhaps the most common. The third form is the `for()` loop, which we will discuss next.

## The *for()* Loop

A common requirement in programming is to perform a loop so that a single variable is incremented over a range of values between two limits. This is frequently provided for by a loop that uses the keyword `for`. Java's `while()` loop can achieve this effect, but it is most commonly achieved using the `for()` loop. However, as with C and C++, the `for()` loop is more general than simply providing for iteration over a sequence of values.

The general form of the `for()` loop is

```
1. for (init_statement ; boolean_condition ; iter_expression)
2.    loop_body
```

Again, a block can be used like this:

```
1. for (init_statement ; boolean_condition ; iter_expression) {
2.    do_something
3.    do_more
4. }
```

The keys to this loop are in the three parts contained in the brackets following the for keyword:

- The init_statement is executed immediately before the loop itself is started. It is often used to set up starting conditions. You will see shortly that it can also contain variable declarations.

- The boolean_condition is treated exactly the same as in the while() loop. The body of the loop will be executed repeatedly until the condition ceases to be true. As with the while() loop, it is possible that the body of a for() loop might never be executed. This occurs if the condition is already false at the start of the loop.

- The iter_expression (short for "iteration expression") is executed immediately after the body of the loop, just before the test is performed again. Commonly, this is used to increment a loop counter.

If you have already declared an int variable x, you can code a simple sequence counting loop like this:

```
1. for (x = 0; x < 10; x++) {
2.    System.out.println("value is " + x);
3. }
```

This would result in 10 lines of output starting with

```
value is 0
```

and ending with

```
value is 9
```

In fact, because for() loops commonly need a counting variable, you are allowed to declare variables in the init_statement part. The scope of such a variable is restricted to the statement or block following the for() statement and the for() part itself. This protects loop counter variables from interfering with each other and prevents leftover loop count values from accidental re-use. This results in code like this:

```
1. for (int x = 0; x < 10; x++) {
2.    System.out.println("value is " + x);
3. }
```

It might be useful to look at the equivalent of this code implemented using a `while()` loop:

```
1. {
2.   int x = 0;
3.   while (x < 10) {
4.     System.out.println("value is " + x);
5.     x++;
6.   }
7. }
```

This version reinforces a couple of points. First, the scope of the variable x, declared in the init_statement part of the for() loop, is restricted to the loop and its control parts (that is, the init_statement, boolean_condition, and iter _expression). Second, the iter_expression is executed after the rest of the loop body, effectively before control comes back to the test condition.

## The *for()* Loop and the Comma Separator

The for() loop allows the use of the comma separator in a special way. The init_statement and iter_expression parts described previously can actually contain a sequence of expressions rather than just a single one. If you want such a sequence, you should separate those expressions, not with a semicolon (which would be mistaken as the separator between the three parts of the for() loop control structure) but with a comma. This behavior is borrowed from C and C++ where the comma is an operator, but in Java the comma serves only as a special case separator for conditions where the semicolon would be unsuitable. This example demonstrates:

```
1. int i, j;
2. for (j = 3, k = 6; j + k < 20; j++, k +=2) {
3.   System.out.println("j is " + j + " k is " + k);
4. }
```

Note that while you can use the comma to separate several expressions, you cannot mix expressions with variable declarations. So this would be illegal:

```
1. int i;
2. for (i = 7, int j = 0; i < 10; j++) { } // illegal !
```

We have now discussed the three loop constructions in their basic forms. The next section looks at more advanced flow control in loops, specifically the use of the break and continue statements.

# The *break* and *continue* Statements in Loops

Sometimes you need to abandon execution of the body of a loop—or perhaps a number of nested loops. The Java development team recognized this situation as a legitimate use for a goto statement. Java provides two statements, break and continue, which can be used instead of goto to achieve this effect.

## Using *continue*

Suppose you have a loop that is processing an array of items that contain two String references. The first String is always non-null, but the second might not be present. To process this, you might decide that you want, in pseudocode, something along these lines:

```
for each element of the array
  process the first String
  if the second String exists
    process the second String
  endif
endfor
```

You will recognize that this can be coded easily by using an if block to control processing of the second String. However, you can also use the continue statement like this:

```
1. for (int i = 0; i < array.length; i++) {
2.   // Process first string
3.   if (array[i].secondString == null) {
4.     continue;
5.   }
6.   // process second string
7. }
```

In this case, the example is sufficiently simple that you probably do not see any advantage over using the if() condition to control the execution of the second part. If the second String processing was long, and perhaps heavily indented in its own right, you might find that the use of `continue` was slightly simpler visually.

The real strength of `continue` is that it is able to skip out of multiple levels of loop. Suppose our example, instead of being two `String` objects, had two arrays of char values. Now we will need to nest our loops. Consider this sample:

```
1. mainLoop: for (int i = 0; i < array.length; i++) {
2.    // Process first array
3.    for (int j = 0; j < array[i].secondArray.length; j++) {
4.       if (array[i].secondArray[j] == '\u0000') {
5.          continue mainLoop;
6.       }
7.    }
8. }
```

Notice particularly the label `mainLoop` that has been applied to the `for()` on line 1. The fact that this is a label is indicated by the trailing colon. You can apply labels of this form to the opening loop statements: `do`, `while()`, or `for()`.

Here, when the processing of the second array comes across a zero value, it abandons the whole processing not just for the second array, but for the current object in the main array. This is equivalent to jumping to the statement `i++` in the first `for()` statement.

You might still think that this is not really any advantage over using `if()` statements, but imagine that further processing was done between lines 6 and 7 and that finding the zero character in the array was required to avoid that further processing, too. To achieve that without using `continue`, you would have to set a flag in the inner loop and use that to abandon the outer loop processing. It can be done, but it is rather messy.

## Using *break*

The `break` statement, when applied to a loop, is somewhat similar to the `continue` statement. However, instead of prematurely completing the current iteration of a loop, `break` causes the entire loop to be abandoned. Consider this example:

```
1. for (int j = 0; j < array.length; j++) {
2.    if (array[j] == null) {
3.       break; //break out of inner loop
```

```
4.  }
5.  // process array[j]
6. }
```

In this case, instead of simply skipping some processing for array[j] and proceeding directly to processing array[j+1], this version quits the entire inner loop as soon as a null element is found.

You can also use labels on break statements, and as before, you must place a matching label on one of the three loop statements of an enclosing loop. The break and continue statements provide a convenient way to make parts of a loop conditional, especially when used in their labeled formats.

In fact, labels may be applied to any statements, but they are only useful, and the exam objectives only require you to understand their use, in the context of break and continue in loop constructions.

The next section discusses the if()/else and switch() constructions, which provide the normal means of implementing conditional code.

# The Selection Statements

**J**ava provides a choice of two selection constructs. These are the if()/else and switch() mechanisms. You can easily write simple conditional code or a choice of two execution paths based on the value of a boolean expression using if()/else. If you need more complex choices between multiple execution paths, and if an appropriate argument is available to control the choice, then you can use switch(); otherwise you can use either nests or sequences of if()/else.

## The *if()/else* Construct

The if()/else construct takes a boolean argument as the basis of its choice. Often you will use a comparison expression to provide this argument, for example:

```
1. if (x > 5)
2.   System.out.println("x is more than 5");
```

This sample executes line 2 provided the test (x > 5) in line 1 returns true. Often you will require more than one line of code to be conditional upon the result of the test, and you can achieve this using a block, just as with the loops discussed earlier.

Additionally, you can use an else part to give code that is executed under the conditions that the test returns false. For example

```
1. if (x > 5) {
2.    System.out.println("x is more than 5");
3. }
4. else {
5.    System.out.println("x is not more than 5");
6. }
```

Beyond this, you can use if()/else in a nested fashion, refining conditions to more specific, or narrower, tests at each point.

The if()/else construction makes a test between only two possible paths of execution, although you can create nests or sequences to select between a greater range of possibilities. The next section discusses the switch() construction, which allows a single value to select between multiple possible execution paths.

## The *switch()* Construct

If you need to make a choice between multiple alternative execution paths, and the choice can be based upon an int value, you can use the switch() construct. Consider this example:

```
1. switch (x) {
2.    case 1:
3.      System.out.println("Got a 1");
4.      break;
5.    case 2:
6.    case 3:
7.      System.out.println("Got 2 or 3");
8.      break;
9.    default:
10.     System.out.println("Got something other then 1, 2, or 3");
11.     break;
12. }
```

Note that, although you cannot determine the fact by inspection of this code, the variable x must be either byte, short, char, or int. It must not be long, either of the floating point types, boolean, or an object reference.

The comparison of values following case labels with the value of the expression supplied as an argument to switch() determines the execution path. The arguments to case labels must be constants, or at least a constant expression that can be fully evaluated at compile time. You cannot use a variable or expression involving variables.

Each case label takes only a single argument, but when execution jumps to one of these labels, it continues downward until it reaches a break statement. This occurs even if it passes another case label or the default label. So in the example shown above, if x has the value 2, execution goes through lines 1, 5, 6, 7, 8, and continues beyond line 12. This requirement for break to indicate the completion of the case part is important. More often than not, you do not want to omit the break, as you do not want execution to "fall through." However, to achieve the effect shown in the example, where more than one particular value of x causes execution of the same block of code, you use multiple case labels with only a single break.

The default statement is comparable to the else part of an if()/else construction. Execution jumps to the default statement if none of the explicit case values matches the argument provided to switch(). Although the default statement is shown at the end of the switch() block in the example (and this is both a conventional and reasonably logical place to put it), there is no rule that requires this placement.

Now that we have examined the constructions that provide for iteration and selection under normal program control, we will look at the flow of control under exception conditions—that is, conditions when some runtime problem has arisen.

# Exceptions

Sometimes when a program is executing, something occurs that is not quite normal from the point of view of the goal at hand. For example, a user might enter an invalid filename, or a file might contain corrupted data, a network link can fail, or there could be a bug in the program that causes it to try to make an illegal memory access, such as referring to an element beyond the end of an array.

Circumstances of this type are called exception conditions in Java. If you take no steps to deal with an exception, execution jumps to the end of the current method. The exception then appears in the caller of that method, and execution jumps to the end of the calling method. This continues until execution reaches the "top" of the affected thread, at which point the thread dies.

The process of an exception "appearing" either from the immediate cause of the trouble, or because a method call is abandoned and passes the exception up to its caller, is called throwing an exception in Java. You will hear other terms used, particularly an exception being raised.

Exceptions are actually objects, and a subtree of the class hierarchy is dedicated to describing them. All exceptions are subclasses of a class called java.lang.Throwable.

# Flow of Control in Exception Conditions

## Using *try{} catch() {}*

To intercept, and thereby control, an exception, you use a try/catch/finally construction. You place lines of code that are part of the normal processing sequence in a try block. You then put code to deal with an exception that might arise during execution of the try block in a catch block. If there are multiple exception classes that might arise in the try block, then several catch blocks are allowed to handle them. Code that must be executed no matter what happens can be placed in a finally block. Let's take a moment to consider an example:

```
1. int x = (int)(Math.random() * 5);
2. int y = (int)(Math.random() * 10);
3. int [] z = new int[5];
4. try {
5.   System.out.println("y/x gives " + (y/x));
6.   System.out.println("y is " + y + " z[y] is " + z[y]);
7. }
8. catch (ArithmeticException e) {
9.   System.out.println("Arithmetic problem " + e);
10. }
11. catch (ArrayIndexOutOfBoundsException e) {
12.   System.out.println("Subscript problem " + e);
13. }
```

In this example, there is a possibility of an exception at line 5 and at line 6. Line 5 has the potential to cause a division by 0, which in integer arithmetic results in an `ArithmeticException` being thrown. Line 6 will sometimes throw an `ArrayIndexOutOfBoundsException`.

If the value of x happens to be 0, then line 5 will result in the construction of an instance of the `ArithmeticException` class that is then thrown. Execution continues at line 8, where the variable e takes on the reference to the newly created exception. At line 9, the message printed includes a description of the problem, which comes directly from the exception itself. A similar flow occurs if line 5 executes without a problem but the value of y is 5 or greater, causing an out-of-range subscript in line 6. In that case, execution jumps directly to line 11.

In either of these cases, where an exception is thrown in a `try` block and is caught by a matching `catch` block, the exception is considered to have been handled: Execution continues after the last `catch` block as if nothing had happened. If, however, there is no `catch` block that names either the class of exception that has been thrown or a class of exception that is a parent class of the one that has been thrown, then the exception is considered to be unhandled. In such conditions, execution generally leaves the method directly, just as if no `try` had been used.

Table 5.1 summarizes the flow of execution that occurs in the exception handling scenarios discussed up to this point. You should not rely on this table for exam preparation, because it is only describes the story so far. You will find a more complete study reference in the summary at the end of this chapter.

| **T A B L E   5.1** | **Exception** | **Try {}** | **Matching Catch() {}** | **Behavior** |
|---|---|---|---|---|
| Outline of Flow in Simple Exception Conditions | No | | | Normal Flow |
| | Yes | No | | Method terminates |
| | Yes | Yes | No | Method terminates |
| | Yes | Yes | Yes | Terminate try {} block. Execute body of matching catch block. Continue normal flow after catch blocks |

## Using *finally*

The generalized exception handling code has one more part to it than you saw in the last example. This is the `finally` block. If you put a `finally` block after a `try` and its associated `catch` blocks, then the code in that `finally` block will definitely be executed whatever the circumstances—well, nearly definitely. If an exception arises with a matching `catch` block, then the `finally` block is executed after the `catch` block. If no exception arises, the `finally` block is executed after the `try` block. If an exception arises for which there is no appropriate `catch` block, then the `finally` block is executed after the `try` block.

The circumstances that can prevent execution of the code in a `finally` block are

- The death of the thread

- The use of `System.exit()`

- Turning off the power to the CPU

- An exception arising in the `finally` block itself

Notice that an exception in the `finally` block behaves exactly like any other exception; it can be handled via a `try/catch`. If no `catch` is found, then control jumps out of the method from the point at which the exception is raised, perhaps leaving the `finally` block incompletely executed.

## Catching Multiple Exceptions

When you define a `catch` block, that block will catch exceptions of the class specified, including any exceptions that are subclasses of the one specified. In this way, you can handle categories of exceptions in a single `catch` block. If you specify one exception class in one particular `catch` block and a parent class of that exception in another `catch` block, you can handle the more specific exceptions—those of the subclass—separately from others of the same general parent class. Under such conditions these rules apply:

- A more specific `catch` block must precede a more general one in the source. Failure to meet this ordering requirement causes a compiler error.

- Only one `catch` block, that is the first applicable one, will be executed.

Now let's look at the overall framework for try, multiple catch blocks, and finally:

```
 1. try {
 2.   // statements....
 3.   // some are safe, some might throw an exception
 4. }
 5. catch (SpecificException e) {
 6.   // do something, perhaps try to recover
 7. }
 8. catch (OtherException e) {
 9.   // handling for OtherException
10. }
11. catch (GeneralException e) {
12.   // handling for GeneralException
13. }
14. finally {
15.   // code that must be executed under
16.   // successful or unsuccessful conditions.
17. }
18. // more lines of method code....
```

In this example, GeneralException is a parent class of Specific-Exception. Several scenarios can arise under these conditions:

- No exceptions occur.

- A SpecificException occurs.

- A GeneralException occurs.

- An entirely different exception occurs, which we will call an UnknownException.

If no exceptions occur, execution completes the try block, lines 1, 2, 3, and 4 and then proceeds to the finally block, lines 14, 15, 16, and 17. The rest of the method, line 18 onward, is then executed.

If a SpecificException occurs, execution abandons the try block at the point the exception is raised and jumps into the SpecificException catch block. Typically, this might result in lines 1 and 2, then 5, 6, and 7 being executed. After the catch block, the finally block and the rest of the method are executed, lines 14–17 and line 18 onward.

If a GeneralException that is not a SpecificException occurs, then execution proceeds out of the try block, into the GeneralException catch block at lines 11, 12, and 13. After that catch block, execution proceeds to the finally block and the rest of the method, just as in the last example.

If an UnknownException occurs, execution proceeds out of the try block directly to the finally block. After the finally block is completed, the rest of the method is abandoned. This is an uncaught exception; it will appear in the caller just as if there had never been any try block in the first place.

Now that we have discussed what happens when an exception is thrown, let's proceed to how exceptions are thrown and the rules that relate to methods that might throw exceptions.

# Throwing Exceptions

The last section discussed how exceptions modify the flow of execution in a Java program. We will now continue by examining how exceptions are issued in the first place, and how you can write methods that use exceptions to report difficulties.

## The *throw* Statement

Throwing an exception, in its most basic form, is simple. You need to do two things. First, you create an instance of an object that is a subclass of java.lang.Throwable. Next you use the throw keyword to actually throw the exception. These two are normally combined into a single statement like this:

```
throw new IOException("File not found");
```

There is an important reason why the throw statement and the construction of the exception are normally combined. The exception builds information about the point at which it was created, and that information is shown in the stack trace when the exception is reported. It is convenient if the line reported as the origin of the exception is the same line as the throw statement, so it is a good idea to combine the two parts, and throw new xxx() becomes the norm.

## The *throws* Statement

You have just seen how easy it is to generate and throw an exception; however, the overall picture is more complex. First, as a general rule, Java requires that any method that might throw an exception must declare the fact. In a way, this is a form of enforced documentation, but you will see that there is a little more to it than just that.

If you write a method that might throw an exception (and this includes unhandled exceptions that are generated by other methods called from your method), then you must declare the possibility using a throws statement. For example, the (incomplete) method shown here can throw a Malformed-URLException or an EOFException.

```
1. public void doSomeIO(String targetUrl)
2. throws MalformedURLException, EOFException {
3.    // the URL constructor can throw MalformedURLException
4.    URL url = new URL(targetUrl);
5.    // open the url and read from it...
6.    // set flag 'completed' when IO is completed satisfactorily
7.    //....
8.    // so if we get here with completed == false, we got
9.    // unexpected end of file.
10.   if (!completed) {
11.      throw new EOFException("Invalid file contents");
12.   }
13. }
```

Line 11 demonstrates the use of the throw statement—it is usual for a throw statement to be conditional in some way; otherwise the method has no way to complete successfully. Line 2 shows the use of the throws statement. In this case, there are two distinct exceptions listed that the method might throw under different failure conditions. The exceptions are given as a comma-separated list.

The section "Catching Multiple Exceptions," earlier in this chapter explained that the class hierarchy of exceptions is significant in catch blocks. The hierarchy is also significant in the throws statement. In this example, line 2 could be shortened to throws IOException. This is because both Malformed-URLException and EOFException are subclasses of IOException.

## Checked Exceptions

So far we have discussed throwing exceptions and declaring methods that might throw exceptions. We have said that any method that throws an exception should use the `throws` statement to declare the fact. The whole truth is slightly subtler than that.

The class hierarchy that exists under the class `java.lang.Throwable` is divided into three parts. One part contains the errors, which are `java.lang` `.Error` and all subclasses. Another part is called the runtime exceptions, which are `java.lang.RuntimeException` and all the subclasses of that. The third part contains the checked exceptions, which are all subclasses of `java.lang` `.Exception` (except for `java.lang.RuntimeException` and its subclasses). Figure 5.1 shows this diagrammatically.

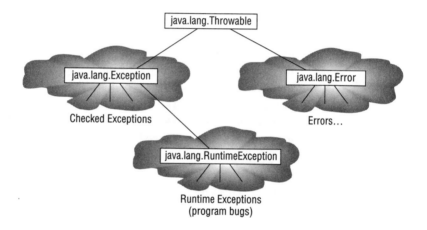

You might well ask why the hierarchy is divided up and what these various names mean.

The `checked exceptions` describe problems that can arise in a correct program, typically difficulties with the environment such as user mistakes or I/O problems. For example, attempting to open a socket to a machine that is not responding can fail if the remote machine does not exist or is not providing the requested service. Neither of these problems indicates a programming error; it's more likely to be a problem with the machine name (the user mistyped it) or with the remote machine (perhaps it is incorrectly configured). Because these conditions can arise at any time, in a commercial-grade program you must write code to handle and recover from them. In fact, the

Java compiler checks that you have indeed stated what is to be done when they arise, and it is because of this checking that they are called checked exceptions.

`Runtime exceptions` describe program bugs. You could use a runtime exception as deliberate flow control, but it would be an odd way to design code and rather poor style. Runtime exceptions generally arise from things like out-of-bounds array accesses, and normally these would be avoided by a correctly coded program. Because runtime exceptions should never arise in a correct program, you are not required to handle them. After all, it would only clutter your program if you had to write code that your design states should never be executed.

An approach to program design and implementation that is highly effective in producing robust and reliable code is known as programming by contract. Briefly, this approach requires clearly defined responsibilities for methods and the callers of those methods. For example, a square-root method could require that it must be called only with a non-negative argument. If called with a negative argument, the method would react by throwing an exception, since the contract between it and its caller has been broken. This approach simplifies code, since methods only attempt to handle properly formulated calls. It also brings bugs out into the open as quickly as possible, thereby insuring they get fixed. You should use runtime exceptions to implement this approach, as it is clearly inappropriate for the caller to have to check for programming errors; the programmer should fix them.

`Errors` generally describe problems that are sufficiently unusual, and sufficiently difficult to recover from, that you are not required to handle them. They might reflect a program bug, but more commonly they reflect environmental problems, such as running out of memory. As with runtime exceptions, Java does not require that you state how these are to be handled.

## Checking Checked Exceptions

We have stated that of the three categories of exceptions, the checked exceptions make certain demands of the programmer: You are obliged to state how the exception is to be handled. In fact you have two choices. You can put a `try` block around the code that might throw the exception and provide a corresponding `catch` block that will apply to the exception in question.

This handles the exception so it effectively goes away. Alternatively, you might decide that if this exception occurs, your method cannot proceed and should be abandoned. In this case, you do not need to provide the try/catch construction, but you must instead make sure that the method declaration includes a throws part that informs potential callers that the exception might arise. Notice that by insisting that the method be declared in this way, the responsibility for handling the exception is explicitly passed to the caller of the method, which must then make the same choice—whether to declare or handle the exception. The following example demonstrates this choice:

```
1. public class DeclareOrHandle {
2.    // this method makes no attempt to recover from the
3.    // exception, rather it declares that it might throw
4.    // it and uses no try block
5.    public void declare(String s) throws IOException {
6.      URL u = new URL(s); // might throw an IOException
7.      // do things with the URL object u...
8.    }
9.
10.    // this method handles the exception that might arise
11.    // when it calls the method declare(). Because of this,
12.    // it does not throw any exceptions and so does not use
13.    // any throws declaration
14.    public void handle(String s) {
15.      boolean success = false;
16.      while (!success) {
17.          try {
18.        declare(s);  // might throw an IOException
19.        success = true;  // execute this if declare() succeeded
20.      }
21.      catch (IOException e) {
22.        // Advise user that String s is somehow unusable
23.        // ask for a new one
24.      }
25.    } // end of while loop, exits when success is true.
26. }
```

Notice that the method declare() does not attempt to handle the exception that might arise during construction of the URL object. Instead, the declare() method states that it might throw the exception. By contrast, the handle() method uses a try/catch construction to insure that control remains inside the handle() method itself until it becomes possible to recover from the problem.

We have now discussed the handling of exceptions and the constructions that allow you to throw exceptions of your own. Before we have finished with exceptions, we must consider a rule relating to overriding methods and exceptions. The next section discusses this rule.

## Exceptions and Overriding

When you extend a class and override a method, Java insists that the new method cannot be declared as throwing checked exceptions of classes other than those that were declared by the original method. Consider these examples (assume they are declared in separate source files; the line numbers are simply for reference):

```
1. public class BaseClass {
2.   public void method() throws IOException {
3.   }
4. }
5.
6. public class LegalOne extends BaseClass {
7.   public void method() throws IOException {
8.   }
9. }
10.
11. public class LegalTwo extends BaseClass {
12.   public void method() {
13.   }
14. }
15.
16. public class LegalThree extends BaseClass {
17.   public void method()
18.     throws EOFException, MalformedURLException {
19.   }
```

```
20. }
21.
22. public class IllegalOne extends BaseClass {
23.   public void method()
24.   throws IOException, IllegalAccessException {
25.   }
26. }
27.
28.
29. public class IllegalTwo extends BaseClass {
30.   public void method()
31.   throws Exception {
32.   }
33. }
```

Notice that the original method() in BaseClass is declared as throwing IOException. This allows it, and any overriding method defined in a subclass, to throw an IOException or any object that is a subclass of IOException. Overriding methods may not, however, throw any checked exceptions that are not subclasses of IOException.

Given these rules, you will see that line 7 in LegalOne is correct, since method() is declared exactly the same way as the original that it overrides. Similarly, line 18 in LegalThree is correct, since both EOFException and MalformedURLException are subclasses of IOException–so this adheres to the rule that nothing may be thrown that is not a subclass of the exceptions already declared. Line 12 in LegalTwo is correct, since it throws no exceptions and therefore cannot throw any exceptions that are not subclasses of IOException.

The methods at lines 23 and 30 are not permissible, since both of them throw checked exceptions that are not subclasses of IOException. In IllegalOne, IllegalAccessException is a superclass of IOException; in IllegalTwo, Exception itself is a superclass of IOException. Both IllegalAccessException and Exception are checked exceptions, so the methods that attempt to throw them are illegal as overriding methods of method() in BaseClass.

The point of this rule relates to the use of base class variables as references to objects of subclass type. Chapter 4 explains that you can declare a variable of a class X and then use that variable to refer to any object that is of class X or any subclass of X.

Imagine that in the examples just described, you had declared a variable myBaseObject of class BaseClass; you can use it to refer to objects of any of the classes LegalOne, LegalTwo and LegalThree. (You couldn't use it to refer to objects of class IllegalOne or IllegalTwo, since those objects cannot be created in the first place: Their code won't compile.) The compiler imposes checks on how you call myBaseObject.method(). Those checks insure that for each call, you have either enclosed the call in a try block and provided a corresponding catch block or you have declared that the calling method itself might throw an IOException. Now suppose that at runtime the variable myBaseObject was used to refer to an object of class IllegalOne. Under these conditions, the compiler would still believe that the only exceptions that must be dealt with are of class IOException. This is because it believes that myBaseObject refers to an object of class BaseClass. The compiler would therefore not insist that you provide a try/catch construct that catches the IllegalAccessException, nor that you declare the calling method as throwing that exception. This means that if the class IllegalOne were permitted, then overriding methods would be able to bypass the enforced checks for checked exceptions.

Because an overriding method cannot throw more exceptions than were declared for the original method, it is important to consider the likely needs of subclasses whenever you define a class. For example, the InputStream class cannot, of itself, actually throw any exceptions, since it doesn't interact with real devices that could fail. However, it is used as the base class for a whole hierarchy of classes that do interact with physical devices: FileInputStream and so forth. It is important that the read() methods of those subclasses be able to throw exceptions, so the corresponding read() methods in the InputStream class itself must be declared as throwing IOException.

We have now looked at all the aspects of exception handling that you will need to prepare for the Certification Exam and to make effective use of exceptions in your programs. The next section summarizes all the key points of flow control and exceptions.

# Chapter Summary

## Loop Constructs

- Three loop constructs are provided: `while()`, `do`, and `for()`.

- Each loop statement is controlled by an expression that must be of `boolean` type.

- In both `while()` and `for()`, the test occurs at the "top" of the loop, so the body might not be executed at all.

- In `do`, the test occurs at the end of the loop so the body of the loop definitely executes at least once.

- The `for()` loop takes three elements in its brackets. The first is executed once only, before the loop starts. Typically you might use it for initializing the loop or for declaring a loop counter variable. The second is the loop control test. The third is executed at the end of the loop body, just prior to performing the test.

- The first element in the brackets of a `for()` construction can declare a variable. In that case, the scope of the variable is restricted to the control parts in the brackets, and the following statement. The following statement is often a block in its own right, in which case the variable remains in scope throughout that block.

- The `continue` statement causes the current iteration of the loop to be abandoned. Flow restarts at the bottom of the loop. For `while()` and `do`, this means the test is executed next. For the `for()` loop, the third statement in the brackets is executed, followed by the test.

- The `break` statement abandons the loop altogether; the test is not performed on the way out.

- Both `break` and `continue` can take a label that causes them to skip out of multiple levels of nested loop. The matching label must be placed at the head of a loop and is indicated by using an identifier followed by a colon (`:`).

## Selection Statements

- The `if()` statement takes a `boolean` argument.

- The `else` part is optional after `if()`.

- The `switch()` statement takes an argument that is assignment compatible to `int` (that is, one of `byte`, `short`, `char`, or `int`).

- The argument to `case` must be a constant or constant expression that can be calculated at compile time.

- The `case` label takes only a single argument. To create a list of values that lead to the same point, use multiple `case` statements and allow execution to "fall through."

- The `default` label may be used in a `switch()` construction to pick up execution where none of the explicit cases match.

## Flow in Exception Handling

- An exception causes a jump to the end of the enclosing `try` block even if the exception occurs within a method called from the `try` block, in which case the called method is abandoned.

- If any of the `catch` blocks associated with the `try` block just terminated specifies an exception class that is the same as, or a parent class of, the exception that was thrown, then execution proceeds to the first such `catch` block. The exception is now considered handled. If no appropriate `catch` block is found, the exception is considered unhandled.

- Regardless of whether or not an exception occurred, or whether or not it was handled, execution proceeds next to the `finally` block associated with the `try` block, if such a `finally` block exists.

- If there was no exception, or if the exception was handled, execution continues after the `finally` block.

- If the exception was unhandled, the process repeats, looking for the next enclosing `try` block. If the search for a `try` block reaches the top of the method call hierarchy (that is, the point at which the thread was created), then the thread is killed and a message and stack trace is dumped to `System.err`.

## Exception Throwing

- To throw an exception, use the construction `throw new XXXException();`.

- Any object that is of class `java.lang.Exception`, or any subclass of `java.lang.Exception` except subclasses of `java.lang.Runtime-Exception`, is a checked exception.

- In any method that contains lines that might throw a checked exception, you must either handle the exception using a `try/catch` construct, or declare that the method throws the exception using a `throws` construct in the declaration of the method.

- An overriding method may not throw a checked exception unless the overridden method also throws that exception or a superclass of that exception.

# Test Yourself

**1.** Consider the following code:

```
1. for (int i = 0; i < 2; i++) {
2.    for (int j = 0; j < 3; j++) {
3.       if (i == j) {
4.          continue;
5.       }
6.       System.out.println("i = " + i + " j = " + j);
7.    }
8. }
```

Which lines would be part of the output?

**A.** `i = 0 j = 0`

**B.** `i = 0 j = 1`

**C.** `i = 0 j = 2`

**D.** `i = 1 j = 0`

**E.** `i = 1 j = 1`

**F.** `i = 1 j = 2`

**2.** Consider the following code:

```
1. outer: for (int i = 0; i < 2; i++) {
2.    for (int j = 0; j < 3; j++) {
3.       if (i == j) {
4.          continue outer;
5.       }
6.       System.out.println("i = " + i + " j = " + j);
7.    }
8. }
```

Which lines would be part of the output?

**A.** i = 0 j = 0

**B.** i = 0 j = 1

**C.** i = 0 j = 2

**D.** i = 1 j = 0

**E.** i = 1 j = 1

**F.** i = 1 j = 2

**3.** Which of the following are legal loop constructions? (Choose one or more.)

**A.** while (int i < 7) { i++; System.out.println("i is " + i); }

**B.** int i = 3; while (i) { System.out.println("i is " + i); }

**C.**
```
1. int j = 0; for (int k = 0; j + k != 10; j++, k++) {
2.    System.out.println("j is " + j + " k is " + k);
3. }
```

**D.**
```
1. int j = 0;
2. do {
3.    System.out.println("j is " + j++);
4.    if (j == 3) { continue loop; }
5. } while (j < 10);
```

**4.** What would be the output from this code fragment?

```
 1. int x = 0, y = 4, z = 5;
 2. if (x > 2) {
 3.   if (y < 5) {
 4.     System.out.println("message one");
 5.   }
 6.   else {
 7.     System.out.println("message two");
 8.   }
 9. }
10. else if (z > 5) {
11.   System.out.println("message three");
12. }
13. else {
14.   System.out.println("message four");
15. }
```

**A.** message one

**B.** message two

**C.** message three

**D.** message four

**5.** Which statement is true about the following code fragment?

```
 1. int j = 2;
 2. switch (j) {
 3.   case 2:
 4.     System.out.println("value is two");
 5.   case 2 + 1:
 6.     System.out.println("value is three");
 7.     break;
 8.   default:
 9.     System.out.println("value is " + j);
10.     break;
11. }
```

    **A.** The code is illegal because of the expression at line 5.

    **B.** The acceptable types for the variable j, as the argument to the switch() construct, could be any of byte, short, int, or long.

    **C.** The output would be only the text value is two.

    **D.** The output would be the text value is two followed by the text value is three.

    **E.** The output would be the text value is two, followed by the text value is three, followed by the text value is 2.

**6.** Consider the following class hierarchy and code fragments:

```
java.lang.Exception
         \
    java.io.IOException
      /            \
java.io.StreamCorruptedException   java.net.MalformedURLException
```

```
1. try {
2.    URL u = new URL(s); // assume s is previously defined
3.    Object o = in.readObject(); // in is an ObjectInputStream
4.    System.out.println("Success");
5. }
6. catch (MalformedURLException e) {
7.    System.out.println("Bad URL");
8. }
9. catch (StreamCorruptedException e) {
10.    System.out.println("Bad file contents");
11. }
12. catch (Exception e) {
13.    System.out.println("General exception");
14. }
15. finally {
16.    System.out.println("doing finally part");
17. }
18. System.out.println("Carrying on");
```

What lines are output if the method at line 2 throws a
MalformedURLException?

**A.** Success

**B.** Bad URL

**C.** Bad file contents

**D.** General exception

**E.** doing finally part

**F.** Carrying on

**7.** Consider the following class hierarchy and code fragments:

```
                     java.lang.Exception
                             \
                      java.io.IOException
                      /               \
java.io.StreamCorruptedException    java.net.MalformedURLException
```

```
1. try {
2.    URL u = new URL(s); // assume s is previously defined
3.    Object o = in.readObject(); // in is an ObjectInputStream
4.    System.out.println("Success");
5. }
6. catch (MalformedURLException e) {
7.    System.out.println("Bad URL");
8. }
9. catch (StreamCorruptedException e) {
10.    System.out.println("Bad file contents");
11. }
12. catch (Exception e) {
13.    System.out.println("General exception");
14. }
15. finally {
16.    System.out.println("doing finally part");
17. }
18. System.out.println("Carrying on");
```

What lines are output if the methods at lines 2 and 3 complete successfully without throwing any exceptions?

**A.** Success

**B.** Bad URL

**C.** Bad file contents

**D.** General exception

**E.** doing finally part

**F.** Carrying on

8. Consider the following class hierarchy and code fragments:

```
                java.lang.Throwable
               /                    \
   java.lang.Error          java.lang.Exception
           /                          \
java.lang.OutOfMemoryError     java.io.IOException
                              /                \
   java.io.StreamCorruptedException   java.net.MalformedURLException
```

```
1. try {
2.   URL u = new URL(s); // assume s is previously defined
3.   Object o = in.readObject(); // in is an ObjectInputStream
4.   System.out.println("Success");
5. }
6. catch (MalformedURLException e) {
7.   System.out.println("Bad URL");
8. }
9. catch (StreamCorruptedException e) {
10.   System.out.println("Bad file contents");
11. }
12. catch (Exception e) {
13.   System.out.println("General exception");
14. }
15. finally {
16.   System.out.println("doing finally part");
17. }
18. System.out.println("Carrying on");
```

What lines are output if the method at line 3 throws an
OutOfMemoryError?

**A.** Success

**B.** Bad URL

**C.** Bad file contents

**D.** General exception

**E.** doing finally part

**F.** Carrying on

9. Which *one* of the following fragments shows the *most* appropriate
way to throw an exception? Assume that any undeclared variables
have been appropriately declared elsewhere and are in scope and have
meaningful values.

**A.** 1. Exception e = new IOException("File not found");

2. if (!f.exists()) { // f is a File object

3.    throw e;

4. }

**B.** 1. if (!f.exists()) { // f is a File object

2.   throw new IOException("File " + f.getName() + " not _
found");

3. }

**C.** 1. if (!f.exists()) {

2.    throw IOException;

3. }

**D.** 1. if (!f.exists()) {

2.    throw "File not found";

3. }

**E.** 1. if (!f.exists()) { // f is a File object

2.    throw new IOException();

3. }

**10.** Given that the method dodgy() might throw a java.io.IOException, java.lang.RuntimeException, or java.net.MalformedURLException (which is a subclass of java.io.IOException), which of the following classes and sets of classes are legal? (Choose one or more.)

**A.**

```
1. public class aClass {
2.   public void aMethod() {
3.     dodgy();
4.   }
5. }
```

**B.**

```
1. public class aClass {
2.   public void aMethod() throws java.io.Exception {
3.     dodgy();
4.   }
5. }
```

**C.**

```
1. public class aClass {
2.   public void aMethod() throws java.lang._
     RuntimeException {
3.     dodgy();
4.   }
5. }
```

**D.**

```
1. public class aClass {
2.   public void aMethod() {
3.     try {
4.       dodgy();
5.     }
6.     catch (IOException e) {
7.       e.printStackTrace();
8.     }
9.   }
10. }
```

**E.**  1. public class aClass {

    2.   public void aMethod() throws java.net._
        MalformedURLException {

    3.    try { dodgy(); }

    4.    catch (IOException e) { /* ignore it */ }

    5.   }

    6. }

    7.

    8. public class anotherClass extends aClass {

    9.   public void aMethod() throws java.io.IOException {

   10.    super.aMethod();

   11.   }

   12. }

# CHAPTER

# 6

Objects and Classes

**T**his chapter covers the following Java Certification Exam objectives:

- State the benefits of encapsulation in object-oriented design, and write code that implements tightly encapsulated classes and the relationships "is a" and "has a."

- State the legal return types for any method given the declarations of all related methods in this or parent classes.

- Write code to invoke overridden or overloaded methods and parental or overloaded constructors; and describe the effect of invoking these methods.

- Declare classes, inner classes, methods, instance variables, static variables, and automatic (method local) variables, making appropriate use of all permitted modifiers (such as public, final, static, abstract, and so forth). State the significance of each of these modifiers both singly and in combination, and state the effect of package relationships on declared items qualified by these modifiers.

- Write code to construct instances of any concrete class, including normal top level classes, inner classes, static inner classes, and anonymous inner classes.

- Identify correctly constructed source files, package declarations, import statements, class declarations (of all forms, including inner classes), interface declarations and implementations (for `java.lang.Runnable` or other interface described in the test), method declarations (including the main method that is used to start execution of a class), variable declarations, and identifiers.

This chapter discusses the object-oriented features of Java. Good coding in Java requires a sound understanding of the object-oriented (OO) paradigm, and this in turn requires a good grasp of the language features that implement objects and classes. The many benefits of object orientation have been the subject of considerable public debate, but for most programmers these benefits have not been realized. In most cases, the reason the promise has not been fulfilled is simply that programmers have not been writing objects. Instead, many C++ programmers have been writing a hybrid form of C with a mixture of procedural and object-oriented code. Unfortunately, such an approach has given rise, not to some of the benefits of OO, but instead to all the disadvantages of both styles.

# Benefits of Object-Oriented Implementation

**B**eginning with the 1.2 examination, you are required to understand the benefits of object-oriented design. These benefits accrue from two particular features of the object-oriented paradigm. The first of these, and perhaps the most important, is the notion of an abstract data type. The second, perhaps better known, of these is the extensibility provided by inheritance.

## Abstract data types

An abstract data type is really just a fancy name for a well-encapsulated aggregate of data and behavior. Consider the primitive data types of any programming language you have ever used. You do not know how these data items are stored and for the most part you do not care. What matters are the operations that you can perform on these data items and the boundary conditions within which you can expect those operations to work properly. These primitive types are in fact abstract data types, albeit not user defined.

Your first goal in defining a good class should be to clearly state the operations that can be applied to instances of that class. Next you consider how to represent the state of the instance, keeping in mind that this should be done only with variables of private accessibility. All behavior should be accessed only via methods. By insisting that the variables inside an object are not accessible outside the object, you ensure that the nature of those variables is irrelevant outside the object. This in turn means that you can change the nature of the storage, for maintenance purposes, for performance improvement, or for any other reason, freely.

Sometimes, perhaps as a consequence of the way you have stored the state in a class, there are boundary conditions that must be applied to its methods. A boundary condition is a limit on the range of arguments for which a method can operate properly. For example, a square root function cannot operate conventionally on a negative number, and an add operation cannot operate if both of its arguments are more than half the maximum representable range for its return type.

When you encounter a boundary condition that results from your choice of storage format, you must make a choice. If you consider that the boundary conditions are reasonable, then you should do two things. First, document the boundary condition. Next, test the boundary conditions at the entry to the method and, if the boundary condition has been exceeded, throw a runtime exception of some kind. Alternatively, you might decide that the boundary condition is not acceptable, in which case you should redesign the storage and used in the class.

Now, consider this: If you had allowed access to any of the variables used to represent the object state, then redefining the way the object's state is stored would immediately cause any other code that uses these variables to have to be rewritten. However, by using only private member variables we have insisted that all interaction with this object is made through methods and never by direct variable access—so we have eliminated this problem. In consequence, we are able to redesign our internal storage freely and, provided the signatures of all the methods remain the same, no other code needs to change.

Sometimes you will realize that the methods you have provided for a class are inadequate. This is not usually a problem, either. You may add new methods to provide additional functionality freely. No client code will break, provided the methods that were already provided remain available, with the same signatures and the same semantics. The only issues that might arise during maintenance are if you realize that a method you have defined has a fundamentally flawed prototype. This should not happen often, since it implies that the operation you defined for the class was conceptually flawed in some way.

### Encapsulation and Perceived Efficiency

Many programmers have such deep-seeded concerns about performance that they cannot bring themselves to force all access to will their objects to be made through methods, and they resist creating classes with entirely private member variables. There are several reasons why this is an unwise approach. First, fully encapsulated classes are more likely to be used correctly, especially if boundary conditions are properly flagged with exceptions— therefore, code using them is more likely to be correct. Second, bug fixes and maintenance changes are less likely to break the program as a whole, since the effects of the change are confined to the effected class. These reasons fall into the broad heading of "Would your customer prefer a slow program that works and is delivered on time (and that can be made faster later) or a program that is delivered late, works incorrectly, but runs quickly?"

There are more reasons why fully encapsulated classes are the right way to start out a design. An optimizing virtual machine such as Sun's Hotspot can transparently optimize simple variable access methods by "inlining." This approach allows the program all the robustness, reliability, and maintainability that results from full encapsulation, while giving the run-time performance associated with it, direct variable access. Furthermore, if you decide that a program's slow performance is attributable to the use of private variables and accessor/mutator methods, then changing the variable to be more accessible does not require any changes to the rest of the code, either inside or outside the class. On the other hand, if you have code that fails to run properly as a result of making direct variable access, you will find that reducing the accessibility of the relevant variable will require considerable collateral changes in many other pieces of code (all code that makes such direct access).

## Reuse

We have discussed how tight encapsulation can make code that is more reliable and robust. Now we will consider the second-most significant advantage of object-oriented programming. This is code reuse.

Writing good, encapsulated classes usually requires more work in the initial stages than would have been required to produce the same functionality with a traditional programming approach. While this is true, you will normally find that using rigorous object-oriented techniques will actually reduce the overall time required to produce finished code. This happens for two reasons. The first reason is that the robust classes you produce actually require less time to integrate into the final program and less time to fix bugs. The second reason is that with careful design you can reuse classes even in some circumstances that are different from the original intent of the class.

This reuse is actually possible in two ways, using either composition (the "has a" relationship) or inheritance (the "is a" relationship). Composition is probably safer and easier to control, although inheritance, because it is perceived as "pure OO," seems to be more interesting and appealing to most programmers.

The Java certification exam does not require you to discuss details of object-oriented design techniques or the relative merits and weaknesses of composition versus inheritance. However, you should appreciate one significant sequence of facts: If a class is well encapsulated, it will be easier to reuse successfully. The more a class is reused, the better tested it will be and the fewer bugs it will have. Better-tested, less buggy classes are easier to reuse. This sequence leads to a positive spiral of quality since the better the class, the easier and safer it becomes to reuse. All this comes from tight encapsulation.

Now that we've discussed why you would want to write object-oriented code, let's look at how this is achieved.

# Implementing Object-Oriented Relationships

This section is not intended to discuss object-oriented design; rather it considers the implementation of classes for which you have been given a basic description.

There are two clauses that are commonly used when describing a class in plain English. These are "is a" and "has a." As a working simplification, these are used to describe the superclass and member variables respectively. For example, consider this description:

"A home is a house which has a family and a pet."

This description would give rise to the outline of a Java class in this form:

```
1. public class Home extends House {
2.     Family inhabitants;
3.     Pet thePet;
4. }
```

Notice the direct correspondence between the "is a" clause and the extends clause. In this example, there is also a direct correspondence between the items listed after "has a" and the member variables. Such a correspondence is representative in simple examples and in a test situation; however, you should be aware that in real examples there are other ways that you can provide a class with attributes. Probably the most important of these alternatives is the approach taken by Java Beans, which is to supply accessor and mutator methods that operate on `private` data members.

# Overloading and Overriding

**A**s you construct classes and add methods to them, there are circumstances when you will want to re-use the same name for a method. There are two ways that you can do this with Java. Reusing the same method name with different arguments and perhaps a different return type is known as *overloading*. Using the same method name with identical arguments and return type is known as *overriding*.

A method name can be reused anywhere, as long as certain conditions are met:

- In an unrelated class, no special conditions apply and the two methods are not considered related in any way.

- In the class that defines the original method, or a subclass of that class, the method name can be reused if the argument list differs in terms of the type of at least one argument. This is overloading. It is important to realize that a difference in return type alone is not sufficient to constitute an overload, and is illegal.

- In a strict subclass of the class that defines the original method, the method name can be reused with identical argument types and order and with identical return type. This is overriding. In this case, additional restrictions apply to the accessibility of, and exceptions that may be thrown by, the method.

In general, a class is considered to be a subclass of itself. That is, if classes A, B, and C are defined so that C extends B, and B extends A, then the subclasses of A are A, B, and C. The term *strict subclass* is used to describe the subclasses excluding the class itself. So the strict subclasses of A are only B and C.

Now let's take a look at these ideas in detail. First, we will consider overloading method names.

## Overloading Method Names

In Java, a method is uniquely identified by the combination of its fully qualified class name, method name, and the exact sequence of its argument types. Overloading is the reuse of a method name in the one class or subclass for a different method. This is not related to object orientation, although there is a purely coincidental correlation that shows that object-oriented languages are more likely to support overloading. Notice that overloading is essentially a trick with names, hence this section's title is "Overloading Method Names" rather than "Overloading Methods." The following are all different methods:

```
1. public void aMethod(String s) { }
2. public void aMethod() { }
3. public void aMethod(int i, String s) { }
4. public void aMethod(String s, int i) { }
```

These methods all have identical return types and names, but their argument lists are different either in the types of the arguments that they take or in the order. Only the argument types are considered, not their names, hence a method

```
public void aMethod(int j, String name) { }
```

would *not* be distinguished from the method defined in line 3 above.

## What is Overloading For?

Why is overloading useful? There are times when you will be creating several methods that perform closely related functions under different conditions. For example, imagine methods that calculate the area of a triangle. One such method might take the Cartesian coordinates of the three vertices and another might take the polar coordinates. A third method might take the lengths of all three sides, while a fourth might take three angles and the length of one side. These would all be performing the same essential function, and so it is entirely proper to use the same name for the methods. In languages that do not permit overloading, you would have to think up four different method names, such as `areaOfTriangleByCoordinate` (`Point p, Point q, Point r`), `areaOfTriangleByPolarCoordinates(PolarPoint p, PolarPoint q, PolarPoint r)`, and so forth.

Overloading is really nothing new. Almost every language that has a type system has used overloading in a way, although most have not allowed the programmer free use of it. Consider the arithmetic operators +, -, *, and /. In most languages these can be used with integer or floating-point operands. The actual implementation of, say, multiplication for integer and floating-point operands generally involves completely different code, and yet the compiler permits the same symbol to be used. Because the operand types are different, the compiler can decide which version of the operation should be used. This is known as operator overloading and is the same principle as method overloading.

So it is quite useful, for thinking up method names and for improving program readability, to be able to use one method name for several related methods requiring different implementations. However, you should restrict your use of overloaded method names to situations where the methods really are performing the same basic function with different data sets. Methods that perform different jobs should have different names.

One last point to consider is the return type of an overloaded method. The language treats methods with overloaded names as totally different methods, and as such they can have different return types (you will see shortly that overriding methods do not have this freedom). However, if two methods are performing the same job with different data sets, shouldn't they produce the same result type? Generally this is true, and you should expect overloaded methods to be defined with the same result types. There is one particular condition, however, under which it is clearly sensible to define different return types for overloaded methods. This is the situation where the return type is derived from the argument type and is exactly parallel with the arithmetic operators discussed earlier. If you define three methods called addUp() which take two arguments, both int, both float, or both double, then it is entirely reasonable for the method to return int, float or double in lines with its arguments.

## Invoking Overloaded Methods

When you write multiple methods that perform the same basic function with different arguments, you often find that it would be useful to call one of these methods as support for another version. Consider a method printRight-Justified() that is to be provided in versions that take a String or an int value. The version that takes an int could most easily be coded so that it converts the int to a String and then calls the version that operates on String objects.

You can do this easily. Remember that the compiler decides which method to call simply by looking at the argument list and that the various overloaded methods are in fact unrelated. All you have to do is write the method call exactly as normal—the compiler will do the rest. Consider this example:

```
1. public class RightJustify {
2.   private static final String padding =
3.     "                                        " +
4.     "                                        "; // 80 spaces
5.   public static void print(String s, int w) {
6.     System.out.print(padding.substring(0, w - s.length()));
7.     System.out.print(s);
8.   }
9.   public static void print(int i, int w) {
10.    print("" + i, w);
11.  }
12. }
```

At line 10 the int argument is converted to a String object by adding it to an empty String. The method call at this same line is then seen by the compiler as a call to a method called print() that takes a String as the first argument, which results in selection of the method at line 5.

To summarize, these are the key points about overloading methods:

- The identity of a method is determined by the combination of its fully qualified class, name, and the type, order, and count of arguments in the argument list.

- Two or more methods in the same class (including methods inherited from a superclass) with the same name but different argument lists are called overloaded.

- Methods with overloaded names are effectively independent methods—using the same name is really just a convenience to the programmer. Return type, accessibility, and exception lists may vary freely.

- Overloaded methods may call one another simply by providing a normal method call with an appropriately formed argument list.

Now that we have considered overloading thoroughly, let's look at overriding.

## Method Overriding

You have just seen that overloading is essentially a trick with names, effectively treating the argument list as part of the method identification. Overriding is somewhat more subtle, relating directly to subclassing and hence to the object-oriented nature of a language.

When you extend one class to produce a new one, you inherit and have access to all the non-private methods of the original class. Sometimes, however, you might need to modify the behavior of one of these methods to suit your new class. In this case, you actually want to redefine the method, and this is the essential purpose of overriding.

There are a number of key distinctions between overloading and overriding:

- Overloaded methods supplement each other; an overriding method (largely) replaces the method it overrides.

- Overloaded methods can exist, in any number, in the same class. Each method in a parent class can be overridden at most once in any one subclass.

- Overloaded methods must have *different* argument lists; overriding methods must have argument lists of *identical* type and order (otherwise they are simply treated as overloaded methods).

- The return type of an overloaded method may be chosen freely; the return type of an overriding method must be *identical* to that of the method it overrides.

## What is Overriding For?

Overloading allows multiple implementations of the same essential functionality to use the same name. Overriding, on the other hand, modifies the implementation of a particular piece of behavior for a subclass.

Consider a class that describes a rectangle. Imaginatively, we'll call it Rectangle. We're talking about an abstract rectangle here, so there is no visual representation associated with it. This class has a method called setSize(), which is used to set width and height values. In the Rectangle class itself, the implementation of the setSize() method simply sets the value of the private width and height variables for later use. Now imagine we create a DisplayedRectangle class which is a subclass of the original Rectangle. Now, when the setSize() method is called, we need to arrange a new behavior. Specifically, the width and height variables must be changed, but also the visual representation must be redrawn. This is achieved by overriding.

If you define a method that has exactly the same name and exactly the same argument types as a method in a parent class, then you are overriding the method. Under these conditions, the method must also have the identical return type to that of the method it overrides. Consider this example:

```
1. class Rectangle {
2.    int x, y, w, h;
3.
4.    public void setSize(int w, int h) {
5.       this.w = w; this.h = h;
6.    }
7. }
8. class DisplayedRectangle extends Rectangle {
9.    public void setSize(int w, int h) {
10.      this.w = w; this.h = h;
11.      redisplay(); // implementation
12.   }
13.   public void redisplay() {
14.      // implementation not shown
```

```
15.    }
16.  }
17.
18.  public class TestRectangle {
19.     public static void main(String args[]) {
20.        Rectangle [] recs = new Rectangle[4];
21.        recs[0] = new Rectangle();
22.        recs[1] = new DisplayedRectangle();
23.        recs[2] = new DisplayedRectangle();
24.        recs[3] = new Rectangle();
25.        for (int r=0; r<4; r++) {
26.          int i = ((int)(Math.random() * 4));
27.          int w = ((int)(Math.random() * 400));
28.          int h = ((int)(Math.random() * 200));
29.          recs[r].setSize(w, h);
30.        }
31.     }
32.  }
```

Clearly this example is incomplete, since no code exists to cause the display of the DisplayedRectangle objects, but it is complete enough for us to discuss.

At line 20 you will see the array recs is created as an array of Rectangle objects, yet at lines 21–24 the array is used to hold not only two instances of Rectangle but also two instances of DisplayedRectangle. Subsequently, when the setSize() method is called, it will be important that the code that is executed should be the code associated with the actual object referred to by the array element, rather than always being the code of the Rectangle class. This is actually exactly what Java does, and this is the essential point of overriding methods. It is as if you ask an object to perform certain behavior and that object makes its own interpretation of that request. This is a point that C++ programmers should take particular note of, as it differs significantly from the default behavior of overriding methods in that language.

In order for any particular method to override another correctly, there are a number of requirements that must be met. Some of these have been mentioned before in comparison with overloading, but all are listed here for completeness:

- The method name and the type and order of arguments must be identical to those of a method in a parent class. If this is the case, then the method is an attempt to override the corresponding parent class method and the remaining points listed here must be adhered to, or a compiler error arises. If these criteria are not met, then the method is not an attempt to override and the following rules are irrelevant.

- The return type must be identical.

- The accessibility must not be more restricted than the original method.

- The method must not throw checked exceptions of classes that are not possible for the original method.

The first two points have been covered, but the last two are new. The accessibility of an overriding method must not be less than that of the method it overrides simply because it is considered to be the replacement method in conditions like those of the rectangles example earlier. So, imagine that the setSize() method of DisplayedRectangle was inaccessible from the main() method of the TestRectangle class. The calls to recs[1].setSize() and recs[2].setSize() would be illegal, but the compiler would be unable to determine this, since it only knows that the elements of the array are Rectangle objects. The extends keyword literally requires that the subclass be an extension of the parent class: If methods could be removed from the class, or made less accessible, then the subclass would not be a simple extension, but would potentially be a reduction. Under those conditions, the idea of treating DisplayedRectangle objects as being Rectangle objects when used as method arguments or elements of a collection would be severely flawed.

A similar logic gives rise to the final rule relating to checked exceptions. Checked exceptions are those that the compiler insures are handled in the source you write. As with accessibility, it must be possible for the compiler to make correct use of a variable of the parent class even if that variable really refers to an object of a derived class. For checked exceptions, this means that an overriding method must not be able to throw exceptions that would not be thrown by the original method. Chapter 5 discusses checked exceptions and this rule in more detail.

## Late Binding or Virtual Method Invocation

Normally, when a compiler for a non-object–oriented language comes across a method (or function or procedure) invocation, it determines exactly what target code should be called and builds machine language to represent that call. In an object-oriented language, this is not possible since the proper code to invoke is determined based upon the class of the object being used to make the call, not the type of the variable. Instead, code is generated that will allow the decision to be made at run time. This delayed decision-making is variously referred to as *late binding* (binding is one term for the job a linker does when it glues various bits of machine code together to make an executable program file) or *virtual method invocation.*

Java's Virtual Machine has been designed from the start to support an object-oriented programming system, so there are machine-level instructions for making method calls. The compiler only needs to prepare the argument list and produce one method invocation instruction; the job of identifying and calling the proper target code is performed by the Virtual Machine.

If the Virtual Machine is to be able to decide what actual code should be invoked by a particular method call, it must be able to determine the class of the object upon which the call is based. Again, the Virtual Machine design has supported this from the beginning. Unlike traditional languages or run-time environments, every time the Java system allocates memory, it marks that memory with the type of the data that it has been allocated to hold. This means that given any object, and without regard to the type associated with the reference variable acting as a handle to that object, the runtime system can determine the real class of that object by inspection. This is the basis of the `instanceof` operator, which allows you to program a test to determine the actual class of an object at run time. The `instanceof` operator is described in Chapter 2.

## Invoking Overridden Methods

When we discussed overloading methods you saw how to invoke one version of a method from another. It is also useful to be able to invoke an overridden method from the method that overrides it. Consider that when you write an overriding method, that method entirely replaces the original method, but sometimes you only wish to add a little extra behavior and want to retain all the original behavior. This can be achieved, although it requires a small trick of syntax to perform. Look at this example:

```
1. class Rectangle {
2.   private int x, y, w, h;
3.   public String toString() {
4.     return "x = " + x + ", y = " + y +
5.        ", w = " + w + ", h = " + h;
```

```
 6.    }
 7.  }
 8.  class DecoratedRectangle extends Rectangle {
 9.    private int borderWidth;
10.    public String toString() {
11.      return super.toString() + ", borderWidth = " + _
         borderWidth;
12.    }
13.  }
```

At line 11 the overriding method in the DecoratedRectangle class uses the parental toString() method to perform the greater part of its work. Note that since the variables x, y, w, and h in the Rectangle class are marked as private, it would have been impossible for the overriding method in DecoratedRectangle to achieve its work directly.

A call of the form super.xxx() always invokes the behavior that would have been used if the current overloading method had not been defined. It does not matter if the parental method is defined in the immediate superclass, or in some ancestor class further up the hierarchy, super invokes the version of this method that is "next up the tree." Be aware that you cannot bypass a level in the hierarchy. That is, if three classes, A, B, and C, all define a method m(), and they are all part of a hierarchy—so that B extends A, and C extends B—then the method m() in class C cannot directly invoke the method m() in class A.

To summarize, these are the key points about overriding methods:

- A method which has an identical name, and identical number, types, and order of arguments as a method in a parent class is an overriding method.

- Each parent class method may be overridden at most once in any one subclass. (That is, you cannot have two identical methods in the same class.)

- Overriding methods must return exactly the same type as the method they override.

- An overriding method must not be less accessible than the method it overrides.

- An overriding method must not throw any checked exceptions that are not declared for the overridden method.

- An overridden method is completely replaced by the overriding method unless the overridden method is deliberately invoked from within the subclass.

- An overridden method can be invoked from within the subclass using the construction `super.xxx()` where `xxx()` is the method name. Methods that are overridden more than once (by chains of subclasses) are not directly accessible.

There is quite a lot to think about in overriding methods, so you might like to have a break before you move on to the next topic: Constructors.

# Constructors and Subclassing

Inheritance generally makes the code and data that are defined in a parent class available for use in a subclass. This is subject to accessibility so that, for example, private items in the parent class are not directly accessible in the methods of the subclass, even though they exist. In fact, constructors are not inherited in the normal way but must be defined in the class itself.

When you write code to construct an instance of any particular class, you write code of the form `new MyClass(arg, list);`. In these conditions there must be a constructor defined for `MyClass`, and that constructor must take arguments of the types (or some superclass) of the variables `arg` and `list`. In the case of a constructor, it is not sufficient for this to have been defined in the parent class; rather, a constructor is generally available for a class only if it is explicitly defined in that class. The exception to this is the default constructor. The default constructor takes no arguments and is created by the compiler if no other constructors are defined for the class. Notice the default constructor is not inherited—It is created for you by the compiler if, and only if, you do not provide any other constructors in the source of the particular class.

Often you will define a constructor that takes arguments and will want to use those arguments to control the construction of the parent part of the object. You can pass control to a constructor in the parent class by using the keyword super(). To control the particular constructor that is used, you simply provide the appropriate arguments. Consider this example:

```
1. class Base {
2.   public Base(String s) {
3.     // initialize this object using s
4.   }
5.   public Base(int i) {
6.     // initialize this object using i
7.   }
8. }
9.
10. class Derived extends Base {
11.   public Derived(String s) {
12.     super(s); // pass control to Base constructor at line 2
13.   }
14.   public Derived(int i) {
15.     super(i); // pass control to Base constructor at line 5
16.   }
17. }
```

The code at lines 12 and 15 demonstrate the use of super() to control the construction of the parent class part of an object. The definitions of the constructors at lines 11 and 14 select an appropriate way to build the parental part of themselves by invoking super() with an argument list that matches one of the constructors for the parent class. It is important to know that the superclass constructor must be called before any reference is made to any part of this object. This rule is imposed to guarantee that nothing is ever accessed in an uninitialized state. Generally the rule means that if super() is to appear at all in a constructor, then it must be the first statement.

Although the example shows the invocation of parental constructors with argument lists that match those of the original constructor, this is not a requirement. It would be perfectly acceptable, for example, if line 15 had read:

```
15.     super("Value is " + i);
```

This would have caused control to be passed to the constructor at line 2, which takes a String argument, rather than the one at line 5.

# Overloading Constructors

Although you have just seen that constructors are not inherited in the same way as methods, the overloading mechanisms apply quite normally. In fact, the example discussing the use of super() to control the invocation of parental constructors showed overloaded constructors. You saw earlier how you could invoke one method from another that overloads its name simply by calling the method with an appropriate parameter list. There are also times when it would be useful to invoke one constructor from another. Imagine you have a constructor that takes five arguments and does considerable processing to initialize the object. You wish to provide another constructor that takes only two arguments and sets the remaining three to default values. It would be nice to avoid re-coding the body of the first constructor and instead simply set up the default values and pass control to the first constructor. This is possible but requires a small trick of syntax to achieve.

Usually you would invoke a method by using its name followed by an argument list in parentheses, and you would invoke a constructor by using the keyword new, followed by the name of the class, followed again by an argument list in parentheses. This might lead you to try to use the new ClassName(args) construction to invoke another constructor of your own class. Unfortunately, although this is legal syntax, it results in an entirely separate object being created. The approach Java takes is to provide another meaning for the keyword this. Look at this example:

```
1. public class AnyClass {
2.    public AnyClass(int a, String b, float c, Date d) {
3.      // complex processing to initialize based on arguments
4.    }
5.    public AnyClass(int a) {
6.      this(a, "default", 0.0F, new Date());
7.    }
8. }
```

The constructor at line 5 takes a single argument and uses that, along with three other default values, to call the constructor at line 2. The call itself is made using the this() construction at line 6. As with super(), this() must be positioned as the first statement of the constructor.

We have said that any use of either super() or this() in a constructor must be placed at the first line. Clearly, you cannot put both on the first line. In fact, this is not a problem. If you write a constructor that has neither a call to super(...) nor a call to this(...), then the compiler automatically inserts a call to the parent class constructor with no arguments. If an explicit call to another constructor is made using this(...), then the superclass constructor is not called until the other constructor runs. It is permitted for that other constructor to start with a call to either this(...) or super(...) if desired. Java insists that the object is initialized from the top of the class hierarchy downward; that is why the call to super(...) or this(...) must occur at the start of a constructor.

Let's summarize the key points about constructors before we move on to inner classes:

- Constructors are not inherited in the same way as normal methods. You can only create an object if a constructor with an argument list that matches the one your new call provides is defined in the class itself.

- If you define no constructors at all in a class, then the compiler provides a default that takes no arguments. If you define even a single constructor, this default is not provided.

- It is common to provide multiple overloaded constructors: that is, constructors with different argument lists. One constructor can call another using the syntax this(arguments...).

- A constructor delays running its body until the parent parts of the class have been initialized. This commonly happens because of an implicit call to super() added by the compiler. You can provide your own call to super(arguments...) to control the way the parent parts are initialized. If you do this, it must be the first statement of the constructor.

- A constructor can use overloaded constructor versions to support its work. These are invoked using the syntax this(arguments...) and if supplied, this call must be the first statement of the constructor. In such conditions, the initialization of the parent class is performed in the overloaded constructor.

# Inner Classes

The material we have looked at so far has been part of Java since its earliest versions. Inner classes are a feature added with the release of JDK 1.1. Inner classes, which are sometimes called nested classes, can give your programs additional clarity and make them more concise.

Fundamentally, an *inner class* is the same as any other class, but is declared inside (that is, between the opening and closing curly braces of) some other class. The complexity of inner classes relates to scope and access, particularly access to variables in enclosing scopes. Before we consider these matters, let's look at the syntax of a basic inner class, which is really quite simple. Consider this example:

```
1. public class OuterOne {
2.    private int x;
3.    public class InnerOne {
4.       private int y;
5.       public void innerMethod() {
6.          System.out.println("y is " + y);
7.       }
8.    }
9.    public void outerMethod() {
10.      System.out.println("x is " + x);
11.   }
12.   // other methods...
13. }
```

In this example, there is no obvious benefit in having declared the class called InnerOne as an inner class; so far we are only looking at the syntax. When an inner class is declared like this, the enclosing class name becomes part of the fully qualified name of the inner class. In this case, the two classes' full names are OuterOne and OuterOne.InnerOne. This format is reminiscent of a class called InnerOne declared in a package called OuterOne. This point of view is not entirely inappropriate, since an inner class belongs to its enclosing class in a fashion similar to the way a class belongs to a package. It is illegal for a package and a class to have the same name, so there can be no ambiguity.

Although the dotted representation of inner class names works for the declaration of the type of an identifier, it does not reflect the real name of the class. If you try to load this class using the `Class.forName()` method, the call will fail. On the disk, and from the point of view of the `Class` class and class loaders, the name of the class is actually `OuterOne$InnerOne`. The dollar-separated name is also used if you print out the class name by using the methods `getClass().getName()` on an instance of the inner class. You probably recall that classes are located in directories that reflect their package names. The dollar ($) separated convention is adopted for inner class names to insure that there is no ambiguity on the disk between inner classes and package members. It also reduces conflicts with filing systems that treat the dot character as special, perhaps limiting the number of characters that can follow it.

Although for the purpose of naming there is some organizational benefit in being able to define a class inside another class, this is not the end of the story. Objects that are instances of the inner class generally retain the ability to access the members of the outer class. This is discussed in the next section.

## The Enclosing *this* Reference and Construction of Inner Classes

When an instance of an inner class is created, there must normally be a pre-existing instance of the outer class acting as context. This instance of the outer class will be accessible from the inner object. Consider this example, which is expanded from the earlier one:

```
1. public class OuterOne {
2.   private int x;
3.   public class InnerOne {
4.     private int y;
5.     public void innerMethod() {
6.       System.out.println("enclosing x is " + x);
7.       System.out.println("y is " + y);
8.     }
9.   }
```

```
10.    public void outerMethod() {
11.      System.out.println("x is " + x);
12.    }
13.    public void makeInner() {
14.      InnerOne anInner = new InnerOne();
15.      anInner.innerMethod();
16.    }
17.    // other methods...
18.  }
```

You will see two changes in this code when you compare it to the earlier version. First, at line 6, innerMethod() now outputs not just the value of y, which is defined in InnerOne, but also the value of x which is defined in OuterOne. The second change is that in lines 13–16, there is code that creates an instance of the InnerOne class and invokes innerMethod() upon it.

The accessibility of the members of the enclosing class is crucial and very useful. It is possible because the inner class actually has a hidden reference to the outer class instance that was the current context when the inner class object was created. In effect, it ensures that the inner class and the outer class belong together, rather than the inner instance being just another member of the outer instance.

Sometimes you might want to create an instance of an inner class from a static method, or in some other situation where there is no this object available. The situation arises in a main() method or if you need to create the inner class from a method of some object of an unrelated class. You can achieve this by using the new operator as though it were a member method of the outer class. Of course you still must have an instance of the outer class. The following code, which is a main() method in isolation, could be added to the code seen so far to produce a complete example:

```
1. public static void main(String args[]) {
2.   OuterOne.InnerOne i = new OuterOne().new InnerOne();
3.   i.innerMethod();
4. }
```

From the point of view of the inner class instance, this use of two new statements on the same line is a compacted way of doing this:

```
1. public static void main(String args[]) {
2.   OuterOne o = new OuterOne();
```

```
3.    OuterOne.InnerOne i = o.new InnerOne();
4.    i.innerMethod();
5. }
```

If you attempt to use the new operation to construct an instance of an inner class without a prefixing reference to an instance of the outer class, then the implied prefix this. is assumed. This behavior is identical to that which you find with ordinary member accesses and method invocations. As with member access and method invocation, it is important that the this reference be valid when you try to use it. Inside a static method there is no this reference, which is why you must take special efforts in these conditions.

### Static Inner Classes

Java's inner class mechanisms allow an inner class to be marked static. When applied to a variable, static means that the variable is associated with the class, rather than with any particular instance of the class. When applied to an inner class, the meaning is similar. Specifically, a static inner class does *not* have any reference to an enclosing instance. Because of this, methods of a static inner class cannot access instance variables of the enclosing class; those methods can, however, access static variables of the enclosing class. This is similar to the rules that apply to static methods in ordinary classes. As you would expect, you can create an instance of a static inner class without the need for a current instance of the enclosing class.

The net result is that a static inner class is really just a top-level class with a modified naming scheme. In fact, you can use static inner classes as an extension to packaging.

Not only can you declare a class inside another class, but you can also declare a class inside a method of another class. We will discuss this next.

## Classes Defined Inside Methods

So far you have seen classes defined inside other classes, but Java also allows you to define a class inside a method. This is superficially similar to what you have already seen, but in this case there are two particular aspects to be considered. First, an object created from an inner class within a method can have some access to the variables of the enclosing method. Second, it is possible to create an anonymous class, literally a class with no specified name, and this can be very eloquent when working with event listeners.

The rule that governs access to the variables of an enclosing method is simple. Any variable, either a local variable or a formal parameter, can be accessed by methods within an inner class, provided that variable is marked final. A final variable is effectively a constant, so this is perhaps quite a severe restriction, but the point is simply this: An object created inside a method is likely to outlive the method invocation. Since local variables and method arguments are conventionally destroyed when their method exits, these variables would be invalid for access by inner class methods after the enclosing method exits. By allowing access only to final variables, it becomes possible to copy the values of those variables into the object itself, thereby extending their lifetime. The other possible approaches to this problem would be writing to two copies of the same data every time it got changed or putting method local variables onto the heap instead of the stack. Either of these approaches would significantly degrade performance.

Let's look at an example:

```
1. public class MOuter {
2.    public static void main(String args[]) {
3.      MOuter that = new MOuter();
4.      that.go((int)(Math.random() * 100),
5.        (int)(Math.random() * 100));
6.    }
7.
8.    public void go(int x, final int y) {
9.      int a = x + y;
10.     final int b = x - y;
11.     class MInner {
12.       public void method() {
13. //       System.out.println("x is " + x); //Illegal!
14.          System.out.println("y is " + y);
15. //       System.out.println("a is " + a); //Illegal!
16.          System.out.println("b is " + b);
17.       }
18.     }
19.
20.     MInner that = new MInner();
21.     that.method();
22.   }
23. }
```

In this example, the class MInner is defined in lines 11–18. Within it, method() has access to the member variables of the enclosing class (as with the previous examples) but also to the final variables of method() itself. Lines 13 and 15 are illegal, because they attempt to refer to non-final variables in method(): If these were included in the source proper, they would cause compiler errors.

## Anonymous Classes

Some classes that you define inside a method do not need a name. A class defined in this way without a name is called an *anonymous class*. Clearly you cannot use new in the usual way to create an instance of a class if you do not know its name. In fact, anonymous classes are defined in the place they are constructed:

```
1. public void aMethod() {
2.   theButton.addActionListener(
3.     new ActionListener() {
4.       public void actionPerformed(ActionEvent e) {
5.         System.out.println("The action has occurred");
6.       }
7.     }
8.   );
9. }
```

In this fragment, theButton at line 2 is a Button object. Notice that the action listener attached to the button is defined in lines 3–7. The entire declaration forms the argument to the addActionListener() method call at line 2; the closing parenthesis that completes this method call is on line 8.

At line 3, the new call is followed immediately by the start of the class definition; the class has no name but is referred to simply using an interface name. The effect of this syntax is to state that you are defining a class and you do not want to think up a name for that class. Further, the class implements the specified interface without using the implements keyword.

An anonymous class gives you a convenient way to avoid having to think up trivial names for classes, but the facility should be used with care. Clearly, you cannot instantiate objects of this class anywhere except in the code shown. Further, anonymous classes should be small. If the class has methods other than those of a simple, well-known interface such as an AWT event listener, it probably should not be anonymous. Similarly, if the class has methods containing more than one or two lines of straightforward code, it probably should not be anonymous. The point here is that if you do not give the class a name, you have only the "self-documenting" nature of the code itself to explain what it is for. If in fact the code is not simple enough to be genuinely self-documenting, then you probably should give it a descriptive name.

These are the points you need to understand about anonymous inner classes to succeed in the Certification Exam:

- The class is instantiated and declared in the same place.

- The declaration and instantiation takes the form

  ```
  new Xxxx () { //body }
  ```

  where Xxxx is an interface name.

- An anonymous class cannot have a constructor. Since you do not specify a name for the class, you cannot use that name to specify a constructor.

## Additional Features of Anonymous Inner Classes

The Certification Exam objectives only discuss anonymous inner classes that implement specific interfaces. There are some additional points that relate to anonymous inner classes that extend specific parent classes. You might find these points useful, even though they do not relate to the exam.

- An anonymous class can be a subclass of another explicit class, or it can implement a single explicit interface. An anonymous class cannot be both an explicit subclass and implement an interface. Note that extending Object is implicit where an interface is implemented.

- If an anonymous class extends an existing class, rather than implementing an interface, then arguments for the superclass constructor may be placed in the argument part of the new expression, like this:

  ```
  new Button("Press Me") { // define some modification of _
  Button }
  ```

Note that for anonymous classes that implement interfaces the parent class is java.lang.Object. The constructor for java.lang.Object takes no arguments, so it is impossible to use any arguments in the new part for these classes.

# Chapter Summary

We have covered a lot of material in this chapter, but all of it is important. Let's look again at the key points.

## Object-Oriented Design and Implementaion

- Tightly encapsulated class designs make for more robust and reusable code. Code reuse involves code retesting, which further improves reliability and robustness.

- Tightly encapsulated classes hide their state variables from outside interference, typically marking all member variables as private and providing appropriate methods for interaction with the instances.

- Code reuse can be achieved by simply reusing classes, by composition (the "has a" relationship) or by inheritance (the "is a" relationship).

- The "is a" relationship is implemented by inheritance, using the Java keyword extends.

- The "has a" relationship is implemented by providing the class with member variables.

## Overloading and Overriding

- A method can have the same name as another method in the same class, providing it forms either a valid overload or override.

- A valid overload differs in the number or type of its arguments. Differences in argument names are not significant. A different return type is permitted, but it is not sufficient by itself to distinguish an overloading method.

- Methods that overload a name are different methods and can coexist in a single class.

- Both overloaded and overloading methods are accessed simply by providing the correct argument types for the method call.

- A valid override has identical argument types and order, identical return type, and is not less accessible than the original method. The overriding method must not throw any checked exceptions that were not declared for the original method.

- Overriding methods completely replace the original method unless the derived class makes specific reference to that original method using the `super.xxx()` construction.

- An overriding method cannot be defined in the same class as the method it overrides; rather, it must be defined in a subclass.

- The `super.xxx()` mechanism gives access to an overridden method from within the subclass that defines the overriding method.

- Overridden methods are not accessible outside the overriding class. Virtual method invocation otherwise insures that the behavior associated with the object class (not with the variable type) will be the behavior that occurs.

## Constructors and Subclassing

- Constructors are not inherited into subclasses; you must define each form of constructor that you require.

- A class that has no constructors defined in the source is given exactly one constructor. This is the default constructor; it takes no arguments and is of `public` accessibility.

- A constructor can call upon other constructors in its class to help with its work. The `this()` construction does this. If you use the `this()` mechanism, it must occur at the start of the constructor.

- A constructor can call the constructor of the parent class explicitly by using the `super()` mechanism. If you use the `super()` mechanism, it must occur at the start of the constructor.

## Inner Classes

- A class can be declared in any scope. Classes defined in other classes, including those defined in methods, are called inner classes.

- An inner class can have any accessibility, including `private`.

- Classes defined in methods can be anonymous, in which case they must be instantiated at the same point they are defined.

- Inner classes, unless `static`, have an implicit reference to the enclosing instance. The enclosing instance must be provided to the new call that constructs the inner class. In many cases, inner classes are constructed inside instance methods of the enclosing class, in which case `this.new` is implied by new.

- Inner classes, unless `static`, have access to the variables of the enclosing class instance. Additionally, inner classes defined in method scope have read access to `final` variables of the enclosing method.

- Anonymous inner classes may implement interfaces or extend other classes.

- Anonymous inner classes cannot have any explicit constructors.

That's it for classes. This summary includes a great deal of information condensed into terminology, so be sure to review the sections of this chapter if you are unsure about any point. Otherwise, you're ready to move on to the test questions. Good luck!

# Test Yourself

1. Consider this class:

```
1. public class Test1 {
2.     public float aMethod(float a, float b) {
3.     }
4.
5. }
```

Which of the following methods would be legal if added (individually) at line 4?

**A.** `public int aMethod(int a, int b) { }`

**B.** `public float aMethod(float a, float b) { }`

**C.** `public float aMethod(float a, float b, int c) throws _
Exception { }`

**D.** `public float aMethod(float c, float d) { }`

**E.** `private float aMethod(int a, int b, int c) { }`

**2.** Consider these classes, defined in separate source files:

```
1. public class Test1 {
2.    public float aMethod(float a, float b) throws _
      IOException {
3.    }
4. }
```

```
1. public class Test2 extends Test1 {
2.
3. }
```

Which of the following methods would be legal (individually) at line 2 in class Test2?

**A.** `float aMethod(float a, float b) { }`

**B.** `public int aMethod(int a, int b) throws Exception { }`

**C.** `public float aMethod(float a, float b) throws _ Exception { }`

**D.** `public float aMethod(float p, float q) { }`

**3.** You have been given a design document for a veterinary registration system for implementation in Java. It states:

"A pet has an owner, a registration date, and a vaccination-due date. A cat is a pet that has a flag indicating if it has been neutered, and a textual description of its markings."

Given that the Pet class has already been defined, which of the following fields would be appropriate for inclusion in the cat class as members?

**A.** `Pet thePet;`

**B.** `Date registered;`

**C.** `Date vaccinationDue;`

**D.** `Cat theCat;`

**E.** `boolean neutered;`

**F.** `String markings;`

**4.** You have been given a design document for a veterinary registration system for implementation in Java. It states:

"A pet has an owner, a registration date, and a vaccination-due date. A cat is a pet that has a flag indicating if it has been neutered, and a textual description of its markings."

Given that the pet class has already been defined and you expect the Cat class to be used freely throughout the application, how would you make the opening declaration of the Cat class, up to but not including the first opening brace? Use only these words and spaces: `boolean`, `Cat`, `class`, `Date`, `extends`, `Object`, `Owner`, `Pet`, `private`, `protected`, `public`, `String`.

**5.** Consider the following classes, declared in separate source files:

```
1. public class Base {
2.    public void method(int i) {
3.       System.out.println("Value is " + i);
4.    }
5. }
```

```
1. public class Sub extends Base {
2.    public void method(int j) {
3.       System.out.println("This value is " + j);
4.    }
5.    public void method(String s) {
6.       System.out.println("I was passed " + s);
7.    }
8.    public static void main(String args[]) {
9.       Base b1 = new Base();
10.      Base b2 = new Sub();
11.      b1.method(5);
12.      b2.method(6);
13.   }
14. }
```

What output results when the main method of the class Sub is run?

**A.** Value is 5Value is 6

**B.** This value is 5This value is 6

**C.** Value is 5This value is 6

**D.** This value is 5Value is 6

**E.** I was passed 5I was passed 6

**6.** Consider the following class definition:

```
1. public class Test extends Base {
2.    public Test(int j) {
3.    }
4.    public Test(int j, int k) {
5.      super(j, k);
6.    }
7. }
```

Which of the following are legitimate calls to construct instances of the Test class?

**A.** Test t = new Test();

**B.** Test t = new Test(1);

**C.** Test t = new Test(1, 2);

**D.** Test t = new Test(1, 2, 3);

**E.** Test t = (new Base()).new Test(1);

**7.** Consider the following class definition:

```
1. public class Test extends Base {
2.    public Test(int j) {
3.    }
4.    public Test(int j, int k) {
5.      super(j, k);
6.    }
7. }
```

Which of the following forms of constructor must exist explicitly in the definition of the Base class?

**A.** Base() { }

**B.** Base(int j) { }

**C.** Base(int j, int k) { }

**D.** Base(int j, int k, int l) { }

8. Which of the following statements are true? (Choose one or more.)

   **A.** An inner class may be declared private.

   **B.** An inner class may be declared static.

   **C.** An inner class defined in a method should always be anonymous.

   **D.** An inner class defined in a method can access all the method local variables.

   **E.** Construction of an inner class may require an instance of the outer class.

9. Consider the following definitions:

```
1. public class Outer {
2.    public int a = 1;
3.    private int b = 2;
4.    public void method(final int c) {
5.      int d = 3;
6.      public class Inner {
7.        private void iMethod(int e) {
8.
9.        }
10.      }
11.    }
12. }
```

Which variables may be referenced correctly at line 8?

**A.** a

**B.** b

**C.** c

**D.** d

**E.** e

**10.** Which of the following statements are true? (Choose one or more.)

**A.** Given that Inner is a non-static class declared inside a public class Outer, and appropriate constructor forms are defined, an instance of Inner may be constructed like this:

```
(new Outer()).new Inner()
```

**B.** If an anonymous inner class inside the class Outer is defined to implement the interface ActionListener, it may be constructed like this:

```
(new Outer()).new ActionListener()
```

**C.** Given that Inner is a non-static class declared inside a public class Outer and appropriate constructor forms are defined, an instance of Inner may be constructed in a static method like this:

```
new Inner()
```

**D.** An anonymous class instance that implements the interface MyInterface may be constructed and returned from a method like this:

```
1. return new MyInterface(int x) {
2.    int x;
3.    public MyInterface(int x) {
4.      this.x = x;
5.    }
6. };
```

# CHAPTER 7

# Threads

his chapter covers aspects of the following Java certification exam objectives:

- Write code to define, instantiate, and start new threads using both `java.lang.Thread` and `java.lang.Runnable`.

- Recognize conditions that might prevent a thread from executing.

- Write code using `synchronized`, `wait`, `notify`, and `notifyAll` to protect against concurrent access problems and to communicate between threads. Define the interaction between threads and between threads and object locks when executing `synchronized`, `wait`, `notify`, or `notifyAll`.

Threads are Java's way of making a single Java Virtual Machine look like many machines, all running at the same time. This effect, usually, is an illusion: There is only one JVM and most often only one CPU; but the CPU switches among the JVM's various projects to give the impression of multiple CPUs.

Java provides you with a number of tools for creating and managing threads. Threads are a valuable tool for simplifying program design, allowing unrelated or loosely related work to be programmed separately, while still executing concurrently. There are system threads that work behind the scenes on your behalf, listening for user input and managing garbage collection. The best way to cooperate with these facilities is to understand what threads really are.

The Certification objectives require that you be familiar with Java's thread support, including the mechanisms for creating, controlling, and communicating between threads.

# Thread Fundamentals

**J**ava's thread support resides in three places:

- The java.lang.Thread class
- The java.lang.Object class
- The Java language and virtual machine

Most (but definitely not all) support resides in the Thread class. In Java, every thread corresponds to an instance of the Thread class. These objects can be in various states: at any moment, at most one object is executing per CPU, while others might be waiting for resources, or waiting for a chance to execute, or sleeping, or dead.

In order to demonstrate an understanding of threads, you need to be able to answer a few questions:

- When a thread executes, what code does it execute?
- What states can a thread be in?
- How does a thread change its state?

The next few sections will look at each of these questions in turn.

## What a Thread Executes

To make a thread execute, you call its start() method. This registers the thread with a piece of system code called the *thread scheduler*. The scheduler might be part of the JVM or it might be part of the host operating system. The scheduler determines which thread is actually running on each available CPU at any given time. Note that calling your thread's start() method doesn't immediately cause the thread to run; it just makes it *eligible* to run. The thread must still contend for CPU time with all the other threads. If all is well, then at some point in the future the thread scheduler will permit your thread to execute.

During its lifetime, a thread spends some time executing and some time in any of several non-executing states. In this section, you can ignore (for the moment) the questions of how the thread is moved between states. The question at hand is: When the thread gets to execute, what does it execute?

The simple answer is that it executes a method called run(). But which object's run() method? You have two choices:

- The thread can execute its own run() method.

- The thread can execute the run() method of some other object.

If you want the thread to execute its own run() method, you need to subclass the Thread class and give your subclass a run(). For example

```
1. public class CounterThread extends Thread {
2.   public void run() {
3.     for (int i=1; i<=10; i++) {
4.       System.out.println("Counting: " + i);
5.     }
6.   }
7. }
```

This run() method just prints out the numbers from 1 to 10. To do this in a thread, you first construct an instance of CounterThread and then invoke its start() method:

```
1. CounterThread ct = new CounterThread();
2. ct.start();      // start(), not run()
```

What you *don't* do is call run() directly; that would just count to 10 in the current thread. Instead, you call start(), which the CounterThread class inherits from its parent class, Thread. The start() method registers the thread (that is, ct) with the thread scheduler; eventually the thread will execute, and at that time its run() method will be called.

If you want your thread to execute the run() method of some object other than itself, you still need to construct an instance of the Thread class. The only difference is that when you call the Thread constructor, you have to specify which object owns the run() method that you want. To do this, you invoke an alternate form of the Thread constructor:

```
public Thread(Runnable target)
```

The Runnable interface describes a single method:

```
public void run();
```

Thus you can pass any object you want into the constructor, provided it implements the Runnable interface (so that it really does have a run() method for the thread scheduler to invoke).

Having constructed an instance of Thread, you proceed as before: You invoke the start() method. As before, this registers the thread with the scheduler, and eventually the run() method of the target will be called.

For example, the following class has a run() method that counts down from 10 to 1:

```
1. public class DownCounter implements Runnable {
2.    public void run() {
3.       for (int i=10; i>=1; i-) {
4.          System.out.println("Counting Down: " + i);
5.       }
6.    }
7. }
```

This class does not extend Thread. However, it has a run() method, and it declares that it implements the Runnable interface. Thus any instance of the DownCounter class is eligible to be passed into the alternative constructor for Thread:

```
1. DownCounter dc = new DownCounter();
2. Thread t = new Thread(dc);
3. t.start();
```

This section has presented two strategies for constructing threads. Superficially, the only difference between these two strategies is the location of the run() method. The second strategy is perhaps a bit more complicated in the case of the simple examples we have considered. However, there are good reasons why you might choose to make this extra effort. The run() method, like any other member method, is allowed to access the private data, and call the private methods, of the class of which it is a member. Putting run() in a subclass of Thread may mean that the method cannot get to features it needs (or cannot get to those features in a clean, reasonable manner).

Another reason that might persuade you to implement your threads using Runnables rather than subclassing Thread is the single implementation inheritance rule. If you write a subclass of Thread, then it cannot be a subclass of anything else. Whereas using Runnable, you can subclass whatever other parent class you choose. Since implementing Runnable is more generally applicable, it might make more sense to do it as a matter of habit, rather than complicate your code with threads created in different ways in different places. Finally, from an object oriented point of view, the "threadiness" of a class is usually peripheral to the essential nature of whatever you are creating, and therefore subclassing Thread, which says in effect "This class 'is a' thread," is probably an inappropriate design choice. Using Runnable, which says "this class is associated with a thread," makes more sense.

To summarize, there are two approaches to specifying which run() method will be executed by a thread:

- Subclass Thread. Define your run() method in the subclass.

- Write a class that implements Runnable. Define your run() method in that class. Pass an instance of that class into your call to the Thread constructor.

## When Execution Ends

When the run() method returns, the thread has finished its task and is considered *dead*. There is no way out of this state. Once a thread is dead, it may not be started again; if you want the thread's task to be performed again, you have to construct and start a new thread instance. The dead thread continues to exist; it is an object like any other object, and you can still access its data and call its methods. You just can't make it run again. In other words

- You *can't* restart a dead thread.

- You *can* call the methods of a dead thread.

The Thread methods include a method called stop(), which forcibly terminates a thread, putting it into the dead state. This method is deprecated since JDK 1.2, because it can cause data corruption or deadlock if you kill a thread that is in a critical section of code. The stop() method is therefore no longer part of the Certification Exam. Instead of using stop(), if a thread might need to be killed from another thread, then you should send it an interrupt() from the killing method.

Although you can't restart a dead thread, if you use runnables, you can submit the old Runnable instance to a new thread. However, it is generally poor design to constantly create, use, and discard threads, because constructing a Thread is a relatively heavyweight operation, involving significant kernel resources. It is better to create a pool of reusable worker threads that can be assigned chores as needed. This is discussed further in Chapter 17 (in the Developer Exam section).

## Thread States

When you call start() on a thread, the thread does not run immediately. It goes into a "ready-to-run" state and stays there until the scheduler moves it to the "running" state. Then the run() method is called. In the course of executing run(), the thread may temporarily give up the CPU and enter some other state for a while. It is important to be aware of the possible states a thread might be in and of the triggers that can cause the thread's state to change.

The thread states are

**Running**   The state that all threads aspire to

**Various waiting states**   Waiting, Sleeping, Suspended, Blocked

**Ready**   Not waiting for anything except the CPU

**Dead**   All done

Figure 7.1 shows the non-dead states. Notice that the figure does not show the Dead state.

At the top of Figure 7.1 is the Running state. At the bottom is the Ready state. In between are the various not-ready states. A thread in one of these intermediate states is waiting for something to happen; when that something eventually happens, the thread moves to the Ready state, and eventually the thread scheduler will permit it to run again. Note that the methods associated with the suspended state are now deprecated; you will not be tested on this state or its associated methods in the exam. For this reason, we will not discuss them in any detail in this book.

The arrows between the bubbles in Figure 7.1 represent state transitions Notice that only the thread scheduler can move a ready thread into the CPU.

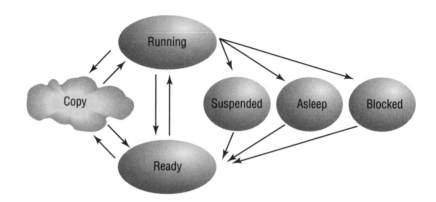

Later in this chapter, you will examine in detail the various waiting states. For now, the important thing to observe in Figure 7.1 is the general flow: A running thread enters an intermediate state for some reason; later, whatever the thread was waiting for comes to pass, and the thread enters the Ready state; later still, the scheduler grants the CPU to the thread. The exceptions to this general flow involve synchronized code and the wait/notify sequence; the corresponding portion of Figure 7.1 is depicted as a vague bubble labeled "Monitor States." These monitor states are discussed later in this chapter, in the section "Monitors, wait(), and notify()."

## Thread Priorities

Every thread has a priority. The priority is an integer from 1 to 10; threads with higher priority get preference over threads with lower priority. The priority is considered by the thread scheduler, when it decides which ready thread should execute. The scheduler generally chooses the highest-priority waiting thread. If there is more than one waiting thread, the scheduler chooses one of them. There is no guarantee that the thread chosen will be the one that has been waiting the longest.

The default priority is 5, but all newly created threads have their priority set to that of the creating thread. To set a thread's priority, call the setPriority() method, passing in the desired new priority. The getPriority() method returns a thread's priority. The code fragment below increments the priority of thread theThread, provided the priority is less than 10. Instead of hardcoding the value

10, the fragment uses the constant MAX_PRIORITY. The Thread class also defines constants for MIN_PRIORITY (which is 1), and NORM_PRIORITY (which is 5).

1. `int oldPriority = theThread.getPriority();`
2. `int newPriority = Math.min(oldPriority+1,`
   `Thread.MAX_PRIORITY);`
3. `theThread.setPriority(newPriority);`

**WARNING**    The specifics of how thread priorities affect scheduling are platform-dependent. The Java specification states that threads must have priorities, but it does not dictate precisely what the scheduler should do about priorities. This vagueness is a problem: Algorithms that rely on manipulating thread priorities might not run consistently on all platforms.

# Controlling Threads

Thread control is the art of moving threads from state to state. You control threads by triggering state transitions. This section examines the various pathways out of the Running state. These pathways are

- Yielding

- Suspending and then resuming

- Sleeping and then waking up

- Blocking and then continuing

- Waiting and then being notified

## Yielding

A thread can offer to move out of the virtual CPU by *yielding*. A call to the yield() method causes the currently executing thread to move to the Ready state if the scheduler is willing to run any other thread in place of the yielding thread. The state transition is shown in Figure 7.2.

A thread that has yielded goes into the Ready state. There are two possible scenarios. If any other threads are in the Ready state, then the thread that just yielded might have to wait a while before it gets to execute again. However,

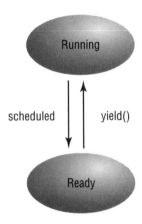

if there are no other waiting threads, then the thread that just yielded will get to continue executing immediately. Note that most schedulers do not stop the yielding thread from running in favor of a thread of lower priority.

The yield() method is a static method of the Thread class. It always causes the currently executing thread to yield.

Yielding allows a time-consuming thread to permit other threads to execute. For example, consider an applet that computes a $300 \times 300$ pixel image using a ray-tracing algorithm. The applet might have a "Compute" button and an "Interrupt" button. The action event handler for the "Compute" button would create and start a separate thread, which would call a traceRays() method. A first cut at this method might look like this:

```
1. private void traceRays() {
2.    for (int j=0; j<300; j++) {
3.       for (int i=0; i<300; i++) {
4.          computeOnePixel(i, j);
5.       }
6.    }
7. }
```

There are 90,000 pixel color values to compute. If it takes 0.1 second to compute the color value of one pixel, then it will take two-and-a-half hours to compute the complete image.

Suppose after half an hour the user looks at the partial image and realizes that something is wrong. (Perhaps the viewpoint or zoom factor is incorrect.) The user will then click the "Interrupt" button since there is no sense in continuing to compute the useless image. Unfortunately, the thread that handles GUI input might not get a chance to execute until the thread that is executing `traceRays()` gives up the CPU. Thus the "Interrupt" button will not have any effect for another two hours.

If priorities are implemented meaningfully in the scheduler, then lowering the priority of the ray-tracing thread will have the desired effect, ensuring that the GUI thread will run when it has something useful to do. However, this is not reliable between platforms (although it is a good course of action anyway, since it will work on most platforms). The reliable approach is to have the ray-tracing thread periodically yield. If there is no pending input when the yield is executed, then the ray-tracing thread will not be moved off the CPU. If, on the other hand, there is input to be processed, the input-listening thread will get a chance to execute.

The ray-tracing thread can have its priority set like this:

```
rayTraceThread.setPriority(Thread.NORM_PRIORITY-1);
```

The `traceRays()` method listed above can yield after each pixel value is computed, after line 4. The revised version looks like this:

```
1. private void traceRays() {
2.    for (int j=0; j<300; j++) {
3.       for (int i=0; i<300; i++) {
4.          computeOnePixel(i, j);
5.          Thread.yield();
6.       }
7.    }
8. }
```

# Suspending

Suspending a thread is a mechanism that allows any arbitrary thread to make another thread un-runnable for an indefinite period of time. The suspended thread becomes runnable when some other thread resumes it. This might feel like a useful mechanism, but it is very easy to cause deadlock in a program using these methods, since a thread has no control over when it is suspended (the control comes from outside the thread) and it might be in a critical section, holding an object lock at the time. The exact effect of suspend and resume is much better implemented using wait and notify and perhaps a small change to your design.

Since `suspend()` and `resume()` are now deprecated and have no place in the certification exam, we will not discuss them any further.

# Sleeping

A *Sleeping* thread passes time without doing anything and without using the CPU. A call to the `sleep()` method requests the currently executing thread to cease executing for (approximately) a specified amount of time. There are two ways to call this method, depending on whether you want to specify the sleep period to millisecond precision or to nanosecond precision:

- `public static void sleep(long milliseconds) throws InterruptedException`
- `public static void sleep(long milliseconds, int nanoseconds) throws InterruptedException`

Note that `sleep()`, like `yield()`, is static. Both methods operate on the currently executing thread.

The state diagram for sleeping is shown in Figure 7.3. Notice that when the thread has finished sleeping, it does not continue execution. As you would expect, it enters the Ready state and will only execute when the thread scheduler allows it to do so. For this reason, you should expect that a `sleep()` call will block a thread for at least the requested time, but it might block for much longer. This suggests that very careful thought should be given to your design before you expect any meaning from the nanosecond accuracy version of the `sleep()` method.

The Thread class has a method called `interrupt()`. A sleeping thread that receives an `interrupt()` call moves immediately into the Ready state; when it gets to run, it will execute its `InterruptedException` handler.

**FIGURE 7.3**

The Sleeping state

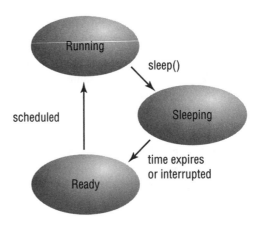

# Blocking

Many methods that perform input or output have to wait for some occurrence in the outside world before they can proceed; this behavior is known as *blocking*. A good example is reading from a socket:

```
1. try {
2.    Socket sock = new Socket("magnesium", 5505);
3.    InputStream istr = sock.getInputStream();
4.    int b = istr.read();
5. }
6. catch (IOException ex) {
7.    // Handle the exception
8. }
```

If you aren't familiar with Java's socket and stream functionality, don't worry: It's all covered in Chapter 13. The discussion here is not complicated.

It looks like line 4 reads a byte from an input stream that is connected to port 5505 on a machine called "magnesium." Actually, line 4 *tries* to read a byte. If a byte is available (that is, if magnesium has previously written a byte), then line 4 can return immediately and execution can continue. If magnesium has not yet written anything, however, the read() call has to wait. If magnesium is busy doing other things and takes half an hour to get around to writing a byte, then the read() call has to wait for half an hour.

Clearly, it would be a serious problem if the thread executing the read() call on line 4 remained in the Running state for the entire half hour. Nothing else could get done. In general, if a method needs to wait an indeterminable amount of time until some I/O occurrence takes place, then a thread executing that method should graciously step out of the Running state. All Java I/O methods behave this way. A thread that has graciously stepped out in this fashion is said to be blocked. Figure 7.4 shows the transitions of the Blocked state.

In general, if you see a method with a name that suggests that it might do nothing until something becomes ready, for example waitForInput(), waitForImages(), you should expect that the caller thread might be blocked, becoming un-runnable and losing the CPU, when the method is called. You do not need to know about all APIs to make this assumption; this is a general principle of APIs, both core and third party, in a Java environment.

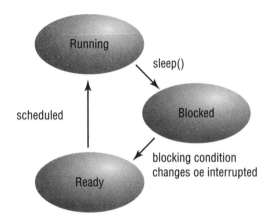

A thread can also become blocked if it fails to acquire the lock for a monitor or if it issues a `wait()` call. Locks and monitors are explained in detail later in this chapter, beginning in the section "Monitors, `wait()`, and `notify()`." Internally, most blocking for I/O, like the `read()` calls just discussed, is implemented using `wait()` and `notify()` calls.

## Monitor States

Figure 7.5 (which is just a rerun of Figure 7.1) shows all the thread state transitions. The intermediate states on the right-hand side of the figure (Suspended, Asleep, and Blocked) have been discussed in previous sections. The Monitor states are drawn all alone on the left-hand side of the figure to emphasize that they are very different from the other intermediate states.

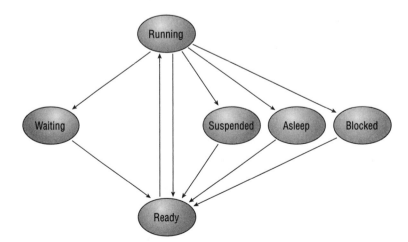

The wait() method puts an executing thread into the *Waiting* state, and the notify() and notifyAll() methods put waiting threads into the Ready state. However, these methods are very different from suspend(), resume(), and yield(). For one thing, they are implemented in the Object class, not in Thread. For another, they may only be called in synchronized code. The Waiting state, and the associated issues and subtleties, are discussed in the final sections of this chapter. But first, there is one more topic to look at concerning thread control.

## Scheduling Implementations

Historically, two approaches have emerged for implementing thread schedulers:

- Preemptive scheduling
- Time-sliced or round robin scheduling

So far, the facilities described in this chapter have been preemptive. In preemptive scheduling, there are only two ways for a thread to leave the Running state without explicitly calling a thread-scheduling method such as wait() or suspend():

- It can cease to be ready to execute (by calling a blocking I/O method, for example).
- It can get moved out of the CPU by a higher-priority thread that becomes ready to execute.

With time slicing, a thread is only allowed to execute for a limited amount of time. It is then moved to the Ready state, where it must contend with all the other ready threads. Time slicing insures against the possibility of a single high-priority thread getting into the Running state and never getting out, preventing all other threads from doing their jobs. Unfortunately, time slicing creates a non-deterministic system; at any moment you can't be certain which thread is executing or for how long it will continue to execute.

It is natural to ask which implementation Java uses. The answer is that it depends on the platform; the Java specification gives implementations a lot of leeway. Solaris machines are preemptive. Macintoshes are time-sliced. Windows platforms were originally preemptive, but changed to time-sliced with the 1.0.2 release of the JDK.

# Monitors, *wait()*, and *notify()*

**A** monitor is an object that can block and revive threads. The concept is simple, but it takes a bit of work to understand what monitors are good for and how to use them effectively.

The reason for having monitors is that sometimes a thread cannot perform its job until an object reaches a certain state. For example, consider a class that handles requests to write to standard output:

```
1. class Mailbox {
2.    public boolean    request;
3.    public String     message;
4. }
```

The intention of this class is that a client can set `message` to some value, then set `request` to `true`:

```
1. myMailbox.message = "Hello everybody.";
2. myMailbox.request = true;
```

There must be a thread that checks `request`; on finding it `true`, the thread should write `message` to `System.out`, and then set `request` to `false`. (Setting `request` to `false` indicates that the mailbox object is ready to handle another request.) It is tempting to implement this thread like this:

```
 1. public class Consumer extends Thread {
 2.    private Mailbox myMailbox;
 3.
 4.    public Consumer(Mailbox box) {
 5.      this.myMailbox = box;
 6.    }
 7.
 8.    public void run() {
 9.      while (true) {
10.        if (myMailbox.request) {
11.          System.out.println(myMailbox.message);
12.          myMailbox.request = false;
13.        }
14.
```

```
15.        try {
16.          sleep(50);
17.        }
18.        catch (InterruptedException e) { }
19.    }
20.  }
```

The consumer thread loops forever, checking for requests every 50 milliseconds. If there is a request (line 10), the consumer writes the message to standard output (line 11) and then sets `request` to `false` to show that it is ready for more requests.

The `Consumer` class may look fine at first glance, but it has two serious problems:

- The `Consumer` class accesses data internal to the `Mailbox` class, introducing the possibility of corruption. On a time-sliced system, the consumer thread could just possibly be interrupted between lines 10 and 11. The interrupting thread could just possibly be a client that sets `message` to its own message (ignoring the convention of checking `request` to see if the handler is available). The consumer thread would send the wrong message.

- The choice of 50 milliseconds for the delay can never be ideal. Sometimes 50 milliseconds will be too long, and clients will receive slow service; sometimes 50 milliseconds will be too frequent, and cycles will be wasted. A thread that wants to send a message has a similar dilemma if it finds the `request` flag set: The thread should back off for a while, but for how long?

Ideally, these problems would be solved by making some modifications to the `Mailbox` class:

- The mailbox should be able to protect its data from irresponsible clients.

- If the mailbox is not available—that is, if the `request` flag is already set—then a client consumer should not have to guess how long to wait before checking the flag again. The handler should tell the client when the time is right.

Java's monitor support addresses these issues by providing the following resources:

- A lock for each object

- The `synchronized` keyword for accessing an object's lock

- The `wait()`, `notify()`, and `notifyAll()` methods, which allow the object to control client threads

The sections below describe locks, synchronized code, and the `wait()`, `notify()`, and `notifyAll()` methods, and show how these can be used to make thread code more robust.

## The Object Lock and Synchronization

Every object has a *lock*. At any moment, that lock is controlled by, at most, one single thread. The lock controls access to the object's synchronized code. A thread that wants to execute an object's synchronized code must first attempt to acquire that object's lock. If the lock is available—that is, if it is not already controlled by another thread—then all is well. If the lock is under another thread's control, then the attempting thread goes into the Seeking Lock state and only becomes ready when the lock becomes available. When a thread that owns a lock passes out of the synchronized code, the thread automatically gives up the lock. All this lock-checking and state-changing is done behind the scenes; the only explicit programming you need to do is to declare code to be synchronized.

Figure 7.6 shows the Seeking Lock state. This figure is the first state in our expansion of the Monitor States as depicted in Figure 7.5.

There are two ways to mark code as synchronized:

- Synchronize an entire method by putting the `synchronized` modifier in the method's declaration. To execute the method, a thread must acquire the lock of the object that owns the method.

- Synchronize a subset of a method by surrounding the desired lines of code with curly brackets (`{}`) and inserting the `synchronized(someObject)` expression before the opening curly. This technique allows you to synchronize the block on the lock of any object at all, not necessarily the object that owns the code.

The first technique is by far the more common; synchronizing on any object other than the object that owns the synchronized code can be extremely

**FIGURE 7.6**

The Seeking
Lock State

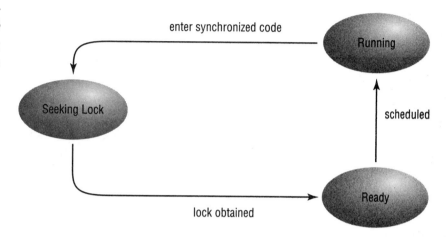

dangerous. The Certification Exam requires you to know how to apply the
second technique, but the exam does not make you think through complicated scenarios of synchronizing on external objects. The second technique
is discussed at the very end of this chapter.

Synchronization makes it easy to clean up some of the problems with the
Mailbox class:

```
1.  class Mailbox {
2.     private boolean   request;
3.     private String    message;
4.
5.     public synchronized void storeMessage(String message) {
6.        request = true;
7.        this.message = message;
8.     }
9.
10.    public synchronized String retrieveMessage() {
11.       request = false;
12.       return message;
13.    }
14. }
```

Now the **request** flag and the message string are private, so they can only
be modified via the public methods of the class. Since **storeMessage()** and

retrieveMessage() are synchronized, there is no danger of a message-producing thread corrupting the flag and spoiling things for a message-consuming thread, or vice versa.

The Mailbox class is now safe from its clients, but the clients still have problems. A message-producing client should only call storeMessage() when the request flag is false; a message-consuming client should only call retrieveMessage() when the request flag is true. In the Consumer class of the previous section, the consuming thread's main loop polled the request flag every 50 milliseconds. (Presumably a message-producing thread would do something similar.) Now the request flag is private, so you must find another way.

It is possible to come up with any number of clever ways for the client threads to poll the mailbox, but the whole approach is backwards. The mailbox becomes available or unavailable based on changes of its own state. The mailbox should be in charge of the progress of the clients. Java's wait() and notify() methods provide the necessary controls, as you will see in the next section.

## *wait()* and *notify()*

The wait() and notify() methods provide a way for a shared object to pause a thread when it becomes unavailable to that thread, and to allow the thread to continue when appropriate. The threads themselves never have to check the state of the shared object.

An object that controls its client threads in this manner is known as a *monitor*. In strict Java terminology, a monitor is any object that has some synchronized code. To be really useful, most monitors make use of wait() and notify() methods. So the Mailbox class is already a monitor; it just is not quite useful yet.

Figure 7.7 shows the state transitions of Wait() and Notify().

Both wait() and notify() must be called in synchronized code. A thread that calls wait() releases the virtual CPU; at the same time, it releases the lock. It enters a pool of waiting threads, which is managed by the object whose wait() method got called. Every object has such a pool. The code below shows how the Mailbox class' retrieveMessage() method could be modified to begin taking advantage of calling wait().

```
1. public synchronized String retrieveMessage() {
2.   while (request == false) {
```

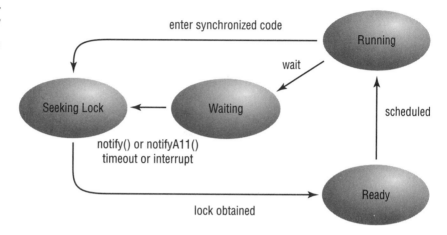

```
3.      try {
4.        wait();
5.      } catch (InterruptedException e) { }
6.    }
7.    request = false;
8.    return message;
9. }
```

Now consider what happens when a message-consuming thread calls this method. The call might look like this:

```
myMailbox.retrieveMessage();
```

When a message-consuming thread calls this method, the thread must first acquire the lock for myMailbox. Acquiring the lock could happen immediately or it could incur a delay if some other thread is executing any of the synchronized code of myMailbox. One way or another, eventually the consumer thread has the lock and begins to execute at line 2. The code first checks the request flag. If the flag is not set, then myMailbox has no message for the thread to retrieve. In this case the wait() method is called at line 4 (it can throw an InterruptedException, so the try/catch code is required, and the while will re-test the condition). When line 4 executes, the consumer thread ceases execution; it also releases the lock for myMailbox and enters the pool of waiting threads managed by myMailbox.

The consumer thread has been successfully prevented from corrupting the myMailbox monitor. Unfortunately, it is stuck in the monitor's pool of waiting threads. When the monitor changes to a state where it can provide the consumer with something to do, then something will have to be done to get the consumer out of the Waiting state. This is done by calling notify() when the monitor's request flag becomes true, which only happens in the storeMessage() method. The revised storeMessage() looks like this:

```
1. public synchronized void storeMessage(String message) {
2.    this.message = message;
3.    request = true;
4.    notify();
5. }
```

On line 4, the code calls notify() just after changing the monitor's state. What notify() does is to select one of the threads in the monitor's waiting pool and move it to the Seeking Lock state. Eventually that thread will acquire the mailbox's lock and can proceed with execution.

Now imagine a complete scenario. A consumer thread calls retrieve-Message() on a mailbox that has no message. It acquires the lock and begins executing the method. It sees that the request flag is false, so it calls wait() and joins the mailbox's waiting pool. (In this simple example, there are no other threads in the pool.) Since the consumer has called wait(), it has given up the lock. Later, a message-producing thread calls storeMessage() on the same mailbox. It acquires the lock, stores its message in the monitor's instance variable, and sets the request flag to true. The producer then calls notify(). At this moment there is only one thread in the monitor's waiting pool: the consumer. So the consumer gets moved out of the waiting pool and into the Seeking Lock state. Now the producer returns from retrieve-Message(); since the producer has exited from synchronized code, it gives up the monitor's lock. Later the patient consumer re-acquires the lock and gets to execute; once this happens, it checks the request flag and (finally!) sees that there is a message available for consumption. The consumer returns the message; upon return it automatically releases the lock.

To briefly summarize this scenario: A consumer tried to consume something, but there was nothing to consume, so the consumer waited. Later a producer produced something. At that point there was something for the consumer to consume, so the consumer was notified; once the producer was done with the monitor, the consumer consumed a message.

As Figure 7.7 shows, a waiting thread has ways to get out of the Waiting state that do not require being notified. One version of the wait() call takes an argument that specifies a timeout in milliseconds; if the timeout expires, the thread moves to the Seeking Lock state even if it has not been notified. No matter what version of wait() is invoked, if the waiting thread receives an interrupt() call it moves immediately to the Seeking Lock state.

This example protected the consumer against the possibility that the monitor might be empty; the protection was implemented with a wait() call in retrieveMessage() and a notify() call in storeMessage(). A similar precaution must be taken in case a producer thread wants to produce into a monitor that already contains a message. To be robust, storeMessage() needs to call wait(), and retrieveMessage() needs to call notify(). The complete Mailbox class looks like this:

```
1.  class Mailbox {
2.     private boolean    request;
3.     private String     message;
4.
5.     public synchronized void storeMessage(String message) {
6.       while(request == true) {  // No room for another message
7.         try {
8.           wait();
9.         } catch (InterruptedException e) { }
10.       }
11.       request = true;
12.       this.message = message;
13.       notify();
14.     }
15.
16.     public synchronized String retrieveMessage() {
17.       while(request == false) {  // No message to retrieve
```

```
18.       try {
19.          wait();
20.       } catch (InterruptedException e) { }
21.       }
22.    request = false;
23.    notify();
24.    return message;
25.  }
26. }
```

 By synchronizing code and judiciously calling wait() and notify(), monitors such as the Mailbox class can insure the proper interaction of client threads and protect shared data from corruption.

Here are the main points to remember about wait():

- The calling thread gives up the CPU.

- The calling thread gives up the lock.

- The calling thread goes into the monitor's waiting pool.

Here are the main points to remember about notify():

- One thread gets moved out of the monitor's waiting pool and into the Ready state.

- The thread that was notified must re-acquire the monitor's lock before it can proceed.

## Beyond the Pure Model

The mailbox example of the previous few sections has been a very simple example of a situation involving one producer and one consumer. In real life things are not always so simple. You might have a monitor that has several methods that do not purely produce or purely consume. All you can say in general about such methods is that they cannot proceed unless the monitor is in a certain state and they themselves can change the monitor's state in ways that could be of vital interest to the other methods.

The notify() method is not precise: You cannot specify which thread is to be notified. In a mixed-up scenario such as the one described above, a thread might alter the monitor's state in a way that is useless to the particular thread that gets notified. In such a case, the monitor's methods should take two precautions:

- Always check the monitor's state in a while loop rather than an if statement.

- After changing the monitor's state, call notifyAll() rather than notify().

The first precaution means that you should not do the following:

```
1. public synchronized void mixedUpMethod() {
2.    if (i<16 || f>4.3f || message.equals("UH-OH") {
3.      try { wait(); } catch (InterruptedException e) { }
4.    }
5.
6.    // Proceed in a way that changes state, and then...
7.    notify();
8. }
```

The danger is that sometimes a thread might execute the test on line 2, then notice that i is (for example) 234, and have to wait. Later, another thread might change the monitor's state by setting i to -23444, and then call notify(). If the original thread is the one that gets notified, it will pick up where it left off, even though the monitor is not in a state where it is ready for mixedUpMethod().

The solution is to change mixedUpMethod() as follows:

```
1. public synchronized void mixedUpMethod() {
2.    while (i<16 || f>4.3f || message.equals("UH-OH") {
3.      try { wait(); } catch (InterruptedException e) { }
4.    }
5.
6.    // Proceed in a way that changes state, and then...
7.    notifyAll();
8. }
```

The monitor's other synchronized methods should be modified in a similar manner.

Now when a waiting thread gets notified, it does not assume that the monitor's state is acceptable. It checks again, in the while-loop check on line 2. If the state is still not conducive, the thread waits again.

On line 8, having made its own modifications to the monitor's state, the code calls notifyAll(); this call is like notify(), but it moves every thread in the monitor's waiting pool to the Ready state. Presumably every thread's wait() call happened in a loop like the one on lines 2–4, so every thread will once again check the monitor's state and either wait or proceed.

Using a while loop to check the monitor's state is a good idea even if you are coding a pure model of one producer and one consumer. After all, you can never be sure that somebody won't try to add an extra producer or an extra consumer.

## Strange Ways to Synchronize

There are two ways to synchronize code that have not been explained yet. They are hardly common and generally should not be used without a very compelling reason. The two approaches are

- Synchronizing on the lock of a different object

- Synchronizing on the lock of a class

It was briefly mentioned in an earlier section ("The Object Lock and Synchronization") that you can synchronize on the lock of any object. Suppose, for example, that you have the following class, which is admittedly a bit contrived:

```
1. class StrangeSync {
2.   Rectangle rect = new Rectangle(11, 13, 1100, 1300);
3.   void doit() {
4.     int x = 504;
5.     int y = x / 3;
6.     rect.width -= x;
7.     rect.height -= y;
8.   }
9. }
```

If you add the `synchronized` keyword at line 3, then a thread that wants to execute the `doit()` method of some instance of `StrangeSync` must first acquire the lock for that instance. That may be exactly what you want. However, perhaps you only want to synchronize lines 7 and 8, and perhaps you want a thread attempting to execute those lines to synchronize on the lock of `rect`, rather than on the lock of the current executing object. The way to do this is shown below:

```
1. class StrangeSync {
2.    Rectangle rect = new Rectangle(11, 13, 1100, 1300);
3.    void doit() {
4.       int x = 504;
5.       int y = x / 3;
6.       synchronized(rect) {
7.          rect.width -= x;
8.          rect.height -= y;
9.       }
10.   }
11. }
```

The code above synchronizes on the lock of some arbitrary object (specified in parentheses after the `synchronized` keyword on line 6), rather than synchronizing on the lock of the current object. Also, the code above synchronizes just two lines, rather than an entire method.

It is difficult to find a good reason for synchronizing on an arbitrary object. However, synchronizing only a subset of a method can be useful; sometimes you want to hold the lock as briefly as possible, so that other threads can get their turn as soon as possible. The Java compiler insists that when you synchronize a portion of a method (rather than the entire method), you have to specify an object in parentheses after the `synchronized` keyword. If you put `this` in the parentheses, then the goal is achieved: You have synchronized a portion of a method, with the lock using the lock of the object that owns the method.

So your options are

- To synchronize an entire method, using the lock of the object that owns the method. To do this, put the `synchronized` keyword in the method's declaration.

- To synchronize part of a method, using the lock of an arbitrary object. To do this, put curly brackets around the code to be synchronized, preceded by `synchronized(theArbitraryObject)`.

- To synchronize part of a method, using the lock of the object that owns the method. To do this, put curly brackets around the code to be synchronized, preceded by synchronized(this).

Classes, as well as objects, have locks. A class lock is used for synchronizing the static methods of a class. The Certification objectives do not reflect a great emphasis on class locks.

# Chapter Summary

**A** Java thread scheduler can be preemptive or time-sliced, depending on the design of the JVM. No matter which design is used, a thread becomes eligible for execution ("Ready") when its start() method is invoked. When a thread begins execution, the scheduler calls the run() method of the thread's target (if there is a target) or the run() method of the thread itself (if there is no target).

In the course of execution, a thread can become ineligible for execution for a number or reasons: A thread can suspend, or sleep, or block, or wait. In due time (one hopes!), conditions will change so that the thread once more becomes eligible for execution; then the thread enters the Ready state and eventually can execute.

When a thread returns from its run() method, it enters the Dead state and cannot be restarted.

You might find the following bulleted lists a useful summary of Java's threads.

Scheduler implementations:

- Preemptive

- Time-sliced

Constructing a thread:

- new Thread(): no target; thread's own run() method is executed

- new Thread(Runnable target): target's run() method is executed

Non-runnable thread states:

- Suspended: caused by suspend(), waits for resume()

- Sleeping: caused by sleep(), waits for timeout

- Blocked: caused by various I/O calls or by failing to get a monitor's lock, waits for I/O or for the monitor's lock

- Waiting: caused by wait(), waits for notify() or notifyAll()

- Dead: caused by stop() or returning from run(), no way out

# Test Yourself

**1.** Which one statement below is true concerning the following code?

```
1. class Greebo extends java.util.Vector implements _
   Runnable {
2.   public void run(String message) {
3.     System.out.println("in run() method: " + message);
4.   }
5. }
6.
7. class GreeboTest {
8.   public static void main(String args[]) {
9.     Greebo g = new Greebo();
10.    Thread t = new Thread(g);
11.    t.start();
12.   }
13. }
```

**A.** There will be a compiler error, because class Greebo does not implement the Runnable interface.

**B.** There will be a compiler error at line 11, because you cannot pass a parameter to the constructor of a Thread.

**C.** The code will compile correctly but will crash with an exception at line 11.

**D.** The code will compile correctly but will crash with an exception at line 12.

**E.** The code will compile correctly and will execute without throwing any exceptions.

**2.** Which one statement below is always true about the following application?

```
1. class HiPri extends Thread {
2.    HiPri() {
3.       setPriority(10);
4.    }
5.
6.    public void run() {
7.       System.out.println("Another thread starting up.");
8.       while (true) { }
9.    }
10.
11.    public static void main(String args[]) {
12.       HiPri hp1 = new HiPri();
13.       HiPri hp2 = new HiPri();
14.       HiPri hp3 = new HiPri();
15.       hp1.start();
16.       hp2.start();
17.       hp3.start();
18.    }
19. }
```

**A.** When the application is run, thread hp1 will execute; threads hp2 and hp3 will never get the CPU.

**B.** When the application is run, all three threads (hp1, hp2, and hp3) will get to execute, taking time-sliced turns in the CPU.

**C.** Either A or B will be true, depending on the underlying platform.

**3.** A thread wants to make a second thread ineligible for execution. To do this, the first thread can call the `yield()` method on the second thread.

   **A.** True

   **B.** False

**4.** A thread wants to make a second thread ineligible for execution. To do this, the first thread can call the `suspend()` method on the second thread.

   **A.** True

   **B.** False

**5.** A thread's `run()` method includes the following lines:

```
1. try {
2.    sleep(100);
3. } catch (InterruptedException e) { }
```

Assuming the thread is not interrupted, which one of the following statements is correct?

   **A.** The code will not compile, because exceptions may not be caught in a thread's `run()` method.

   **B.** At line 2, the thread will stop running. Execution will resume in at most 100 milliseconds.

   **C.** At line 2, the thread will stop running. It will resume running in exactly 100 milliseconds.

   **D.** At line 2, the thread will stop running. It will resume running some time after 100 milliseconds have elapsed.

**6.** A monitor called `mon` has 10 threads in its waiting pool; all these waiting threads have the same priority. One of the threads is `thr1`. How can you notify `thr1` so that it alone moves from the Waiting state to the Ready state?

   **A.** Execute `notify(thr1);` from within synchronized code of `mon`.

    **B.** Execute `mon.notify(thr1);` from synchronized code of any object.

    **C.** Execute `thr1.notify();` from synchronized code of any object.

    **D.** Execute `thr1.notify();` from any code (synchronized or not) of any object.

    **E.** You cannot specify which thread will get notified.

**7.** Which one statement below is true concerning the following application?

```
1. class TestThread extends Thread {
2.   public void run() {
3.     System.out.println("Starting");
4.     suspend();
5.     resume();
6.     System.out.println("Done");
7.   }
8.
9.   public static void main(String args[]) {
10.     TestThread tt = new TestThread();
11.     tt.start();
12.   }
13. }
```

    **A.** Compilation will fail at line 4, because `suspend()` must be called in synchronized code.

    **B.** Compilation will fail at line 5, because `resume()` must be called in synchronized code.

    **C.** Compilation will succeed. On execution, nothing will be printed out.

    **D.** Compilation will succeed. On execution, only one line of output (`Starting`) will be printed out.

    **E.** Compilation will succeed. On execution, both lines of output (`Starting` and `Done`) will be printed out.

**8.** Which one statement below is true concerning the following application?

```
1. class TestThread2 extends Thread {
2.   public void run() {
3.     System.out.println("Starting");
4.     yield();
5.     resume();
6.     System.out.println("Done");
7.   }
8.
9.   public static void main(String args[]) {
10.     TestThread2 tt = new TestThread2();
11.     tt.start();
12.   }
13. }
```

**A.** Compilation will fail at line 4, because `yield()` must be called in synchronized code.

**B.** Compilation will fail at line 5, because `resume()` must be called in synchronized code.

**C.** Compilation will succeed. On execution, nothing will be printed out.

**D.** Compilation will succeed. On execution, only one line of output (`Starting`) will be printed out.

**E.** Compilation will succeed. On execution, both lines of output (`Starting` and `Done`) will be printed out.

**9.** If you attempt to compile and execute the application listed below, will it ever print out the message In xxx?

```
1. class TestThread3 extends Thread {
2.   public void run() {
3.     System.out.println("Running");
4.     System.out.println("Done");
5.   }
6.
```

```
 7.    private void xxx() {
 8.      System.out.println("In xxx");
 9.    }
10.
11.    public static void main(String args[]) {
12.      TestThread3 ttt = new TestThread3();
13.      ttt.xxx();
14.      ttt.start();
12.    }
13.  }
```

**10.** A Java monitor must either extend `Thread` or implement `Runnable`.

**A.** True

**B.** False

# CHAPTER

# 8

## The *java.lang* and *java.util* Packages

This chapter covers aspects of the following certification exam objectives:

- Determine the result of applying the `boolean equals(Object)` method to objects of any combination of the classes `java.lang.String`, `java.lang.Boolean`, and `java.lang.Object`.

- Write code using the following methods of the `java.lang.Math` class: `abs`, `ceil`, `floor`, `max`, `min`, `random`, `round`, `sin`, `cos`, `tan`, `sqrt`.

- Determine the result of applying any operator, including assignment operators and `instanceof`, to operands of any type, class, scope, or accessibility, or any combination of these.

- Describe the significance of the immutability of `String` objects.

The `java.lang` package contains classes that are central to the operation of the Java language and environment. Very little can be done without the `String` class, for example, and the `Object` class is completely indispensable. The Java compiler automatically imports all the classes in the package into every source file.

This chapter examines some of the most important classes of the `java.lang` package:

- `Object`
- `Math`
- The wrapper classes
- `String`
- `StringBuffer`

# The *Object* Class

The Object class is the ultimate ancestor of all Java classes. If a class does not contain the extends keyword in its declaration, the compiler builds a class that extends directly from Object.

All the methods of Object are inherited by every class. Three of these methods (wait(), notify(), and notifyAll()) support thread control; they are discussed in detail in Chapter 7. Two other methods, equals() and toString(), provide little functionality on their own. The intention is that programmers who develop re-usable classes can override equals() and toString() in order to provide class-specific useful functionality.

The signature of equals() is

```
public boolean equals(Object object)
```

The method is supposed to provide "deep" comparison, in contrast to the "shallow" comparison provided by the == operator. To see the difference between the two types of comparison, consider the java.util.Date class, that represents a moment in time. Suppose you have two references of type Date: d1 and d2. One way to compare these two is with the following line of code:

```
if (d1 == d2)
```

The comparison will be true if the reference in d1 is equal to the reference in d2: that is, if both variables contain identical patterns. Of course, this is only the case when both variables refer to the same object.

Sometimes you want a different kind of comparison. Sometimes you don't care whether d1 and d2 refer to the same Date object. Sometimes you know they are different objects; what you care about is whether the two objects represent the same moment in time. In this case you don't want the shallow reference-level comparison of ==; you need to look deeply into the objects themselves. The way to do it is with the equals() method:

```
if (d1.equals(d2))
```

The version of equals() provided by the Object class is not very useful; in fact, it just does an == comparison. All classes should override equals() so that it performs a useful comparison. That is, what most of the standard Java classes do, compare the relevant instance variables of two objects.

The purpose of the toString() method is to provide a string representation of an object's state. This is especially useful for debugging.

The toString() method is similar to equals() in that the version provided by the Object class is not especially useful. (It just prints out the object's class name, followed by a hash code.) Many JDK classes override toString() to provide more useful information. Java's string concatenation facility makes use of this method, as you will see later in this chapter, in the "String Concatenation" section.

# The *Math* Class

Java's Math class contains a collection of methods and two constants that support mathematical computation. The class is final, so you cannot extend it. The constructor is private, so you cannot create an instance. Fortunately, the methods and constants are static, so they can be accessed through the class name without having to construct a Math object. (See Chapter 3 for an explanation of Java's modifiers, including final, static, and private.)

The two constants of the Math class are

- Math.PI
- Math.E

They are declared to be public, static, final, and double.

The methods of the Math class cover a broad range of mathematical functionality, including trigonometry, logarithms and exponentiation, and rounding. The intensive number-crunching methods are generally native, to take advantage of any math acceleration hardware that might be present on the underlying machine.

The Certification Exam requires you to know about the following methods of the Math class:

- int abs(int i): returns the absolute value of i
- long abs(long l): returns the absolute value of l
- float abs(float f): returns the absolute value of f
- double abs(double d): returns the absolute value of d

- double ceil(double d): returns as a double the smallest integer that is not less than d

- double floor(double d): returns as a double the largest integer that is not greater than d

- int max(int i1, int i2): returns the greater of i1 and i2

- long max(long l1, long l2): returns the greater of l1 and l2

- float max(float f1, float f2): returns the greater of f1 and f2

- double max(double d1, double d2): returns the greater of d1 and d2

- int min(int i1, int i2): returns the smaller of i1 and i2

- long min(long l1, long l2): returns the smaller of l1 and l2

- float min(float f1, float f2): returns the smaller of f1 and f2

- double min(double d1, double d2): returns the smaller of d1 and d2

- double random(): returns a random number between 0.0 and 1.0

- int round(float f): returns the closest int to f

- long round(double f): returns the closest long to d

- double sin(double d): returns the sine of d

- double cos(double d): returns the cosine of d

- double tan(double d): returns the tangent of d

- double sqrt(double d): returns the square root of d

# The Wrapper Classes

**E**ach Java primitive data type has a corresponding *wrapper class*. A wrapper class is simply a class that encapsulates a single, immutable value. For example, the Integer class wraps up an int value, and the Float class wraps up a float value. The wrapper class names do not perfectly match the corresponding primitive data type names. Table 8.1 lists the primitives and wrappers.

| **T A B L E  8.1** | **Primitive Data Type** | **Wrapper Class** |
| --- | --- | --- |
| Primitives and Wrappers | boolean | Boolean |
| | byte | Byte |
| | char | Character |
| | short | Short |
| | int | Integer |
| | long | Long |
| | float | Float |
| | double | Double |

All the wrapper classes can be constructed by passing the value to be wrapped into the appropriate constructor. The code fragment below shows how to construct an instance of each wrapper type:

```
 1. boolean    primitiveBoolean = true;
 2. Boolean    wrappedBoolean = new Boolean(primitiveBoolean);
 3.
 4. byte       primitiveByte = 41;
 5. Byte       wrappedByte = new Byte(primitiveByte);
 6.
 7. char       primitiveChar = 'M';
 8. Character  wrappedChar = new Character(primitiveChar);
 9.
10. short      primitiveShort = 31313;
11. Short      wrappedShort = new Short(primitiveShort);
12.
13. int        primitiveInt = 12345678;
14. Integer    wrappedInt = new Integer(primitiveInt);
15.
16. long       primitiveLong = 12345678987654321;
```

```
17. Long        wrappedLong = new Long(primitiveLong);
18.
19. float       primitiveFloat = 1.11f;
20. Float       wrappedFloat = new Float(primitiveFloat);
21.
22. double      primitiveDouble = 1.11111111;
23. Double      wrappedDouble = new Double(primitiveDouble);
```

There is another way to construct any of these classes, with the exception of Character. You can pass into the constructor a string that represents the value to be wrapped. Most of these constructors throw NumberFormatException, because there is always the possibility that the string will not represent a valid value. Only Boolean does not throw this exception: the constructor accepts any String input, and wraps a true value if the string (ignoring case) is "true". The code fragment below shows how to construct wrappers from strings:

```
1. Boolean wrappedBoolean = new Boolean("True");
2.   try {
3.       Byte wrappedByte = new Byte("41");
4.       Short wrappedShort = new Short("31313");
5.       Integer wrappedInt = new Integer("12345678");
6.       Long wrappedLong = new Long("12345678987654321");
7.       Float wrappedFloat = new Float("1.11f");
8.       Double wrappedDouble = new Double("1.11111111");
9.   }
10.  catch (NumberFormatException e) {
11.      System.out.println("Bad Number Format");
12. }
```

The values wrapped inside two wrappers of the same type can be checked for equality by using the equals() method discussed in the previous section. For example, the code fragment below checks two instances of Double:

```
1. Double d1 = new Double(1.01055);
2. Double d2 = new Double("1.11348");
3. if (d1.equals(d2)) {
4.   // Do something.
5. }
```

After a value has been wrapped, it may eventually be necessary to extract it. For an instance of `Boolean`, you can call `booleanValue()`. For an instance of `Character`, you can call `charValue()`. The other six classes extend from the abstract superclass `Number`, which provides methods to retrieve the wrapped value as a byte, a short, an int, a long, a float, or a double. In other words, the value of any wrapped number can be retrieved as any numeric type. The retrieval methods are

- `public byte byteValue()`
- `public short shortValue()`
- `public int byteValue()`
- `public long longValue()`
- `public float floatValue()`
- `public double doubleValue()`

The wrapper classes are useful whenever it would be convenient to treat a piece of primitive data as if it were an object. A good example is the `Vector` class, which is a dynamically growing collection of objects of arbitrary type. The method for adding an object to a vector is

```
public void addElement(Object ob)
```

Using this method, you can add any object of any type to a vector; you can even add an array (you saw why in Chapter 4). You cannot, however, add an int, a long, or any other primitive to a vector. There are no special methods for doing so, and `addElement(Object ob)` will not work because there is no automatic conversion from a primitive to an object. Thus the code below will not compile:

```
1. Vector vec = new Vector();
2. boolean boo = false;
3. vec.addElement(boo);// Illegal
```

The solution is to wrap the boolean primitive, as shown below:

```
1. Vector vec = new Vector();
2. boolean boo = false;
3. Boolean wrapper = new Boolean(boo);
4. vec.addElement(wrapper); // Legal
```

The wrapper classes are useful in another way: they provide a variety of utility methods, most of which are static. For example, the `Character.isDigit(char ch)` static method returns a boolean that tells whether the character represents a base-10 digit. All the wrapper classes except `Character` have a static method called `valueOf(String s)`, which parses a string and constructs and returns a wrapper instance of the same type as the class whose method was called. So, for example, `Long.valueOf("23L")` constructs and returns an instance of the `Long` class that wraps the value 23.

To summarize the major facts about the primitive wrapper classes

- Every primitive type has a corresponding wrapper class type.

- All wrapper types can be constructed from primitives; all except `Character` can also be constructed from strings.

- Wrapped values can be tested for equality with the `equals()` method.

- Wrapped values can be extracted with various `XXXvalue()` methods. All six numeric wrapper types support all six numeric `XXXvalue()` methods.

- Wrapper classes provide various utility methods, including the static `valueOf()` method; ch parses an input string.

# Strings

**J**ava uses the `String` and `StringBuffer` classes to encapsulate strings of characters. Java uses 16-bit Unicode characters in order to support a broader range of international alphabets than would be possible with traditional 8-bit characters. Both strings and string buffers contain sequences of 16-bit Unicode characters. The next several sections examine these two classes, as well as Java's string concatenation feature.

## The *String* Class

The `String` class represents an immutable string. Once an instance is created, the string it contains cannot be changed. There are numerous forms of constructor, allowing you to build an instance out of an array of bytes or chars, a subset of an array of bytes or chars, another string, or a string buffer. Many of these constructors give you the option of specifying a character encoding, specified as a string; however, the Certification Exam does not require you to know the details of character encodings.

Probably the most common string constructor simply takes another string as its input. This is useful when you want to specify a literal value for the new string:

```
String s1 = new String("immutable");
```

An even easier abbreviation could be

```
String s1 = "immutable";
```

It is important to be aware of what happens when you use a String literal ("immutable" in both examples). Every string literal is represented internally by an instance of String. Java classes may have a pool of such strings. When a literal is compiled, the compiler adds an appropriate string to the pool. However, if the same literal already appeared as a literal elsewhere in the class, then it is already represented in the pool. The compiler does not create a new copy; instead, it uses the existing one from the pool. This saves on memory and can do no harm. Since strings are immutable, there is no way that a piece of code can harm another piece of code by modifying a shared string.

Earlier in this chapter, you saw how the equals() method can be used to provide a deep equality check of two objects. With strings, the equals() method does what you would expect—it checks the two contained collections of characters. The code below shows how this is done:

```
1. String s1 = "Compare me";
2. String s2 = "Compare me";
3. if (s1.equals(s2)) {
4.   // whatever
5. }
```

Not surprisingly, the test at line 3 succeeds. Given what you know about how String literals work, you can see that if line 3 is modified to use the == comparison, as shown below, the test still succeeds:

```
1. String s1 = "Compare me";
2. String s2 = "Compare me";
```

```
3. if (s1 == s2)) {
4.   // whatever
5. }
```

The == test is true because s2 refers to the String in the pool that was created in line 1. Figure 8.1 shows this graphically.

**FIGURE 8.1**

Identical literals

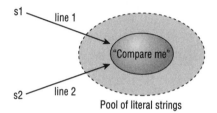

You can also construct a String by explicitly calling the constructor as shown below; however, this causes extra memory allocation for no obvious advantage.

```
String s2 = new String("Constructed");
```

When this line is compiled, the String literal "Constructed" is placed into the pool. At runtime, the new String() statement is executed and a fresh instance of String is constructed, duplicating the String in the literal pool. Finally, a reference to the new String is assigned to s2. Figure 8.2 shows the chain of events.

**FIGURE 8.2**

Explicitly calling the String constructor

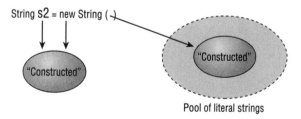

Figure 8.2 shows that explicitly calling new String() results in the existence of two objects, one in the literal pool and the other in the program's space.

You have just seen that if you create a new String instance at runtime, it will not be in the pool, but really will be a new and distinct object. You can arrange for your new String to be placed into the pool for possible reuse, or to reuse an existing identical String from the pool, by using the intern() method of the String class. In programs that use a great many strings that might be similar, this can reduce memory requirements. More importantly in programs that make a lot of String equality comparisons, ensuring that all strings are interen()ed allows you to use the == reference comparison in place of the slower equals() method.

There are several convenient methods in the String class. A number of these methods perform a transformation on a string. For example, toUpper() converts all the characters of a string to upper case. It is important to remember that the original string is not modified. That would be impossible, since strings are immutable. What really happens is a new string is constructed and returned. Generally, this new string will not be in the pool unless you explicitly call intern() to put it there.

The methods listed below are just some of the most useful methods of the String class. There are more methods than those listed here, and some of those listed have overloaded forms that take different inputs. This list includes all the methods that you are required to know for the Certification Exam, plus a few additional useful ones:

- `char charAt(int index)`: This returns the indexed character of a string, where the index of the initial character is 0.

- `String concat(String addThis)`: This returns a new string consisting of the old string followed by addThis.

- `int compareTo(String otherString)`: This performs a lexical comparison; returns an int that is less than 0 if the current string is less than otherString, equal to 0 if the strings are identical, and greater than 0 if the current string is greater than otherString.

- `boolean endsWith(String suffix)`: This returns true if the current string ends with suffix, otherwise returns false.

- `boolean equals(Object ob)`: This returns true if ob instance of String, and the string encapsulated by ob matches the string encapsulated by the executing object.

- boolean equalsIgnoreCase(String s): This is like equals(), but the argument is a String, and the comparison ignores case.

- int indexOf(char ch): This returns the index within the current string of the first occurrence of ch. Alternative forms return the index of a string, and begin searching from a specified offset.

- int lastIndexOf(char ch): This returns the index within the current string of the last occurrence of ch. Alternative forms return the index of a string, and end searching at a specified offset from the end of the string.

- int length(): This returns the number of characters in the current string.

- replace(char oldChar, char newChar): This returns a new string, generated by replacing every occurrence of oldChar with newChar.

- boolean startsWith(String prefix): This returns true if the current string begins with suffix, otherwise returns false.

- String substring(int startIndex): This returns the substring, beginning at startIndex, of the current string and extending to the end of the current string. An alternate form specifies starting and ending offsets.

- String toLowerCase(): This converts the executing object to lower case and returns a new string.

- String toString(): This returns the executing object.

- String toUpperCase(): This converts the executing object to upper case and returns a new string.

- String trim(): This returns the string that results from removing whitespace characters from the beginning and ending of the current string.

The code below shows how to use two of these methods to "modify" a string. The original string is " 5 + 4 = 20". The code first strips off the leading blank space, then converts the addition sign to a multiplication sign.

```
1. String s = " 5 + 4 = 20";
2. s = s.trim();              // "5 + 4 = 20"
3. s = s.replace('+', 'x');   // "5 x 4 = 20"
```

After line 3, s refers to a string whose appearance is shown in the line 3 comment. Of course, the modification has not taken place within the original string. Both the `trim()` call in line 2 and the `replace()` call of line 3 construct and return new strings; the address of each new string in turn gets assigned to the reference variable s. Figure 8.3 shows this sequence graphically.

**F I G U R E 8.3**

Trimming and replacing

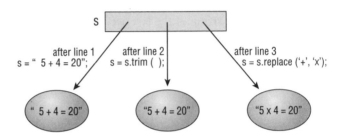

Figure 8.3 shows that the original string only seems to be modified. It is actually replaced, because strings are immutable. If much modification is required, then this becomes very inefficient, as it stresses the garbage collector cleaning up all the old strings and it takes time to copy the contents of the old strings into the new ones. The next section discusses a class that helps alleviate these problems because it represents a mutable string: the `String-Buffer` class.

## The *StringBuffer* Class

An instance of Java's `StringBuffer` class represents a string that can be dynamically modified.

The most commonly used constructor takes a `String` instance as input. You can also construct an empty string buffer (probably with the intention of adding characters to it later). An empty string buffer can have its initial capacity specified at construction time. The three constructors are

- `StringBuffer()`: This constructs an empty string buffer.

- `StringBuffer(int capacity)`: This constructs an empty string buffer with the specified initial capacity.

- `StringBuffer(String initialString)`: This constructs a string buffer that initially contains the specified string.

A string buffer has a `capacity`, which is the maximum-length string it can represent without needing to allocate more memory. A string buffer can grow beyond this as necessary, so usually you do not have to worry about capacity.

The list below presents some of the methods that modify the contents of a string buffer. All of them return the original string buffer itself.

- `StringBuffer append(String str)`: This appends `str` to the current string buffer. Alternative forms support appending primitives and character arrays; these are converted to strings before appending.

- `StringBuffer append(Object obj)`: This calls `toString()` on `obj` and appends the result to the current string buffer

- `StringBuffer insert(int offset, String str)`: This inserts `str` into the current string buffer at position `offset`. There are numerous alternative forms.

- `StringBuffer reverse()`: This reverses the characters of the current string buffer.

- `StringBuffer setCharAt(int offset, char newchar)`: This replaces the character at position `offset` with `newchar`.

- `StringBuffer setLength(int newLength)`: This sets the length of the string buffer to `newLength`. If `newLength` is less than the current length, the string is truncated. If `newLength` is greater than the current length, the string is padded with null characters.

The code below shows the effect of using several of these methods in combination.

```
1. StringBuffer sbuf = new StringBuffer("12345");
2. sbuf.reverse();              // "54321"
3. sbuf.insert(3, "aaa");       // "543aaa21"
4. sbuf.append("zzz");          // "543aaa21zzz"
```

The method calls above actually modify the string buffer they operate on (unlike the `String` class example of the previous section). Figure 8.4 graphically shows what this code does.

One last string buffer method that bears mentioning is `toString()`. You saw earlier in this chapter that every class has one of these methods. Not surprisingly, the string buffer's version just returns the encapsulated string, as

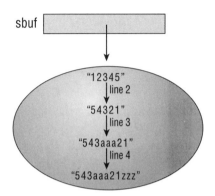

**FIGURE 8.4**

Modifying a
StringBuffer

an instance of class `String`. You will see in the next section that this method plays a crucial role in string concatenation.

Both the `String` and `StringBuffer` classes have `equals()` methods that compare two encapsulated strings. Neither version can be used for mixed comparison. You can compare a string to a string, or a string buffer to a string buffer, but you cannot compare a string to a string buffer. Such a method call would always return `false`, even if the two strings were identical.

## String Concatenation the Easy Way

The `concat()` method of the `String` class and the `append()` method of the `StringBuffer` class glue two strings together. An easier way to concatenate strings is to use Java's overloaded + operator. String concatenation with the + operator and the arithmetic operations are situations in which Java provides built-in operator overloading. However, don't forget that you, the programmer, can not define additional operator overloads.

String concatenation is useful in many situations, for example, in debugging print statements. So, to print the value of a double called `radius`, all you have to do is this:

```
System.out.println("radius = " + radius);
```

This technique also works for object data types. To print the value of a Dimension called dimension, all you have to do is

```
System.out.println("dimension = " + dimension);
```

It is important to understand how the technique works. At compile time, if either operand of a + operator (that is, if what appears on either side of a + sign) is a String object, then the compiler recognizes that it is in a string context. In a string context, the + sign is interpreted as calling for string concatenation, rather than arithmetic addition.

A string context is simply an arbitrary run of additions, where one of the operands is a string. For example, if variable aaa is a string, then the following partial line of code is a string context, regardless of the types of the other operands:

```
aaa + bbb + ccc
```

The Java compiler treats the code above as if it were the following:

```
new StringBuffer().append(aaa).append(bbb).append(ccc)._
toString();
```

If any of the variables (aaa, bbb, or ccc) is a primitive, the append() method computes an appropriate string representation. For an object variable, the append() method uses the string returned from calling toString() on the object. The conversion begins with an empty string buffer, then appends each element in turn to the string buffer, and finally calls toString() to convert the string buffer to a string.

The code below implements a class with its own toString() method.

```
1.  class Abc {
2.     private int a;
3.     private int b;
4.     private int c;
5.
6.     Abc(int a, int b, int c) {
7.        this.a = a;
8.        this.b = b;
9.        this.c = c;
10.    }
11.
```

```
12.    public String toString() {
13.      return "a = " + a + ", b = " + b + ", c = " + c;
14.    }
15. }
```

Now the toString() method (lines 12–14) can be used by any code that wants to take advantage of string concatenation. For example

```
Abc theAbc = new Abc(11, 13, 48);
System.out.println("Here it is: " + theAbc);
```

The output is

```
Here it is: a = 11, b = 13, c = 48
```

To summarize, the sequence of events for a string context is:

1. An empty string buffer is constructed.

2. Each argument in turn is concatenated to the string buffer, using the append() method.

3. The string buffer is converted to a string with a call to toString().

That is all you need to know about string manipulation for the Certification Exam, and probably all you need to know to write effective and efficient code too. Next, we're going to look at collections.

# The Collections API

**M**any, if not most, programs need to keep track of groups of related data items. One of the most basic mechanisms for doing this is the array. Java has always had arrays and also some additional classes, such as the Vector and Hashtable classes, to allow you to manipulate such groups of items. Since JDK 1.2, however, there is a significant API feature to support much more generalized collection management. The Certification Exam objectives now also require that you have a grasp of the concepts of this API.

The Collections API is often referred to as a *framework*. That is, the classes have been designed with a common abstraction of data container behavior in mind, insuring uniform semantics wherever possible. At the same time, each implemented collection type is free to optimize its own operations. The factory class `java.util.Collections` supplements support for these types, which are discussed below, with a variety of static helper and factory methods. These methods support operations such as synchronizing the container, establishing immutability, executing binary searches, and so on. With these classes in place, programmers are no longer required to build their own basic data structures from scratch.

# Collection Types

There are several different collections. They vary, for example, in the storage mechanisms used, in the way they can access data, and in the rules about what data might be stored. The Collections API provides a variety of interfaces, and some concrete implementation classes, covering these variations.

There is a general interface, `java.util.Collection`, that defines the basic framework for all collections. This interface stipulates the methods that allow you to add items, remove items, determine if items are in the collection, and count the number of items in the collection. A collection is sometimes known as a *bag* or a *multiset*. A simple collection places no constraints on the type of elements, order of elements, or repetition of elements within the collection.

Some collections are ordered, that is to say there is a clear notion of one item following another. A collection of this kind is commonly known as a *list* or a *sequence*. In some lists, the order is the order in which items are added to the collection; in others, the elements themselves are assumed to have a natural order, and that order is understood by the list. In the Java Collections API, the interface `java.util.List` defines a basic framework for collections of this sort.

If a collection imposes the specific condition that it cannot contain the same value more than once, then it is known as a *set*. The interface `java.util.Set` defines the basic framework for this type of collection. In some sets, the null value is a legitimate entry, but if it is allowed, null can only occur once in a set.

The final type of specialized behavior directly supported by the Collections API is known as a *map*. A map uses a set of key values to look up, or index, the stored data. For example, if you store an object representing a person, then as the key value you could either use that person's name or some other unique identifier such as a social security number. Maps are particularly appropriate for implementing small online databases, especially if the data being stored will usually be accessed via the unique identifier. It is a requirement for a map that the key be unique, and for this reason if you were storing data about a person in a map, the name would not make a very good key since it is quite possible for two people to have the same name.

Let's take a moment to recap these points:

- A collection has no special order and does not reject duplicates.

- A list is ordered and does not reject duplicates.

- A set has no special order but rejects duplicates.

- A map supports searching on a key field, values of which must be unique.

Of course it is possible for combinations of these behaviors to be meaningful. For example, a map might also be ordered. However, the certification exam only requires you to understand these four fundamental types of collection.

There are many ways in which the storage associated with any one collection can be implemented, but the Collections API implements the four that are most widely used. These are using an array, using a linked list, using a tree, or using hashing. Each of these techniques has benefits and constraints. Let's consider these benefits and constraints for each storage technique in turn.

*Array storage* tends to be fast to access, but it is relatively inefficient as the number of elements in the collection grows or if elements need to be inserted or deleted in the middle of a list. These limitations occur because the array itself is a fixed sequence. Adding or removing elements in the middle requires that all the elements from that point onward must be moved up or down by one position. Adding more data once the array is full requires a whole new array to be allocated, and the entire contents copied over to the new array. Another limitation of an array is that it provides no special search mechanism. Despite these weaknesses, an array can still be an appropriate choice for data that are ordered, do not change often, and do not need to be searched much.

A *linked list* allows elements to be added to, or removed from, the collection at any location in the container, and allows the size of the collection to grow arbitrarily without the penalties associated with array copying. This improvement occurs because each element is an individual object that refers to the next (and sometimes previous, in a double-linked list) element in the list. However, it is significantly slower to access by index than an array, and still provides no special search mechanism. Because linked lists can insert new elements at arbitrary locations, however, they can apply ordering very easily, making it a simple (if not always efficient) matter to search a subset, or range, of data.

A tree, like a linked list, allows easy addition and deletion of elements and arbitrary growth of the collection. Unlike a list, trees insist on a means of ordering. In fact, constructing a tree requires that there be some comparison mechanism to the data being stored—although this can be created artificially in some cases. A tree will usually provide more efficient searching than either an array or a linked list, but this benefit may be obscured if unevenly distributed data is being stored.

Hashing requires that some unique identifying key can be associated with each data item, which in turn provides efficient searching. Hashes still allow a reasonably efficient access mechanism and arbitrary collection growth. Hashing may be inappropriate for small data sets, however, since there is typically some overhead associated with calculating the hash values and maintaining the more complex data structure associated with this type of storage. Without a sufficiently large number of elements that would justify the operational costs, the overhead of a hashing scheme may cancel out or outweigh the benefits of indexed access.

To work properly in the various collection types, data items may need to exhibit certain specific behavior. If you wish to search for an item, for example, that item's class must correctly implement the `equals()` method. Searching in ordered collections may also require that the data implement the interface `java.lang.Comparable`, which defines `compareTo()`, a method for determining the inherent order of two items of the same type. Most implementations of Map will also require a correct implementation of the `hashCode()` method. It is advisable to keep these three methods in mind whenever you define a new class, even if you do not anticipate storing instances of this class in collections.

## Collection Implementations in the API

A variety of concrete implementation classes are supplied in the Collections API to implement the different interfaces Collection, List, Set, and Map, using different storage types. These are listed here:

**HashMap/Hashtable**   These two classes are very similar, using hash based storage to implement a map. The Hashtable has been in the Java API since the earliest releases, and the HashMap was added at JDK 1.2. The main difference between the two is that Hashtable does not allow the null value to be stored, although it makes some efforts to support multi-threaded use.

Note that the interfaces List, Set, and Map each extend the Collection interface.

**HashSet**   This is a set, so it does not permit duplicates and it uses hashing for storage.

**LinkedList**   This is an implementation of a list, based on a linked list storage.

**TreeMap**   This class provides an ordered map. The elements must be orderable, either by implementing the `Comparable` interface or by providing a `Comparator` class to perform the comparisons.

**TreeSet**   This class provides an ordered set, using a tree for storage. As with the TreeMap, the elements must have an order associated with them.

**Vector**   This class, which has been in the Java API since the first release, implements a list using an array internally for storage. The array is dynamically reallocated as necessary, as the number of items in the vector grows.

## Summary of Collections

The essential points in this section have been:

- Collections impose no order, nor restrictions, on content duplication
- Lists maintain an order (possibly inherent in the data, possibly externally imposed)
- Sets reject duplicate entries
- Maps use unique keys to facilitate lookup of their contents

For storage:

- Using arrays makes insertion, deletion, and growing the store more difficult
- Using a linked list supports insertion, deletion, and growing the store, but makes indexed access slower.
- Using a tree supports insertion, deletion, and growing the list, indexed access is slow, but searching is faster

- Using hashing supports insertion, deletion, and growing the store, indexed access is slow, but searching is particularly fast. However, hashing requires the use of unique keys for storing data elements.

# Chapter Summary

The java.lang package contains classes that are indispensable to Java's operation, so all the classes of the package are automatically imported into all source files. Some of the most important classes in the package are:

- Object

- Math

- The wrapper classes

- String

- StringBuffer

In a string context, addition operands are appended in turn to a string buffer, which is then converted to a string; primitive operands are converted to strings, and objects are converted by having their toString() methods invoked.

The java.util package contains many utilities, but for the certification exam, the collections API is of interest. Collections provide ways to store and retrieve data in a program. Different types of collection provide different rules for storage, and different collection implementations optimize different access and update behaviors.

# Test Yourself

1. Given a string constructed by calling s = new String("xyzzy"), which of the calls listed below modify the string? (Choose all that apply.)

   **A.** s.append("aaa");

   **B.** s.trim();

   **C.** s.substring(3);

   **D.** s.replace('z', 'a');

   **E.** s.concat(s);

**2.** Which one statement is true about the code below?

```
1. String s1 = "abc" + "def";
2. String s2 = newString(S1);
3. if (s1 == s2)
4.   System.out.println("== succeeded");
5. if (s1.equals(s2))
6.   System.out.println(".equals() succeeded");
```

**A.** Lines 4 and 6 both execute.

**B.** Line 4 executes, and line 6 does not.

**C.** Line 6 executes, and line 4 does not.

**D.** Neither line 4 nor line 6 executes.

**3.** Suppose you want to write a class that offers static methods to compute hyperbolic trigonometric functions. You decide to subclass java.lang.Math and provide the new functionality as a set of static methods. Which one statement below is true about this strategy?

**A.** The strategy works.

**B.** The strategy works, provided the new methods are public.

**C.** The strategy works, provided the new methods are not private.

**D.** The strategy fails, because you cannot subclass java.lang.Math.

**E.** The strategy fails, because you cannot add static methods to a subclass.

**4.** Which one statement is true about the code fragment below?

```
1. import java.lang.Math;
2. Math myMath = new Math();
3. System.out.println("cosine of 0.123 = " + _
   myMath.cos(0.123));
```

**A.** Compilation fails at line 2.

**B.** Compilation fails at line 3.

   **C.** Compilation succeeds, although the import on line 1 is not necessary. During execution, an exception is thrown at line 3.

   **D.** Compilation succeeds. The import on line 1 is necessary. During execution, an exception is thrown at line 3.

   **E.** Compilation succeeds, and no exception is thrown during execution.

**5.** Which one statement is true about the code fragment below?

```
1. String s = "abcde";
2. StringBuffer s1 = new StringBuffer("abcde");
3. if (s.equals(s1))
4.   s1 = null;
5. if (s1.equals(s))
6.   s = null;
```

   **A.** Compilation fails at line 1, because the String constructor must be called explicitly.

   **B.** Compilation fails at line 3, because s and s1 have different types.

   **C.** Compilation succeeds. During execution, an exception is thrown at line 3.

   **D.** Compilation succeeds. During execution, an exception is thrown at line 5.

   **E.** Compilation succeeds. No exception is thrown during execution.

**6.** In the code fragment below, after execution of line 1, sbuf references an instance of the StringBuffer class. After execution of line 2, sbuf still references the same instance.

```
1. StringBuffer sbuf = new StringBuffer("abcde");
2. sbuf.insert(3, "xyz");
```

   **A.** True

   **B.** False

**7.** In the code fragment below, after execution of line 1, sbuf references an instance of the `StringBuffer` class. After execution of line 2, sbuf still references the same instance.

```
1. StringBuffer sbuf = new StringBuffer("abcde");
2. sbuf.append("xyz");
```

**A.** True

**B.** False

**8.** In the code fragment below, line 4 is executed.

```
1. String s1 = "xyz";
2. String s2 = "xyz";
3. if (s1 == s2)
4.    System.out.println("Line 4");
```

**A.** True

**B.** False

**9.** In the code fragment below, line 4 is executed.

```
1. String s1 = "xyz";
2. String s2 = new String(s1);
3. if (s1 == s2)
System.out.println("Line 4");
```

Which would be most suitable for storing data elements that must not appear in the store more than once, if searching is not a priority?

**A.** Collection

**B.** List

**C.** Set

**D.** Map

**E.** Vector

# CHAPTER

# 9

Layout Managers

This chapter covers the following Java certification exam objective:

- Write code using component, container, and layout manager classes of the java.awt package to present a GUI with specified appearance and resize behavior, and distinguish the responsibilities of layout managers from those of containers.

Java's layout manager approach to Graphical User Interfaces is a novelty. Many GUI systems encourage GUI programmers to think in terms of precise specification of the size and location of interface components. Java changes all that. The Abstract Windowing Toolkit (AWT) provides a handful of layout managers, each of which implements its own layout policy. In Java, you create a GUI by choosing one or more layout managers and letting them take care of the details.

When you started working with layout managers, you probably had two impressions:

- You no longer bore the burden of specifying the exact position and dimensions of each component.

- You no longer had the power to specify the exact position and dimensions of each component.

Some people enjoy working with layout managers, and others resent them. They are here to stay, so the job at hand is to master this feature of the language. Acquiring this competence requires three things:

- An understanding of why Java uses layout managers

- An understanding of the layout policies of the more basic layout managers

- Some practice

The next section explains why Java uses layout managers. Then, after some intervening theory about how layout managers work, the last three sections of this chapter describe Java's three simplest layout managers: Flow Layout, Grid Layout, and Border Layout. (A fourth layout manager, Grid Bag Layout, is more complex than these three by an order of magnitude. Grid Bag Layout is mentioned briefly in this chapter, then discussed in detail in the context of the developer's exam; please see the "Using Layout Managers" section in Chapter 18.) As for the practice, once you successfully work through the questions at the end of the chapter and move through the relevant material in the simulated tester on the CD, you should be in good shape. The polish is up to you.

# Why Java Uses Layout Managers

There are two reasons why Java's AWT uses layout managers. The first reason is a bit theoretical, and you may or may not find yourself convinced by it. The second reason is thoroughly practical.

The theory lies in the position that precise layout (that is, specification in pixels of each component's size and position) is a repetitious and often-performed task; therefore, according to the principles of object-oriented programming, layout functionality ought to be encapsulated into one or more classes to automate the task. Certainly the layout managers eliminate a lot of development tedium. Many programmers dislike the idea of layout managers at first, but come to appreciate them more and more as tedious chores are eliminated.

The practical reason for having layout managers stems from Java's platform independence. Java components borrow their behavior from the window system of the underlying hardware on which the Java Virtual Machine is running. Thus on a Macintosh, an AWT button looks like any other Mac button; on a Motif platform, a Java button looks like any other Motif button, and so on. The problem here is that buttons and other components have different sizes when instantiated on different platforms.

For example, consider the button that is constructed by the following line of code:

```
Button b = new Button("OK");
```

On a Windows 95 machine, this button will be 32 pixels wide by 21 pixels high. On a Motif platform, the button will still be 32 pixels wide, but it will be 22 pixels high, even though it uses the same font. The difference seems small until you consider the effect such a difference would have on a column of many buttons. Other components can also vary in size from platform to platform. If Java encouraged precise pixel-level sizing and positioning, there would be a lot of Java GUIs that looked exquisite on their platform of origin—and terrible on other hosts.

There is no guarantee that fonts with identical names will truly be 100 percent identical from platform to platform; there could be minute differences. Therefore, Java cannot even guarantee that two Strings drawn with the same text and font will display at the same size across platforms. Similarly, there is no way to achieve size consistency among components, which have to deal with font differences and with decoration differences.

Java deals with this problem by delegating precision layout work to layout managers. The rest of this chapter investigates what layout managers are and explores the three most common managers.

# Layout Manager Theory

There are five layout manager classes in the AWT toolkit. You might expect that there would be a common abstract superclass, called something like LayoutManager, from which these five layout managers would inherit common functionality. In fact, there is a java.awt.LayoutManager, but it is an interface, not a class, because the layout managers are so different from one another that they have nothing in common except a handful of method names. (There is also a java.awt.LayoutManager2 interface, which the GridBag, Border, and Card layout managers implement. The certification exam does not cover the GridBag and Card layout managers, although these two are discussed in the developer's section as noted above.)

Layout managers work in partnership with containers. In order to understand layout managers, it is important to understand what a container is and what happens when a component gets inserted into a container. The next two sections explore these topics; the information is not directly addressed by the certification exam, but some relevant theory at this point will make it much easier to understand the material that is required for the exam.

## Containers and Components

Containers are Java components that can contain other components. There is a `java.awt.Container` class which, like `java.awt.Button` and `java.awt` `.Choice`, inherits from the `java.awt.Component` superclass. This inheritance relationship is shown in Figure 9.1.

**FIGURE 9.1**

Inheritance of
`java.awt.Container`

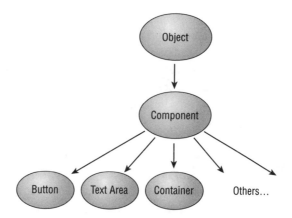

The `Container` class is abstract; its most commonly used concrete subclasses are `Applet`, `Frame`, and `Panel`, as shown in Figure 9.2. (Note that `Applet` is a subclass of `Panel`.)

Java GUIs reside in applets or in frames. For simple applets, you just put your components in your applet; for simple applications, you just put your components in your frame. (In both cases, you might wonder how the components end up where they do; layout managers are lurking in the background, taking care of details.) For more complicated GUIs, it is convenient to divide the applet or frame into smaller regions. These regions might constitute, for example, a toolbar or a matrix of radio buttons. In Java, GUI subregions are implemented most commonly with the `Panel` container. Panels,

**F I G U R E 9.2**

Common subclasses of
`java.awt.Container`

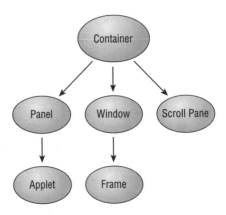

just like applets and frames, can contain other components: buttons, canvases, check boxes, scroll bars, scroll panes, text areas, text fields, and of course other panels. Complicated GUIs sometimes have very complicated containment hierarchies of panels within panels within panels within panels, and so on, down through many layers of containment.

In Java, the term *hierarchy* is ambiguous. When discussing classes, *hierarchy* refers to the hierarchy of inheritance from superclass to subclass. When discussing GUIs, *hierarchy* refers to the containment hierarchy of applets or frames, which contain panels containing panels containing panels.

The GUI in Figure 9.3 is a moderate-size frame for specifying a color. You can see at a glance that the panel contains labels, scroll bars, text fields, and buttons. You have probably guessed that the frame also contains some panels, even though they cannot be seen. In fact, the frame contains five panels. Each of the six containers (the five panels, plus the frame itself) has its own layout manager—there are four instances of Grid layout managers, one Flow layout manager, and one Border layout manager. Don't worry if you're not yet familiar with any of these managers—they will all be discussed shortly.

Figure 9.4 schematically shows the frame's containment hierarchy. A Java GUI programmer must master the art of transforming a proposed GUI into

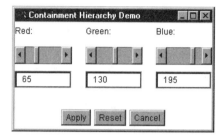

a workable and efficient containment hierarchy. This is a skill that comes
with experience, once the fundamentals are understood. The Programmer's
Java Certification Exam does not require you to develop any complicated
containments, but it does require you to understand the fundamentals.

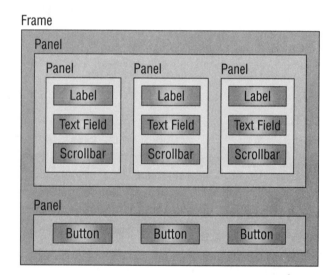

The code that implements the color chooser is listed below:

```
1. import java.awt.*;
2.
3. public class Hier extends Frame {
4.   Hier() {
```

```
5.      super("Containment Hierarchy Demo");
6.      setBounds (20, 20, 300, 180);
7.      setLayout(new BorderLayout(0, 25));
8.
9.      // Build upper panel with 3 horizontal "strips".
10.     String strings[] = {"Red:", "Green:", "Blue:"};
11.     Panel bigUpperPanel = new Panel();
12.     bigUpperPanel.setLayout(new GridLayout(1, 3, 20, 0));
13.     for (int i=0; i<3; i++) {
14.       // Add strips. Each strip is a panel within _
          bigUpperPanel.
15.       Panel levelPanel = new Panel();
16.       levelPanel.setLayout(new GridLayout(3, 1, 0, 10));
17.       levelPanel.add(new Label(strings[i]));
18.       levelPanel.add(new Scrollbar(Scrollbar.HORIZONTAL, i,
19.                                       10, 0, 255));
20.       levelPanel.add(new TextField("0"));
21.       bigUpperPanel.add(levelPanel);
22.     }
23.     add(bigUpperPanel, BorderLayout.CENTER);
24.
25.     // Build lower panel containing 3 buttons.
26.     Panel lowerPanel = new Panel();
27.     lowerPanel.add(new Button("Apply"));
28.     lowerPanel.add(new Button("Reset"));
29.     lowerPanel.add(new Button("Cancel"));
30.     add(lowerPanel, BorderLayout.SOUTH);
31.   }
32. }
```

As you can see from the listing, there is no code anywhere that specifies exactly where the labels, scroll bars, text fields, buttons, or panels should go. Instead, there are a number of calls (lines 7, 12, and 16) to layout manager constructors. In those same lines, the new layout managers are set as the managers for the corresponding containers. The lower panel constructed in line 26 uses its default layout manager, so it is not necessary to give it a new one.

A component inside a container receives certain properties from the container. For example, if a component is not explicitly assigned a font, it uses the same font that its container uses. The same principle holds true for foreground and background color. Layout managers, however, are different. A panel's default layout manager is always Flow. An applet's default layout manager is also always Flow. A frame's default layout manager is always Border.

After each panel is constructed and assigned an appropriate layout manager, the panel is populated with the components it is to contain. For example, the lower panel, constructed in line 26, is populated with buttons in lines 27, 28, and 29. Finally, the now-populated panel is added to the container that is to hold it (line 30).

The add() method call in line 30 does not specify which object is to execute the call. That is, the form of the call is add(params), and not some-Object.add(params). In Java, every non-static method call is executed by some object; if you don't specify one, Java assumes that you intended the method to be executed by this. So line 30 is executed by the instance of Hier, which is the outermost container in the hierarchy. Line 23, which adds the big upper panel, is similar: No executing object is specified in the add()call, so the panel is added to this.

In lines 17–20, and also in lines 27–29, a container is specified to execute the add() call. In those lines, components are added to intermediate containers.

Each panel in the sample code is built in four steps:

1. Construct the panel.

2. Give the panel a layout manager.

3. Populate the panel.

4. Add the panel to its own container.

When a container is constructed (step 1), it is given a default layout manager. For panels, the default is a flow layout manager, and step 2 can be skipped if this is the desired manager. In step 3, populating the panel involves constructing components and adding them to the panel; if any of these components is itself a panel, steps 1–4 must be recursed.

A container confers with its layout manager to determine where components will be placed and (optionally) how they will be resized. If the container subsequently gets resized, the layout manager again lays out the container's components (probably with different results, since it has a different area to work with). This "conference" between the container and the layout manager is the subject of the next section.

## Component Size and Position

Components know where they are and how big they are. That is to say, the `java .awt.Component` class has instance variables called x, y, `width`, and `height`. The x and y variables specify the position of the component's upper-left corner (as measured from the upper-left corner of the container that contains the component), and `width` and `height` are in pixels. Figure 9.5 illustrates the x, y, `width`, and `height` of a text field inside a panel inside an applet.

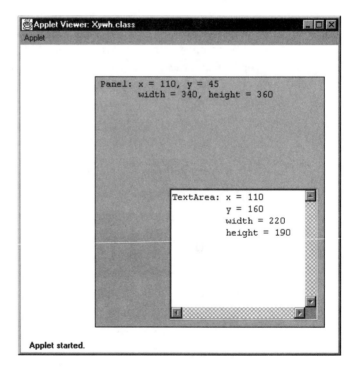

Panel: x = 110, y = 45
       width = 340, height = 360

TextArea: x = 110
          y = 160
          width = 220
          height = 190

A component's position and size can be changed by calling the component's setBounds() method. (In releases of the JDK before 1.1, the method was called reshape(); this has been deprecated in favor of setBounds().) It seems reasonable to expect that the following code, which calls setBounds() on a button, would create an applet with a fairly big button:

```
1. import java.awt.Button;
2. import java.applet.Applet;
3.
4. public class AppletWithBigButton extends Applet {
5.    public void init() {
6.       Button b = new Button("I'm enormous!");
7.       b.setBounds(3, 3, 333, 333);  // Should make _
          button really big
8.       add(b);
9.    }
10. }
```

If you have tried something like this, you know that the result is disappointing. A screen shot appears in Figure 9.6.

**FIGURE 9.6**

A disappointing button

It seems that line 7 should force the button to be 333 pixels wide by 333 pixels tall. In fact, the button is just the size it would be if line 7 were omitted or commented out.

Line 7 has no effect because after it executes, the button is added to the applet (line 8). Eventually (after a fairly complicated sequence of events), the applet calls on its layout manager to enforce its layout policy on the button. The layout manager decides where and how big the button should be; in this case, the layout manager wants the button to be just large enough to accommodate its label. When this size has been calculated, the layout manager calls `setBounds()` on the button, clobbering the work you did in line 7.

In general, it is futile to call `setBounds()` on a component, because layout managers always get the last word; that is, their call to `setBounds()` happens after yours. There are ways to defeat this functionality, but they tend to be complicated, difficult to maintain, and not in the spirit of Java. Java's AWT toolkit wants you to let the layout managers do the layout work. Java impels you to use layout managers, and the Certification Exam expects you to know the layout policies of the more basic managers. These policies are covered in the next several sections.

# Layout Policies

**E**very Java component has a *preferred size*. The preferred size expresses how big the component would like to be, barring conflict with a layout manager. Preferred size is generally the smallest size necessary to render the component in a visually meaningful way. For example, a button's preferred size is the size of its label text, plus a little border of empty space around the text, plus the shadowed decorations that mark the boundary of the button. Thus a button's preferred size is "just big enough."

Preferred size is platform-dependent, since component boundary decorations vary from system to system.

When a layout manager lays out its container's child components, it has to balance two considerations: the layout policy and each component's preferred size. First priority goes to enforcing layout policy. If honoring a component's preferred size would mean violating the layout policy, then the layout manager overrules the component's preferred size.

Understanding a layout manager means understanding where it will place a component, and also how it will treat a component's preferred size. The next several sections discuss some of the some of the simpler layout managers: FlowLayout, GridLayout, and BorderLayout. These are the three managers that you must know for the Certification Exam.

## The Flow Layout Manager

The Flow layout manager arranges components in horizontal rows. It is the default manager type for panels and applets, so it is usually the first layout manager that programmers encounter. It is a common experience for new Java developers to add a few components to an applet and wonder how they came to be arranged so neatly. The following code is a good example:

```
1. import java.awt.*;
2. import java.applet.Applet;
3.
4. public class NeatRow extends Applet {
5.    public void init() {
6.       Label label = new Label("Name:");
7.       add(label);
8.       TextField textfield = new TextField("Beowulf");
9.       add(textfield);
10.      Button button = new Button("OK");
11.      add(button);
12.   }
13. }
```

The resulting applet is shown in Figure 9.7.

If the same three components appear in a narrower applet, as shown in Figure 9.8, there is not enough space for all three to fit in a single row. The Flow layout manager fits as many components as possible into the top row and spills the remainder into a second row. The components always appear, left to right, in the order in which they were added to their container.

**FIGURE 9.8**

A narrower applet using Flow layout manager

If the applet is thinner still, as in Figure 9.9, then the Flow layout manager creates still another row.

**FIGURE 9.9**

A very narrow applet using Flow layout manager

Within every row, the components are evenly spaced, and the cluster of components is centered. The justification of the clustering can be controlled by passing a parameter to the `FlowLayout` constructor. The possible values are `FlowLayout.LEFT`, `FlowLayout.CENTER`, and `FlowLayout.RIGHT`. The applet listed below explicitly constructs a Flow layout manager to right-justify three buttons:

```
1. import java.awt.*;
2. import java.applet.Applet;
3.
```

```
4. public class FlowRight extends Applet {
5.    public void init() {
6.      setLayout(new FlowLayout(FlowLayout.RIGHT));
7.      for (int i=0; i<4; i++) {
8.        add(new Button("Button #" + i));
9.      }
10.   }
11. }
```

Figure 9.10 shows the resulting applet with a wide window.

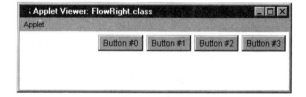

Figure 9.11 uses the same layout manager and components as Figure 9.10, but the applet is narrower.

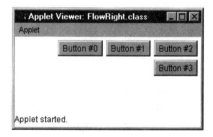

By default, the Flow layout manager leaves a gap of five pixels between components in both the horizontal and vertical directions. This default can be changed by calling an overloaded version of the FlowLayout constructor, passing in the desired horizontal and vertical gaps. All layout managers have this capability. Gaps are not covered in the certification exam, but they are certainly good to know about. A small gap modification can greatly improve a GUI's appearance. In the sample program in this chapter's section titled "Containers and Components," gaps were used in lines 12 and 16.

## The Grid Layout Manager

The Flow layout manager always honors a component's preferred size. The *Grid layout manager* takes the opposite extreme: It always *ignores* a component's preferred size.

The Grid layout manager subdivides its territory into a matrix of rows and columns. The number of rows and number of columns are specified as parameters to the manager's constructor:

```
GridLayout(int nRows, int Ncolumns)
```

The code listed below uses a Grid layout manager to divide an applet into 5 rows and 3 columns, and then puts a button in each grid cell:

```
1. import java.awt.*;
2. import java.applet.Applet;
3.
4. public class ThreeByFive extends Applet {
5.   public void init() {
6.     setLayout(new GridLayout(5, 3));
7.     for (int row=0; row<5; row++) {
8.       add(new Label("Label " + row));
9.       add(new Button("Button " + row));
10.      add(new TextField("TextField " + row));
11.    }
12.  }
13. }
```

Note that the constructor in line 6 yields five rows and three columns, not the other way around. After so many years of programming with Cartesian coordinates, it is probably second nature for most programmers to specify horizontal sorts of information before the comma, and vertical sorts of information after the comma. The GridLayout constructor uses "row-major" notation, which is sometimes confusing for humans.

As you can see in Figure 9.12, every component in the applet is exactly the same size. Components appear in the order in which they were added, from left to right, row by row.

If the same components are to be laid out in a taller, narrower applet, then every component is proportionally taller and narrower, as shown in Figure 9.13.

F I G U R E 9.12

Grid layout

Grid layout managers behave strangely when you have them manage very few components (that is, significantly fewer than the number of rows times the number of columns) or very many components (that is, more than the number of rows times the number of columns).

F I G U R E 9.13

Tall, narrow
Grid layout

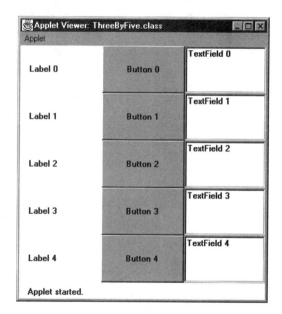

## The Border Layout Manager

The *Border layout manager* is the default manager for frames, so sooner or later application programmers are certain to come to grips with it. It enforces a much less intuitive layout policy than either the Flow or Grid managers.

The Flow layout manager always honors a component's preferred size; the Grid layout manager never does. The Border layout manager does something in between.

The Border layout manager divides its territory into five regions. The names of these regions are North, South, East, West, and Center. Each region may contain a single component (but no region is *required* to contain a component).

The component at North gets positioned at the top of the container, and the component at South gets positioned at the bottom. The layout manager honors the preferred height of the North and South components, and forces them to be exactly as wide as the container.

The North and South regions are useful for toolbars, status lines, and any other controls that ought to be as wide as possible, but no higher than necessary. Figure 9.14 shows an applet that uses a Border layout manager to position a toolbar at North and a status line at South. The font of the status line is set large to illustrate that the height of each of these regions is dictated by the preferred height of the component in the region. (For simplicity, the toolbar is just a panel containing a few buttons.)

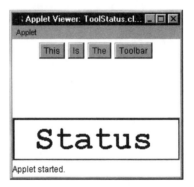

**F I G U R E 9.14**

Border layout for toolbar and status line

Figure 9.15 shows what happens if the same code is used to lay out a larger applet. Notice that the toolbar is still at the top, and the status line is still at the bottom. The toolbar and the status line are as tall as they were in Figure 9.14, and they are automatically as wide as the applet itself.

**F I G U R E  9.15**

Larger Border layout
for toolbar and
status line

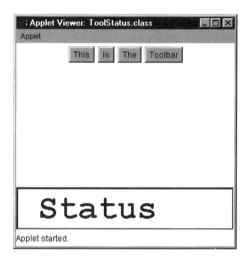

The code that produced these screen shots appears below:

```
1. import java.awt.*;
2. import java.applet.Applet;
3.
4. public class ToolStatus extends Applet {
5.   public void init() {
6.     setLayout(new BorderLayout());
7.
8.     // Build, populate, and add toolbar.
9.     Panel toolbar = new Panel();
10.    toolbar.add(new Button("This"));
11.    toolbar.add(new Button("Is"));
12.    toolbar.add(new Button("The"));
13.    toolbar.add(new Button("Toolbar"));
14.    add(toolbar, BorderLayout.NORTH);
15.
16.    // Add status line.
17.    TextField status = new TextField("Status line.");
18.    status.setFont(new Font("Courier", Font.BOLD, 48));
19.    add(status, BorderLayout.SOUTH);
20.  }
21. }
```

Notice that in lines 14 and 19, an overloaded form of the add() method is used. The border layout is not affected by the order in which you add components. Instead, you must specify which of the five regions will receive the component you are adding. The overloaded version of add() takes two parameters—first the component being added, and second an Object. Proper use of the Border layout manager requires that the second parameter be a String that specifies the name of the region; the valid values for this String are

- "North"
- "South"
- "East"
- "West"
- "Center"

The string must be spelled exactly as in shown above. The BorderLayout class has defined constants that you can use instead of the strings (the constants are defined to be the strings themselves). It is a good idea to use the defined constants rather than the strings, because if you misspell the name of a constant, the compiler will let you know. (On the other hand, if you use a misspelled String literal, a runtime exception will be thrown.) The five constants are

- BorderLayout.NORTH
- BorderLayout.SOUTH
- BorderLayout.EAST
- BorderLayout.WEST
- BorderLayout.CENTER

The East and West regions are the opposite of North and South: In East and West, a component gets to be its preferred width but has its height constrained. Here a component extends vertically up to the bottom of the North component (if there is one) or to the top of the container (if there is no North component). A component extends down to the top of the South component (if there is one) or to the bottom of the container (if there is no South component). Figures 9.16 through 9.19 show applets that use a Border layout manager to lay out two scroll bars, one at East and one at West. In Figure 9.16, there are no components at North or South to contend with.

**FIGURE 9.16**

East and West

In Figure 9.17, there is a label at North.

**FIGURE 9.17**

East and West, with North

In Figure 9.18, there is a label at South. The label has white text on black background so that you can see exactly where the South region is.

In Figure 9.19, there are labels at both North and South. The labels have white text on black background so that you can see exactly where the North and South regions are.

The code that generated these four applets is listed below—there is only one program. The code, as shown, generates Figure 9.19 (both North and South); lines 19 and 24 were judiciously commented out to generate the other figures:

```
1. import java.awt.*;
2. import java.applet.Applet;
3.
4. public class EastWest extends Applet {
5.    public void init() {
6.       setLayout(new BorderLayout());
7.
8.       // Scrollbars at East and West.
9.       Scrollbar sbRight = new Scrollbar(Scrollbar.VERTICAL);
10.      add(sbRight, BorderLayout.EAST);
11.      Scrollbar sbLeft = new Scrollbar(Scrollbar.VERTICAL);
12.      add(sbLeft, BorderLayout.WEST);
13.
14.      // Labels at North and South.
15.      Label labelTop = new Label("This is North");
16.      labelTop.setFont(new Font("TimesRoman", Font.ITALIC, 36));
17.      labelTop.setForeground(Color.white);
18.      labelTop.setBackground(Color.black);
19.      add(labelTop, BorderLayout.NORTH);
20.      Label labelBottom = new Label("This is South");
21.      labelBottom.setFont(new Font("Courier", Font.BOLD, 18));
22.      labelBottom.setForeground(Color.white);
23.      labelBottom.setBackground(Color.black);
24.      add(labelBottom, BorderLayout.SOUTH);
25.   }
26. }
```

The fifth region that a Border layout manager controls is called *Center*. Center is simply the part of a container that remains after North, South, East, and West have been allocated. Figure 9.20 shows an applet with buttons at North, South, East, and West, and a panel at Center. The panel is the white region.

**F I G U R E  9.20**

Center

The code that generated Figure 9.20 is listed below:

```
1. import java.awt.*;
2. import java.applet.Applet;
3.
4. public class Center extends Applet {
5.    public void init() {
6.       setLayout(new BorderLayout());
7.       add(new Button("N"), BorderLayout.NORTH);
8.       add(new Button("S"), BorderLayout.SOUTH);
9.       add(new Button("E"), BorderLayout.EAST);
10.      add(new Button("W"), BorderLayout.WEST);
11.      Panel p = new Panel();
12.      p.setBackground(Color.white);
13.      add(p, BorderLayout.CENTER);
14.   }
15. }
```

In line 13, the white panel is added to the Center region. When adding a component to Center, it is legal to omit the second parameter to the add() call; the Border layout manager will assume that you meant Center. However, it is easier for other people to understand your code if you explicitly specify the region, as in line 13 above.

Figures 9.21 and 9.22 show what happens to the Center region in the absence of various regions. The applets are generated by commenting out line 7 (for Figure 9.21) and lines 8–10 (for Figure 9.22). The figures show that Center (the white panel) is simply the area that is left over after space has been given to the other regions.

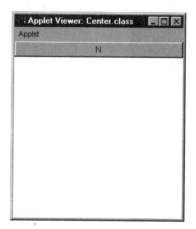

# Other Layout Options

The certification exam only requires you to know about the Flow, Grid, and Border layout managers. However, it is useful to know a little bit about the other options. If you are in a situation where Flow, Grid, and Border will not create the layout you need, your choices are

- To use a GridBag layout manager

- To use a Card layout manager

- To use no layout manager

- To create your own layout manager

GridBag is by far the most complicated layout manager. It divides its container into an array of cells, but (unlike the cells of a Grid layout manager) different cell rows can have different heights, and different cell columns can have different widths. A component can occupy a single cell or it can span a number of cells. A GridBag layout manager requires a lot of information to know where to put a component. A helper class called GridBagConstraints is used to hold all the layout position information. When you add a component, you use the add(Component, Object) version of the add() method, passing an instance of GridBagConstraints as the Object parameter.

The Card layout manager lays out its components in time rather than in space. At any moment, a container using a Card layout manager is displaying one or another of its components; all the other components are unseen. A method call to the layout manager can tell it to display a different component. All the components (which are usually panels) are resized to occupy the entire container. The result is similar to a tabbed panel without the tabs.

You always have the option of using no layout manager at all. To do this, just call

```
myContainer.setLayout(null);
```

If a container has no layout manager, it honors each component's x, y, width, and height values. Thus you can call setBounds() on a component, add it to a container which has no layout manager, and have the component end up where you expect it to be. This is certainly tempting, but hopefully the first part of this chapter has convinced you that layout managers are simple and efficient to work with. Moreover, if your container resides in a larger container (a frame, for example) that gets resized, your layout may need to be redone to save components from being overlaid or clipped away. People who set a container's layout manager to null find that they have to write code to detect when the container resizes, and more code to do the right thing when resizing occurs. This ends up being more complicated than creating your own layout manager.

It is beyond the scope of this book to show you how to concoct your own layout manager, but for simple layout policies it is not especially difficult to do so. The advantage of creating a custom layout manager over setting a container's layout manager to null is that you no longer have to write code to detect resizing of the container; you just have to write code to implement the layout policy, and the system will make the right calls at the right time. Writing your own layout manager class involves implementing the Layout-Manager interface (or possibly the LayoutManager2 interface). For a good reference with examples on how to do this, see Java 2 Developer's Handbook (Sybex, 1999).

# Improving Your Chances

**M**ore than any other Java-related topic, layout managers require you to use your ability to visualize in two dimensions. When you take the certification exam, you will be given the perfect tool to support two-dimensional thinking: a blank sheet of scratch paper. This is the only thing you will be allowed to bring into your test cubicle (and you will have to give it back when you leave).

Aside from layout manager problems, it is difficult to imagine what the scratch paper is good for. Consider drawing a picture of *every* layout manager problem, whether or not it feels like you need one. You won't run out of paper. Your picture might not convince you to choose a different answer than you would otherwise, but if this trick helps you get the right answer to even one extra layout manager problem, then it has done its job.

# Test Yourself

**1.** A Java program creates a check box using the code listed below. The program is run on two different platforms. Which of the statements following the code are true? (Choose one or more.)

```
1. Checkbox cb = new Checkbox("Autosave");
2. Font f = new Font("Courier", Font.PLAIN, 14);
3. cb.setFont(f);
```

**A.** The check box will be the same size on both platforms, because Courier is a standard Java font.

**B.** The check box will be the same size on both platforms, because Courier is a fixed-width font.

**C.** The check box will be the same size on both platforms, provided both platforms have identical 14-point plain Courier fonts.

**D.** The check box will be the same size on both platforms, provided both platforms have identical check-box decorations.

**E.** There is no way to guarantee that the buttons will be the same size on both platforms.

**2.** What is the result of attempting to compile and execute the following application?

```
1.  import java.awt.*;
2.
3.  public class Q2 extends Frame {
4.    Q2() {
5.      setSize(300, 300);
6.      Button b = new Button("Apply");
7.      add(b);
8.    }
9.
10.   public static void main(String args[]) {
11.     Q2 that = new Q2();
```

12.      that.setVisible(true);
13.    }
14.  }

**A.** There is a compiler error at line 11, because the constructor on line 4 is not public.

**B.** The program compiles but crashes with an exception at line 7, because the frame has no layout manager.

**C.** The program displays an empty frame.

**D.** The program displays the button, using the default font for the button label. The button is just large enough to encompass its label.

**E.** The program displays the button, using the default font for the button label. The button occupies the entire frame.

**3.** What is the result of compiling and running the following application?

```
1. import java.awt.*;
2.
3. public class Q3 extends Frame {
4.   Q3() {
5.     // Use Grid layout manager.
6.     setSize(300, 300);
7.     setLayout(new GridLayout(1, 2));
8.
9.     // Build and add 1st panel.
10.     Panel p1 = new Panel();
11.     p1.setLayout(new FlowLayout(FlowLayout.RIGHT));
12.     p1.add(new Button("Hello"));
13.     add(p1);
14.
15.     // Build and add 2nd panel.
16.     Panel p2 = new Panel();
17.     p2.setLayout(new FlowLayout(FlowLayout.LEFT));
18.     p2.add(new Button("Goodbye"));
19.     add(p2);
```

```
20.    }
21.
22.    public static void main(String args[]) {
23.      Q3 that = new Q3();
24.      that.setVisible(true);
25.    }
26. }
```

**A.** The program crashes with an exception at line 7, because the frame's default layout manager cannot be overridden.

**B.** The program crashes with an exception at line 7, because a Grid layout manager must have at least two rows and two columns.

**C.** The program displays two buttons, which are just large enough to encompass their labels. The buttons appear at the top of the frame. The "Hello" button is just to the left of the vertical midline of the frame; the "Goodbye" button is just to the right of the vertical midline of the frame.

**D.** The program displays two large buttons. The "Hello" button occupies the entire left half of the frame, and the "Goodbye" button occupies the entire right half of the frame.

**E.** The program displays two buttons, which are just wide enough to encompass their labels. The buttons are as tall as the frame. The "Hello" button is just to the left of the vertical midline of the frame; the "Goodbye" button is just to the right of the vertical midline of the frame.

**4.** What is the result of compiling and running the following application?

```
1. import java.awt.*;
2.
3. public class Q4 extends Frame {
4.   Q4() {
5.     // Use Grid layout manager.
6.     setSize(300, 300);
7.     setLayout(new GridLayout(3, 1));
8.
9.     // Build and add 1st panel.
```

```
10.      Panel p1 = new Panel();
11.      p1.setLayout(new BorderLayout());
12.      p1.add(new Button("Alpha"), BorderLayout.NORTH);
13.      add(p1);
14.
15.      // Build and add 2nd panel.
16.      Panel p2 = new Panel();
17.      p2.setLayout(new BorderLayout());
18.      p2.add(new Button("Beta"), BorderLayout.CENTER);
19.      add(p2);
20.
21.      // Build and add 3rd panel.
22.      Panel p3 = new Panel();
23.      p3.setLayout(new BorderLayout());
24.      p3.add(new Button("Gamma"), BorderLayout.SOUTH);
25.      add(p3);
26.   }
27.
28.   public static void main(String args[]) {
29.     Q4 that = new Q4();
30.     that.setVisible(true);
31.   }
32. }
```

**A.** Each button is as wide as the frame and is just tall enough to encompass its label. The "Alpha" button is at the top of the frame. The "Beta" button is in the middle. The "Gamma" button is at the bottom.

**B.** Each button is as wide as the frame. The "Alpha" button is at the top of the frame and is just tall enough to encompass its label. The "Beta" button is in the middle of the frame; its height is approximately 1/3 the height of the frame. The "Gamma" button is at the bottom of the frame and is just tall enough to encompass its label.

**C.** Each button is just wide enough and just tall enough to encompass its label. All three buttons are centered horizontally. The "Alpha" button is at the top of the frame. The "Beta" button is in the middle. The "Gamma" button is at the bottom.

**D.** Each button is just wide enough to encompass its label. All three buttons are centered horizontally. The "Alpha" button is at the top of the frame and is just tall enough to encompass its label. The "Beta" button is in the middle of the frame; its height is approximately 1/3 the height of the frame. The "Gamma" button is at the bottom of the frame and is just tall enough to encompass its label.

**E.** Each button is as tall as the frame and is just wide enough to encompass its label. The "Alpha" button is at the left of the frame. The "Beta" button is in the middle. The "Gamma" button is at the right.

**5.** You would like to compile and execute the following code. After the frame appears on the screen (assuming you get that far), you would like to resize the frame to be approximately twice its original width and approximately twice its original height. Which of the statements following the code is correct? (Choose one.)

```
1. import java.awt.*;
2.
3. public class Q5 extends Frame {
4.    Q5() {
5.      setSize(300, 300);
6.      setFont(new Font("Helvetica", Font.BOLD, 36));
7.      Button b = new Button("Abracadabra");
8.      add(b, BorderLayout.SOUTH);
9.    }
10.
11.   public static void main(String args[]) {
12.     Q5 that = new Q5();
13.     that.setVisible(true);
14.   }
15. }
```

**A.** Compilation fails at line 8, because the frame has not been given a layout manager.

**B.** Before resizing, the button appears at the top of the frame and is as wide as the frame. After resizing, the button retains its original width and is still at the top of the frame.

**C.** Before resizing, the button appears at the bottom of the frame and is as wide as the frame. After resizing, the button retains its original width and is the same distance from the top of the frame as it was before resizing.

**D.** Before resizing, the button appears at the bottom of the frame and is as wide as the frame. After resizing, the button is as wide as the frame's new width and is still at the bottom of the frame.

**E.** Before resizing, the button appears at the bottom of the frame and is as wide as the frame. After resizing, the button retains its original width and is about twice as tall as it used to be. It is still at the bottom of the frame.

**6.** The following code builds a GUI with a single button. Which one statement is true about the button's size?

```
1. import java.awt.*;
2.
3. public class Q6 extends Frame {
4.    Q6() {
5.       setSize(500, 500);
6.       setLayout(new FlowLayout());
7.
8.       Button b = new Button("Where am I?");
9.       Panel p1 = new Panel();
10.      p1.setLayout(new FlowLayout(FlowLayout.LEFT));
11.      Panel p2 = new Panel();
12.      p2.setLayout(new BorderLayout());
13.      Panel p3 = new Panel();
14.      p3.setLayout(new GridLayout(3, 2));
15.
16.      p1.add(b);
17.      p2.add(p1, BorderLayout.NORTH);
```

```
18.        p3.add(p2);
19.        add(p3);
20.    }
21.
22.    public static void main(String args[]) {
23.      Q6 that = new Q6();
24.      that.setVisible(true);
25.    }
26. }
```

    **A.** The button is just wide enough and tall enough to encompass its label.

    **B.** The button is just wide enough to encompass its label; its height is the entire height of the frame.

    **C.** The button is just tall enough to encompass its label; its width is the entire width of the frame.

    **D.** The button is just wide enough to encompass its label, and its height is approximately half the frame's height.

    **E.** The button's height is approximately half the frame's height. Its width is approximately half the frame's width.

**7.** An application has a frame that uses a Border layout manager. Why is it probably not a good idea to put a vertical scroll bar at North in the frame?

    **A.** The scroll bar's height would be its preferred height, which is not likely to be high enough.

    **B.** The scroll bar's width would be the entire width of the frame, which would be much wider than necessary.

    **C.** Both A and B.

    **D.** Neither A nor B. There is no problem with the layout as described.

8. What is the default layout manager for an applet? for a frame? for a panel?

9. If a frame uses a Grid layout manager and does not contain any panels, then all the components within the frame are the same width and height.

   **A.** True

   **B.** False

10. If a frame uses its default layout manager and does not contain any panels, then all the components within the frame are the same width and height.

    **A.** A.True

    **B.** B.False

11. With a Border layout manager, the component at Center gets all the space that is left over, after the components at North and South have been considered.

    **A.** True

    **B.** False

12. With a Grid layout manager, the preferred width of each component is honored, while height is dictated; if there are too many components to fit in a single row, additional rows are created.

    **A.** True

    **B.** False

# CHAPTER

# 10

Events

**T**his chapter covers aspects of the following Java certification exam objective:

- Write code to implement listener classes and methods, and in listener methods, extract information from the event to determine the affected component, mouse position, nature, and time of the event. State the event classname for any specified event listener interface in the `java.awt.event` package.

Java's original "outward rippling" event model proved to have some short-comings. A new "event delegation" model was introduced in release 1.1 of the JDK. Both models are supported in Java 2, but eventually the old model will disappear. For now, all methods that support the old event model are deprecated.

The two models are mutually incompatible. A Java program that uses both models is likely to fail, with events being lost or incorrectly processed.

This chapter reviews the new model in detail.

# Motivation for the Event Delegation Model

**C**ertain flaws in the original event model became apparent after Java had been in the world long enough for large programs to be developed.

The major problem was that an event could only be handled by the component that originated the event or by one of the containers that contained the originating component. This restriction violated one of the fundamental principles of object-oriented programming: Functionality should reside in the most appropriate class. Often the most appropriate class for handling an event is not a member of the originating component's containment hierarchy.

Another drawback of the original model was that a large number of CPU cycles were wasted on uninteresting events. Any event in which a program had no interest would ripple all the way through the containment hierarchy before eventually being discarded. The original event model provided no way to disable processing of irrelevant events.

In the event delegation model, a component may be told which object or objects should be notified when the component generates a particular kind of event. If a component is not interested in an event type, then events of that type will not be propagated.

The delegation model is based on four concepts:

- Event classes

- Event listeners

- Explicit event enabling

- Adapters

This chapter explains each of these concepts in turn.

# The Event Class Hierarchy

The event delegation model defines a large number of new event classes. The hierarchy of event classes is shown in Figure 10.1. Most of the event classes reside in the `java.awt.event` package.

The topmost superclass of all the new event classes is `java.util.Event-Object`. It is a very general class, with only one method of interest:

- `Object getSource()`: returns the object that originated the event

One subclass of `EventObject` is `java.awt.AWTEvent`, which is the superclass of all the delegation model event classes. Again, there is only one method of interest:

- `int getID()`: returns the ID of the event

An event's ID is an int that specifies the exact nature of the event. For example, an instance of the `MouseEvent` class can represent one of seven occurrences: a click, a drag, an entrance, an exit, a move, a press, or a release.

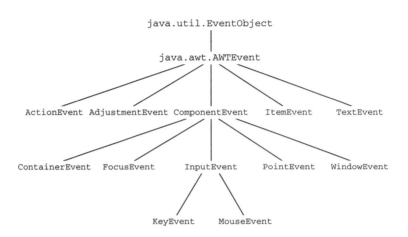

All classes belong to `java.awt.event` package unless otherwise noted.

Each of these possibilities is represented by an int: MouseEvent.MOUSE_ CLICKED, MouseEvent.MOUSE_DRAGGED, and so on.

The subclasses of `java.awt.AWTEvent` represent the various event types that can be generated by the various AWT components. These event types are

- ActionEvent: generated by activation of components

- AdjustmentEvent: generated by adjustment of adjustable components such as scroll bars

- ContainerEvent: generated when components are added to or removed from a container

- FocusEvent: generated when a component receives input focus

- ItemEvent: generated when an item is selected from a list, choice, or check box

- KeyEvent: generated by keyboard activity

- MouseEvent: generated by mouse activity

- PaintEvent: generated when a component is painted

- MouseEvent: generated when a text component is modified

- WindowEvent: generated by window activity (such as iconifying or de-iconifying)

The InputEvent superclass has a getWhen() method that returns the time when the event took place; the return type is long. The MouseEvent class has getX() and getY() methods that return the position of the mouse within the originating component at the time the event took place; the return types are both int.

There are two ways to handle the events listed previously. The first way is to delegate event handling to a listener object. The second way is to explicitly enable the originating component to handle its own events. These two strategies are discussed in the next two sections.

# Event Listeners

An *event listener* is an object to which a component has delegated the task of handling a particular kind of event. When the component experiences input, an event of the appropriate type is constructed; the event is then passed as the parameter to a method call on the listener. A listener must implement the interface that contains the event-handling method.

For example, consider a button in an applet. When the button is clicked, an action event is to be sent to an instance of class MyActionListener. The code for MyActionListener is as follows:

```
1. class MyActionListener implements ActionListener {
2.   public void actionPerformed(ActionEvent ae) {
3.     System.out.println("Action performed.");
4.   }
5. }
```

The class implements the ActionListener interface, thus guaranteeing the presence of an actionPerformed() method. The applet code looks like this:

```
1. public class ListenerTest extends Applet {
2.   public void init() {
3.     Button btn = new Button("OK");
4.     MyActionListener listener = new MyActionListener();
```

```
5.      btn.addActionListener(listener);
6.      add(btn);
7.    }
8.  }
```

On line 4, an instance of MyActionListener is created. On line 5, this instance is set as one of the button's action listeners. The code follows a standard formula for giving an action listener to a component; the formula can be summarized as follows:

1. Create a listener class that implements the ActionListener interface.

2. Construct the component.

3. Construct an instance of the listener class.

4. Call addActionListener() on the component, passing in the listener object.

In all, there are 11 listener types, each represented by an interface. Table 10.1 lists the listener interfaces, along with the interface methods and the addXXX-Listener() methods.

**T A B L E 10.1:** Listener interfaces

| Interface | Interface Methods | Add Method |
|-----------|-------------------|------------|
| ActionListener | actionPerformed(ActionEvent) | addActionListener() |
| AdjustmentListener | adjustmentValueChanged (AdjustmentEvent) | addAdjustmentListener() |
| ComponentListener | componentHidden(ComponentEvent) | addComponentListener() |
|  | componentMoved(ComponentEvent) | |
|  | componentResized (ComponentEvent) | |
|  | componentShown (ComponentEvent) | |
| ContainerListener | componentAdded(ContainerEvent) | addContainerListener() |
|  | componentRemoved(ContainerEvent) | |

**T A B L E  10.1:**  Listener interfaces *(Continued)*

| Interface | Interface Methods | Add Method |
|---|---|---|
| FocusListener | focusGained(FocusEvent) | addFocusListener() |
| | focusLost(FocusEvent) | |
| ItemListener | itemStateChanged(ItemEvent) | addItemListener() |
| KeyListener | keyPressed(KeyEvent) | addKeyListener() |
| | keyReleased(KeyEvent) | |
| | keyTyped(KeyEvent) | |
| MouseListener | mouseClicked(MouseEvent) | addMouseListener() |
| | mouseEntered(MouseEvent) | |
| | mouseExited(MouseEvent) | |
| | mousePressed(MouseEvent) | |
| | mouseReleased(MouseEvent) | |
| MouseMotionListener | mouseDragged(MouseEvent) | addMouseMotionListener() |
| | mouseMoved(MouseEvent) | |
| TextListener | textValueChanged(TextEvent) | addTextListener() |
| WindowListener | windowActivated(WindowEvent) | addWindowListener() |
| | windowClosed(WindowEvent) | |
| | windowClosing(WindowEvent) | |
| | windowDeactivated(WindowEvent) | |
| | windowDeiconified(WindowEvent) | |
| | windowIconified(WindowEvent) | |
| | windowOpened(WindowEvent) | |

A component may have multiple listeners for any event type. There is no guarantee that listeners will be notified in the order in which they were added. There is also no guarantee that all listener notification will occur in the same thread; thus listeners must take precautions against corrupting shared data.

An event listener may be removed from a component's list of listeners by calling a removeXXXListener() method, passing in the listener to be removed. For example, the code below removes action listener al from button btn:

```
btn.removeActionListener(al);
```

The techniques described in this section represent the standard way to handle events in the delegation model. Event delegation is sufficient in most situations; however, there are times when it is preferable for a component to handle its own events, rather than delegating its events to listeners. The next section describes how to make a component handle its own events.

# Explicit Event Enabling

There is an alternative to delegating a component's events. It is possible to subclass the component and override the method that receives events and dispatches them to listeners. For example, components that originate action events have a method called processActionEvent(ActionEvent), which dispatches its action event to each action listener. The following code implements a subclass of Button that overrides processActionEvent():

```
1. class MyBtn extends Button  {
2.    public MyBtn(String label) {
3.      super(label);
4.      enableEvents(AWTEvent.ACTION_EVENT_MASK);
5.    }
6.
7.    public void processActionEvent(ActionEvent ae) {
8.      System.out.println("Processing an action event.");
```

```
 9.       super.processActionEvent(ae);
10.    }
11. }
```

On line 4, the constructor calls enableEvents(), passing in a constant that enables processing of action events. The AWTEvent class defines 11 constants that can be used to enable processing of events; these constants are listed in Table 10.2. (Event processing is automatically enabled when event listeners are added, so if you restrict yourself to the listener model, you never have to call enableEvents().)

Line 7 is the beginning of the subclass' version of the processAction-Event() method. Notice the call on line 9 to the superclass' version. This call is necessary because the superclass' version is responsible for calling action-Performed() on the button's action listeners; without line 9, action listeners would be ignored.

Of course, you can always make a component subclass handle its own events by making the subclass an event listener of itself, as shown in the listing below:

```
 1. class MyBtn extends Button implements ActionListener {
 2.    public MyBtn(String label) {
 3.      super(label);
 4.      addActionListener(this);
 5.    }
 6.
 7.    public void actionPerformed(ActionEvent ae) {
 8.      // Handle the event here.
 9.    }
10. }
```

The only difference between this strategy and the enableEvents() strategy is the order in which event handlers are invoked. When you explicitly call enableEvents(), the component's processActionEvent() method will be called before any action listeners are notified. When the component sub-subclass is its own event listener, there is no guarantee as to order of notification.

Each of the 11 listener types has a corresponding XXX_EVENT_MASK constant defined in the AWTEvent class, and corresponding processXXXEvent() methods. Table 10.2 lists the mask constants and the processing methods.

| **T A B L E  10.2** | **Mask** | **Method** |
|---|---|---|
| Event masks | AWTEvent.ACTION_EVENT_MASK | processActionEvent() |
| | AWTEvent.ADJUSTMENT_EVENT_MASK | processAdjustmentEvent() |
| | AWTEvent.COMPONENT_EVENT_MASK | processComponentEvent() |
| | AWTEvent.CONTAINER_EVENT_MASK | processContainerEvent() |
| | AWTEvent.FOCUS_EVENT_MASK | processFocusEvent() |
| | AWTEvent.ITEM_EVENT_MASK | processItemEvent() |
| | AWTEvent.KEY_EVENT_MASK | processKeyEvent() |
| | AWTEvent.MOUSE_EVENT_MASK | processMouseEvent() |
| | AWTEvent.MOUSE_MOTION_EVENT_MASK | processMouseMotionEvent() |
| | AWTEvent.TEXT_EVENT_MASK | processTextEvent() |
| | AWTEvent.WINDOW_EVENT_MASK | processWindowEvent() |

The strategy of explicitly enabling events for a component can be summarized as follows:

1. Create a subclass of the component.

2. In the subclass constructor, call enableEvents(AWTEvent.XXX_EVENT_MASK).

3. Provide the subclass with a processXXXEvent() method; this method should call the superclass' version before returning.

# Adapters

If you look at Table 10.1, which lists the methods of the 11 event listener interfaces, you will see that several of the interfaces have only a single method, while others have several methods. The largest interface, Window-Listener, has seven methods.

Suppose you want to catch iconified events on a frame. You might try to create the following class:

```
1. class MyIkeListener implements WindowListener {
2.   public void windowIconified(WindowEvent we) {
3.     // Process the event.
4.   }
5. }
```

Unfortunately, this class will not compile. The WindowListener interface defines seven methods, and class MyIkeListener needs to implement the other six before the compiler will be satisfied.

Typing in the remaining methods and giving them empty bodies is tedious. The java.awt.event package provides seven *adapter* classes, one for each listener interface that defines more than just a single method. An adapter is simply a class that implements an interface by providing do-nothing methods. For example, the WindowAdapter class implements the Window-Listener interface with seven do-nothing methods. Our example can be modified to take advantage of this adapter:

```
1. class MyIkeListener extends WindowAdapter {
2.   public void windowIconified(WindowEvent we) {
3.     // Process the event.
4.   }
5. }
```

Table 10.3 lists all the adapter classes, along with the event-listener interfaces that they implement.

| | Adapter Class | Listener Interface |
|---|---|---|
| **T A B L E  10.3**<br>Adapters | ComponentAdapter | ComponentListener |
| | ContainerAdapter | ContainerListener |
| | FocusAdapter | FocusListener |

| **TABLE 10.3** *(cont.)* | **Adapter Class** | **Listener Interface** |
|---|---|---|
| Adapters | KeyAdapter | KeyListener |
| | MouseAdapter | MouseListener |
| | MouseMotionAdapter | MouseMotionListener |
| | WindowAdapter | WindowListener |

# Chapter Summary

The event delegation model allows you to designate any object as a listener for a component's events. A component may have multiple listeners for any event type. All listeners must implement the appropriate interface. If the interface defines more than one method, the listener may extend the appropriate adapter class.

A component subclass may handle its own events by calling enable-Events(), passing in an event mask. With this strategy, a processXXXEvent() method is called before any listeners are notified.

# Test Yourself

**1.** The event delegation model, introduced in release 1.1 of the JDK, is fully compatible with the 1.0 event model.

**A.** True

**B.** False

**2.** Which statement or statements are true about the code listed below?

```
1. public class MyTextArea extends TextArea {
2.    public MyTextArea(int nrows, int ncols) {
3.       enableEvents(AWTEvent.TEXT_EVENT_MASK);
4.    }
5.
```

```
6.    public void processTextEvent(TextEvent te) {
7.      System.out.println("Processing a text event.");
8.    }
9.  }
```

**A.** The source code must appear in a file called `MyTextArea.java`.

**B.** Between lines 2 and 3, a call should be made to `super(nrows, ncols)` so that the new component will have the correct size.

**C.** At line 6, the return type of `processTextEvent()` should be declared `boolean`, not `void`.

**D.** Between lines 7 and 8, the following code should appear: `return true;`.

**E.** Between lines 7 and 8, the following code should appear: `super.ProcessTextEvent(te);`.

**3.** Which statement or statements are true about the code listed below?

```
1. public class MyFrame extends Frame {
2.   public MyFrame(String title) {
3.     super(title);
4.     enableEvents(AWTEvent.WINDOW_EVENT_MASK);
5.   }
6.
7.   public void processWindowEvent(WindowEvent we) {
8.     System.out.println("Processing a window event.");
9.   }
10. }
```

**A.** Adding a window listener to an instance of `MyFrame` will result in a compiler error.

**B.** Adding a window listener to an instance of `MyFrame` will result in the throwing of an exception at run time.

**C.** Adding a window listener to an instance of `MyFrame` will result in code that compiles cleanly and executes without throwing an exception.

**D.** A window listener added to an instance of `MyFrame` will never receive notification of window events.

**4.** Which statement or statements are true about the code fragment listed below? (Assume that classes F1 and F2 both implement the FocusListener interface.)

```
1. TextField tf = new TextField("Not a trick question");
2. FocusListener flis1 = new F1();
3. FocusListener flis2 = new F2();
4. tf.addFocusListener(flis1);
5. tf.addFocusListener(flis2);
```

**A.** Lines 2 and 3 generate compiler errors.

**B.** Line 5 throws an exception at run time.

**C.** The code compiles cleanly and executes without throwing an exception.

**5.** Which statement or statements are true about the code fragment listed below? (Assume that classes F1 and F2 both implement the FocusListener interface.)

```
1. TextField tf = new TextField("Not a trick question");
2. FocusListener flis1 = new F1();
3. FocusListener flis2 = new F2();
4. tf.addFocusListener(flis1);
5. tf.addFocusListener(flis2);
6. tf.removeFocusListener(flis1);
```

**A.** Lines 2 and 3 generate compiler errors.

**B.** Line 6 generates a compiler error.

**C.** Line 5 throws an exception at run time.

**D.** Line 6 throws an exception at run time.

**E.** The code compiles cleanly and executes without throwing an exception.

**6.** Which statement or statements are true about the code fragment listed below?

```
1. class MyListener extends MouseAdapter implements _
   MouseListener {
2.   public void mouseEntered(MouseEvent mev) {
3.     System.out.println("Mouse entered.");
4.   }
5. }
```

**A.** The code compiles without error and defines a class that could be used as a mouse listener.

**B.** The code will not compile correctly, because the class does not provide all the methods of the MouseListener interface.

**C.** The code compiles without error. The words implements MouseListener can be removed from line 1 without affecting the code's behavior in any way.

**D.** The code compiles without error. During execution, an exception will be thrown if a component uses this class as a mouse listener and receives a mouse exited event.

**7.** Which statement or statements are true about the code fragment listed below? (Hint: The ActionListener and ItemListener interfaces each define a single method.)

```
1. class MyListener implements ActionListener, ItemListener {
2.   public void actionPerformed(ActionEvent ae) {
3.     System.out.println("Action.");
4.   }
5.
6.   public void itemStateChanged(ItemEvent ie) {
7.     System.out.println("Item");
8.   }
9. }
```

**A.** The code compiles without error and defines a class that could be used as an action listener or as an item listener.

**B.** The code generates a compiler error on line 1.

**C.** The code generates a compiler error on line 6.

**8.** Which statement or statements are true about the code fragment listed below?

```
1. class MyListener extends MouseAdapter, KeyAdapter {
2.    public void mouseClicked(MouseEvent mev) {
3.      System.out.println("Mouse clicked.");
4.    }
5.
6.    public void keyPressed(keyEventEvent kev) {
7.      System.out.println("KeyPressed.");
8.    }
9. }
```

**A.** The code compiles without error and defines a class that could be used as a mouse listener or as a key listener.

**B.** The code generates a compiler error on line 1.

**C.** The code generates a compiler error on line 6.

**9.** A component subclass that has executed `enableEvents()` to enable processing of a certain kind of event cannot also use an adapter as a listener for the same kind of event.

**A.** True

**B.** False

**10.** Assume that the class `AcLis` implements the `ActionListener` interface. The code fragment below constructs a button and gives it four action listeners. When the button is pressed, which action listener is the first to get its `actionPerformed()` method invoked?

```
1. Button btn = new Button("Hello");
2. AcLis a1 = new AcLis();
3. AcLis a2 = new AcLis();
4. AcLis a3 = new AcLis();
5. AcLis a4 = new AcLis();
6. btn.addActionListener(a1);
7. btn.addActionListener(a2);
```

```
 8. btn.addActionListener(a3);
 9. btn.addActionListener(a4);
10. btn.removeActionListener(a2);
11. btn.removeActionListener(a3);
12. btn.addActionListener(a3);
13. btn.addActionListener(a2);
```

**A.** a1 gets its `actionPerformed()` method invoked first.

**B.** a2 gets its `actionPerformed()` method invoked first.

**C.** a3 gets its `actionPerformed()` method invoked first.

**D.** a4 gets its `actionPerformed()` method invoked first.

**E.** It is impossible to know which listener will be first.

# CHAPTER

# 11

## Components

**C**omponents are Java's building blocks for creating graphical user interfaces. Some component types, such as buttons and scroll bars, are used directly for GUI control. Other kinds of components (those that inherit from the abstract `Container` class) provide spatial organization.

GUIs are an important part of any program. Java's Abstract Windowing Toolkit (AWT) provides extensive functionality. Chapter 9 discussed how to organize GUI components in two-dimensional space. Chapter 10 looked at how to respond to user input. This chapter reviews components.

While this chapter, and the two chapters that follow it, do not directly address topics that are explicitly mentioned in the Java Certification Exam Objectives, this material is essential to a full understanding of the subjects you need to know for the exam.

# Components in General

**J**ava's components are implemented by the many subclasses of the `java.awt.Component` and `java.awt.MenuComponent` superclasses. There are 19 non-superclass components in all, and you should know the basics of all the component classes. One way to organize this fairly large number of classes is to divide them into categories:

- Visual components
- Container components
- Menu components

These category names are not official Java terminology, but they serve to organize a fairly large number of component classes. This chapter discusses 16 classes—11 visual components, four containers, and four menu components.

There are several methods that are implemented by all the visual and container components, by virtue of inheritance from java.awt.Component. (The menu components extend from java.awt.MenuComponent, so they do not inherit the same superclass functionality.) These methods are discussed below.

### getSize()

The getSize() method returns the size of a component. The return type is Dimension, which has public data members height and width.

### setForeground() and setBackground()

The setForeground() and setBackground() methods set the foreground and background colors of a component. Each method takes a single argument, which is an instance of java.awt.Color. Chapter 12 discusses how to use the Color class.

Generally the foreground color of a component is used for rendering text, and the background color is used for rendering the non-textual area of the component. Thus a label with blue as its foreground color and black as its background color will show up as blue text on a black background.

**WARNING**

The last paragraph describes how things are supposed to be, but some components on some platforms resist having their colors changed.

If you do not explicitly set a component's foreground or background color, the component uses the foreground and background color of its immediate container. Thus if you have an applet whose foreground color is white and whose background color is red, and you add a button to the applet without calling setForeground() or setBackground() on the button, then the button's label will be white on red.

### setFont()

The setFont() method determines the font that a component will use for rendering any text that it needs to display. The method takes a single argument, which is an instance of java.awt.Font.

If you do not explicitly set a component's font, the component uses the font of its container, in the same way that the container's foreground and background colors are used if you do not explicitly call `setForeground()` or `setBackground()`. Thus if you have an applet whose font is 48-point bold Serif, and you add a check box to the applet without calling `setFont()` on the check box, you will get a check box whose label appears in 48-point bold Serif.

### setEnabled()

The `setEnabled()` method takes a single argument of type `boolean`. If this argument is `true`, then the component has its normal appearance. If the argument is `false`, then the component is grayed out and does not respond to user input. This method replaces the 1.0 methods `enable()` and `disable()`, which are deprecated.

### setSize() and setBounds()

These methods set a component's geometry—or rather, they `attempt` to set geometry. They replace the deprecated 1.0 methods `resize()` and `reshape()`. The `setSize()` method takes two int arguments: width and height; an overloaded form takes a single dimension. The `setBounds()` method takes four int arguments: x, y, width, and height; an overloaded form takes a single rectangle.

If you have tried calling these methods, you know that it is usually futile. Chapter 9 explains that the size and position that you attempt to give a component is overruled by a layout manager. In fact, these two methods exist mostly for the use of layout managers. The major exception to this rule is the `Frame` class, which is not under the thumb of a layout manager and is perfectly willing to have you set its size or bounds. This is explained below in the *Frame* section.

### setVisible()

This method takes a `boolean` argument that dictates whether the component is to be seen on the screen. This is another method that only works for frames, unless you learn some techniques that are beyond the scope of this book or the Certification Exam. Again, this method is explained in detail in the Frame section later in this chapter.

# The Visual Components

The visual components are the ones that users can actually see and interact with. The 11 visual components are

- Button
- Canvas
- Checkbox
- Choice
- FileDialog
- Label
- List
- ScrollPane
- Scrollbar
- TextArea
- TextField

To use one of these components in a GUI, you first create an instance by calling the appropriate constructor. Then you add the component to a container. Adding a component to a container is decidedly non-trivial; in fact, this topic was covered in Chapter 9. For the sake of this chapter, you will be asked to take it on faith that the components shown in the screen shots below have all been added to their containing applets in straightforward ways.

The next 11 sections show you how to construct each of the visual components. Of course to really learn how to use components, you also have to know how to position them (see Chapter 9) and how to receive event notification from them (see Chapter 10).

Not all forms of the component constructors are given; the intention here is not to provide you with an exhaustive list (you can always refer to the API pages for that), but to expose you to what you will need to know for the Certification Exam.

All the screen shots in this chapter were taken from a Windows 95 platform. Component appearance varies from machine to machine. All the applets were assigned a 24-point italic Serif font; most of the components were not sent `setFont()` method calls, so they inherited this font.

### Button

The `Button` class, of course, implements a push button. The button shown in Figure 11.1 was constructed with the following line of code:

```
new Button("Apply");
```

This constructor takes a string parameter that specifies the text of the button's label.

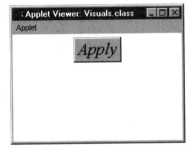

---

**F I G U R E   11.1**

A button

When a button is pushed, it sends an Action event. Action events, and indeed the entire event delegation model, are explained in detail in Chapter 10.

### Canvas

A canvas is a component that has no default appearance or behavior. You can subclass `Canvas` to create custom drawing regions, work areas, components, and so on. Canvases receive input events from the mouse and the keyboard; it is up to the programmer to transform those inputs into a meaningful look and feel.

The default size (or, more properly, the *preferred size*, as you saw in Chapter 9) of a canvas is uselessly small. One way to deal with this problem is to use a layout manager that will resize the canvas. Another way is to call `setSize()` on the canvas yourself; canvases are a rare case where this will actually work. Figure 11.2 shows a canvas that was created with the following code:

```
1. Canvas canv = new Canvas();
2. canv.setBackground(Color.black);
3. canv.setSize(100, 50);
```

**FIGURE 11.2**

A canvas

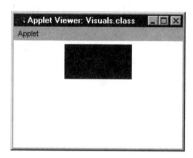

Canvases send Mouse, MouseMotion, and Key events, as explained in Chapter 10.

## Checkbox

A check box is a two-state button. The two states are `true` (checked) and `false` (not checked). The two basic forms of the `Checkbox` constructor are

```
Checkbox(String label)
Checkbox(String label, boolean initialState)
```

If you do not specify an initial state, the default is `false`. Two methods support reading and setting the state of a check box:

- `boolean getState()`
- `void setState(boolean state)`

Figure 11.3 shows a check box in the true state.

Check boxes can be grouped together into check-box groups, which have radio behavior. With radio behavior, only one member of a check-box group can be true at any time; selecting a new member changes the state of the previously selected member to false. Many window systems (Motif and NextStep, for example) implement radio groups as components in their own

FIGURE 11.3

A check box

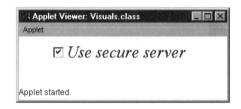

FIGURE 11.3

A check box

right. In Java, the `java.awt.CheckboxGroup` class is not a component; it is simply a non-visible class that organizes check boxes. This means that Java imposes no restrictions on the spatial relationships among members of a check-box group. If you wanted to, you could put one member of a group in the upper-left corner of a frame, another member in the lower-right corner, and a third member in a different frame altogether. Of course, the result would hardly be useful.

To use a check-box group, you first create an instance of `CheckboxGroup`, and then pass the instance as a parameter to the `Checkbox` constructor. The code below adds three check boxes to a group called `cbg`. The result is shown in Figure 11.4.

```
1. CheckboxGroup cbg = new CheckboxGroup();
2. p.add(new Checkbox("Cinnamon", false, cbg));
3. p.add(new Checkbox("Nutmeg", false, cbg));
4. p.add(new Checkbox("Allspice", true, cbg));
```

FIGURE 11.4

Check boxes with
radio behavior

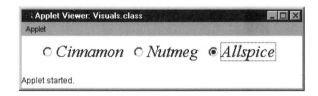

Two methods of the `CheckboxGroup` class support reading and setting the currently selected member of the group:

- `Checkbox getSelectedCheckbox()`
- void setSelectedCheckbox(Checkbox newSelection)

Check boxes send Item events when they are selected, as explained in Chapter 10.

## Choice

A choice is a pull-down list, as shown in Figure 11.5. This figure shows two choices, both of which present the same options. The choice on the left is in its normal state; the choice on the right has been mouse-clicked.

To create a choice, first call the constructor, and then populate the choice by repeatedly calling addItem(). The code fragment below shows how to create one of the choices shown in Figure 11.5.

```
1. Choice ch1 = new Choice();
2. ch1.addItem("Alligators");
3. ch1.addItem("Crocodiles");
4. ch1.addItem("Gila Monsters");
5. ch1.addItem("Dragons");
```

Choices, like check boxes, send Item events when they are selected. Item events are explained in Chapter 10.

**F I G U R E  11.5**

Two choices

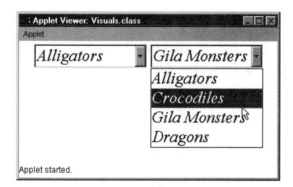

## FileDialog

The FileDialog class represents a file open or file save dialog. The appearance of these dialogs varies greatly from platform to platform. A file dialog is modal; this means that input from the dialog's parent frame will be directed exclusively to the dialog, as long as the dialog remains visible on the screen. The dialog is automatically removed when the user specifies a file or clicks the Cancel button.

The most useful `FileDialog` constructor has the following form:

- `FileDialog(Frame parent, String title, int mode)`

The dialog's parent is the frame over which the dialog will appear. The title string appears in the dialog's title bar (on most platforms). The mode should be either `FileDialog.LOAD` or `FileDialog.SAVE`.

After the user has specified a file, the name of the file or its directory can be retrieved with the following methods:

- `String getFile()`
- `String getDirectory()`

The code fragment below constructs a file dialog, and displays it above frame f. After the user has specified a file, the file name is retrieved and displayed.

```
1. FileDialog fidi =
2.    new FileDialog(f, "Choose!", FileDialog.LOAD);
3. fidi.setVisible(true);
4. System.out.println(fidi.getFile());
```

## Label

The simplest AWT component is the label. Labels do not respond to user input, and they do not send out any events.

There are three ways to construct a label:

- `Label()`
- `Label(String text)`
- `Label(String text, int alignment)`

The default alignment for labels is to the left. To set the alignment, use the third form of the constructor and pass in one of the following:

- `Label.LEFT`
- `Label.CENTER`
- `Label.RIGHT`

Two methods support reading and setting the text of a label:

- `String getText()`
- `void setText(String newText)`

**NOTE**   If you use the no-arguments version of the label constructor, you will undoubtedly want to setText() at some point.

Figure 11.6 shows a label that was created with the following call:

```
new Label("I'm a label, Mabel");
```

**FIGURE 11.6**

A label

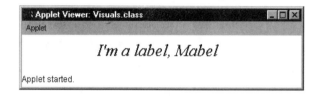

## List

A list is a collection of text items, arranged vertically. If a list contains more items than it can display, it acquires a vertical scroll bar. There are three forms of constructor:

- `List()`
- `List(int nVisibleRows)`
- `List(int nVisibleRows, boolean multiSelectOk)`

The number of visible rows (parameter nVisibleRows) dictates the height of a list. The first version of the constructor does not specify a number of visible rows, so presumably the height of such list will be dictated by a layout manager.

If the version of the third constructor is used and multiSelectOk is true, then the list supports multiple selection. If multiple selection is not enabled, then selecting a new item causes the old selected item to be deselected.

The code listed below creates the list shown in Figure 11.7:

```
1. List list = new List(4, true);
2. list.addItem("Augustus");
3. list.addItem("Tiberius");
```

4. list.addItem("Caligula");

5. list.addItem("Claudius");

6. list.addItem("Nero");

7. list.addItem("Otho");

8. list.addItem("Galba");

The list has seven items but only four visible rows, so a scroll bar is automatically provided to give access to the bottom three items. Multiple selection is enabled, as shown in the figure: Both barbarian (non-Roman) emperors are selected.

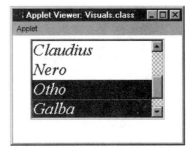

**FIGURE 11.7**

A scrolled list with multiple selection

The List class provides a large number of support methods. A partial list of these methods appears below. The methods are intended to give you a feel for how the List class operates.

- void addItem(String text): adds an item to the bottom of the list

- void addItem(String text, int index): inserts an item at the specified index

- String getItem(int index): returns the item with the specified index

- int getItemCount(): returns the number of items in the list

- int getRows(): returns the number of visible lines in the list

- int getSelectedIndex(): returns the index of the currently selected item (the list should be in single-selection mode)

- `int[] getSelectedIndexes()`: returns an array containing the index of every currently selected item (the list should be in multiple-selection mode)

- `String getSelectedItem()`: returns a string that reflects the currently selected item (the list should be in single-selection mode)

- `String[]getSelectedItems()`: returns an array containing a string for every currently selected item (the list should be in multiple-selection mode)

Selecting an item in a list causes the list to send an Item event; double-clicking an item sends an Action event.

## ScrollPane

The `ScrollPane` is an extremely useful class that was introduced in 1.1. A scroll pane can contain a single component, which may be taller or wider than the scroll pane itself. If the contained component is larger than the scroll pane, then the default behavior of the scroll pane is to acquire horizontal and/or vertical scroll bars as needed.

There are two constructors for this class:

- `ScrollPane()`: constructs a scroll pane with default scroll bar behavior

- `ScrollPane(int scrollbarPolicy)`: constructs a scroll pane with the specified scroll bar behavior

If you use the second form of the constructor, then `scrollbarPolicy` should be one of

- `ScrollPane.SCROLLBARS_AS_NEEDED`
- `ScrollPane.SCROLLBARS_ALWAYS`
- `ScrollPane.SCROLLBARS_NEVER`

The code listed below creates a scroll pane with default (as-needed) scroll bar behavior. The scroll pane contains a very large button, so the scroll bars will definitely be needed.

```
1. ScrollPane spane = new ScrollPane();
2. Button reallyBigButton =
3.    new Button("What big teeth you have, Grandmother");
```

4. reallyBigButton.setFont(new Font("Serif", Font.ITALIC, 80));

5. spane.add(reallyBigButton);

Figure 11.8 shows the resulting scroll pane.

**FIGURE 11.8**

A scroll pane

Scroll panes send Mouse and MouseMotion events.

## Scrollbar

The scroll bar component that adjusts lists and scroll panes is available as a component in its own right. There are three constructors:

- Scrollbar(): constructs a vertical scroll bar

- Scrollbar(int orientation): constructs a scroll bar with the specified orientation

- Scrollbar(int orientation, int initialValue, int slider-Size, int minValue, int maxValue): constructs a scroll bar with the specified parameters

For constructors that take an orientation parameter, this value should be one of

- Scrollbar.HORIZONTAL

- Scrollbar.VERTICAL

In the third form of the constructor, the sliderSize parameter is a bit confusing. The Java terminology for the piece of the scroll bar that slides is the *slider*, which in itself is confusing because in some window systems the entire component is called a slider. The sliderSize parameter controls the size of the slider, but not in pixel units. The units of sliderSize parameter are the units defined by the spread between the minimum and maximum value of the scroll bar.

For example, consider a horizontal scroll bar whose minimum value is 600 and maximum value is 700. The spread covered by the scroll bar is the difference between these two numbers, or 100. A sliderSize value of 50 would represent half the spread, and the slider would be half the width of the scroll bar. A sliderSize value of 10 would represent half the spread, and the slider would be one-tenth the width of the scroll bar.

If the scroll bar's minimum and maximum were 1400 and 1500, the spread would still be 100; a sliderSize value of 50 would still represent half the spread, and the slider would still be half the width of the scroll bar. A sliderSize value of 10 would still result in a slider one-tenth the width of the scroll bar.

The line of code below creates a horizontal scroll bar with a range from 600 to 700. The initial value is 625. The slider size is 25 out of a range of 700 – 600 = 100, so the slider should be one-fourth the width of the scroll bar. Figure 11.8 shows that this is indeed the case. The scroll bar is shown in Figure 11.9.

```
Scrollbar sbar = new Scrollbar(Scrollbar.HORIZONTAL, 625, _
25, 600, 700);
```

Scroll bars generate Adjustment events, as explained in Chapter 10.

**FIGURE 11.9**

A horizontal scroll bar

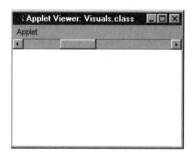

## *TextField* and *TextArea*

The TextField and TextArea classes implement one-dimensional and two-dimensional components for text input, display, and editing. Both classes extend from the TextComponent superclass, as shown in Figure 11.10.

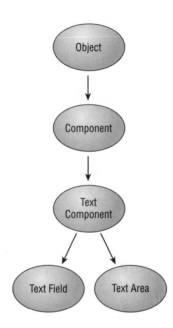

Both classes have a variety of constructors, which offer the option of specifying or not specifying an initial string or a size. That constructors that do not specify size are for use with layout managers that will enforce a size.

The constructors for TextField are listed below:

- TextField(): constructs an empty text field

- TextField(int nCols): constructs an empty text field with the specified number of columns

- TextField(String text): constructs a text field whose initial content is text

- TextField(String text, int nCols): constructs a text field whose initial content is text, with the specified number of columns

The constructors for TextArea are listed below:

- TextArea(): constructs an empty text area

- TextArea(int nRows, int nCols): constructs an empty text area with the specified number of rows and columns

- `TextArea(String text)`: constructs a text area whose initial content is `text`

- `TextArea(String text, int nRows, int nCols)`: constructs a text area whose initial content is `text`, with the specified number of rows and columns

- `TextArea(String text, int nRows, int nCols, int scrollbar-Policy)`: same as above, but the scroll bar placement policy is determined by the last parameter, which should be one of

  - `TextArea.SCROLLBARS_BOTH`

  - `TextArea.SCROLLBARS_NONE`

  - `TextArea.SCROLLBARS_HORIZONTAL_ONLY`

  - `TextArea.SCROLLBARS_VERTICAL_ONLY`

For both classes, there are some surprising issues to the number-of-columns parameter.

First, the number of columns is a measure of width in terms of columns of text, *as rendered in a particular font*. A 25-column text area with a tiny font will be very narrow, while a 5-column text area with a huge font will be extremely wide.

Next, there is the problem of proportional fonts. For a fixed-width font, it is obvious what the column width should be. For a proportional font, the column width is taken to be the average of all the font's character widths.

A final issue is the question of what happens when a user types beyond the rightmost character column in one of these components. In both cases, the visible text scrolls to the left. The insertion point remains in place, at the rightmost column. The component now contains more text than it can display, so scrolling is required. Text areas support scroll bars. Text fields can be scrolled by using the ← and → keys.

Both classes inherit some functionality from their common superclass, `TextComponent`. These methods include

- `String getSelectedText()`: returns the currently selected text

- `String getText()`: returns the text contents of the component

- `void setEditable(boolean editable)`: if `editable` is `true`, permits the user to edit the component

- `void setText(String text)`: sets the text contents of the component

A common experience among beginning AWT programmers who need, for example, to retrieve the contents of a text field, is to look for some promising name among the methods listed on the API page for TextField. There is nothing promising to be found there, and suddenly text fields seem useless. The problem, of course, is inheritance: The desired methods are available, but they are inherited from TextComponent and documented on a different page. If you know that a class must implement a certain method (because you have heard that it does, or because you remember using the method long ago, or because the class would otherwise be useless), don't give up if you don't find what you want on the class' API page. Use the superclass links near the top of the page to check from inherited methods.

The code below creates three text fields. Each is five columns wide, but they all use different fonts. (The fonts are all 24 points, so differences will be subtle).

```
1. TextField tf1 = new TextField(5);
2. tf1.setFont(new Font("Serif", Font.PLAIN, 24));
3. tf1.setText("12345");
4. TextField tf2 = new TextField(5);
5. tf2.setFont(new Font("SansSerif", Font.PLAIN, 24));
6. tf2.setText("12345");
7. TextField tf3 = new TextField(5);
8. tf3.setFont(new Font("Monospaced", Font.PLAIN, 24));
9. tf3.setText("12345");
```

Figure 11.11 shows the text fields. Surprisingly, only four characters appear in each field (although the dot near the right of the first field looks suspiciously like the truncated tail of the "5"). This is not a bug. The fields really are five columns wide, but some of the space is taken up by leading and inter-character whitespace.

**FIGURE 11.11**

Three text fields

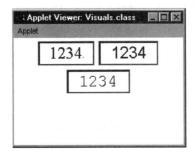

The code below implements three text areas, each with six rows and five columns. Again, each component has a different family of 24-point fonts. (The font name appears in the first row of each component.) The first two fonts are proportional, so a lot more *i*'s than *w*'s can fit into a row. Again, the components really do have five columns, but whitespace reduces the number of visible characters.

```
1. TextArea ta1 = new TextArea(6, 5);
2. ta1.setFont(new Font("Serif", Font.PLAIN, 24));
3. ta1.setText("Serif\n12345\nabcde\niiiiiiiiiii\nWWWWW");
4. TextArea ta2 = new TextArea(6, 5);
5. ta2.setFont(new Font("SansSerif", Font.PLAIN, 24));
6. ta2.setText("Sans\n12345\nabcde\niiiiiiiiiii\nWWWWW");
7. TextArea ta3 = new TextArea(6, 5);
8. ta3.setFont(new Font("Monospaced", Font.PLAIN, 24));
9. ta3.setText("Mono\n12345\nabcde\niiiiiiiiiii\nWWWWW");
```

Figure 11.12 shows the resulting text areas.

**FIGURE 11.12**

Three text areas

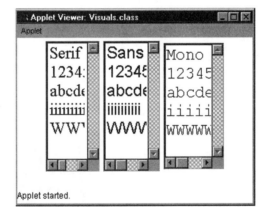

Both text fields and text areas generate Text events. Additionally, text fields generate Action events on receipt of an Enter keystroke.

# The Container Components

The four non-superclass container component classes are

- Applet
- Frame
- Panel
- Dialog

Technically, ScrollPane is also a container, because it inherits from the Container superclass, but it does not present the issues that the other three do. Figure 11.13 shows the inheritance hierarchy of these classes.

*Containers* are components capable of holding other components within their boundaries. Every screen shot so far in this chapter has shown an applet acting as a container for the component being illustrated. Adding components to containers requires interacting with layout managers; this entire topic was covered in depth in Chapter 9. The next three sections are brief.

**FIGURE 11.13**

Inheritance of Applet, Frame, and Panel

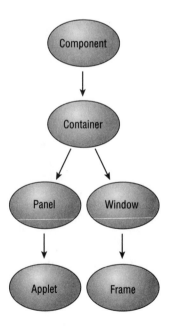

## *Applet*

The only issue that needs attention here is the problem of resizing. Applets, by virtue of inheriting from Component, have setSize() and setBounds() methods. Applets only exist in browsers. Changing the size of an applet is permitted or forbidden by the applet's browser, and during the development cycle you cannot know which brand of browser will be running your applet. The easiest browser for development is the applet viewer, which allows resizing of applets. It is common for an applet to have a temporary set-Size() call in its init() method, because this provides an easy way to play with different sizes. If you use this technique, remember to delete the set-Size() call before final delivery, and set the size in your HTML tag.

## *Frame*

A frame is an independent window, decorated by the underlying window system and capable of being moved around on the screen independent of other GUI windows. Any application that requires a GUI must use one or more frames to contain the desired components.

There are only two forms of the Frame constructor:

- Frame(): constructs a frame with an empty title bar

- Frame(String title): constructs a frame with the specified title

When a frame is constructed, it has no size and is not displayed on the screen. To give a frame a size, call one of the inherited methods setSize() or setBounds(). (If you call setBounds(), the x and y parameters tell the frame where it will appear on the screen.) Once a frame has been given a size, you can display it by calling setVisible(true).

To remove an unwanted frame from the screen, you can call set-Visible(false). This does not destroy the frame or damage it in any way; you can always display it again by calling setVisible(true).

When you are finished with a frame, you need to recycle its non-memory resources. (Memory will be harvested by the garbage collector.) Non-memory resources are system-dependent; suffice it to say that it takes a lot to connect a Java GUI to an underlying window system. On a UNIX/Motif platform, for example, a frame's non-memory resources would include at least one file descriptor and X window.

To release the non-memory resources of a frame, just call its `dispose()` method. The code below builds and displays a 500×350 frame; 30 seconds later the frame is removed from the screen and disposed.

```
1. // Construct and display
2. Frame f = new Frame("This is a frame");
3. f.setBounds(10, 10, 500, 350);
4. f.setVisible(true);
5.
6. // Delay
7. try {
8.   Thread.sleep(30*1000);
9. } catch (InterruptedException e) { }
10.
11. // Remove and dispose
12. f.setVisible(false);
13. f.dispose();
```

**WARNING**  If an applet attempts to display a frame, the applet's browser confers with the local security manager. Most browsers have security managers that impose a restriction on frames. Display of the frame is permitted, but the frame unexpectedly contains a label that marks the frame as "untrusted." The rationale is that the frame might have been displayed by an applet which was loaded from the Internet, so any sensitive information entered into the frame's components might possibly be transmitted to parties of dubious moral fiber.

## *Panel*

Applets and frames serve as top-level or outermost GUI components. Panels provide an intermediate level of spatial organization for GUIs. You are free to add all the components of a GUI directly into an applet or a frame, but you can provide additional levels of grouping by adding components to panels and adding panels to a top-level applet or frame. This process is recursive: The components that you add to panels can themselves be panels, and so on, to whatever depth of containment you like. Getting components to go exactly where you want them within a panel was the subject of the oft-mentioned Chapter 9.

### Dialog

A dialog is a pop-up window that accepts user input. Dialogs may optionally be made modal. The `Dialog` class is the superclass of the `FileDialog` class. The default layout manager for this class is border layout.

# The Menu Components

**J**ava supports two kinds of menu: pull-down and pop-up. The certification exam does not cover pop-up menus.

Pull-down menus are accessed via a menu bar, which may contain multiple menus. Menu bars may only appear in frames. (Therefore pull-down menus also may only appear in frames.)

To create a frame with a menu bar containing a pull-down menu, you need to go through the following steps:

1. Create a menu bar and attach it to the frame.

2. Create and populate the menu.

3. Attach the menu to the menu bar.

To create a menu bar, just construct an instance of the `MenuBar` class. To attach it to a frame, pass it into the frame's `setMenuBar()` method.

To create a menu, just construct an instance of the `Menu` class. The most common constructor takes a string that is the menu's label; this label appears on the menu bar. There are four kinds of element that can be mixed and matched to populate a menu:

- Menu items
- Check-box menu items
- Separators
- Menus

A menu item is an ordinary textual component available on a menu. The basic constructor for the `MenuItem` class is

```
MenuItem(String text)
```

where `text` is the label of the menu item. A menu item is very much like a button that happens to live in a menu. Like buttons, menu items generate Action events.

A check-box menu item looks like a menu item with a check box to the left of its label. When a check-box menu item is selected, the check box changes its state. The basic constructor for the `CheckboxMenuItem` class is

```
CheckboxMenuItem(String text)
```

where `text` is the label of the item. A check-box menu item is very much like a check box that happens to live in a menu; you can read and set an item's state by calling `getState()` and `setState()` just as you would with a plain check box. Check-box menu items generate Item events.

A separator is just a horizontal mark used for visually dividing a menu into sections. To add a separator to a menu, call the menu's `addSeparator()` method.

When you add a menu to another menu, the first menu's label appears in the second menu, with a pull-right icon. Pulling the mouse to the right causes the sub-menu to appear.

After a menu is fully populated, you attach it to a menu bar by calling the menu bar's `add()` method. If you want the menu to appear in the Help menu position to the right of all other menus, call instead the `setHelpMenu()` method.

The code below creates and displays a frame with a menu bar and two menus. The first menu contains one of each kind of menu constituent (menu item, check-box menu item, separator, and submenu). The second menu is a Help menu and just contains two menu items.

```
1. Frame          frame;
2. MenuBar        bar;
3. Menu           fileMenu, subMenu, helpMenu;
4.
5. // Create frame and install menu bar.
6. frame = new Frame("Menu demo");
7. frame.setSize(400, 300);
```

```
 8. bar = new MenuBar();
 9. frame.setMenuBar(bar);
10.
11. // Create submenu.
12. subMenu = new Menu("Pull me");
13. subMenu.add(new MenuItem("Sub-This"));
14. subMenu.add(new MenuItem("Sub-That"));
15.
16. // Create and add file menu.
17. fileMenu = new Menu("File");
18. fileMenu.add(new MenuItem("New"));
19. fileMenu.add(new MenuItem("Open"));
20. fileMenu.addSeparator();
21. fileMenu.add(new CheckboxMenuItem("Print Preview Mode"));
22. fileMenu.add(subMenu);
23. bar.add(fileMenu);
24.
25. // Create help menu.
26. helpMenu = new Menu("Help");
27. helpMenu.add(new MenuItem("Contents ..."));
28. helpMenu.add(new MenuItem("About this program ..."));
29. bar.setHelpMenu(helpMenu);
30.
31. // Now that the frame is completely built, display it.
32. frame.setVisible(true);
```

Figure 11.14 shows the frame with the File menu and the submenu visible.

**F I G U R E   11.14**

Frame with file menu
and submenu

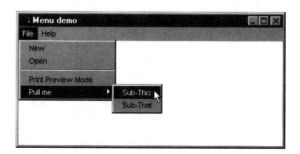

Figure 11.15 shows the frame with the Help menu visible.

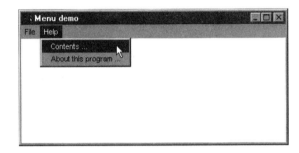

# Chapter Summary

This chapter has introduced three categories of components:

- Visual components
- Container components
- Menu components

Visual components are the components that the user interacts with. Container components contain other components. Menu components support menus in frames.

# Test Yourself

1.  A text field is constructed and then given a foreground color of white and a 64-point bold serif font. The text field is then added to an applet that has a foreground color of red, background color of blue, and 7-point plain sans-serif font. Which one statement below is true about the text field?

    **A.** Foreground color is black, background color is white, font is 64-point bold serif.

    **B.** Foreground color is red, background color is blue, font is 64-point bold serif.

C. Foreground color is red, background color is blue, font is 7-point bold serif.

D. Foreground color is white, background color is blue, font is 7-point bold serif.

E. Foreground color is white, background color is blue, font is 64-point bold serif.

2. You have a check box in a panel; the panel is in an applet. The applet contains no other components. Using setFont(), you give the applet a 100-point font, and you give the panel a 6-point font. Which statement or statements below are correct?

A. The check box uses a 12-point font.

B. The check box uses a 6-point font.

C. The check box uses a 100-point font.

D. The check box uses the applet's font, because you can't set a font on a panel.

E. The check box uses the panel's font, because you did not explicitly set a font for the check box.

3. You have a check box in a panel; the panel is in an applet. The applet contains no other components. Using setFont(), you give the applet a 100-point font. Which statement or statements below are correct?

A. The check box uses a 12-point font.

B. The check box uses a 6-point font.

C. The check box uses a 100-point font.

D. The check box uses the applet's font.

E. The check box uses the panel's font, because you did not explicitly set a font for the check box.

4. You want to construct a text area that is 80 character-widths wide and 10 character-heights tall. What code do you use?

   **A.** `new TextArea(80, 10)`

   **B.** `new TextArea(10, 80)`

5. You construct a list by calling `new List(10, false)`. Which statement or statements below are correct? (Assume that layout managers do not modify the list in any way.)

   **A.** The list has 10 items.

   **B.** The list supports multiple selection.

   **C.** The list has 10 visible items.

   **D.** The list does not support multiple selection.

   **E.** The list will acquire a vertical scroll bar if needed.

6. A text field has a variable-width font. It is constructed by calling `new TextField("iiiii")`. What happens if you change the contents of the text field to `"wwwww"`? (Bear in mind that `i` is one of the narrowest characters, and `w` is one of the widest.)

   **A.** The text field becomes wider.

   **B.** The text field becomes narrower.

   **C.** The text field stays the same width; to see the entire contents you will have to scroll by using the ← and → keys.

   **D.** The text field stays the same width; to see the entire contents you will have to scroll by using the text field's horizontal scroll bar.

7. Which of the following may a menu contain? (Choose all that apply.)

   **A.** A separator

   **B.** A check box

   **C.** A menu

   **D.** A button

   **E.** A panel

**8.** Which of the following may contain a menu bar? (Choose all that apply.)

   **A.** A panel

   **B.** A frame

   **C.** An applet

   **D.** A menu bar

   **E.** A menu

**9.** Your application constructs a frame by calling `Frame f = new Frame();` but when you run the code, the frame does not appear on the screen. What code will make the frame appear? (Choose one.)

   **A.** `f.setSize(300, 200);`

   **B.** `f.setFont(new Font("SansSerif", Font.BOLD, 24));`

   **C.** `f.setForeground(Color.white);`

   **D.** `f.setVisible(true);`

   **E.** `f.setSize(300, 200); f.setVisible(true);`

**10.** The `CheckboxGroup` class is a subclass of the `Component` class.

   **A.** True

   **B.** False

# CHAPTER

# 12

## Painting

**C**hapter 11 discussed the various components of the AWT toolkit. Many types of AWT components (buttons and scroll bars, for example) have their appearance dictated by the underlying window system. Other component types, notably applets, frames, panels, and canvases, have no intrinsic appearance. If you use any of these classes and want your component to look at all useful, you will have to provide the code that implements the component's appearance.

Java's painting mechanism provides the way for you to render your components. The mechanism is robust, and if you use it correctly you can create good, scaleable, re-usable code. The best approach is to understand how Java's painting really works. The fundamental concepts of painting are

- The paint() method and the graphics context
- The GUI thread and the repaint() method
- Spontaneous painting
- Painting to images

This chapter will take you through the steps necessary to understand and apply these concepts. And while the topics covered here are not explicitly mentioned in any exam objectives, you may well find this information useful or essential.

# The *paint()* Method and the Graphics Context

**M**ost programmers encounter the paint() method in the early chapters of an introductory Java book. The applet listed below is a simple example of this method:

```
1. import java.applet.Applet;
2. import java.awt.*;
```

```
 3.
 4. public class SimplePaint extends Applet {
 5.    public void paint(Graphics g) {
 6.       g.setColor(Color.black);
 7.       g.fillRect(0, 0, 300, 300);
 8.       g.setColor(Color.white);
 9.       g.fillOval(30, 30, 50, 50);
10.    }
11. }
```

Figure 12.1 shows a screen shot of this applet.

**F I G U R E   12.1**

A very simple
painting applet

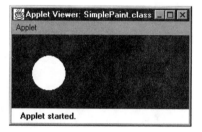

One interesting point about this applet is that no calls are made to the
paint() method. The method is simply *provided*. The environment seems to
do a good job of calling paint() at the right moment. Exactly when the environment chooses to call paint() is the subject of "Spontaneous Painting,"
later in this chapter. For now, the topic at hand is the paint() method itself.

Painting on a component is accomplished by making calls to a *graphics
context*, which is an instance of the Graphics class. A graphics context
knows how to render onto a single target. The three media a graphics context can render onto are

- Components

- Images

- Printers

Most of this chapter discusses graphics contexts that render onto components; at the end of the chapter is a section that discusses how to render onto
an image.

Any kind of component can be associated with a graphics context. The association is permanent; a context cannot be reassigned to a new component. Although you can use graphics contexts to paint onto any kind of component, it is unusual to do so with components that already have an appearance. Buttons, choices, check boxes, labels, scroll bars, text fields, and text areas do not often require programmer-level rendering. Most often, these components just use the version of paint() that they inherit from the Component superclass. This version does nothing; the components are rendered by the underlying window system. However, there are four classes of "blank" components that have no default appearance and will show up as empty rectangles unless they are subclassed and given paint() methods. These four component classes are

- Applet
- Canvas
- Frame
- Panel

If you look at line 5 of the applet code sample earlier in this section, you will see that a graphics context is passed into the paint() method. When you subclass a component class and give the subclass its own paint() method, the environment calls that method at appropriate times, passing in an appropriate instance of Graphics.

The four major operations provided by the Graphics class are

- Selecting a color
- Selecting a font
- Drawing and filling
- Clipping

## Selecting a Color

Colors are selected by calling the setColor() method. The argument is an instance of the Color class. There are 13 pre-defined colors, accessible as static final variables of the Color class. (The variables are themselves instances of the Color class, which makes some people uneasy, but Java has no trouble with such things.) The pre-defined colors are

- Color.red
- Color.yellow

- `Color.blue`
- `Color.green`
- `Color.orange`
- `Color.magenta`
- `Color.cyan`
- `Color.pink`
- `Color.lightGray`
- `Color.darkGray`
- `Color.gray`
- `Color.white`
- `Color.black`

If you want a color that is not on this list, you can construct your own. There are several versions of the `Color` constructor; the simplest is

```
Color(int redLevel, int greenLevel, int blueLevel)
```

The three parameters are intensity levels for the primary colors, with a range of 0–255. The code fragment below lists the first part of a `paint()` method that sets the color of its graphics context to pale green:

```
1. public void paint(Graphics g) {
2. Color c = new Color(170, 255, 170);
3. g.setColor(c);
      . . .
```

After line 3 above, all graphics will be painted in pale green, until the next `g.setColor()` call. Calling `g.setColor()` does not change the color of anything that has already been drawn; it only affects *subsequent* operations.

## Selecting a Font

Setting the font of a graphics context is like setting the color: Subsequent string-drawing operations will use the new font, while previously drawn strings are not affected.

Before you can set a font, you have to create one. The constructor for the Font class looks like this:

```
Font(String fontname, int style, int size)
```

The first parameter is the name of the font. Font availability is platform-dependent. You can get a list of available font names, returned as an array of strings, by calling the getFontList() method on your toolkit; an example follows:

```
String fontnames[] = Toolkit.getDefaultToolkit().getFontList()
```

There are three font names that you can always count on, no matter what platform you are running on:

- "Serif"

- "SansSerif"

- "Monospaced"

On releases of the JDK before 1.1, these were called, respectively, "Times-Roman," "Helvetica," and "Courier."

The style parameter of the Font constructor should be one of the following three ints:

- Font.PLAIN

- Font.BOLD

- Font.ITALIC

The code fragment below sets the font of graphics context gc to 24-point bold sans serif:

```
1. Font f = new Font("SansSerif", Font.BOLD, 24);
2. gc.setFont(f);
```

You can specify a bold italic font by passing Font.BOLD+Font.ITALIC as the style parameter to the Font constructor.

## Drawing and Filling

All the rendering methods of the Graphics class specify pixel coordinate positions for the shapes they render. Every component has its own coordinate space, with the origin in the component's upper-left corner, x increasing to the right, and y increasing downward. Figure 12.2 shows the component coordinate system.

**FIGURE 12.2**

The component
coordinate system

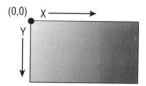

Graphics contexts do not have an extensive repertoire of painting methods. (Sophisticated rendering is handled by non-core APIs such as 2D, 3D, and Animation.) The ones to know about are

- drawLine()
- drawRect() and fillRect()
- drawOval() and fillOval()
- drawArc() and fillArc()
- drawPolygon() and fillPolygon()
- drawPolyline()
- drawString()

These methods are covered in detail in the next several sections.

### drawLine()

The drawLine() method draws a line from point (x0, y0) to point (x1, y1). The method's signature is

```
public void drawLine(int x0, int y0, int x1, int y1);
```

Figure 12.3 shows a simple applet whose paint() method makes the following call:

```
g.drawLine(20, 120, 100, 50);
```

**FIGURE 12.3**

drawLine()

## drawRect() and fillRect()

The drawRect() and fillRect() methods respectively draw and fill rectangles. The methods' signatures are

```
public void drawRect(int x, int y, int width, int height);
public void fillRect(int x, int y, int width, int height);
```

The x and y parameters are the coordinates of the upper-left corner of the rectangle. Notice that the last two parameters are width and height—not the coordinates of the opposite corner. Width and height must be positive numbers, or nothing will be drawn. (This is true of all graphics-context methods that take a width and a height.)

Figure 12.4 shows a simple applet whose paint() method makes the following call:

```
g.drawRect(20, 20, 100, 80);
```

**FIGURE 12.4**

drawRect()

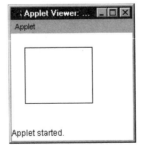

Figure 12.5 shows a simple applet whose `paint()` method makes the following call:

```
g. fillRect(20, 20, 100, 80);
```

**FIGURE 12.5**

`fillRect()`

## drawOval() and fillOval()

The `drawOval()` and `fillOval()` methods respectively draw and fill ovals. An oval is specified by a rectangular bounding box. The oval lies inside the bounding box and is tangent to each of the box's sides at the midpoint, as shown in Figure 12.6. To draw a circle, use a square bounding box.

**FIGURE 12.6**

Bounding box for
an oval

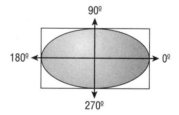

The two oval-drawing methods require you to specify a bounding box in exactly the same way that you specified a rectangle in the `drawRect()` and `fillRect()` methods:

```
public void drawOval(int x, int y, int width, int height);
public void fillOval(int x, int y, int width, int height);
```

Here x and y are the coordinates of the upper-left corner of the bounding box, and `width` and `height` are the width and height of the box.

Figure 12.7 shows a simple applet whose paint() method makes the following call:

g.drawOval(10, 10, 150, 100);

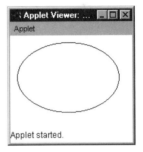

Figure 12.8 shows an applet whose paint() method calls

g. fillOval(10, 10, 150, 100);

## *drawArc()* and *fillArc()*

An arc is a segment of an oval. To specify an arc, you first specify the oval's bounding box, just as you do with drawOval() and fillOval(). You also need to specify the starting and ending points of the arc, which you do by specifying a starting angle and the angle swept out by the arc. Angles are measured in degrees. For the starting angle, 0 degrees is to the right, 90 degrees is upward, and so on, increasing counterclockwise.

A filled arc is the region bounded by the arc itself and the two radii from the center of the oval to the endpoints of the arc.

The method signatures are

```
public void drawArc(int x, int y, int width, int height,
                    int startDegrees, int arcDegrees);
public void fillArc(int x, int y, int width, int height,
                    int startDegrees, int arcDegrees);
```

Figure 12.9 shows an applet whose paint() method calls

g. drawArc(10, 10, 150, 100, 45, 180);

**F I G U R E   12.9**

drawArc()

Figure 12.10 shows an applet whose paint() method calls

g. fillArc(10, 10, 150, 100, 45, 180);

**F I G U R E   12.10**

fillArc()

### *drawPolygon* and *fillPolygon*

A *polygon* is a closed figure with an arbitrary number of vertices. The vertices are passed to the drawPolygon() and fillPolygon() methods as two int arrays. The first array contains the x coordinates of the vertices; the second array contains the y coordinates. A third parameter specifies the number of vertices. The method signatures are

```
public void drawPolygon(int xs[], int ys[], int numPoints);
public void fillPolygon(int xs[], int ys[], int numPoints);
```

Figure 12.11 shows an applet whose `paint()` method calls

1. `int polyXs[] = {20, 150, 150};`
2. `int polyYs[] = {20, 20,  120};`
3. `g.drawPolygon(polyXs, polyYs, 3);`

**F I G U R E  12.11**

drawPolygon()

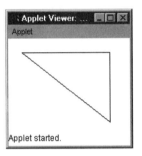

Figure 12.12 shows an applet whose `paint()` method calls

1. `int polyXs[] = {20, 150, 150};`
2. `int polyYs[] = {20, 20,  120};`
3. `g.fillPolygon(polyXs, polyYs, 3);`

**F I G U R E  12.12**

fillPolygon()

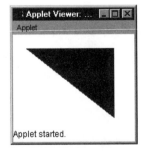

### drawPolyline()

A *polyline* is similar to a polygon, but it is open rather than closed: There is no line segment connecting the last vertex to the first. The parameters to drawPolyline() are the same as those to drawPolygon(): a pair of int arrays representing vertices, and an int that tells how many vertices there are. There is no fillPolyline() method, since fillPolygon() achieves the same result.

The signature for drawPolyline() is

```
public void drawPolyline(int xs[], int ys[], int numPoints);
```

Figure 12.13 shows an applet whose paint() method calls

```
1. int polyXs[] = {20, 150, 150};
2. int polyYs[] = {20, 20,  120};
3. g.drawPolyline (polyXs, polyYs, 3);
```

**F I G U R E  12.13**

drawPolyline()

### drawString()

The drawString() method paints a string of text. The signature is

```
public  void drawString(String s, int x, int y);
```

The x and y parameters specify the left edge of the baseline of the string. Characters with descenders (g, j, p, q, and y in most fonts) extend below the baseline.

By default, a graphics context uses the font of the associated component. However, you can set a different font by calling the graphics context's set-Font() method, as you saw in the section "Selecting a Font."

Figure 12.14 shows an applet whose paint() method calls

```
1. Font font = new Font("Serif", Font.PLAIN, 24);
2. g.setFont(font);
3. g.drawString("juggle quickly", 20, 50);
4. g.setColor(Color.darkGray);
5. g.drawLine(20, 50, 150, 50);
```

The string in line 3 contains five descender characters. Lines 4 and 5 draw the baseline, so you can see it in relation to the rendered string.

**FIGURE 12.14**

drawString()

### drawImage()

An image is an off-screen representation of a rectangular collection of pixel values. Java's image support is complicated, and a complete description would go well beyond the scope of this book. The last section of this chapter, "Images," discusses what you need to know about creating and manipulating images.

For now, assume that you have somehow obtained an image (that is, an instance of class java.awt.Image) that you want to render to the screen using a certain graphics context. The way to do this is to call the graphics context's drawImage() method, which has the following signature:

```
void drawImage(Image im, int x, int y, ImageObserver observer);
```

There are other versions of the method, but this is the most common form. Obviously, im is the image to be rendered, and x and y are the coordinates within the destination component of the upper-left corner of the image. The image observer must be an object that implements the ImageObserver interface.

> **NOTE** Image observers are part of Java's complicated image-support system; the point to remember is that your image observer can always be the component into which you are rendering the image. For a complete discussion of images, please refer to the *Java 2 Developer's Handbook* (Sybex, 1999).

## Clipping

Most calls that programmers make on graphics contexts involve color selection or drawing and filling. A less common operation is *clipping*. Clipping is simply restricting the region that a graphics context can modify.

Every graphics context—that is, every instance of the Graphics class—has a *clip region*, which defines all or part of the associated component. When you call one of the drawXXX() or fillXXX() methods of the Graphics class, only those pixels that lie within the graphics context's clip region are modified. The default clip region for a graphics context is the entire associated component. There are methods that retrieve and modify a clip region.

In a moment you will see an example of clipping, but to set things up, consider the following paint() method:

```
1. public void paint(Graphics g) {
2.   for (int i=10; i<500; i+=20)
3.     for (int j=10; j<500; j+=20)
4.       g.fillOval(i, j, 15, 15);
5. }
```

This method draws a polka-dot pattern. Consider what happens when this is the paint() method of an applet that is 300 pixels wide by 300 pixels high. Because the loop counters go all the way up to 500, the method attempts to draw outside the bounds of the applet. This is not a problem, because the graphics context by default has a clip region that coincides with the applet itself. Figure 12.15 shows the applet.

To set a rectangular clip region for a graphics context, you can call the setClip (x, y, width, height) method, passing in four ints that describe

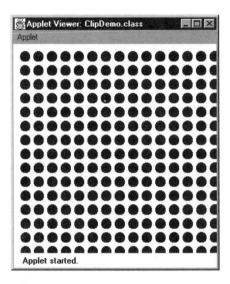

the position and size of the desired clip rectangle. For example, the code above could be modified as follows:

```
1. public void paint(Graphics g) {
2.    g.setClip(100, 100, 100, 100);
3.    for (int i=10; i<500; i+=20)
4.       for (int j=10; j<500; j+=20)
5.          g.fillOval(i, j, 15, 15);
6. }
```

Now painting is clipped to a 100×100 rectangle in the center of the 300 × 300 applet, as Figure 12.16 shows.

Clipping is good to know about in its own right. Clipping also comes into play when the environment needs to repair exposed portions of a component, as described in "Spontaneous Painting," later in this chapter.

## Painting a Contained Component

If an applet or a frame contains components that have their own `paint()` methods, then all the `paint()` methods will be called by the environment

**FIGURE 12.16**

Applet with
default clipping

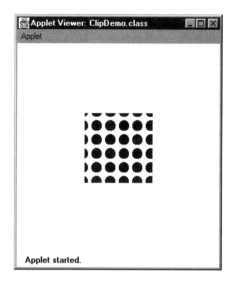

**FIGURE 12.16**

Applet with
default clipping

when necessary. For example, if a frame contains a panel and a canvas, then at certain times the environment will call the frame's paint(), the panel's paint(), and the canvas' paint().

The code listed below implements a frame that contains a panel and a canvas. The frame uses a Grid layout manager with three rows and one column. The panel is added to the frame first, so it appears in the top third of the frame. The canvas is added second, so it appears in the middle third. Since there is no component in the last grid cell, what you see in the bottom third of the frame is the frame itself (that is, you see whatever the frame itself draws in its own paint() method).

The panel draws concentric ovals. The canvas draws concentric rectangles. The frame draws text.

```
1. import java.awt.*;
2.
3. public class ThingsInFrame extends Frame {
4.   public ThingsInFrame() {
5.     super("Panel and Canvas in a Frame");
6.     setSize(350, 500);
```

```
7.      setLayout(new GridLayout(3, 1));
8.      add(new RectsPanel());
9.      add(new OvalsCanvas());
10.   }
11.
12.   public static void main(String args[]) {
13.     ThingsInFrame tif = new ThingsInFrame();
14.     tif.setVisible(true);
15.   }
16.
17.   public void paint(Graphics g) {
18.   Rectangle bounds = getBounds();
19.     int y = 12;
20.     while (y < bounds.height) {
21.       g.drawString("frame frame frame frame frame _
              frame", 60, y);
22.       y += 12;
23.     }
24.   }
25. }
26.
27.
28.
29. class RectsPanel extends Panel {
30.   public RectsPanel() {
31.     setBackground(Color.lightGray);
32.   }
33.
34.   public void paint(Graphics g) {
35.     Rectangle bounds = getBounds();
36.     int x = 0;
37.     int y = 0;
38.     int w = bounds.width - 1;
39.     int h = bounds.height - 1;
40.     for (int i=0; i<10; i++) {
```

```
41.          g.drawRect(x, y, w, h);
42.          x += 10;
43.          y += 10;
44.          w -= 20;
45.          h -= 20;
46.      }
47.  }
48. }
49.
50.
51. class OvalsCanvas extends Canvas {
52.    public OvalsCanvas() {
53.      setForeground(Color.white);
54.      setBackground(Color.darkGray);
55.    }
56.
57.    public void paint(Graphics g) {
58.      Rectangle bounds = getBounds();
59.      int x = 0;
60.      int y = 0;
61.      int w = bounds.width - 1;
62.      int h = bounds.height - 1;
63.      for (int i=0; i<10; i++) {
64.        g.drawOval(x, y, w, h);
65.        x += 10;
66.        y += 10;
67.        w -= 20;
68.        h -= 20;
69.      }
70.    }
71. }
```

Figure 12.17 shows the frame.

On line 31, the constructor for RectsPanel called setBackground(). On lines 53 and 54, the constructor for OvalsCanvas called both setBackground()

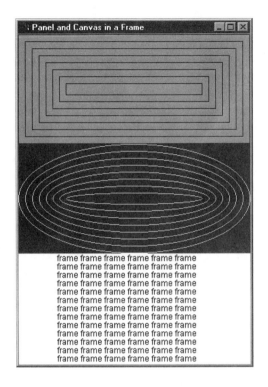

and setForeground(). The screen shot in Figure 12.15 shows that the foreground and background colors seem to have taken effect without any effort on the part of the paint() methods. The environment is not only making paint() calls at the right times; it is also doing the right thing with the foreground and background colors.

The next several sections discuss what the environment is really up to. But first, to summarize what you have learned so far about the paint() method and the graphics context:

- A graphics context is dedicated to a single component.

- To paint on a component, you call the graphics context's drawXXX() and fillXXX() methods.

- To change the color of graphics operations, you call the graphics context's setColor() method.

# The GUI thread and the *repaint()* method

In Chapter 7, you reviewed Java's facilities for creating and controlling threads. The runtime environment creates and controls its own threads that operate behind the scenes, and one of these threads is responsible for GUI management.

This *GUI thread* is the environment's tool for accepting user input events and (more importantly for this chapter) for calling the paint() method of components that need painting.

Calls to paint() are not all generated by the environment. Java programs can of course make their own calls, either directly (which is not recommended) or indirectly (via the repaint() method). The next two sections cover the two ways that paint() calls can be generated:

- Spontaneous painting, initiated by the environment

- Programmer-initiated painting

## Spontaneous Painting

*Spontaneous Painting* is not an official Java term, but it gets the point across. Some painting happens all by itself, with no impetus from the program. For example, as every introductory Java book explains, when a browser starts up an applet, shortly after the init() method completes, a call is made to the paint() method. Also, when part or all of a browser or a frame is covered by another window and then becomes exposed, a call is made to the paint() method.

It is the GUI thread that makes these calls to paint(). Every applet, and every application that has a GUI, has a GUI thread. The GUI thread spontaneously calls paint() under four circumstances, two of which are only applicable for applets:

- After exposure

- After de-iconification

- Shortly after init() returns (applets only)

- When a browser returns to a previously displayed page containing an applet, provided the applet is at least partially visible

When the GUI thread calls paint(), it must supply a graphics context, since the paint() method's input parameter is an instance of the Graphics class. An earlier section ("Clipping") discussed the fact that every graphics context has a clip region. The GUI thread makes sure that the graphics contexts that get passed to paint() have their clip regions appropriately set. Most often, the default clip region is appropriate. (Recall that the default clip region is the entire component.) However, when a component is exposed, the clip region is set to be just that portion of the component that requires repair. If only a small piece of the component was exposed, then the clip region insures that no time is wasted on drawing pixels that are already the correct color.

## The *repaint()* method

There are times when the program, not the environment, should initiate painting. This usually happens in response to input events.

Suppose you have an applet that wants to draw a red dot at the point of the most recent mouse click. The remainder of the applet should be yellow. Assume that the applet is handling its own mouse-motion events. Your event handler might look like this:

```
1. public void mouseClicked(MouseEvent e) {
2.     Graphics g = getGraphics();              // Obtain _
       graphics context
3.     g.setColor(Color.yellow);                // Yellow _
       background
4.     g.fillRect(0, 0, getSize().width, getSize().height);
5.     g.setColor(Color.red);                   // Red dot
6.     g.fillOval(e.getX()-10, e.getY()-10, 20, 20);
7. }
```

There are two reasons why this approach is far from optimal.

First, if the applet ever gets covered and exposed, the GUI thread will call paint(). Unfortunately, paint() does not know about the red circle that was drawn in mouseClicked(), so the red circle will not be repaired. It is a good rule of thumb to do *all* drawing operations in paint(), or in methods called from paint(), so that the GUI thread will be able to repair exposure damage. The GUI thread expects paint() to be able to correctly reconstruct the screen at any arbitrary moment.

The way to give the GUI thread what it expects is to remove all drawing code from event handlers. Event handlers such as mouseClicked() above should store state information in instance variables, and then cause a call to paint(). The paint() method should use the values of the instance variables as instructions on what to draw. In our example, mouseClicked() should be modified as shown below, assuming that the class has instance variables mouseX and mouseY:

```
1. public void mouseClicked(MouseEvent e) {
2.    mouseX = e.getX();
3.    mouseY = e.getY();
4.    Graphics g = getGraphics();
5.    paint(g);
6. }
```

The paint() method should be as follows:

```
1. public void paint(Graphics g) {
2.    g.setColor(Color. yellow);          // Yellow background
3.    g.fillRect(0, 0, getSize().width, getSize().height);
4.    g.setColor(Color.red);              // Red dot
5.    g.fillOval(mouseX-10, mouseY-10, 20, 20);
6. }
```

Much better! Now if a dot gets covered and exposed, the damage will be repaired automatically. There remains, however, a second problem, and it is a bit subtler than the spontaneous painting issue.

The program can be simplified a bit. There is a method of the Component class called update(), which clears the component to its background color and then calls paint(). The input parameter to update() is a graphics context. The applet's init() method could set the background color to yellow:

```
setBackground(Color.yellow);
```

Now the event handler should call update() rather than paint(), and update() only needs to draw the red dot:

```
1. public void mouseClicked(MouseEvent e) {
2.    mouseX = e.getX();
3.    mouseY = e.getY();
4.    Graphics g = getGraphics();
5.    update(g);
```

```
6. }
7.
8. public void paint(Graphics g) {
9.    g.setColor(Color.red);
10.   g.fillOval(mouseX-10, mouseY-10, 20, 20);
11. }
```

This code works just fine as it is. It is a simple program that only cares about mouse-click events. In the real world, programs often need to track many different kinds of events: action events, adjustment events, key events, focus events, mouse events, mouse-motion events, and so on. It may be that every event requires painting the screen anew.

Consider what happens if a large number of events of different types are generated in rapid succession. (This is not unusual; moving or dragging the mouse can create a lot of mouse-moved and mouse-dragged events in very short order.) Time after time, an event will be generated, event handlers will modify instance variables, and paint() will modify the screen, only to have the cycle repeat and repeat. Most of the screen-drawing operations will instantly get clobbered by other screen-drawing operations triggered by more recent events. Many compute cycles will be wasted. The more compute-intensive the paint() method is, the worse the situation becomes. If the user can generate events faster than paint() can handle them, then the program will fall farther and farther behind.

It would be ideal if the event handlers could just modify the instance variables and have paint() run from time to time, often enough that the screen stays up to date, but not so often that compute cycles are wasted. This is where the repaint() method comes in.

The repaint() method *schedules* a call to the update() method. All this means is that a request flag is set in the GUI thread. Every 100 milliseconds (on most platforms), the GUI thread checks the flag. If the flag is set, the GUI thread calls update() and clears the flag. No matter how many requests are made during any 100-millisecond period, only a single call is made to update(). The example code can be modified one last time, as shown below:

```
1. public void mouseClicked(MouseEvent e) {
2.    mouseX = e.getX();
3.    mouseY = e.getY();
4.    repaint();
5. }
```

```
 6.
 7. public void paint(Graphics g) {
 8.    g.setColor(Color.red);
 9.    g.fillOval(mouseX-10, mouseY-10, 20, 20);
10. }
```

The repaint() call at line 4 has replaced the calls to getGraphics() and update(). Now even if the world's fastest kangaroo hops up and down on the mouse at 50 khops per second, there will still be only 10 calls to paint() per second, and the system cannot possibly fall behind.

The code above shows the preferred approach to handling events that cause the screen to be changed: Event handlers store information in instance variables and then call repaint(), and paint() draws the screen according to the information in the instance variables. The two benefits of this approach are

- The screen is correctly repaired when the environment spontaneously calls paint().

- The Virtual Machine never gets overwhelmed by events.

If you want to accumulate dots, rather than have each dot cleared away when a new one is to be drawn, you can always override update() so that it does not clear. All update() needs to do in this case is call paint(), as shown below:

```
1. public void update(Graphics g) {
2.    paint(g);
3. }
```

This is a standard technique.

# Images

**I**mages are off-screen representations of rectangular pixel patterns. There are three things you can do with images:

- Create them

- Modify them

- Draw them to the screen or to other images

There are two ways to create an image. You can create an empty one, or you can create one that is initialized from a .gif or a .jpeg file.

To create an empty image, call the createImage() method of the Component class and pass in the desired width and height. For example, the following line creates an image called im1 that is 400 pixels wide and 250 pixels high; it might appear in the init() method of an applet:

```
Image im1 = createImage(400, 250);
```

An image can be created based on the information in a .gif or a .jpeg file. The Applet and Toolkit classes both have a method called getImage(), which has two common forms:

```
getImage(URL fileURL)

getImage(URL dirURL, String path)
```

The first form takes a URL that references the desired image file. The second form takes a URL that references a directory and the path of the desired image file, relative to that directory. The code fragment below shows an applet's init() method; it loads an image from a file that resides in the same server directory as the page that contains the applet:

```
1. public void init() {
2.    Image im = getImage(getDocumentBase(), "thePicture.gif");
3. }
```

If you load an image from a file, you may want to modify it; you will definitely want to modify any image that you create via createImage(). Fortunately, images have graphics contexts. All you need to do is obtain a graphics context for the image you wish to modify and make the calls that were discussed earlier in this chapter in "Drawing and Filling." To obtain a graphics context, just call getGraphics(). The code below implements an applet whose init() method creates an image and then obtains a graphics context in order to draw a blue circle on a yellow background. The applet's paint() method renders the image onto the screen using the drawImage() method, which is documented earlier in this chapter.

```
1. import java.applet.Applet;
2. import java.awt.*;
3.
4. public class PaintImage extends Applet {
```

```
5.    Image im;
6.
7.    public void init() {
8.       im = createImage(300, 200);
9.       Graphics imgc = im.getGraphics();
10.      imgc.setColor(Color.yellow);
11.      imgc.fillRect(0, 0, 300, 200);
12.      imgc.setColor(Color.blue);
13.      imgc.fillOval(50, 50, 100, 100);
14.   }
15.
16.   public void paint(Graphics g) {
17.      g.drawImage(im, 25, 80, this);
18.   }
19. }
```

Notice that in lines 9–13, imgc is a graphics context that draws to the off-screen image im. In lines 16–17, g is a graphics context that draws to the applet's screen.

# Chapter Summary

The paint() method provides a graphics context for drawing. The functionality of the graphics context (class Graphics) includes

- Selecting a color
- Selecting a font
- Drawing and filling
- Clipping

Calls to paint() can be generated spontaneously by the system, under four circumstances:

- After exposure
- After de-iconification

- Shortly after `init()` returns (applets only)

- When a browser returns to a previously displayed page containing an applet (applets only)

In all cases, the clip region of the graphics context will be set appropriately. Event handlers that need to modify the screen can store state information in instance variables, and then call `repaint()`. This method schedules a call to `update()`, which clears the component to its background color and then calls `paint()`.

Images can be created from scratch or loaded from external files. An image can be modified by using a graphics context.

# Test Yourself

**1.** How would you set the color of a graphics context called g to cyan?

**A.** `g.setColor(Color.cyan);`

**B.** `g.setCurrentColor(cyan);`

**C.** `g.setColor("Color.cyan");`

**D.** `g.setColor("cyan");`

**E.** `g.setColor(new Color(cyan));`

**2.** The code below draws a line. What color is the line?

```
1. g.setColor(Color.red.green.yellow.red.cyan);
2. g.drawLine(0, 0, 100, 100);
```

**A.** Red

**B.** Green

**C.** Yellow

**D.** Cyan

**E.** Black

**3.** What does the following code draw?

```
1. g.setColor(Color.black);
2. g.drawLine(10, 10, 10, 50);
3. g.setColor(Color.red);
4. g.drawRect(100, 100, 150, 150);
```

**A.** A red vertical line that is 40 pixels long and a red square with sides of 150 pixels

**B.** A black vertical line that is 40 pixels long and a red square with sides of 150 pixels

**C.** A black vertical line that is 50 pixels long and a red square with sides of 150 pixels

**D.** A red vertical line that is 50 pixels long and a red square with sides of 150 pixels

**E.** A black vertical line that is 40 pixels long and a red square with sides of 100 pixels

**4.** Figure 12.18 shows two shapes. Which shape (A or B) is drawn by the following line of code?

```
g.fillArc(10, 10, 100, 100, 0, 90);
```

**F I G U R E  12.18**

Question 4

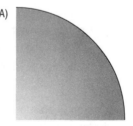

A)

B)

**5.** Which of the statements below are true? (Choose one or more.)

**A.** A polyline is always filled.

**B.** A polyline cannot be filled.

**C.** A polygon is always filled.

**D.** A polygon is always closed.

**E.** A polygon may be filled or not filled.

**6.** When the GUI thread calls `paint()` in order to repair exposure damage, the `paint()` method must determine what was damaged and set its clip region appropriately.

**A.** True

**B.** False

**7.** Your `mouseDragged()` event handler and your `paint()` method look like this:

```
1. public void mouseDragged(MouseEvent e) {
2.     mouseX = e.getX();
3.     mouseY = e.getY();
4.     repaint();
5. }
6.
7. public void paint(Graphics g) {
8.     g.setColor(Color.cyan);
9.     g.drawLine(mouseX, mouseY, mouseX+10, mouseY+10);
10. }
```

You want to modify your code so that the cyan lines accumulate on the screen, rather than getting erased every time `repaint()` calls `update()`. What is the simplest way to proceed?

**A.** On line 4, replace `repaint()` with `paint()`.

**B.** On line 4, replace `repaint()` with `update()`.

**C.** After line 7, add this: `super.update(g);`

**D.** Add the following method:

```
public void update(Graphics g) {paint(g);}
```

**8.** What code would you use to construct a 24-point bold serif font?

**A.** `new Font(Font.SERIF, 24, Font.BOLD);`

**B.** `new Font("Serif", 24, "Bold");`

**C.** `new Font("Bold", 24, Font.SERIF);`

**D.** `new Font("Serif", Font.BOLD, 24);`

**E.** `new Font(Font.SERIF, "Bold", 24);`

**9.** What does the following `paint()` method draw?

```
1. public void paint(Graphics g) {
2.   g.drawString("question #9", 10, 0);
3. }
```

**A.** The string "question #9", with its top-left corner at 10, 0

**B.** A little squiggle coming down from the top of the component, a little way in from the left edge

**10.** What does the following `paint()` method draw?

```
1. public void paint(Graphics g) {
2.   g.drawOval(100, 100, 44);
3. }
```

**A.** A circle at (100, 100) with radius of 44

**B.** A circle at (100, 44) with radius of 100

**C.** A circle at (100, 44) with radius of 44

**D.** The code does not compile.

# C H A P T E R

# 13

## Input and Output

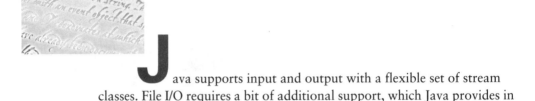

**J**ava supports input and output with a flexible set of stream classes. File I/O requires a bit of additional support, which Java provides in the File and RandomAccessFile classes.

All I/O operations into and out of a Java Virtual Machine are contingent on approval by the security manager. Most browsers forbid all file access, so the File and RandomAccessFile classes are generally for use in applications.

All the classes discussed in this chapter reside in the java.io package.

As with Chapters 11 and 12, the information discussed here is not explicitly mentioned in the objectives, but should be considered essential background.

# File Input and Output

**J**ava's File and RandomAccessFile classes provide functionality for navigating the local file system, describing files and directories, and accessing files in non-sequential order. (Accessing files sequentially is done with streams, readers, and writers, which are described later in this chapter.)

Files often contain text. Java's text representation goes far beyond traditional ASCII. Since the Certification Exam requires you to be familiar with how Java represents text, it is worthwhile to review this topic before looking at file I/O.

## Text Representation and Character Encoding

Java uses two kinds of text representation:

- Unicode for internal representation of characters and strings
- UTF for input and output

Unicode uses 16 bits to represent each character. If the high-order 9 bits are all zeros, then the encoding is simply standard ASCII, with the low-order byte containing the character representation. Otherwise, the bits represent a character that is not represented in 7-bit ASCII. Java's char data type uses Unicode encoding, and the String class contains a collection of Java chars.

Unicode's 16 bits are sufficient to encode most alphabets, but pictographic Asian languages present a problem. Standards committees have developed compromises to allow limited but useful subsets of Chinese, Japanese, and Korean to be represented in Unicode, but it has become clear that an ideal global text representation scheme must use more than 16 bits per character.

The answer is UTF. The abbreviation stands for "UCS Transformation Format," and UCS stands for "Universal Character Set." Many people believe that UTF is short for "Universal Text Format," and while they are wrong, their version is more descriptive than the true version.

UTF encoding uses as many bits as needed to encode a character: fewer bits for smaller alphabets, more bits for the larger Asian alphabets. Since every character can be represented, UTF is a truly global encoding scheme.

A character encoding is a mapping between a character set and a range of binary numbers. Every Java platform has a default character encoding, which is used to interpret between internal Unicode and external bytes. The default character encoding reflects the local language and culture. Every encoding has a name. For example, "8859_1" is common ASCII, "8859_8" is ISO Latin/Hebrew, and "Cp1258" is Vietnamese.

When an I/O operation is performed in Java, the system needs to know which character encoding to use. The various I/O support classes use the local default encoding, unless they are explicitly instructed to use a different encoding. For most operations, the local default encoding is perfectly adequate. However, when communicating across a network with another computer, both machines need to use the same encoding, even if they reside in different countries. In such cases, it is a good idea to explicitly request "8859_1."

# The *File* Class

The java.io.File class represents the name of a file or directory that might exist on the host machine's file system. The simplest form of the constructor for this class is

```
File(String pathname);
```

It is important to know that constructing an instance of File does not create a file on local file system. Calling the constructor simply creates an instance that encapsulates the specified string. Of course, if the instance is to be of any use, most likely it should encapsulate a string that represents an existing file or directory, or one that will shortly be created. However, at construction time no checks are made.

There are two other versions of the File constructor:

```
File(String dir, String subpath);
File(File dir, String subpath);
```

Both versions require you to provide a directory and a relative path (the subpath argument) within that directory. In one version you use a string to specify the directory; in the other, you use an instance of File. (Remember that the File class can represent a directory as well as a file.) You might, for example, execute the following code on a UNIX machine:

```
1. File f = new File("/tmp", "xyz");    // Assume /tmp is _
   a directory
```

You might execute the following code on a Windows platform:

```
1. File f1 = new File("C:\a");          // Assume C:\a is _
   a directory
2. File f2 = new File(f1, "Xyz.java");
```

Of course, there is no theoretical reason why you could not run the first example on a Windows machine and the second example on a UNIX platform. Up to this point you are doing nothing more than constructing objects that encapsulate strings. In practice, however, there is nothing to be gained from using the wrong pathname semantics.

After constructing an instance of File, you can make a number of method calls on it. Some of these calls simply do string manipulation on the file's pathname, while others access or modify the local file system.

The methods that support navigation are listed below:

- boolean exists(): This returns true if the file or directory exists, otherwise returns false.

- String getAbsolutePath(): This returns the absolute (i.e., not relative path of the file or directory.

- `String getCanonicalPath()`: This returns the canonical path of the file or directory. This is similar to `getAbsolutePath()`, but the symbols . and .. are resolved.

- `String getName()`: This returns the name of the file or directory. The name is the last element of the path.

- `String getParent()`: This returns the name of the directory that contains the `File`.

- `boolean isDirectory()`: This returns `true` if the `File` describes a directory that exists on the file system.

- `boolean isFile()`: This returns `true` if the `File` describes a file that exists on the file system.

- `String[] list()`: This returns an array containing the names of the files and directories within the `File`. The `File` must describe a directory, not a file.

The methods listed above are not the entirety of the class' methods. Some non-navigation methods are

- `boolean canRead()`: This returns `true` if the file or directory may be read.

- `boolean canWrite()`: This returns `true` if the file or directory may be modified.

- `boolean delete()`: This attempts to delete the file or directory.

- `long length()`: This returns the length of the file.

- `boolean mkdir()`: This attempts to create a directory whose path is described by the `File`.

- `boolean renameTo(File newname)`: This renames the file or directory. Returns `true` if the renaming succeeded, otherwise returns `false`.

The program listed below uses some of the navigation methods to create a recursive listing of a directory. The application expects the directory to be specified in the command line. The listing appears in a text area within a frame.

```
1. import java.awt.*;
2. import java.io.File;
3.
```

```
4. public class Lister extends Frame {
5.    TextArea     ta;
6.
7.    public static void main(String args[]) {
8.      // Get path or dir to be listed. Default to cwd if
9.      // no command line arg.
10.      String path = ".";
11.      if (args.length >= 1)
12.        path = args[0];
13.
14.      // Make sure path exists and is a directory.
15.      File f = new File(path);
16.      if (!f.isDirectory()) {
17.        System.out.println("Doesn't exist or not dir: _
         " + path);
18.        System.exit(0);
19.      }
20.
21.      // Recursively list contents.
22.      Lister lister = new Lister(f);
23.      lister.setVisible(true);
24.    }
25.
26.    Lister(File f) {
27.      setSize(300, 450);
28.      ta = new TextArea();
29.      ta.setFont(new Font("Monospaced", Font.PLAIN, 14));
30.      add(BorderLayout.CENTER, ta);
31.      recurse(f, 0);
32.    }
33.
34.    //
35.    // Recursively list the contents of dirfile. Indent _
         5 spaces for
36.    // each level of depth.
37.    //
38.    void recurse(File dirfile, int depth) {
```

```
39.        String contents[] = dirfile.list();
40.        for (int i=0; i<contents.length; i++) {
           // For each child...
41.          for (int spaces=0; spaces<depth; spaces++)
             // Indent
42.            ta.append("     ");
43.          ta.append(contents[i] + "\n");
             // Print name
44.          File child = new File(dirfile, contents[i]);
45.          if (child.isDirectory())
46.            recurse(child, depth+1);
             // Recurse if dir
47.        }
48.      }
49. }
```

Figure 13.1 shows a sample of this program's output.

The program first checks for a command-line argument (lines 10–12). If one is supplied, it is assumed to be the name of the directory to be listed; if there is no argument, the current working directory will be listed. Note the call to isDirectory() on line 16. This call returns true only if path represents an existing directory.

After establishing that the thing to be listed really is a directory, the code constructs an instance of Lister, which makes a call to recurse(), passing in the File to be listed in the parameter dirfile.

The recurse() method makes a call to list() (line 39) to get a listing of the contents of the directory. Each file or subdirectory is printed (line 43) after appropriate indentation (5 spaces per level, lines 41 and 42). If the child is a directory (tested on line 45), its contents are listed recursively.

The Lister program shows one way to use the methods of the File class to navigate the local file system. These methods do not modify the contents of files in any way; to modify a file you must use either the RandomAccess-File class or Java's stream, reader, and writer facilities. All these topics are covered in the sections that follow, but first here is a summary of the key points concerning the File class:

- An instance of File describes a file or directory.

- The file or directory might or might not exist.

- Constructing/garbage collecting an instance of File has no effect on the local file system.

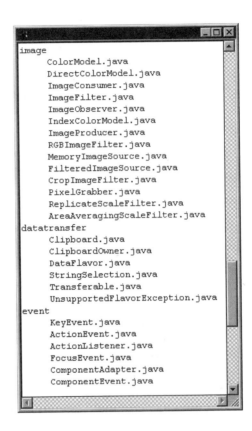

```
image
        ColorModel.java
        DirectColorModel.java
        ImageConsumer.java
        ImageFilter.java
        ImageObserver.java
        IndexColorModel.java
        ImageProducer.java
        RGBImageFilter.java
        MemoryImageSource.java
        FilteredImageSource.java
        CropImageFilter.java
        PixelGrabber.java
        ReplicateScaleFilter.java
        AreaAveragingScaleFilter.java
datatransfer
        Clipboard.java
        ClipboardOwner.java
        DataFlavor.java
        StringSelection.java
        Transferable.java
        UnsupportedFlavorException.java
event
        KeyEvent.java
        ActionEvent.java
        ActionListener.java
        FocusEvent.java
        ComponentAdapter.java
        ComponentEvent.java
```

## The *RandomAccessFile* Class

One way to read or modify a file is to use the java.io.RandomAccessFile class. This class presents a model of files that is incompatible with the stream/ reader/writer model described later in this chapter. The stream/reader/writer model was developed for general I/O, while the RandomAccessFile class takes advantage of a particular behavior of files that is not found in general I/O devices.

With a random-access file, you can seek to a desired position within a file, and then read or write a desired amount of data. The RandomAccessFile class provides methods that support seeking, reading, and writing.

The constructors for the class are

- RandomAccessFile(String file, String mode)
- RandomAccessFile(File file, String mode)

The mode string should be either "r" or "rw." Use "r" to open the file for reading only, and use "rw" to open for both reading and writing.

The second form of the constructor is useful when you want to use some of the methods of the File class before opening a random-access file, so that you already have an instance of File at hand when it comes time to call the RandomAccessFile constructor. For example, the code fragment below constructs an instance of File in order to verify that the string path represents a file that exists and may be written. If this is the case, the RandomAccessFile constructor is called; otherwise an exception is thrown.

```
1. File file = new File(path);
2. if (!file.isFile() || !file.canRead() ||
      !file.canWrite()) {
3.    throw new IOException();
4. }
5. RandomAccessFile raf = new RandomAccessFile(file, "rw");
```

Constructing an instance of RandomAccessFile is like constructing an instance of File: No file is created on the file system. Similarly, unreferencing and garbage collecting an instance of RandomAccessFile does not cause deletion of the corresponding file on the file system.

After a random-access file is constructed, you can seek to any byte position within the file and then read or write. Pre-Java systems (the C standard I/O library, for example) have supported seeking to a position relative to the beginning of the file, the end of the file, or the current position within the file. Java's random-access files only support seeking relative to the beginning of the file, but there are methods that report the current position and the length of the file, so you can effectively perform the other kinds of seek as long as you are willing to do the arithmetic.

The methods that support seeking are

- long getFilePointer() throws IOException: This returns the current position within the file, in bytes. Subsequent reading and writing will take place starting at this position.

- long length() throws IOException: This returns the length of the file, in bytes.

- void seek(long position) throws IOException: This sets the current position within the file, in bytes. Subsequent reading and writing will take place starting at this position. Files start at position 0.

The code listed below is a subclass of RandomAccessFile that adds two new methods to support seeking from the current position or the end of the file. The code illustrates the use of the methods listed above.

```
1. class GeneralRAF extends RandomAccessFile {
2. public GeneralRAF(File path, String mode) throws _
    IOException {
3.   super(path, mode);
4. }
5.
6.   public GeneralRAF(String path, String mode) throws _
    IOException {
7.     super(path, mode);
8.   }
9.
10.   public void seekFromEnd(long offset) throws _
    IOException {
11.     seek(length() - offset);
12.   }
13.
14.   public void seekFromCurrent(long offset) throws _
    IOException {
15.     seek(getFilePointer() + offset);
16.   }
17. }
```

The whole point of seeking, of course, is to read from or write to a desired position within a file. Files are ordered collections of bytes, and the Random-AccessFile class has several methods that support reading and writing of bytes. However, the bytes in a file often combine to represent richer data formats. For example, two bytes could represent a Unicode character; four bytes could represent a float or an int. All the reading and writing methods advance the current file position.

The more common methods that support byte reading and writing are

- int read() throws IOException: This returns the next byte from the file (stored in the low-order 8 bits of an int), or -1 if at end of file.

- `int read(byte dest[]) throws IOException`: This attempts to read enough bytes to fill array `dest[]`. Returns the number of bytes read, or -1 if the file was at end of file.

- `int read(byte dest[], int offset, int len) throws IOException`: This attempts to read `len` bytes into array `dest[]`, starting at `offset`. Returns the number of bytes read, or -1 if the file was at end of file.

- `void write(int b) throws IOException`: This writes the low-order byte of b.

- `void write(int b[]) throws IOException`: writes all of byte array b[].

- `void write(int b[], int offset, int len) throws IOException`: This writes `len` bytes from byte array b[], starting at `offset`.

Random-access files support reading and writing of all primitive data types. Each read or write operation advances the current file position by the number of bytes read or written. Table 13.1 presents the various primitive-oriented methods, all of which throw `IOException`.

**T A B L E  13.1:**   Random-access file methods for primitive data types

| Data Type | Read Method | Write Method |
|-----------|-------------|--------------|
| boolean | boolean readBoolean() | void writeBoolean(boolean b) |
| byte | byte readByte() | void writeByte(int b) |
| short | short readShort() | void writeShort(int s) |
| char | char readChar() | void writeChar(int c) |
| int | int readInt() | void writeInt(int i) |
| long | long readLong() | void writeLong(long l) |
| float | float readFloat() | void writeFloat(float f) |
| double | double readDouble() | void writeDouble(double d) |

**T A B L E 13.1:** Random-access file methods for primitive data types *(Continued)*

| Data Type | Read Method | Write Method |
|---|---|---|
| unsigned byte | int readUnsignedByte() | None |
| unsigned short | int readUnsignedShort() | None |
| line of text | String readLine() | None |
| UTF string | String readUTF() | void writeUTF(String s) |

There are several more random access file methods to support reading and writing of not-quite-primitive data types. These methods deal with unsigned bytes, unsigned shorts, lines of text, and UTF strings, as shown in Table 13.1.

When a random-access file is no longer needed it should be closed:

- `void close()throws IOException`

The `close()` method releases non-memory system resources associated with the file.

To summarize, random-access files offer the following functionality:

- Seeking to any position within a file

- Reading and writing single or multiple bytes

- Reading and writing groups of bytes, treated as higher-level data types

- Closing

# Streams, Readers, and Writers

Java's stream, reader, and writer classes view input and output as ordered sequences of bytes. Of course, dealing strictly with bytes would be tremendously bothersome, because data appears sometimes as bytes, sometimes as ints, sometimes as floats, and so on. You have already seen how the `RandomAccessFile` class allows you to read and write all of Java's primitive data types. The `readInt()` method, for example, reads four bytes from a file, pieces them together, and returns an int. Java's general I/O classes provide a similar structured approach:

- A low-level output stream receives bytes and writes bytes to an output device.

- A high-level `filter` output stream receives general-format data, such as primitives, and writes bytes to a low-level output stream or to another filter output stream.

- A `writer` is similar to a filter output stream but is specialized for writing Java strings in units of Unicode characters.

- A low-level input stream reads bytes from an input device and returns bytes to its caller.

- A high-level `filter` input stream reads bytes from a low-level input stream, or from another filter input stream, and returns general-format data to its caller.

- A `reader` is similar to a filter input stream but is specialized for reading UTF strings in units of Unicode characters.

The stream, reader, and writer classes are not very complicated. The easiest way to review them is to begin with the low-level streams.

## Low-Level Streams

*Low-level input streams* have methods that read input and return the input as bytes. *Low-level output streams* have methods that are passed bytes, and write the bytes as output. The `FileInputStream` and `FileOutputStream` classes are excellent examples.

The two most common file input stream constructors are

- `FileInputStream(String pathname)`

- `FileInputStream(File file)`

After a file input stream has been constructed, you can call methods to read a single byte, an array of bytes, or a portion of an array of bytes. The functionality is similar to the byte-input methods you have already seen in the `RandomAccessFile` class:

- `int read() throws IOException`: This returns the next byte from the file (stored in the low-order 8 bits of an int) or -1 if at end of file.

- `int read(byte dest[]) throws IOException`: This attempts to read enough bytes to fill array `dest[]`. Returns the number of bytes read or -1 if the file was at end of file.

- `int read(byte dest[], int offset, int len) throws IOException`: This attempts to read `len` bytes into array `dest[]`, starting at `offset`. Returns the number of bytes read, or -1 if the file was at end of file.

The code fragment below illustrates the use of these methods by reading a single byte into byte b, then enough bytes to fill byte array `bytes[]`, and finally 20 bytes into the first 20 locations of byte array `morebytes[]`.

```
1.  byte b;
2.  byte bytes[] = new byte[100];
3.  byte morebytes[] = new byte[50];
4.  try {
5.    FileInputStream fis = new FileInputStream("some_file_
      name");
6.    b = (byte) fis.read();        // Single byte
7.    fis.read(bytes);               // Fill the array
8.    fis.read(morebytes, 0, 20);    // 1st 20 elements
9.    fis.close();
10. } catch (IOException e) { }
```

The `FileInputStream` class has a few very useful utility methods:

- `int available() throws IOException`: This returns the number of bytes that can be read without blocking.

- `void close() throws IOException`: This releases non-memory system resources associated with the file. A file input stream should always be closed when no longer needed.

- `long skip(long nbytes) throws IOException`: This attempts to read and discard `nbytes` bytes. Returns the number of bytes actually skipped.

It is not surprising that file output streams are almost identical to file input streams. The commonly used constructors are

- `FileOutputStream(String pathname)`
- `FileOutputStream(File file)`

There are methods to support writing a single byte, an array of bytes, or a subset of an array of bytes:

- `void write(int b) throws IOException`: This writes the low-order byte of b.

- `void write(byte bytes[]) throws IOException`: This writes all members of byte array `bytes[]`.

- `void write(byte bytes[], int offset, int len) throws IOException`: This writes `len` bytes from array `bytes[]`, starting at `offset`.

The `FileOutputStream` class also has a `close()` method, which should always be called when a file output stream is no longer needed.

In addition to the two classes described above, the `java.io` package has a number of other low-level input and output stream classes:

- `InputStream` and `OutputStream`: These are the superclasses of the other low-level stream classes. They can be used for reading and writing network sockets.

- `ByteArrayInputStream` and `ByteArrayOutputStream`: These classes read and write arrays of bytes. Byte arrays are certainly not hardware I/O devices, but the classes are useful when you want to process or create sequences of bytes.

- `PipedInputStream` and `PipedOutputStream`: These classes provide a mechanism for thread communication.

## High-Level Filter Streams

It is all very well to read bytes from input devices and write bytes to output devices, if bytes are the unit of information you are interested in. However, more often than not the bytes to be read or written constitute higher-level information such as ints or strings.

Java supports high-level I/O with high-level streams. The most common of these (and the ones covered in this chapter) extend from the abstract super-classes `FilterInputStream` and `FilterOutputStream`. *High-level input streams* do not read from input devices such as files or sockets; rather, they read from other streams. *High-level output streams* do not write to output devices, but to other streams.

A good example of a high-level input stream is the data input stream. There is only one constructor for this class:

- `DataInputStream(InputStream instream)`

The constructor requires you to pass in an input stream. This instance might be a file input stream (because `FileInputStream` extends `Input-Stream`), an input stream from a socket, or any other kind of input stream. When the instance of `DataInputStream` is called on to deliver data, it will make some number of `read()` calls on `instream`, process the bytes, and return an appropriate value. The commonly used input methods of the `DataInputStream` class are

- `boolean readBoolean() throws IOException`
- `byte readByte() throws IOException`
- `char readChar () throws IOException`
- `double readDouble () throws IOException`
- `float readFloat () throws IOException`
- `int readInt() throws IOException`
- `long readLong() throws IOException`
- `short readShort() throws IOException`
- `String readUTF() throws IOException`

There is, of course, a `close()` method.

When creating chains of streams, it is recommended that you close all streams when you no longer need them, making sure to close in the opposite order of the order in which the streams were constructed.

The code fragment below illustrates a small input chain:

```
1. try {
2.    // Construct the chain
3.    FileInputStream fis = new FileInputStream("a_file");
4.    DataInputStream dis = new DataInputStream(fis);
5.
6.    // Read
```

```
7.   double d = dis.readDouble();
8.   int i = dis.readInt();
9.   String s = dis.readUTF();
10.
11.  // Close the chain
12.  dis.close();// Close dis first, because it
13.  fis.close();        // Was created last
14.  }
15.  catch (IOException e) { }
```

Figure 13.2 shows the hierarchy of the input chain.

The code expects that the first eight bytes in the file represent a double, the next four bytes represent an int, and the next who-knows-how-many bytes represent a UTF string. This means that the code that originally created the file must have been writing a double, an int, and a UTF string. The file need not have been created by a Java program, but if it was, the easiest approach would be to use a data output stream.

The DataOutputStream class is the mirror image of the DataInputStream class. The constructor is

- DataOutputStream(OutputStream ostream)

The constructor requires you to pass in an output stream. When you write to the data output stream, it converts the parameters of the write methods to bytes, and writes them to ostream. The commonly used input methods of the DataOutputStream class are

- void writeBoolean(boolean b) throws IOException
- void writeByte(int b) throws IOException
- void writeBytes(String s) throws IOException
- void writeChar(int c) throws IOException
- void writeDouble(double d) throws IOException
- void writeFloat(float b) throws IOException
- void writeInt(int i) throws IOException
- void writeLong(long l) throws IOException
- void writeShort(short s) throws IOException
- void writeUTF(String s) throws IOException

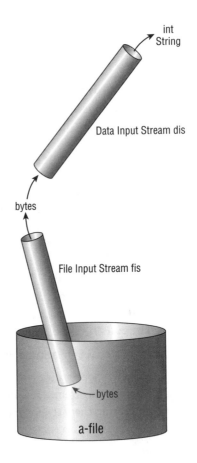

All these methods convert their input to bytes in the obvious way, with the exception of `writeBytes()`, which writes out only the low-order byte of each character in its string. As usual, there is a `close()` method. Again, chains of output streams should be closed in reverse order from their order of creation.

With the methods listed above in mind, you can now write code that creates a file like the one read in the previous example. In that example, the file contained a double, an int, and a string. The file might be created as follows:

```
1. try {
2.    // Create the chain
3.    FileOutputStream fos = new FileOutputStream("a_file");
```

```
4.   DataOutputStream dos = new DataOutputStream(fos);
5.
6.   // Write
7.   dos.writeDouble(123.456);
8.   dos.writeInt(55);
9.   dos.writeUTF("The moving finger writes");
10.
11.  // Close the chain
12.  dos.close();
13.  fos.close();
14. }
15. catch (IOException e) { }
```

In addition to data input streams and output streams, the java.io package offers several other high-level stream classes. The constructors for all high-level input streams require you to pass in the next-lower input stream in the chain; this will be the source of data read by the new object. Similarly, the constructors for the high-level output streams require you to pass in the next-lower output stream in the chain; the new object will write data to this stream. Some of the high-level streams are listed below:

- BufferedInputStream and BufferedOutputStream: These classes have internal buffers so that bytes can be read or written in large blocks, thus minimizing I/O overhead.

- PrintStream: This class can be asked to write text or primitives. Primitives are converted to character representations. The System.out and System.err objects are examples of this class.

- PushbackInputStream: This class allows the most recently read byte to be put back into the stream, as if it had not yet been read. This functionality is very useful for certain kinds of parsers.

It is possible to create stream chains of arbitrary length. For example, the code fragment below implements a data input stream that reads from a buffered input stream, which in turn reads from a file input stream:

```
1. FileInputStream fis = new FileInputStream("read_this");
2. BufferedInputStream bis = new BufferedInputStream(fis);
3. DataInputStream dis = new DataInputStream(bis);
```

The chain that this code creates is shown in Figure 13.3.

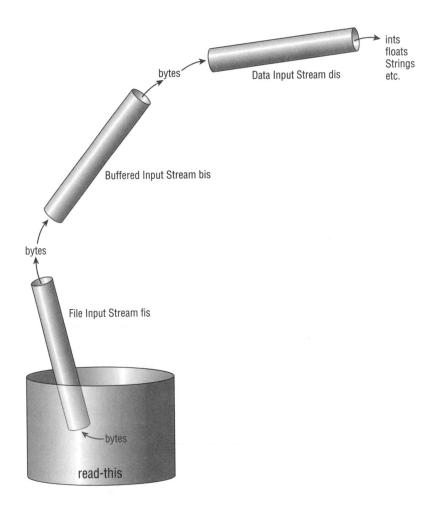

## Readers and Writers

*Readers* and *writers* are like input and output streams: The low-level varieties communicate with I/O devices, while the high-level varieties communicate with low-level varieties. What makes readers and writers different is that they are exclusively oriented to Unicode characters.

A good example of a low-level reader is the `FileReader` class. Its commonly used constructors are

- `FileReader(String pathname)`
- `FileReader(File file)`

Of course, any file passed into these constructors must genuinely contain UTF strings.

The corresponding writer is the `FileWriter` class:

- `FileWriter(String pathname)`
- `FileWriter(File file)`

The other low-level reader and writer classes are

- `CharArrayReader` and `CharArrayWriter`: These classes read and write char arrays.

- `PipedReader` and `PipedWriter`: These classes provide a mechanism for thread communication.

- `StringReader` and `StringWriter`: These classes read and write strings.

The low-level readers all extend from the abstract `Reader` superclass. This class offers the now-familiar trio of `read()` methods for reading a single char, an array of chars, or a subset of an array of chars. Note, however, that the unit of information is now the char, not the byte. The three methods are

- `int read() throws IOException`: This returns the next char (stored in the low-order 16 bits of the int return value), or -1 if at end of input.

- `int read(char dest[]) throws IOException`: This attempts to read enough chars to fill array `dest[]`. Returns the number of chars read, or -1 if at end of input.

- `abstract int read(char dest[], int offset, int len) throws IOException`: This attempts to read `len` chars into array `dest[]`, starting at `offset`. Returns the number of chars read, or -1 if at end of input.

The low-level writers all extend from the abstract `Writer` superclass. This class provides methods that are a bit different from the standard trio of `write()` methods:

- `void write(int ch) throws IOException`: writes the char that appears in the low-order 16 bits of ch

- void write(String str) throws IOException: writes the string str

- void write(String str, int offset, int len) throws IOException: writes the substring of str that begins at offset and has length len

- void write(char chars[]) throws IOException: writes the char array chars[]

- void write(char chars[], int offset, int len) throws IOException: writes len chars from array chars[], beginning at offset

The high-level readers and writers all inherit from the Reader or Writer superclass, so they also support the methods listed above. As with high-level streams, when you construct a high-level reader or writer you pass in the next-lower object in the chain. The high-level classes are

- BufferedReader and BufferedWriter: These classes have internal buffers so that data can be read or written in large blocks, thus minimizing I/O overhead. They are similar to buffered input streams and buffered output streams.

- InputStreamReader and OutputStreamWriter: These classes convert between streams of bytes and sequences of Unicode characters. By default, the classes assume that the streams use the platform's default character encoding; alternative constructors provide any desired encoding.

- LineNumberReader: This class views its input as a sequence of lines of text. A method called readLine() returns the next line, and the class keeps track of the current line number.

- PrintWriter: This class is similar to PrintStream, but it writes chars rather than bytes.

- PushbackReader: This class is similar to PushbackInputStream, but it reads chars rather than bytes.

The code fragment below chains a line number reader onto a file reader. The code prints each line of the file, preceded by a line number.

```
1. try {
2.    FileReader fr = new FileReader("data");
3.    LineNumberReader lnr = new LineNumberReader(fr);
```

```
4.    String s;
5.    int lineNum;
6.    while ((s = lnr.readLine()) != null) {
7.        System.out.println(lnr.getLineNumber() + ": " + s);
8.    }
9.    lnr.close();
10.   fr.close();
11. }
12. catch (IOException x) { }
```

Figure 13.4 shows the reader chain implemented by this code.

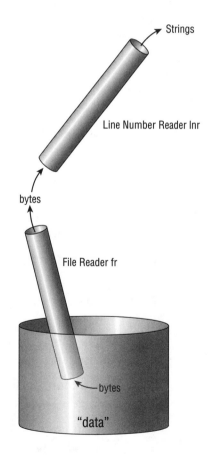

# Chapter Summary

This chapter has covered the four big ideas of Java's I/O support:

- Inside a Java Virtual Machine, text is represented by 16-bit Unicode characters and strings. For I/O, text may alternately be represented by UTF strings.

- The File class is useful for navigating the local file system.

- The RandomAccessFile class lets you read and write at arbitrary places within a file.

- Input streams, output streams, readers, and writers provide a mechanism for creating input and output chains. Input and output streams operate on bytes; readers and writers operate on chars.

# Test Yourself

**1.** Which of the statements below are true? (Choose none, some, or all.)

   **A.** UTF characters are all 8 bits.

   **B.** UTF characters are all 16 bits.

   **C.** UTF characters are all 24 bits.

   **D.** Unicode characters are all 16 bits.

   **E.** Bytecode characters are all 16 bits.

**2.** Which of the statements below are true? (Choose none, some, or all.)

   **A.** When you construct an instance of File, if you do not use the file-naming semantics of the local machine, the constructor will throw an IOException.

   **B.** When you construct an instance of File, if the corresponding file does not exist on the local file system, one will be created.

   **C.** When an instance of File is garbage collected, the corresponding file on the local file system is deleted.

**3.** The File class contains a method that changes the current working directory.

  **A.** True

  **B.** False

**4.** It is possible to use the File class to list the contents of the current working directory.

  **A.** True

  **B.** False

**5.** How many bytes does the following code write to file destfile?

```
1. try {
2.    FileOutputStream fos = new FileOutputStream("destfile");
3.    DataOutputStream dos = new DataOutputStream(fos);
4.    dos.writeInt(3);
5.    dos.writeDouble(0.0001);
6.    dos.close();
7.    fos.close();
8. }
9. catch (IOException e) { }
```

  **A.** 2

  **B.** 8

  **C.** 12

  **D.** 16

  **E.** The number of bytes depends on the underlying system.

**6.** What does the following code fragment print out at line 9?

```
1. FileOutputStream fos = new FileOutputStream("xx");
2. for (byte b=10; b<50; b++)
3.    fos.write(b);
4. fos.close();
```

```
5. RandomAccessFile raf = new RandomAccessFile("xx", "r");
6. raf.seek(10);
7. int i = raf.read();
8. raf.close()
9. System.out.println("i = " + i);
```

**A.** The output is i = 30.

**B.** The output is i = 20.

**C.** The output is i = 10.

**D.** There is no output because the code throws an exception at line 1.

**E.** There is no output because the code throws an exception at line 5.

**7.** A file is created with the following code:

```
1. FileOutputStream fos = new FileOutputStream("datafile");
2. DataOutputStream dos = new DataOutputStream(fos);
3. for (int i=0; i<500; i++)
4.    dos.writeInt(i);
```

You would like to write code to read back the data from this file. Which solutions listed below will work? (Choose none, some, or all.)

**A.** Construct a FileInputStream, passing the name of the file. Onto the FileInputStream, chain a DataInputStream, and call its readInt() method.

**B.** Construct a FileReader, passing the name of the file. Call the file reader's readInt() method.

**C.** Construct a PipedInputStream, passing the name of the file. Call the piped input stream's readInt() method.

**D.** Construct a RandomAccessFile, passing the name of the file. Call the random access file's readInt() method.

**E.** Construct a FileReader, passing the name of the file. Onto the FileReader, chain a DataInputStream, and call its readInt() method.

**8.** Readers have methods that can read and return floats and doubles.

   **A.** True

   **B.** False

**9.** You execute the code below in an empty directory. What is the result?

```
1. File f1 = new File("dirname");
2. File f2 = new File(f1, "filename");
```

   **A.** A new directory called `dirname` is created in the current working directory.

   **B.** A new directory called `dirname` is created in the current working directory. A new file called `filename` is created in directory `dirname`.

   **C.** A new directory called `dirname` and a new file called `filename` are created, both in the current working directory.

   **D.** A new file called `filename` is created in the current working directory.

   **E.** No directory is created, and no file is created.

**10.** What is the result of attempting to compile and execute the code fragment below? Assume that the code fragment is part of an application that has write permission in the current working directory. Also assume that before execution, the current working directory does not contain a file called `datafile`.

```
1. try {
2.    RandomAccessFile raf = new RandomAccessFile _
      ("datafile") ,"rw";
3.    BufferedOutputStream bos = new BufferedOutput _
      Stream(raf);
4.    DataOutputStream dos = new DataOutputStream(bos);
5.    dos.writeDouble(Math.PI);
6.    dos.close();
```

```
7.    bos.close();
8.    raf.close();
9. } catch (IOException e) { }
```

**A.** The code fails to compile.

**B.** The code compiles, but throws an exception at line 3.

**C.** The code compiles and executes, but has no effect on the local file system.

**D.** The code compiles and executes; afterward, the current working directory contains a file called datafile.

# PART

# II

## The Developer's Exam

# CHAPTER

# 14

## Taking the Developer's Exam

The first thing you should know about the Java 2 Developer's Exam is that it is practical rather than objective. In an industry where certification testing almost always boils down to multiple-choice questions, term/definition matching, short answers, and true/false statements—the mainstays of evaluating competence cost-effectively—practical exams are rare. But there are good reasons for them beyond cost. In a timed multiple-choice test, for example, the answer to each question can be "normalized," or designed so it not only provides the correct answer but also elicits it, unambiguously, with the right question. The average response time (difficulty level) can be assessed in trials so that the candidate faces a reasonable number of questions for the time allotted, receives the same opportunity as everyone else, and so on.

In a practical exam, the test candidate aims for a more general result: "Make this thing work." A few application vendors use such exams for their resellers or field engineers as a test of applied skills, but typically the time given in such cases is liberal or even left to the candidate's discretion. Certain skills or resources such as *keyboard thinking* that a timed, restricted environment might negate or prohibit become more useful, allowing some candidates greater comfort while under stress to perform. These exams are not evenhanded in the sense of being rigidly standardized and always applied under the same conditions, but at the same time, each candidate is generally free to draw upon familiar tools to solve a problem. Of course, there is a catch. Practical exams, particularly project assignments, have more requirements to fulfill and depend on a broader range of skills—rather than knowledge and reasoning—to fulfill them. Candidates must rehearse the kinds of skills expected in field situations and similar to the ones the practical test suggests. Moreover, as is often true in the field, process matters just as much as the finished product. Guessing strategies are far less helpful.

For people who feel more comfortable with projects over knowledge-based examinations, the developer's exam is ideal. Because it is broad in scope and because there are few industry exams like it, we will review the concepts and expectations of the exam in some detail. We'll use a scenario similar to the one the developer's exam offers as a guide to understanding what is required and how to approach the test—by breaking down its component parts and building them into a working whole. The certification process at this level costs a few hundred dollars, so it is certainly worth your while to assess your readiness.

# Are You Ready for the Exam?

**Y**ou can deduce from the guides to the Programmer's Exam in this book that Sun does not want to confer pro forma certifications. The candidates for that exam are expected to know the core libraries, operators, and compile-time and runtime behaviors well enough to recognize flawed code when they read it and to anticipate the errors such code will generate. In an era when many of us get lazy and use the compiler to point out flaws in our code, that's a skill that may require honing at first. Most programmers don't set out to write lots of flawed code and see what happens; however, they accomplish this readily in everyday practice. But it is everyday practice that will best complement the use of this guide.

Again, this certification exam is a practical one. The test challenges your ability to use Java in conjunction with the skills, experience, and discipline required of any competent programmer. If Java has been your sole focus for more than a year and you have a bit more experience on development projects using Java or some other language—ideally an object-oriented one—little of what you see in the programming assignment or follow-up exam should be too surprising. Even if some requirements represent new territory, there's no time limit, so the opportunity to learn one or two things as you go should not represent a hardship.

It should therefore come as no surprise that getting the code to execute correctly merely initiates the grading process. Professional developers must be able to justify their designs, recognize strengths and weaknesses in their solutions, translate those principles correctly into code, and document their work clearly for the benefit of future programmers and maintainers. In that spirit, this guide focuses on strategy and design choices more than fully coded solutions, in order to demonstrate the various tasks the exam presents and provide a conceptual model for developing the solution. Your ability to write the code is assumed, and in fact, several code exercises are left to the reader as preparatory exercises.

The reason code-level solutions are not always included is simple: The exam itself has as many right answers as there are justifiable ways of solving it. The exam does not hint at or beg for an ideal solution. Rather, you must design and implement the assignment project in a manner sufficient to you. The code must pass a mechanical test, which, as anyone might guess, cannot possibly verify all possible solutions. Finally, you must explain how your code works in two ways: by demonstrating knowledge of some other approaches and by explaining what benefits and penalties derive from the one applied.

If you are confident in your experience and only want a feel for the structure of the assignment, feel free to browse the chapters now and get the lay of the land. Chapter 15 introduces a sample project (we will say more about this in a bit) and offers a means for analyzing and breaking down the requirements. Chapters 16 through 18 each address the major topics—the database/server, networking, and creating a client module. Chapter 19 poses several questions to stimulate your thinking about design. The focus in this final chapter is oriented toward tenable design. Of course, you are free to write an implementation as practice; it is certainly less expensive to practice here than on the exam itself.

Listed below are a few general questions to help you assess your readiness:

- Do you write Java code three or more days a week?

- How many applications have you completed based only on written instructions?

- Name one or two principles of effective user interface design.

- How many threaded applications have you written? Client-server? Database-oriented?

- Recall your last experience being assigned an incomplete project, including undocumented code and missing source files. How did you work through those problems?

- What risks are involved with a remote client locking a record on a database?

- For storing data in memory, when does it make sense to use an array? A Vector? A Hashtable? A List?

- What are the relative merits of using Remote Method Invocation (RMI), Object Serialization, or some ad hoc data format for network communication?

- How is a two-tier client-server scheme different from three-tier?

Some of these questions are the basis for discussion in the following chapters. If they seem intimidating, review the following chapters with some care. The exam may prove to be quite a challenge if many of the discussions you see ahead are unfamiliar. Precise knowledge of Java's core operations and class libraries, which is required to pass the Programmer's Exam, will carry you some of the way. The single best preparation for getting certified as a Developer, however, is meaningful experience with Java development, ideally by completing tasks put to you by someone else. We cannot emphasize enough the value of good programming habits and experience in taking on a moderately complex programming task with only written instructions for guidance, and no real-world pressure to finish (other than forfeiting the registration fee).

Sun offers a five-day course, called Java Programming Workshop, which is well suited to preparing students for this certification. The course is numbered SL-285 for programmers who wish to learn on a Unix platform and SL-286 for Windows. The course description can be viewed by pointing your browser to http://suned.sun.com/courses/SL-285.html.

Sun also offers courses specific to major areas of the exam, but are not defined as certification courses. You may also wish to browse SL-320, GUI Construction with Swing and JFC, and SL-301, Distributed Programming with Java, which treats RMI in detail.

# Formalities of the Exam

This certification exam has two parts: a project assignment and a follow-up exam. The assignment describes a programming task that starts with some code supplied with the project description; you are then asked to finish the intended project. Some portions of the final code are to be written from scratch, some must extend or apply provided interfaces or classes, and some must modify incomplete or rudimentary classes. The requirements will also indicate areas of the application that you are not required to finish; to keep the test within reasonable limits, no one will be asked to create a robust, user-tolerant, business-grade application using the code provided. In fact, solving more problems than the assignment requires may actually create problems in the mechanical testing of your work, and if the application does not satisfy the checkpoints imposed by the test harness, it fails automatically. To keep testing simple, the assignment may also constrain some areas by disallowing certain approaches (for example, CORBA) or by simply mandating others (say, RMI). As a further discouragement against going too far afield, a solution that works but duplicates resources readily available in the core libraries may be marked against the final score.

The follow-up exam, which takes place in a timed and proctored test facility, has at least three aspects. The objective side deals with knowledge of Java's features and libraries. For example, you might be asked to list some data structures useful for storing an indeterminate number of runtime objects and then asked to explain the advantages each of those structures offers relative to the others. The practical side of the exam focuses on your knowledge and understanding of your own code (yes, this is a check to make sure you've done the work), asking you to offer one or two cases where you made a certain choice and what you decided on. Finally, from the subjective view, you may be asked to justify that choice. Perhaps you did not pick the fastest or most efficient data structure. What did you pick, and why? The right answer, in this last case, will be one that demonstrates that your choices were made in a conscious and reasonable way, regardless of whether the grader of the test might have done the same thing. It's important to bear in mind that this is not an exercise in anticipating what Sun wants Java programmers to think. So you should not second-guess your own judgment if your design suits you.

Nonetheless, the reality of open-ended practical exams is that grading can become subjective. Process does matter. So while getting your application to run properly doesn't guarantee certification, it's a bare minimum for getting to that point. But it isn't worthwhile dwelling for very long on the idea of "subjective grading." There are a few compensating factors:

- A test harness is provided with the exam. You should ensure the code passes all mechanical testing before submitting it.

- The weight allotted to each part of the assignment evaluation, and the categories of evaluation, will be included in the assignment.

- The time limit of the exam is the life of the exam's administration.

- This guide will help you to broaden your inquiry into the skills needed to succeed.

## Downloading the Assignment

Once you pay the registration fee for the Developer's Exam, Sun will enter your name in their Certification Database—you may have to wait a day for this to process.

At the time this guide went to press, Sun had not yet posted details on the Developer's Exam for Java 2. It's highly unlikely, however, that the process will change substantially from the 1.1 Exam. Full details for the 1.1 Exam are available by browsing http://suned.sun.com/usa/cert_test.html or by calling Sun Educational Services at (800) 422-8020.

Once the assignment is ready, you can download it by logging into the database through your browser. Once downloaded, be sure to save the bundle to a backup right away; the site is not set up to allow repeated downloads. The bundle you receive will include the project description, some source and class files, and instructions for submitting the finished work back to Sun.

You'll need your assigned student ID as a password. The login page is located at http://merchant.hibbertco.com/sun_certification. You can verify your Programmer's Exam score and certification here as well. While you are there, you may also want to check the contact information this database has for you and make sure it is correct.

## Taking the Follow-up Exam

Sun does not review your assignment until you complete the essay examination. This portion requires an additional fee payable to Sun, which will issue you an exam voucher. The voucher is used to reserve testing space at any Sylvan Prometric center, which administers the exam. As seating is limited in most centers, and the exams are scheduled ahead of time for download to a testing computer, reservations are essential (call 1-800-795-3926). The time limit is 90 minutes. See the above section "Formalities of the Exam" for an overview of what this exam is like. The finished assignment will be relatively complex, and you will not have the luxury of bringing any notes you may have into the exam room. It's a good idea to submit the assignment as soon as you have it working and to take the follow-up quickly thereafter, while the code is still fresh in your mind.

## What the Assignment Covers

Chapter 15 illustrates through a mock assignment what the actual project might address. In short, you'll be asked to take an existing database scheme and possibly enhance its features by adding one or more new functions. The database may require support for user access (local, remote, or both), concurrent users, and a client GUI to facilitate ease-of-use. To accomplish these tasks—to integrate them and design something flexible enough to make future improvements easy to implement—requires a practical command of these areas:

- TCP/IP networking
- I/O Streams
- Swing
- The AWT event model
- Object Serialization
- RMI
- javadoc
- Packages
- Threads
- Interfaces

Some of the elements listed here may not appear on the exam or may have already been established for you; familiarity in that topic area may be all that you need. For example, one or two interfaces may be provided that you are simply required to implement. On other elements, the assignment may dictate how you may apply them to the project, typically to help standardize the grading process or to ensure the finished code complies with the test harness.

## How the Assignment and Exam Are Graded

Review of the assignment begins once the follow-up exam is completed and forwarded to a Sun-appointed grader. The grader tests the submitted application code using the same test harness provided with the assignment distribution; failure to clear this phase automatically concludes the evaluation. If you have tested your code before submitting it, however, this step is a formality. The grader then examines the source code along and the answers given in the follow-up exam. Good source-writing style, adequate documentation, clarity of design, judicious use of the core libraries, and the consistency of the follow-up essays with the assignment all fall under review here. Sun estimates the process to take four weeks from the date they receive the follow-up exam. The values assigned to each part of the grading criteria are listed in the downloaded assignment documentation, but here are the general parameters:

- `API-style` documentation; proper use of comment code

- Use of standard library features and algorithms

- Applying conventional object-oriented programming techniques

- GUI meets requirements, follows principles for effective human-computer interaction

- Event-handling mechanisms are appropriate

- Data operations are threadsafe

- Code layout is clear, maintainable, and consistent and follows expected formatting guidelines

## JDK 1.2 Specifics

If you have taken the Developer's Exam for JDK 1.1, the structure of the exam does not change that much for you in this version. The change from

Java 1.1 to 2, however, is a different matter. The new additions, like Swing, add considerable depth and richness to areas where the JDK has been perceived as anemic. Improvements to existing facilities are broad as well. The following list describes those areas most relevant to the exam, including topics that will be required to complete the exam.

## Swing

The most anticipated and widely beta-tested module in the Java Foundation Classes (JFC), Swing has been included as a requirement to writing the client GUI. Swing's dependence on the AWT Component class, layout managers, and event-handling structure means those skills are still necessary (we include discussions of important topics on both packages). If you have paid relatively little attention to Swing so far, bear in mind that it is more than a larger library of widgets unencumbered by the AWT native-peer component strategy. The internal architecture of Swing components is quite different from the AWT; this design pattern is widely referred to as a Model-View-Controller (MVC) implementation. For the sake of argument, in Chapter 18 we refer to this structure as "View-Model-Controller" because we believe it clarifies the relationship between these three pieces

To make the inclusion of Swing meaningful and to make grading manageable, the requirements for building the GUI will be more general than in previous test versions. Rather than build a menu that looks exactly as the one pictured or decipher which layout managers are involved in a picture of a sample frame resizing, you will assume responsibility for good design. These points are also discussed in Chapter 18. You will still control your aesthetic choices, in addition to demonstrating your knowledge of the components available.

## Collections

Java 2 has stepped up considerably in its offering of container classes in java.util. The package now includes a number of classes, initially made available as an add-on to the JDK 1.1, called the Collections framework. This framework abstracts the major operations of all container classes and provides a mechanism for, among other things, moving data from one container type to another with very little programming effort. Vector and Hashtable have been retrofitted into the Collections scheme as well, and a new class, Arrays, now supports methods for sorting, filling, and treating an array like a list. The Enumeration interface has an eventual successor, Iterator, which maps back to the container, offering a tighter binding during most element-level operations. Certain other classes like `Dictionary` are still around but slated for oblivion.

One key issue to examine with respect to these classes is how to implement multi-threading. There are at least two schools of thought on performance and multi-threading. One school suggests that serializing access to these containers—which requires a single method call—offers credible performance. Other imminent developments to increase VM performance on lower-level operations will justify trading optimal performance designs for the ease of maintaining synchronized-container code. The other school wants to realize the full efficiency of multi-threaded performance wherever it can. Synchronizing on the container is fine for small structures with few records, but as the data scales to large proportions, the only feasible solution to keeping performance high is record-level access.

We cover the issues concerning both camps in Chapters 16 and 17.

## Data Formatting for Communications

The assignment will require that you fashion some means for communicating between the server and the client. The only constant principle in the exam, with respect to networking, is that the client must operate in a separate VM from the server and the back-end application it supports. There are really three choices to consider: use serialization, RMI, or a combination of the two. In the guide, these techniques will be demonstrated simply and on their own, to help illustrate their differences and to stimulate further thinking on which approach offers the greatest advantage for a given task. Much like the discussion surrounding containers and multi-threading, this approach design can mostly be reduced to choosing flexibility or ease of coding and maintenance, along a few lines.

Object Serialization and RMI have both undergone important changes. Given the practical limits and expectations of testing, it is unlikely most of these new features will be involved in completing the programming assignment.

The change history for the Java Object Serialization Specification is available with the documentation download. From the base docs directory, the path to the index is /docs/guide/serialization/index.html. The documents are also available online. Put http://java.sun.com/products/jdk/1.2 in front of the previous path to access it.

On the slight chance that the assignment requires an "activatable" object (a new RMI extension) or a custom socket factory to enable protocols like SSL, the JDK tutorials are both detailed and populated with sample code. These tutorials are recommended for experienced RMI users, however, so they are worth reviewing in advance. Remember that the aim of the Developer's Exam is to test your skills on a reasonably sized problem set, not to make you write code on every new feature.

Browse docs/guide/rmi/index.html relative to a local or online documentation set, as shown above, for details on RMI enhancements.

With that qualification in mind, the follow-up exam may be an ideal place to express awareness of these features and apply that awareness to your justification of a design solution for the project assignment. If knowing that distributed garbage collection or the ability to activate an RMI server from a remote VM is reason enough to design a solution that can take advantage of them, then by all means proceed. In open-ended assignments such as this one, some developers will go beyond the stated requirements of the exam to write something "meaningful." That is OK to a point—that point being to make sure the test harness can certify your code, so long as the effort is qualified by correct facts and justified by the proper view in the follow-up exam. In Chapter 17, however, the discussion will stay focused on the modest boundaries of completing the project to satisfaction.

## Documentation and *javadoc*

There are five new documentation tags to be aware of. Three in particular help to document object serialization code for those who employ object serialization in their designs.

**@link**   Links a name (package, class, interface, constructor, field, method) to a label, or hyperlinked text. Unlike the @see tag, {link} formats the label where it occurs in the comment code, instead of moving it to a "See Also" subheading.

**@serial**   For use in documenting a field that is already serialized.

**@serialData**   For use in documenting the order and type of objects in a serial stream. Recommended particularly for use with writeObject(), readObject(), writeExternal(), and readExternal() calls.

**@serialField**    For use in documenting objects of type ObjectStreamField, a descriptor class that identifies the characteristics of a each serializable field for a given class.

**@throws**    Synonymous with the @exception tag, provided for semantic convenience.

Not to be left behind in the quest for ubiquitous flexibility and choice, javadoc now supports a pluggable output scheme called *doclets*, intended for technical writers who want to target another document format, such as XML, for their standard. Expect no requirement in this area.

# CHAPTER 15

## Assignment: Room Reservation System

**T**his chapter describes a programming assignment similar in style to the actual project assignment. The assignment itself is intended to be neither a mystery nor an exercise in reading between the lines of the project description. The scenario is provided as a motivation to write the code and offer a basis for justifying your implementation. At the same time, you should not try to infer much beyond what you see on the page. No portion of the exam will ask if you considered this or that aspect of the business case given when you devised your threading model. On the other hand, you should know if your code fares well or poorly if, say, the data model scales from one or two hundred to tens of thousands of records.

The stated objectives of the developer's exam will read something like the following:

- Write an application program using Java 2, with the following component parts:

  - A user interface utilizing specified component elements and conforming to general principles of human interaction.

  - A network connection, using a specified protocol, to connect to an information server that supplies the data for display in the user interface.

  - A multi-threaded, threadsafe network server, which connects to a previously specified Java database.

  - An application created by extending the functionality of a previously written piece of code, for which only limited documentation is available. This application may take the form of a flat-file database or some other application that can be modeled simply in pure Java.

- Test your code against the provided validation harness.

- List a number of the significant design choices to be made during the implementation of the application.

- List a number of the main advantages and disadvantages of each of these design choices.

- Briefly justify choices made in terms of the comparison of design and implementation objectives with the advantages and disadvantages of each.

Our purpose here is simply to familiarize you with the conditions of the exam. It starts out with some nearly completed code for a database scheme, based on a business scenario. Your job is broken down into a series of tasks, which may include some or all of the following:

- The "missing feature" to the database scheme may be a field-level search capability, a sort routine to support advanced queries, or possibly a record locking mechanism.

- Write a debugging or conversion tool that will output the current contents into human-readable text and/or import a valid text file into the data format.

- Implement the network protocol without benefit of the underlying source. This "protocol" may be nothing more than the pre-compiled interface file and an API-style HTML page made available.

- Write a GUI-based client to access the database. Count on using only Swing components. Since we can certainly expect to display records, a JTable is an obvious consideration.

Certain variations may occur from one assignment to the next, and certain underlying files may vary accordingly. This step is a check against sharing with or receiving assignment files and tasks from other candidates, as there is no time limit and no way to monitor the work before submission.

In short, the assignment's test of functional proficiency is in completing a project with multiple, interrelated tasks, despite any limitations imposed by the initial code. The test of overall proficiency is in writing code that is clear, concise, and relatively easy to interpret through its generated API documentation. One aim the candidate should have in mind is to produce code that a less-experienced programmer could read and maintain with a working knowledge of the language and the use of standard Java references and conventions.

The actual assignment will provide scoring criteria, instructions for submitting the exam, and other administrative details that this chapter does not cover for obvious reasons. Those sections relevant to our discussion are:

- A business scenario to create the assignment's context
- Some project specifics to stimulate thoughts on design
- An overall project goal
- A requirements breakdown for each portion of the assignment

# Business Scenario

**M**obile Conferencing Services is a startup firm that leases meeting rooms by the day. The meeting rooms vary in type, number, and housing facility from location to location, and are currently available to subscribing customers by calling a sales rep and making a reservation. In response to customer requests for faster service, Mobile Conferencing wants to automate their reservation process. They ultimately want to develop a kiosk that their representatives and clients can use on-site to reserve and confirm meeting rooms and dates. Clients have also expressed interest in being able to schedule rooms from their desks, home offices, or hotel rooms. To provide that level of service but avoid the cost of an expensive network infrastructure, the company wants to explore using the Internet, but prefers to develop a dedicated client tool.

Mobile Conferencing's current IT employee has already written a rudimentary database scheme in Java, as a way to familiarize himself with the language and prove Java's usability for the overall development effort. This scheme was suitable for stub-testing. However, inexperience with object-oriented development and more urgent projects has made it necessary for him to outsource the next phase of development. Mindful of the cost of outside development, the company president wants the project to incorporate all the code written so far. Meanwhile, the IT "staff" will be engaged in a rollout of desktop systems at several remote facilities, so a developer who can work independently, using only written instructions as a guide, is a must.

# Project Specifics

To make the exam manageable and testable, some advisories that narrow the scope of the assignment may appear in or after the scenario. Here we've included a likely set of constraints as a part of the business rationale.

Through the client tool, the user should be able to determine, for any one location, how many rooms are available, what type of meeting rooms that facility has, and the daily lease rate. In this phase of the project, each facility will offer one type of room, all at the same lease rate, and customer information will not be included. User/password login validation will be implemented at a later date.

The initial database schema assumes single-user access to the kiosk (and therefore the local database) at one time. Strong customer demand for remote access to the reservation tool has added a requirement for a network server to front the database. The developer will have to devise the protocol for network communications and implement it from scratch. Since funding for this phase of the project is limited, the company expresses no technological preference for the implementation method.

Like many startups, Mobile Conferencing is unsure of its future growth projections. Currently they have as many as four dozen rooms at one site and about 100 facilities they currently administer. They may decide to host all databases on a single server at some point, using their current kiosks as remote clients.

In discussing interface design meetings, the IT staff expressed dissatisfaction with the limited components available in the AWT library. They avoided third-party libraries to keep the code in-house. The project was finally shelved until Swing came out of beta testing. Now that Swing is ready, they want certain components included in the interface. They also intend to review the completed GUI to ensure they can easily maintain and extend it.

# Code & APIs Provided

The code supplied with the project assignment will largely consist of concrete code, rather than a skeletal design that must first be implemented. With respect to the database scheme, this means that certain choices, such as

the underlying container type, will be pre-determined, along with the fundamental methods for reading from and writing to the database. Method signatures for the enhancements you are required to add may already be defined
as well. You may have to subclass the code provided or add the missing code
to it, so we'll address both situations in the next chapter.

Here is what an implementation-independent schema might look like:

```
public interface DataBase {
    public Field[] getFields();
    public int recordTotal();
    public Record getRecord(int recID);
    public Record[] find(String matchItem);
    public void addRecord(String [] newData);
    public void modifyRecord(Record changes);
    public void deleteRecord(Record delete);
    public void close();
}
```

This prototype view is for the sake of illustration. Obviously, we cannot
define important constructors or protected methods—which could nonetheless be designed independent of implementation—in an interface; but we
wanted to keep this preview tight and defer fleshing out an abstract or concrete class until the next chapter. Even though you won't have to develop
schema code of your own, you can see in the above interface what a simple
Java schema might amount to. The object types' names are self-explanatory.
Those who want more flexibility may balk at defining an int for a record
number in getRecord(). We could of course specify recID as an Object,
arguing that it makes more sense to use a wrapper class to get an int. Alternatively, we might overload getRecord() in a concrete subclass and call the
provided method signature from there. These are both useful observations to
apply to the follow-up exam, so keep a critical eye toward such factors as
you consider how you will complete the project. Chapter 16 includes a walk-
through of building the initial database scheme, then goes about a method
for fulfilling the current requirements, as a guide for anticipating the problems you'll inherit from the supplied code.

The project will also incorporate a package structure to logically divide
the functional areas of the project. Packaging should pose no particular difficulties with respect to the scope of existing code; you should observe the
vanilla rules of encapsulation unless there is an unavoidable reason to do

otherwise (performance or the ease of direct field access would not be good reasons to offer). In case you are consulting a variety of materials to prepare for the exam, note that the terms "friendly" and "package private" both refer to the same thing: a field, method, or class with no explicit scope keyword. "Package private" is far more descriptive, but the term "friendly," something of a holdover from Java's applet-mania days, still gets some use. Certain classes that must be developed may already be named in the assignment to assure compatibility with the test harness.

# Functional Goals

The next three chapters concern themselves with delving into the design and implementation issues for each major assignment task. Included below we offer an overview of the strategic choices you will need to make before jumping into writing the code.

## Write a User Interface

The user interface has a twofold task. The first is to provide users with an interactive tool that they can learn easily. An interface should draw on a user's experience with other client interfaces by providing a clear, familiar visual layout with predictable graphic elements. The graphics library toolkit must supply the visual aesthetics and appeal that invite clicking or scrolling, but the GUI developer still must deploy them properly. It is just as easy today to frustrate or confuse a user with poor layout or uncoordinated graphic elements as it ever was. A random survey of a several dozen business and personal Web sites will demonstrate the point.

For the purposes of building the GUI client for this project, keeping things simple and following the instructions provided should be sufficient. In fact, if the project instructions are very precise, dictating the behavior on resizing and which components to use, the task actually gets easier. There are only so many layout managers that don't resize a component along with the parent container (`FlowLayout`, or possibly `GridBagLayout`) and only so many ways to ensure that another component gets all the horizontal space its container has to offer but only as much vertical space as it requires (`BorderLayout`).

Even with Swing, only so many components recommend themselves if the instructions are very specific. If they aren't, keep things simple. There are four facilities you can provide to promote interaction with the user:

- Menu choices

- Widgets that toggle a feature or initiate action when clicked

- Important data fields a user is inclined to treat as a widget

- Keystroke combinations to match core menu choices, especially file and edit operations

Chapter 18 focuses on describing how the Swing framework clarifies the structure for adding multiple types of access to the same underlying events and data models associated with each component type. Studying the data models of those Swing components we are most likely to use will supplement that discussion.

This brings us to the second task of the user interface: to handle data flow so that graphic presentation is consistent with the exchange of data between client and server programs. Although the AWT supports this ably through event-handling, Swing components separate the actors out explicitly so that the programmer has a little bit more to understand about the internals of a Swing component, but ultimately can complete the objectives with a bit more elegance and in fewer lines of code.

The foundation for this elegance in the Swing package is a variation on a design pattern known as Model-View-Controller (MVC). In this pattern, the model is state data. In a `List` component, for example, the *Model* comprises all the elements contained by the component internally along with their current states. The *View* refers to any perspective of that model; for a human user, the view is the graphical representation of a list—all or some of the elements, limited by the viewing area's constraints, with selected elements highlighted and the rest not. The *Controller* (event handler) is then responsible for updating the Model's state.

The conventional relationship between these three actors is triangular. With respect to Swing, there's really only one View we are concerned with, and that's the GUI. The Model's data updates the View as expected. The View, by way of an event object, passes state change information to the Controller, which in turn updates the Model. Given the user-centric approach we take to GUI development, saying "view-controller-model" seems a little more intuitively clear, but that still isn't quite what Swing does.

Put another way, the View is the screen, or the "read-only" attribute of every Swing component. Using the data contained in the Model that expresses the visual state of the component, the View applies its set of drawing instructions and rules for component behavior to render what the user sees. Users may of course form the impression that they are manipulating the View when they click a button or resize a frame, but the View's only responsibility is to paint its share of the screen with information provided by the Model. Gathering and interpreting user input are actions the Controller performs. The Controller has nothing the user may read, even though it accepts all user input to the component. This makes it easy to confuse the two actors; because they often share pixel space on-screen, the intuitive guess is that the View itself presents the graphic layer and accepts all change requests sent to it.

It's important to outline these issues early so that we can see how Swing makes it easy to support multiple views with the same data model or possibly just change the view if the current one doesn't satisfy. Once you get your data model the way you want it, there's no need to revise it. Managing appearances is a completely separate task.

## Enable Network Access (Client-Server)

Building the connection between client and server for this assignment is perhaps the most straightforward—if potentially most tedious—portion of the overall exercise. Unless the plans for the project assignment change at the last minute, each candidate will have the option of using object serialization to communicate across the wire or using Remote Method Invocation (RMI) as a transport. Like many other choices in object-oriented development, making this decision boils down to an accurate analysis of the given requirements and forecast of how the application is best suited for future growth. A concrete implementation (straight serialization) can be done quickly, but if there are frequent changes to what goes on the stream, the cost of ongoing maintenance may be high. A more flexible, open-ended architecture will make maintenance less of a problem over the long run, but if no changes are in the plan, is the initial effort up front justified? These are real-world considerations that don't influence this testing environment much, since the time spent to complete the project is up to each candidate.

For the purpose of staking out territory for these two choices, though, it's worth saying here that object serialization as a standalone technique is vulnerable to some amount of criticism. The developer has to define the objects that will go over the stream and in what order for each request, and ensure that client and server adhere to that format. Protocols like HTTP, FTP, telnet, and others operate this way, but in these cases a community of developers have agreed on how standard services will work. This makes it possible for everyone to implement their own applications, while fully expecting they will work with any other application built to the standard. Any standardized browser should be able to contact any HTTP server and expect the service to function correctly.

For small or custom applications this is not much of a problem, unless you plan to build on top of it, tie it in to other applications that perform a supplementary service, or make a wholesale changes to the protocol when new services need to be added. Maintaining backward compatibility complicates the matter, particularly if the client and server are developed independently. Barring some shrewd design choices, foresight, and luck, maintaining an independent protocol may be a dead-end for design over time. Then again, depending on the circumstances, these problems may be safe to ignore.

RMI is Sun's approach to distributed computing among Java VMs. Its feature set continues to develop rapidly as the user community demands increasingly sophisticated operations from it. The idea of RMI is to make the network imposed between client and server seem like a semantic detail, requiring one extra layer of handling compared to operations taking place within a single VM. This means the actions of two separate VMs have to be coordinated. The client and server code must be developed in tandem and kept in sync.

 RMI uses object serialization to *marshal* data between VMs, so objects that use RMI still must implement the java.io.Serializable interface. *Marshal* is Java's term for converting an object first into its component arguments, then into a serialized byte stream, suitable for transport over the network.

When running, the RMI server exports objects that are available to clients at a well-known port; the client only has to know where to ask and what to ask for, using stub references to call on each server-side object it wants. RMI's built-in "wire protocol," or *transport*, then handles the exchange between the two VMs.

RMI has technical limitations of its own. Because the execution trace moves back and forth between VMs, debugging client-server problems can be difficult. More importantly, when dealing with a multi-threaded server, care has to be taken that the single channel between the client VM and server VM does not block on a thread that prevents the server-side from completing related process via an `update()` call. This typically entails some kind of thread-moderating process. It is also possible for the client to get an object from the server and pass it back so that the server considers it a remote object, not a local one. This is similar to having phone calls forwarded to an office that then forwards them back, incurring a usage charge each way. It will work, but the cost will continue to add up until someone notices.

These of course are consequences of incorrect implementation. The chief point to bear in mind is that RMI may add a noticeable amount of complexity. As with any design choice, the benefits should be clear and compelling before adopting it.

## Add Features to an Existing Database

The work required here will depend largely on the code provided with the project assignment. There are several ways a simple database scheme could be implemented, centering on what structure is used to store the data. Each approach will pose some ground-level obstacles to ensuring threadsafe operation. Our discussion will examine several of these angles, taking a comprehensive view as the best preparation.

Assuming the assignment may pose some feature to be implemented at the record-object level, there will be another strategic decision to make—similar to the one between object serialization and RMI. There are several ways to ensure a data store will not be corrupted by multiple accesses: the two broad approaches include synchronizing on the data structure itself and designing a threading scheme that synchronizes at the record level. The latter approach is of course far more efficient and levies a proportionally greater burden on the developer to design it correctly.

The central consideration is scalability. Serializing access to the entire data store, while effectively guaranteeing data integrity, erodes performance as the record count and user demand (threaded access) increase. But against a database with no thread safety, the vulnerability to corruption also increases. Let's say Thread A is totaling a column of fields, which requires accessing that field in each record. Thread B enters the data store to insert a record. If no mechanism for thread safety is available to order these processes, the resulting behavior is uncertain. If Thread B inserts a record that Thread A has not accessed yet, then Thread A will include that value in its sum once it gets there. But if Thread B inserts a record in an area Thread A has already passed by, Thread A will omit the value, and its record count will be off by one. If Thread A enters a record Thread B is in the middle of writing, the result is uncertain. This problem is termed a *race condition*, suggesting that one thread is "racing" to finish before another can cause trouble.

In a small bank with two tellers, it might be far easier on the bank if it closes while each teller balances their cash drawer in turn, and the impact on customer service might be negligible. But in a large branch with a dozen tellers, the same policy would generate no small number of complaints. Each kind of bank must take into account the way it intends to operate and structure its procedures accordingly. Where threading and data are concerned, a "one-size-fits-all" approach to data access could mean over-developed code on one end of the scale and unacceptable performance on the other.

In the following chapter, we'll review the potential container strategies for a data scheme built in Java, then focus on one to further explore these two approaches to thread safety.

# Other Requirements

The following elements address how the grader appointed by Sun will review the source code and documentation submitted with your working program. In the assignment documentation you receive, the relative weight of each category will be provided.

## Adherence to Supplied Naming

Following the naming scheme given for packages, classes, and methods primarily ensures that the test harness will check the code properly. Beyond that, there is no set limit on the number of support classes that may be created for the finished assignment. Choose names for any such classes you supply that evoke their purpose or type. Naming subclasses so that they refer to the parent helps to create an immediate association for the code reader and is good policy where it is practical.

# Other Design Issues

## Stress readability

Javasoft recommends a few conventions for programmers to follow. These guidelines promote a common visual appearance for source code that makes it easier for other programmers to identify the elements and form a clear impression of the code's operation. Some guidelines to bear in mind are:

- Begin all class names with an uppercase letter.

- Begin all method and field names with a lowercase letter.

- Use mixed-case for multiple-word names (like `getResourceAsStream()`).

- Avoid using one-character field names (o, l, i, and e) beyond counter variables in a loop.

- Indent three or four spaces per code block.

- Avoid using multiple `System.out.println()` calls to concatenate a long string. Use the '+' operator instead and span the strings over multiple lines.

As with any coding style, the key is a consistent application of form the intended readers know. One habit we have seen in sample code on the Web is beginning class names with a lowercase letter. While legal, it can make a class reference hard to distinguish from a variable in a long code list. Avoid this practice.

## Use *javadoc*-style comments

The source code bundled with the download will include `javadoc`-ready comments. Employing the same style and format in the code you submit should offer some form of immunity. If you intend on using object serialization on its own, you might apply the three serial tags that are new with Java 2. Note that `javadoc` now supports HTML output for API overview and package-level documentation by including properly named files in the same directory as the source. `javadoc`'s command-line argument options have expanded considerably and are worth a look.

New tags and other changes to javadoc are included with the documentation bundle for JDK 2 that can be downloaded from `http://java.sun.com`. If installed locally, the relative path to `javadoc` is `docs/tooldocs/solaris/javadoc.html`.

**Don't comment the obvious**   Good form is part of the grading process, as is your best understanding of the level of information other programmers need to know to grasp your code quickly. Anyone who is going to read source code for meaning—as opposed to seeing what it looks like—will find a comment on an assignment operation or what object type a method returns distracting rather than helpful. Limit source file commentary to complex operations that may be unclear from the code block itself or to defining the role of methods that contribute to a larger design scheme. `javadoc` commentary should inform the API browser what service each documented field and method offers.

**Use standard design patterns**   Design patterns describe a relationship within a class or among several classes that serve a fundamental purpose to applications without regard to their "domain." The JDK makes ample use of design patterns throughout its core libraries: Swing uses a variation of the MVC pattern to support multiple graphic views of one data model. The `Applet` class uses an Observer pattern to monitor any `Image` instances it may contain. These abstractions also allow developers to communicate their ideas in terms of architecture, rather than implementation. Once consensus is achieved on the structure of an application, the individual programmers can then focus on building the elements needed to complete it.

Design patterns by themselves are not magic. They simply express a consistently useful approach to some common problem. It's quite likely that some experienced programmers use them without knowing their given names. But knowing these patterns by name and structure can greatly reduce the time it takes to recognize the tools that use them. Classes like `java.net` `.ContentHandlerFactory`, for example, embed the design model directly in their name. If you know what a Factory design is good for, you'll be able to identify a factory class' role quickly and put it to use. Other classes, such as `java.util.Observer` and `Observable` get their names directly from the patterns they implement, so the pattern-aware programmer can save time otherwise spent researching classes and reading method lists. It is worth your while to research the patterns most commonly used and learn to apply them to your projects.

# CHAPTER

# 16

## Enhancing and Extending
## the Database

**T**his chapter discusses the first part of the project assignment by tracing the design steps for building a small database application. The specific objective is to design a model suitable to the scenario presented in the last chapter and to build out enough code to illustrate one implementation. Based on our own development, we will be able to anticipate some of the issues the project assignment will present. After that walk-through, we'll encounter several issues in extending the application, for example, securing the database from the hazards of concurrent access ("thread safety").

The assignment may contain a requirement that the candidate cannot (or may not) solve in an ideal way. The idea behind this condition is to require each candidate to weigh the relative merits of the remaining choices. It is possible that none of them will be attractive, which is arguably real world enough. To simulate that environment, we will also discuss some likely constraints on enhancing our own code and possible workarounds along with their costs and benefits.

# Two-Tier Databases

**T**his chapter does not assume you know a lot about databases or have studied the JDBC API. This chapter concentrates on an application structure that adheres to a simple *client-server* architecture. In a client-server structure, the database system is integrated with or running in the same process space as the mechanism that handles client requests and serves data back. The next few paragraphs cover common terms relating to database design and structure and supplies a context to aid our approach to design.

The most widely used database model today is the *relational* database. Relational databases are composed of multiple *tables* of information. A single table comprises any number of *records* of a specific kind. A table stores each record in its own *row*, which consists of ordered *fields* of data. Each field is, in turn, defined by its *column*, which declares what *type* of data it will store and the maximum space (*width*) available to each field in the column.

Relational design, as the name suggests, makes it possible to declare relationships between tables that share columns of the same type. There are several potential benefits. For example, highly redundant field data can be replaced by lookup references to another table. On a more sophisticated level, a database programmer can develop new relationships from existing tables to meet a new user requirement. This functionality comes at the price of substantial complexity, certainly enough to justify the vast industry behind relational database management systems (RDBMS) seen on the market today. In fact, the JDBC API merely addresses a vendor-neutral way to incorporate an existing RDBMS package into a Java application.

For the purposes of discussing the project assignment, we will use a "flat" data model in this chapter. The database model offered in the project is *two-tiered* in structure. Simply put, this means that the server and database portions of the project are integrated and running on the same virtual machine. The user (*client*) runs on a separate VM, which might be located on the same machine or a remote machine accessible via a network. This relationship between the two processes is one variation of the *client-server* computing model.

The explosion of commercial interest in the Internet over the last few years has brought the *three-tier* (alternatively, *n-tier*) model into more widespread use, particularly in areas where client interaction is intense and response times are critical. This arrangement logically separates the server component from the database and allows the server component to focus on managing client demands so that the database can be optimized for storage and retrieval performance. The advantages of *n*-tier models extend in several potential directions. A common strategy is to deploy multiple servers between the clients and the back-end application. The server portion may spend more time interpreting or preparing client requests than submitting them. In this case, having multiple servers speaking to one database may be the best solution. If there is some concern that the server application could crash and take the database with it, this separation also achieves some amount of data protection.

There could also be a need for a few servers to support a wide variety of request types that the servers must then route to the correct data server. This could easily be the case for the Mobile Conferencing scenario described in the previous chapter. We might prefer to build a number of distributed databases but access them through a common server. The server itself then handles the various incoming requests, making maintenance and updating easier, and avoiding any elaborate client-side coding for determining which database to connect to. N-tier architectures provide a wealth of other strategies on top of these more common approaches, including the introduction of architectural concepts such as *application partitioning*, a means for moving application demand loads from one server to another as a form of load-balancing. Many companies interested in adjusting for the volatility of Internet demand look to these schemes as a way of scaling their ability to serve customers without bringing systems down to refit their hardware; as with many strategies for increasing flexibility, the key is advance planning and design.

# Designing a Basic Scheme

**A** flat data model simply implies that the scheme for organizing data records is largely, if not completely, self-describing. Relational or other data indexing schemes can be very powerful, but they impose complexities, not the least of which is a separate language to access the scheme's feature set. A flat file is ideal for small databases that do not require a complete subsystem to facilitate searching and/or organizing data.

There are only so many meaningful ways to write a scheme that is little more than the data itself. Some of the most common types include the following:

- An ASCII-based file of human-readable information, in which the rules for delimiting or parsing data are often hard-coded in the application logic or self-evident in the layout of the file itself.

- A binary file, written with an encoded definition of its own structure, called a header or *metadata*, and followed by data records adhering to that structure.

- Multiple data files indexed by a control file. Schemes of this type (such as a browser's disk cache) often use the file system's directory structure as a ready-made structure for facilitating searches.

- A data structure that resides completely in memory but is saved to a file on regular intervals.

Simple text files are, of course, easiest to read and edit directly. Binary files can be read faster, obscure the contained information (which may or may not be desirable), and are ideal for arbitrary or "random" access.

## Using Interfaces

Establishing the design by writing interfaces has multiple advantages. One advantage is that writing only the abstractions first helps to determine what actions and class relationships are necessary without committing to a specific means of achieving them. Interfaces achieve the broadest sense of polymorphic behavior, because they supply the definition of the behavior that is wanted but not the means to implement behavior. They can also provide a bridge for using the same underlying data in several concrete classes that share the same high-level design, in the same way Java 2's Collections framework allows several container types to store one set of data.

One risk in any development effort that begins with concrete coding is the potential for implementation obstacles that are no less expensive to throw away than they are to solve. Once in that regrettable situation of facing a rewrite, there is the further risk of scrapping otherwise useful design elements because the specific code in which they are obscured failed to work. By using an interface design at the start, the possibilities for implementation remain open and some investment is preserved.

The simplest structure we have to create is a field type. A field is a member in a record that contains one type of data. The type and width of the field are defined by a column, which is the representation of one field type across multiple records. To leave open the possibilities of using the column in some meaningful way, we decide to define it abstractly:

```
/**
 * GenericColumn describes the behavior of a general data
 * column.
 *
 * @author Mobile Conferencing IT
 */
public interface GenericColumn {

    /**
```

```
    * getTitle() returns the name of the column.
    *
    * @returns String - the name assigned to the column
    */
   public String getTitle();

   /**
    * getWidth() gives the maximum length one column entry
    * can take.
    *
    * @return int - the width allotted to any entry.
    */
   public int getWidth();
}
```

A record consists of an ordered set of fields, each of which is described by a column. Given the simplicity of our scheme, we decide somewhat arbitrarily that we want records to be able to report their own organization; therefore, we need a method to return the list of columns the record contains. A record will also have to have some form of unique identification within the table. The identification type should not be limited to a primitive such as int in case the data container implemented allows a non-numeric ID:

```
/**
 * GenericRecord defines any record that knows its own
 * schema and the unique identifier given to it in a table.
 *
 * @author Mobile Conferencing IT
 */
public interface GenericRecord {

   /**
    * getSchema() returns the list of columns that compose
    * a record.
    *
    * @returns GenericColumn[] - the abstract type of a
```

```
    * column that reports its name and width.
    * @see GenericColumn
    */
   public GenericColumn[] getSchema();

   /**
    * getID() returns the Object representation of the
    * class used to store a record's unique ID.
    *
    * @returns java.lang.Object
    */
   public Object getID();
}
```

Defining a field, a cell that is part of every record, can be tricky in this scheme. Following simple rules of thumb may not always determine a best choice. We can say every field has a column; the phrase "has a" then signifies that a field object should include a column member in its class definition. On the other hand, a field "is a" kind of column—one with a single row—which suggests that subclassing makes intuitive sense. Rather than commit to a design choice for either one, we'll leave the decision to a subsequent stage of development.

You may also be wondering if a method, like getData() should be included in the interface. There are at least two schools of thought on this matter. A minimalist approach suggests the interface should only declare methods this type must support for the benefit of other classes. Assuming we only want to publicly define our records within our framework by their schema and unique ID, this interface is arguably sufficient—for now. We may determine later that GenericRecord should enforce getData()—if for no other reason than to ensure consistent naming and type return—and simply include it. The need to apply further methods to the interface is therefore compelled by demonstration rather than intuition. If we do include getdata() now, we will have to decide on (and fix) its return type. The benefit is that we can start drawing on this part of the interface right away, since a record's data could then be returned through its abstract type. The only real question is whether to defer specifying getData() until the best implementation presents itself or put it in now and worry about any needed changes to its signature later.

Finally, we want to define a `Database` interface, to specify the real work. As a description of data control, it must account for the following tasks:

- Manipulating records: adding, modifying, deleting
- Counting records
- Finding a record by a field value it contains
- Saving data to a backing store
- Knowing the scheme of the database

The Database interface shown below declares all the methods we want to insure are employed. By describing them here, we document the methods other programmers may rely on when they write related or dependent classes.

```
/**
 * DataBase outlines the basic services required of any
 * implementing database.
 *
 * @author Mobile Conferencing IT
 */
public interface DataBase {

    /**
     * recordTotal() should return the number of records
     * currently residing in the database.
     *
     * @returns long - number of database records
     * currently stored
     */
    public long recordTotal();

    /**
     * getRecord() returns the Record matching a unique
     * ID. The ID value and type are determined by the
     * implementing class.
     *
```

```
 * @param Object - a key or ID value in an object
 * wrapper.
 * @returns String[] - the full record matched to the
 * unique ID.
 */
public String[] getRecord(Object ID);


/**
 * find() searches through the available records and
 * returns all records that match Column data to the
 * String provided.
 *
 * @param String - a text value that matches data in
 * a Record
 * @returns String[][] - an array of matching Record
 * objects
 */
public String[][] find(String matchItem);


/**
 * add() accepts a String array which is assumed to
 * conform to the Record type in use.  Means for
 * handling an improper parameter is left to
 * implementation.  Client validation or
 * exception-handling are possible avenues.
 *
 * @param String[] - Data values conforming to the
 * record scheme.
 */
public void add(String[] newData);


/**
 * modify() allows Record update.
 *
```

```
     * @param Object - the key or wrapped ID of the original
     * Record
     * @param Record - the original Record with updated values
         */
       public void modify(Object ID, String[] changes);


         /**
          * deleteRecord() removes a Record from the
          * database.
          *
          * @param Object - ID of the object to be removed.
          */
       public void delete(Object ID);


       /**
        * Commit current state of database to file.
        */
       public void save();


       /**
     * listScheme() allows caller to see the layout of a Record.
     *
     * @returns GenericColumn[] - Ordered list of column names
     * and widths used in the current scheme.
     */
       public GenericColumn[] listScheme();
   }
```

Part of the task in reading code that's been given to you, particularly in a test situation, is to read for what's missing as well as what's explicitly troublesome. In the previous case, there is something missing: None of the previous methods throw exceptions. Unlike adding methods to an interface, which is a matter of adding on and then tracing through any existing implementations, adding exceptions later on is not a simple option. Consider the following:

```
public interface Commit {
```

```
        public void save();
}

public class Persistent implements Commit {

        public void save() throws CommitException {…}
}
```

The class will not compile under the rule that an overriding method cannot add to a parent method's declared list of exceptions. Therefore, an interface that provides a series of process-sensitive methods must include the semantics of those exceptions up front. Otherwise, implementing the interface becomes very awkward. An interface's methods must also be public, and overriding methods cannot further restrict a method's scope. If a developer were forced to work under such constraints, it would still be possible to include some kind of precondition within each method that disallowed access to all but the instance itself. Having done that, the developer could then supply other new public methods that throw the required exceptions, but it would be a seriously compromised and confusing implementation at best. If we want to support exception handling, we must incorporate it at the design level. Backtracking, in this regard, is not difficult, but it does involve revising all implemented methods, which can be tedious. For further discussion on why the interface should not throw generic exceptions, see the "Issues in Implementation" section later in this chapter.

## Using Abstract Classes

In designing and reviewing a set of interfaces over time, it is likely that some new requirements will emerge and others will boil out. The effort to achieve efficient abstractions can also get lost in generalities, with lots of methods taking Object parameters and returning Object types. In extreme cases, so many options are left completely open that it becomes unclear how to implement the model meaningfully or how to avoid constant casting and type checking down the line.

By the same token, anticipating a concrete solution can also cause problems in design. Adding methods that point overtly to one implementation may obscure the interface's usefulness to a feasible set of alternatives. Moreover, an interface that tempts developers to null-code a number of methods in order to get at what they want becomes, at best, tedious. Unless the interface methods are specifically designed to be ignored safely (such as the listener classes in java.awt.event), the implementing class may be of limited use.

A good way to remain partial to abstractions while nailing down some important details is to write an abstract class. Since abstract classes can include constructors and non-public methods and add or defer method implementations as desired, they are an effective means for signaling insights and intended approaches to a given design. An ideal use for an abstract class models the style of abstract implementations shown throughout the JDK. In the bulk of those implementations, the abstract class implements some amount of code that all its subclasses can use. But, one or more of those implemented methods then call on the abstract methods in the class, which the developer must implement in order to complete the subclass for use. The Component and Container classes in the AWT are stock examples of this technique. However, abstract classes needn't be confined to this toolkit-oriented interpretation of their use.

Partial coding gives us a way to address the previously raised question about whether to write a Field class that subclasses a column or includes an object of that type. Using an abstract class, we could have it both ways. The following example leaves out any additional abstract methods that might be useful, such as package-private methods for setting the width or title, to keep the illustration simple. Comment code is also omitted for this and other brief examples:

```java
public abstract class ModelColumn implements GenericColumn {
    private String title;
    private int width;

    ModelColumn(String name, int width) {
        title = name;
        this.width = width;
    }

    public String getTitle() {
        return title();
    }
```

```
        public int getWidth() {
            return width;
        }
        …
    }
```

With the constructor and methods already written, a concrete version of Column, suitable for use in a Field class, is trivial.

```
public class Column extends ModelColumn {

    public Column(String name, int width) {
        super(name, width);
    }
}

public class Field extends Serializable {
    private String datum;
    private Column col;

    public Field(String datum) {
        this.datum = datum;
    }
}
```

Or Field could simply use a Column in one of its constructors and extend the abstract class.

```
public class Field extends ModelColumn implements _
Serialiazable {
    private String datum;

    public Field(Column col, String datum) {
        super(col.getTitle(), col.getWidth());
        this.datum = datum;
    }

    public Field(String column, int width, String datum) {
```

```
        super(column, width);
        this.datum = datum);
    }
}
```

Abstract classes are also useful for pointing out implementation strategies that, by definition, an interface cannot convey. Any developer who wants to implement Database, for example, will write a constructor to read in an existing data file. It may be less obvious to create a second constructor in order to create new data files as needed and self-document the layout data files must conform to.

```java
public abstract class ModelDatabase implements Database {

public ModelDatabase(String datafile) {
        FileInputStream fis = new FileInputStream(new _
File(datafile));
        // Read metadata or index from datafile
        // Verify file integrity
        // Read in records
    }

    public ModelDatabase(String file, GenericColumn[] _
    newScheme) {
        // Read in newScheme array
        // Use newScheme metrics to determine metadata
        FileOutputStream fos = new FileOutputStream(new _
        File(file));
        // Write metadata to newfile
    }
    ...
    protected String[] getMetadata(){…}
    void close();
}
```

This skeleton code illustrates the most likely implementation of a backing store for a database—reading information to and from files. Just as important, it describes a way to create a new data file and automatically build its metadata. Now the developer does not have to track these details; a short program to generate new data files is reduced to passing a name for a file and the columns it will contain.

These two sections that illustrate interfaces and abstract classes are by no means complete. They are merely intended to suggest that some conceptual work prior to writing an application can help to clarify common elements. The result may be the development of a more flexible framework that can be applied to other problems, or simply recognizing that certain well-known patterns have emerged through conceptual realization and can be applied with better understanding now that the application goals have been laid out.

More importantly, well-designed applications promote more effective maintenance. Programmers assigned to maintain an existing application can read its interfaces first to cleanly separate issues of design from implementation in their own minds. Code reuse, with respect to other projects, is not always a practical objective, particularly for tasks such as this project assignment. Nonetheless, maintenance is not a great factor in this test either, aside from defending your code as maintainable. Where they are practical, worth the effort, and justifiable in the time required to design them, interfaces offer a lot of benefit.

# Issues in Implementation

The fact that we have no assignment code in hand gave us a means to introduce the use of design abstractions. We can anticipate what a simple database application might look like simply by considering what elements are required and by avoiding the specifics of implementation other than surveying common tactics. There are a variety of articles available on the Web. These articles address specific techniques in great detail.

The actual code you receive will spell things out soon enough. There are enough variations to make a comprehensive discussion here fairly tedious and not necessarily helpful—there is no assurance the assignment will even center on using a low-level database. In that area, each candidate must rely on their general experience to adapt to the assignment specifics as best they can.

Our focus here is the general set of implementation problems the exam will pose, which should revolve around one or more of the following topical areas:

- Exception handling

- Design flaws

- Thread safety

- Supporting new features

Thread safety will almost certainly be a central issue in all assignment variations, and the exam objectives will certainly influence other potential problem areas, such as writing in new features or dealing with deliberate design flaws. Nonetheless, we'll handle these topics point by point, referring to the potential impact on thread safety and its server counterpart, concurrent access, as we go.

## Exception Handling

Exceptions in Java define the conditions in normal program operation that would otherwise interrupt execution, based on nonroutine circumstances. There are as many as four objectives to pursue when dealing with aberrant but nonfatal processing in a program:

- Determine if modifying the existing code will eliminate the problem.

- Inform the user.

- Save the data whenever possible.

- Offer the user a choice of subsequent action.

A fundamental exception type might preclude one or more of these objectives being met. Other exceptions may be benign and require no action from the user. If normal operation can be resumed with no threat to data loss, the exception might be noted in a log for someone who maintains the application. But the user should not be alerted to circumstances beyond their control and that do not affect their work. Beyond these two cases, however, a robust program will provide any user with clear problem reports, data safety, and the courses of action open to them.

The parent class of all these operations is `Throwable`. From Throwable, there are three major branches in which exception classes are defined:

- `Error`
- `RuntimeException`
- `Exception`

Descendants of `Error` represent system- or VM-level interruptions (such as `OutOfMemoryError`) in which the question of recovering user access is probably a moot point. It is possible to briefly catch some of these exception types, but what level of service is then available may be indeterminate. These classes are therefore intended simply to name the specific error, when possible, and provide a stack trace of execution as an aid to ruling out fundamental bugs in the underlying VM or other low-level resource.

`RuntimeException` subclasses define type violations and other faults that cannot be trapped at compile-time, such as a `NullPointerException`. The VM will use these classes to specify the fault type and also are not types a programmer should intentionally throw. While they can be caught, it's a fundamental mistake to conditionally handle problems that originate with faulty code. Consider the following:

```
public class MathWhiz {

    …

    public long add (String num1, String num2) {
        long n1 = Integer.parseInt(num1);
        long n2 = Integer.parseInt(num2);
        return (n1 + n2);
    }

    public static void main(String args[]) {
        MathWhiz mw = new MathWhiz();
        try {
            mw.add("3","FOOD");
        }
        catch(NumberFormatException nfe) {
            …
        }
    }
}
```

This is not a subtle example, but it illustrates the burden placed on a catch clause that would attempt to rectify the situation. This clause could report the error by name, but the VM already provides that service. It could report the specific input values that were used when the exception was thrown, but that merely shifts attention from the problem to its symptoms. Finally, the catch code could perform the work expected of the original method, but that would merely underscore how poorly the original method handles its assigned task. Runtime exception conditions should be traced and solved, treating them as program bugs. Any handling in this regard can only be considered a short-term hack that must be applied each time the class is used.

Classes that directly extend Exception lay between system faults and code flaws, usually dealing with events that reflect the necessary risks of the activities they relate to. Dealing with stream or thread operations, as two examples, require some means for anticipating IOException and InterruptedException objects, respectively. When a method executes a "risky" operation, it has the option of dealing with it, by catching the potential exception, or deferring its handling to a calling method, by throwing (or rethrowing) the exception. The key criteria is the portion of the resulting program that is best able to inform the user, preserve data integrity, and provide alternatives to the intended operation, including repeat attempts.

Every exception object knows three things: its name, the trace of execution leading to the point it was constructed from the top of its thread, and any data that was passed to its constructor (usually a String). An exception's name is provided by its toString() method, which is useful when a try block only captures a parent exception. It is therefore always a good idea to develop a family of exceptions for any application of substance, much like a list of error codes is compiled for an elaborate C program. Often these exceptions simply add a naming scheme for context. Extending Exception is all that's required. To support message passing, the parent class of an application's exception hierarchy then provides two constructors: one to accept a String message and a default that either requires no message or passes along a generic one.

```
public class ReservationException extends Exception {

    public static final String generic = "General _
    exception fault.";

    public Reservation {
        this(generic);
    }
```

```
public Reservation(String message) {
    super(message);
}
}
```

Problems in adequate exception handling are typically noted by their absence rather than poor deployment. Look for meaningful points in process control where adding exception handling makes sense. If the sample code provides an exception class, consider whether extending it would clarify risky operations specific to the application. If it does not, provide at least one for context. Finally, as a general rule, avoid using exceptions to handle data validation, unless the code gives you no other reasonable choice. Exception handling, by definition, is a controlled deviation from the normal flow of control followed by code that only runs in the event of that deviation. Consequently, exception code may run up to an order of magnitude slower than inline code covering the same operations and using expected entry and return points.

## Design Impediments

You may find in the application code you receive one or two methods that, based on the instructions you are given, pose more hindrance than help in completing the assignment. Obstacles of this sort may be the result of hastily written code, where the central principles of object-oriented programming—data encapsulation, polymorphism, access control, inheritance—were not given adequate forethought, leaving subsequent programmers some form of maintenance headache. The easiest way to approach such problems is to break them down in four steps. First, identify the ideal or conventional technique to complete the code. Second, determine it cannot be used. Third, consider the less attractive options. And fourth, implement the least of those evils. Chances are there won't be a right choice, simply two or more bad ones that sacrifice different virtues.

Consider a parent class whose public methods make frequent use of a variety of private methods, which are intended to spare any programmer who wants to write a subclass some burdensome details of implementation:

```
public class DoDirtyWork {

    // record key
    private Object key;
```

```
public void addRecord() {
// private method
    checkDataIntegrity();
// private method
    handle = getObjectID();
    try {
        // code that changes fields the subclass
        // wants left alone
    }
    catch(Exception ex) {}
}
}
```

Let's say a subclass of DoDirtyWork needs the two private methods at the beginning of addRecord(), but wants to override the processing within the try block.

```
public class MyWork extends DoDirtyWork {

    public void addRecord() {
        super.addRecord();
// now what?
        ...
    }
}
```

The desired actions are private and, from the point of view of the subclass, impossible to get at without executing the unwanted code. Assuming that the work of the parent class within the try block could be reversed, the subclass has two ugly choices:

- Call the parent's addRecord() method to first perform the integrity check and get a copy of the record's key. Then set the values altered by the parent's try block back to their original state in the remainder of the overriding method.

- Copy the private methods into the subclass using the parent source code, including any necessary private fields and other dependencies to make the calls work.

Neither of these choices represents inspired object-oriented work. They may be all the more difficult to realize because they require abusive programming to solve the problem. But they do pose very different potential problems, and the justification chosen for either approach will depend on which problems are deemed least severe.

In the first approach, the chief danger is exposure to concurrent accesses. Assume for one reason or another that the overriding version of addRecord() cannot be made synchronized. Thread R calls the overridden method in the parent class, which changes state data and then returns. Before Thread R can revert state back to the original values, it is preempted by Thread W, which accesses those values through a different method and writes them to another record. In this specific case, Thread W's subsequent behavior may be indeterminate. In the best case, it is preempted again by Thread R, which then has a chance to rectify the situation. In the worst case, data gets corrupted in one record or possibly all subsequent records.

The second approach, copying the relevant source from DoDirtyWork into MyWork, severs the chain of inheritance. The parent class has its private methods modified, possibly to account for the use of a more efficient data structure or to introduce other hidden fields that expand the versatility of the class. Because the changes occur to private members and methods, there is no reason MyWork shouldn't compile, and it could be a long time before the disconnect in logic is detected. Any attempt to subclass MyWork leads to the same dismal choice as before.

There is no good answer in a case like this, much less a right one. It is more likely that the solution you choose here will influence the remainder of the project. A problem of this type may well be covered in the follow-up exam; examine the problem carefully and choose from the alternatives you can devise, rather than take the first workaround that comes to mind.

# Thread Safety

Making data threadsafe is just one of two considerations in implementing an effective multithreading strategy. Achieving thread safety means guaranteeing serial access to the data on some level. Serial or *synchronized* access to data guarantees that any number of concurrent operations, which share access to the data and may modify it, do not interfere with each other. Another way of saying this is that the object that contains or wraps the data usually assumes a passive or defensive role against concurrent access. In a two-tier database model, the database portion assumes this role. Based on how data is safeguarded, the server code is responsible for managing and applying incoming client requests to data retrieval and storage in a manner that acknowledges such limits.

In practice, the balance between these processes can shift considerably, depending on the design goals of the application. If the database permits only one access at a time of any kind to the entire data structure, then there is no possibility of corrupting the data through conflicts in concurrent requests. But global enforcement of data safety comes at a price—a very limited potential for performance, which may become unacceptable as data operations take more time to process. There's no advantage to improving server efficiency if requests are prepared faster than the database can accept and process them. But for small databases supporting very basic requests, serially ordered access to all data is easy to program and maintain and is a viable approach for many situations.

Achieving greater performance requires data access below the level of the entire data structure coupled with a technique for processing requests that corresponds to how deeply the data is exposed. The finer the granularity of the access, the more sophisticated the techniques available to exploit it. And of course the more complex the strategy, the greater the burden on the developer to ensure it is implemented and maintained correctly. Simply put, a scheme for multithreading that offers optimal performance is not right for all occasions. The cost of such a scheme must be justified by the potential benefits it can return. Some of those schemes are covered in the following chapter.

## Synchronizing on the Data Structure

Synchronizing data access has to occur on some level, but it can take a variety of forms. Some container types guarantee threadsafe access as part of their structure. For other containers, the same result can be achieved within a code block that invokes synchronization on the data object as a precondition to the block's execution.

```
...
public void modifyRecord() {
    synchronized (theData) {
        //modify the record
    }
    ...
}
...
```

This approach is not as stifling to performance as it might first seem. Calls to the Thread class' wait() and notify() methods within a synchronized block can be used to defer operation as desired, allowing thread control to change hands based on some conditional state. By using a series of wait/notify conditions with each potential data change, some degree of thread interleaving is possible, again depending on which threads are subsequently eligible to run. Without the use of wait() and notify() (and notifyAll()), the synchronized qualifier confers exclusive access to the executing thread on the lock of any object (or class) it operates in or declares. If that declared object encapsulates the data, serialized access is achieved for the duration of that block.

The programmer also has the option of synchronizing the methods that access the data structure to achieve the same effect; methods and blocks both acquire the object lock before they operate. Synchronizing on the method may seem to make simpler and "cleaner" code, but there are, as always, trade-offs. A long method that is synchronized may wrap process-intensive code that doesn't need an object lock. In extreme cases, such methods that access a number of major resources can create a deadlock condition by calling on competing processes. But employing a large number of synchronized blocks could be just as inefficient. Acquiring the lock over several code blocks in the same method is certainly slower than acquiring it once, but the difference may be marginal. The bigger danger is in synchronizing on objects other than the one represented by this, which can also create deadlock. However, in choosing to synchronize methods rather than code blocks, the programmer must ensure that non-synchronized method operations don't rely on data that synchronized methods actively manipulate. Conversely, non-synchronized methods can't be allowed to change data that synchronized methods are supposed to handle.

Other rules to bear in mind about synchronized methods:

- Calls to other synchronized methods in the same object do not block.

- Calls to a non-synchronized method, in the same object or elsewhere, also do not affect the atomic execution of the calling method.

- Synchronization is not inherited, nor does the compiler require the keyword in an overriding method. An abstract class that supports a synchronized abstract method will compile, but the declaration is not meaningful. The abstract synchronized method aside, a super.method() call to a synchronized parent can create a block the programmer is not expecting.

## Data Structure

Java 2's Collections Framework, located in `java.util`, offers a number of containers that by default are not threadsafe. Each of these containers is supported by a static method in the Collections class that returns serialized control in the form of an interface reference that wraps and "backs" the original container type.

```java
public class DataStore {
    private Hashmap hm;
    private Map map;

    public DataStore() {
    // "raw" access
        hm = new Hashmap();
    // threadsafe access
        map = Collections.synchronizedMap(hm);
        ...
    }
}
```

The key to ensuring serial access is to eliminate any reference to the "raw" class. Otherwise the means for accessing the container is open to a developer's determination.

```java
public class DataStore2 {
    private Map map;

    public DataStore2() {
        map = Collections.synchronizedMap(new HashMap());
        // threadsafe access only
        ...
    }
}
```

The philosophy behind this support is twofold. If protection against concurrent access is not required, the container form can be used as is; to make it threadsafe, the entire object should be synchronized. In fact, the API documentation goes so far as to insist on using a synchronized reference to the container whenever multithreaded operations will rely on it.

This does *not* mean that synchronizing on a container protects it completely at all times, only that individual operations are guaranteed to be atomic. Most of the time, in practice, we rely on multiple operations to complete a single task, e.g., reading a record, modifying it, and writing back to the data store. The programmer must still devise a strategy for how records are handled during compound operations: whether the record is locked for the duration or may change asynchronously, whether the user is notified of other current locks or the latest change simply writes over any previous modifications, etc.

This all-or-nothing rationale behind container synchronization merely rests on the idea that requiring the developer to design a more granular thread safety scheme, in the name of optimal performance, is not typically justified by an application's actual requirements. It may be better to achieve performance through other means, such as faster hardware or a more efficient VM. Less complicated programming strategies that do not involve defensive techniques can also aid performance. These include reducing file accesses, partitioning data structures in memory, or perhaps applying a design that would permit read-only threads to run asynchronously, while write-oriented threads are queued and scheduled for execution. But if optimal performance remains a central concern, nothing beyond advice prevents developers from writing their own interleaving schemes and applying them to native container types.

## Data Elements

Each thread can be required to synchronize on the record objects they want to write or modify. As a general rule, synchronizing on an object other than the one currently executing can be dangerous. Any code block that synchronizes on one autonomous object and then calls a method that threads its own attempt to synchronize on that same object runs the risk of creating a deadlock condition, hanging the system.

The alternative is to synchronize all the methods in a record object (and maintain complete encapsulation), but again this is only part of the entire scheme needed. The developer must still guarantee that each new record will receive a unique ID and will get written to a location in the container that is not already in use. Some container types inherently guarantee this, based on the record ID as a key, which then maps to its value pair; other structures do not. An ordered container, such as a linked list or a low-level file using a random-access pointer, should be wrapped so that acquiring the record's unique ID and adding the record are atomically executed, ensuring no conflicts with other record inserts. With respect to an actual file, the programmer must then also account for the space left by a deleted record and determine when best to reorganize files that fill up with null records.

## Supporting New Features

Any feature you are expected to add to the existing code may imply through their own requirements a preferred way to implement threadsafe operations and still provide scalable performance. The considerations for achieving performance in the project assignment are, again, a decision each candidate will have to make based on the solution they feel most comfortable justifying. The following examples are intended to suggest potential threading strategies for the assignment based on supporting features such as

- Search and replace

- Sorting

- A record "lock"

Each one of these feature rests on a means for getting a list of records from the database, ignoring elements that fail to match the search criteria, and modifying those that succeed. In the case of a search-and-replace request, it isn't possible to know ahead of time whether the executing thread will only read (no matches), sometimes write, or always write. To avoid blocking the entire database, we need some way to list through the data and release records once they are no longer needed. An optimal solution for performance would also permit other threads to act on records the current thread does not yet need but are still on the list.

This kind of job has been supported by Enumeration interface, which can be used to list the contents of a Vector or other ad-hoc container type that implements it. The Collections framework provides an eventual successor to Enumeration called Iterator, which offers a tighter binding to all the container types in java.util. An Iterator knows how to remove elements from the container type and updates itself accordingly; an Enumeration has no such association with its container. But an Iterator cannot cope with modifications made by another Iterator or any other process that modifies the database; the program must ensure that records cannot be added or deleted while a list is running.

Sorting can be even more demanding, inasmuch as elements are required until the sort is complete. One workaround that avoids blocking for the duration of the process is to copy the contents to sort into a temporary container and return the results from there. Using this same technique to holds records pending an update, sometimes called a "dirty buffer," can lead to improved performance. Write processes must be confined to using the dirty buffer, which only offers synchronous access. The original buffer is always readable. A copy of all dirty records remains in the original buffer but is marked "read-only" until the dirty buffer writes it back. Such writes must then take place while client write requests are blocked.

Ultimately, adding some type of state reference to the record object is required to track interested threads, iteration lists, buffer assignments, or even simple locks on a record while it is being added, updated, or deleted. This can take the form of a wrapper around the record that includes, for example, a `Vector` of thread references. The methods of the controlling database must be updated to wait or notify based on record state, including a means to update the set of active references.

# Chapter Summary

The programming assignment requires each candidate to extend code that is supplied with the project and make it threadsafe. In our example, illustrating the potential development of a simple database, we've shown how some very simple oversights in design can lead to problematic development for future programmers—a context very close in purpose to what the assignment poses. In particular, when multithreaded design is not considered as a factor in initial design, the developer assumes a burden in retrofitting an effective scheme.

Achieving thread safety can be as simple as guaranteeing synchronous access to the entire data structure. Providing it in such a way as to optimize concurrent access increases the potential for performance but at the cost of adding considerable complexity to the overall project. There is such a thing as "too much" performance, from the perspective of the cost in time and future maintenance to achieve it.

# CHAPTER

# 17

## Writing the Network Protocol

**O**ne simple way to address the requirement for making a threadsafe database is to synchronize on it as a whole. The data cannot be corrupted by concurrent write requests if they're all forced to stand in line. At the same time, it's clear that the "bullet-proof" approach comes at a high price. If the database grows to any appreciable size, or if many requests require iterating over the entire record set, performance perception may suffer. And if the project assignment requires adding a feature that depends on "granular" access, some accommodation will have to be made for a complex scheme anyway. To that end, the previous chapter outlined some general points for designing such a system. The code bundled with the assignment may also influence those choices, so the best defense is a broad view of the options.

Whatever method you choose to manage the application, it's always good design to maintain independence between the server that encapsulates the database (or any application it will serve) and the database itself. Ideally, the application and all classes related to its operation present themselves in as few references as practically attainable within the server code. As the exchange point between all possible clients and the data, the application server already has plenty of functionaries to manage. The initial design goal for it should be to maintain the cleanest possible separation of role-players. One assumption we will maintain in this chapter is that the database has been "wrapped" in such a manner.

Concurrency is only part of the puzzle. We have to make our decision early as to how we are going to institute inter-VM operations. If we want to build incrementally, we can define a network communication protocol, set up a loop to handle incoming requests, and add a scheduling system for the actual jobs. In the world of "request-response" internet services, this is solid and well-trod ground. Java's Object Serialization facility lightens the load a bit, making it possible to send single objects over the network that contain all the details of a given request. There are lots of details to implement and document in this manner, but the developer then can build in new services one by one, verifying operation along the way. With a little advance planning, new request types can be written as classes that conform to a general interface contract, making it a simple matter to incorporate new jobs into the client-server scheme.

But if we want to avoid the details of how services are provided and focus solely on what services to provide, we need another approach. To make one VM's call on another VM's resources appear as a matter of detail—an important concept in distributed computing—we need an API that renders the need for a communications protocol transparent to the programmer. That convenience of course exacts its own costs, the first of which is defining client requirements in advance. To take advantage of RMI's services, a de facto network protocol and object transport system, we forego the ability to tinker with and refine services. Redefining a client service with RMI would mean rewriting and recompiling the service objects and the client code, which would get tedious quickly. We have to know what we want in advance so that RMI is doing what it does best—hiding the details of remote resources and expediting requests.

We'll discuss each method in turn in this chapter, weaving the discussion of threading in where appropriate, and saving for last some approaches to job scheduling that would apply equally well to both models.

# Client-Server from Scratch

**J**ava makes building the network aspect of a simple client-server application easy. The explosive rise in Web server deployment has made communicating over the network, by way of requesting "pages" of data, such a pervasive model that the JDK provides an entire library of tools to adopt it. This rapid change in the way most of us use computers has brought with it some devaluation of the term "client-server." A client-server system signifies the potential for a persistent connection between two machines; the dividing line between who processes what is somewhat negotiable. Basic Web servers are arguably better described as "request-response" information servers. Electronic commerce and other forms of facilitating browser access to a back-end database or other interactive facility are blurring this distinction more and more, but HTTP servers are so widespread and cheap to implement that people will continue to develop and extend them—and live with their restrictions. Until Web servers that can track clients across their individual requests come in to wide use, development efforts to implement "true" client-server will largely remain the effort of individual development efforts.

One product that integrates "session tracking" into its client handling now is Java Web Server. If the browser permits the server to write "cookies," or state information to the browser's local disk, the server can then track the status of the client throughout a multi-stage request. More information is available online at `http://www.sun.com/software/jwebserver`.

## Server Operation

A server's fundamental job is to run indefinitely, listening for and servicing requests. To reach the server, a client must know the name of the machine the server runs on, the *port* or channel it listens to, and the correct way to state a request. For widely popular service types, these last two elements usually assume the status of convention by way of a standards committee, such as the Internet Engineering Task Force (IETF). The user community relies on such committees to provide consensus or an authoritative message for agreed-upon standards and to make the information available to the public. You usually don't have to find a Web server by its port number, for example, because a "well-known" port (80) has been agreed upon and is even assumed by browsers unless you direct them explicitly to another port.

HTTP servers also use a standardized protocol that clients must adhere to in order to receive the services they want. It is common for these types of servers to "speak" across the network in clear text, which makes testing and debugging much easier. The minimum request that a Web server would honor, once a client connects to it, looks like this:

```
GET /
<A blank line and carriage return signal a completed request.>
...
```

Here the server is instructed to transmit the default, or "home" page in its root document directory, using version 1.0 of the HTTP protocol. If we were to telnet into a Web server instead of using a browser and submit this request, we'd get a stream of raw HTML code as a response. The browser simply formats the response according to the HTML tags that are part of the response.

This paradigm is so widely used that most of the needed behavior is already encapsulated in the java.net classes:

```java
import java.net.*;
import java.io.*;

public class Server implements Runnable {
    public final static int WK_PORT = 2012;
    protected int port;
    protected ServerSocket service;
private String message = "Hello client!";

    public Server(int port_request) {
        if (port_request < 1024 || port_request > 65535) {
            port = WK_PORT;
        }
        this.port = port_request;
        try {
            service = new ServerSocket(port);
        }
        catch (IOException ioe) {
            System.out.println("Error: Port " + port +
                               "was not available.");
        }
        System.out.println("Port " + port + " is up and _
        running.");
    }

    public void run() {
InputStream receiving;
        OutputStream sending;
        while (true) {
            try {
                Socket client = service.accept();
                sending = client.getOutputStream();
```

```
                        receiving = client.getInputStream();
                        // accept client input, if any
                        sending(message.getBytes());
                        //return request information, if any
                    }
                    catch (IOException ioe) {
                        System.out.println("Could not accept _
                        client request or establish streams.");
                    }
                }
            }

        public static void main(String args[]) {
            Server svr = new Server(WK_PORT);
        }
    }
```

After establishing itself as a port listener, a Server creates and maintains incoming connections within its own thread of execution. At the same time, it's also possible to run multiple Server instances on different ports of the same machine. Our code checks to see if a legal port number is entered: on Unix systems, ports below 1024 are reserved for the super-user. A TCP/IP stack supports 64K ports, making 65535 the upper limit. We also chose to catch the IOException that would be thrown if a Server instance attempted to start on a port already in use, in order to clarify the nature of this fault to the user. We could do more, of course, if we did not want the instance to terminate on this error. We also want to think about how we might protect the database itself; not a straightforward task to accomplish while also maintaining platform independence.

Within the run()method itself we've written just enough client-response code to test correct run-time behavior; no attempt at threading client requests has been made yet. Once a request does connect, ServerSocket returns an object that encapsulates the client's connection and the means for opening lines of communication between the two. This information is then managed by the Socket reference client, which invokes input and output streams to facilitate client-server communication. There is of course no need to open an InputStream if the socket has no reason to listen to the client.

To test this initial version, there's no need to write any Java at all. Java's networking library runs over TCP/IP as the transport protocol, which means Java network code can communicate with other TCP/IP-based applications, like telnet. Telnet is a mainstay tool of Unix systems and is more than likely available and in your command path. You can then do the following:

```
$ javac Server.java
$ java Server &
$ telnet localhost 2012
Hello client!
```

On a Windows machine, you must start the Server in its own window, then telnet to it through another window. Also, be sure a TCP/IP stack has been configured and is currently active among the list of network drivers. You can check this in the Control Panel by clicking the Network icon and browsing the Configuration panel's list of drivers.

## Connecting Clients to the Server

Our bare-bones server code above is not very interesting, but it gives us the first building block we need. As we further define the model for connecting multiple clients and threading the requests they carry, we want to think about mapping out the various tasks and developing a working set of class relationships. One of the first things to consider, since we know we will have to thread client requests, is to encapsulate each client connection in its own object running on its own thread. The server code must then provide a way to

- Remember each client.

- Check the state of each client and its request regularly.

- Restore resources used by the client when done.

As each of these tasks appears to grow more complex or involve more than one basic job, you want to think again about forming classes to divide responsibilities economically. Before we get too deeply engrossed in class design, however, we want to establish how the client will call for the services provided by the application.

## Communications Protocol

An HTTP server supports a variety of calls, like GET and POST, which any browser client may issue—along with the relevant arguments the call requires such as a filename or query data. The server recognizes these keywords as signals to invoke the corresponding service. Or, in more complex cases, the call keyword introduces subsequent information needed relevant to clarify or fulfill the request. If we were in fact writing our own application from the ground up, this is probably where we would want to start. By determining what services our application should provide, we may quickly define a language, however small, that specifies how to communicate service requests. In a well-disciplined design environment, making such decisions early makes it possible for some aspects of client and server development to continue in parallel.

### Define the Operations

In the project assignment, should we decide to build the client-server from scratch, we will need to document

- The action represented by each service code.

- The data, if any, that must follow the code.

- The data, if any, that the server should return.

- Expected behavior if the data are inconsistent with the request or response.

- What to do in "corner cases," or events that result from system operation the request cannot control.

This last point is especially important from a maintenance perspective. Anticipating odd but plausible situations early in design helps future maintainers to avoid patching problematic situations with exception handling or some other cumbersome workaround, when no one wants to alter an otherwise acceptable design. How will the program behave if a find operation returns a null pointer? What if a record we want to delete has already been purged? The more specific and detailed our understanding of system behavior in these cases, the plainer the coding tasks become.

Let's assume our database application wants to make available a minimum complement of services, for the sake of illustration. Some of the issues addressed in the list above are only noted in part here and in the subsequent code example. The assignment documentation should strive to be thorough in this respect.

**Add**   Given a `String` array that conforms to the record type, this command prompts the database to convert the array into a record and return the unique ID assigned to it. The client is responsible for knowing the record layout and providing appropriate data.

**Modify**   Given a `String` array that conforms to the record type, this command prompts the database to update a record that is specified by its ID. Modify does not protect against multiple concurrent updates—the last change supercedes all previous changes.

**Delete**   Given a unique ID, removes the associated record from the database. Requests to delete a record that has already been purged are ignored.

**Find**   Given a single `String`, returns a list of all records that have matching data in one of their fields.

**Scheme**   Returns the type and width of all columns used by records in the database to the requesting client.

## Implement the Protocol

Interfaces are an ideal repository for static data such as codes that specify the legal calls a client can make to the server. Any class that implements the interface gains access to its list of constants, which in this example are nothing more than "named" integer values, similar to what one would expect in a C language header file.

```
/**
 * Services specifies the various operations the client may
 * call on the application to provide.
 *
 * @author Mobile Conferencing IT, 10/98.
 */
public interface DataServices {

    /**
     * The ADD_RECORD command prompts the database to
     * include the data that follows it as a new record.
```

```
      * The client is responsible for the data provided
      * conforms to the record's fields.
      */
     public static final int ADD_RECORD = 0xA0A1;

     /**
      * MODIFY_RECORD must be followed by an existing record
      * ID and the intended modifications.
      */
     public static final int MODIFY_RECORD = 0xB0B1;

     /**
      * DELETE_RECORD must be followed by a record ID.  It
      * prompts the database to purge the indicated record, or
      * ignore the request if the record is no longer resident.
      */
     public static final int DELETE_RECORD = 0xD0D1;

     /**
      * FIND_RECORDS is followed by a String representing the
      * match criteria. The database is prompted to find every
      * match among the available records and return a list of
      * "hits" or a null pointer.
      */
     public static final int FIND_RECORDS = 0xF0F1;

     /**
      * SCHEME requires no arguments and prompts the database to
      * list the column names and widths that compose each record.
      */
     public static final int SCHEME = 0xFFFF;
 }
```

Thinking ahead for just a second, an additional benefit of the interface is that it gives us a document from which to extrapolate "job" classes, which might operate on a separate thread from client that initiates it. Each type of operation could be contained in a class which implements something like a "job" interface, and the job itself could run as a thread in a group along with other threads that perform the same function. We can look for ways to achieve some kind of threading economy, in one scenario, if we somehow bundle certain jobs to run concurrently against the data store (because they don't change anything) while others must observe a strict queue. We'll develop this is idea further once we have had a chance to explore both this approach and RMI in full.

# The Client/Request Structure

As mentioned above, the server should keep an account of all current client connections, check their connection status and the progress of their requests, and recoup server resources once a connection terminates. An intuitive first step on the first objective is to separate out client connections and requests and giving them their own classes. Using the Socket reference returned by accept(), we can construct a Client instance and read the service call written by the remote machine to form a Request. Setting up the server to juggle concurrent instances is simple. All the Client class has to do is implement Runnable, construct a thread for itself, call its own start()method, and execute its central processes from that point, thereby keeping the listener loop free of the details and self-documenting a map of the object's life.

The Client class can absorb more detail by managing the creation of its associated Request object. A Request should consist of the action the remote client wants to perform along with the data needed to support it. On its face, it may seem extraneous to form a separate object that uncouples the client's connection from its own request; it certainly isn't essential. But in this case, we are thinking ahead a little to how we will handle a data request. The request itself is only one part of the client object, so is it necessary to include posting the request within the same thread that governs the client's connection state? One advantage of breaking out the request as a separate object is that the full client object won't have to participate fully in a scheduling model the server might employ to expedite or regulate requests. A Client object could, in one configuration, simply observe its Request and wait for notification of the request thread's termination, indicating it has run its course. The Client then receives any return data by way of the notification update, which is passed back over the stream to the remote client. See Figure 17.1 for a diagram of this relationship.

**F I G U R E  17.1**

The client/request
structure

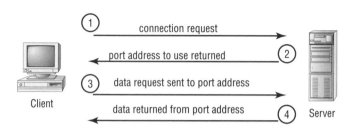

An alternative approach might be to make Request an inner class of Client, avoiding the overhead of the Observer notification model and the burden of negotiating field access between the two. Once data has been sent back to the remote client, the Client can close its data streams and flag itself for removal. The request object, focussed solely on getting processed and passing return data back, can be scoped and dereferenced by the server during a routine check.

This brings us to our second objective, to have the server support some form of client tracking. A container suffices to store object references, but we will also want to query each stored element to determine its current state. The least cumbersome way of accomplishing this is to add a boolean flag to the contained elements that indicates if their purpose has been served. Client objects will close their own streams, so in normal processing we don't have to worry about connections staying open. If this were a full-fledged application, we would need to check for client connections that fail while their requests are in progress and respond accordingly.

The elements of the Server class that derive from our discussion are included in this code fragment:

```
public class Server implements Runnable{
    private Vector connections;
    private Vector jobs;
    private Client clientTmp;
    private Request request;
    private DataBase dbs;
    private ServerSocket listener;
    ...

    public Server(int port) {
        listener = new ServerSocket(port);
```

```
        //stores client connection
        connections = new Vector();
        //stores request portion of client
        jobs = new Vector();
        //loads the database into memory
        dbs = new Database("reservations.ser");
        this.start();
    }

    public void run() {
        while(true) {
            try {
                clientTmp = new Client(listener.accept(), dbs);
                request = clientTmp.getRequest();
                connections.add(clientTmp);
                jobs.add(request);
                clientTmp = null;
                request = null;
            }
            catch(IOException ioe) {
                System.out.println("Listener aborted _
                irregularly");
                ioe.printStackTrace();
            }

            Iterator connectList = connections.iterator();
            Iterator jobList = jobs.iterator();

            while (connectList.hasMoreElements()) {
                clientTmp = (Client)connections.next();
                if (clientTmp.isDone()) {
                    connectList.remove(clientTmp);
                }
            }
            while (jobList.hasMoreElements()) {
                request = (Request)jobs.next();
```

```
                    if (request.isComplete()) {
                        jobList.remove(request);
                    }
                }
            }
        }
        ...
    }
```

There are more than a few blanks to fill in for this class. They are left as development exercises for those who wish to complete the code. To keep this illustration brief, we have left a few things undone that would make the overall design more elegant. We are currently maintaining Client and Request objects in separate vectors; as intimately related as the two objects are, a tighter association between the two is a necessity.

The last portion of the run() method satisfies our third objective, to provide some form of cleanup for expired connections and jobs. If we wanted to keep the server's the loop focussed on efficient listening, we could perform vector monitoring through a separate Cleanup class and run it on its own thread. Vectors are already internally synchronized, so we wouldn't have to worry about removing elements while the listener is trying to add a new one. But if we wanted to use wait() and notifyAll() to pre-empt the cleanup thread when either vector is unavailable, we'd still have to synchronize on them. Neither the compiler nor the runtime allows wait() and notifyAll()except within a synchronized block of code; there is no cross-check in the compiler to see whether the object in question "really" needs it.

The Client class below is also incomplete, but illustrates the features that have been discussed. It encapsulates the streams connecting the server's machine to the remote client, instantiates its request as a discrete object, and implements an Observer for keeping tabs on the request's progress. This is by no means the only choice. Using a Beans-oriented approach, our connection object could implement an event listener to be notified of changes in the request object, thereby taking advantage of Java's built-in event handling mechanism. In the sense that the request portion of a client represents its "model," and the connection portion a type of "view," there are really a variety of ways to consider capturing the relationship effectively—one of which would be an MVC-type of pattern. These techniques have the advantage of being more flexible. The Observer/Observable interface/class pair has the advantage of being easy to implement and ideally suited to the immediate problem. The boolean flag done can be set to true once the data returned from the database call, if any, has been written back to the remote machine. With a few basic modifications, however, this class could also support a persistent connection to the server, using its run() method as a loop for handling successive service requests.

```java
public class Client implements Runnable, Observer {
    protected Thread runner;
    private InputStream incoming;
    private OutputStream outgoing;
    private Request req;
    private boolean done = false;
    private Object returnData;
    private Database db;

    public Client(Socket connection, Database db) {
        try {
            incoming = connection.getInputStream();
            outgoing = connection.getOutputStream();
            req = new Request(this, incoming.readObject(), db);
            runner = new Thread(this);
            runner.start();
        }
        catch(IOException ioe) {
            System.out.println("Failed to open socket streams");
        }
    }

    public Request getRequest() {
        return req;
    }

    public boolean isDone() {
        return done;
    }
```

```
public void update(Observable request, Object retData) {
    returnData = retData;
}

protected void finalize() {
    incoming = null;
    outgoing = null;
    runner = null;
}

public void run() {
    while (!isDone())
    {
        try {
            outgoing.writeObject(returnData);
            outgoing.flush();
        }
        catch (IOException ioe) {
            System.out.println("Could not write return _
            data back to the client.");
            ioe.printStackTrace();
        }
        done = true;
    }
    ...
}
```

This class implements the Observer method update(), which is then called by any Observable that has added this class to its list of listeners. As design patterns go, it is similar to the way event handlers work and is very useful when one object needs to base its behavior on the state change in another object. Also notice the assumption that the client's request is sent as a single Request object, reducing the "protocol" for client-server communication to a single read-Object() call. Since this class has no role in dealing with data other than as a middleman, it only requires an Object reference to pass it back and forth.

The last class fragment we have roughed out in this preliminary sketch is Request itself. This class extends Observable so it can register its "owner's" interest in knowing when the job has completed. DataServices is implemented for access to the service codes. At the end of the thread run, the request notifies its client of any data that may have been returned when the call to the database finished. The boolean field completed is also set to true to expedite dereferencing the thread used by this object.

```
public class Request extends Observable implements Runnable,
  DataServices, Serializable {
    protected int command;
    protected Object data;
    protected boolean completed = false;
    protected transient Thread runJob;

    public Request(Client owner, Object obj, Database db) {
        Request req = (Request)obj;
        command = req.getCommand();
        data = req.getData();
        runJob = new Thread(this);
        addObserver(owner);
        runJob.start();
    }

    public int getCommand() {
        return command;
    }

    public Object getData() {
        return data;
    }

    protected void setData(Object dbReturn) {
        data = dbReturn;
    }

    public boolean isComplete() {
        return completed;
    }
```

```
public void run(){
    switch(getCommand()) {
        case ADD_DATA: db.add((String[])getData());
                        break;
        case SCHEME:   Object obj = db.getListScheme();
                        break;
        // remainder of service calls
        }
        setChanged();
        notifyObservers(getData());
        completed = true;
    }
}
```

Since we have a limited number of data calls, a simple switch on getCom-
mand() will suffice. But if the command list is going to grow to any size, it
makes sense to start thinking about a parent class that all requests can subclass
or perhaps even an interface they can all implement. See Figure 17.2 for one
such arrangement. Another way to maintain uniform communication between
client and server, regardless of the service requested, is to encapsulate all the
relevant objects into one, perhaps in a Response object. This technique almost
trivializes the argument that straight VM-to-VM communication over streams
requires the developer to maintain a special protocol. Allowances have to be
made for threads and other objects that do not serialize—notice that Request
implements Serializable but marks its Thread reference transient—but
hiding the details of transmitting objects over the wire is worth it.

**F I G U R E   17.2**

A flexible parent class.

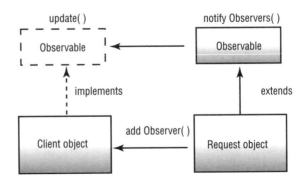

# Limitations of the Model

Before object serialization was added to Java, one of the chief complaints about the JDK, regardless of its newcomer status, was its lack of a ready-to-use persistence model. Prior to the arrival of an object serialization facility, in order to commit an object type to a stream, programmers had to break the object into its constituent parts. Once an object was "unrolled" into integers, floats, byte arrays, and so on, they could be placed on the stream, one writeUTF() call at a time. Reading those values back in was of course the same call-intensive and order-sensitive process. The methods that were written to handle this were little more than hand-coded "object protocols." The process wasn't ugly just because it was tedious and prone to error; it was ugly because there was no way to assure that any two people would even write the same class to the stream in the same way. Every object mapping was a potential exercise in lengthy, detail-oriented, throwaway code. Most workarounds, such as trying to share object-serial maps in advance of the classes themselves, simply defeated the benefits that a "network-aware" language was supposed to offer.

Now, object serialization makes the task relatively easy. Where it is possible to abstract the types sent over the network so that as few objects as possible are part of the transmission, the resulting code is very straightforward and easy to read. With a small application, such as one like the project assignment will require you to write, building a quick-and-dirty protocol and defining a few object types to communicate to send back and forth may be all you really need. But there is a limit to how effective a "state-oriented" communication scheme can be. In general, the constraints of passing objects between autonomous VMs are the constraints of version control and updating.

Once we commit an object to the stream, its state is fixed. It's like sending a letter, in the sense that the information it contains is only current for so long. The more volatile the information, the less useful the letter is, especially if its delivery is slow or the recipient doesn't read it right away. If that object is being sent to a file, our only concern is keeping the stored data current. But if it is going to another VM, keeping both VMs in sync on the object means either limiting object communication to state-oriented updates, making sure neither VM would need to change the object while it is in transit, or making sure that the changes aren't material to inter-VM communication.

The usual style of communicating through streams is a procedural one: the client sends a request, the server sends a response. If we want to develop an exchange that feels more interactive or reflect several turns the exchange might take, the script might be made more elaborate, but it remains tied to a synchronous model. As the communication becomes more complex, we end up with a new protocol on our hands. This has been a predominant objection among developers who see the ease of serializing individual objects but remember the lesson of writing individual objects into serial form by hand. Serialization alone relies on the programmer to maintain the protocol for communicating. Eliminating one layer of tedium, the atomic level of persistence, merely shifts the problem to higher ground. In the absence of a set way to communicate multiple objects between any two machines, we must still distribute the protocol, and the class files that embody them, to cast serialized objects back to their correct type.

# Remote Method Invocation (RMI)

The end goal of Java's serialization facility is to simplify the task of persisting objects. Saving objects to a file or to another VM is now a straightforward, standardized, sometimes even trivial process. To call RMI, an alternative networking approach serves our immediate purpose in discussing the developer's exam assignment, but ultimately there's no qualitative comparison worth making. Object serialization is a useful but one-dimensional facility; RMI, on the other hand, is a full-grown architecture for distributed computing and it is scalable to far more complex tasks than the request-response style of programming our project requires at a minimum.

Serialization handles the details of writing object-level protocols so the programmer can send objects to a stream without worrying about their elemental structure or ordering. In much the same way, RMI provides a means for distributing objects as services so that a remote service request looks as much like a local one as we can manage. This bridges at least one potential limitation in the approach we just discussed. Rather than send an object back and forth between VMs, we station it in one place. The VM responsible for serving the object declares it "exportable" and puts it where an RMI "object server" can call on it when a request comes in.

To use the object's services, the remote client must first obtain a reference to it. In order to do that, the client must of course know where to find the object, what it is called, and what method calls it provides. Once that information is acquired, however, RMI takes care of the rest:

- Object serialization

- Object transport, using its own "wire protocol"

- Exception handling specific to network errors

- Security management

Taking advantage of all these services requires some forethought. The developer must consider which objects to serve based on the applicability of their services to remote access. Although the risks of distributed computing are similar in nature to straightforward protocol-based communication, trying to make these variances transparent through RMI casts some murkiness over the exception process, arguably making it seem complex. Network connections can be severed physically or logically. The client or server may go down or drop the connection. The occasional extreme latency in network transmissions may signal a timeout condition just prior to fulfilling a request—any of these can disrupt the expected flow, leaving the server's current state and the client's understanding of it uncertain. The elegance of RMI is a fine thing, but we do not want to inherit a spate of exceptions on every remote call just to achieve it.

# A Model RMI Transaction

For a client to be able to call on an object that resides on a remote machine, it must first have a reference to it. To retrieve the reference and use it, the client has to know substantially more about the object than we need to know to find a Web page. The only concise way to do this is to embed that lookup information in the client code. It is possible to find and determine remote services at runtime, but short of wanting to write an object browser in and of itself, we do not want to explore remotely-available services and determine their facilities in runtime, prior to using them.. We just want to use them, so advance knowledge of the available method calls is essential. Prior to changes in the JDK 1.2, RMI facilitated this discovery through a custom pair of classes called *skeletons* and *stubs*. These two classes derived directly from the class file of the remote object.

When the remote client calls on an object, it does so by way of a lookup. This lookup is coded into the client, as are the explicit calls to the object's methods. If the lookup succeeds, the RMI server returns the remote object's stub, which acts as a stand-in for the remote object's class and methods. Upon a call to any one of these methods in pre-1.2 code, the stub sends the request to the skeleton reference, which resides on the server side. The skeleton retrieves the operations of the local object that the client is interested in and maintains a dispatch() method to coordinate routing the object's response back through the stub. This method of internal communication-by-proxy is still available in the JDK 1.2, but RMI changes in the current release have brought the skeleton's role into the RemoteObject class.

The current JDK release changes the structure of RMI to make room for new features such as activatable objects. Prior to Java 2, the skeleton retrieved methods from the remote object as Operation objects, which are now deprecated. The tool that creates the skeleton and stub classes, the rmic compiler, now provides a flag (rmic -v1.2) to create stubs that are not backward compatible with 1.1 RMI code.

The communication between stub and skeleton (whether discrete or part of RemoteObject) takes place over RMI's remote reference layer, the "wire protocol" we referred to earlier, which in turn relies on the transport layer already provided by TCP/IP. But the point of all this layering is to render the mechanics of network communication as transparent as possible, freeing the programmer to focus on the semantics of routine method calls. Figure 17.3 shows a logical view of an RMI-based interaction. In this diagram, the remote object is a Request, through which the client can call the same services we provided through the protocol interface shown earlier in the chapter.

**F I G U R E  17.3**

An RMI-based
interaction

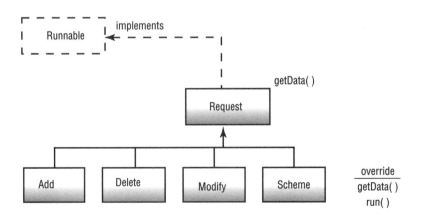

## Implementing RMI

Once the questions surrounding proper design have been settled, writing the code for RMI requires several steps, but it is not overly complicated. In this example, we'll redesign the Request class as an object our client will access to enter a transaction request. We need to provide both the client and server resources. The Request class now assumes the dimensions of a protocol similar to DataServices, but has the advantage of being self-describing in its implementation:

```
import java.rmi.*;
public interface RemoteRequest extends Remote {
    public void add(String[] newRecord) throws _
RemoteException;
    public void modify(Object id, String[] changes) throws _
RemoteException;
    public void delete(Object id) throws RemoteException;
    public void String[][] find(String match) throws _
RemoteException;
}
```

Remote is a "tagging" interface, like Serializable. All it does is identify implementers of this interface to the VM as objects that are eligible for remote access. It's also necessary for each abstract method to declare throwing RemoteException, the parent class for all the processes that can go wrong during a remote invocation.

The class that implements RemoteRequest, which we will name Request, has three conditions to meet. First, it needs the semantics that are peculiar to identifying an object in a remote contextits hashcode, toString() representation, and so on. Second, it must be give the host VM a way to export it to the object server providing its lookup service. The easiest way to satisfy both requirements is by extending UnicastRemoteObject. UnicastRemoteObject provides an export method the VM can call automatically when binding the object to its object server. This class also inherits its remote identification semantics from its parent, RemoteObject. Third, Request must explicitly provide a default constructor that throws RemoteException:

```
import java.rmi.*;
import java.rmi.server.*;
```

```
public class Request extends UnicastRemoteObject _
implements RemoteRequest {

    public Request() throws RemoteException {
        super();
    }

    public void add(String[] newRecord) {
    // code to add a record to the local database
    }
    …

}
```

If this class for some reason must extend something else, UnicastRemote-Object also supports a static **export()** method that takes the current object as an argument. This call can be added to the constructor:

```
UnicastRemoteObject.export(this);
```

Once the remote interface and implementing class are complete, we can generate the skeleton and stub classes that will be used to manage the communication endpoints between client and server. The tool that does this, rmic, takes the implementing class (not the .java source) as its argument and produces class files using the same name, but with _Skel.class and _Stub.class suffixes:

```
$ javac RemoteRequest.java Request.java
$ rmic Request
$ ls *.class
RemoteRequest.class
Request.class
Request_Skel.class
Request_Stub.class
```

RMI respectively calls on or distributes each class once a remote request occurs. The only requirement for these classes is that they reside in the same package space as the class they are generated from. To accommodate classes that are part of a package, the -d flag for rmic works the same as it does for javac.

The server code that sponsors the `Request` object is responsible for binding it to an RMI server. This service is launched through a tool bundled with the JDK called `rmiregistry`. This registry is really just another server like the one built early in this chapter. It sets itself up on an available port and waits for request from any client, local or remote. It functions as a registry by tracking all remote objects that any local VM binds to it. Since it operates autonomously from any VM on the same system, the VM must be given the port address of the registry. By default, `rmiregistry` attempts to use 1099 as its service port, but an optional one can be provided by passing the appropriate argument.

RMI for Java 2 adds a very interesting feature to its repertoire: the ability to launch the registry of one machine on demand, by way of a remote object request. The current registry has to run all the time, potentially taking up resources when it has no work to do. The JDK provides another tool, `rmid`, which behaves similarly to a Unix daemon or NT service, polling for requests to start up the registry when needed. A tutorial on acitvation is supplied with the JDK documentation. From the root directory for the documentation, locally or online, it is available at `docs/guide/rmi/activation.html`.

To bind a remote object to the registry, the server must first implement security. This step is a precaution against the client trying to pass an argument type with less than honorable intentions through the object server back to the application server. RMI does not mandate the use of a security manager, but it will refuse to load new classes coming from the client without one.

If we wanted the `Request` class to host its own registration code, we could add a main method to implement security and call `Naming.rebind()`. `rebind()` takes two arguments, a URL-style `String` representing the remote object's location, followed by a reference to the remote object itself:

```
public class Request extends UnicastRemoteObject _
implements RemoteRequest {
...

    public static void main(String args[]) {
        System.setSecurityManager(new RMISecurityManager());
        try {
```

```
                    // assume port 1099
                    String URL = "rmi://www.objserver.net/ DataRequest";
                    // Naming.rebind(URL, new Request());
                }
                catch(IOException ioe) {
                    // the parent exception to both RemoteException
                    // and MalformedURLException;
                    // rebind() throws both
                    ioe.printStackTrace();
                }
            }
```

The Naming class has a static bind() method, but in practice it is not often used. bind() throws one more exception than rebind() does, called AlreadyBoundException, which directly subclasses Exception. rebind(), but on the other hand, does not complain if its object wasn't already bound prior to being called, so it's used to refresh either a "null" or existing object registration.

The registration process by no means limits us to a single instance of the remote object type, but each instance does have to be uniquely named and individually registered.

In a system of any complexity, it would make sense to compose a single remote object through which other server resources could then be accessed. This "single resource" could even be the application server itself, providing a remote public interface to clients while reserving its internal operations—calls to the database, thread-scheduling and other local tasks—behind the scenes. This would certainly reduce name-space confusion when writing the client code. Under less than ideal circumstances, client-side programmers would have to document all of the object URLs required or add them and recompile code as they become available. This can get tedious quickly. The server-side developer, with good planning and design, could encapsulate all the required services through one remote reference and avoid that situation. Any way it's handled, using an incremental approach to adding RMI services means extra work. The new services have to be written and compiled, new stubs and skeletons generated, new registration code added, and client code modified to use them. We're almost back to where we started with creating elaborate protocols! Design and include all the necessary remote objects before implementing them, and there will be less to remember and maintain.

All this work on the server side translates to a relatively trivial coding task for the client. The client must be able to cast a remote reference to its class, although it may not use the class reference to instantiate objects of that type; it must instead use the Naming class to look up the object via an RMI protocol handler and the correct URL:

```
public class ClientSide {
    Request myRequest;
    String [][] schema;
    ...
    public void issueRequest() {
        try {
            myRequest =
            (Request)Naming.lookup("rmi://www.objserver.net/_
            DataRequest");
            // port 1099 assumed
            schema = myRequest.listScheme();
        }
        catch(AccessException re) {
        // A RemoteException subclass - shown for illustration
        }
        catch(RemoteException ae) {
         // all remote accesses throw this
        }
        catch(NotBoundException nbe){
        // an Exception subclass thrown if the lookup fails
        }
        ...
    }
    ...
}
```

The client code then calls methods on the `myRequest` reference just as if were a local object. RMI handles all the subsequent details. Here we've also laid out in detail the exceptions that a call to `lookup()` requires us to catch. Often these are ignored in example code by catching `RemoteException`, the parent class to most exceptions thrown when using RMI. Taking this shortcut also obscures the opportunity to recover from specific faults. On an `AccessException`, for example, a specific message pertaining to what action was denied could be crucial information to debugging. If we just catch the parent class, we can get an exception name and a stack trace if we want them, but no further information that could be provided in an exception-specific catch clause.

## Limitations of RMI

Glossing over exceptions in complex, distributed code is a mild symptom of one of the more severe limitations of choosing RMI in any project: it can be exceptionally hard to debug a complex distributed application, particularly if the client and server are multithreaded. RMI renders many underlying operations transparent to the application code, which is a great advantage in many ways. It's not RMI's fault that it's easy to defeat proper exception-handling by catching parents and super-parents. Nonetheless, that fact that runtime bugs can be obscured by the lack of a robust reporting mechanism may influence the perception that somehow RMI is at fault. However transparent RMI renders remote services at the code level, there is a deeper responsibility that the developer must take for a proper and thorough implementation of RMI's services. It is not a "pop-in" replacement for a more straightforward, if less robust technique, that writing proprietary serialization schemes.

Step-tracing through an RMI problem can be a technically overwhelming task without the right tools—assuming anyone has them. A debug walk-through in this environment means being able to walk through the stacks of two (or more) independent VM's, each of which is running simultaneously and quite possibly threading its activities among local and remote tasks. That said, there's no reason RMI programming must be overly complex, but it's easy to slip into bad habits and take a few shortcuts just to get something up and running. If multithreading is added as an afterthought, the application could well be at risk. The protocol-based approach we took earlier in the chapter makes us write more of the ground-level code by hand, but there is always only one VM acting on a serialized object at a time, which is easier to isolate.

Read Java Software's current FAQ on RMI and Object Serialization for a rundown on common misunderstandings developers encounter when deploying RMI. The FAQ is available locally or online, relative to the documentation's root directory, at `/docs/guide/rmi/faq.html`.

Another condition any RMI implementation has to look out for is in the way remote requests enter the server's local threading scheme. It's possible for Client A to look up Remote Reference B, which calls on Server object C, on which some other server-local object is synchronizing. Without carefully negotiating the asynchronous requests of remote clients with what the server wants to execute locally, the potential for deadlocking the server and hanging the VM is high. Again this problem goes back to design and properly accounting for interaction on the server side.

On various newsgroups and mailing lists that discuss RMI, there has been a fair amount of discussion about RMI's performance. The range of experiences reported in these forums are almost exclusively comparative and seem to vary from much faster than CORBA to a degree or two slower, depending on the design and type of implementation. But it's difficult to determine where the true mean in experiences lie: it's far easier to write toy code and benchmark it than it is to invest in a full-fledged example and gauge experience in production.

We can certainly infer that serializing entire objects, when only a small part of the data needed to be sent plays a part in reports of sluggish performance, a point which brings us to a major difference between RMI and CORBA. RMI can pass objects by value, whereas CORBA, a model predicated on distributed code among heterogenous systems, only offers passing values by reference. The developer has to be aware that passing a 10 MB Vector is just as easy as passing a 15-character byte array, where RMI is concerned. Careful design, again, is imperative, to keep track of exactly what kind of information (and how much of it) the completed system will send over the wire.

A full appreciation of RMI starts with understanding the functional differences between a local object and a remote one. With those characteristics fully understood, the benefits of the architecture can be weighed more effectively against its potential costs. At the same time, RMI is not so complex that experimenting with it will take substantially longer than writing straight "object protocol" code, once the functional steps are committed to memory.

# More on Threads

**U**p to this point in our discussions about the developer's exam, we've addressed threading on a tactical level, suggesting a few possible ways to deploy them, but without creating a robust, working model of any one type. These hints and code fragments reflect an underlying philosophy to provide ideas and initial explorations that will help set the stage for the requirements of the project assignment. Providing some ready-made templates for implementation toward a generic project might be more to the point, but it would not help you to justify your work, as will be required on the follow-up exam. You must be able to articulate the relative merits of your work against other possible choices, and for that, a survey of possible answers is better preparation than a given few.

At the same time, concurrent programming, and Java threads in particular, are respectively multiple-volume and book-length subjects in their own right. It's not easy to simply "survey" threading strategies, so in this chapter's final section we will take a look at one thread-pooling strategy that may prove a useful complement to building the network server.

## Sharing Threads

One complex aspect of writing a multi-threaded application server is choosing a way to define how client requests will run. A request to the server implies a temporary need for its resources, which can be restored and allocated to subsequent requests—if we remember to reclaim them. But when that resource is a thread, a notably finite resource on any system, extra caution is warranted. Threads are not intended, by their nature, to be instanced, run, and dereferenced without some regard for the system-level resources involved in maintaining them. We can demonstrate this by creating a thread *pool*, or a collection of thread references that are continually "re-referenced" as their current tasks run their course, and compare that technique side by side with an application that creates new threads on demand and de-allocates them when their execution tasks complete.

Intuitively, we should expect to conserve a substantial amount of resources. As the need for more threads increases, the cost of object creation and garbage-collection should increase, perhaps rising proportionately with the number of threaded tasks submitted. In a pooled-resource model, our thread creation costs are incurred up front. After that, we reuse those resources continually, avoiding object creation and destruction in favor of referencing and dereferencing Runnable objects. It also stands to reason that the more efficient the arrangement for managing the thread pool, the more time or system-level resources can be conserved, up to some hard limit.

Another important point to make about threading: just because an object is Runnable doesn't mean it needs a thread. Runnable is just an interface. It is a contract to implement a run() method, and an agreement into which any class may enter. By itself, the run() method is not especially significant. If a subclass of Applet were to implement Runnable, calling its start() method would not invoke threaded behavior. What makes a Runnable object so potentially powerful is that one of the Thread class' constructors will accept one as an argument. It is the Thread class itself that contains the tools necessary to endow a Runnable with its own line of execution, and only a thread construction that ties up system resources.

To demonstrate all of these points, and to give you something more to think about in preparation for the project assignment, we've provided the Share-Thread class. This is a very simple subclass of Thread with just four methods and one constructor. All the constructor does is call setDaemon() and set it to true. Daemon threads are a special case; any application that has them may exit if only daemon threads are currently running. There are two methods that attempt to run a submitted job, execute() and executeIfAvailable(). Both synchronize on the current ShareThread instance. execute() waits until workToDo loses its current reference, then assigns it a new one. execute-IfAvailable(), on the other hand, tests workToDo to see if it is set to null during the current synchronized execution. If so, workToDo is given a new job. This is a one-shot attempt that makes the method appear clumsy. At the same time, it returns a boolean indicating success or failure in assigning a new job, so the responsibility is on the programmer to write a proper loop and test it.

Then ShareThread's run() method does an interesting thing. It synchronizes on its own instance, immediately returning if any thread other than the correct instance of ShareThread tries to run it. The method then waits until workToDo acquires a reference, rather than loses one. When that condition occurs, the new job is immediately reassigned to a temporary variable created within run(). Just before calling notifyAll(), workToDo is dereferenced again so that either execute method can assign a waiting job to it. But outside the synchronized block, the temporary variable calls run() directly on the Runnable object it now refers to. Since the current instance of Share-Thread is already a thread, the job does not require a thread of its own:

```java
/**
 * ShareThread is a poolable thread resource capable of
 * accepting and and executing small Runnable jobs repeatedly.
 *
 * @author Sybex Certification Study Guide authors
 */
public class ShareThread extends Thread {
    private Runnable workToDo;

    /**
 * Sets this "pooled thread" instance as a daemon so the program
 * can exit if this is the only thing left.
 */
    public ShareThread() {
        setDaemon(true);
    }

    /**
     * execute() waits until the internal Runnable reference is
 * null, then assigns it a new job.
     *
 * @param Runnable - an object that requires a thread resource
 */
    public void execute(Runnable job) {
        synchronized(this) {
            while(workToDo != null) {
                try {
                    wait();
                }
                catch(InterruptedException ie) { }
            }
            workToDo = job;
            notifyAll();
        }
```

```
    }
/**
 * executeIfAvailable() checks once to see if no job is
 * pending. If not, a job is assigned, the boolean flag set to
 * true, and all waiting threads notified.
 *
 * @param Runnable - an object that needs its run() method
 * called.
 * @returns boolean - indicating whether a job was
 * successfully assigned
 */
public boolean executeIfAvailable(Runnable job) {
    boolean executed = false;

    synchronized(this) {
        if (workToDo == null) {
            workToDo = job;
            executed = true;
            notifyAll();
        }
    }
    return executed;
}


/**
 * A "snapshot" check whether a job is currently assigned.
 * Not reliable beyond the moment of the test.
 *
 * @return boolean - indicates whether a job is assigned.
 */
public boolean available() {
    return (workToDo == null);
}

/**
```

```
 * Rejects any thread that is not owned by the current
 * instance. Waits until a Runnable job is assigned, then
 * calls its run() method directly, acting as its surrogate
 * Thread instance. Signals for another job by dereferencing
 * the current one. Terminates when no more user-level jobs
 * are available.
 */
public void run() {
    if (Thread.currentThread() == this) {
        Runnable job = null;
        for (;;) {
            synchronized(this) {
                while (workToDo == null) {
                    try {
                        wait();
                    }
                    catch(InterruptedException ie) {}
                }
                r = workToDo;

                notifyAll();
            }
             job.run();
            workToDo = null;
        }
    }
}
```

The call to job.run() illustrates that the run method itself has no inherently threaded properties. If a job is called and executed within another threaded instance, it performs the same way as if it had constructed its own thread instance, minus the costs of object creation. The jobs that are submitted to this class could be any object that implements Runnable, such as the Request class, minus its thread instantiation code. This class lends itself well to a round-robin approach to satisfying data requests. Round-robin is a technique that isn't known to scale well, unless more "robins" can be added easily. In this situation, that's precisely the case. The larger the number of requests expected, the more ShareThread objects that could be created to meet demand. Of course, the limiting factor will still lie in the ability of the database to expedite requests.

As a final demonstration, the code below is suitable for ShareThread's main() method. It compares the time needed for a given number of Share-Thread objects to execute a number of "joblets" against the time needed for the same number of jobs to instance their own threads and run individually. Use this code and experiment with a variety of pooled thread and joblet-count combinations. When you are satisfied that there is a clear difference in performance between the two, consider applying this model to your future project assignment.

```java
public class ShareThread {
...

  /**
   * Test facility that compares pooled threading to straight
   * threading of every submitted job.  Launch this program with
   * the following syntax:
   * <PRE>java ShareThread <num_threads> <num_jobs> <job>
   * num_threads is how many threads to pool.
   * num_jobs is the total number of Runnable jobs to queue.
   * job is a class that implements Runnable</PRE>
   */
  public static void main(String args[]) throws Exception {

          //timing variables
      long startPool, startThreads, stopPool, stopThreads;

      final int totalJobs = Integer.parseInt(args[0]);
      final int threadPool = Integer.parseInt(args[1]);
      // runnables accounts for multiple job types submitted
      final int runnables = Integer.parseInt(args.length - 2);

      Runnable[] joblets = new Runnable[totalJobs * runnables];
```

```java
// populates the joblets array with the number of jobs
// requested times the total Runnable types given
for (int i = 0; i < runnables; i++){
    Class class = Class.forName(args[i + 2]);
    for (int j = 0; j < totalJobs; j++) {
        joblets[i + j * runnables] = (Runnable) _
        (class.newInstance());
    }
}

System.out.println("Running " + joblets.length + " jobs _
in " +
    threadPool + "worker threads.\n");
//begin timer on threadpool
startPool = System.currentTimeMillis();

ShareThread[] workers = new ShareThread[threadpool];
for (int i = 0; I < workers.length; i++) {
    workers[i] = new ShareThread();
    workers[i].start();
}

// simple looping strategy to assign a job to any
// available worker instance
int iLoop = 0;
int jLoop = 0;
while (iLoop < joblets.length) {
    while (!workers[jLoop].executeIfAvailable(joblets _
    [iLoop])) {
        jLoop++;
        if (jLoop = workers.length) jLoop = 0;
    }
    Thread.yield();
    jLoop = 0;
    iLoop++;
}
```

```
        // another simple loop to see if all workers are idle
        // if so, we're done
        for (iLoop = 0; iLoop < workers.length; i++) {
            while(!workers[iLoop].available()){
                Thread.yield();
            }
        }
        stopPool = System.currentTimeMillis();
        System.out.println("Pooling all joblets took: " +
            (stopPool - startPool) + " milliseconds.\n");


        System.out.println("Now giving each job a thread.\n");


        // Use a threadgroup to monitor all threads
        ThreadGroup group = new ThreadGroup("Threaded joblets");
        startThreads = System.currentTimeMillis();


        // Launch a thread for each joblet, and track all joblet
        // completions as a group to stop the clock.
        for (int i = 0; i < joblets.length; i++) {
            Thread thr = new Thread(group, joblets[i]);
            t.start();
        }
        while(group.activeCount() > 0) {
            Thread.yield();
        }


        stopThreads = System.currentTimeMillis();
        System.out.println("Threading all joblets took: " +
            (stopThreads - startThreads) + " milliseconds.\n");
    }
}
```

The test class doesn't need to be much, just enough to cause a tick or two. As the number of jobs scales, the threaded test won't have any problem chewing up time. With pooled threads, make sure the sample Runnable can burn a few cycles, or you may get a few test runs that report taking no time. Here's an example test:

```
public class Tester implements Runnable {
    public void run() {
        double val = getX() * getY();
    }

    private double getX() {
        return 3;
    }

    private double getY() {
        return 4;
    }
}
```

# Chapter Summary

**B**uilding the application server brings together at least one aspect of each of the major components in a client-server environment. While the choices for network communication are relatively few, they are very different—and each technique has its own range of strengths and limitations. Building a network protocol between client and server is easy, but is limited to a synchronous exchange of objects between the two VMs and doesn't allow for interaction between them beyond what has already been scripted into the code. Object serialization hides the details of committing objects to a stream, but still requires us to handle writing objects in over the network in a sequence we have to define: there's no getting away from writing a proprietary protocol.

RMI makes everything look very simple from the client perspective. Instead of instantiating objects that exist on a remote server, we simply look them up to start using them. Each object we work with is otherwise transparent in its remoteness. Each object always resides on one machine, virtually eliminating the problem of state inconsistency that could arise with overly complex interactions in which objects themselves are being passed back and forth over the wire in serial form. At the same time, RMI hides so many layers of detail, that when something goes wrong it can be difficult to find. Not the least of the obstacles is determining which VM originated the problem. RMI requires considerably more planning and design consideration before implementing. Casual oversights in RMI means lots of maintenance later on, and lots of class rewrites and recompiles if we try to fix problems wholesale.

Once the choice of network technique has been made, however, we can give more thought to how threading plays a role in the whole scheme. This is admittedly a lot trickier to contend with in an RMI scheme, and multithreading questions should be pursued early in an RMI scheme rather than later.

As a final note, when looking for an efficient way to deal with lots of short requests to the application, consider using a thread pool to conserve on object creation and destruction.

# CHAPTER

# 18

## Designing the User Interface

ots of programmers whose efforts focus on writing business applications like to write the user interface first. The simple fact is that most people can absorb far more information in less time from a well-designed picture than they can from a well-written technical document. End-users, particularly those who are removed from the process of programming, usually see a program's effectiveness in the form of the interaction it offers. Screen shots still sell far more programs than any other single marketing tool.

One of the more important decisions made within many corporate development efforts is not just the choice of a programming platform, but which "builder tool" to standardize on. The rise of rapid application development (RAD) tools, fourth-generation languages (4GL), and "integrated development environments" (IDE) is all based on the perception that direct visual feedback promotes faster and easier code writing than the code-compile-test cycle of a pure text environment. One end result of these developments seems to be that developers as well as users are just as interested in what programs will look like as what features they offer.

The GUI doesn't mean much, of course, unless it helps get the work done. Nor does it make sense to write application logic based on how the presentation will be structured. Java's Swing library addresses this issue in a very smart way, by decoupling the responsibilities of data presentation and manipulation into two different class groups. One outcome is that the data model, once developed, places no real constraints on the potential views for it and vice versa. Since the cohesion between data and graphic elements have already been spelled out, development of the GUI in Swing could begin with either part or it could progress in parallel in a team environment, without generating any fundamental concern for bringing the two together.

Another beauty of Swing is that this fundamental design pattern, often described as "loosely based on Model-View-Controller (MVC)," is repeated throughout the library. Once you understand Swing's particular take on this pattern, which we call "model-delegate," most of what's left to know is a question of details. We won't worry about a comprehensive class review; exhaustive treatments of Swing are available if you want one. We will focus instead on four topics we do not see covered in detail elsewhere and that will directly benefit you in preparing for the project assignment. Once you have the basics down, you can reference the Swing library as necessary and absorb the details you need to write the client you want.

See the section in Chapter 15, "Write a User Interface," for a brief definition of the MVC design pattern and how Swing departs from it.

Assuming you'll have to build the client the same way you did the network server—from the ground up—there are five points to address that will assist you in writing your GUI and defending it on the follow-up exam:

- Defining the GUI requirements

- How Swing components and models work

- Using layout managers

- Event-handling and coding style

- Event-handling and threading

# Defining the GUI's Requirements

There's an even better tool for modeling a graphic interface than a drag-and-drop code builder—pencil and paper. The single best recommendation we can make on designing your program's appearance is to just draw what you'd like to see on the screen. You can create a sketch for one or two GUI layouts in the time it takes your computer to boot. They are likely to capture more of your requirements and create less of a distraction than finding the proper widget in a draw program (unless, of course, you are already expert with one). Since there is usually less investment in designing on paper, it's easier to throw away bad ideas (one of the more important design principles we know). Unless you already have the digital art skills or an existing template for the kind of display you want in hand, a legible drawing makes a very reasonable initial reference document.

Here's a simple four-step plan:

1. Identify needed components.

2. Sketch the GUI and a resizing.

3. Isolate regions of behavior.

4. Choose layout managers.

## Identify Needed Components

However austere the AWT's list of components might seem, it does have the advantage of economically describing the graphic objects in use on the most popular windowing systems today—Motif, Windows, and MacOS. It's therefore quite simple for virtually all GUI developers to express basic visual ideas in those terms: buttons for actions, checkboxes for toggles, lists for specified choices, text fields for arbitrary input, and so on. A microwave control panel, for example, is easy to conceive as one or more groups of buttons and a display for the time. The front of a tower computer translates easily—were we inclined to design one graphically—into a grid of 5$^{1/4}$" device faces; a tall, thin panel of status lights; a column of 3$^{1/2}$" wide device faces; a power button; and so on.

User interfaces are not that much different once the requirements are defined. But it can be difficult, once having identified the needed pieces, to verbalize how they should lay on the page and how they should respond to a window resizing. The menu belongs at the top—we know that. Generally speaking, if there is a primary display area—whether graphic, tabular, or document-oriented in presentation—we will want to devote any extra available space to it on a resize. Beyond those two principles, we need more information about what our application is. Let's assume for the sake of an illustration that we want to build a mail client in Java and our first design review will concern the visual layout for a large number of departmental users. We know we will want to display a directory structure for sorting stored mail. Users will expect a table or list element to show mail items in the current directory; a text display for the current item being read; and a "status" area for updates on the client's background actions—downloading new messages, signaling new mail, and so forth.

## Sketching the GUI

In our example in Figure 18.1, we profile the appearance of a typical mail client. The interface requires an area where we can review our directory tree of sorted mail, which we placed to the left. We also want an area at the bottom of the frame for displaying status messages on the client's current attempt to send or retrieve mail. A dynamic display area for the list of current incoming mail is located to the right of the tree structure and on top of another dynamic area that displays the current mail item. We want the detailed list of pending mail to be laid out by column and to show the column names in a button. We expect that experienced users will get the idea to click on a column name and infer from the results that a sort has taken place. As a provision for user preferences, we also want to allow the column size to be modified by dragging the column button's border.

**FIGURE 18.1**

Mail Client window resized

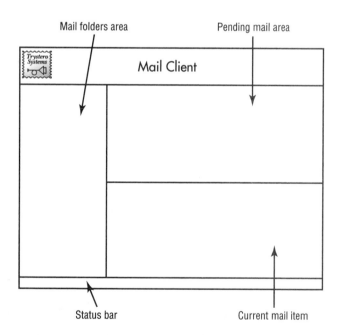

To get these ideas to paper, we sketched out a fairly conventional diagram with a menu bar on top, a flush-left panel with a tree-like figure drawn in, and a bottom bar with some sample text. The dynamic space we have split in two regions, showing the columnar support for the mail list but a blank border area for the current mail. We have split this area in equal parts so that a resize will better demonstrate who is acquiring the new space and in which direction.

Figure 18.2 shows the intended effect of the resize. In our example we wanted the mail item currently being read to assume as much available area as it can, on the presumption that the user resizes the window to get as much text to show as possible. While some users may in fact want a larger font for status messages or a dynamic font for the menu, we've chosen not to tie such preferences to the default behavior of dragging a window corner.

**FIGURE 18.2**

Mail Client window

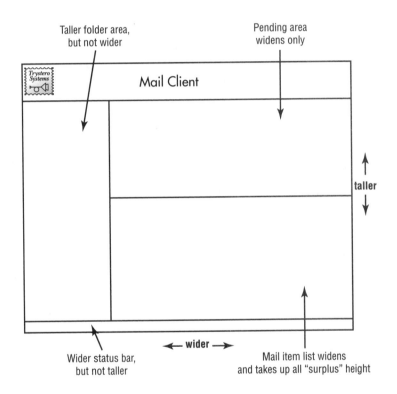

Along the horizontal axis, we want the bottom section to allow the status message area to use as much space as available, but without usurping the minimum space needed by the small icons. In the menu, we've followed the universal convention that the "Help" or "About" menu list appears flush right on the frame. Both of the displays of the mail item and mail list grow to the right but do not impinge on the tree view. Along the vertical axis, our tree-area takes all the space the menu and status bars will allow. In our display area the current mail item view resizes; the mail list remains fixed.

## Isolating Regions of Behavior

Hopefully the description given of the behavior shown in the figures, combined with your knowledge of the AWT layout managers, already tipped you off to some appropriate layout choices. There is, of course, no single answer or "right" choice to make for the entire screen. Any reasonably sophisticated interface requires multiple layout managers and panels to contain the management behavior to its prescribed area, and there is no one formula for ordering or nesting those panels to get the desired effect. Yet neither is there a completely neutral way to describe the behavior we want. It probably wasn't hard to tell we already were thinking in terms of BorderLayout when we wrote the description above, in particular by our attempt to avoid saying "north," "south," "center," and so on. And this result is, in fact, exactly what we should expect—if we can articulate the screen behavior we want, the isolation of one region from the next and the tool needed to achieve the intent should be virtually self-evident.

This mail client breaks down very cleanly into the geographical areas provided by BorderLayout, the default management scheme for an AWT or Swing frame or window. The south will contain a status bar and small icons and the tree will go in the west, leaving the center with the two dynamic areas. The center and south need a little more work to negotiate space allocation among the contained elements. In the south, the message bar and icons can first be contained by a panel. The panel, which is then added to the south, can adopt its own BorderLayout (instead of its default FlowLayout), putting the message element in the panel's center and the icons in the east. Putting the icons in the east ensures that the icons get as much horizontal space as they require, and the center grabs all remaining space for messages. In the center we add another panel with a BorderLayout manager, putting the mail list in its north and mail item in the center.

This is a decent first cut, but a second look will tell us we might have to rethink things as we refine the scheme. Just because we do not want the mail list to resize on a window control doesn't necessarily mean we don't want the user to have some control over setting the height requirement altogether. Also, if this window can't fit the messages listed in it, we'd like to have a scrollbar. If it has more space than it needs, a scrollbar that can't move but takes up space is a bit of an annoyance, but a price we pay with AWT components. The remaining option, prior to Swing, was to write our own.

The west can hold the tree we want without further help, but adding a panel first and then adding the tree to the panel is not a bad idea. It is one way of leaving options open to modifying that area of the border scheme rather than just the contained component itself. Getting in the habit of composing graphic areas this way so that they can be added to a larger "component-container" frame and hooked in—we're whispering a loose definition for a JavaBean here—is an honorable way to build task-specific, reusable components. As we're about to discuss, however, Swing components already do that work for us.

## Choosing Layout Managers

When you do come across limitations in the layout model, it's not a time to worry. The default layout managers, along with `Grid`, are widely applicable to a number of visual design objectives and relatively simple to use. Whether they will suffice to handle a particular requirement well is a good first question to ask. In most cases, you should probably consider several alternative layout schemes to ensure you are choosing a simple approach that provides enough flexibility for some foreseeable changes. It's very nice to have choices for future improvements, but there is also a limit to how much versatility is a benefit. For example, if a programmer is required to survey a variety of open-ended alternatives that could just as easily been left static with no real loss of benefit, the value of having so many of "pluggables" may get lost in forcing many subtle decisions.

If you do have complex requirements and a compelling reason to implement them fully—for example, to successfully complete a certification exam—there are very powerful layout tools already available in the JDK. The Programmer's Exam already tests your understanding of the fundamentals of the AWT layout managers,. Chapter 10 provides some background and Java philosophy on layout management, then explores these three managers in detail. In this chapter's "Using Layout Managers" section, we complement that discussion by looking at another special-purpose manager, `CardLayout`, and then the Swiss-army knife of layout managers, `GridBagLayout`.

# Using Swing

As mentioned in Chapters 14 and 15, the Swing library brings several new dimensions to graphic programming in Java. The first structural feature worth noticing is Swing's adaptation of a design pattern known as Model-View-Controller (MVC). In that pattern, the data, presentation, and data controls are decoupled from each other. Separating these roles into discrete classes allows the data to provide a generic interface to all possible views so that any number of views can form their data descriptions from a single centralized source. Each one can then visually describe the model according to the set or subset of data that it is most interested in. The term that is catching on with respect to Swing's recast of this arrangement is "model-delegate." The important concept to enforce by this renaming is that Swing employs a two-role version of MVC, the data model, and the view-controller.

The controller function is already built into Java by way of its event-handling facility, but Swing even takes that a step further by taking full advantage of JavaBeans' architecture in its components. For the purposes of our discussion, Beans can be oversimplified a little; they are characterized by a series of "properties " that are simply a class' existing field members supplied with a pair of formulaic get/set method signatures. Should you pick up a comprehensive book on Swing, you'll undoubtedly notice numerous references to the "properties" of each component. Beans are also designed to communicate state changes to their properties, not just that they've passed over by a mouse or been iconified. Other interested Beans can listen to these "fired" changes and behave appropriately. For example, if the listening Bean has an identical property, it can match the change. This might result in a change to the color of one component that would cause a whole group of components to change together. The advantage of this scheme is that changes in one Bean can be *bound* to changes in another, making it possible for one Bean to act as a "controller" for any component that wants to subscribe to the service.

As a further step, Beans can be configured to veto changes sent to them, rejecting values that exceed a normal range for the target Bean or whatever rule that Bean institutes. Of course, this process only has value to the sending Bean if it can learn whether its target accepts or rejects a change, and then it can respond. The sending Bean may wish to "roll back" to the previous state if the target Bean cannot comply or, in the case of multiple targets, attempt to set all target Beans to the last agreed-upon state. See Figure 18.3 for an illustration of each of these Bean-style events.

There's more to the total make-up of a Bean, but much of the rest deals with managing them in a builder tool, which we don't have to worry about. The following sections discuss two component types that are particularly important to us: tables and lists. In keeping with Swing's model-delegate paradigm, we'll examine both aspects of these components—the way they present themselves and the way they hold the data that is used to create the presentation. It's also worth noting how Swing takes advantage of a structural model we discussed in Chapter 16. Swing relies heavily on interfaces and abstract classes in promoting its components, often providing a reference implementation model either for recommended use or as a guide in building your own. As for toolkit design, this is a practice of the first quality. Take time to look around the source code for some of these classes and take some notes on how it's been implemented.

**FIGURE 18.3**

Three Bean event
models

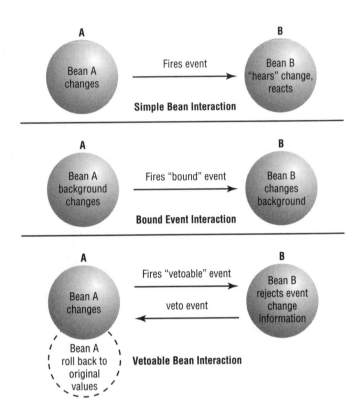

In the following sections, we take a look at two of three data-intensive Swing component types: tables and lists. As it stands, the organization of these two types is very similar. We're confident a structural overview of these two types and their support classes will fill in the blanks for you on the third component type, trees, leaving the implementation details of that type for you to master at your convenience.

## Tables

The organization of classes for representing tabular data breaks down into three principal subgroups: the widget JTable, the table model, and the table column model. A list of the support classes for each, particularly the models, will give you a sense of the consistency of structure that will also apply to lists and trees. The following lists are not all-inclusive lists of relationships.

### *JTable* (Class)

- JTableHeader (class)
- TableCellEditor (interface)
- TableCellRenderer (interface)
- DefaultTableCellRenderer (class) (implements TableCellRenderer)

### *TableModel* (Interface)

- AbstractTableModel (abstract class) (implements TableModel)
- DefaultTableModel (class) (extends AbstractTableModel)
- TableModelEvent (class)
- TableModelListener (interface)

### *TableColumnModel* (Interface)

- TableColumn (class)
- DefaultTableColumnModel (class) (implements TableColumnModel)
- TableColumnModelEvent (class)
- TableColumnModelListener (interface)

A table in Swing uses the column as its smallest organizing unit; a table does not model itself at the cell level. Columns make sense, because they organize a specific data type, give it a descriptive name, and track important properties (such as field width). The TableColumn class itself represents a column. The interface TableColumnModel, as the name implies, provides the semantics for collecting a series of TableColumn objects together to represent a table row or record. This interface requires altogether implementation for nineteen methods; fortunately, DefaultTableColumnModel provides a standard implementation and includes event "firing" methods that broadcast changes in column behavior—deletion, addition, order change, selection change, and margin change. The event and listener classes associated with table columns are what you would expect—a means for generating column-oriented event objects and getting notifications when they occur.

The general and more important model is TableModel itself. TableModel adds a layer of control on top of column objects, which allows an implementation of the interface to return information on its table—row count, column count, and column names among them. Information reported on columns is not tied to what TableColumnModel reports, which makes it possible to report columns with non-unique names or hide columns. TableModel also adds methods for accessing rows and cells.

One aspect of model-view relationships that may take some getting used to is that data model representations maintain column order independent of the view. When we want to rearrange data on the view level, for example, we don't want to be restricted to the model's internal arrangement of columns. We may decide we would rather have last names before first names or states before zip codes. Conversely, we do not want casual reorganization of the display to generate work for the model, forcing it to rearrange itself to reflect what the user sees. Therefore, there are always two accounts of what the data looks like—the order in which the widget table presents it and the order in which the underlying model maintains it. There is no obligation for either to match its arrangement to the other. The good news is that TableModel doesn't have to listen to events in the view regarding column activity. The better news is that indexing by column or row through any of the supporting classes follows the view. The mapping between the view and the model is hidden from the programmer so that the view can serve as a guide. Be wary of the three exceptions where the model's index order is maintained rather than the view's index order. If you decide to dig around a bit, bear in mind that the model's indexing of columns is kept in three places:

- TableModel in its entirety

- The TableColumn field modelIndex

- TableModelEvent constructors that get their values from TableModel

It's not required that you explicitly build models to create a JTable. You have the option to do so, of course, and it will make sense when you are thinking ahead to multiple types of presentation that can be based on one model of data. Otherwise, JTable is smart enough to accept hard-coded data or row-column dimensions in integer or Vector form and then construct default models using the inferred dimensions. One element that may not be immediately apparent is that JTable can also be constructed with a ListSelectionModel to support row selection. Details on ListSelectionModel are included with the discussion on lists.

## Lists

There are three big changes between AWT and Swing lists. First, JList can contain any object as an item. The only requirement is some means must be provided for drawing a representation of the object if a toString conversion would not suffice. This is a vast improvement over the Strings-only support of List. Second, where the AWT List enforces "pick-style" or multiple selections at random points on the list, JList supports range selection. Range selection is defined by its *anchor* (or initial selection) and its *lead* (or the last element pointed to when a selection is completed). Third, like all other Swing components, JList has no built-in scrollbar. To incorporate one, an instance of JList must be passed as the argument to a JScrollPane constructor. From that point forward, JScrollPane acts as a viewport to the list view, only providing scroll elements to the pane if the horizontal or vertical reach of the list's contents exceeds the viewable area.

The pattern of support classes for lists are quite similar to that for tables. However, lists have one less dimension to manage, so there are fewer roles to flesh out into classes. Nonetheless, these should look very familiar:

### *JList* (Class)

- ListCellRenderer (interface)
- DefaultListCellRenderer (class)

### *ListModel* (Interface)

- AbstractListModel (abstract class) (implements ListModel)
- DefaultListModel (class) (extends AbstractListModel)
- ListDataEvent (class)
- ListDataListener (interface)

### *ListSelectionModel* (interface)

- DefaultListSelectionModel (class) (implements ListSelectionModel)
- ListSelectionEvent (class)
- ListSelectionListener (interface)

Providing modeling support for lists is quite simple, but it's good design form to model the list's selection state separately from the arrangement of list data itself in the same manner that column behavior is de-coupled from the overall data management for tables. A few properties are worth noting when dealing with selection behavior. selectionMode allows the programmer to define single element, single range, or multiple range selection as the allowed behavior. Naturally, a selection of one item is just a special case of a range, one whose anchor and lead point to the same index value. valueIsAdjusting indicates whether the list object is currently firing events. This can be a useful state check condition if you want to wait on new actions to the list until the current changes have been broadcast.

As with AWT List events, the broadcast of an event change does not necessarily mean a list selection has changed from its previous value. The only thing we can infer from receiving a list selection event is that some action took place on the JList and the item state might have changed as a result. In order to learn exactly what happened, we have to look at the event object itself; we cannot rely on the fact of an event alone to make decisions.

ListModel looks suspiciously like the beginnings of a Vector, as it supports two properties—elementAt and size. It's method list only supports these properties and the requisite methods for the Beans registration model—addListDataEventListener() and removeListDataEventListener(). As expected, the abstract class implementation AbstractListModel augments this with methods for firing changes to interested listeners. The DefaultList-Model class bears out our hunch—it's almost a pure Vector. If you can handle questions on Vector for the Programmer's Exam, you'll have no problem mastering the DefaultListModel.

There are suggestions in the API and Sun Web sites that this implementation may change for future releases of Swing. One motivation is to tie Swing in more tightly with the Collections framework. In the meantime, any Java programmer who works with data structures or Beans has come across a Vector before, so it's familiar territory. To keep up to date on this and other Swing developments, you can browse http://java.sun.com/products/jfc/tsc/.

# Using Layout Managers

**A**pplying layout managers is all about matching the component behavior required with the manager that best provides it. As mentioned above, the only purpose of this section is to make sure your kit of layout managers is complete. Here we fully describe the use of the two more advanced layout managers from the AWT, and show some sample code for demonstrating CardLayout, and the beginnings of a scheme for learning how to manage a GridBagLayout. If you have already taken the time to learn the default layout managers, you're aware that it takes a few coding attempts to get a full sense of each layout manager's capabilities. With CardLayout, things are straightforward—just off the beaten path of layout managers. Learning GridBagLayout is an investment of your time and focus. It is something you should definitely look at twice before you think about applying it to your project assignment.

# CardLayout

CardLayout differs from the other layout management in the ways it works. Instead of negotiating the screen's real estate among the contending preferred sizes of all the components, it organizes in layers. Though component overlap represents a misstep in layout among the other four managers, in CardLayout it's expected behavior. Consequently, it's the only layout manager that supplies a navigation scheme to flip through the number of cards made in a given container. Cards also link tail-to-head, so that flipping past the last card brings up the first in the series. The methods first(), last(), next(), and previous() each take the layout's parent container as an argument and are self-evident in action.

To add each component to a card, both the component and its constraints object must be specified in the add() argument of the container. In the case of CardLayout, the constraints object must be a String object; if it isn't, the method will throw an IllegalArgumentException. This String name is entered into a table as a key to the card with which it is associated. Calling on the show() method with this key then allows for direct access to any card in the set. Listed below is a brief program to display a random card in the stack. Each card is a button with its number as a label. The program shows a card, waits an interval, and then picks another at random. The horizontal and vertical insets as well as the number of buttons wanted are entered at the command line like so:

```
$ java CardShow 5 5 25

import javax.swing.*;
import java.awt.*;

public class CardShow extends JPanel implements Runnable {
    private CardLayout clo;
    JButton jb[];

    public CardShow(int hgap, int vgap, int nbut) {
```

```
            clo = new CardLayout(hgap,vgap);
            setLayout(clo);
            jb = new JButton[nbut];

            for (int i = 0; i < jb.length; i++) {
                jb[i] = new JButton("Button: " + i);
                String number = new String(""+i);
                add(jb[i],number);
            }
        }

        public void run() {
            while (true) {
                try {
                    Thread.sleep(1250);
                }
                catch(InterruptedException ie) {}
                String rand = "" + (int)(Math.random() * jb.length);
                clo.show(this, rand);
            }
        }

        public static void main(String args[]) {
            // horizontal gap
            int horGap = Integer.parseInt(args[0]);
            // vertical gap
            int verGap = Integer.parseInt(args[1]);
            // # of buttons
            int numButtons = Integer.parseInt(args[2]);
            CardShow cs = new CardShow(horGap, verGap, numButtons);

            JFrame jf = new JFrame("Flash Card");
            Container con = jf.getContentPane();
            con.add(cs, BorderLayout.CENTER);
            jf.pack();
            jf.setVisible(true);
            Thread t = new Thread(cs);
            t.start();
        }
    }
```

# GridBagLayout

Getting accustomed to layout managers is sometimes a chore. Spending the time to mentally associate a layout class' methods and field controls with its presentation takes a fair amount of practice and patience, especially when the components or their containers manifest what seems like competing behavior. GridBagLayout, of all the layout managers, is the one that is the most demanding in this regard. It is often deemed overly complex, hard to get accustomed to, and difficult to manage. It is the only layout manager with a separate helper class, GridBagConstraints, for dealing with the thirteen different behavioral variables it adds to the usual constraints of preferred size and minimum size. Unfortunately, GridBagConstraints only provides two constructors, a no-arg constructor that sets default values for all the layout variables and another that requires the implementer to provide a default for every one of them. The latter, of course, is recommended for use only with a GUI builder tool that automates the process of setting those values. But in order to deal with each of these variables individually, a Grid-BagConstraints object must be constructed and default values changed by setting field-values as desired. It sounds bad.

The value of GridBag is that it provides a way to achieve highly specific layout designs that the other existing managers might roughly approximate but only at the cost of a far more complex arrangement of containers and components. The various constraints are not difficult to understand in the proper context; they take getting used to, of course. However, with a few helper classes of your own, learning to use GridBag by experimentation can become a very manageable process. As with any tool that provides a disarming number of controls, the key to using GridBag effectively is to first turn only the knobs that do work in broad strokes before resorting to the controls that provide fine adjustments.

GridBagLayout divides its given area into a number of abstract cells (regions). Unlike GridLayout, which allots the same amount of space to each cell and one cell to each component, GridBag's components may vary in width and height, respectively, by occupying an arbitrary number of rows and columns. The height of each row is then determined by the height of the tallest component in it. The width of each column is the width as its widest component. This can get tricky, because the developer does *not* get to define the dimensions of a unit cell—the required size of the largest component gets to define that.

Each component occupies a cell "region" or some number of contiguous columns and rows. The resulting shape is a solid rectangle—ells, snakes, and hollow boxes are not supported. The upper-leftmost cell it will occupy defines a component's location. This value is set using the `GridBagConstraints` fields `gridx` and `gridy`. The component's `width` (number of columns) and `height` (number of rows) are stored in variables with those names.

Some care has to be taken to assign components with incompatible needs to different columns or rows—if it's practical. It's quite possible that a desired arrangement will, nonetheless, create a sizing conflict; the result being that some components will get more space than they want. To alleviate the problem, there are further controls that separate a component's size from the size of its allotted region. If a component gets more space than it wants, it can set the variable `fill` to indicate its preference—accept surplus horizontal or vertical space, accept both, or accept none. None (keeping the current size) is the default. Furthermore, if the component should stick to one edge or corner of its region, a second variable, `anchor`, will set its alignment to one of eight compass points or center it.

So far we've covered the "broad-stroke" variables `GridBagConstraint` offers. These include setting the cell of origin, the component's dimension in rows and columns (remember, these are arbitrarily sized), and the instructions for sizing and positioning the component if its region is too large. The four grid variables can be set to one of two more possible values we have not mentioned yet—RELATIVE and REMAINDER. A component whose grid variables are set to RELATIVE will be next to last in its column or row. REMAINDER is then the final component for a given row or column. These options return some measure of convenience to developers. The extent of travel along either axis can be set without having to count out discrete cell units. By the same token, adding a new component can be much simpler.

In a `GridBag`, rows and columns maintain responsibility for resizing behavior. To change that behavior, the programmer must use `GridBag-Constraints`, which is tied to the definition of one or more components. Each time a component wants to set the behavior of its row and column through `GridBagConstraints` there is a potential for conflict with other components that want the same row or column to behave differently. But since there is no master control, there must be a way to determine which component's instructions are heeded. With `GridBag`, it's the last component to set row and column sizing behavior that gets heard.

To visualize what this means, imagine a dozen audio speakers in a movie theater with six speakers on each wall to either side of the screen. Each speaker has its own equalizer and volume controls. There's also a master volume control for the left and right walls in the projection room, but the knob's been broken off. Rather than replace the knob, the theater's electrician elected to wire every speaker on the left to adjust the master volume for the left. The master volume, in turn, now adjusts all the speakers on the left. With respect to resizing, the situation is similar.

When a resize occurs and there is more space than the sum of all the widest and tallest components for each column and row require, the surplus is divided according to the relative `weight` of each row and column. We say "relative" because the values that are assigned as "weight" only matter with respect to the values assigned to every other column or row. If we assigned a relative weight of 5 to all columns, they will divide surplus space equally, just as if every number given was 100. The potential confusion that arises comes from the fact that weight is set through a component—there's no way to do it from a "master" row or column object. In practice, this means you should set a non-zero `weighty` for, at most, one component in each row and leave `weighty` at zero for all other components in the same row. Similarly, set a non-zero `weightx` on, at most, one component in each column and leave it at zero for all the others. Furthermore, make sure that you choose components that occupy only a single row (when setting `weighty`) and column (when setting `weightx`). If you choose to leave all the weights at zero for a row or column, then that row or column will not change size at all when the available space changes.

The remaining applicable values available through `GridBagConstraints` do the fine-tuning. The value `insets` sets a pad of pixels around the component relative to its containing region. The variables for internal padding, `ipaddx` and `ipaddy`, set the number of pad pixels relative to the component's border.

Assuming you want to use a `GridBag`—and you should if it offers the services you need—one way to cut down the workload of setting up constraints is, write a number of small arrays that keep associated values together (`gridx` and `gridy`, `height` and `width`, `anchor` and `fill`). This is also a case where a short substitution for typing out `GridBagConstraints.HORIZONTAL` and the like will make it far easier to read the resulting code.

```
public class GBC {

    public GBC(int location[], int area[], int size[]) {
        GridBagConstraints gbc = new GridBagConstraints();
```

```
        gbc.gridx = location[0];
        gbc.gridy = location[1];
        gbc.width = area[0];
        gbc.height = area[1];
        gbc.fill = size[0];
        gbc.anchor = size[1];
    }
}
```

If some amount of fine-tuning is expected for each component or the developer simply wants more flexibility, other options can be added in the form of overloaded constructors. We recommend that weight (because it is not specific to a component but to a column or row) be set explicitly in the main body of code, where it will be noticed. Alternatively, it could also be invoked with a special constructor.

In the main class defining the class, setting up an array that groups associated values together make maintenance and fudging the numbers a lot easier.

```
public class BentoBox {
    public static void main(String args[]) {
        final int NONE = GridBagConstraints.NONE;
        final int BOTH = GridBagConstraints.BOTH;
        final int NORT = GridBagConstraints.NORTH;
        final int VERT = GridBagConstraints.VERTICAL;
        GBC gbc = null;
        JButton jb1 = null;
        JButton jb2 = null;
        ...

        // gridder lays out location, area, and size in
        // two-element integer arrays; this is cosmetic to
        // allow the programmer to eyeball the values for
        // each component.
        public int gridder[][] =
            { {0, 0}, {3, 2}, {VERT, NORT},
              {3, 0}, {2, 2}, {VERT, NORT},
```

```
               {0, 1}, {4, 4}, {HORZ, CENT},
          ...
        };

        JFrame jf = new JFrame("Bento Box Designer");
        Container box = jf.contentPane();
        box.setLayout(new GridBagLayout());

        // sample additions
        gbc = new GBC{gridder[0], gridder[1], gridder[2]};
        jb1 = new JButton("Tskimono");
        // fine-tuning for jb1 here
        box.add(jb1, gbc);

        gbc = new GBC(gridder[3], gridder[4], gridder[5]);
        jb2 = new JButton("Rice");
        // fine-tuning for jb2 here
        box.add(jb2, gbc);

        gbc = new GBC(gridder[6], gridder[7], gridder[8];
        jb3 = new JButton("Tempura");
        // fine-tuning here
        box.add(jb3, gbc);
        ...
        jf.setSize(300, 400);
        jf.setVisible(true);
    }
  }
```

This technique is not an example to put to regular use; it merely illustrates a quick technique for experimenting with GridBagLayout to get familiar with its basic behavior. We've taken several shortcuts here. To avoid repetitive recompiling, the ideal solution would be to set up the grid data in a file and build a library of templates. Using a basic component like a JButton makes it simple to rough out the desired dimensions through experimentation. The messiness of the setup code is a reflection of the priority placed on presenting the grid data in as readable a format as possible.

Notice for example that the first row of data in the `gridder` array shows a component located at (0,0), taking up three columns and extending down two rows. Following that, another component is placed at (3,0), taking up the next four columns and extending down five rows. The result so far is depicted in Figure 18.4. With a grid of values visually presented like this, we can check for overlap fairly easily, and verify the integrity of the layout. Once assured of a proper arrangement, adding in consideration for weight and pixel padding are far easier to manage.

**FIGURE 18.4**

Preliminary grid layout of Bento box

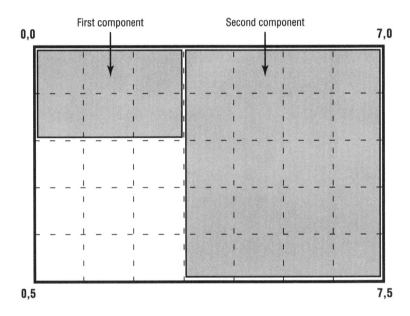

Notice — First component — Second component — 0,0 — 7,0 — 0,5 — 7,5

# Event-Handling and Style

**B**eginning with the change in event-handling introduced in the JDK 1.1, the style of event-handling code has been a matter of some discussion in various circles. Talk about Java GUI development does not seem to generate a lot of thoughts on the question of code reuse, which doesn't seem altogether unreasonable. Application interfaces are often complex and customized enough that they don't lend themselves to a great deal of extension. If some effort has been invested up front in creating Bean-style components that could then be reapplied as modular units to other design requests, this might not be the case. But, as noted at the beginning of this chapter, many interfaces are written right away, so people can begin discussion on the topic of visual presentation right away. Quite often they are built from toolboxes provided by a RAD program. When they are built by hand, the focus on quick development usually precludes modular building, in most cases.

To expedite this sort of development in event-handling, but also in other areas where the ability to write quick helper classes saves a lot of time, the JDK 1.1 introduced the concept of inner classes. Inner classes allow the programmer to embed one or more classes inside a "top-level" class. The benefits include the following:

- Convenient and elegant way to expose multiple implementations of the same interface (typically listeners) from what is superficially a single class

- Common access to import and package statements

- Common access to private variables across classes

- Self-describing class relationships

- Perceived reduction in name space cluttering (especially with anonymous inner classes)

- Some reduction in class file size

Inner classes may also appeal intuitively to students of Alonzo Church's lambda-calculus, the underlying mathematical model for the Lisp programming language.

For custom event-handlers, as one example, it makes sense to allow the developer to separate the class that contains event-handling code away from the rest of the class but at the same time show the tight relationship between the two by inserting one inside the another. A brief example might look like this:

```
public class MyFrame {
    private JFrame jf;
    private Container cont;
    private JButton jb;
```

```
public MyFrame() {
    jf = new JFrame("Inner Class Model");
    cont = jf.getContentPane();
    jb = new JButton("Send Query");
    jb.addActionListener(new EventHandle ());
    cont.add(jb);
}

// inner class to deal with this one little thing...
class EventHandle implements ActionListener {
    public void actionPerformed(ActionEvent ae) {
        System.out.println("Query Sent.");
    }
}

public static void main(String args[]) {
    MyFrame mf = new MyFrame();
    mf.pack();
    mf.setVisible(true);
}
}
```

This implementation is straightforward and clean, and its conveniences clear. The separator between GUI code and event-handling code clarifies the source code a bit, and would also allow us to incorporate another inner class implementing the same kind of listener, but with different behavior for another component. Moreover, if the programmer were using an event adapter class, the benefit would be even more apparent. We don't want to implement, say, all five methods of MouseListener if we're only interested in mouseClicked(), but we don't want our main class to extend MouseEventAdapter for the privilege of avoiding null methods either.

But just as we have room in Java for static (anonymous method blocks, which have their uses and abuses), we also have a provision for anonymous inner classes (classes that are defined as part of their instantiation). Here is a partial example drawing on the complete code model from above. In this case, an anonymous inner class is used three times: once to define the ActionEvent class, once to define a Thread that would execute a query on a remote database, and once more to define a Runnable that restores a label from "Working" to "Ready" and reenables the container.

```
...
JLabel status = new JLabel("Ready");
JButton button = new JButton("Query me");

// anonymous class 1
button.addActionListener(ActionEvent ae {
    status.setText("Query is pending");
    setEnabled(false);

    // anonymous class 2
    Thread queryJob = new Thread() {
        public void run() {
            try {
                //invoke query on remote VM
            }
            catch(InterruptedException ie) {}
            SwingUtilities.invokeLater(new Runnable() _
            {   // #3
                public void run() {
                    status.setText("Ready");
                    setEnabled(true);
                }
            });
        }
    };
    queryJob.start();
}
...
```

The application this code was excerpted from works fine, but it is a bit lengthier. We replaced several lines of code with our comment "invoke query on remote VM," which mitigates the concern we felt, wondering how quickly a programmer could find a bug in this code if a bracket or semi-colon were accidentally deleted. While the code has managed to convey a variety of processes in a few lines, the thing that has been ignored is the readability and maintainability of this code. In return for a marginal savings in memory, file space, and number of code lines, the code here has sacrificed a simple style that would be far easier to read and modify when necessary. As it stands, the first thing a new programmer to this code must do is assure themselves that all the brackets match up and that this code will in fact compile.

Style matters. Clarity matters. It's possible to do a little worse than the snippet above, with a few anonymous array instantiations, but for purposes other than entertainment, this is a style that doesn't read well and is unusually fragile. When used as a crutch rather than a complement, anonymous inner class code can quickly get out of hand.

The secret of a powerful tool is in its proper use. When anonymous inner classes are kept short and to an immediate purpose, they can be quite beneficial. Having the ability to write one on the fly to capture a listener definition saves the programmer a considerable amount of time in choosing a name, writing a separate class, and working out the issues of variable access. The following code

```
...
button.addActionListener(ActionEvent ae {
    status.setText("Query is pending");
    setEnabled(false);
    runQueryOnThread();})
...
```

is easy to read, understand, and maintain, and it takes nothing away from the example code above. We have immediate access to top-level references and methods, and we remove what could rightly be called the baggage of naming something that realizes no advantage from being named. Furthermore, all the important elements of a class' behavior ends up in a single source file. In the final analysis, anonymous classes are open to abuse precisely because they are so powerful. When their use is backed by a compelling programming need, there is no need to avoid them.

# Event-Handling and Threads

**S**o far, we have discussed threads in conjunction with each major application component of the project assignment. Threading has a place in the GUI as well, and as with the database and the network server, there are certain caveats we must be aware of when adding threaded functionality to the client program. Let's imagine we are thinking about the application from the end-user's viewpoint. We see a button that sends an already-formed query to the server. Knowing that the request may take some time, we'd like to have the GUI able to accept other types of input while that process churns in the background. Thinking we know something about threading, we might suggest that a separate thread be used to manage the remote request while another allows us to continue working. We come to the conclusion that allotting a thread to each functionally independent button would make for a very efficient interface.

It sounds right in concept, but it doesn't necessarily translate directly into correct implementation. So far, it hasn't been part of our objective to read deeply into Swing's architecture, but adding some context here is helpful in understanding why threading with AWT or Swing components is risky. We want to justify the correct implementation with a refresher on the mechanics of paint routines. Refer back to Chapter 12, "Painting," for the full background.

In the AWT, all paint requests route through a single AWT thread. Either the system or the user can signal a call to paint the screen through various mechanisms. The system does so to initialize the screen or when it detects damage to the graphics area. The user can interject by way of a call to `repaint()`, which calls `update()`, which in turn "schedules" a paint request on the same thread the system uses to refresh or repaint. The upshot of all this is that screen appearance is kept up to date by the most recent request to update the screen it receives. In a special case, if the overloaded version of `update()` is called, (which allows the user to specify a clip region for painting), then the `update()` call taken up by the painting thread composes a union of all clips to be painted, not just a "whitewash" request to cover all previous requests. In a very large or complex screen area, this approach may save some processing time.

It's a little different with Swing. A Swing component calls attention to itself as a painting target when any of three calls are invoked on it: `paint()`, `setVisible(true)`, or `pack()`. Obviously, `pack()` is not a paint call, but because it does perform a recalculation of a component's size, which is prefaced by a call to `invalidate()`, a subsequent system call to `paint()` is inevitable. Without going in to detail here, paint order is important to Swing components; lightweight components have issues dealing with overlap and neighboring with heavyweight components that become more complicated if one component paints out of turn. If one component's call to be painted goes on a separate thread, it runs the risk of violating the order the Repaint-Manager wants to follow. If the RepaintManager happens to do its part at the right time, no problem will manifest. It's when the autonomous thread paint request kicks in out of turn that screen behavior may be indeterminate. Let the underlying paint system do its own work.

There is a second issue with threading and Swing that has to do with sending off requests that may not return at a convenient interval to the event dispatch thread, such as a request to a remote database. The SwingUtilities class provides two key static methods to support cases where we don't want to hold things up while our job is in state, and where we do. invokeAnd-Wait() and invokeLater() each take a Runnable argument. While the former method blocks on the event dispatch thread until it completes its Runnable assignment, invokeLater() returns immediately once it posts its job, so that local processing can proceed while the Runnable contends normally for process time.

The trick to running a proper request using invokeLater() is shown in the previous code snippet. In that example, once the query button is pressed, a thread is defined and instanced to handle the actual query. This is followed by a call to invokeLater(), which defines a Runnable process that restores GUI interaction and sets the label back to its "Ready" message. The job to reset the GUI returns immediately, restoring the event dispatch's control of its own process queue, while the query thread itself is started and sent on its way. If we were to lock up the dispatch thread for the duration of our database call, our GUI would not be able to repaint or update in any way until that call returned.

Since a remote network connection plays a significant part in your project, it's worthwhile to investigate these two methods in detail and familiarize yourself with their operations.

# Chapter Summary

**P**utting together a sketch of what a GUI should look like, along with the desired behavior on a window resizing, is an excellent tool for articulating the exact screen requirements you want. For a basic interface, the component choices are fairly simple, and should be. Choose the components, assess how the overall window should behave, assign behavior to each region of the screen, and choose the layout managers that can implement that behavior. As a general rule, putting components into panels before they are added to layout regions adds a layer of flexibility to controlling layout management.

Although they were not discussed at length in this chapter, you should plan, at a minimum, to write some kind of menu system for your GUI, taking advantage of keyboard accelerators and other Swing features to provide a reasonable ease-of-use experience to your client.

If you are not already conversant with the model Swing uses to structure components and underlying behavior, defer the project assignment for a time. Get familiar with, at the very least, the differences between AWT components and their Jxxx counterparts. Do not consider yourself ready until you feel you can articulate the structural differences between AWT and Swing architecture, which is bound to come up in the follow-up exam for certification. You should be able to do the following:

- Explain Swing's "model-delegate" structure.

- Identify the roles of a model, listener, event and view.

- Describe each layout manager.

- Offer a scenario for which each layout manager would be ideally suited.

- Explain the importance of the event dispatch thread.

- Apply anonymous and inner classes appropriately.

Unless the requirements for writing the GUI are rigorously defined, it's unlikely a mechanical check will suffice as an evaluation. With that in mind, you should be prepared to justify your solution on aesthetic, as well as functional, terms.

# CHAPTER

# 19

## Thinking About the Follow-Up Exam

In this last chapter, we review some key topics presented in the last four chapters and present a short, FAQ-style list of questions and answers. The spirit of the mock exam questions presented in the programmer's exam guide is to acquaint you with the style and difficulty level of those test questions. In this case, we're posing questions to help prepare you to defend your project implementation, which of course will vary with each developer and will invariably involve making some subjective judgments.

# Preparation Questions

Rather than attempt to mirror the exam questions, we have more or less fed ourselves a list of questions that hopefully will broaden your sense of what you should be prepared to discuss. Some of the discussion here will raise awareness on points that, strictly speaking, aren't tested in the project assignment, but may provide an explicit way to justify a design choice or two, that the developer has intuitively grasped.

## What are the choices for data structures?

Review the classes in `java.util` and consider using arrays where practical. The conventional wisdom is that the better you understand your data, the clearer the choices become for a type of storage. With the addition of the Collections framework to Java 2, however, switching container types to meet new requirements has become very simple. It's now possible to move data from one kind of container to another with a minimum of conversion work. Knowing the benefits of each container type aids the selection processing, but it's also important to know that such decisions can be changed more readily if necessary.

Each container type has its own most suitable usage. Arrays are fast, but once their length is set, they're fixed for the life of the program run. It's possible to copy from one array to another with more room using `System.array-Copy()`, but if that turns out to be a common operation, a `Vector`, which does the copying for you, is a tidier choice. `Vectors` will acquire memory space for more elements each time they reach capacity, but they don't trim themselves automatically; in a volatile storage environment, Vectors may require a lot of checking, and tuning for capacity and expansion may prove problematic.

Key-value structures like `HashMap` offer constant-time performance, meaning the time needed to add or access records doesn't scale along with the size of the table, assuming it is proportioned correctly. As long as operations against the table are predominantly simple ones, `HashMaps` perform well. Upon a non-key search, however, the developer must typically iterate through the entire structure, which does take time proportional to the number of elements. A structure such as a linked list may take time up front to sort elements as they are added. This work greatly speeds up the time taken to iterate over the list. The pre-sorting of the elements makes it possible to select a small range of the list's contents in cases where the search follows the sorting criteria of the structure itself.

While each container type has specific advantages, it may not be clear in some cases how one is a better choice than another. In such cases, the best defense is to know the strengths of each type and justify your choice based on the features you find most useful for the task at hand. Simplicity is a reasonable justification, too, provided you acknowledge that simplicity is important to you, and the performance price you might have to pay, acceptable. Ease of maintenance is an even better reason in many situations.

## Is implementing Runnable better than extending Thread?

Because threading is built into Java, there may be some confusion among programmers about the relationship between the `Thread` class and the `Runnable` interface. It's not uncommon to come across classes that extend `Thread` and do nothing more than override the `run()` method. Compared to classes that merely implement `Runnable` and provide a code body for `run()`, these operations may seem synonymous in every important regard.

However, consider that we normally subclass to alter or specialize the function of a parent class. In cases where we extend JDK classes just to override a method or two, it's typically because the class is designed to be used that way, such as an exception or the `Applet` class. With respect to `Thread`, which merely houses a null implementation of the `Runnable` interface, there's no practical motivation to extend the class if all that's intended is to add `run()` code. It's just one method, and, if no other behavior in `Thread` is going to be changed, it's not worth sacrificing the one opportunity we have to extend a parent class.

## Isn't comparing object serialization to RMI an apples-to-oranges analysis?

Yes... and no. As technologies, they do not compete with each other for attention. Object serialization is a fundamental Java facility; RMI is Java's architecture for distributed computing. Both are bound to evolve a bit more. For object serialization, evolution most likely means improvements of its basic features. For RMI, it means cooperating in the larger, industrial world of distributed computing that includes not only heterogeneous systems, but heterogeneous code as well. The fact that RMI makes ample use of serialization demonstrates the different playing fields in which they both operate.

But so far as choosing a way to talk VM-to-VM is concerned, both are likely candidates for the job, until some requirements are established. Serializing objects by hand and establishing the patterns for sending them back and forth between two machines is neither elegant nor necessarily reusable work. It can, however, be quickly implemented, tested, and deployed on limited-scale projects with short build times. If it's determined that there will be future needs to address through inter-VM communication, it's easy enough to add a method to the proper class that encapsulates a new "object protocol" for communication with other machines. It's not difficult, other than checking to ensure that all values intending to cross the wire are serializable.

RMI is a means for establishing object control from a single location. It avoids the potentially messy effects of simply passing around state information from machine to machine and risking version control. Since the remote user's semantics for invoking a remote reference are very similar to calling a local one, most of the details are hidden once RMI is implemented. But RMI's power comes at a very definite cost: Among those issues, the one that arguably damages perception of RMI's efficacy the most is its ability to pass objects by value, rather than by reference. The very convenience that makes us think nothing of a remote method invocation may also lure us into passing a huge object across the wire without thinking twice about where the subsequent slowdown in performance is coming from.

If the care in design for proper RMI is not something a project assignment can tolerate, ground-level object serialization is available. Like the many dumb terminals we see still heavily populating shop floors and financial desks, object serialization may not be ground-breaking stuff, but it does the job at a reasonable price. Good enough is good engineering.

## How elaborate should an exception class structure get?

It's possible to create as many shell exceptions as one wants, as a cheap and easy way to describe the variant conditions that represent non-routine code execution for an application. It might be easy to infer from the cumbersome naming of certain JDK classes, such as `ArrayIndexOutOfBoundsException`, that naming is in fact important enough to support, that the expense of developer convenience is not too high a price to pay for it. Bearing in mind that some of these classes were never intended to be caught or managed by users— all exceptions that extend `RuntimeException` fall into this category—we have to take any emphatic importance on naming with a grain of salt. Yes, we want to know what an exception is about, and ideally we can get the idea from the name alone. A more substantive policy, however, might be to simply name unique exceptions when there is a potential need to catch them and write alternate code to execute when it occurs.

Provide new exceptions whenever the application should, under unusual conditions: inform the user, save current data, and offer alternate ways to continue or exit. This helps to define exceptions by necessity rather than using them merely to spell out a problem through a class name. Also consider the possibility that the exception class itself might add methods to enable context-specific processing, thus avoiding rewrites of the same catch code over several related classes.

## How many ways can you set up "listener" relationships? Which one is best?

There are several patterns already implemented in Java, including:

- Observer/Observable
- Event-handling, as implemented in the AWT package.
- "Model-delegate" (an MVC variant) in Swing, which is 50 percent event-handling.

- Beans' style change listeners, which are nothing more than a standardized set of event handlers.

The proliferation of these patterns in Java shows the increased use of objects that rely on event notification to monitor changes. Three of these listener schemes deal primarily with GUI components in one form or another, although model-view-controller as a pattern needn't be strictly defined as having a visual component. Views can just as easily be called filters where they offer a narrow perspective on the model at hand, and the filter could just as easily be an interpreter or parser. Whatever the case, there are several available strategies to incorporate listening in one form or another, and if you're persuaded that it works well enough that the graphic components shouldn't hog all the fun, a little research will show you how these techniques work.

One place you may be inclined to experiment with "callbacks," as they are often informally termed, is between the client and server in your project assignment. Assuming the assignment's main objectives don't prohibit this, the easiest thing to experiment with is the `Observer/Observable` interface/ class pair in `java.util`. The class that implements `Observable` does most of the work, tying its inherited methods to state changes elsewhere in the class so that ultimately a call its own `notifyObservers()` is made, which then calls `update()` in any class that implements `Observer` and has registered interest in the notifying `Observable`. The two knocks on this pattern are that the observed class must extend `Observable`, which may not be feasible if it must subclass something else, and that the use of events and listeners is more widely accepted and accomplishes the same goal.

The event-handling model for the AWT and the change-listener format for Beans follow the same pattern. Swing, with its model-delegate structure, also takes advantage of the Beans specification by instituting change listeners and event-firing mechanisms as a way to bind changes in one part of a component's supporting tools to another. The nice part about the Beans model (which is essentially the AWT's) is that it doesn't require you to create full-fledged Beans to take advantage of it. At the same time, the features that allow the developer to create modular components are easy enough to adopt so that maintaining compatibility with Bean adaptation is usually a good idea. If there is no best way to establish listening between classes, there certainly seems to be a most popular one: the Beans model.

## How do I know which layout manager to use?

Consider the type of behavior each layout manager supports. Consider the possibilities of mixing each with the behavior of different components. Then consider the additional permutations of nesting one container within another, each with its own layout manager. There are lots of variations, some of which ultimately produce the same effect. So far as the end-user is concerned, whatever brings the GUI to its most effective presentation is suitable. End-user satisfaction should be a developer goal as well, but also find a way to remember that someone has to maintain the resulting code.

The only recommendation to be made is to offer all the required functionality in the most maintainable form possible, for applications that may be in service for a while. The overlap in behavior between one layout manager and another is often accounted for by the constrained situation in which a choice will be made. Border layouts are ideal where each set of components wants to occupy a fixed peripheral space and "serve" what's going on in the center. Flow layouts confer each component with its added order. Grid layouts offer a quick "control console" feeling and automatic equal-weight distribution to every column and row. Card layout is clearly different, useful for information that may "stack" well, but don't overlook the TabbedPane in Swing, which gives the user control of the tabs. Gridbag offers a great deal of flexibility, but mastering its behavior is by far the most challenging of the five layout managers.

If the topmost layout strategy is unclear, one simple strategy is to build up to the containing frame. Components that share space or work together in some cohesive way will typically suggest by their function an appropriate layout scheme. As these groups are placed in panels, it may make sense to combine two or more panels into another panel; multiple nested containers are honorable. Once the major panels are assembled, it's very likely that one of two schemes will apply to the topmost container: Border or GridBag. GridBag, in a nutshell, allows you to vary component dimension by the rows and columns they reside in; if you have no need for this kind of flexibility, use Border.

## Which design patterns are most useful in this kind of project?

At the risk of sounding evasive, whichever design patterns help you get the job done are most useful. While using design patterns competently to complete the project assignment will most likely lead to tighter code that an experienced programmer can readily appreciate, it's hard to say abstractly when to apply one. Using design patterns in a formal sense requires some foreknowledge of them. If you know what they are, how they're commonly referred to, and how they solve specific problems, that is a good start. With some advance preparations and experience, it's more likely that articulating a specific objective may lead to a design pattern you know of and can apply to the situation. Looking for a place to plug one isn't likely to help produce better code. But there are plenty of opportunities, just by reading some source in the JDK itself. Observer/Observable represent a class design pattern, as does MVC. Any time you come across a class with the term *factory* in its name, you're looking at a class built with that pattern in mind. Studying these classes along with a primer on design patterns will help you understand what's going on: Design patterns are simply solutions to very common problems in object-oriented programming.

That said, it's not necessarily true that formal schooling with design patterns is the only way to learn how to use them. For experienced programmers, many design patterns may seem to be generic articulations of code they've had in their toolboxes for years. Giving them specific names merely makes it easier to talk about them; it's the proper application of design patterns in code that makes them powerful.

Some knowledge of the formal conventions for design patterns may make it easier for some candidates to discuss their programming rationale on the follow-up exam. A working knowledge of the patterns mentioned above will go a long way toward preparing the candidate, as they are among the most prevalent patterns in the JDK. Look for signs of often-repeated words in class names: It's your best hint that a pattern is lurking underneath.

The seminal book on design patterns is called "Design Patterns: Elements of Reusable Object-Oriented Software" by a group of authors known as the "Gang of Four"—Erich Gamma, Richard Helm, Ralph Johnson, and John Vlissides. More and more literature on Java and design patterns is coming out regularly, including design patterns that take particular advantage of Java.

## When does it make sense to use *protected* and "package-private" scope?

Look for a compelling need to use either. Even though the project assignment may employ a package structure for the code provided, it's unlikely you'll be looking at a problem in choosing the best scope for a certain variable or method. Variables and methods that are `protected` are only accessible to subclasses and other classes sharing the same package. Package-private members and variables, which is signified by the absence of a scope modifier, means the identifier is only visible to other package members. Subclasses outside the package do not have access to package-private resources, while subclasses inside the package do.

The value of these scopes is to allow direct access for "local" classes into important package resources, while blocking access to out-of-package programmers altogether, or blocking those that aren't extending the class in question. Typically, a package-private identifier is available within a package to allow some package-specific operations to take place more readily than they could through the normal public interface.

A good place to study the use of `protected` identifiers is the AWT, where there are a lot of class interrelationships. Unless you intend to write something as complex as a windowing toolkit or similar package, chances are you won't have a real need for either scope. If it shouldn't be `public`, make it `private`. If `private` seems restrictive, keep it private. If being `private` prevents related classes from doing their job without adding a lot of code, consider whether access outside the package would ever be warranted. If so, choose `protected`. Otherwise, choose package-private.

What we really want to challenge is the nature of the question. Learning programmers want to know how best to use the tools they encounter, and so will ask questions in the form written above. The better question we want programmers to ask is "Why should I make all fields private?"

Our first objective in developing new classes is to preserve encapsulation. A class is properly encapsulated when its data are only available through the class' public "interface." When we say interface in this context, we mean the methods that permit access to the state of a class instance or object. Consider what happens to a class that uses a vector for internal storage and allows direct access to it, possibly in the name of greater performance. Along comes a better type of storage for the class developer's purpose. Now if the developer wants to swap out the vector for this new type, all the subsequent code that relies on this class will break. If, instead, some methods, such as `get-Container()` and `setContainer()`, are used to govern access to the data container, the developer is free to internally implement fields at will, leaving other programmers with a consistent, unchanging interface.

So encapsulation promotes maintenance. You can find several Java articles that demonstrate how much faster a field access is than a method call, but if you want to keep code maintenance simple, you'll acknowledge the difference and stick to proper encapsulation. A class can add methods to the interface without breaking its contract to existing users, and it can change the body of a method. So long as method signatures remain consistent, encapsulated classes provide the greatest protection to their users.

Why would we take a hit in performance, especially if our code seems to run unacceptably slow? First, of course, we have to determine whether it's method calls that are really holding things up. Knowing that field accesses are faster than method calls is a dangerous bit of information if it's regarded in a vacuum. We have to know through profiling or other analysis where our compute time is being spent. Even if method calls proved to be our biggest expense, we still must consider whether breaking the public interface—a drastic step—is warranted. But it's a simple matter if access is initially more restrictive than not. We can simply change a private member to the appropriate scope and document this variance. If fields start out as public or protected, however, and we make them private, we've now broken the public interface, and our users to date have to address the consequences of that. Maintenance is easier if we start out with a conservative view of encapsulating fields.

In various portions of the guide, we've stated our case that you can't overuse interfaces to declare method calls when designing your application. Assuming you've been persuaded, you're also aware that an interface has no support for instance variables, since an interface bears no relation to any one instance. The point of an interface is to separate design from the details of implementation. Once you've fixed on a specific field type and given access to other classes, you've anchored your design in a specific implementation. If there's never a case for changing that specific field type, there's no problem. In this situation, we must admit that performance outweighs flexibility of design.

In short, keep fields private. If the application runs correctly but is too slow, and performance is critical, consider allowing field access. If you can afford to wait, however, the best of all worlds is coming in the form of improved VMs, which include a just-in-time (JIT) compiler to execute code faster. Sun's much-anticipated HotSpot will include features such as the ability to "inline" simple accessor/mutator methods. From a design point of view, the long-term problem is creating an engine that runs with proper efficiency, rather than "tricking out" the design to achieve better performance by forsaking ease of maintenance.

## Doesn't an abstract class let the developer specify more behavior than an interface?

If specific behavior is what you want, yes. The point of an interface, in one respect, is that it really doesn't tie you down to very much. Earlier in this chapter, we discussed the run() method in Thread that is merely a null implementation of the Runnable interface. The fact is, run() has next to nothing to do with the Thread class. We can implement run() in any class we want. We can also call any object's run() method directly from another thread; bypassing Thread.start() simply means that we don't set this process off on its own execution context.

If you're unsure about this assertion, review the section "Sharing Threads" at the end of Chapter 17. In the code sample for that section, look closely at the run() method of ShareThread and the call to job.run() near the end of that method. Notice that no call is made to job.start(). Yet job references an object that implements Runnable. Walk through the code until you see the logic behind this call.

One view on the abstract class is that it should contain the code that will be common to every subclass, but leave abstract those methods that rely on a local implementation to fulfill its commitments to other implemented methods in that class. If we have an abstract class Currency, for example, all methods pertaining to exchange for goods or services may be implemented. The methods that describe the local currency, however, which are called by the methods that describe exchange, still must be implemented locally for the class to be useful. This is the idea behind classes like the AWT's Container and Component, which define the vast majority of AWT operations, but leave some important methods the completed methods call to be defined by actual components. Outside of toolkit development, abstract classes could also be used as a "convenience class" to capture information interfaces cannot—implementations of non-public methods, constructors, overrides of inherited methods—and could be useful as a kind of "concrete reference" for an intended subset of extending classes.

But this type of usage should not necessarily be construed as affording the kind of control that interfaces lack. The true power of interfaces lies in remaining as abstract as possible. Consider this:

```java
public interface Payment {
    public Double getAmount();
```

```
        public Account getAccountInfo();
    }
    public interface Account {
        public Double getBalance();
        public String getName();
    }
    public interface Payable {
        public Account deductPayment(Payment pmtOut);
    }
    public interface Receivable {
        public Account addPayment(Payment pmtIn);
    }
```

With three exceptions, these preliminary interfaces rely completely on abstract definitions to describe a rudimentary ledger-entry system. If we need to add behavior as we further define the details, all we have to do is add the name of that method to the interface list, and we've broken no code. What we have done is set the stage to describe relationships for the classes that implement these interfaces. We've also started declaring their responsibilities for participating in this framework appropriately in a minimum of time. In this manner, we could go through a couple of design passes without every worrying about updating concrete code as we make potentially sweeping changes.

Abstract classes are convenient for conveying ideas that are more concrete than design-oriented. Interfaces, by contrast, keep details from bogging down the design effort. Chances are an interface that seems to do nothing but name methods simply hasn't been developed aggressively enough. Some schools of thought go so far as to propose that *every* parameter and return type in a method be represented by an interface, for both maximum flexibility and to preserve the precious single opportunity each class has to inherit from another.

# Summary

The follow-up exam determines whether candidates can demonstrate their command of Java's core libraries and submitted code well enough to defend it in a series of essay questions. The above questions are simply intended to provoke some thoughts on what kinds of topics might be fair game for the exam itself. Candidates might be expected to offer several alternatives to a problem that is posed generally, and to state the various attractions and drawbacks of each alternative. The candidate then might be asked to correlate the previous question to a situation in the exam itself, detail how the problem was solved, and explain why they chose that approach.

The best preparation for this kind of exam is to have a reasonably broad overview of how the project assignment might be solved, as well as a particular interest in completing it in a manner that suits the candidate's style. The easiest way to answer subjective questions is to stick your natural inclination to problem solving. In the context of an exam like this, there are wrong factual answers: It would be bad to conclude that synchronized methods are faster than synchronized blocks, or that arrays take up more memory than Vectors. But in justifying an approach that has proven to work, the remaining element is whether the code as it appears on paper corresponds to the candidate's accounting for it, and whether its implementation remains consistent with their judgment.

# APPENDICES

# APPENDIX

# A

## Answers

# Chapter 1: Language Fundamentals

1. False. The range of negative numbers is greater by 1 than the range of positive numbers.

2. All of the identifiers are valid.

3. B and D are both acceptable. Answer A will compile but will not be called.

4. D is correct. This order must be strictly observed.

5. A and E are true. The array has 25 elements, indexed from 0 through 24. All elements are initialized to zero.

6. D is correct. A holder is constructed on line 6. A reference to that holder is passed into method bump() on line 5. Within the method call, the holder's held variable is bumped from 100 to 101.

7. C is correct. The decrement() method is passed a copy of the argument d; the copy gets decremented, but the original is untouched.

8. A is correct. Garbage collection cannot be forced. Calling System.gc() or Runtime.gc() is not 100 percent reliable, since the garbage-collection thread might defer to a thread of higher priority; thus B and D are incorrect. C is incorrect because the two gc() methods do not take arguments; in fact, if you still have a reference to pass into the method, the object is not yet eligible to be collected. E will make the object eligible for collection the next time the garbage collector runs.

9. D is correct. The range for a 16-bit short is –215 through 215 – 1. This range is part of the Java specification, regardless of the underlying hardware.

10. D is correct. The range for an 8-bit short is –27 through 27 – 1. Table 1.3 lists the ranges for Java's integral primitive data types.

# Chapter 2: Operators and Assignments

**1.** C is correct. The assignment statement is evaluated as if it were

```
x = a + b; a = a + 1; b = b + 1;
```

Therefore the assignment to x is made using the sum of 6 + 7 giving 13. After the addition, the values of a and b are actually incremented, the new values, 7 and 8, are stored in the variables.

**2.** B and C are correct. In A the use of ! is inappropriate, since x is of int type, not boolean. This is a common mistake among C and C++ programmers, since the expression would be valid in those languages. In B, the comparison is inelegant (being a cumbersome equivalent of if (x <= 3), but valid, since the expression (x > 3) is a boolean type, and the ! operator can properly be applied to it. In C the bitwise inversion operator is applied to an integral type. The bit pattern of 6 looks like 0...0110 where the ellipsis represents 27 0 bits. The resulting bit pattern looks like 1...1001 where the ellipsis represents 27 1 bits.

**3.** A is correct. In every case, the bit pattern for –1 is "all ones." In A this is shifted five places to the right with the introduction of 0 bits at the most significant positions. The result is 27 1 bits in the less significant positions of the int value. Since the most significant bit is 0, this represents a positive value (actually 134217727). In B the shift value is 32 bits. This will result in no change at all to x, since the shift is actually performed by (32 mod 32) bits, which is 0. So in B the value of x is unchanged at –1. C is actually illegal since the result of x >>> 5 is of type int, and cannot be assigned into the byte variable x without explicit casting. Even if the cast were added, giving byte x = –1; x = (byte)(x >>> 5); the result of the expression x >>> 5 would be calculated like this:

**A.** First promote x to an int. This gives a sign-extended result, that is an int –1 with 32 1 bits.

**B.** Perform the shift; this behaves the same as in A above, giving 134217727,which is the value of 27 1 bits in the less significant positions.

**C.** Casting the result of the expression simply "chops off" the less significant eight bits, since these are all ones, the resulting `byte` represents –1.

Finally, D performs a signed shift, which propagates 1 bits into the most significant position. So, in this case, the resulting value of x is unchanged at –1.

**4.** A, C, and E are all legal. In A the use of `+=` is treated as a shorthand for the expression in C. This attempts to "add" an `int` to a `String` which results in conversion of the `int` to a `String`–`"9"` in this case— and the concatenation of the two `String` objects. So in this case, the value of x after the code is executed is "Hello9".

In B the comparison (x `==` y) is not legal, since only the `+` operator performs implicit conversion to a `String` object. The variable y is an `int` type and cannot be compared with a reference value. Don't forget that comparison using `==` tests the values and that for objects, the "value" is the reference value and not the contents.

C is identical to A without the use of the shorthand assignment operator.

D calculates y + x, which is legal in itself, because it produces a `String` in the same way as did x + y. It then attempts to assign the result, which is "9Hello", into an `int` variable. Since the result of y + x is a `String`, this is not permitted.

E is rather different from the others. The important points are the use of the short-circuit operator `&&` and the ternary operator `?:`. The left-hand operand of the `&&` operator is always evaluated and in this case the condition (x `!=` null) is `false`. Because this is `false`, the right-hand part of the expression (x.length() > 0) need not be evaluated, as the result of the `&&` operator is known to be `false`. This short-circuit effect neatly avoids executing the method call x.length(), which would fail with a `NullPointerException` at run time. This `false` result is then used in the evaluation of the ternary expression. As the `boolean` value is `false`, the result of the overall expression is the value to the right of the colon, that is 0.

5. A and E are correct. Although int and float are not assignment compatible, they can generally be mixed on either side of an operator. Since == is not assignment but is a comparison operator, it simply causes normal promotion, so that the int value 9 is promoted to a float value 9.0 and compared successfully with the other float value 9.0F. For this reason A is true.

   The code in B actually fails to compile. This is because of the mismatch between the int and the Integer object. The value of an object is its reference, and no conversions are ever possible between references and numeric types. This applies to any conversion, not just assignment compatibility.

   In C, the code compiles successfully, since the comparison is between two object references. However, the test for equality compares the value of the references (the memory address typically) and since the variables x and y refer to two different objects, the test returns false. The code in D behaves exactly the same way.

   Comparing E with D might persuade you that E should probably not print "Equal". In fact it does so because of a required optimization. Since String objects are immutable, literal strings are inevitably constant strings, so the compiler re-uses the same String object if it sees the same literal value occur more than once in the source. This means that the variables x and y actually do refer to the same object; so the test (x == y) is true and the "Equal" message is printed. It is particularly important that you do not allow this special behavior to persuade you that the == operator can be used to compare the contents of objects in any general way.

6. A is correct. The effect of the && operator is first to evaluate the left-hand operand. That is the expression (s.length() > 5). Since the length of the StringBuffer object s is actually 5, this test returns false. Using the logical identity false AND X = false, the value of the overall conditional is fully determined, and the && operator therefore skips evaluation of the right-hand operand. As a result, the value in the StringBuffer object is still simply "Hello" when it is printed out.

   If the test on the left-hand side of && had returned true, as would have occurred had the StringBuffer contained a longer text segment, then the right-hand side would have been evaluated. Although it might look a little strange, that expression, (`s.append("there").equals("False")`), is valid and returns a `boolean`. In fact, the value of the expression is guaranteed to be `false`, since it is clearly impossible for any `StringBuffer` to contain exactly "False" when it has just had the `String` " there" appended to it. This is irrelevant however—the essence of this expression is that, if it is evaluated, it has the side effect of changing the original `StringBuffer` by appending the text " there".

7. B is correct. The Exclusive-OR operator ^ works on the pairs of bits in equivalent positions in the two operands. In this example this produces:

```
     00001010
     00001111
XOR  --------
     00000101
```

Notice that the only 1 bits in the answer are in those columns where exactly one of the operands has a 1 bit. If neither, or both, of the operands has a 1, then a 0 bit results.

The value 00000101 binary corresponds to 5 decimal.

It is worth remembering that, although this example has been shown as a `byte` calculation, the actual working is done using `int` (32-bit) values. This is why the explicit cast is required before the result is assigned back into the variable b in line 5.

8. C is correct. In this code the optional result values for the ternary operator, 99.99 (a `double`) and 9 (an `int`), are of different types. The result type of a ternary operator must be fully determined at compile time, and in this case the type chosen, using the rules of promotion for binary operands, is `double`. Because the result is a `double`, the output value is printed in a floating point format.

The choice of which of the two values to output is made on the basis of the `boolean` value that precedes the ?. Since x is 4, the test (x > 4) is `false`. This causes the overall expression to take the second of the possible values, which is 9 rather than 99.99. Because the result type is promoted to a `double`, the output value is actually written as 9.0, rather than the more obvious 9.

If the two possible argument types had been entirely incompatible, for example (x > 4) ? "Hello" : 9, then the compiler would have issued an error at that line.

9. B shows the correct output. In this case, the calculation is relatively straightforward since only positive integers are involved. Dividing 10 by 3 gives 3 remainder 1, and this 1 forms the result of the modulo expression. Another way to think of this calculation is 10 – 3 = 7, 7 – 3 = 4, 4 – 3 = 1, 1 is less than 3 therefore the result is 1. The second approach is actually more general, since it handles floating-point calculations, too. Don't forget that for negative numbers, you should ignore the signs during the calculation part, and simply attach the sign of the left-hand operand to the result.

10. A is correct. The assignment operators of the form op= only evaluate the left-hand expression once. So the effect of decrementing x, in —x, occurs only once, resulting in a value of 0 and not –1. Therefore no out-of-bounds array accesses are attempted. The array element that is affected by this operation is "Fred", since the decrement occurs before the += operation is performed. Although String objects themselves are immutable, the references that are the array elements are not. It is entirely possible to cause the value name[0] to be modified to refer to a newly constructed String, which happens to be "Fred."

# Chapter 3: Modifiers

1. A, D, and E are illegal. A is illegal because "friendly" is not a keyword. B is a legal transient declaration. C is strange but legal. D is illegal because only methods and classes may be abstract. E is illegal because abstract and final are contradictory.

2. B is true: A final class may not have any abstract methods. Any class with abstract methods must itself be abstract, and a class may not be both abstract and final. Statement A says that an abstract class may not have final methods, but there is nothing wrong with this. The abstract class will eventually be subclassed, and the subclass must

avoid overriding the parent's final methods. Any other methods can be freely overridden.

3. A is the correct answer. The code will not compile because on line 1 class Aaa is declared final and may not be subclassed. Lines 10 and 15 are fine. The instance variable `finalref` is final, so it may not be modified; it can only reference the object created on line 10. However, the data within that object is not final, so there is nothing wrong with line 15.

4. E is correct. A, B, and C don't mean anything, because only variables may be transient, not methods or classes. D is false because transient variables may never be static. E is a good one-sentence definition of transient.

5. E is correct. Multiple static initializers (lines 5 and 12) are legal. All static initializer code is executed at class-load time, so before `main()` is ever run, the value of x is initialized to 10 (line 3), then bumped to 15 (line 5), then divided by 5 (line 12).

6. E is correct. The program compiles fine; the "static reference to a private variable" stuff in answers A and B is nonsense. The static variable x gets incremented four times, on lines 8, 10, 12, and 13.

7. On line 3, the method may be declared private. The method access of the subclass version (line 8) is friendly, and only a private or friendly method may be overridden to be friendly. The basic principle is that a method may not be overridden to be more private. (See Figure 3.2.) On line 8 (assuming line 3 is left alone), the superclass version is friendly, so the subclass version may stand as it is (and be friendly), or it may be declared protected or public.

8. The correct answer is D (`transient`). The other modifiers control access from other objects within the Java Virtual Machine. Answer E (`private transient`) also works but is not minimal.

9. C is correct: Static methods may not be overridden to be non-static. B is incorrect because it states the case backwards: Methods actually may be overridden to be more public, not more private. Answers A, D, and E make no sense.

10. A is correct. There is nothing wrong with `Nightingale`. The static `referenceCount` is bumped twice: once on line 4 of `Nightingale`, and once on line 5 of `Bird`. (The no-argument constructor of the superclass is always implicitly called at the beginning of a class' constructor, unless a different superclass constructor is requested. This has nothing to do with the topic of this chapter, but is covered in Chapter 6, *Objects and Classes*.) Since `referenceCount` is bumped twice and not just once, answer B is wrong. C says that statics cannot be overridden, but no static method is being overridden on line 4; all that is happening is an increment of an inherited static variable. D is wrong, since `protected` is precisely the access modifier we want `Bird.fly()` to have: We are calling `Bird.fly()` from a subclass in a different package. Answer E is ridiculous, but it uses credible terminology.

# Chapter 4: Converting and Casting

1. D is correct. C is wrong because objects do not take part in arithmetic operations. E is wrong because only casting of object references potentially requires a runtime check.

2. Line 6 (`b = s`) will not compile because converting a short to a byte is a narrowing conversion, which requires an explicit cast. The other assignments in the code are widening conversions.

3. Surprisingly, the code will fail to compile at line 3. The two operands, which are originally bytes, are converted to ints before the multiplication. The result of the multiplication is an int, which cannot be assigned to byte `b`.

4. E is correct. The result of the calculation on line 2 is an int (because all arithmetic results are ints or wider). An int can be assigned to an int, long, float, or double.

5. D is correct. At line 8, the char argument ch is widened to type int (a method-call conversion), and passed to the int version of method crunch().

6. D is correct.

7. Line 7 will not compile. Changing an Object to a Float is going "down" the inheritance hierarchy tree, so an explicit cast is required.

8. D is correct. The code will compile and run; the cast in line 6 is required, because changing an Animal to a Dog is going "down" the tree.

9. E is correct. The cast in line 7 is required. Answer D is a preposterous statement expressed in a tone of authority.

10. B is correct. The conversion in line 6 is fine (class to interface), but the conversion in line 7 (interface to class) is not allowed. A cast in line 7 will make the code compile, but then at runtime a ClassCastException will be thrown, because Washer and Raccoon are incompatible.

# Chapter 5: Flow Control and Exceptions

1. B, C, D, and F are correct. The loops iterate i from 0 to 1 and j from 0 to 2. However, the inner loop executes a continue statement whenever the values of i and j are the same. Since the output is generated inside the inner loop, after the continue statement, this means that no output is generated when the values are the same. Therefore, the outputs suggested by answers A and E are skipped.

**2.** D is correct. The values of i appear set to take the values 0 to 1 and for each of these values, j takes values 0, 1 and 2. However, whenever i and j have the same value, the outer loop is continued before the output is generated. Since the outer loop is the target of the continue statement, the whole of the inner loop is abandoned. The only line to be output is that shown in D as the starting condition, i = 0 and j = 0 immediately causes i to take on the value 1, and as soon as both i and j are set to 1 after the first inner iteration, the continue again serves to terminate the remaining values.

**3.** C is correct. In A the variable declaration for i is illegal. This type of declaration is permitted only in the first part of a for() loop. The absence of initialization should also be a clue here. In B the loop control expression—the variable i in this case—is of type int. A boolean expression is required. C is valid. Despite the complexity of declaring one value inside the for() construction, and one outside (along with the use of the comma operator in the end part) this is entirely legitimate. D would have been correct, except that the label has been omitted from line 2 which should have read loop: do {.

**4.** D is correct. The first test at line 2 fails, which immediately causes control to skip to line 10, bypassing both the possible tests that might result in the output of message one or message two. So, even though the test at line 3 would be true, it is never made; A is not correct. At line 10, the test is again false, so the message at line 11 is skipped, but message four, at line 14, is output.

**5.** D is correct. A is incorrect because the code is legal despite the expression at line 5. This is because the expression itself is a constant. B is incorrect because it states that the switch() part can take a long argument. Only byte, short, char, and int are acceptable. The output results from the value 2 like this: First, the option case 2: is selected, which outputs value is two. However, there is no break statement between lines 4 and 5, so the execution falls into the next case and outputs value is three from line 6. The default: part of a switch() is only executed when no other options have been selected, or if there is no break preceding it. In this case, neither of these situations holds true, so the output consists only of the two messages listed in D.

**6.** B, E, and F are correct. The exception causes a jump out of the `try` block, so the message `Success` from line 4 is not printed. The first applicable catch is at line 6, which is an exact match for the thrown exception. This results in the message at line 7 being printed, so B is one of the required answers. Only one `catch` block is ever executed, so control passes to the `finally` block which results in the message at line 16 being output; so E is part of the correct answer. Since the exception was caught, it is considered to have been handled and execution continues after the `finally` block. This results in the output of the message at line 18, so F is also part of the correct answer.

**7.** A, E, and F are correct. With no exceptions the `try` block executes to completion, so the message `Success` from line 4 is printed and A is part of the correct answer. No `catch` is executed, so B, C, and D are incorrect. Control then passes to the `finally` block, which results in the message at line 16 being output, so E is part of the correct answer. Because no exception was thrown, execution continues after the `finally` block, resulting in the output of the message at line 18, so F is also part of the correct answer.

**8.** E is correct. The thrown error prevents completion of the `try` block, so the message `Success` from line 4 is not printed. No catch is appropriate, so B, C, and D are incorrect. Control then passes to the `finally` block, which results in the message at line 16 being output; so option E is part of the correct answer. Because the error was not caught, execution exits the method and the error is rethrown in the caller of this method, so F is not part of the correct answer.

**9.** B is correct. A would give misleading line number information in the stack trace of the exception, reporting that the exception arose at line 1, which is where the exception object was created. C is illegal since you must throw an object that is a subclass of `java.lang.Throwable`, and you cannot throw a class, only an object. D is also illegal, as it attempts to throw a `String` which is not a subclass of `java.lang.Throwable`. E is entirely legal, but it is not as good as B since E doesn't take the effort to clarify the nature of the problem by providing a string of explanation.

**10.** B and D are correct. A does not handle the exceptions, so the method aMethod might throw any of the exceptions that dodgy() might throw. However the exceptions are not declared with a throws construction. In B, declaring "throws IOException" is sufficient, because java.lang .RuntimeException is not a checked exception and because IOException is a superclass of MalformedURLException, it is unnecessary to mention the MalformedURLException explicitly (although it might make better "self-documentation" to do so). C is unacceptable because its throws declaration fails to mention the checked exceptions—it is not an error to declare the runtime exception, although it is strictly redundant. D is also acceptable, since the catch block handles IOException, which include MalformedURLException. RuntimeException will still be thrown by the method aMethod() if it is thrown by dodgy(), but as Runtime-Exception is not a checked exception, this is not an error. E is not acceptable, since the overriding method in anotherClass is declared as throwing IOException, while the overridden method in aClass was only declared as throwing MalformedURLException. It would have been correct for the base class to declare that it throws IOException and then the derived class to throw MalformedURLException, but as it is, the overriding method is attempting to throw exceptions not declared for the original method. The fact that the only exception that actually can arise is the MalformedURLException is not enough to rescue this, because the compiler only checks the declarations, not the semantics of the code.

# Chapter 6: Objects and Classes

**1.** A, C, and E are correct. In each of these answers, the argument list differs from the original, so the method is an overload. Overloaded methods are effectively independent, and there are no constraints on the accessibility, return type, or exceptions that may be thrown. B would be a legal overriding method, except that it cannot be defined in the same class as the original method; rather, it must be declared in a subclass. D is also an override, since the *types* of its arguments are the same: Changing the parameter names is not sufficient to count as overloading.

**2.** B and D are correct. A is illegal because it is less accessible than the original method; the fact that it throws no exceptions is perfectly acceptable. B is legal because it overloads the method of the parent class, and as such it is not constrained by any rules governing its return value, accessibility, or argument list. The exception thrown by C is sufficient to make that method illegal. D is legal because the accessibility and return type are identical, and the method is an override because the types of the arguments are identical—remember that the names of the arguments are irrelevant. The absence of an exception list in D is not a problem: An overriding method may legitimately throw fewer exceptions than its original, but it may not throw more.

**3.** E and F are correct. The Cat class is a subclass of the Pet class, and as such should extend Pet, rather than containing an instance of Pet. B and C should be members of the Pet class and as such are inherited into the Cat class; therefore, they should not be declared in the Cat class. D would declare a reference to an instance of the Cat class, which is not generally appropriate inside the Cat class itself (unless, perhaps, you were asked to give the Cat a member that refers to its mother). Finally, the neutered flag and markings descriptions, E and F, are the items called for by the specification; these are correct items.

**4.** Answer: `public class Cat extends Pet`. The class should be `public` since it is to be used freely throughout the application. The statement "A cat is a pet" tells us that the Cat class should subclass Pet. The other words offered are required for the body of the definitions of either Cat or Pet–for use as member variables—but are not part of the opening declaration.

**5.** C is correct. The first message is produced by the Base class when b1 `.method(5)` is called and is therefore `Value is 5`. Despite variable b2 being declared as being of the Base class, the behavior that results when `method()` is invoked upon it is the behavior associated with class of the actual object, not with the type of the variable. Since the object is of class Sub, not of class Base, the second message is generated by line 3 of class Sub: `This value is 6`.

**6.** B and C are correct. Since the class has explicit constructors defined, the default constructor is suppressed, so A is not possible. B and C have argument lists that match the constructors defined at lines 2 and 4 respectively, and so are correct constructions. D has three integer arguments, but there are no constructors that take three arguments of any kind in the Test class, so D is incorrect. Finally, E is a syntax used for construction of inner classes and is therefore wrong.

**7.** A and C are correct. In the constructor at lines 2 and 3, there is no explicit call to either this() or super(), which means that the compiler will generate a call to the zero argument superclass constructor, as in A. The explicit call to super() at line 5 requires that the Base class must have a constructor as in C. This has two consequences. First, C must be one of the required constructors and therefore one of the answers. Second, the Base class must have at least that constructor defined explicitly, so the default constructor is not generated, but must be added explicitly. Therefore the constructor of A is also required and must be a correct answer. At no point in the Test class is there a call to either a superclass constructor with one or three arguments, so B and D need not explicitly exist.

**8.** A, B, and E are correct. Inner classes may be defined with any accessibility, so private is entirely acceptable and A is correct. Similarly, the static modifier is permitted on an inner class, which causes it not to be associated with any particular instance of the outer class. This means that B is also correct. Inner classes defined in methods may be anonymous—and indeed often are—but this is not required, so C is wrong. D is wrong because it is not possible for an inner class defined in a method to access the local variables of the method, except for those variables that are marked as final. Constructing an instance of a static inner class does not need an instance of the enclosing object, but all non-static inner classes do require such a reference, and that reference must be available to the new operation. The reference to the enclosing object is commonly implied as this, which is why it is commonly not explicit. These points make E true.

**9.** A, B, C, and E are correct. Since `Inner` is not a `static` inner class, it has a reference to an enclosing object, and all the variables of that object are accessible. Therefore A and B are correct, despite the fact that b is marked `private`. Variables in the enclosing method are only accessible if those variables are marked `final`, so the method argument c is correct, but the variable d is not. Finally, the parameter e is of course accessible, since it is a parameter to the method containing line 8 itself.

**10.** A is correct. Construction of a normal (that is, a named and non-static) inner class requires an instance of the enclosing class. Often this enclosing instance is provided via the implied `this` reference, but an explicit reference may be used in front of the new operator, as shown in A.

Anonymous inner classes can only be instantiated at the same point they are declared, like this:

```
return new ActionListener() {
  public void actionPerformed(ActionEvent e); { }
};
```

Hence B is illegal—it actually attempts to instantiate the interface `ActionListener` as if that interface were itself an inner class inside `Outer`.

C is illegal since `Inner` is a non-static inner class, and so it requires a reference to an enclosing instance when it is constructed. The form shown suggests the implied `this` reference, but since the method is `static`, there is no `this` reference and the construction is illegal.

D is illegal since it attempts to use arguments to the constructor of an anonymous inner class that implements an interface. The clue is in the attempt to define a constructor at line 3. This would be a constructor for the interface `MyInterface` not for the inner class—this is wrong on two counts. First, interfaces do not define constructors, and second we need a constructor for our anonymous class, not for the interface.

# Chapter 7: Threads

1. A is correct. The Runnable interface defines a run() method with void return type and no parameters. The method given in the problem has a String parameter, so the compiler will complain that class Greebo does not define void run() from interface Runnable. B is wrong, because you can definitely pass a parameter to a thread's constructor; the parameter becomes the thread's target. C, D, and E are nonsense.

2. C is correct. A is true on a preemptive platform, B is true on a time-sliced platform. The moral is that such code should be avoided, since it gives such different results on different platforms.

3. False. The yield() method is static and always causes the current thread to yield. In this case, ironically, it is the first thread that will yield.

4. True. The second thread will remain in the Suspended state until it receives a resume() call.

5. D is true. The thread will sleep for 100 milliseconds (more or less, given the resolution of the JVM being used). Then the thread will enter the Ready state; it will not actually run until the scheduler permits it to run.

6. E is correct. When you call notify() on a monitor, you have no control over which waiting thread gets notified.

7. D is correct. Although wait() and notify() must be called from synchronized code, there is no corresponding rule for suspend() and resume(). The code will run until line 4, at which point the executing thread will become suspended. Since it is suspended, it will never be able to execute line 5. A suspended thread can never resume itself, since to do so it has to be running; a suspended thread can only be resumed by a different thread.

8. This time E is correct. The only difference between this problem and the previous one is that line 4 yields rather than suspending. The executing thread moves into the Ready state; soon afterward, the scheduler moves it back into the Running state. It then executes line 5, making a `resume()` call to itself. This call has no effect, because the thread was not suspended.

9. Yes. The call to xxx() occurs before the thread is registered with the thread scheduler, so the question has nothing to do with threads.

10. False. A monitor is an instance of any class that has synchronized code.

# Chapter 8: The *java.lang* Package

1. None of the answers is correct. Strings are immutable.

2. C is correct. Since s1 and s2 are references to two different objects, the == test fails. However, the strings contained within the two string objects are identical, so the `equals()` test passes.

3. D is correct. The `java.lang.Math` class is final, so it cannot be subclassed.

4. A is correct. The constructor for the `Math` class is private, so it cannot be called. The `Math` class methods are static, so it is never necessary to construct an instance. The import at line 1 is not required, since all classes of the `java.lang` package are automatically imported.

5. E is correct. A is wrong because line 1 is a perfectly acceptable way to create a string, and is actually more efficient than explicitly calling the constructor. B is wrong because the argument to the `equals()` method is of type `Object`; thus any object reference or array variable may be passed. The calls on lines 3 and 5 return `false` without throwing exceptions.

**6.** True. The `StringBuffer` class is mutable. After execution of line 2, `sbuf` refers to the same object, although the object has been modified.

**7.** True. See answer 6 above.

**8.** True. Line 1 constructs a new instance of `String` and stores it in the string pool. In line 2, `_xyz_` is already represented in the pool, so no new instance is constructed.

**9.** False. Line 1 constructs a new instance of String and stores it in the string pool. Line 2 explicitly constructs another instance.

**10.** C is correct. A set prohibits duplication while a list or collection does not. A map also prohibits duplication of the key entries, but maps are primarily for looking up data based on the unique key. So, in this case, we could have used a map, storing the data as the key and leaving the data part of the map empty. However, we are told that searching is not a priority, so the proper answer is a set.

# Chapter 9: Components

**1.** E is correct. Since the button does not specify a background, it gets the same background as the applet: blue. The button's foreground color and font are explicitly set to white and 64-point bold serif, so these settings take effect rather than the applet's values.

**2.** B and E are correct. Since you have not explicitly set a font for the check box, it uses the font of its immediate container.

**3.** C, D, and E are correct. The panel does not explicitly get its font set, so it uses the applet's font. The check box does not explicitly get its font set, so it uses the panel's font, which is the applet's font.

**4.** B. The number of rows comes first, then the number of columns.

**5.** C, D, and E are correct. The first parameter (10) specifies the number of *visible* items. The second parameter (`false`) specifies whether multiple selection is supported. A list always acquires a vertical scroll bar if the number of items exceeds the number of visible items.

**6.** C is correct. If a text field is too narrow to display its contents, you need to scroll using the arrow keys.

**7.** A and C are correct. A menu may contain menu items, check-box menu items (*not* check boxes!), separators, and (sub)menus.

**8.** B is correct. Only a frame may contain a menu bar.

**9.** E is correct. A newly constructed frame has zero-by-zero size and is not visible. You have to call both `setSize()` (or `setBounds()`) and `setVisible()`.

**10.** False. The `java.awt.CheckboxGroup` class is not a kind of component.

# Chapter 10: Layout Managers

**1.** E is correct. Java makes no guarantees about component size from platform to platform, because it uses each platform's own fonts and component appearance. The whole point of layout managers is that you don't have to worry about platform-to-platform differences in component appearance.

**2.** E is correct. A is wrong because the constructor is called from within its own class; the application would compile even if the constructor were private. B is wrong because the frame has a default layout manager, which is an instance of `BorderLayout`. If you `add()` a component to a container that uses a Border layout manager, and you don't specify a region as a second parameter, then the component is added at Center, just as if you had specified `BorderLayout.CENTER` as a second parameter. (Note, however, that explicitly providing the parameter is much better programming style than relying on default behavior.) C is wrong because the button does appear; it takes up the entire frame, as described in E. Answer D would be true if frames used Flow layout managers by default.

3. C is correct. A is wrong because *any* container's default layout manager can be replaced; that is the only way to get things done if the default manager isn't what you want. B is wrong because there is no restriction against having a single row or a single column. What really happens is this: The frame contains two panels—p1 occupies the entire left half of the frame and p2 occupies the entire right half (because the frame uses a grid with one row and two columns). Each panel uses a Flow layout manager, so within the panels every component gets to be its preferred size. Thus the two buttons are just big enough to encompass their labels. Panel p1 uses a right-aligning Flow layout manager, so its single component is aligned to the far right of that panel, just left of the vertical center line. Panel p2 uses a left-aligning Flow layout manager, so its single component is aligned to the far left of that panel, just right of the vertical center line. The two buttons end up as described in answer C. D and E are incorrect because the buttons get to be their preferred sizes.

4. B is correct. The frame is laid out in a grid with three rows and one column. Thus each of the three panels p1, p2, and p3 is as wide as the frame and 1/3 as high. The "Alpha" button goes at North of the top panel, so it is as wide as the panel itself (thus as wide as the frame), and it gets to be its preferred height. The "Beta" button goes at Center of the middle panel, so it occupies the entire panel (since there is nothing else in the panel). The "Gamma" button goes at South of the bottom panel, so it is as wide as the panel itself (thus as wide as the frame), and it gets to be its preferred height.

5. D is correct. A is wrong because every frame gets a default Border layout manager. Since the button is placed at South, it is always as wide as the frame, and it gets resized when the frame gets resized. Its height is always its preferred height. Note that of the three plausible answers (C, D, and E), the correct answer is the simplest. The point of this question is that when a container gets resized, its layout manager lays out all the components again.

6. A is correct. The only lines of code that matter are 9, 10, and 16. The button is added to a panel that uses a Flow layout manager. Therefore the button gets to be its preferred size.

7. With a Border layout manager, any component at North (or South) is as wide as the container and as high as its own preferred height. A vertical scroll bar needs plenty of play in the vertical direction, but it does not need to be very wide. The problem produces a scroll bar that is both too wide and too short to be useful, so the correct answer is C. With a Border layout manager, vertical scroll bars are most useful at East and West; horizontal scroll bars are most useful at North and South.

8. The default layout manager for panels and applets is Flow. The default for frames is Border.

9. True. The Grid layout manager ignores the preferred size of its components and makes all components the same size. If the frame contained any panels, then the components within those panels would be likely to be smaller than those directly contained by the panel. However, the question explicitly states that the frame does not contain any panels.

10. False. The default layout manager is Border. Components at North and South will be the same width; components at East and West will be the same height. No other generalizations are possible.

11. False. Almost, but not quite. The component at Center gets all the space that is left over, after the components at North, South, *East and West* have been considered.

12. False. The question describes a hodgepodge of layout manager attributes.

# Chapter 11: Events

1. False. The two event models are incompatible, and they should not appear in the same program.

2. A, B and E are correct. Since the class is public, it must reside in a file whose name corresponds to the class name. If the call to super(nrows, ncols) is omitted, the no-arguments constructor for TextArea will be

invoked, and the desired number of rows and columns will be ignored. C and D are attempts to create confusion by introducing concepts from the 1.0 model; in the delegation model, all event handlers have void return type. E is correct because if the suggested line is omitted, text listeners will be ignored.

3. C and D are correct. The code will compile and execute cleanly. However, without a call to super.processWindowEvent(we), the component will fail to notify its window listeners.

4. C is correct. Lines 2 and 3 construct instances of the listener classes, and store references to those instances in variables with interface types; such assignment is perfectly legal. The implication of answer B is that adding a second listener might create a problem; however, the delegation model supports multiple listeners. The code compiles cleanly and runs without throwing an exception.

5. E is correct. This problem is just like the previous one, with the addition of a perfectly legal removeFocusListener() call.

6. A and C are correct. Since the class extends MouseAdapter, and MouseAdapter implements the MouseListener interface, the MyListener class implicitly implements the interface as well; it does no harm to declare the implementation explicitly. The class can serve as a mouse listener. In response to mouse events other than mouse entered, the listener executes the handler methods that it inherits from its superclass; these methods do nothing.

7. A is correct. Multiple interface implementation is legal in Java. The class must implement all methods of both interfaces, and this is indeed the case. Since the class implements the ActionListener interface, it is a legal action listener; since it also implements the ItemListener interface, it is also a legal item listener.

8. B is correct. This class attempts multiple class inheritance, which is illegal in Java.

**9.** False. A component, whether or not it has explicitly called `enable-Events()`, can have an unlimited number of listeners, and those listeners may be adapter subclasses.

**10.** E is correct. There are no guarantees about the order of invocation of event listeners.

# Chapter 12: Painting

**1.** A is correct. The 13 pre-defined colors are static variables in class `Color`, so you access them via the class name as you would any other static variable. The name of the color-setting method is `setColor()`, not `setCurrentColor()`.

**2.** D (cyan) is correct. This question tests your knowledge of static variables as well as the `Color` class. The `Color` class has 13 final static variables, named `red`, `green`, `yellow`, and so on. These variables happen to be of type `Color`. So `Color.red` is the name of an instance of `Color`. Recall from Chapter 3 (*Modifiers*) that there are two ways to access a static variable: via the class name, which is the preferred way, or via a reference to any instance of the class. Thus one (non-preferred) way to access the `green` static variable is via `Color.red`, because `Color.red` is a reference to an instance. Thus `Color .red.green` is a legal way to refer to the `green` static variable. Similarly, the preferred way to refer to the `yellow` static variable is `Color.yellow`, but it is legal (although very strange) to reference it as `Color.red.green.yellow`, because `Color.red.green` is a reference to an instance. And so on. The answer would still be cyan if the color were set to `Color.red.white.red .black.cyan.magenta .blue.pink.orange.cyan`.

**3.** B is correct (a black vertical line that is 40 pixels long, and a red square with sides of 150 pixels). The `setColor()` method affects only *subsequently drawn* graphics; it does not affect *previously drawn* graphics. Thus the line is black and the square is red. The arguments to `set-Line()` are coordinates of endpoints, so the line goes from (10, 10) to (10, 50) and its length is 40 pixels. The arguments to `drawRect()` are x position, y position, width, and height, so the square's side is 150 pixels.

Some readers may feel that a different answer is appropriate: "None of the above, because you never said that g was an instance of Graphics." This is legitimate; the real issue is what to do when you have this reaction during the Certification Exam. Always bear in mind that the exam questions are about Java, not about rhetoric. The exam tests your knowledge of Java, not your ability to see through tricky phrasing.

**4.** A is correct. The fillArc() method draws pie pieces, not chords.

**5.** B, D, and E are correct. A polyline is never filled or closed; it is just an open run of line segments. A polygon may be filled (the fill-Polygon() method) or not filled (the drawPolygon() method).

**6.** False. When there is damage to be repaired, the GUI thread passes to paint() a graphics context whose clip region is already set to the damaged region. Java was built this way to make sure that programmers never have to determine damaged clip regions. In fact, programmers never have to do anything at all about exposure damage, provided all drawing is done in paint() or in methods called by paint().

**7.** D is correct, and is a standard technique whenever you don't want update() to wipe the screen before calling paint(). All the diagonal cyan lines will remain on the screen; the effect will be like drawing with a calligraphy pen. Answers A and B (on line 4, replace repaint() with paint() or repaint()) will not compile, because both paint() and repaint() require a Graphics as an input. Answer C is serious trouble: super.update(g) will clear the screen and call paint(g), which will call super.update(g), and so on forever.

**8.** D is correct. The signature for the Font constructor is Font(String fontname, int style, int size). The font name can be one of "Serif", "SansSerif", or "Monospaced". The style should be one of Font.PLAIN, Font.BOLD, or Font.ITALIC.

**9.** B is correct. The y-coordinate parameter passed into drawString() is the vertical position of the baseline of the text. Since the baseline is at 0 (that is, the top of the component) only descenders will be visible. The string "question #9" contains one descender, so only a single descending squiggle from the *q* will be seen.

**10.** D is correct. The signature for drawOval() is drawOval(int x, int y, int width, int height), where x and y define the upper-left corner of the oval's bounding box, and width and height define the bounding box's size. The question points out the common misconception that x and y define the center of the oval.

# Chapter 13: Applets and HTML

**1.** There is a problem in line 1. The value of CODE is case-sensitive, so capitalizing the first letter of the .class extension is not valid. The browser will ignore the entire applet tag.

**2.** False. If the value is an URL, then the class file could even reside on a different machine.

**3.** False. A String variable can be assigned a value of null.

**4.** False. An ARCHIVE tag may specify a comma-separated list of JAR files.

**5.** E is correct. The call to getParameter() ignores the case of its argument and returns "Secondo", which is the exact value from the HTML page, with capitalization intact. The call to toUpperCase() converts to upper case.

**6.** B is correct. The call to getParameter() ignores the case of its argument, and returns "3a6", which is the exact value from the HTML page, with capitalization intact. The parseInt() call throws a number-format exception, so the assignment to i on line 5 never happens. Thus i retains its original value of 100.

7. False. The class file might reside in `big.jar`, or it might reside in the same directory as the HTML file.

8. Yes. The value of `CODEBASE` may be an URL.

9. The value is `null`. The `getParameter()` call is looking for a parameter named "`pearl`", and no such parameter is defined in the HTML code. The only parameter defined in the HTML is "`gem`".

10. D is correct. Since the parameter aa is not defined, `null` is passed into the `toUpperCase()` call at line 6, resulting in a null pointer exception. The exception handler assigns a value of 400 to `i`.

# Chapter 14: Input and Output

1. Only D is correct. UTF characters are as big as they need to be. Unicode characters are all 16 bits. There is no such thing as a Bytecode character; bytecode is the format generated by the Java compiler.

2. All three statements are false. Construction and garbage collection of a `File` have no effect on the local file system.

3. False. The `File` class does not provide a way to change the current working directory.

4. True. The code below shows how this is done:
   ```
   1. File f = new File(".");
   2. String contents[] = f.list();
   ```

5. C is correct. The `writeInt()` call writes out an int, which is 4 bytes long; the `writeDouble()` call writes out a double, which is 8 bytes long, for a total of 12 bytes.

6. B is correct. All the code is perfectly legal, so no exceptions are thrown. The first byte in the file is 10, the next byte is 11, the next is 12, and so on. The byte at file position 10 is 20, so the output is i = 20.

7. A and D are correct. Solution A chains a data input stream onto a file input stream. Solution D simply uses the RandomAccessFile class. B fails because the FileReader class has no readInt() method; readers and writers only handle text. Solution C fails because the PipedInputStream class has nothing to do with file I/O. (Piped input and output streams are used in inter-thread communication.) Solution E fails because you cannot chain a data input stream onto a file reader. Readers read chars, and input streams handle bytes.

8. False. Readers and writers only deal with character I/O.

9. E is correct. Constructing an instance of the File class has no effect on the local file system.

10. A is correct. Compilation fails at line 3, because there is no constructor for BufferedOutputStream that takes a RandomAccessFile object as a parameter. You can be sure of this even if you are not familiar with buffered output streams, because random-access files are completely incompatible with the stream/reader/writer model.

# APPENDIX B

## Using the Test Program

The CD-ROM supplied with this book contains a Java program that allows you to test yourself. Our tester uses some of the questions from each chapter and allows you to simulate taking the real Java Certification Exam and to make a reasonable estimate of whether you are sufficiently prepared for the exam.

# The Real Test

First, we'll discuss the real test program, since it differs somewhat from our tester, but is the one you will have to use when you take the exam "for real." You will see immediately that the user interface is different. The real test uses a native Windows 3.1 interface that differs in appearance from any variation that our tester will offer. However, in addition to the inevitable differences of windowing system, the overall layout differs a little. We will take a little time to describe the overall appearance of the real test system.

The real test uses a single, scrollable area to present the question and the answer choices. This question area occupies most of the screen. Beneath the question area are three buttons: Next, Previous, and Help. The Help button gives help on using the test system, not on the questions. Next and Previous step between questions, but the Next button sometimes changes to More. This change occurs when a question is long enough to require scrolling, for you to see the whole question and all the answers. After you have pressed the More button, or have scrolled down the page far enough to have seen the whole question with all its answers, the button changes back to Next. The diagram in Figure B.1 shows the approximate layout of the real test system's main screen.

When you have stepped through all the questions the real test system offers, you see a review page which shows all the questions and indicates any you have left unanswered. This page provides facilities for you to return to these unanswered questions to complete them.

Upon completion of the real test, which is strictly timed, you are presented with your mark on paper. You do not find out the correct answers, or even what specific questions you got wrong. The 1.1 version of the test does give you a breakdown of your scores by each group of objectives, so that you get some indication of the areas you should study further before you retake the exam.

**FIGURE B.1**

Sketch of the main screen of the real test

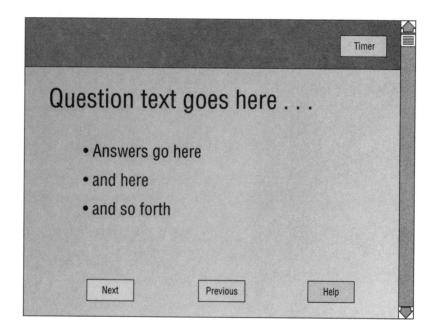

In addition to the main test system, the real test allows you to have a "trial run" working with the test system to become familiar with it. During that phase you are given questions that are entirely unrelated to Java, so do not worry about getting them right!

Another facility allows you to make comments about the questions, if you wish, although you will probably want to concentrate on your answers.

Now that you have a sense of the format of the real test, let's discuss the tester that is provided on the CD with this book.

# The Tester

There are several differences between the real test and the tester. First and foremost, the questions are different! While we have sought to cover the same ground as the real test and to make the questions of comparable difficulty, you must appreciate that this is not the "real thing." There is no point in learning the answers to these questions by rote—that will only give you inappropriate confidence and will not provide you with actual answers to the real test.

The appearance of the tester main window on a Windows 95 system is shown in Figure B.2.

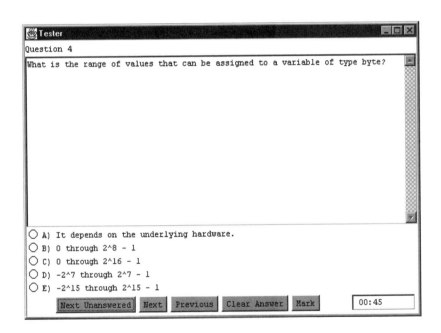

In the tester, the questions are presented in a scrollable text area in the upper part of the main window, with the answer options presented in the lower part.

The tester provides five buttons at the bottom of the window, and to the right is a timer. The timer can operate in either count-up mode, allowing you to determine how long you took to answer a set of questions, or in count-down mode, in which case it will force the tester into marking mode, preventing you from answering any more questions when the time reaches zero.

The buttons provided are marked Next Unanswered, Next, Previous, Clear Answer, and Mark. The first three of these buttons are for navigating the question set, Next and Previous are self-evident, while Next Unanswered checks the question set to find the next question that you have not yet answered.

The Clear Answer button removes all marks from a question so that the Next Unanswered button will consider it to be unanswered. You can use this if you decide to skip a question for now but want to be able to come back to it easily.

The Mark button stops the test and the timer and marks the questions. Unlike the real test, the tester gives you complete feedback on all the questions, including the correct answers and explanations. To give this feedback, the tester uses two additional windows. One pops up automatically when you press the Mark button. A screen shot of this window is shown in Figure B.3.

**FIGURE B.3**

The marking window

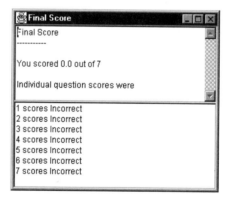

Notice that the marking window is divided into two regions. At the top is a text area that states your mark and the total number of questions you were asked. Beneath this is a scrollable list that indicates your score on a question-by-question basis. If you select one of the lines in this list, you are presented with a second window containing a text area that tells you either that you got the question correct, or what the correct answer is. An example of this is shown in Figure B.4.

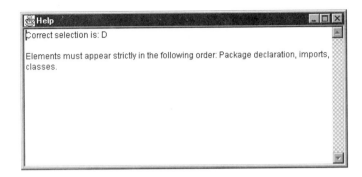

Notice how the first line indicates the correct answer or answers. If you got the question right, this line simply says so. The explanation text appears on the following lines.

Now that you know broadly what to expect when you run the tester, let's take a look at how to start the program and the options that it offers.

# Running the Tester

The tester is written to run under JDK 1.2 and can be run directly from the CD-ROM. To do this, simply issue the command

```
java -jar d:\tester.jar
```

and substitute the identifier of your CD-ROM drive for "d:" if necessary. Alternatively, you can simply double-click on the icon for tester.jar in the Windows Explorer. This starts the tester program, giving you unlimited time to complete the test and a random selection of about 65 questions. When you press the Mark button, the timer at the bottom right-hand corner of the display will stop, showing you how long you spent on the questions.

## Imposing a Time Limit

You can also run the test in timed mode; the tester will move forcibly into marking mode if you take too long. To invoke this behavior in the tester, define the property `testTime` when you start the program. This value should be specified in minutes, and to approximate the conditions of the real exam you should give yourself between one-and-a-half and two minutes per question. To define this property, start the tester with a command like this:

```
java -jar -DtestTime=90 d:\tester.jar
```

This will give you one-and-a-half hours to complete the test.

## Controlling the Number of Questions

If for any reason you do not want to run a test with the default number of questions, you can specify a particular number by setting the property `questionCount`. So, for example, to request only 20 questions, start the tester like this:

```
java -jar -DquestionCount=20 d:\tester.jar
```

Of course, you can ask for more questions than the default if you wish. If you ask for more questions than are available, however, you will only get each question once.

## Controlling the Question Categories

By default, the tester reads all the questions from the file `Questions.ser`, which contains questions for all chapters, but you can direct it to specific files if you wish. The questions for each chapter are in separate files. The filenames are the chapter number as a two-digit value followed by an underscore, a short hint at the chapter name, and finally the extension `.ser`. You can select one or more of these by specifying the property `questionFiles`. For example, to select questions from chapters 4 and 7 issue the command:

```
java -jar -DquestionFiles="04_Cast.ser|07_Threads.ser" _
d:\tester.jar
```

Notice the use of the pipe character (`|`) to separate the files in the list. If you want questions from only one chapter, you don't need to use the pipe at all.

# Answering the Questions

The questions presented by the tester are all multiple choice; some take only a single correct answer, and some allow zero or more selections. You can tell if you are allowed only a single answer to a question because the answers will be presented to you with round radio buttons.

If you see square check boxes, you can select any number of options, from none to all that are shown. You can think of this type of question as a collection of true/false questions based on the same topic. Because true/false is generally considered to be pretty easy—giving you a 50 percent chance of success simply by guessing—you will not be surprised to know that you must get *all* parts of the question correct to score the mark.

As with any test, you must read each question carefully. We have tried to make the questions unambiguous, but inevitably some uncertainties will remain. Although it is practically impossible to eliminate ambiguity from natural language (if it weren't, then lawyers would be unemployed), the questions on the Java Certification Exam have been subjected to extensive review and correction by many people; therefore, you can reasonably expect your interpretation of a question to match the intended one.

Good luck!

# APPENDIX

# C

## Java 2 API Reference

This appendix documents the inheritances, fields, constructors and methods of the most useful classes in the Java 2 Applications Programming Interface. Here's a list:

- java.applet.*

- java.awt.*

- java.beans.*

- java.io.*

- java.lang.*

- java.math.*

- java.net.*

- java.rmi.*

- java.security.*

- java.sql.*

- java.text.*

- java.util.*

# AbstractAction

public abstract class javax.swing.
AbstractAction
implements javax.swing.Action
implements java.lang.Cloneable
implements java.io.Serializable
extends java.lang.Object

## Fields

protected javax.swing.event.
SwingPropertyChangeSupport
changeSupport
protected boolean enabled

## Constructors

public  AbstractAction()
public  AbstractAction(String name)
public  AbstractAction(String name,Icon
icon)

## Methods

public synchronized void
addPropertyChangeListener(
PropertyChangeListener listener)
protected Object clone()
protected void firePropertyChange(String
propertyName,Object oldValue,Object
newValue)
public Object getValue(String key)
public boolean isEnabled()
public synchronized void putValue(String
key,Object newValue)
public synchronized void
removePropertyChangeListener(
PropertyChangeListener listener)
public synchronized void setEnabled(
boolean newValue)

# AbstractBorder

public abstract class javax.swing.border.
AbstractBorder
implements javax.swing.border.Border
implements java.io.Serializable
extends java.lang.Object

## Methods

public Insets getBorderInsets(Component
c)
public Insets getBorderInsets(Component
c,Insets insets)
public Rectangle getInteriorRectangle(
Component c,int x,int y,int width,int
height)
public static Rectangle
getInteriorRectangle(Component c,Border
b,int x,int y,int width,int height)
public boolean isBorderOpaque()
public void paintBorder(Component c,
Graphics g,int x,int y,int width,int
height)

# AbstractButton

public abstract class javax.swing.
AbstractButton
implements java.awt.ItemSelectable
implements javax.swing.SwingConstants
extends javax.swing.JComponent
extends java.awt.Container
extends java.awt.Component
extends java.lang.Object

## Fields

protected java.awt.event.ActionListener
actionListener
public final static java.lang.String
BORDER_PAINTED_CHANGED_PROPERTY
protected transient javax.swing.event.
ChangeEvent changeEvent
protected javax.swing.event.
ChangeListener changeListener
public final static java.lang.String
CONTENT_AREA_FILLED_CHANGED_PROPERTY
public final static java.lang.String
DISABLED_ICON_CHANGED_PROPERTY
public final static java.lang.String
DISABLED_SELECTED_ICON_CHANGED_PROPERTY
public final static java.lang.String
FOCUS_PAINTED_CHANGED_PROPERTY
public final static java.lang.String
HORIZONTAL_ALIGNMENT_CHANGED_PROPERTY
public final static java.lang.String
HORIZONTAL_TEXT_POSITION_CHANGED_
PROPERTY
public final static java.lang.String
ICON_CHANGED_PROPERTY
protected java.awt.event.ItemListener
itemListener
public final static java.lang.String
MARGIN_CHANGED_PROPERTY
public final static java.lang.String
MNEMONIC_CHANGED_PROPERTY
protected javax.swing.ButtonModel model
public final static java.lang.String
MODEL_CHANGED_PROPERTY
public final static java.lang.String
PRESSED_ICON_CHANGED_PROPERTY
public final static java.lang.String
ROLLOVER_ENABLED_CHANGED_PROPERTY
public final static java.lang.String
ROLLOVER_ICON_CHANGED_PROPERTY
public final static java.lang.String
ROLLOVER_SELECTED_ICON_CHANGED_PROPERTY
public final static java.lang.String
SELECTED_ICON_CHANGED_PROPERTY
public final static java.lang.String
TEXT_CHANGED_PROPERTY
public final static java.lang.String
VERTICAL_ALIGNMENT_CHANGED_PROPERTY
public final static java.lang.String
VERTICAL_TEXT_POSITION_CHANGED_PROPERTY

## Methods

public void addActionListener(
ActionListener l)

```
public void addChangeListener(
ChangeListener l)
public void addItemListener(ItemListener
l)
protected int checkHorizontalKey(int key,
String exception)
protected int checkVerticalKey(int key,
String exception)
protected ActionListener
createActionListener()
protected ChangeListener
createChangeListener()
protected ItemListener
createItemListener()
public void doClick()
public void doClick(int pressTime)
protected void fireActionPerformed(
ActionEvent event)
protected void fireItemStateChanged(
ItemEvent event)
protected void fireStateChanged()
public String getActionCommand()
public Icon getDisabledIcon()
public Icon getDisabledSelectedIcon()
public int getHorizontalAlignment()
public int getHorizontalTextPosition()
public Icon getIcon()
public String getLabel()
public Insets getMargin()
public int getMnemonic()
public ButtonModel getModel()
public Icon getPressedIcon()
public Icon getRolloverIcon()
public Icon getRolloverSelectedIcon()
public Icon getSelectedIcon()
public synchronized Object
getSelectedObjects()
public String getText()
public ButtonUI getUI()
public int getVerticalAlignment()
public int getVerticalTextPosition()
protected void init(String text,Icon
icon)
public boolean isBorderPainted()
public boolean isContentAreaFilled()
public boolean isFocusPainted()
public boolean isRolloverEnabled()
public boolean isSelected()
protected void paintBorder(Graphics g)
protected String paramString()
public void removeActionListener(
ActionListener l)
public void removeChangeListener(
ChangeListener l)
public void removeItemListener(
ItemListener l)
public void setActionCommand(String
actionCommand)
public void setBorderPainted(boolean b)
public void setContentAreaFilled(boolean
b)
public void setDisabledIcon(Icon
disabledIcon)
```

```
public void setDisabledSelectedIcon(Icon
disabledSelectedIcon)
public void setEnabled(boolean b)
public void setFocusPainted(boolean b)
public void setHorizontalAlignment(int
alignment)
public void setHorizontalTextPosition(
int textPosition)
public void setIcon(Icon defaultIcon)
public void setLabel(String label)
public void setMargin(Insets m)
public void setMnemonic(int mnemonic)
public void setMnemonic(char mnemonic)
public void setModel(ButtonModel
newModel)
public void setPressedIcon(Icon
pressedIcon)
public void setRolloverEnabled(boolean b)
public void setRolloverIcon(Icon
rolloverIcon)
public void setRolloverSelectedIcon(Icon
rolloverSelectedIcon)
public void setSelected(boolean b)
public void setSelectedIcon(Icon
selectedIcon)
public void setText(String text)
public void setUI(ButtonUI ui)
public void setVerticalAlignment(int
alignment)
public void setVerticalTextPosition(int
textPosition)
public void updateUI()
```

## AbstractCollection

```
public abstract class java.util.
AbstractCollection
implements java.util.Collection
extends java.lang.Object
```

### Constructors
```
protected  AbstractCollection()
```

### Methods
```
public boolean add(Object o)
public boolean addAll(Collection c)
public void clear()
public boolean contains(Object o)
public boolean containsAll(Collection c)
public boolean isEmpty()
public abstract Iterator iterator()
public boolean remove(Object o)
public boolean removeAll(Collection c)
public boolean retainAll(Collection c)
public abstract int size()
public Object toArray()
public Object toArray(Object a)
public String toString()
```

## AbstractColorChooserPanel

```
public abstract class javax.swing.
colorchooser.AbstractColorChooserPanel
extends javax.swing.JPanel
extends javax.swing.JComponent
```

extends java.awt.Container
extends java.awt.Component
extends java.lang.Object

### Methods
protected abstract void buildChooser()
protected Color getColorFromModel()
public ColorSelectionModel
getColorSelectionModel()
public abstract String getDisplayName()
public abstract Icon getLargeDisplayIcon(
)
public abstract Icon getSmallDisplayIcon(
)
public void installChooserPanel(
JColorChooser enclosingChooser)
public void paint(Graphics g)
public void uninstallChooserPanel(
JColorChooser enclosingChooser)
public abstract void updateChooser()

## AbstractDocument
public abstract class javax.swing.text.
AbstractDocument
implements javax.swing.text.Document
implements java.io.Serializable
extends java.lang.Object

### Fields
protected final static java.lang.String
BAD_LOCATION
public final static java.lang.String
BidiElementName
public final static java.lang.String
ContentElementName
public final static java.lang.String
ElementNameAttribute
protected javax.swing.event.
EventListenerList listenerList
public final static java.lang.String
ParagraphElementName
public final static java.lang.String
SectionElementName

### Constructors
protected  AbstractDocument(Content data)
protected  AbstractDocument(Content data,
AttributeContext context)

### Methods
public void addDocumentListener(
DocumentListener listener)
public void addUndoableEditListener(
UndoableEditListener listener)
protected Element createBranchElement(
Element parent,AttributeSet a)
protected Element createLeafElement(
Element parent,AttributeSet a,int p0,int
p1)
public synchronized Position
createPosition(int offs)
public void dump(PrintStream out)
protected void fireChangedUpdate(
DocumentEvent e)

protected void fireInsertUpdate(
DocumentEvent e)
protected void fireRemoveUpdate(
DocumentEvent e)
protected void fireUndoableEditUpdate(
UndoableEditEvent e)
public int getAsynchronousLoadPriority()
protected final AttributeContext
getAttributeContext()
public Element getBidiRootElement()
protected final Content getContent()
protected final synchronized Thread
getCurrentWriter()
public abstract Element
getDefaultRootElement()
public Dictionary getDocumentProperties()
public final Position getEndPosition()
public int getLength()
public abstract Element
getParagraphElement(int pos)
public final Object getProperty(Object
key)
public Element getRootElements()
public final Position getStartPosition()
public String getText(int offset,int
length)
public void getText(int offset,int
length,Segment txt)
public void insertString(int offs,String
str,AttributeSet a)
protected void insertUpdate(
DefaultDocumentEvent chng,AttributeSet
attr)
protected void postRemoveUpdate(
DefaultDocumentEvent chng)
public final void putProperty(Object key,
Object value)
public final synchronized void readLock()
public final synchronized void
readUnlock()
public void remove(int offs,int len)
public void removeDocumentListener(
DocumentListener listener)
public void removeUndoableEditListener(
UndoableEditListener listener)
protected void removeUpdate(
DefaultDocumentEvent chng)
public void render(Runnable r)
public void setAsynchronousLoadPriority(
int p)
public void setDocumentProperties(
Dictionary x)
protected final synchronized void
writeLock()
protected final synchronized void
writeUnlock()

## AbstractLayoutCache
public abstract class javax.swing.tree.
AbstractLayoutCache
implements javax.swing.tree.RowMapper
extends java.lang.Object

## Fields

```
protected NodeDimensions nodeDimensions
protected boolean rootVisible
protected int rowHeight
protected javax.swing.tree.TreeModel
treeModel
protected javax.swing.tree.
TreeSelectionModel treeSelectionModel
```

## Methods

```
public abstract Rectangle getBounds(
TreePath path,Rectangle placeIn)
public abstract boolean getExpandedState(
TreePath path)
public TreeModel getModel()
public NodeDimensions getNodeDimensions()
protected Rectangle getNodeDimensions(
Object value,int row,int depth,boolean
expanded,Rectangle placeIn)
public abstract TreePath
getPathClosestTo(int x,int y)
public abstract TreePath getPathForRow(
int row)
public int getPreferredHeight()
public int getPreferredWidth(Rectangle
bounds)
public abstract int getRowCount()
public abstract int getRowForPath(
TreePath path)
public int getRowHeight()
public int getRowsForPaths(TreePath
paths)
public TreeSelectionModel
getSelectionModel()
public abstract int getVisibleChildCount(
TreePath path)
public abstract Enumeration
getVisiblePathsFrom(TreePath path)
public abstract void
invalidatePathBounds(TreePath path)
public abstract void invalidateSizes()
public abstract boolean isExpanded(
TreePath path)
protected boolean isFixedRowHeight()
public boolean isRootVisible()
public abstract void setExpandedState(
TreePath path,boolean isExpanded)
public void setModel(TreeModel newModel)
public void setNodeDimensions(
NodeDimensions nd)
public void setRootVisible(boolean
rootVisible)
public void setRowHeight(int rowHeight)
public void setSelectionModel(
TreeSelectionModel newLSM)
public abstract void treeNodesChanged(
TreeModelEvent e)
public abstract void treeNodesInserted(
TreeModelEvent e)
public abstract void treeNodesRemoved(
TreeModelEvent e)
public abstract void
treeStructureChanged(TreeModelEvent e)
```

## AbstractList

```
public abstract class java.util.
AbstractList
implements java.util.List
extends java.util.AbstractCollection
extends java.lang.Object
```

### Fields

```
protected transient int modCount
```

### Constructors

```
protected  AbstractList()
```

### Methods

```
public boolean add(Object o)
public void add(int index,Object element)
public boolean addAll(int index,
Collection c)
public void clear()
public boolean equals(Object o)
public abstract Object get(int index)
public int hashCode()
public int indexOf(Object o)
public Iterator iterator()
public int lastIndexOf(Object o)
public ListIterator listIterator()
public ListIterator listIterator(int
index)
public Object remove(int index)
protected void removeRange(int fromIndex,
int toIndex)
public Object set(int index,Object
element)
public List subList(int fromIndex,int
toIndex)
```

## AbstractListModel

```
public abstract class javax.swing.
AbstractListModel
implements javax.swing.ListModel
implements java.io.Serializable
extends java.lang.Object
```

### Fields

```
protected javax.swing.event.
EventListenerList listenerList
```

### Methods

```
public void addListDataListener(
ListDataListener l)
protected void fireContentsChanged(
Object source,int index0,int index1)
protected void fireIntervalAdded(Object
source,int index0,int index1)
protected void fireIntervalRemoved(
Object source,int index0,int index1)
public void removeListDataListener(
ListDataListener l)
```

## AbstractMap

```
public abstract class java.util.
AbstractMap
```

```
implements java.util.Map
extends java.lang.Object
```

**Constructors**
```
protected  AbstractMap()
```

**Methods**
```
public void clear()
public boolean containsKey(Object key)
public boolean containsValue(Object
value)
public abstract Set entrySet()
public boolean equals(Object o)
public Object get(Object key)
public int hashCode()
public boolean isEmpty()
public Set keySet()
public Object put(Object key,Object
value)
public void putAll(Map t)
public Object remove(Object key)
public int size()
public String toString()
public Collection values()
```

# AbstractMethodError
```
public class java.lang.
AbstractMethodError
extends java.lang.
IncompatibleClassChangeError
extends java.lang.LinkageError
extends java.lang.Error
extends java.lang.Throwable
extends java.lang.Object
```

**Constructors**
```
public  AbstractMethodError()
public  AbstractMethodError(String s)
```

# AbstractSequentialList
```
public abstract class java.util.
AbstractSequentialList
extends java.util.AbstractList
extends java.util.AbstractCollection
extends java.lang.Object
```

**Constructors**
```
protected  AbstractSequentialList()
```

**Methods**
```
public void add(int index,Object element)
public boolean addAll(int index,
Collection c)
public Object get(int index)
public Iterator iterator()
public abstract ListIterator
listIterator(int index)
public Object remove(int index)
public Object set(int index,Object
element)
```

# AbstractSet
```
public abstract class java.util.
AbstractSet
implements java.util.Set
extends java.util.AbstractCollection
extends java.lang.Object
```

**Constructors**
```
protected  AbstractSet()
```

**Methods**
```
public boolean equals(Object o)
public int hashCode()
```

# AbstractTableModel
```
public abstract class javax.swing.table.
AbstractTableModel
implements java.io.Serializable
implements javax.swing.table.TableModel
extends java.lang.Object
```

**Fields**
```
protected javax.swing.event.
EventListenerList listenerList
```

**Methods**
```
public void addTableModelListener(
TableModelListener l)
public int findColumn(String columnName)
public void fireTableCellUpdated(int row,
int column)
public void fireTableChanged(
TableModelEvent e)
public void fireTableDataChanged()
public void fireTableRowsDeleted(int
firstRow,int lastRow)
public void fireTableRowsInserted(int
firstRow,int lastRow)
public void fireTableRowsUpdated(int
firstRow,int lastRow)
public void fireTableStructureChanged()
public Class getColumnClass(int
columnIndex)
public String getColumnName(int column)
public boolean isCellEditable(int
rowIndex,int columnIndex)
public void removeTableModelListener(
TableModelListener l)
public void setValueAt(Object aValue,int
rowIndex,int columnIndex)
```

# AbstractUndoableEdit
```
public class javax.swing.undo.
AbstractUndoableEdit
implements java.io.Serializable
implements javax.swing.undo.
UndoableEdit
extends java.lang.Object
```

**Fields**
```
protected final static java.lang.String
RedoName
```

```
protected final static java.lang.String
UndoName
```

### Constructors

```
public AbstractUndoableEdit()
```

### Methods

```
public boolean addEdit(UndoableEdit
anEdit)
public boolean canRedo()
public boolean canUndo()
public void die()
public String getPresentationName()
public String getRedoPresentationName()
public String getUndoPresentationName()
public boolean isSignificant()
public void redo()
public boolean replaceEdit(UndoableEdit
anEdit)
public String toString()
public void undo()
```

## AbstractWriter

```
public abstract class javax.swing.text.
AbstractWriter
extends java.lang.Object
```

### Fields

```
protected final static char NEWLINE
```

### Constructors

```
protected AbstractWriter(Writer w,
Document doc)
protected AbstractWriter(Writer w,
Document doc,int pos,int len)
protected AbstractWriter(Writer w,
Element root)
protected AbstractWriter(Writer w,
Element root,int pos,int len)
```

### Methods

```
protected void decrIndent()
protected Document getDocument()
protected ElementIterator
getElementIterator()
protected String getText(Element elem)
protected void incrIndent()
protected void indent()
protected boolean inRange(Element next)
protected void setIndentSpace(int space)
protected void setLineLength(int l)
protected void text(Element elem)
protected abstract void write()
protected void write(char ch)
protected void write(String str)
protected void writeAttributes(
AttributeSet attr)
```

## AccessControlContext

```
public final class java.security.
AccessControlContext
extends java.lang.Object
```

### Constructors

```
public AccessControlContext(
ProtectionDomain context)
 AccessControlContext()
```

### Methods

```
public void checkPermission(Permission
perm)
public boolean equals(Object obj)
public int hashCode()
```

## AccessControlException

```
public class java.security.
AccessControlException
extends java.lang.SecurityException
extends java.lang.RuntimeException
extends java.lang.Exception
extends java.lang.Throwable
extends java.lang.Object
```

### Constructors

```
public AccessControlException(String s)
public AccessControlException(String s,
Permission p)
```

### Methods

```
public Permission getPermission()
```

## AccessController

```
public final class java.security.
AccessController
extends java.lang.Object
```

### Constructors

```
private AccessController()
```

### Methods

```
public static void checkPermission(
Permission perm)
public static native Object doPrivileged(
PrivilegedAction action)
public static native Object doPrivileged(
PrivilegedAction action,
AccessControlContext context)
public static native Object doPrivileged(
PrivilegedExceptionAction action)
public static native Object doPrivileged(
PrivilegedExceptionAction action,
AccessControlContext context)
public static AccessControlContext
getContext()
```

## AccessException

```
public class java.rmi.AccessException
extends java.rmi.RemoteException
extends java.io.IOException
extends java.lang.Exception
extends java.lang.Throwable
extends java.lang.Object
```

**Constructors**
```
public  AccessException(String s)
public  AccessException(String s,
Exception ex)
```

## AccessibleBundle

```
public abstract class javax.
accessibility.AccessibleBundle
extends java.lang.Object
```

### Fields
```
protected java.lang.String key
```

### Methods
```
protected String toDisplayString(String
resourceBundleName,Locale locale)
public String toDisplayString(Locale
locale)
public String toDisplayString()
public String toString()
```

## AccessibleContext

```
public abstract class javax.
accessibility.AccessibleContext
extends java.lang.Object
```

### Fields
```
protected java.lang.String
accessibleDescription
protected java.lang.String
accessibleName
protected javax.accessibility.Accessible
accessibleParent
public final static java.lang.String
ACCESSIBLE_ACTIVE_DESCENDANT_PROPERTY
public final static java.lang.String
ACCESSIBLE_CARET_PROPERTY
public final static java.lang.String
ACCESSIBLE_CHILD_PROPERTY
public final static java.lang.String
ACCESSIBLE_DESCRIPTION_PROPERTY
public final static java.lang.String
ACCESSIBLE_NAME_PROPERTY
public final static java.lang.String
ACCESSIBLE_SELECTION_PROPERTY
public final static java.lang.String
ACCESSIBLE_STATE_PROPERTY
public final static java.lang.String
ACCESSIBLE_TEXT_PROPERTY
public final static java.lang.String
ACCESSIBLE_VALUE_PROPERTY
public final static java.lang.String
ACCESSIBLE_VISIBLE_DATA_PROPERTY
```

### Methods
```
public void addPropertyChangeListener(
PropertyChangeListener listener)
public void firePropertyChange(String
propertyName,Object oldValue,Object
newValue)
public AccessibleAction
getAccessibleAction()
public abstract Accessible
getAccessibleChild(int i)
public abstract int
getAccessibleChildrenCount()
public AccessibleComponent
getAccessibleComponent()
public String getAccessibleDescription()
public abstract int
getAccessibleIndexInParent()
public String getAccessibleName()
public Accessible getAccessibleParent()
public abstract AccessibleRole
getAccessibleRole()
public AccessibleSelection
getAccessibleSelection()
public abstract AccessibleStateSet
getAccessibleStateSet()
public AccessibleText getAccessibleText()
public AccessibleValue
getAccessibleValue()
public abstract Locale getLocale()
public void removePropertyChangeListener(
PropertyChangeListener listener)
public void setAccessibleDescription(
String s)
public void setAccessibleName(String s)
public void setAccessibleParent(
Accessible a)
```

## AccessibleHyperlink

```
public abstract class javax.
accessibility.AccessibleHyperlink
implements javax.accessibility.
AccessibleAction
extends java.lang.Object
```

### Methods
```
public abstract boolean
doAccessibleAction(int i)
public abstract Object
getAccessibleActionAnchor(int i)
public abstract int
getAccessibleActionCount()
public abstract String
getAccessibleActionDescription(int i)
public abstract Object
getAccessibleActionObject(int i)
public abstract int getEndIndex()
public abstract int getStartIndex()
public abstract boolean isValid()
```

## AccessibleObject

```
public class java.lang.reflect.
AccessibleObject
extends java.lang.Object
```

### Constructors
```
protected  AccessibleObject()
```

### Methods
```
public boolean isAccessible()
public static void setAccessible(
AccessibleObject array,boolean flag)
public void setAccessible(boolean flag)
```

## AccessibleResourceBundle

public class javax.accessibility.
AccessibleResourceBundle
extends java.util.ListResourceBundle
extends java.util.ResourceBundle
extends java.lang.Object

### Methods
public Object getContents()

## AccessibleRole

public class javax.accessibility.
AccessibleRole
extends javax.accessibility.
AccessibleBundle
extends java.lang.Object

### Fields
public final static javax.accessibility.
AccessibleRole ALERT
public final static javax.accessibility.
AccessibleRole AWT_COMPONENT
public final static javax.accessibility.
AccessibleRole CHECK_BOX
public final static javax.accessibility.
AccessibleRole COLOR_CHOOSER
public final static javax.accessibility.
AccessibleRole COLUMN_HEADER
public final static javax.accessibility.
AccessibleRole COMBO_BOX
public final static javax.accessibility.
AccessibleRole DESKTOP_ICON
public final static javax.accessibility.
AccessibleRole DESKTOP_PANE
public final static javax.accessibility.
AccessibleRole DIALOG
public final static javax.accessibility.
AccessibleRole DIRECTORY_PANE
public final static javax.accessibility.
AccessibleRole FILE_CHOOSER
public final static javax.accessibility.
AccessibleRole FILLER
public final static javax.accessibility.
AccessibleRole FRAME
public final static javax.accessibility.
AccessibleRole GLASS_PANE
public final static javax.accessibility.
AccessibleRole INTERNAL_FRAME
public final static javax.accessibility.
AccessibleRole LABEL
public final static javax.accessibility.
AccessibleRole LAYERED_PANE
public final static javax.accessibility.
AccessibleRole LIST
public final static javax.accessibility.
AccessibleRole MENU
public final static javax.accessibility.
AccessibleRole MENU_BAR
public final static javax.accessibility.
AccessibleRole MENU_ITEM
public final static javax.accessibility.
AccessibleRole OPTION_PANE

public final static javax.accessibility.
AccessibleRole PAGE_TAB
public final static javax.accessibility.
AccessibleRole PAGE_TAB_LIST
public final static javax.accessibility.
AccessibleRole PANEL
public final static javax.accessibility.
AccessibleRole PASSWORD_TEXT
public final static javax.accessibility.
AccessibleRole POPUP_MENU
public final static javax.accessibility.
AccessibleRole PROGRESS_BAR
public final static javax.accessibility.
AccessibleRole PUSH_BUTTON
public final static javax.accessibility.
AccessibleRole RADIO_BUTTON
public final static javax.accessibility.
AccessibleRole ROOT_PANE
public final static javax.accessibility.
AccessibleRole ROW_HEADER
public final static javax.accessibility.
AccessibleRole SCROLL_BAR
public final static javax.accessibility.
AccessibleRole SCROLL_PANE
public final static javax.accessibility.
AccessibleRole SEPARATOR
public final static javax.accessibility.
AccessibleRole SLIDER
public final static javax.accessibility.
AccessibleRole SPLIT_PANE
public final static javax.accessibility.
AccessibleRole SWING_COMPONENT
public final static javax.accessibility.
AccessibleRole TABLE
public final static javax.accessibility.
AccessibleRole TEXT
public final static javax.accessibility.
AccessibleRole TOGGLE_BUTTON
public final static javax.accessibility.
AccessibleRole TOOL_BAR
public final static javax.accessibility.
AccessibleRole TOOL_TIP
public final static javax.accessibility.
AccessibleRole TREE
public final static javax.accessibility.
AccessibleRole UNKNOWN
public final static javax.accessibility.
AccessibleRole VIEWPORT
public final static javax.accessibility.
AccessibleRole WINDOW

### Constructors
protected  AccessibleRole(String key)

## AccessibleState

public class javax.accessibility.
AccessibleState
extends javax.accessibility.
AccessibleBundle
extends java.lang.Object

## Fields

public final static javax.accessibility.
AccessibleState ACTIVE
public final static javax.accessibility.
AccessibleState ARMED
public final static javax.accessibility.
AccessibleState BUSY
public final static javax.accessibility.
AccessibleState CHECKED
public final static javax.accessibility.
AccessibleState COLLAPSED
public final static javax.accessibility.
AccessibleState EDITABLE
public final static javax.accessibility.
AccessibleState ENABLED
public final static javax.accessibility.
AccessibleState EXPANDABLE
public final static javax.accessibility.
AccessibleState EXPANDED
public final static javax.accessibility.
AccessibleState FOCUSABLE
public final static javax.accessibility.
AccessibleState FOCUSED
public final static javax.accessibility.
AccessibleState HORIZONTAL
public final static javax.accessibility.
AccessibleState ICONIFIED
public final static javax.accessibility.
AccessibleState MODAL
public final static javax.accessibility.
AccessibleState MULTISELECTABLE
public final static javax.accessibility.
AccessibleState MULTI_LINE
public final static javax.accessibility.
AccessibleState OPAQUE
public final static javax.accessibility.
AccessibleState PRESSED
public final static javax.accessibility.
AccessibleState RESIZABLE
public final static javax.accessibility.
AccessibleState SELECTABLE
public final static javax.accessibility.
AccessibleState SELECTED
public final static javax.accessibility.
AccessibleState SHOWING
public final static javax.accessibility.
AccessibleState SINGLE_LINE
public final static javax.accessibility.
AccessibleState TRANSIENT
public final static javax.accessibility.
AccessibleState VERTICAL
public final static javax.accessibility.
AccessibleState VISIBLE

## Constructors

protected  AccessibleState(String key)

# AccessibleStateSet

public class javax.accessibility.
AccessibleStateSet
extends java.lang.Object

## Fields

protected java.util.Vector states

## Constructors

public  AccessibleStateSet()
public  AccessibleStateSet(
AccessibleState states)

## Methods

public boolean add(AccessibleState state)
public void addAll(AccessibleState
states)
public void clear()
public boolean contains(AccessibleState
state)
public boolean remove(AccessibleState
state)
public AccessibleState toArray()
public String toString()

# AclNotFoundException

public class java.security.acl.
AclNotFoundException
extends java.lang.Exception
extends java.lang.Throwable
extends java.lang.Object

## Constructors

public  AclNotFoundException()

# ActionEvent

public class java.awt.event.ActionEvent
extends java.awt.AWTEvent
extends java.util.EventObject
extends java.lang.Object

## Fields

public final static int ACTION_FIRST
public final static int ACTION_LAST
public final static int ACTION_
PERFORMED
public final static int ALT_MASK
public final static int CTRL_MASK
public final static int META_MASK
public final static int SHIFT_MASK

## Constructors

public  ActionEvent(Object source,int id,
String command)
public  ActionEvent(Object source,int id,
String command,int modifiers)

## Methods

public String getActionCommand()
public int getModifiers()
public String paramString()

# Activatable

public abstract class java.rmi.
activation.Activatable
extends java.rmi.server.RemoteServer
extends java.rmi.server.RemoteObject
extends java.lang.Object

## Constructors

```
protected  Activatable(String location,
MarshalledObject data,boolean restart,
int port)
protected  Activatable(String location,
MarshalledObject data,boolean restart,
int port,RMIClientSocketFactory csf,
RMIServerSocketFactory ssf)
protected  Activatable(ActivationID id,
int port)
protected  Activatable(ActivationID id,
int port,RMIClientSocketFactory csf,
RMIServerSocketFactory ssf)
```

## Methods

```
public static ActivationID exportObject(
Remote obj,String location,
MarshalledObject data,boolean restart,
int port)
public static ActivationID exportObject(
Remote obj,String location,
MarshalledObject data,boolean restart,
int port,RMIClientSocketFactory csf,
RMIServerSocketFactory ssf)
public static Remote exportObject(Remote
obj,ActivationID id,int port)
public static Remote exportObject(Remote
obj,ActivationID id,int port,
RMIClientSocketFactory csf,
RMIServerSocketFactory ssf)
protected ActivationID getID()
public static boolean inactive(
ActivationID id)
public static Remote register(
ActivationDesc desc)
public static boolean unexportObject(
Remote obj,boolean force)
public static void unregister(
ActivationID id)
```

# ActivateFailedException

```
public class java.rmi.activation.
ActivateFailedException
extends java.rmi.RemoteException
extends java.io.IOException
extends java.lang.Exception
extends java.lang.Throwable
extends java.lang.Object
```

## Constructors

```
public  ActivateFailedException(String s)
public  ActivateFailedException(String s,
Exception ex)
```

# ActivationDesc

```
public final class java.rmi.activation.
ActivationDesc
implements java.io.Serializable
extends java.lang.Object
```

## Constructors

```
public  ActivationDesc(String className,
String location,MarshalledObject data)
```

```
public  ActivationDesc(String className,
String location,MarshalledObject data,
boolean restart)
public  ActivationDesc(ActivationGroupID
groupID,String className,String location,
MarshalledObject data)
public  ActivationDesc(ActivationGroupID
groupID,String className,String location,
MarshalledObject data,boolean restart)
```

## Methods

```
public boolean equals(Object obj)
public String getClassName()
public MarshalledObject getData()
public ActivationGroupID getGroupID()
public String getLocation()
public boolean getRestartMode()
public int hashCode()
```

# ActivationException

```
public class java.rmi.activation.
ActivationException
extends java.lang.Exception
extends java.lang.Throwable
extends java.lang.Object
```

## Fields

```
public java.lang.Throwable detail
```

## Constructors

```
public  ActivationException()
public  ActivationException(String s)
public  ActivationException(String s,
Throwable ex)
```

## Methods

```
public String getMessage()
public void printStackTrace(PrintStream
ps)
public void printStackTrace()
public void printStackTrace(PrintWriter
pw)
```

# ActivationGroup

```
public abstract class java.rmi.
activation.ActivationGroup
implements java.rmi.activation.
ActivationInstantiator
extends java.rmi.server.
UnicastRemoteObject
extends java.rmi.server.RemoteServer
extends java.rmi.server.RemoteObject
extends java.lang.Object
```

## Constructors

```
protected  ActivationGroup(
ActivationGroupID groupID)
```

## Methods

```
public abstract void activeObject(
ActivationID id,Remote obj)
protected void activeObject(ActivationID
id,MarshalledObject mobj)
```

```
public static synchronized
ActivationGroup createGroup(
ActivationGroupID id,ActivationGroupDesc
desc,long incarnation)
public static synchronized
ActivationGroupID currentGroupID()
public static synchronized
ActivationSystem getSystem()
protected void inactiveGroup()
public boolean inactiveObject(
ActivationID id)
public static synchronized void
setSystem(ActivationSystem system)
```

## ActivationGroupDesc

```
public final class java.rmi.activation.
ActivationGroupDesc
implements java.io.Serializable
extends java.lang.Object
```

### Constructors

```
public  ActivationGroupDesc(Properties
overrides,CommandEnvironment cmd)
public  ActivationGroupDesc(String
className,String location,
MarshalledObject data,Properties
overrides,CommandEnvironment cmd)
```

### Methods

```
public boolean equals(Object obj)
public String getClassName()
public CommandEnvironment
getCommandEnvironment()
public MarshalledObject getData()
public String getLocation()
public Properties getPropertyOverrides()
public int hashCode()
```

## ActivationGroupID

```
public class java.rmi.activation.
ActivationGroupID
implements java.io.Serializable
extends java.lang.Object
```

### Constructors

```
public  ActivationGroupID(
ActivationSystem system)
```

### Methods

```
public boolean equals(Object obj)
public ActivationSystem getSystem()
public int hashCode()
```

## ActivationID

```
public class java.rmi.activation.
ActivationID
implements java.io.Serializable
extends java.lang.Object
```

### Constructors

```
public  ActivationID(Activator activator)
```

### Methods

```
public Remote activate(boolean force)
public boolean equals(Object obj)
public int hashCode()
```

## AdjustmentEvent

```
public class java.awt.event.
AdjustmentEvent
extends java.awt.AWTEvent
extends java.util.EventObject
extends java.lang.Object
```

### Fields

```
public final static int ADJUSTMENT_
FIRST
public final static int ADJUSTMENT_LAST
public final static int ADJUSTMENT_VALUE_
CHANGED
public final static int BLOCK_DECREMENT
public final static int BLOCK_INCREMENT
public final static int TRACK
public final static int UNIT_DECREMENT
public final static int UNIT_INCREMENT
```

### Constructors

```
public  AdjustmentEvent(Adjustable
source,int id,int type,int value)
```

### Methods

```
public Adjustable getAdjustable()
public int getAdjustmentType()
public int getValue()
public String paramString()
```

## Adler32

```
public class java.util.zip.Adler32
implements java.util.zip.Checksum
extends java.lang.Object
```

### Constructors

```
public static  Adler32()
```

### Methods

```
public long getValue()
public void reset()
public void update(int b)
public void update(byte b,int off,int
len)
public void update(byte b)
```

## AffineTransform

```
public class java.awt.geom.
AffineTransform
implements java.lang.Cloneable
implements java.io.Serializable
extends java.lang.Object
```

### Fields

```
public final static int TYPE_FLIP
public final static int TYPE_GENERAL_
ROTATION
```

```
public final static int TYPE_GENERAL_
SCALE
public final static int TYPE_GENERAL_
TRANSFORM
public final static int TYPE_IDENTITY
public final static int TYPE_MASK_
ROTATION
public final static int TYPE_MASK_SCALE
public final static int TYPE_QUADRANT_
ROTATION
public final static int TYPE_
TRANSLATION
public final static int TYPE_UNIFORM_
SCALE
```

### Constructors
```
private  AffineTransform()
public  AffineTransform()
public  AffineTransform(AffineTransform
Tx)
public  AffineTransform(float m00,float
m10,float m01,float m11,float m02,float
m12)
public  AffineTransform(float flatmatrix)
public  AffineTransform(double m00,
double m10,double m01,double m11,double
m02,double m12)
public  AffineTransform(double
flatmatrix)
```

### Methods
```
public Object clone()
public void concatenate(AffineTransform
Tx)
public AffineTransform createInverse()
public Shape createTransformedShape(
Shape pSrc)
public Point2D deltaTransform(Point2D
ptSrc,Point2D ptDst)
public void deltaTransform(double srcPts,
int srcOff,double dstPts,int dstOff,int
numPts)
public boolean equals(Object obj)
public double getDeterminant()
public void getMatrix(double flatmatrix)
public static AffineTransform
getRotateInstance(double theta)
public static AffineTransform
getRotateInstance(double theta,double x,
double y)
public static AffineTransform
getScaleInstance(double sx,double sy)
public double getScaleX()
public double getScaleY()
public static AffineTransform
getShearInstance(double shx,double sy)
public double getShearX()
public double getShearY()
public static AffineTransform
getTranslateInstance(double tx,double ty)
public double getTranslateX()
public double getTranslateY()
public int getType()
public int hashCode()
```

```
public Point2D inverseTransform(Point2D
ptSrc,Point2D ptDst)
public void inverseTransform(double
srcPts,int srcOff,double dstPts,int
dstOff,int numPts)
public boolean isIdentity()
public void preConcatenate(
AffineTransform Tx)
public void rotate(double theta)
public void rotate(double theta,double x,
double y)
public void scale(double sx,double sy)
public void setToIdentity()
public void setToRotation(double theta)
public void setToRotation(double theta,
double x,double y)
public void setToScale(double sx,double
sy)
public void setToShear(double shx,double
shy)
public void setToTranslation(double tx,
double ty)
public void setTransform(AffineTransform
Tx)
public void setTransform(double m00,
double m10,double m01,double m11,double
m02,double m12)
public void shear(double shx,double shy)
public String toString()
public Point2D transform(Point2D ptSrc,
Point2D ptDst)
public void transform(Point2D ptSrc,int
srcOff,Point2D ptDst,int dstOff,int
numPts)
public void transform(float srcPts,int
srcOff,float dstPts,int dstOff,int
numPts)
public void transform(double srcPts,int
srcOff,double dstPts,int dstOff,int
numPts)
public void transform(float srcPts,int
srcOff,double dstPts,int dstOff,int
numPts)
public void transform(double srcPts,int
srcOff,float dstPts,int dstOff,int
numPts)
public void translate(double tx,double
ty)
```

## AffineTransformOp
```
public class java.awt.image.
AffineTransformOp
implements java.awt.image.
BufferedImageOp
implements java.awt.image.RasterOp
extends java.lang.Object
```

### Fields
```
public final static int TYPE_BILINEAR
public final static int TYPE_NEAREST_
NEIGHBOR
```

## Constructors

```
public AffineTransformOp(
AffineTransform xform,RenderingHints
hints)
public AffineTransformOp(
AffineTransform xform,int
interpolationType)
```

## Methods

```
public BufferedImage
createCompatibleDestImage(BufferedImage
src,ColorModel destCM)
public WritableRaster
createCompatibleDestRaster(Raster src)
public final BufferedImage filter(
BufferedImage src,BufferedImage dst)
public final WritableRaster filter(
Raster src,WritableRaster dst)
public final Rectangle2D getBounds2D(
BufferedImage src)
public final Rectangle2D getBounds2D(
Raster src)
public final int getInterpolationType()
public final Point2D getPoint2D(Point2D
srcPt,Point2D dstPt)
public final RenderingHints
getRenderingHints()
public final AffineTransform
getTransform()
```

# AlgorithmParameterGenerator

```
public class java.security.
AlgorithmParameterGenerator
extends java.lang.Object
```

## Constructors

```
protected AlgorithmParameterGenerator(
AlgorithmParameterGeneratorSpi
paramGenSpi,Provider provider,String
algorithm)
```

## Methods

```
public final AlgorithmParameters
generateParameters()
public final String getAlgorithm()
public static
AlgorithmParameterGenerator getInstance(
String algorithm)
public static
AlgorithmParameterGenerator getInstance(
String algorithm,String provider)
public final Provider getProvider()
public final void init(int size)
public final void init(int size,
SecureRandom random)
public final void init(
AlgorithmParameterSpec genParamSpec)
public final void init(
AlgorithmParameterSpec genParamSpec,
SecureRandom random)
```

# AlgorithmParameterGeneratorSpi

```
public abstract class java.security.
AlgorithmParameterGeneratorSpi
extends java.lang.Object
```

## Methods

```
protected abstract AlgorithmParameters
engineGenerateParameters()
protected abstract void engineInit(int
size,SecureRandom random)
protected abstract void engineInit(
AlgorithmParameterSpec genParamSpec,
SecureRandom random)
```

# AlgorithmParameters

```
public class java.security.
AlgorithmParameters
extends java.lang.Object
```

## Constructors

```
protected AlgorithmParameters(
AlgorithmParametersSpi paramSpi,Provider
provider,String algorithm)
```

## Methods

```
public final String getAlgorithm()
public final byte getEncoded()
public final byte getEncoded(String
format)
public static AlgorithmParameters
getInstance(String algorithm)
public static AlgorithmParameters
getInstance(String algorithm,String
provider)
public final AlgorithmParameterSpec
getParameterSpec(Class paramSpec)
public final Provider getProvider()
public final void init(
AlgorithmParameterSpec paramSpec)
public final void init(byte params)
public final void init(byte params,
String format)
public final String toString()
```

# AlgorithmParametersSpi

```
public abstract class java.security.
AlgorithmParametersSpi
extends java.lang.Object
```

## Methods

```
protected abstract byte engineGetEncoded(
)
protected abstract byte engineGetEncoded(
String format)
protected abstract
AlgorithmParameterSpec
engineGetParameterSpec(Class paramSpec)
protected abstract void engineInit(
AlgorithmParameterSpec paramSpec)
```

```
protected abstract void engineInit(byte
params)
protected abstract void engineInit(byte
params,String format)
protected abstract String engineToString(
)
```

## AllPermission

```
public final class java.security.
AllPermission
extends java.security.Permission
extends java.lang.Object
```

### Constructors

```
public  AllPermission()
public  AllPermission(String name,String
actions)
```

### Methods

```
public boolean equals(Object obj)
public String getActions()
public int hashCode()
public boolean implies(Permission p)
public PermissionCollection
newPermissionCollection()
```

## AlphaComposite

```
public final class java.awt.
AlphaComposite
implements java.awt.Composite
extends java.lang.Object
```

### Fields

```
public final static int CLEAR
public final static java.awt.
AlphaComposite Clear
public final static java.awt.
AlphaComposite DstIn
public final static java.awt.
AlphaComposite DstOut
public final static java.awt.
AlphaComposite DstOver
public final static int DST_IN
public final static int DST_OUT
public final static int DST_OVER
public final static int SRC
public final static java.awt.
AlphaComposite Src
public final static java.awt.
AlphaComposite SrcIn
public final static java.awt.
AlphaComposite SrcOut
public final static java.awt.
AlphaComposite SrcOver
public final static int SRC_IN
public final static int SRC_OUT
public final static int SRC_OVER
```

### Constructors

```
private  AlphaComposite()
private  AlphaComposite()
```

### Methods

```
public CompositeContext createContext(
ColorModel srcColorModel,ColorModel
dstColorModel,RenderingHints hints)
public boolean equals(Object obj)
public float getAlpha()
public static AlphaComposite getInstance(
int rule)
public static AlphaComposite getInstance(
int rule,float alpha)
public int getRule()
public int hashCode()
```

## AlreadyBoundException

```
public class java.rmi.
AlreadyBoundException
extends java.lang.Exception
extends java.lang.Throwable
extends java.lang.Object
```

### Constructors

```
public  AlreadyBoundException()
public  AlreadyBoundException(String s)
```

## AncestorEvent

```
public class javax.swing.event.
AncestorEvent
extends java.awt.AWTEvent
extends java.util.EventObject
extends java.lang.Object
```

### Fields

```
public final static int ANCESTOR_ADDED
public final static int ANCESTOR_MOVED
public final static int ANCESTOR_
REMOVED
```

### Constructors

```
public  AncestorEvent(JComponent source,
int id,Container ancestor,Container
ancestorParent)
```

### Methods

```
public Container getAncestor()
public Container getAncestorParent()
public JComponent getComponent()
```

## Annotation

```
public class java.text.Annotation
extends java.lang.Object
```

### Constructors

```
public  Annotation(Object value)
```

### Methods

```
public Object getValue()
public String toString()
```

## Applet

```
public class java.applet.Applet
extends java.awt.Panel
extends java.awt.Container
```

extends java.awt.Component
extends java.lang.Object

## Methods
public void destroy()
public AppletContext getAppletContext()
public String getAppletInfo()
public AudioClip getAudioClip(URL url)
public AudioClip getAudioClip(URL url,
String name)
public URL getCodeBase()
public URL getDocumentBase()
public Image getImage(URL url)
public Image getImage(URL url,String
name)
public Locale getLocale()
public String getParameter(String name)
public String getParameterInfo()
public void init()
public boolean isActive()
public final static AudioClip
newAudioClip(URL url)
public void play(URL url)
public void play(URL url,String name)
public void resize(int width,int height)
public void resize(Dimension d)
public final void setStub(AppletStub
stub)
public void showStatus(String msg)
public void start()
public void stop()

# Arc2D
public abstract class java.awt.geom.
Arc2D
extends java.awt.geom.RectangularShape
extends java.lang.Object

## Fields
public final static int CHORD
public final static int OPEN
public final static int PIE

## Constructors
protected  Arc2D(int type)

## Methods
public boolean contains(double x,double
y)
public boolean contains(double x,double
y,double w,double h)
public boolean contains(Rectangle2D r)
public boolean containsAngle(double
angle)
public abstract double getAngleExtent()
public abstract double getAngleStart()
public int getArcType()
public Rectangle2D getBounds2D()
public Point2D getEndPoint()
public PathIterator getPathIterator(
AffineTransform at)
public Point2D getStartPoint()

public boolean intersects(double x,
double y,double w,double h)
protected abstract Rectangle2D
makeBounds(double x,double y,double w,
double h)
public abstract void setAngleExtent(
double angExt)
public void setAngles(double x1,double
y1,double x2,double y2)
public void setAngles(Point2D p1,Point2D
p2)
public abstract void setAngleStart(
double angSt)
public void setAngleStart(Point2D p)
public abstract void setArc(double x,
double y,double w,double h,double angSt,
double angExt,int closure)
public void setArc(Point2D loc,
Dimension2D size,double angSt,double
angExt,int closure)
public void setArc(Rectangle2D rect,
double angSt,double angExt,int closure)
public void setArc(Arc2D a)
public void setArcByCenter(double x,
double y,double radius,double angSt,
double angExt,int closure)
public void setArcByTangent(Point2D p1,
Point2D p2,Point2D p3,double radius)
public void setArcType(int type)
public void setFrame(double x,double y,
double w,double h)

# Area
public class java.awt.geom.Area
implements java.lang.Cloneable
implements java.awt.Shape
extends java.lang.Object

## Constructors
public  Area()
public  Area(Shape g)
 Area()

## Methods
public void add(Area rhs)
public Object clone()
public boolean contains(double x,double
y)
public boolean contains(Point2D p)
public boolean contains(double x,double
y,double w,double h)
public boolean contains(Rectangle2D r)
public Area createTransformedArea(
AffineTransform t)
public boolean equals(Area rhs)
public void exclusiveOr(Area rhs)
public Rectangle getBounds()
public Rectangle2D getBounds2D()
public PathIterator getPathIterator(
AffineTransform t)
public PathIterator getPathIterator(
AffineTransform t,double f)
public void intersect(Area rhs)

```
public boolean intersects(double x,
double y,double w,double h)
public boolean intersects(Rectangle2D r)
public boolean isEmpty()
public boolean isPolygonal()
public boolean isRectangular()
public boolean isSingular()
public void reset()
public void subtract(Area rhs)
public void transform(AffineTransform t)
```

## AreaAveragingScaleFilter

```
public class java.awt.image.
AreaAveragingScaleFilter
extends java.awt.image.
ReplicateScaleFilter
extends java.awt.image.ImageFilter
extends java.lang.Object
```

### Constructors
```
public  AreaAveragingScaleFilter(int
width,int height)
```

### Methods
```
public void setHints(int hints)
public void setPixels(int x,int y,int w,
int h,ColorModel model,byte pixels,int
off,int scansize)
public void setPixels(int x,int y,int w,
int h,ColorModel model,int pixels,int
off,int scansize)
```

## ArithmeticException

```
public class java.lang.
ArithmeticException
extends java.lang.RuntimeException
extends java.lang.Exception
extends java.lang.Throwable
extends java.lang.Object
```

### Constructors
```
public  ArithmeticException()
public  ArithmeticException(String s)
```

## Array

```
public final class java.lang.reflect.
Array
extends java.lang.Object
```

### Constructors
```
private  Array()
```

### Methods
```
public static native Object get(Object
array,int index)
public static native boolean getBoolean(
Object array,int index)
public static native byte getByte(Object
array,int index)
public static native char getChar(Object
array,int index)
```

```
public static native double getDouble(
Object array,int index)
public static native float getFloat(
Object array,int index)
public static native int getInt(Object
array,int index)
public static native int getLength(
Object array)
public static native long getLong(Object
array,int index)
public static native short getShort(
Object array,int index)
public static Object newInstance(Class
componentType,int length)
public static Object newInstance(Class
componentType,int dimensions)
public static native void set(Object
array,int index,Object value)
public static native void setBoolean(
Object array,int index,boolean z)
public static native void setByte(Object
array,int index,byte b)
public static native void setChar(Object
array,int index,char c)
public static native void setDouble(
Object array,int index,double d)
public static native void setFloat(
Object array,int index,float f)
public static native void setInt(Object
array,int index,int i)
public static native void setLong(Object
array,int index,long l)
public static native void setShort(
Object array,int index,short s)
```

## ArrayIndexOutOfBoundsException

```
public class java.lang.
ArrayIndexOutOfBoundsException
extends java.lang.
IndexOutOfBoundsException
extends java.lang.RuntimeException
extends java.lang.Exception
extends java.lang.Throwable
extends java.lang.Object
```

### Constructors
```
public  ArrayIndexOutOfBoundsException()
public  ArrayIndexOutOfBoundsException(
int index)
public  ArrayIndexOutOfBoundsException(
String s)
```

## ArrayList

```
public class java.util.ArrayList
implements java.lang.Cloneable
implements java.util.List
implements java.io.Serializable
extends java.util.AbstractList
extends java.util.AbstractCollection
extends java.lang.Object
```

### Constructors
```
public  ArrayList(int initialCapacity)
```

```
public  ArrayList()
public  ArrayList(Collection c)
```

### Methods
```
public boolean add(Object o)
public void add(int index,Object element)
public boolean addAll(Collection c)
public boolean addAll(int index,
Collection c)
public void clear()
public Object clone()
public boolean contains(Object elem)
public void ensureCapacity(int
minCapacity)
public Object get(int index)
public int indexOf(Object elem)
public boolean isEmpty()
public int lastIndexOf(Object elem)
public Object remove(int index)
protected void removeRange(int fromIndex,
int toIndex)
public Object set(int index,Object
element)
public int size()
public Object toArray()
public Object toArray(Object a)
public void trimToSize()
```

# Arrays
```
public class java.util.Arrays
extends java.lang.Object
```

### Constructors
```
private  Arrays()
```

### Methods
```
public static List asList(Object a)
public static int binarySearch(long a,
long key)
public static int binarySearch(int a,int
key)
public static int binarySearch(short a,
short key)
public static int binarySearch(char a,
char key)
public static int binarySearch(byte a,
byte key)
public static int binarySearch(double a,
double key)
public static int binarySearch(float a,
float key)
public static int binarySearch(Object a,
Object key)
public static int binarySearch(Object a,
Object key,Comparator c)
public static boolean equals(long a,long
a2)
public static boolean equals(int a,int
a2)
public static boolean equals(short a,
short a2)
public static boolean equals(char a,char
a2)
```

```
public static boolean equals(byte a,byte
a2)
public static boolean equals(boolean a,
boolean a2)
public static boolean equals(double a,
double a2)
public static boolean equals(float a,
float a2)
public static boolean equals(Object a,
Object a2)
public static void fill(long a,long val)
public static void fill(long a,int
fromIndex,int toIndex,long val)
public static void fill(int a,int val)
public static void fill(int a,int
fromIndex,int toIndex,int val)
public static void fill(short a,short
val)
public static void fill(short a,int
fromIndex,int toIndex,short val)
public static void fill(char a,char val)
public static void fill(char a,int
fromIndex,int toIndex,char val)
public static void fill(byte a,byte val)
public static void fill(byte a,int
fromIndex,int toIndex,byte val)
public static void fill(boolean a,
boolean val)
public static void fill(boolean a,int
fromIndex,int toIndex,boolean val)
public static void fill(double a,double
val)
public static void fill(double a,int
fromIndex,int toIndex,double val)
public static void fill(float a,float
val)
public static void fill(float a,int
fromIndex,int toIndex,float val)
public static void fill(Object a,Object
val)
public static void fill(Object a,int
fromIndex,int toIndex,Object val)
public static void sort(long a)
public static void sort(long a,int
fromIndex,int toIndex)
public static void sort(int a)
public static void sort(int a,int
fromIndex,int toIndex)
public static void sort(short a)
public static void sort(short a,int
fromIndex,int toIndex)
public static void sort(char a)
public static void sort(char a,int
fromIndex,int toIndex)
public static void sort(byte a)
public static void sort(byte a,int
fromIndex,int toIndex)
public static void sort(double a)
public static void sort(double a,int
fromIndex,int toIndex)
public static void sort(float a)
public static void sort(float a,int
fromIndex,int toIndex)
public static void sort(Object a)
```

```
public static void sort(Object a,int
fromIndex,int toIndex)
public static void sort(Object a,
Comparator c)
public static void sort(Object a,int
fromIndex,int toIndex,Comparator c)
```

## ArrayStoreException

```
public class java.lang.
ArrayStoreException
extends java.lang.RuntimeException
extends java.lang.Exception
extends java.lang.Throwable
extends java.lang.Object
```

### Constructors

```
public  ArrayStoreException()
public  ArrayStoreException(String s)
```

## AttributedString

```
public class java.text.AttributedString
extends java.lang.Object
```

### Constructors

```
public  AttributedString(String text)
public  AttributedString(String text,Map
attributes)
public  AttributedString(
AttributedCharacterIterator text)
public  AttributedString(
AttributedCharacterIterator text,int
beginIndex,int endIndex)
public  AttributedString(
AttributedCharacterIterator text,int
beginIndex,int endIndex,Attribute
attributes)
```

### Methods

```
public void addAttribute(Attribute
attribute,Object value)
public void addAttribute(Attribute
attribute,Object value,int beginIndex,
int endIndex)
public void addAttributes(Map attributes,
int beginIndex,int endIndex)
public AttributedCharacterIterator
getIterator()
public AttributedCharacterIterator
getIterator(Attribute attributes)
public AttributedCharacterIterator
getIterator(Attribute attributes,int
beginIndex,int endIndex)
```

## AttributeList

```
public final class javax.swing.text.html.
parser.AttributeList
implements javax.swing.text.html.parser.
DTDConstants
implements java.io.Serializable
extends java.lang.Object
```

### Fields

```
public int modifier
public java.lang.String name
public javax.swing.text.html.parser.
AttributeList next
public int type
public java.lang.String value
public java.util.Vector values
```

### Constructors

```
 AttributeList()
public  AttributeList(String name)
public  AttributeList(String name,int
type,int modifier,String value,Vector
values,AttributeList next)
```

### Methods

```
public int getModifier()
public String getName()
public AttributeList getNext()
public int getType()
public String getValue()
public Enumeration getValues()
public static int name2type(String nm)
public String toString()
public static String type2name(int tp)
```

## Attributes

```
public class java.util.jar.Attributes
implements java.lang.Cloneable
implements java.util.Map
extends java.lang.Object
```

### Fields

```
protected java.util.Map map
```

### Constructors

```
public  Attributes()
public  Attributes(int size)
public  Attributes(Attributes attr)
```

### Methods

```
public void clear()
public Object clone()
public boolean containsKey(Object name)
public boolean containsValue(Object
value)
public Set entrySet()
public boolean equals(Object o)
public Object get(Object name)
public String getValue(String name)
public String getValue(Name name)
public int hashCode()
public boolean isEmpty()
public Set keySet()
public Object put(Object name,Object
value)
public void putAll(Map attr)
public String putValue(String name,
String value)
public Object remove(Object name)
public int size()
public Collection values()
```

# Authenticator

```
public abstract class java.net.
Authenticator
extends java.lang.Object
```

## Methods

```
protected PasswordAuthentication
getPasswordAuthentication()
protected final int getRequestingPort()
protected final String
getRequestingPrompt()
protected final String
getRequestingProtocol()
protected final String
getRequestingScheme()
protected final InetAddress
getRequestingSite()
public static PasswordAuthentication
requestPasswordAuthentication(
InetAddress addr,int port,String
protocol,String prompt,String scheme)
public static synchronized void
setDefault(Authenticator a)
```

# AWTError

```
public class java.awt.AWTError
extends java.lang.Error
extends java.lang.Throwable
extends java.lang.Object
```

## Constructors

```
public  AWTError(String msg)
```

# AWTEvent

```
public abstract class java.awt.AWTEvent
extends java.util.EventObject
extends java.lang.Object
```

## Fields

```
public final static long ACTION_EVENT_
MASK
public final static long ADJUSTMENT_
EVENT_MASK
public final static long COMPONENT_EVENT_
MASK
protected boolean consumed
public final static long CONTAINER_EVENT_
MASK
public final static long FOCUS_EVENT_
MASK
protected int id
public final static long INPUT_METHOD_
EVENT_MASK
public final static long ITEM_EVENT_
MASK
public final static long KEY_EVENT_MASK
public final static long MOUSE_EVENT_
MASK
public final static long MOUSE_MOTION_
EVENT_MASK
public final static int RESERVED_ID_MAX
public final static long TEXT_EVENT_
MASK
```

```
public final static long WINDOW_EVENT_
MASK
```

## Constructors

```
public  AWTEvent(Event event)
public  AWTEvent(Object source,int id)
```

## Methods

```
protected void consume()
protected void finalize()
public int getID()
protected boolean isConsumed()
public String paramString()
public String toString()
```

# AWTEventMulticaster

```
public class java.awt.
AWTEventMulticaster
implements java.awt.event.
ActionListener
implements java.awt.event.
AdjustmentListener
implements java.awt.event.
ComponentListener
implements java.awt.event.
ContainerListener
implements java.awt.event.FocusListener
implements java.awt.event.
InputMethodListener
implements java.awt.event.ItemListener
implements java.awt.event.KeyListener
implements java.awt.event.MouseListener
implements java.awt.event.
MouseMotionListener
implements java.awt.event.TextListener
implements java.awt.event.
WindowListener
extends java.lang.Object
```

## Fields

```
protected final java.util.EventListener
a
```

## Constructors

```
protected  AWTEventMulticaster(
EventListener a,EventListener b)
```

## Methods

```
public void actionPerformed(ActionEvent
e)
public static ComponentListener add(
ComponentListener a,ComponentListener b)
public static ContainerListener add(
ContainerListener a,ContainerListener b)
public static FocusListener add(
FocusListener a,FocusListener b)
public static KeyListener add(
KeyListener a,KeyListener b)
public static MouseListener add(
MouseListener a,MouseListener b)
public static MouseMotionListener add(
MouseMotionListener a,
MouseMotionListener b)
```

public static WindowListener add(
WindowListener a,WindowListener b)
public static ActionListener add(
ActionListener a,ActionListener b)
public static ItemListener add(
ItemListener a,ItemListener b)
public static AdjustmentListener add(
AdjustmentListener a,AdjustmentListener
b)
public static TextListener add(
TextListener a,TextListener b)
public static InputMethodListener add(
InputMethodListener a,
InputMethodListener b)
protected static EventListener
addInternal(EventListener a,
EventListener b)
public void adjustmentValueChanged(
AdjustmentEvent e)
public void caretPositionChanged(
InputMethodEvent e)
public void componentAdded(
ContainerEvent e)
public void componentHidden(
ComponentEvent e)
public void componentMoved(
ComponentEvent e)
public void componentRemoved(
ContainerEvent e)
public void componentResized(
ComponentEvent e)
public void componentShown(
ComponentEvent e)
public void focusGained(FocusEvent e)
public void focusLost(FocusEvent e)
public void inputMethodTextChanged(
InputMethodEvent e)
public void itemStateChanged(ItemEvent e)
public void keyPressed(KeyEvent e)
public void keyReleased(KeyEvent e)
public void keyTyped(KeyEvent e)
public void mouseClicked(MouseEvent e)
public void mouseDragged(MouseEvent e)
public void mouseEntered(MouseEvent e)
public void mouseExited(MouseEvent e)
public void mouseMoved(MouseEvent e)
public void mousePressed(MouseEvent e)
public void mouseReleased(MouseEvent e)
protected EventListener remove(
EventListener oldl)
public static ComponentListener remove(
ComponentListener l,ComponentListener
oldl)
public static ContainerListener remove(
ContainerListener l,ContainerListener
oldl)
public static FocusListener remove(
FocusListener l,FocusListener oldl)
public static KeyListener remove(
KeyListener l,KeyListener oldl)
public static MouseListener remove(
MouseListener l,MouseListener oldl)

public static MouseMotionListener remove(
MouseMotionListener l,
MouseMotionListener oldl)
public static WindowListener remove(
WindowListener l,WindowListener oldl)
public static ActionListener remove(
ActionListener l,ActionListener oldl)
public static ItemListener remove(
ItemListener l,ItemListener oldl)
public static AdjustmentListener remove(
AdjustmentListener l,AdjustmentListener
oldl)
public static TextListener remove(
TextListener l,TextListener oldl)
public static InputMethodListener remove(
InputMethodListener l,
InputMethodListener oldl)
protected static EventListener
removeInternal(EventListener l,
EventListener oldl)
protected static void save(
ObjectOutputStream s,String k,
EventListener l)
protected void saveInternal(
ObjectOutputStream s,String k)
public void textValueChanged(TextEvent e)
public void windowActivated(WindowEvent
e)
public void windowClosed(WindowEvent e)
public void windowClosing(WindowEvent e)
public void windowDeactivated(
WindowEvent e)
public void windowDeiconified(
WindowEvent e)
public void windowIconified(WindowEvent
e)
public void windowOpened(WindowEvent e)

## AWTException
public class java.awt.AWTException
extends java.lang.Exception
extends java.lang.Throwable
extends java.lang.Object

### Constructors
public AWTException(String msg)

## AWTPermission
public final class java.awt.
AWTPermission
extends java.security.BasicPermission
extends java.security.Permission
extends java.lang.Object

### Constructors
public AWTPermission(String name)
public AWTPermission(String name,String
actions)

## BadLocationException
public class javax.swing.text.
BadLocationException

```
extends java.lang.Exception
extends java.lang.Throwable
extends java.lang.Object
```

### Constructors
```
public  BadLocationException(String s,
int offs)
```

### Methods
```
public int offsetRequested()
```

# BandCombineOp
```
public class java.awt.image.
BandCombineOp
implements java.awt.image.RasterOp
extends java.lang.Object
```

### Constructors
```
public  BandCombineOp(float matrix,
RenderingHints hints)
```

### Methods
```
public WritableRaster
createCompatibleDestRaster(Raster src)
public WritableRaster filter(Raster src,
WritableRaster dst)
public final Rectangle2D getBounds2D(
Raster src)
public final float getMatrix()
public final Point2D getPoint2D(Point2D
srcPt,Point2D dstPt)
public final RenderingHints
getRenderingHints()
```

# BandedSampleModel
```
public final class java.awt.image.
BandedSampleModel
extends java.awt.image.
ComponentSampleModel
extends java.awt.image.SampleModel
extends java.lang.Object
```

### Constructors
```
public  BandedSampleModel(int dataType,
int w,int h,int numBands)
public  BandedSampleModel(int dataType,
int w,int h,int scanlineStride,int
bankIndices,int bandOffsets)
```

### Methods
```
public SampleModel
createCompatibleSampleModel(int w,int h)
public DataBuffer createDataBuffer()
public SampleModel
createSubsetSampleModel(int bands)
public Object getDataElements(int x,int
y,Object obj,DataBuffer data)
public int getPixel(int x,int y,int
iArray,DataBuffer data)
public int getPixels(int x,int y,int w,
int h,int iArray,DataBuffer data)
```

```
public int getSample(int x,int y,int b,
DataBuffer data)
public int getSamples(int x,int y,int w,
int h,int b,int iArray,DataBuffer data)
public void setDataElements(int x,int y,
Object obj,DataBuffer data)
public void setPixel(int x,int y,int
iArray,DataBuffer data)
public void setPixels(int x,int y,int w,
int h,int iArray,DataBuffer data)
public void setSample(int x,int y,int b,
int s,DataBuffer data)
public void setSamples(int x,int y,int w,
int h,int b,int iArray,DataBuffer data)
```

# BasicArrowButton
```
public class javax.swing.plaf.basic.
BasicArrowButton
implements javax.swing.SwingConstants
extends javax.swing.JButton
extends javax.swing.AbstractButton
extends javax.swing.JComponent
extends java.awt.Container
extends java.awt.Component
extends java.lang.Object
```

### Fields
```
protected int direction
```

### Constructors
```
public  BasicArrowButton(int direction)
```

### Methods
```
public int getDirection()
public Dimension getMaximumSize()
public Dimension getMinimumSize()
public Dimension getPreferredSize()
public boolean isFocusTraversable()
public void paint(Graphics g)
public void paintTriangle(Graphics g,int
x,int y,int size,int direction,boolean
isEnabled)
public void setDirection(int dir)
```

# BasicBorders
```
public class javax.swing.plaf.basic.
BasicBorders
extends java.lang.Object
```

# BasicButtonListener
```
public class javax.swing.plaf.basic.
BasicButtonListener
implements javax.swing.event.
ChangeListener
implements java.awt.event.FocusListener
implements java.awt.event.MouseListener
implements java.awt.event.
MouseMotionListener
implements java.beans.
PropertyChangeListener
extends java.lang.Object
```

### Constructors
```
public BasicButtonListener(
AbstractButton b)
```

### Methods
```
protected void checkOpacity(
AbstractButton b)
public void focusGained(FocusEvent e)
public void focusLost(FocusEvent e)
public void installKeyboardActions(
JComponent c)
public void mouseClicked(MouseEvent e)
public void mouseDragged(MouseEvent e)
public void mouseEntered(MouseEvent e)
public void mouseExited(MouseEvent e)
public void mouseMoved(MouseEvent e)
public void mousePressed(MouseEvent e)
public void mouseReleased(MouseEvent e)
public void propertyChange(
PropertyChangeEvent e)
public void stateChanged(ChangeEvent e)
public void uninstallKeyboardActions(
JComponent c)
```

## BasicButtonUI
```
public class javax.swing.plaf.basic.
BasicButtonUI
extends javax.swing.plaf.ButtonUI
extends javax.swing.plaf.ComponentUI
extends java.lang.Object
```

### Fields
```
protected int defaultTextIconGap
protected int defaultTextShiftOffset
```

### Methods
```
protected void clearTextShiftOffset()
protected BasicButtonListener
createButtonListener(AbstractButton b)
public static ComponentUI createUI(
JComponent c)
public int getDefaultTextIconGap(
AbstractButton b)
public Dimension getMaximumSize(
JComponent c)
public Dimension getMinimumSize(
JComponent c)
public Dimension getPreferredSize(
JComponent c)
protected String getPropertyPrefix()
protected int getTextShiftOffset()
protected void installDefaults(
AbstractButton b)
protected void installKeyboardActions(
AbstractButton b)
protected void installListeners(
AbstractButton b)
public void installUI(JComponent c)
public void paint(Graphics g,JComponent
c)
protected void paintButtonPressed(
Graphics g,AbstractButton b)
```

```
protected void paintFocus(Graphics g,
AbstractButton b,Rectangle viewRect,
Rectangle textRect,Rectangle iconRect)
protected void paintIcon(Graphics g,
JComponent c,Rectangle iconRect)
protected void paintText(Graphics g,
JComponent c,Rectangle textRect,String
text)
protected void setTextShiftOffset()
protected void uninstallDefaults(
AbstractButton b)
protected void uninstallKeyboardActions(
AbstractButton b)
protected void uninstallListeners(
AbstractButton b)
public void uninstallUI(JComponent c)
```

## BasicCheckBoxMenuItemUI
```
public class javax.swing.plaf.basic.
BasicCheckBoxMenuItemUI
extends javax.swing.plaf.basic.
BasicMenuItemUI
extends javax.swing.plaf.MenuItemUI
extends javax.swing.plaf.ButtonUI
extends javax.swing.plaf.ComponentUI
extends java.lang.Object
```

### Methods
```
public static ComponentUI createUI(
JComponent c)
protected String getPropertyPrefix()
protected void installDefaults()
public void processMouseEvent(JMenuItem
item,MouseEvent e,MenuElement path,
MenuSelectionManager manager)
```

## BasicCheckBoxUI
```
public class javax.swing.plaf.basic.
BasicCheckBoxUI
extends javax.swing.plaf.basic.
BasicRadioButtonUI
extends javax.swing.plaf.basic.
BasicToggleButtonUI
extends javax.swing.plaf.basic.
BasicButtonUI
extends javax.swing.plaf.ButtonUI
extends javax.swing.plaf.ComponentUI
extends java.lang.Object
```

### Methods
```
public static ComponentUI createUI(
JComponent b)
public String getPropertyPrefix()
```

## BasicColorChooserUI
```
public class javax.swing.plaf.basic.
BasicColorChooserUI
extends javax.swing.plaf.ColorChooserUI
extends javax.swing.plaf.ComponentUI
extends java.lang.Object
```

## Fields

protected javax.swing.colorchooser.
AbstractColorChooserPanel
defaultChoosers
protected javax.swing.event.
ChangeListener previewListener
protected java.beans.
PropertyChangeListener
propertyChangeListener

## Methods

protected AbstractColorChooserPanel
createDefaultChoosers()
protected PropertyChangeListener
createPropertyChangeListener()
public static ComponentUI createUI(
JComponent c)
protected void installDefaults()
protected void installListeners()
protected void installPreviewPanel()
public void installUI(JComponent c)
protected void uninstallDefaultChoosers()
protected void uninstallDefaults()
protected void uninstallListeners()
public void uninstallUI(JComponent c)

# BasicComboBoxEditor

public class javax.swing.plaf.basic.
BasicComboBoxEditor
implements javax.swing.ComboBoxEditor
implements java.awt.event.FocusListener
extends java.lang.Object

## Fields

protected javax.swing.JTextField editor

## Constructors

public  BasicComboBoxEditor()

## Methods

public void addActionListener(
ActionListener l)
public void focusGained(FocusEvent e)
public void focusLost(FocusEvent e)
public Component getEditorComponent()
public Object getItem()
public void removeActionListener(
ActionListener l)
public void selectAll()
public void setItem(Object anObject)

# BasicComboBoxRenderer

public class javax.swing.plaf.basic.
BasicComboBoxRenderer
implements javax.swing.ListCellRenderer
implements java.io.Serializable
extends javax.swing.JLabel
extends javax.swing.JComponent
extends java.awt.Container
extends java.awt.Component
extends java.lang.Object

## Fields

protected static javax.swing.border.
Border noFocusBorder

## Constructors

public  BasicComboBoxRenderer()

## Methods

public Component
getListCellRendererComponent(JList list,
Object value,int index,boolean
isSelected,boolean cellHasFocus)

# BasicComboBoxUI

public class javax.swing.plaf.basic.
BasicComboBoxUI
extends javax.swing.plaf.ComboBoxUI
extends javax.swing.plaf.ComponentUI
extends java.lang.Object

## Fields

protected javax.swing.JButton
arrowButton
protected java.awt.Dimension
cachedMinimumSize
protected javax.swing.JComboBox
comboBox
protected javax.swing.CellRendererPane
currentValuePane
protected java.awt.Component editor
protected java.awt.event.FocusListener
focusListener
protected boolean hasFocus
protected boolean isMinimumSizeDirty
protected java.awt.event.ItemListener
itemListener
protected java.awt.event.KeyListener
keyListener
protected javax.swing.JList listBox
protected javax.swing.event.
ListDataListener listDataListener
protected javax.swing.plaf.basic.
ComboPopup popup
protected java.awt.event.KeyListener
popupKeyListener
protected java.awt.event.MouseListener
popupMouseListener
protected java.awt.event.
MouseMotionListener
popupMouseMotionListener
protected java.beans.
PropertyChangeListener
propertyChangeListener

## Methods

public void addEditor()
public void configureArrowButton()
protected void configureEditor()
protected JButton createArrowButton()
protected ComboBoxEditor createEditor()
protected FocusListener
createFocusListener()

```
protected ItemListener
createItemListener()
protected KeyListener createKeyListener()
protected LayoutManager
createLayoutManager()
protected ListDataListener
createListDataListener()
protected ComboPopup createPopup()
protected PropertyChangeListener
createPropertyChangeListener()
protected ListCellRenderer
createRenderer()
public static ComponentUI createUI(
JComponent c)
public Accessible getAccessibleChild(
JComponent c,int i)
public int getAccessibleChildrenCount(
JComponent c)
protected Dimension getDefaultSize()
protected Dimension getDisplaySize()
protected Insets getInsets()
public Dimension getMaximumSize(
JComponent c)
public Dimension getMinimumSize(
JComponent c)
public Dimension getPreferredSize(
JComponent c)
protected void installComponents()
protected void installDefaults()
protected void installKeyboardActions()
protected void installListeners()
public void installUI(JComponent c)
public boolean isFocusTraversable(
JComboBox c)
protected boolean isNavigationKey(int
keyCode)
public boolean isPopupVisible(JComboBox
c)
public void paint(Graphics g,JComponent
c)
public void paintCurrentValue(Graphics g,
Rectangle bounds,boolean hasFocus)
public void paintCurrentValueBackground(
Graphics g,Rectangle bounds,boolean
hasFocus)
protected Rectangle
rectangleForCurrentValue()
public void removeEditor()
protected void selectNextPossibleValue()
protected void
selectPreviousPossibleValue()
public void setPopupVisible(JComboBox c,
boolean v)
protected void toggleOpenClose()
public void unconfigureArrowButton()
protected void unconfigureEditor()
protected void uninstallComponents()
protected void uninstallDefaults()
protected void uninstallKeyboardActions()
protected void uninstallListeners()
public void uninstallUI(JComponent c)
```

# BasicComboPopup

```
public class javax.swing.plaf.basic.
BasicComboPopup
implements javax.swing.plaf.basic.
ComboPopup
extends javax.swing.JPopupMenu
extends javax.swing.JComponent
extends java.awt.Container
extends java.awt.Component
extends java.lang.Object
```

### Fields

```
protected javax.swing.Timer
autoscrollTimer
protected javax.swing.JComboBox
comboBox
protected boolean hasEntered
protected boolean isAutoScrolling
protected java.awt.event.ItemListener
itemListener
protected java.awt.event.KeyListener
keyListener
protected javax.swing.JList list
protected javax.swing.event.
ListDataListener listDataListener
protected java.awt.event.MouseListener
listMouseListener
protected java.awt.event.
MouseMotionListener
listMouseMotionListener
protected javax.swing.event.
ListSelectionListener
listSelectionListener
protected java.awt.event.MouseListener
mouseListener
protected java.awt.event.
MouseMotionListener mouseMotionListener
protected java.beans.
PropertyChangeListener
propertyChangeListener
protected int scrollDirection
protected javax.swing.JScrollPane
scroller
protected final static int SCROLL_DOWN
protected final static int SCROLL_UP
protected boolean valueIsAdjusting
```

### Constructors

```
public  BasicComboPopup(JComboBox combo)
```

### Methods

```
protected void autoScrollDown()
protected void autoScrollUp()
protected Rectangle computePopupBounds(
int px,int py,int pw,int ph)
protected void configureList()
protected void configurePopup()
protected void configureScroller()
protected MouseEvent convertMouseEvent(
MouseEvent e)
protected ItemListener
createItemListener()
protected KeyListener createKeyListener()
```

```
protected JList createList()
protected ListDataListener
createListDataListener()
protected MouseListener
createListMouseListener()
protected MouseMotionListener
createListMouseMotionListener()
protected ListSelectionListener
createListSelectionListener()
protected MouseListener
createMouseListener()
protected MouseMotionListener
createMouseMotionListener()
protected PropertyChangeListener
createPropertyChangeListener()
protected JScrollPane createScroller()
protected void delegateFocus(MouseEvent
e)
public KeyListener getKeyListener()
public JList getList()
public MouseListener getMouseListener()
public MouseMotionListener
getMouseMotionListener()
protected int getPopupHeightForRowCount(
int maxRowCount)
public void hide()
protected void installComboBoxListeners()
protected void
installComboBoxModelListeners(
ComboBoxModel model)
protected void installKeyboardActions()
protected void installListListeners()
public boolean isFocusTraversable()
public void show()
protected void startAutoScrolling(int
direction)
protected void stopAutoScrolling()
protected void togglePopup()
protected void
uninstallComboBoxModelListeners(
ComboBoxModel model)
public void uninstallingUI()
protected void uninstallKeyboardActions()
protected void
updateListBoxSelectionForEvent(
MouseEvent anEvent,boolean shouldScroll)
```

## BasicDesktopIconUI

```
public class javax.swing.plaf.basic.
BasicDesktopIconUI
extends javax.swing.plaf.DesktopIconUI
extends javax.swing.plaf.ComponentUI
extends java.lang.Object
```

### Fields

```
protected JInternalFrame.JDesktopIcon
desktopIcon
protected javax.swing.JInternalFrame
frame
```

### Constructors

```
public  BasicDesktopIconUI()
```

### Methods

```
protected MouseInputListener
createMouseInputListener()
public static ComponentUI createUI(
JComponent c)
public void deiconize()
public Insets getInsets(JComponent c)
public Dimension getMaximumSize(
JComponent c)
public Dimension getMinimumSize(
JComponent c)
public Dimension getPreferredSize(
JComponent c)
protected void installComponents()
protected void installDefaults()
protected void installListeners()
public void installUI(JComponent c)
protected void uninstallComponents()
protected void uninstallDefaults()
protected void uninstallListeners()
public void uninstallUI(JComponent c)
```

## BasicDesktopPaneUI

```
public class javax.swing.plaf.basic.
BasicDesktopPaneUI
extends javax.swing.plaf.DesktopPaneUI
extends javax.swing.plaf.ComponentUI
extends java.lang.Object
```

### Fields

```
protected javax.swing.KeyStroke
closeKey
protected javax.swing.JDesktopPane
desktop
protected javax.swing.DesktopManager
desktopManager
protected javax.swing.KeyStroke
maximizeKey
protected javax.swing.KeyStroke
minimizeKey
protected javax.swing.KeyStroke
navigateKey
```

### Constructors

```
public  BasicDesktopPaneUI()
```

### Methods

```
public static ComponentUI createUI(
JComponent c)
public Dimension getMaximumSize(
JComponent c)
public Dimension getMinimumSize(
JComponent c)
public Dimension getPreferredSize(
JComponent c)
protected void installDefaults()
protected void installDesktopManager()
protected void installKeyboardActions()
public void installUI(JComponent c)
public void paint(Graphics g,JComponent
c)
protected void registerKeyboardActions()
protected void uninstallDefaults()
```

protected void uninstallDesktopManager()
protected void uninstallKeyboardActions()
public void uninstallUI(JComponent c)
protected void unregisterKeyboardActions(
)

## BasicDirectoryModel

public class javax.swing.plaf.basic.
BasicDirectoryModel
implements java.beans.
PropertyChangeListener
extends javax.swing.AbstractListModel
extends java.lang.Object

### Constructors

public  BasicDirectoryModel(JFileChooser
filechooser)

### Methods

public boolean contains(Object o)
public void fireContentsChanged()
public Vector getDirectories()
public Object getElementAt(int index)
public Vector getFiles()
public int getSize()
public int indexOf(Object o)
public void intervalAdded(ListDataEvent
e)
public void intervalRemoved(
ListDataEvent e)
public void invalidateFileCache()
protected boolean lt(File a,File b)
public void propertyChange(
PropertyChangeEvent e)
protected void sort(Vector v)
public void validateFileCache()

## BasicEditorPaneUI

public class javax.swing.plaf.basic.
BasicEditorPaneUI
extends javax.swing.plaf.basic.
BasicTextUI
extends javax.swing.plaf.TextUI
extends javax.swing.plaf.ComponentUI
extends java.lang.Object

### Constructors

public  BasicEditorPaneUI()

### Methods

public static ComponentUI createUI(
JComponent c)
public EditorKit getEditorKit(
JTextComponent tc)
protected String getPropertyPrefix()

## BasicFileChooserUI

public class javax.swing.plaf.basic.
BasicFileChooserUI
extends javax.swing.plaf.FileChooserUI
extends javax.swing.plaf.ComponentUI
extends java.lang.Object

### Fields

protected int cancelButtonMnemonic
protected java.lang.String
cancelButtonText
protected java.lang.String
cancelButtonToolTipText
protected javax.swing.Icon computerIcon
protected javax.swing.Icon
detailsViewIcon
protected javax.swing.Icon
directoryIcon
protected javax.swing.Icon fileIcon
protected javax.swing.Icon
floppyDriveIcon
protected javax.swing.Icon
hardDriveIcon
protected int helpButtonMnemonic
protected java.lang.String
helpButtonText
protected java.lang.String
helpButtonToolTipText
protected javax.swing.Icon
homeFolderIcon
protected javax.swing.Icon listViewIcon
protected javax.swing.Icon
newFolderIcon
protected int openButtonMnemonic
protected java.lang.String
openButtonText
protected java.lang.String
openButtonToolTipText
protected int saveButtonMnemonic
protected java.lang.String
saveButtonText
protected java.lang.String
saveButtonToolTipText
protected int updateButtonMnemonic
protected java.lang.String
updateButtonText
protected java.lang.String
updateButtonToolTipText
protected javax.swing.Icon upFolderIcon

### Constructors

public  BasicFileChooserUI(JFileChooser
b)

### Methods

public void clearIconCache()
protected MouseListener
createDoubleClickListener(JFileChooser
fc,JList list)
public ListSelectionListener
createListSelectionListener(JFileChooser
fc)
protected void createModel()
public PropertyChangeListener
createPropertyChangeListener(
JFileChooser fc)
public void ensureFileIsVisible(
JFileChooser fc,File f)
public FileFilter getAcceptAllFileFilter(
JFileChooser fc)
public JPanel getAccessoryPanel()

protected JButton getApproveButton(
JFileChooser fc)
public int getApproveButtonMnemonic(
JFileChooser fc)
public String getApproveButtonText(
JFileChooser fc)
public String
getApproveButtonToolTipText(JFileChooser
fc)
public Action getApproveSelectionAction()
public Action getCancelSelectionAction()
public Action
getChangeToParentDirectoryAction()
public String getDialogTitle(
JFileChooser fc)
public String getDirectoryName()
public JFileChooser getFileChooser()
public String getFileName()
public FileView getFileView(JFileChooser
fc)
public Action getGoHomeAction()
public BasicDirectoryModel getModel()
public Action getNewFolderAction()
public Action getUpdateAction()
public void installComponents(
JFileChooser fc)
protected void installDefaults(
JFileChooser fc)
protected void installIcons(JFileChooser
fc)
protected void installListeners(
JFileChooser fc)
protected void installStrings(
JFileChooser fc)
public void installUI(JComponent c)
public void rescanCurrentDirectory(
JFileChooser fc)
public void setDirectoryName(String
dirname)
public void setFileName(String filename)
public void uninstallComponents(
JFileChooser fc)
protected void uninstallDefaults(
JFileChooser fc)
protected void uninstallIcons(
JFileChooser fc)
protected void uninstallListeners(
JFileChooser fc)
protected void uninstallStrings(
JFileChooser fc)
public void uninstallUI(JComponent c)

## BasicGraphicsUtils

public class javax.swing.plaf.basic.
BasicGraphicsUtils
extends java.lang.Object

### Methods

public static void drawBezel(Graphics g,
int x,int y,int w,int h,boolean
isPressed,boolean isDefault,Color shadow,
Color darkShadow,Color highlight,Color
lightHighlight)

public static void drawDashedRect(
Graphics g,int x,int y,int width,int
height)
public static void drawEtchedRect(
Graphics g,int x,int y,int w,int h,Color
shadow,Color darkShadow,Color highlight,
Color lightHighlight)
public static void drawGroove(Graphics g,
int x,int y,int w,int h,Color shadow,
Color highlight)
public static void drawLoweredBezel(
Graphics g,int x,int y,int w,int h,Color
shadow,Color darkShadow,Color highlight,
Color lightHighlight)
public static void drawString(Graphics g,
String text,int underlinedChar,int x,int
y)
public static Insets getEtchedInsets()
public static Insets getGrooveInsets()
public static Dimension
getPreferredButtonSize(AbstractButton b,
int textIconGap)

## BasicIconFactory

public class javax.swing.plaf.basic.
BasicIconFactory
implements java.io.Serializable
extends java.lang.Object

### Methods

public static Icon createEmptyFrameIcon()
public static Icon getCheckBoxIcon()
public static Icon
getCheckBoxMenuItemIcon()
public static Icon getMenuArrowIcon()
public static Icon getMenuItemArrowIcon()
public static Icon getMenuItemCheckIcon()
public static Icon getRadioButtonIcon()
public static Icon
getRadioButtonMenuItemIcon()

## BasicInternalFrameTitlePane

public class javax.swing.plaf.basic.
BasicInternalFrameTitlePane
extends javax.swing.JComponent
extends java.awt.Container
extends java.awt.Component
extends java.lang.Object

### Fields

protected javax.swing.Action
closeAction
protected javax.swing.JButton
closeButton
protected javax.swing.Icon closeIcon
protected final static java.lang.String
CLOSE_CMD
protected javax.swing.JInternalFrame
frame
protected javax.swing.JButton
iconButton
protected javax.swing.Icon iconIcon

protected javax.swing.Action
iconifyAction
protected final static java.lang.String
ICONIFY_CMD
protected javax.swing.JButton maxButton
protected javax.swing.Icon maxIcon
protected javax.swing.Action
maximizeAction
protected final static java.lang.String
MAXIMIZE_CMD
protected javax.swing.JMenuBar menuBar
protected javax.swing.Icon minIcon
protected javax.swing.Action moveAction
protected final static java.lang.String
MOVE_CMD
protected java.awt.Color
notSelectedTextColor
protected java.awt.Color
notSelectedTitleColor
protected java.beans.
PropertyChangeListener
propertyChangeListener
protected javax.swing.Action
restoreAction
protected final static java.lang.String
RESTORE_CMD
protected java.awt.Color
selectedTextColor
protected java.awt.Color
selectedTitleColor
protected javax.swing.Action sizeAction
protected final static java.lang.String
SIZE_CMD
protected javax.swing.JMenu windowMenu

## Constructors
public BasicInternalFrameTitlePane(
JInternalFrame f)

## Methods
protected void addSubComponents()
protected void addSystemMenuItems(JMenu
systemMenu)
protected void assembleSystemMenu()
protected void createActions()
protected void createButtons()
protected LayoutManager createLayout()
protected PropertyChangeListener
createPropertyChangeListener()
protected JMenu createSystemMenu()
protected JMenuBar createSystemMenuBar()
protected void enableActions()
protected void installDefaults()
protected void installListeners()
protected void installTitlePane()
public void paintComponent(Graphics g)
protected void postClosingEvent(
JInternalFrame frame)
protected void setButtonIcons()
protected void showSystemMenu()
protected void uninstallDefaults()

# BasicInternalFrameUI
public class javax.swing.plaf.basic.
BasicInternalFrameUI
extends javax.swing.plaf.
InternalFrameUI
extends javax.swing.plaf.ComponentUI
extends java.lang.Object

## Fields
protected javax.swing.event.
MouseInputAdapter borderListener
protected java.awt.event.
ComponentListener componentListener
protected javax.swing.JComponent
eastPane
protected javax.swing.JInternalFrame
frame
protected javax.swing.event.
MouseInputListener glassPaneDispatcher
protected java.awt.LayoutManager
internalFrameLayout
protected javax.swing.JComponent
northPane
protected javax.swing.KeyStroke
openMenuKey
protected java.beans.
PropertyChangeListener
propertyChangeListener
protected javax.swing.Jcomponent
southPane
protected javax.swing.plaf.basic.
BasicInternalFrameTitlePane titlePane
protected javax.swing.JComponent
westPane

## Constructors
public BasicInternalFrameUI(
JInternalFrame b)

## Methods
protected void activateFrame(
JInternalFrame f)
protected void closeFrame(JInternalFrame
f)
protected MouseInputAdapter
createBorderListener(JInternalFrame w)
protected ComponentListener
createComponentListener()
protected DesktopManager
createDesktopManager()
protected JComponent createEastPane(
JInternalFrame w)
protected MouseInputListener
createGlassPaneDispatcher()
protected void
createInternalFrameListener()
protected LayoutManager
createLayoutManager()
protected JComponent createNorthPane(
JInternalFrame w)
protected PropertyChangeListener
createPropertyChangeListener()

protected JComponent createSouthPane(
JInternalFrame w)
public static ComponentUI createUI(
JComponent b)
protected JComponent createWestPane(
JInternalFrame w)
protected void deactivateFrame(
JInternalFrame f)
protected void deiconifyFrame(
JInternalFrame f)
protected void deinstallMouseHandlers(
JComponent c)
protected DesktopManager
getDesktopManager()
public JComponent getEastPane()
public Dimension getMaximumSize(
JComponent x)
public Dimension getMinimumSize(
JComponent x)
public JComponent getNorthPane()
public Dimension getPreferredSize(
JComponent x)
public JComponent getSouthPane()
public JComponent getWestPane()
protected void iconifyFrame(
JInternalFrame f)
protected void installComponents()
protected void installDefaults()
protected void installKeyboardActions()
protected void installListeners()
protected void installMouseHandlers(
JComponent c)
public void installUI(JComponent c)
public final boolean isKeyBindingActive()
protected final boolean
isKeyBindingRegistered()
protected void maximizeFrame(
JInternalFrame f)
protected void minimizeFrame(
JInternalFrame f)
protected void replacePane(JComponent
currentPane,JComponent newPane)
public void setEastPane(JComponent c)
protected final void setKeyBindingActive(
boolean b)
protected final void
setKeyBindingRegistered(boolean b)
public void setNorthPane(JComponent c)
public void setSouthPane(JComponent c)
protected void setupMenuCloseKey()
protected void setupMenuOpenKey()
public void setWestPane(JComponent c)
protected void uninstallComponents()
protected void uninstallDefaults()
protected void uninstallKeyboardActions()
protected void uninstallListeners()
public void uninstallUI(JComponent c)

## BasicLabelUI

public class javax.swing.plaf.basic.
BasicLabelUI
implements java.beans.
PropertyChangeListener

extends javax.swing.plaf.LabelUI
extends javax.swing.plaf.ComponentUI
extends java.lang.Object

### Fields
protected static javax.swing.plaf.basic.
BasicLabelUI labelUI

### Methods
public static ComponentUI createUI(
JComponent c)
public Dimension getMaximumSize(
JComponent c)
public Dimension getMinimumSize(
JComponent c)
public Dimension getPreferredSize(
JComponent c)
protected void installComponents(JLabel
c)
protected void installDefaults(JLabel c)
protected void installKeyboardActions(
JLabel l)
protected void installListeners(JLabel c)
public void installUI(JComponent c)
protected String layoutCL(JLabel label,
FontMetrics fontMetrics,String text,Icon
icon,Rectangle viewR,Rectangle iconR,
Rectangle textR)
public void paint(Graphics g,JComponent
c)
protected void paintDisabledText(JLabel
l,Graphics g,String s,int textX,int
textY)
protected void paintEnabledText(JLabel l,
Graphics g,String s,int textX,int textY)
public void propertyChange(
PropertyChangeEvent e)
protected void uninstallComponents(
JLabel c)
protected void uninstallDefaults(JLabel
c)
protected void uninstallKeyboardActions(
JLabel c)
protected void uninstallListeners(JLabel
c)
public void uninstallUI(JComponent c)

## BasicListUI

public class javax.swing.plaf.basic.
BasicListUI
extends javax.swing.plaf.ListUI
extends javax.swing.plaf.ComponentUI
extends java.lang.Object

### Fields
protected int cellHeight
protected int cellHeights
protected final static int
cellRendererChanged
protected int cellWidth
protected final static int
fixedCellHeightChanged

```
protected final static int
fixedCellWidthChanged
protected java.awt.event.FocusListener
focusListener
protected final static int fontChanged
protected javax.swing.JList list
protected javax.swing.event.
ListDataListener listDataListener
protected javax.swing.event.
ListSelectionListener
listSelectionListener
protected final static int modelChanged
protected javax.swing.event.
MouseInputListener mouseInputListener
protected java.beans.
PropertyChangeListener
propertyChangeListener
protected final static int
prototypeCellValueChanged
protected javax.swing.CellRendererPane
rendererPane
protected final static int
selectionModelChanged
protected int updateLayoutStateNeeded
```

### Methods

```
protected int convertRowToY(int row)
protected int convertYToRow(int y0)
protected FocusListener
createFocusListener()
protected ListDataListener
createListDataListener()
protected ListSelectionListener
createListSelectionListener()
protected MouseInputListener
createMouseInputListener()
protected PropertyChangeListener
createPropertyChangeListener()
public static ComponentUI createUI(
JComponent list)
public Rectangle getCellBounds(JList
list,int index1,int index2)
public Dimension getMaximumSize(
JComponent c)
public Dimension getMinimumSize(
JComponent c)
public Dimension getPreferredSize(
JComponent c)
protected int getRowHeight(int row)
public Point indexToLocation(JList list,
int index)
protected void installDefaults()
protected void installKeyboardActions()
protected void installListeners()
public void installUI(JComponent c)
public int locationToIndex(JList list,
Point location)
protected void maybeUpdateLayoutState()
public void paint(Graphics g,JComponent
c)
protected void paintCell(Graphics g,int
row,Rectangle rowBounds,ListCellRenderer
cellRenderer,ListModel dataModel,
ListSelectionModel selModel,int
leadIndex)
```

```
protected void selectNextIndex()
protected void selectPreviousIndex()
protected void uninstallDefaults()
protected void uninstallKeyboardActions()
protected void uninstallListeners()
public void uninstallUI(JComponent c)
protected void updateLayoutState()
```

## BasicLookAndFeel

```
public abstract class javax.swing.plaf.
basic.BasicLookAndFeel
implements java.io.Serializable
extends javax.swing.LookAndFeel
extends java.lang.Object
```

### Methods

```
public UIDefaults getDefaults()
protected void initClassDefaults(
UIDefaults table)
protected void initComponentDefaults(
UIDefaults table)
protected void initSystemColorDefaults(
UIDefaults table)
protected void loadSystemColors(
UIDefaults table,String systemColors,
boolean useNative)
```

## BasicMenuBarUI

```
public class javax.swing.plaf.basic.
BasicMenuBarUI
extends javax.swing.plaf.MenuBarUI
extends javax.swing.plaf.ComponentUI
extends java.lang.Object
```

### Fields

```
protected javax.swing.event.
ChangeListener changeListener
protected java.awt.event.
ContainerListener containerListener
protected javax.swing.JMenuBar menuBar
```

### Methods

```
protected ChangeListener
createChangeListener()
protected ContainerListener
createContainerListener()
public static ComponentUI createUI(
JComponent x)
public Dimension getMaximumSize(
JComponent c)
public Dimension getMinimumSize(
JComponent c)
public Dimension getPreferredSize(
JComponent c)
protected void installDefaults()
protected void installKeyboardActions()
protected void installListeners()
public void installUI(JComponent c)
protected void uninstallDefaults()
protected void uninstallKeyboardActions()
protected void uninstallListeners()
public void uninstallUI(JComponent c)
```

# BasicMenuItemUI

public class javax.swing.plaf.basic.
BasicMenuItemUI
extends javax.swing.plaf.MenuItemUI
extends javax.swing.plaf.ButtonUI
extends javax.swing.plaf.ComponentUI
extends java.lang.Object

## Fields

protected java.awt.Font acceleratorFont
protected java.awt.Color
acceleratorForeground
protected java.awt.Color
acceleratorSelectionForeground
protected javax.swing.Icon arrowIcon
protected javax.swing.Icon checkIcon
protected int defaultTextIconGap
protected java.awt.Color
disabledForeground
protected javax.swing.event.
MenuDragMouseListener
menuDragMouseListener
protected javax.swing.JMenuItem
menuItem
protected javax.swing.event.
MenuKeyListener menuKeyListener
protected javax.swing.event.
MouseInputListener mouseInputListener
protected boolean oldBorderPainted
protected java.awt.Color
selectionBackground
protected java.awt.Color
selectionForeground

## Methods

protected MenuDragMouseListener
createMenuDragMouseListener(JComponent c)
protected MenuKeyListener
createMenuKeyListener(JComponent c)
protected MouseInputListener
createMouseInputListener(JComponent c)
public static ComponentUI createUI(
JComponent c)
public Dimension getMaximumSize(
JComponent c)
public Dimension getMinimumSize(
JComponent c)
public MenuElement getPath()
protected Dimension
getPreferredMenuItemSize(JComponent c,
Icon checkIcon,Icon arrowIcon,int
defaultTextIconGap)
public Dimension getPreferredSize(
JComponent c)
protected String getPropertyPrefix()
protected void installDefaults()
protected void installKeyboardActions()
protected void installListeners()
public void installUI(JComponent c)
public void paint(Graphics g,JComponent
c)
protected void paintMenuItem(Graphics g,
JComponent c,Icon checkIcon,Icon

arrowIcon,Color background,Color
foreground,int defaultTextIconGap)
protected void uninstallDefaults()
protected void uninstallKeyboardActions()
protected void uninstallListeners()
public void uninstallUI(JComponent c)
public void update(Graphics g,JComponent
c)

# BasicMenuUI

public class javax.swing.plaf.basic.
BasicMenuUI
extends javax.swing.plaf.basic.
BasicMenuItemUI
extends javax.swing.plaf.MenuItemUI
extends javax.swing.plaf.ButtonUI
extends javax.swing.plaf.ComponentUI
extends java.lang.Object

## Fields

protected javax.swing.event.
ChangeListener changeListener
protected javax.swing.event.MenuListener
menuListener
protected java.beans.
PropertyChangeListener
propertyChangeListener

## Methods

protected ChangeListener
createChangeListener(JComponent c)
protected MenuDragMouseListener
createMenuDragMouseListener(JComponent c)
protected MenuKeyListener
createMenuKeyListener(JComponent c)
protected MenuListener
createMenuListener(JComponent c)
protected MouseInputListener
createMouseInputListener(JComponent c)
protected PropertyChangeListener
createPropertyChangeListener(JComponent
c)
public static ComponentUI createUI(
JComponent x)
public Dimension getMaximumSize(
JComponent c)
protected String getPropertyPrefix()
protected void installDefaults()
protected void installKeyboardActions()
protected void installListeners()
protected void setupPostTimer(JMenu menu)
protected void uninstallDefaults()
protected void uninstallKeyboardActions()
protected void uninstallListeners()

# BasicOptionPaneUI

public class javax.swing.plaf.basic.
BasicOptionPaneUI
extends javax.swing.plaf.OptionPaneUI
extends javax.swing.plaf.ComponentUI
extends java.lang.Object

## Fields

protected boolean hasCustomComponents
protected java.awt.Component
initialFocusComponent
protected javax.swing.JComponent
inputComponent
public final static int MinimumHeight
protected java.awt.Dimension
minimumSize
public final static int MinimumWidth
protected javax.swing.JOptionPane
optionPane
protected java.beans.
PropertyChangeListener
propertyChangeListener

## Methods

protected void addButtonComponents(
Container container,Object buttons,int
initialIndex)
protected void addIcon(Container top)
protected void addMessageComponents(
Container container,GridBagConstraints
cons,Object msg,int maxll,boolean
internallyCreated)
protected void burstStringInto(Container
c,String d,int maxll)
public boolean containsCustomComponents(
JOptionPane op)
protected ActionListener
createButtonActionListener(int
buttonIndex)
protected Container createButtonArea()
protected LayoutManager
createLayoutManager()
protected Container createMessageArea()
protected PropertyChangeListener
createPropertyChangeListener()
protected Container createSeparator()
public static ComponentUI createUI(
JComponent x)
protected Object getButtons()
protected Icon getIcon()
protected Icon getIconForType(int
messageType)
protected int getInitialValueIndex()
protected int
getMaxCharactersPerLineCount()
public Dimension getMaximumSize(
JComponent c)
protected Object getMessage()
public Dimension
getMinimumOptionPaneSize()
public Dimension getMinimumSize(
JComponent c)
public Dimension getPreferredSize(
JComponent c)
protected boolean
getSizeButtonsToSameWidth()
protected void installComponents()
protected void installDefaults()
protected void installKeyboardActions()
protected void installListeners()
public void installUI(JComponent c)

protected void resetInputValue()
public void selectInitialValue(
JOptionPane op)
protected void uninstallComponents()
protected void uninstallDefaults()
protected void uninstallKeyboardActions()
protected void uninstallListeners()
public void uninstallUI(JComponent c)

## BasicPanelUI

public class javax.swing.plaf.basic.
BasicPanelUI
extends javax.swing.plaf.PanelUI
extends javax.swing.plaf.ComponentUI
extends java.lang.Object

### Methods

public static ComponentUI createUI(
JComponent c)
protected void installDefaults(JPanel p)
public void installUI(JComponent c)
protected void uninstallDefaults(JPanel
p)
public void uninstallUI(JComponent c)

## BasicPasswordFieldUI

public class javax.swing.plaf.basic.
BasicPasswordFieldUI
extends javax.swing.plaf.basic.
BasicTextFieldUI
extends javax.swing.plaf.basic.
BasicTextUI
extends javax.swing.plaf.TextUI
extends javax.swing.plaf.ComponentUI
extends java.lang.Object

### Methods

public View create(Element elem)
public static ComponentUI createUI(
JComponent c)
protected String getPropertyPrefix()

## BasicPermission

public abstract class java.security.
BasicPermission
implements java.io.Serializable
extends java.security.Permission
extends java.lang.Object

### Constructors

public BasicPermission(String name)
public BasicPermission(String name,
String actions)

### Methods

public boolean equals(Object obj)
public String getActions()
public int hashCode()
public boolean implies(Permission p)
public PermissionCollection
newPermissionCollection()

## BasicPopupMenuSeparatorUI

public class javax.swing.plaf.basic.
BasicPopupMenuSeparatorUI
extends javax.swing.plaf.basic.
BasicSeparatorUI
extends javax.swing.plaf.SeparatorUI
extends javax.swing.plaf.ComponentUI
extends java.lang.Object

### Methods

public static ComponentUI createUI(
JComponent c)
public Dimension getPreferredSize(
JComponent c)
public void paint(Graphics g,JComponent
c)

## BasicPopupMenuUI

public class javax.swing.plaf.basic.
BasicPopupMenuUI
extends javax.swing.plaf.PopupMenuUI
extends javax.swing.plaf.ComponentUI
extends java.lang.Object

### Fields

protected javax.swing.JPopupMenu
popupMenu

### Methods

public static ComponentUI createUI(
JComponent x)
public Dimension getMaximumSize(
JComponent c)
public Dimension getMinimumSize(
JComponent c)
public Dimension getPreferredSize(
JComponent c)
public void installDefaults()
protected void installKeyboardActions()
protected void installListeners()
public void installUI(JComponent c)
protected void uninstallDefaults()
protected void uninstallKeyboardActions()
protected void uninstallListeners()
public void uninstallUI(JComponent c)

## BasicProgressBarUI

public class javax.swing.plaf.basic.
BasicProgressBarUI
extends javax.swing.plaf.ProgressBarUI
extends javax.swing.plaf.ComponentUI
extends java.lang.Object

### Fields

protected javax.swing.event.
ChangeListener changeListener
protected javax.swing.JProgressBar
progressBar

### Methods

public static ComponentUI createUI(
JComponent x)

protected int getAmountFull(Insets b,int
width,int height)
protected int getCellLength()
protected int getCellSpacing()
public Dimension getMaximumSize(
JComponent c)
public Dimension getMinimumSize(
JComponent c)
protected Dimension
getPreferredInnerHorizontal()
protected Dimension
getPreferredInnerVertical()
public Dimension getPreferredSize(
JComponent c)
protected Color getSelectionBackground()
protected Color getSelectionForeground()
protected Point getStringPlacement(
Graphics g,String progressString,int x,
int y,int width,int height)
protected void installDefaults()
protected void installListeners()
public void installUI(JComponent c)
public void paint(Graphics g,JComponent
c)
protected void paintString(Graphics g,
int x,int y,int width,int height,int
amountFull,Insets b)
protected void setCellLength(int cellLen)
protected void setCellSpacing(int
cellSpace)
protected void uninstallDefaults()
protected void uninstallListeners()
public void uninstallUI(JComponent c)

## BasicRadioButtonMenuItemUI

public class javax.swing.plaf.basic.
BasicRadioButtonMenuItemUI
extends javax.swing.plaf.basic.
BasicMenuItemUI
extends javax.swing.plaf.MenuItemUI
extends javax.swing.plaf.ButtonUI
extends javax.swing.plaf.ComponentUI
extends java.lang.Object

### Methods

public static ComponentUI createUI(
JComponent b)
protected String getPropertyPrefix()
protected void installDefaults()
public void processMouseEvent(JMenuItem
item,MouseEvent e,MenuElement path,
MenuSelectionManager manager)

## BasicRadioButtonUI

public class javax.swing.plaf.basic.
BasicRadioButtonUI
extends javax.swing.plaf.basic.
BasicToggleButtonUI
extends javax.swing.plaf.basic.
BasicButtonUI
extends javax.swing.plaf.ButtonUI
extends javax.swing.plaf.ComponentUI
extends java.lang.Object

### Fields

```
protected javax.swing.Icon icon
```

### Methods

```
public static ComponentUI createUI(
JComponent b)
public Icon getDefaultIcon()
public Dimension getPreferredSize(
JComponent c)
protected String getPropertyPrefix()
protected void installDefaults(
AbstractButton b)
public synchronized void paint(Graphics
g,JComponent c)
protected void paintFocus(Graphics g,
Rectangle textRect,Dimension size)
protected void uninstallDefaults(
AbstractButton b)
```

## BasicScrollBarUI

```
public class javax.swing.plaf.basic.
BasicScrollBarUI
implements java.awt.LayoutManager
implements javax.swing.SwingConstants
extends javax.swing.plaf.ScrollBarUI
extends javax.swing.plaf.ComponentUI
extends java.lang.Object
```

### Fields

```
protected ArrowButtonListener
buttonListener
protected javax.swing.JButton
decrButton
protected final static int DECREASE_
HIGHLIGHT
protected javax.swing.JButton
incrButton
protected final static int INCREASE_
HIGHLIGHT
protected boolean isDragging
protected java.awt.Dimension
maximumThumbSize
protected java.awt.Dimension
minimumThumbSize
protected ModelListener modelListener
protected final static int NO_HIGHLIGHT
protected java.beans.
PropertyChangeListener
propertyChangeListener
protected javax.swing.JScrollBar
scrollbar
protected ScrollListener scrollListener
protected javax.swing.Timer scrollTimer
protected java.awt.Color thumbColor
protected java.awt.Color
thumbDarkShadowColor
protected java.awt.Color
thumbHighlightColor
protected java.awt.Color
thumbLightShadowColor
protected java.awt.Rectangle thumbRect
protected java.awt.Color trackColor
protected int trackHighlight
```

```
protected java.awt.Color
trackHighlightColor
protected TrackListener trackListener
protected java.awt.Rectangle trackRect
```

### Methods

```
public void addLayoutComponent(String
name,Component child)
protected void configureScrollBarColors()
protected ArrowButtonListener
createArrowButtonListener()
protected JButton createDecreaseButton(
int orientation)
protected JButton createIncreaseButton(
int orientation)
protected ModelListener
createModelListener()
protected PropertyChangeListener
createPropertyChangeListener()
protected ScrollListener
createScrollListener()
protected TrackListener
createTrackListener()
public static ComponentUI createUI(
JComponent c)
public Dimension getMaximumSize(
JComponent c)
protected Dimension getMaximumThumbSize()
public Dimension getMinimumSize(
JComponent c)
protected Dimension getMinimumThumbSize()
public Dimension getPreferredSize(
JComponent c)
protected Rectangle getThumbBounds()
protected Rectangle getTrackBounds()
protected void installComponents()
protected void installDefaults()
protected void installKeyboardActions()
protected void installListeners()
public void installUI(JComponent c)
public void layoutContainer(Container
scrollbarContainer)
protected void layoutHScrollbar(
JScrollBar sb)
protected void layoutVScrollbar(
JScrollBar sb)
public Dimension minimumLayoutSize(
Container scrollbarContainer)
public void paint(Graphics g,JComponent
c)
protected void paintDecreaseHighlight(
Graphics g)
protected void paintIncreaseHighlight(
Graphics g)
protected void paintThumb(Graphics g,
JComponent c,Rectangle thumbBounds)
protected void paintTrack(Graphics g,
JComponent c,Rectangle trackBounds)
public Dimension preferredLayoutSize(
Container scrollbarContainer)
public void removeLayoutComponent(
Component child)
protected void scrollByBlock(int
direction)
```

```
protected void scrollByUnit(int
direction)
protected void setThumbBounds(int x,int
y,int width,int height)
protected void uninstallComponents()
protected void uninstallDefaults()
protected void uninstallKeyboardActions()
protected void uninstallListeners()
public void uninstallUI(JComponent c)
```

## BasicScrollPaneUI

```
public class javax.swing.plaf.basic.
BasicScrollPaneUI
implements javax.swing.
ScrollPaneConstants
extends javax.swing.plaf.ScrollPaneUI
extends javax.swing.plaf.ComponentUI
extends java.lang.Object
```

### Fields

```
protected javax.swing.event.
ChangeListener hsbChangeListener
protected javax.swing.JScrollPane
scrollpane
protected java.beans.
PropertyChangeListener
spPropertyChangeListener
protected javax.swing.event.
ChangeListener viewportChangeListener
protected javax.swing.event.
ChangeListener vsbChangeListener
```

### Methods

```
protected ChangeListener
createHSBChangeListener()
protected PropertyChangeListener
createPropertyChangeListener()
public static ComponentUI createUI(
JComponent x)
protected ChangeListener
createViewportChangeListener()
protected ChangeListener
createVSBChangeListener()
public Dimension getMaximumSize(
JComponent c)
public Dimension getMinimumSize(
JComponent c)
public Dimension getPreferredSize(
JComponent c)
protected void installDefaults(
JScrollPane scrollpane)
protected void installKeyboardActions(
JScrollPane c)
protected void installListeners(
JScrollPane c)
public void installUI(JComponent x)
public void paint(Graphics g,JComponent
c)
protected void
syncScrollPaneWithViewport()
protected void uninstallDefaults(
JScrollPane c)
```

```
protected void uninstallKeyboardActions(
JScrollPane c)
protected void uninstallListeners(
JComponent c)
public void uninstallUI(JComponent c)
protected void updateColumnHeader(
PropertyChangeEvent e)
protected void updateRowHeader(
PropertyChangeEvent e)
protected void
updateScrollBarDisplayPolicy(
PropertyChangeEvent e)
protected void updateViewport(
PropertyChangeEvent e)
```

## BasicSeparatorUI

```
public class javax.swing.plaf.basic.
BasicSeparatorUI
extends javax.swing.plaf.SeparatorUI
extends javax.swing.plaf.ComponentUI
extends java.lang.Object
```

### Fields

```
protected java.awt.Color highlight
protected java.awt.Color shadow
```

### Methods

```
public static ComponentUI createUI(
JComponent c)
public Dimension getMaximumSize(
JComponent c)
public Dimension getMinimumSize(
JComponent c)
public Dimension getPreferredSize(
JComponent c)
protected void installDefaults(
JSeparator s)
protected void installListeners(
JSeparator s)
public void installUI(JComponent c)
public void paint(Graphics g,JComponent
c)
protected void uninstallDefaults(
JSeparator s)
protected void uninstallListeners(
JSeparator s)
public void uninstallUI(JComponent c)
```

## BasicSliderUI

```
public class javax.swing.plaf.basic.
BasicSliderUI
extends javax.swing.plaf.SliderUI
extends javax.swing.plaf.ComponentUI
extends java.lang.Object
```

### Fields

```
protected javax.swing.event.
ChangeListener changeListener
protected java.awt.event.
ComponentListener componentListener
protected java.awt.Rectangle
contentRect
protected java.awt.Insets focusInsets
```

```
protected java.awt.event.FocusListener
focusListener
protected java.awt.Rectangle focusRect
protected java.awt.Insets insetCache
protected java.awt.Rectangle labelRect
public final int MAX_SCROLL
public final int MIN_SCROLL
public final int NEGATIVE_SCROLL
public final int POSITIVE_SCROLL
protected java.beans.
PropertyChangeListener
propertyChangeListener
protected ScrollListener scrollListener
protected javax.swing.Timer scrollTimer
protected javax.swing.JSlider slider
protected java.awt.Rectangle thumbRect
protected java.awt.Rectangle tickRect
protected int trackBuffer
protected TrackListener trackListener
protected java.awt.Rectangle trackRect
```

## Constructors
```
public  BasicSliderUI(JSlider b)
```

## Methods
```
protected void calculateContentRect()
protected void calculateFocusRect()
protected void calculateGeometry()
protected void calculateLabelRect()
protected void calculateThumbLocation()
protected void calculateThumbSize()
protected void calculateTickRect()
protected void calculateTrackBuffer()
protected void calculateTrackRect()
protected ChangeListener
createChangeListener(JSlider slider)
protected ComponentListener
createComponentListener(JSlider slider)
protected FocusListener
createFocusListener(JSlider slider)
protected PropertyChangeListener
createPropertyChangeListener(JSlider
slider)
protected ScrollListener
createScrollListener(JSlider slider)
protected TrackListener
createTrackListener(JSlider slider)
public static ComponentUI createUI(
JComponent b)
protected Color getFocusColor()
protected int getHeightOfHighValueLabel()
protected int getHeightOfLowValueLabel()
protected int getHeightOfTallestLabel()
protected Component getHighestValueLabel(
)
protected Color getHighlightColor()
protected Component getLowestValueLabel()
public Dimension getMaximumSize(
JComponent c)
public Dimension
getMinimumHorizontalSize()
public Dimension getMinimumSize(
JComponent c)
```

```
public Dimension getMinimumVerticalSize()
public Dimension
getPreferredHorizontalSize()
public Dimension getPreferredSize(
JComponent c)
public Dimension
getPreferredVerticalSize()
protected Color getShadowColor()
protected Dimension getThumbSize()
protected int getTickLength()
protected int getWidthOfHighValueLabel()
protected int getWidthOfLowValueLabel()
protected int getWidthOfWidestLabel()
protected void installDefaults(JSlider
slider)
protected void installKeyboardActions(
JSlider slider)
protected void installListeners(JSlider
slider)
public void installUI(JComponent c)
public void paint(Graphics g,JComponent
c)
public void paintFocus(Graphics g)
protected void paintHorizontalLabel(
Graphics g,int value,Component label)
public void paintLabels(Graphics g)
protected void
paintMajorTickForHorizSlider(Graphics g,
Rectangle tickBounds,int x)
protected void
paintMajorTickForVertSlider(Graphics g,
Rectangle tickBounds,int y)
protected void
paintMinorTickForHorizSlider(Graphics g,
Rectangle tickBounds,int x)
protected void
paintMinorTickForVertSlider(Graphics g,
Rectangle tickBounds,int y)
public void paintThumb(Graphics g)
public void paintTicks(Graphics g)
public void paintTrack(Graphics g)
protected void paintVerticalLabel(
Graphics g,int value,Component label)
protected void
recalculateIfInsetsChanged()
public void scrollByBlock(int direction)
public void scrollByUnit(int direction)
protected void scrollDueToClickInTrack(
int dir)
public void setThumbLocation(int x,int y)
protected void uninstallKeyboardActions(
JSlider slider)
protected void uninstallListeners(
JSlider slider)
public void uninstallUI(JComponent c)
public int valueForXPosition(int xPos)
public int valueForYPosition(int yPos)
protected int xPositionForValue(int
value)
protected int yPositionForValue(int
value)
```

## BasicSplitPaneDivider
public class javax.swing.plaf.basic.
BasicSplitPaneDivider
implements java.beans.
PropertyChangeListener
extends java.awt.Container
extends java.awt.Component
extends java.lang.Object

### Fields
protected int dividerSize
protected DragController dragger
protected java.awt.Component
hiddenDivider
protected javax.swing.JButton
leftButton
protected MouseHandler mouseHandler
protected final static int ONE_TOUCH_
OFFSET
protected final static int ONE_TOUCH_
SIZE
protected int orientation
protected javax.swing.JButton
rightButton
protected javax.swing.JSplitPane
splitPane
protected javax.swing.plaf.basic.
BasicSplitPaneUI splitPaneUI

### Constructors
public  BasicSplitPaneDivider(
BasicSplitPaneUI ui)

### Methods
protected Jbutton
createLeftOneTouchButton()
protected JButton
createRightOneTouchButton()
protected void dragDividerTo(int
location)
protected void finishDraggingTo(int
location)
public BasicSplitPaneUI
getBasicSplitPaneUI()
public int getDividerSize()
public Dimension getPreferredSize()
protected void oneTouchExpandableChanged(
)
public void paint(Graphics g)
protected void prepareForDragging()
public void propertyChange(
PropertyChangeEvent e)
public void setBasicSplitPaneUI(
BasicSplitPaneUI newUI)
public void setDividerSize(int newSize)

## BasicSplitPaneUI
public class javax.swing.plaf.basic.
BasicSplitPaneUI
extends javax.swing.plaf.SplitPaneUI
extends javax.swing.plaf.ComponentUI
extends java.lang.Object

### Fields
protected int beginDragDividerLocation
protected javax.swing.plaf.basic.
BasicSplitPaneDivider divider
protected javax.swing.KeyStroke
dividerResizeToggleKey
protected int dividerSize
protected javax.swing.KeyStroke downKey
protected boolean draggingHW
protected javax.swing.KeyStroke endKey
protected java.awt.event.FocusListener
focusListener
protected javax.swing.KeyStroke homeKey
protected java.awt.event.ActionListener
keyboardDownRightListener
protected java.awt.event.ActionListener
keyboardEndListener
protected java.awt.event.ActionListener
keyboardHomeListener
protected java.awt.event.ActionListener
keyboardResizeToggleListener
protected java.awt.event.ActionListener
keyboardUpLeftListener
protected static int KEYBOARD_DIVIDER_
MOVE_OFFSET
protected BasicHorizontalLayoutManager
layoutManager
protected javax.swing.KeyStroke leftKey
protected java.awt.Component
nonContinuousLayoutDivider
protected final static java.lang.String
NON_CONTINUOUS_DIVIDER
protected java.beans.
PropertyChangeListener
propertyChangeListener
protected javax.swing.KeyStroke
rightKey
protected javax.swing.JSplitPane
splitPane
protected javax.swing.KeyStroke upKey

### Methods
public BasicSplitPaneDivider
createDefaultDivider()
protected Component
createDefaultNonContinuousLayoutDivider()
protected FocusListener
createFocusListener()
protected ActionListener
createKeyboardDownRightListener()
protected ActionListener
createKeyboardEndListener()
protected ActionListener
createKeyboardHomeListener()
protected ActionListener
createKeyboardResizeToggleListener()
protected ActionListener
createKeyboardUpLeftListener()
protected PropertyChangeListener
createPropertyChangeListener()
public static ComponentUI createUI(
JComponent x)
protected void dragDividerTo(int
location)

```
protected void finishDraggingTo(int
location)
public void finishedPaintingChildren(
JSplitPane jc,Graphics g)
public BasicSplitPaneDivider getDivider()
protected int getDividerBorderSize()
public int getDividerLocation(JSplitPane
jc)
public Insets getInsets(JComponent jc)
public int getLastDragLocation()
public int getMaximumDividerLocation(
JSplitPane jc)
public Dimension getMaximumSize(
JComponent jc)
public int getMinimumDividerLocation(
JSplitPane jc)
public Dimension getMinimumSize(
JComponent jc)
public Component
getNonContinuousLayoutDivider()
public int getOrientation()
public Dimension getPreferredSize(
JComponent jc)
public JSplitPane getSplitPane()
protected void installDefaults()
protected void installKeyboardActions()
protected void installListeners()
public void installUI(JComponent c)
public boolean isContinuousLayout()
public void paint(Graphics g,JComponent
jc)
protected void resetLayoutManager()
public void resetToPreferredSizes(
JSplitPane jc)
public void setContinuousLayout(boolean
b)
public void setDividerLocation(
JSplitPane jc,int location)
public void setLastDragLocation(int l)
protected void
setNonContinuousLayoutDivider(Component
newDivider)
protected void
setNonContinuousLayoutDivider(Component
newDivider,boolean rememberSizes)
public void setOrientation(int
orientation)
protected void startDragging()
protected void uninstallDefaults()
protected void uninstallKeyboardActions()
protected void uninstallListeners()
public void uninstallUI(JComponent c)
```

## BasicStroke

```
public class java.awt.BasicStroke
implements java.awt.Stroke
extends java.lang.Object
```

### Fields

```
public final static int CAP_BUTT
public final static int CAP_ROUND
public final static int CAP_SQUARE
public final static int JOIN_BEVEL
```

```
public final static int JOIN_MITER
public final static int JOIN_ROUND
```

### Constructors

```
public BasicStroke(float width,int cap,
int join,float miterlimit,float dash,
float dash_phase)
public BasicStroke(float width,int cap,
int join,float miterlimit)
public BasicStroke(float width,int cap,
int join)
public BasicStroke(float width)
public BasicStroke()
```

### Methods

```
public Shape createStrokedShape(Shape s)
public boolean equals(Object obj)
public float getDashArray()
public float getDashPhase()
public int getEndCap()
public int getLineJoin()
public float getLineWidth()
public float getMiterLimit()
public int hashCode()
```

## BasicTabbedPaneUI

```
public class javax.swing.plaf.basic.
BasicTabbedPaneUI
implements javax.swing.SwingConstants
extends javax.swing.plaf.TabbedPaneUI
extends javax.swing.plaf.ComponentUI
extends java.lang.Object
```

### Fields

```
protected java.awt.Insets
contentBorderInsets
protected java.awt.Color darkShadow
protected javax.swing.KeyStroke downKey
protected java.awt.Color focus
protected java.awt.event.FocusListener
focusListener
protected java.awt.Color highlight
protected javax.swing.KeyStroke leftKey
protected java.awt.Color lightHighlight
protected int maxTabHeight
protected int maxTabWidth
protected java.awt.event.MouseListener
mouseListener
protected java.beans.
PropertyChangeListener
propertyChangeListener
protected java.awt.Rectangle rects
protected javax.swing.KeyStroke
rightKey
protected int runCount
protected int selectedRun
protected java.awt.Insets
selectedTabPadInsets
protected java.awt.Color shadow
protected java.awt.Insets tabAreaInsets
protected javax.swing.event.
ChangeListener tabChangeListener
protected java.awt.Insets tabInsets
```

protected javax.swing.JTabbedPane
tabPane
protected int tabRunOverlay
protected int tabRuns
protected int textIconGap
protected javax.swing.KeyStroke upKey

## Methods
protected void assureRectsCreated(int
tabCount)
protected int calculateMaxTabHeight(int
tabPlacement)
protected int calculateMaxTabWidth(int
tabPlacement)
protected int calculateTabAreaHeight(int
tabPlacement,int horizRunCount,int
maxTabHeight)
protected int calculateTabAreaWidth(int
tabPlacement,int vertRunCount,int
maxTabWidth)
protected int calculateTabHeight(int
tabPlacement,int tabIndex,int fontHeight)
protected int calculateTabWidth(int
tabPlacement,int tabIndex,FontMetrics
metrics)
protected ChangeListener
createChangeListener()
protected FocusListener
createFocusListener()
protected LayoutManager
createLayoutManager()
protected MouseListener
createMouseListener()
protected PropertyChangeListener
createPropertyChangeListener()
public static ComponentUI createUI(
JComponent c)
protected void expandTabRunsArray()
protected Insets getContentBorderInsets(
int tabPlacement)
protected FontMetrics getFontMetrics()
protected Icon getIconForTab(int
tabIndex)
public Dimension getMaximumSize(
JComponent c)
public Dimension getMinimumSize(
JComponent c)
protected int getNextTabIndex(int base)
public Dimension getPreferredSize(
JComponent c)
protected int getPreviousTabIndex(int
base)
protected int getRunForTab(int tabCount,
int tabIndex)
protected Insets getSelectedTabPadInsets(
int tabPlacement)
protected Insets getTabAreaInsets(int
tabPlacement)
public Rectangle getTabBounds(
JTabbedPane pane,int i)
protected Insets getTabInsets(int
tabPlacement,int tabIndex)

protected int getTabLabelShiftX(int
tabPlacement,int tabIndex,boolean
isSelected)
protected int getTabLabelShiftY(int
tabPlacement,int tabIndex,boolean
isSelected)
public int getTabRunCount(JTabbedPane
pane)
protected int getTabRunIndent(int
tabPlacement,int run)
protected int getTabRunOffset(int
tabPlacement,int tabCount,int tabIndex,
boolean forward)
protected int getTabRunOverlay(int
tabPlacement)
protected Component getVisibleComponent()
protected void installDefaults()
protected void installKeyboardActions()
protected void installListeners()
public void installUI(JComponent c)
protected int lastTabInRun(int tabCount,
int run)
protected void layoutLabel(int
tabPlacement,FontMetrics metrics,int
tabIndex,String title,Icon icon,
Rectangle tabRect,Rectangle iconRect,
Rectangle textRect,boolean isSelected)
protected void navigateSelectedTab(int
direction)
public void paint(Graphics g,JComponent
c)
protected void paintContentBorder(
Graphics g,int tabPlacement,int
selectedIndex)
protected void
paintContentBorderBottomEdge(Graphics g,
int tabPlacement,int selectedIndex,int x,
int y,int w,int h)
protected void
paintContentBorderLeftEdge(Graphics g,
int tabPlacement,int selectedIndex,int x,
int y,int w,int h)
protected void
paintContentBorderRightEdge(Graphics g,
int tabPlacement,int selectedIndex,int x,
int y,int w,int h)
protected void paintContentBorderTopEdge(
Graphics g,int tabPlacement,int
selectedIndex,int x,int y,int w,int h)
protected void paintFocusIndicator(
Graphics g,int tabPlacement,Rectangle
rects,int tabIndex,Rectangle iconRect,
Rectangle textRect,boolean isSelected)
protected void paintIcon(Graphics g,int
tabPlacement,int tabIndex,Icon icon,
Rectangle iconRect,boolean isSelected)
protected void paintTab(Graphics g,int
tabPlacement,Rectangle rects,int
tabIndex,Rectangle iconRect,Rectangle
textRect)
protected void paintTabBackground(
Graphics g,int tabPlacement,int tabIndex,
int x,int y,int w,int h,boolean
isSelected)

```
protected void paintTabBorder(Graphics g,
int tabPlacement,int tabIndex,int x,int
y,int w,int h,boolean isSelected)
protected void paintText(Graphics g,int
tabPlacement,Font font,FontMetrics
metrics,int tabIndex,String title,
Rectangle textRect,boolean isSelected)
protected static void rotateInsets(
Insets topInsets,Insets targetInsets,int
targetPlacement)
protected void selectAdjacentRunTab(int
tabPlacement,int tabIndex,int offset)
protected void selectNextTab(int current)
protected void selectPreviousTab(int
current)
protected void setVisibleComponent(
Component component)
protected boolean shouldPadTabRun(int
tabPlacement,int run)
protected boolean shouldRotateTabRuns(
int tabPlacement)
public int tabForCoordinate(JTabbedPane
pane,int x,int y)
protected void uninstallDefaults()
protected void uninstallKeyboardActions()
protected void uninstallListeners()
public void uninstallUI(JComponent c)
```

## BasicTableHeaderUI

```
public class javax.swing.plaf.basic.
BasicTableHeaderUI
extends javax.swing.plaf.TableHeaderUI
extends javax.swing.plaf.ComponentUI
extends java.lang.Object
```

### Fields

```
protected javax.swing.table.JTableHeader
header
protected javax.swing.event.
MouseInputListener mouseInputListener
protected javax.swing.CellRendererPane
rendererPane
```

### Methods

```
protected MouseInputListener
createMouseInputListener()
public static ComponentUI createUI(
JComponent h)
public Dimension getMaximumSize(
JComponent c)
public Dimension getMinimumSize(
JComponent c)
public Dimension getPreferredSize(
JComponent c)
protected void installDefaults()
protected void installKeyboardActions()
protected void installListeners()
public void installUI(JComponent c)
public void paint(Graphics g,JComponent
c)
protected void uninstallDefaults()
protected void uninstallKeyboardActions()
protected void uninstallListeners()
public void uninstallUI(JComponent c)
```

## BasicTableUI

```
public class javax.swing.plaf.basic.
BasicTableUI
extends javax.swing.plaf.TableUI
extends javax.swing.plaf.ComponentUI
extends java.lang.Object
```

### Fields

```
protected java.awt.event.FocusListener
focusListener
protected java.awt.event.KeyListener
keyListener
protected javax.swing.event.
MouseInputListener mouseInputListener
protected javax.swing.CellRendererPane
rendererPane
protected javax.swing.JTable table
```

### Methods

```
protected FocusListener
createFocusListener()
protected KeyListener createKeyListener()
protected MouseInputListener
createMouseInputListener()
public static ComponentUI createUI(
JComponent c)
public Dimension getMaximumSize(
JComponent c)
public Dimension getMinimumSize(
JComponent c)
public Dimension getPreferredSize(
JComponent c)
protected void installDefaults()
protected void installKeyboardActions()
protected void installListeners()
public void installUI(JComponent c)
public void paint(Graphics g,JComponent
c)
protected void uninstallDefaults()
protected void uninstallKeyboardActions()
protected void uninstallListeners()
public void uninstallUI(JComponent c)
```

## BasicTextAreaUI

```
public class javax.swing.plaf.basic.
BasicTextAreaUI
extends javax.swing.plaf.basic.
BasicTextUI
extends javax.swing.plaf.TextUI
extends javax.swing.plaf.ComponentUI
extends java.lang.Object
```

### Constructors

```
public  BasicTextAreaUI()
```

### Methods

```
public View create(Element elem)
public static ComponentUI createUI(
JComponent ta)
protected String getPropertyPrefix()
protected void propertyChange(
PropertyChangeEvent evt)
```

# BasicTextFieldUI

public class javax.swing.plaf.basic.
BasicTextFieldUI
extends javax.swing.plaf.basic.
BasicTextUI
extends javax.swing.plaf.TextUI
extends javax.swing.plaf.ComponentUI
extends java.lang.Object

## Constructors
public BasicTextFieldUI()

## Methods
public View create(Element elem)
protected Caret createCaret()
public static ComponentUI createUI(
JComponent c)
protected String getPropertyPrefix()

# BasicTextPaneUI

public class javax.swing.plaf.basic.
BasicTextPaneUI
extends javax.swing.plaf.basic.
BasicEditorPaneUI
extends javax.swing.plaf.basic.
BasicTextUI
extends javax.swing.plaf.TextUI
extends javax.swing.plaf.ComponentUI
extends java.lang.Object

## Constructors
public BasicTextPaneUI()

## Methods
public static ComponentUI createUI(
JComponent c)
public EditorKit getEditorKit(
JTextComponent tc)
protected String getPropertyPrefix()
protected void propertyChange(
PropertyChangeEvent evt)

# BasicTextUI

public abstract class javax.swing.plaf.
basic.BasicTextUI
implements javax.swing.text.ViewFactory
extends javax.swing.plaf.TextUI
extends javax.swing.plaf.ComponentUI
extends java.lang.Object

## Constructors
public BasicTextUI()

## Methods
public View create(Element elem)
public View create(Element elem,int p0,
int p1)
protected Caret createCaret()
protected Highlighter createHighlighter()
protected Keymap createKeymap()
public void damageRange(JTextComponent
tc,int p0,int p1)

public void damageRange(JTextComponent t,
int p0,int p1,Bias p0Bias,Bias p1Bias)
protected final JTextComponent
getComponent()
public EditorKit getEditorKit(
JTextComponent tc)
protected String getKeymapName()
public Dimension getMaximumSize(
JComponent c)
public Dimension getMinimumSize(
JComponent c)
public int getNextVisualPositionFrom(
JTextComponent t,int pos,Bias b,int
direction,Bias biasRet)
public Dimension getPreferredSize(
JComponent c)
protected abstract String
getPropertyPrefix()
public View getRootView(JTextComponent
tc)
protected Rectangle getVisibleEditorRect(
)
protected void installDefaults()
protected void installKeyboardActions()
protected void installListeners()
public void installUI(JComponent c)
protected void modelChanged()
public Rectangle modelToView(
JTextComponent tc,int pos)
public Rectangle modelToView(
JTextComponent tc,int pos,Bias bias)
public final void paint(Graphics g,
JComponent c)
protected void paintBackground(Graphics
g)
protected void paintSafely(Graphics g)
protected void propertyChange(
PropertyChangeEvent evt)
protected final void setView(View v)
protected void uninstallDefaults()
protected void uninstallKeyboardActions()
protected void uninstallListeners()
public void uninstallUI(JComponent c)
public int viewToModel(JTextComponent tc,
Point pt)
public int viewToModel(JTextComponent tc,
Point pt,Bias biasReturn)

# BasicToggleButtonUI

public class javax.swing.plaf.basic.
BasicToggleButtonUI
extends javax.swing.plaf.basic.
BasicButtonUI
extends javax.swing.plaf.ButtonUI
extends javax.swing.plaf.ComponentUI
extends java.lang.Object

## Methods
public static ComponentUI createUI(
JComponent b)
protected String getPropertyPrefix()
public void paint(Graphics g,JComponent
c)

```
protected void paintButtonPressed(
Graphics g,AbstractButton b)
protected void paintFocus(Graphics g,
AbstractButton b,Rectangle viewRect,
Rectangle textRect,Rectangle iconRect)
protected void paintIcon(Graphics g,
AbstractButton b,Rectangle iconRect)
protected void paintText(Graphics g,
AbstractButton b,Rectangle textRect,
String text)
```

## BasicToolBarSeparatorUI

```
public class javax.swing.plaf.basic.
BasicToolBarSeparatorUI
extends javax.swing.plaf.basic.
BasicSeparatorUI
extends javax.swing.plaf.SeparatorUI
extends javax.swing.plaf.ComponentUI
extends java.lang.Object
```

### Methods

```
public static ComponentUI createUI(
JComponent c)
public Dimension getMaximumSize(
JComponent c)
public Dimension getMinimumSize(
JComponent c)
public Dimension getPreferredSize(
JComponent c)
protected void installDefaults(
JSeparator s)
public void paint(Graphics g,JComponent
c)
```

## BasicToolBarUI

```
public class javax.swing.plaf.basic.
BasicToolBarUI
implements javax.swing.SwingConstants
extends javax.swing.plaf.ToolBarUI
extends javax.swing.plaf.ComponentUI
extends java.lang.Object
```

### Fields

```
protected java.awt.Color
dockingBorderColor
protected java.awt.Color dockingColor
protected javax.swing.event.
MouseInputListener dockingListener
protected javax.swing.KeyStroke downKey
protected DragWindow dragWindow
protected java.awt.Color
floatingBorderColor
protected java.awt.Color floatingColor
protected int focusedCompIndex
protected javax.swing.KeyStroke leftKey
protected java.beans.
PropertyChangeListener propertyListener
protected javax.swing.KeyStroke
rightKey
protected javax.swing.JToolBar toolBar
protected java.awt.event.
ContainerListener toolBarContListener
```

```
protected java.awt.event.FocusListener
toolBarFocusListener
protected javax.swing.KeyStroke upKey
```

### Methods

```
public boolean canDock(Component c,Point
p)
protected MouseInputListener
createDockingListener()
protected DragWindow createDragWindow(
JToolBar toolbar)
protected JFrame createFloatingFrame(
JToolBar toolbar)
protected WindowListener
createFrameListener()
protected PropertyChangeListener
createPropertyListener()
protected ContainerListener
createToolBarContListener()
protected FocusListener
createToolBarFocusListener()
public static ComponentUI createUI(
JComponent c)
protected void dragTo(Point position,
Point origin)
protected void floatAt(Point position,
Point origin)
public Color getDockingColor()
public Color getFloatingColor()
public Dimension getMaximumSize(
JComponent c)
public Dimension getMinimumSize(
JComponent c)
public Dimension getPreferredSize(
JComponent c)
protected void installComponents()
protected void installDefaults()
protected void installKeyboardActions()
protected void installListeners()
public void installUI(JComponent c)
public boolean isFloating()
protected void navigateFocusedComp(int
direction)
public void setDockingColor(Color c)
public void setFloating(boolean b,Point
p)
public void setFloatingColor(Color c)
public void setFloatingLocation(int x,
int y)
public void setOrientation(int
orientation)
protected void uninstallComponents()
protected void uninstallDefaults()
protected void uninstallKeyboardActions()
protected void uninstallListeners()
public void uninstallUI(JComponent c)
```

## BasicToolTipUI

```
public class javax.swing.plaf.basic.
BasicToolTipUI
extends javax.swing.plaf.ToolTipUI
extends javax.swing.plaf.ComponentUI
extends java.lang.Object
```

## Constructors
```
public BasicToolTipUI()
```

## Methods
```
public static ComponentUI createUI(
JComponent c)
public Dimension getMaximumSize(
JComponent c)
public Dimension getMinimumSize(
JComponent c)
public Dimension getPreferredSize(
JComponent c)
protected void installDefaults(
JComponent c)
protected void installListeners(
JComponent c)
public void installUI(JComponent c)
public void paint(Graphics g,JComponent
c)
protected void uninstallDefaults(
JComponent c)
protected void uninstallListeners(
JComponent c)
public void uninstallUI(JComponent c)
```

# BasicTreeUI
```
public class javax.swing.plaf.basic.
BasicTreeUI
extends javax.swing.plaf.TreeUI
extends javax.swing.plaf.ComponentUI
extends java.lang.Object
```

## Fields
```
protected transient javax.swing.tree.
TreeCellEditor cellEditor
protected transient javax.swing.Icon
collapsedIcon
protected boolean createdCellEditor
protected boolean createdRenderer
protected transient javax.swing.tree.
TreeCellRenderer currentCellRenderer
protected int depthOffset
protected java.util.Hashtable
drawingCache
protected java.awt.Component
editingComponent
protected javax.swing.tree.TreePath
editingPath
protected int editingRow
protected boolean
editorHasDifferentSize
protected transient javax.swing.Icon
expandedIcon
protected boolean largeModel
protected int lastSelectedRow
protected int leftChildIndent
protected AbstractLayoutCache.
NodeDimensions nodeDimensions
protected java.awt.Dimension
preferredMinSize
protected java.awt.Dimension
preferredSize
```

```
protected javax.swing.CellRendererPane
rendererPane
protected int rightChildIndent
protected boolean
stopEditingInCompleteEditing
protected int totalChildIndent
protected javax.swing.JTree tree
protected javax.swing.tree.TreeModel
treeModel
protected javax.swing.tree.
TreeSelectionModel treeSelectionModel
protected javax.swing.tree.
AbstractLayoutCache treeState
protected boolean
validCachedPreferredSize
```

## Constructors
```
public BasicTreeUI()
```

## Methods
```
public void cancelEditing(JTree tree)
protected void
checkForClickInExpandControl(TreePath
path,int mouseX,int mouseY)
protected void completeEditing()
protected void completeEditing(boolean
messageStop,boolean messageCancel,
boolean messageTree)
protected void completeUIInstall()
protected void completeUIUninstall()
protected void configureLayoutCache()
protected CellEditorListener
createCellEditorListener()
protected CellRendererPane
createCellRendererPane()
protected ComponentListener
createComponentListener()
protected TreeCellEditor
createDefaultCellEditor()
protected TreeCellRenderer
createDefaultCellRenderer()
protected FocusListener
createFocusListener()
protected KeyListener createKeyListener()
protected AbstractLayoutCache
createLayoutCache()
protected MouseListener
createMouseListener()
protected NodeDimensions
createNodeDimensions()
protected PropertyChangeListener
createPropertyChangeListener()
protected PropertyChangeListener
createSelectionModelProperty
ChangeListener()
protected TreeExpansionListener
createTreeExpansionListener()
protected TreeModelListener
createTreeModelListener()
protected TreeSelectionListener
createTreeSelectionListener()
public static ComponentUI createUI(
JComponent x)
```

protected void drawCentered(Component c,
Graphics graphics,Icon icon,int x,int y)
protected void drawDashedHorizontalLine(
Graphics g,int y,int x1,int x2)
protected void drawDashedVerticalLine(
Graphics g,int x,int y1,int y2)
protected void ensureRowsAreVisible(int
beginRow,int endRow)
protected TreeCellEditor getCellEditor()
protected TreeCellRenderer
getCellRenderer()
public TreePath
getClosestPathForLocation(JTree tree,int
x,int y)
public Icon getCollapsedIcon()
public TreePath getEditingPath(JTree
tree)
public Icon getExpandedIcon()
protected Color getHashColor()
protected int getHorizontalLegBuffer()
protected TreePath getLastChildPath(
TreePath parent)
public int getLeftChildIndent()
public Dimension getMaximumSize(
JComponent c)
public Dimension getMinimumSize(
JComponent c)
protected TreeModel getModel()
public Rectangle getPathBounds(JTree
tree,TreePath path)
public TreePath getPathForRow(JTree tree,
int row)
public Dimension getPreferredMinSize()
public Dimension getPreferredSize(
JComponent c)
public Dimension getPreferredSize(
JComponent c,boolean checkConsistancy)
public int getRightChildIndent()
public int getRowCount(JTree tree)
public int getRowForPath(JTree tree,
TreePath path)
protected int getRowHeight()
protected TreeSelectionModel
getSelectionModel()
protected boolean getShowsRootHandles()
protected int getVerticalLegBuffer()
protected void handleExpandControlClick(
TreePath path,int mouseX,int mouseY)
protected void installComponents()
protected void installDefaults()
protected void installKeyboardActions()
protected void installListeners()
public void installUI(JComponent c)
protected boolean isEditable()
public boolean isEditing(JTree tree)
protected boolean isLargeModel()
protected boolean isLeaf(int row)
protected boolean
isLocationInExpandControl(TreePath path,
int mouseX,int mouseY)
protected boolean isMultiSelectEvent(
MouseEvent event)
protected boolean isRootVisible()

protected boolean isToggleEvent(
MouseEvent event)
protected boolean isToggleSelectionEvent(
MouseEvent event)
public void paint(Graphics g,JComponent
c)
protected void paintExpandControl(
Graphics g,Rectangle clipBounds,Insets
insets,Rectangle bounds,TreePath path,
int row,boolean isExpanded,boolean
hasBeenExpanded,boolean isLeaf)
protected void paintHorizontalLine(
Graphics g,JComponent c,int y,int left,
int right)
protected void paintHorizontalPartOfLeg(
Graphics g,Rectangle clipBounds,Insets
insets,Rectangle bounds,TreePath path,
int row,boolean isExpanded,boolean
hasBeenExpanded,boolean isLeaf)
protected void paintRow(Graphics g,
Rectangle clipBounds,Insets insets,
Rectangle bounds,TreePath path,int row,
boolean isExpanded,boolean
hasBeenExpanded,boolean isLeaf)
protected void paintVerticalLine(
Graphics g,JComponent c,int x,int top,
int bottom)
protected void paintVerticalPartOfLeg(
Graphics g,Rectangle clipBounds,Insets
insets,TreePath path)
protected void pathWasCollapsed(TreePath
path)
protected void pathWasExpanded(TreePath
path)
protected void prepareForUIInstall()
protected void prepareForUIUninstall()
protected void selectPathForEvent(
TreePath path,MouseEvent event)
protected void setCellEditor(
TreeCellEditor editor)
protected void setCellRenderer(
TreeCellRenderer tcr)
public void setCollapsedIcon(Icon newG)
protected void setEditable(boolean
newValue)
public void setExpandedIcon(Icon newG)
protected void setHashColor(Color color)
protected void setLargeModel(boolean
largeModel)
public void setLeftChildIndent(int
newAmount)
protected void setModel(TreeModel model)
public void setPreferredMinSize(
Dimension newSize)
public void setRightChildIndent(int
newAmount)
protected void setRootVisible(boolean
newValue)
protected void setRowHeight(int
rowHeight)
protected void setSelectionModel(
TreeSelectionModel newLSM)
protected void setShowsRootHandles(
boolean newValue)

```
protected boolean
shouldPaintExpandControl(TreePath path,
int row,boolean isExpanded,boolean
hasBeenExpanded,boolean isLeaf)
protected boolean startEditing(TreePath
path,MouseEvent event)
public void startEditingAtPath(JTree
tree,TreePath path)
public boolean stopEditing(JTree tree)
protected void toggleExpandState(
TreePath path)
protected void uninstallComponents()
protected void uninstallDefaults()
protected void uninstallKeyboardActions()
protected void uninstallListeners()
public void uninstallUI(JComponent c)
protected void updateCachedPreferredSize(
)
protected void updateCellEditor()
protected void updateDepthOffset()
protected void updateExpandedDescendants(
TreePath path)
protected void
updateLayoutCacheExpandedNodes()
protected void updateRenderer()
protected void updateSize()
```

## BasicViewportUI

```
public class javax.swing.plaf.basic.
BasicViewportUI
extends javax.swing.plaf.ViewportUI
extends javax.swing.plaf.ComponentUI
extends java.lang.Object
```

### Methods

```
public static ComponentUI createUI(
JComponent c)
protected void installDefaults(
JComponent c)
public void installUI(JComponent c)
protected void uninstallDefaults(
JComponent c)
public void uninstallUI(JComponent c)
```

## BatchUpdateException

```
public class java.sql.
BatchUpdateException
extends java.sql.SQLException
extends java.lang.Exception
extends java.lang.Throwable
extends java.lang.Object
```

### Constructors

```
public  BatchUpdateException(String
reason,String SQLState,int vendorCode,
int updateCounts)
public  BatchUpdateException(String
reason,String SQLState,int updateCounts)
public  BatchUpdateException(String
reason,int updateCounts)
public  BatchUpdateException(int
updateCounts)
public  BatchUpdateException()
```

### Methods

```
public int getUpdateCounts()
```

## BeanContextChildSupport

```
public class java.beans.beancontext.
BeanContextChildSupport
implements java.beans.beancontext.
BeanContextChild
implements java.beans.beancontext.
BeanContextServicesListener
implements java.io.Serializable
extends java.lang.Object
```

### Fields

```
protected transient java.beans.
beancontext.BeanContext beanContext
public java.beans.beancontext.
BeanContextChild beanContextChildPeer
protected java.beans.
PropertyChangeSupport pcSupport
protected transient boolean
rejectedSetBCOnce
protected java.beans.
VetoableChangeSupport vcSupport
```

### Constructors

```
public  BeanContextChildSupport()
public  BeanContextChildSupport(
BeanContextChild bcc)
```

### Methods

```
public void addPropertyChangeListener(
String name,PropertyChangeListener pcl)
public void addVetoableChangeListener(
String name,VetoableChangeListener vcl)
public void firePropertyChange(String
name,Object oldValue,Object newValue)
public void fireVetoableChange(String
name,Object oldValue,Object newValue)
public synchronized BeanContext
getBeanContext()
public BeanContextChild
getBeanContextChildPeer()
protected void
initializeBeanContextResources()
public boolean isDelegated()
protected void
releaseBeanContextResources()
public void removePropertyChangeListener(
String name,PropertyChangeListener pcl)
public void removeVetoableChangeListener(
String name,VetoableChangeListener vcl)
public void serviceAvailable(
BeanContextServiceAvailableEvent bcsae)
public void serviceRevoked(
BeanContextServiceRevokedEvent bcsre)
public synchronized void setBeanContext(
BeanContext bc)
public boolean
validatePendingSetBeanContext(
BeanContext newValue)
```

## BeanContextEvent

public abstract class java.beans.
beancontext.BeanContextEvent
extends java.util.EventObject
extends java.lang.Object

### Fields

protected java.beans.beancontext.
BeanContext propagatedFrom

### Constructors

protected  BeanContextEvent(BeanContext
bc)

### Methods

public BeanContext getBeanContext()
public synchronized BeanContext
getPropagatedFrom()
public synchronized boolean isPropagated(
)
public synchronized void
setPropagatedFrom(BeanContext bc)

## BeanContextMembershipEvent

public class java.beans.beancontext.
BeanContextMembershipEvent
extends java.beans.beancontext.
BeanContextEvent
extends java.util.EventObject
extends java.lang.Object

### Fields

protected java.util.Collection children

### Constructors

public  BeanContextMembershipEvent(
BeanContext bc,Collection changes)
public  BeanContextMembershipEvent(
BeanContext bc,Object changes)

### Methods

public boolean contains(Object child)
public Iterator iterator()
public int size()
public Object toArray()

## BeanContextServiceAvailableEvent

public class java.beans.beancontext.
BeanContextServiceAvailableEvent
extends java.beans.beancontext.
BeanContextEvent
extends java.util.EventObject
extends java.lang.Object

### Fields

protected java.lang.Class serviceClass

### Constructors

public  BeanContextServiceAvailableEvent(
BeanContextServices bcs,Class sc)

### Methods

public Iterator
getCurrentServiceSelectors()
public Class getServiceClass()
public BeanContextServices
getSourceAsBeanContextServices()

## BeanContextServiceRevokedEvent

public class java.beans.beancontext.
BeanContextServiceRevokedEvent
extends java.beans.beancontext.
BeanContextEvent
extends java.util.EventObject
extends java.lang.Object

### Fields

protected java.lang.Class serviceClass

### Constructors

public  BeanContextServiceRevokedEvent(
BeanContextServices bcs,Class sc,boolean
invalidate)

### Methods

public Class getServiceClass()
public BeanContextServices
getSourceAsBeanContextServices()
public boolean
isCurrentServiceInvalidNow()
public boolean isServiceClass(Class
service)

## BeanContextServicesSupport

public class java.beans.beancontext.
BeanContextServicesSupport
implements java.beans.beancontext.
BeanContextServices
extends java.beans.beancontext.
BeanContextSupport
extends java.beans.beancontext.
BeanContextChildSupport
extends java.lang.Object

### Fields

protected transient java.util.ArrayList
bcsListeners
protected transient
BCSSProxyServiceProvider proxy
protected transient int serializable
protected transient java.util.HashMap
services

### Constructors

public  BeanContextServicesSupport(
BeanContextServices peer,Locale lcle,
boolean dTime,boolean visible)
public  BeanContextServicesSupport(
BeanContextServices peer,Locale lcle,
boolean dtime)
public  BeanContextServicesSupport(
BeanContextServices peer,Locale lcle)
public  BeanContextServicesSupport(
BeanContextServices peer)

```
public  BeanContextServicesSupport()
```

## Methods
```
public void
addBeanContextServicesListener(
BeanContextServicesListener bcsl)
public boolean addService(Class
serviceClass,BeanContextServiceProvider
bcsp)
protected boolean addService(Class
serviceClass,BeanContextServiceProvider
bcsp,boolean fireEvent)
protected synchronized void
bcsPreDeserializationHook(
ObjectInputStream ois)
protected synchronized void
bcsPreSerializationHook(
ObjectOutputStream oos)
protected void childJustRemovedHook(
Object child,BCSChild bcsc)
protected BCSChild createBCSChild(Object
targetChild,Object peer)
protected BCSSServiceProvider
createBCSSServiceProvider(Class sc,
BeanContextServiceProvider bcsp)
protected final void fireServiceAdded(
Class serviceClass)
protected final void fireServiceAdded(
BeanContextServiceAvailableEvent bcssae)
protected final void fireServiceRevoked(
BeanContextServiceRevokedEvent bcsre)
protected final void fireServiceRevoked(
Class serviceClass,boolean revokeNow)
public BeanContextServices
getBeanContextServicesPeer()
protected final static
BeanContextServicesListener
getChildBeanContextServicesListener(
Object child)
public Iterator getCurrentServiceClasses(
)
public Iterator
getCurrentServiceSelectors(Class
serviceClass)
public Object getService(
BeanContextChild child,Object requestor,
Class serviceClass,Object
serviceSelector,
BeanContextServiceRevokedListener bcsrl)
public synchronized boolean hasService(
Class serviceClass)
public void initialize()
protected synchronized void
initializeBeanContextResources()
protected synchronized void
releaseBeanContextResources()
public void releaseService(
BeanContextChild child,Object requestor,
Object service)
public void
removeBeanContextServicesListener(
BeanContextServicesListener bcsl)
```

```
public void revokeService(Class
serviceClass,BeanContextServiceProvider
bcsp,boolean revokeCurrentServicesNow)
public void serviceAvailable(
BeanContextServiceAvailableEvent bcssae)
public void serviceRevoked(
BeanContextServiceRevokedEvent bcssre)
```

# BeanContextSupport
```
public class java.beans.beancontext.
BeanContextSupport
implements java.beans.beancontext.
BeanContext
implements java.beans.
PropertyChangeListener
implements java.io.Serializable
implements java.beans.
VetoableChangeListener
extends java.beans.beancontext.
BeanContextChildSupport
extends java.lang.Object
```

## Fields
```
protected transient java.util.ArrayList
bcmListeners
protected transient java.util.HashMap
children
protected boolean designTime
protected java.util.Locale locale
protected boolean okToUseGui
```

## Constructors
```
public  BeanContextSupport(BeanContext
peer,Locale lcle,boolean dTime,boolean
visible)
public  BeanContextSupport(BeanContext
peer,Locale lcle,boolean dtime)
public  BeanContextSupport(BeanContext
peer,Locale lcle)
public  BeanContextSupport(BeanContext
peer)
public  BeanContextSupport()
```

## Methods
```
public boolean add(Object targetChild)
public boolean addAll(Collection c)
public void
addBeanContextMembershipListener(
BeanContextMembershipListener bcml)
public boolean avoidingGui()
protected Iterator bcsChildren()
protected void bcsPreDeserializationHook(
ObjectInputStream ois)
protected void bcsPreSerializationHook(
ObjectOutputStream oos)
protected void childDeserializedHook(
Object child,BCSChild bcsc)
protected void childJustAddedHook(Object
child,BCSChild bcsc)
protected void childJustRemovedHook(
Object child,BCSChild bcsc)
protected final static boolean
classEquals(Class first,Class second)
```

```
public void clear()
public boolean contains(Object o)
public boolean containsAll(Collection c)
public boolean containsKey(Object o)
protected final Object copyChildren()
protected BCSChild createBCSChild(Object
targetChild,Object peer)
protected final void deserialize(
ObjectInputStream ois,Collection coll)
public synchronized void dontUseGui()
protected final void fireChildrenAdded(
BeanContextMembershipEvent bcme)
protected final void fireChildrenRemoved(
BeanContextMembershipEvent bcme)
public BeanContext getBeanContextPeer()
protected final static BeanContextChild
getChildBeanContextChild(Object child)
protected final static
BeanContextMembershipListener
getChildBeanContextMembershipListener(
Object child)
protected final static
PropertyChangeListener
getChildPropertyChangeListener(Object
child)
protected final static Serializable
getChildSerializable(Object child)
protected final static
VetoableChangeListener
getChildVetoableChangeListener(Object
child)
protected final static Visibility
getChildVisibility(Object child)
public synchronized Locale getLocale()
public URL getResource(String name,
BeanContextChild bcc)
public InputStream getResourceAsStream(
String name,BeanContextChild bcc)
protected synchronized void initialize()
public Object instantiateChild(String
beanName)
public synchronized boolean isDesignTime(
)
public boolean isEmpty()
public boolean isSerializing()
public Iterator iterator()
public synchronized boolean needsGui()
public synchronized void okToUseGui()
public void propertyChange(
PropertyChangeEvent pce)
public final void readChildren(
ObjectInputStream ois)
public boolean remove(Object targetChild)
protected boolean remove(Object
targetChild,boolean callChildSetBC)
public boolean removeAll(Collection c)
public void
removeBeanContextMembershipListener(
BeanContextMembershipListener bcml)
public boolean retainAll(Collection c)
protected final void serialize(
ObjectOutputStream oos,Collection coll)
public synchronized void setDesignTime(
boolean dTime)
```

```
public synchronized void setLocale(
Locale newLocale)
public int size()
public Object toArray()
public Object toArray(Object arry)
protected boolean validatePendingAdd(
Object targetChild)
protected boolean validatePendingRemove(
Object targetChild)
public void vetoableChange(
PropertyChangeEvent pce)
public final void writeChildren(
ObjectOutputStream oos)
```

## BeanDescriptor

```
public class java.beans.BeanDescriptor
extends java.beans.FeatureDescriptor
extends java.lang.Object
```

### Constructors

```
public  BeanDescriptor(Class beanClass)
public  BeanDescriptor(Class beanClass,
Class customizerClass)
 BeanDescriptor()
```

### Methods

```
public Class getBeanClass()
public Class getCustomizerClass()
```

## Beans

```
public class java.beans.Beans
extends java.lang.Object
```

### Methods

```
public static Object getInstanceOf(
Object bean,Class targetType)
public static Object instantiate(
ClassLoader cls,String beanName)
public static Object instantiate(
ClassLoader cls,String beanName,
BeanContext beanContext)
public static Object instantiate(
ClassLoader cls,String beanName,
BeanContext beanContext,
AppletInitializer initializer)
public static boolean isDesignTime()
public static boolean isGuiAvailable()
public static boolean isInstanceOf(
Object bean,Class targetType)
public static void setDesignTime(boolean
isDesignTime)
public static void setGuiAvailable(
boolean isGuiAvailable)
```

## BevelBorder

```
public class javax.swing.border.
BevelBorder
extends javax.swing.border.
AbstractBorder
extends java.lang.Object
```

## Fields
```
protected int bevelType
protected java.awt.Color highlightInner
protected java.awt.Color highlightOuter
public final static int LOWERED
public final static int RAISED
protected java.awt.Color shadowInner
protected java.awt.Color shadowOuter
```

## Constructors
```
public  BevelBorder(int bevelType)
public  BevelBorder(int bevelType,Color
highlight,Color shadow)
public  BevelBorder(int bevelType,Color
highlightOuter,Color highlightInner,
Color shadowOuter,Color shadowInner)
```

## Methods
```
public int getBevelType()
public Insets getBorderInsets(Component
c)
public Insets getBorderInsets(Component
c,Insets insets)
public Color getHighlightInnerColor(
Component c)
public Color getHighlightOuterColor(
Component c)
public Color getShadowInnerColor(
Component c)
public Color getShadowOuterColor(
Component c)
public boolean isBorderOpaque()
public void paintBorder(Component c,
Graphics g,int x,int y,int width,int
height)
protected void paintLoweredBevel(
Component c,Graphics g,int x,int y,int
width,int height)
protected void paintRaisedBevel(
Component c,Graphics g,int x,int y,int
width,int height)
```

# BigDecimal
```
public class java.math.BigDecimal
implements java.lang.Comparable
extends java.lang.Number
extends java.lang.Object
```

## Fields
```
public final static int ROUND_CEILING
public final static int ROUND_DOWN
public final static int ROUND_FLOOR
public final static int ROUND_HALF_DOWN
public final static int ROUND_HALF_EVEN
public final static int ROUND_HALF_UP
public final static int ROUND_
UNNECESSARY
public final static int ROUND_UP
```

## Constructors
```
public  BigDecimal(String val)
public  BigDecimal(double val)
public  BigDecimal(BigInteger val)
```

```
public  BigDecimal(BigInteger
unscaledVal,int scale)
```

## Methods
```
public BigDecimal abs()
public BigDecimal add(BigDecimal val)
public int compareTo(BigDecimal val)
public int compareTo(Object o)
public BigDecimal divide(BigDecimal val,
int scale,int roundingMode)
public BigDecimal divide(BigDecimal val,
int roundingMode)
public double doubleValue()
public boolean equals(Object x)
public float floatValue()
public int hashCode()
public int intValue()
public long longValue()
public BigDecimal max(BigDecimal val)
public BigDecimal min(BigDecimal val)
public BigDecimal movePointLeft(int n)
public BigDecimal movePointRight(int n)
public BigDecimal multiply(BigDecimal
val)
public BigDecimal negate()
public int scale()
public BigDecimal setScale(int scale,int
roundingMode)
public BigDecimal setScale(int scale)
public int signum()
public BigDecimal subtract(BigDecimal
val)
public BigInteger toBigInteger()
public String toString()
public BigInteger unscaledValue()
public static BigDecimal valueOf(long
unscaledVal,int scale)
public static BigDecimal valueOf(long
val)
```

# BigInteger
```
public class java.math.BigInteger
implements java.lang.Comparable
extends java.lang.Number
extends java.lang.Object
```

## Fields
```
public final static java.math.BigInteger
ONE
public final static java.math.BigInteger
ZERO
```

## Constructors
```
public  BigInteger(byte val)
public  BigInteger(int signum,byte
magnitude)
public  BigInteger(String val,int radix)
public  BigInteger(String val)
public  BigInteger(int numBits,Random
rnd)
public  BigInteger(int bitLength,int
certainty,Random rnd)
private  BigInteger()
```

## Methods
```
public BigInteger abs()
public BigInteger add(BigInteger val)
public BigInteger and(BigInteger val)
public BigInteger andNot(BigInteger val)
public int bitCount()
public int bitLength()
public BigInteger clearBit(int n)
public int compareTo(BigInteger val)
public int compareTo(Object o)
public BigInteger divide(BigInteger val)
public BigInteger divideAndRemainder(
BigInteger val)
public double doubleValue()
public boolean equals(Object x)
public BigInteger flipBit(int n)
public float floatValue()
public BigInteger gcd(BigInteger val)
public int getLowestSetBit()
public int hashCode()
public int intValue()
public boolean isProbablePrime(int
certainty)
public long longValue()
public BigInteger max(BigInteger val)
public BigInteger min(BigInteger val)
public BigInteger mod(BigInteger m)
public BigInteger modInverse(BigInteger
m)
public BigInteger modPow(BigInteger
exponent,BigInteger m)
public BigInteger multiply(BigInteger
val)
public BigInteger negate()
public BigInteger not()
public BigInteger or(BigInteger val)
public BigInteger pow(int exponent)
public BigInteger remainder(BigInteger
val)
public BigInteger setBit(int n)
public BigInteger shiftLeft(int n)
public BigInteger shiftRight(int n)
public int signum()
public BigInteger subtract(BigInteger
val)
public boolean testBit(int n)
public byte toByteArray()
public String toString(int radix)
public static String toString()
public static BigInteger valueOf(long
val)
public BigInteger xor(BigInteger val)
```

## BindException
```
public class java.net.BindException
extends java.net.SocketException
extends java.io.IOException
extends java.lang.Exception
extends java.lang.Throwable
extends java.lang.Object
```

### Constructors
```
public  BindException(String msg)
public  BindException()
```

## BitSet
```
public class java.util.BitSet
implements java.lang.Cloneable
implements java.io.Serializable
extends java.lang.Object
```

### Constructors
```
public  BitSet()
public  BitSet(int nbits)
```

### Methods
```
public void and(BitSet set)
public void andNot(BitSet set)
public void clear(int bitIndex)
public Object clone()
public boolean equals(Object obj)
public boolean get(int bitIndex)
public int hashCode()
public int length()
public void or(BitSet set)
public void set(int bitIndex)
public int size()
public String toString()
public void xor(BitSet set)
```

## BlockView
```
public class javax.swing.text.html.
BlockView
extends javax.swing.text.BoxView
extends javax.swing.text.CompositeView
extends javax.swing.text.View
extends java.lang.Object
```

### Constructors
```
public  BlockView(Element elem,int axis)
```

### Methods
```
public float getAlignment(int axis)
public AttributeSet getAttributes()
public int getResizeWeight(int axis)
protected StyleSheet getStyleSheet()
public void paint(Graphics g,Shape
allocation)
protected void
setPropertiesFromAttributes()
```

## Book
```
public class java.awt.print.Book
implements java.awt.print.Pageable
extends java.lang.Object
```

### Constructors
```
public  Book()
```

### Methods
```
public void append(Printable painter,
PageFormat page)
public void append(Printable painter,
PageFormat page,int numPages)
public int getNumberOfPages()
public PageFormat getPageFormat(int
pageIndex)
```

public Printable getPrintable(int pageIndex)
public void setPage(int pageIndex, Printable painter,PageFormat page)

## Boolean

public final class java.lang.Boolean
implements java.io.Serializable
extends java.lang.Object

### Fields

public final static java.lang.Boolean FALSE
public final static java.lang.Boolean TRUE
public final static java.lang.Class TYPE

### Constructors

public  Boolean(boolean value)
public  Boolean(String s)

### Methods

public boolean booleanValue()
public boolean equals(Object obj)
public static boolean getBoolean(String name)
public int hashCode()
public String toString()
public static Boolean valueOf(String s)

## BorderFactory

public class javax.swing.BorderFactory
extends java.lang.Object

### Constructors

private  BorderFactory()

### Methods

public static Border createBevelBorder( int type)
public static Border createBevelBorder( int type,Color highlight,Color shadow)
public static Border createBevelBorder( int type,Color highlightOuter,Color highlightInner,Color shadowOuter,Color shadowInner)
public static CompoundBorder createCompoundBorder()
public static CompoundBorder createCompoundBorder(Border outsideBorder,Border insideBorder)
public static Border createEmptyBorder()
public static Border createEmptyBorder( int top,int left,int bottom,int right)
public static Border createEtchedBorder()
public static Border createEtchedBorder( Color highlight,Color shadow)
public static Border createLineBorder( Color color)
public static Border createLineBorder( Color color,int thickness)

public static Border createLoweredBevelBorder()
public static MatteBorder createMatteBorder(int top,int left,int bottom,int right,Color color)
public static MatteBorder createMatteBorder(int top,int left,int bottom,int right,Icon tileIcon)
public static Border createRaisedBevelBorder()
public static TitledBorder createTitledBorder(String title)
public static TitledBorder createTitledBorder(Border border)
public static TitledBorder createTitledBorder(Border border,String title)
public static TitledBorder createTitledBorder(Border border,String title,int titleJustification,int titlePosition)
public static TitledBorder createTitledBorder(Border border,String title,int titleJustification,int titlePosition,Font titleFont)
public static TitledBorder createTitledBorder(Border border,String title,int titleJustification,int titlePosition,Font titleFont,Color titleColor)

## BorderLayout

public class java.awt.BorderLayout
implements java.awt.LayoutManager2
implements java.io.Serializable
extends java.lang.Object

### Fields

public final static java.lang.String AFTER_LAST_LINE
public final static java.lang.String AFTER_LINE_ENDS
public final static java.lang.String BEFORE_FIRST_LINE
public final static java.lang.String BEFORE_LINE_BEGINS
public final static java.lang.String CENTER
public final static java.lang.String EAST
public final static java.lang.String NORTH
public final static java.lang.String SOUTH
public final static java.lang.String WEST

### Constructors

public  BorderLayout()
public  BorderLayout(int hgap,int vgap)

## Methods

```
public void addLayoutComponent(Component
comp,Object constraints)
public void addLayoutComponent(String
name,Component comp)
public int getHgap()
public float getLayoutAlignmentX(
Container parent)
public float getLayoutAlignmentY(
Container parent)
public int getVgap()
public void invalidateLayout(Container
target)
public void layoutContainer(Container
target)
public Dimension maximumLayoutSize(
Container target)
public Dimension minimumLayoutSize(
Container target)
public Dimension preferredLayoutSize(
Container target)
public void removeLayoutComponent(
Component comp)
public void setHgap(int hgap)
public void setVgap(int vgap)
public String toString()
```

## BorderUIResource

```
public class javax.swing.plaf.
BorderUIResource
implements javax.swing.border.Border
implements java.io.Serializable
implements javax.swing.plaf.UIResource
extends java.lang.Object
```

### Constructors

```
public BorderUIResource(Border delegate)
```

### Methods

```
public static Border
getBlackLineBorderUIResource()
public Insets getBorderInsets(Component
c)
public static Border
getEtchedBorderUIResource()
public static Border
getLoweredBevelBorderUIResource()
public static Border
getRaisedBevelBorderUIResource()
public boolean isBorderOpaque()
public void paintBorder(Component c,
Graphics g,int x,int y,int width,int
height)
```

## Box

```
public class javax.swing.Box
implements javax.accessibility.
Accessible
extends java.awt.Container
extends java.awt.Component
extends java.lang.Object
```

### Fields

```
protected javax.accessibility.
AccessibleContext accessibleContext
```

### Constructors

```
public Box(int axis)
```

### Methods

```
public static Component createGlue()
public static Box createHorizontalBox()
public static Component
createHorizontalGlue()
public static Component
createHorizontalStrut(int width)
public static Component createRigidArea(
Dimension d)
public static Box createVerticalBox()
public static Component
createVerticalGlue()
public static Component
createVerticalStrut(int height)
public AccessibleContext
getAccessibleContext()
public void setLayout(LayoutManager l)
```

## BoxLayout

```
public class javax.swing.BoxLayout
implements java.awt.LayoutManager2
implements java.io.Serializable
extends java.lang.Object
```

### Fields

```
public final static int X_AXIS
public final static int Y_AXIS
```

### Constructors

```
public BoxLayout(Container target,int
axis)
 BoxLayout()
```

### Methods

```
public void addLayoutComponent(String
name,Component comp)
public void addLayoutComponent(Component
comp,Object constraints)
public float getLayoutAlignmentX(
Container target)
public float getLayoutAlignmentY(
Container target)
public void invalidateLayout(Container
target)
public void layoutContainer(Container
target)
public Dimension maximumLayoutSize(
Container target)
public Dimension minimumLayoutSize(
Container target)
public Dimension preferredLayoutSize(
Container target)
public void removeLayoutComponent(
Component comp)
```

# BoxView

    public class javax.swing.text.BoxView
    extends javax.swing.text.CompositeView
    extends javax.swing.text.View
    extends java.lang.Object

## Constructors
    public BoxView(Element elem,int axis)

## Methods
    protected void baselineLayout(int
    targetSpan,int axis,int offsets,int
    spans)
    protected SizeRequirements
    baselineRequirements(int axis,
    SizeRequirements r)
    protected SizeRequirements
    calculateMajorAxisRequirements(int axis,
    SizeRequirements r)
    protected SizeRequirements
    calculateMinorAxisRequirements(int axis,
    SizeRequirements r)
    public void changedUpdate(DocumentEvent
    e,Shape a,ViewFactory f)
    protected void childAllocation(int index,
    Rectangle alloc)
    protected boolean flipEastAndWestAtEnds(
    int position,Bias bias)
    public float getAlignment(int axis)
    public final int getHeight()
    public float getMaximumSpan(int axis)
    public float getMinimumSpan(int axis)
    protected final int getOffset(int axis,
    int childIndex)
    public float getPreferredSpan(int axis)
    public int getResizeWeight(int axis)
    protected final int getSpan(int axis,int
    childIndex)
    protected View getViewAtPoint(int x,int
    y,Rectangle alloc)
    public final int getWidth()
    public void insertUpdate(DocumentEvent e,
    Shape a,ViewFactory f)
    protected boolean isAfter(int x,int y,
    Rectangle innerAlloc)
    protected boolean isAllocationValid()
    protected boolean isBefore(int x,int y,
    Rectangle innerAlloc)
    protected void layout(int width,int
    height)
    protected void layoutMajorAxis(int
    targetSpan,int axis,int offsets,int
    spans)
    protected void layoutMinorAxis(int
    targetSpan,int axis,int offsets,int
    spans)
    public Shape modelToView(int pos,Shape a,
    Bias b)
    public void paint(Graphics g,Shape
    allocation)
    protected void paintChild(Graphics g,
    Rectangle alloc,int index)

    public void preferenceChanged(View child,
    boolean width,boolean height)
    public void removeUpdate(DocumentEvent e,
    Shape a,ViewFactory f)
    public void replace(int offset,int
    length,View elems)
    public void setSize(float width,float
    height)
    public int viewToModel(float x,float y,
    Shape a,Bias bias)

# BreakIterator

    public abstract class java.text.
    BreakIterator
    implements java.lang.Cloneable
    extends java.lang.Object

## Fields
    public final static int DONE

## Constructors
    protected BreakIterator()

## Methods
    public Object clone()
    public abstract int current()
    public abstract int first()
    public abstract int following(int offset)
    public static synchronized Locale
    getAvailableLocales()
    public static BreakIterator
    getCharacterInstance()
    public static BreakIterator
    getCharacterInstance(Locale where)
    public static BreakIterator
    getLineInstance()
    public static BreakIterator
    getLineInstance(Locale where)
    public static BreakIterator
    getSentenceInstance()
    public static BreakIterator
    getSentenceInstance(Locale where)
    public abstract CharacterIterator
    getText()
    public static BreakIterator
    getWordInstance()
    public static BreakIterator
    getWordInstance(Locale where)
    public boolean isBoundary(int offset)
    public abstract int last()
    public abstract int next(int n)
    public abstract int next()
    public int preceding(int offset)
    public abstract int previous()
    public void setText(String newText)
    public abstract void setText(
    CharacterIterator newText)

# BufferedImage

    public class java.awt.image.
    BufferedImage
    implements java.awt.image.
    WritableRenderedImage

```
extends java.awt.Image
extends java.lang.Object
```

**Fields**
```
public final static int TYPE_3BYTE_BGR
public final static int TYPE_4BYTE_ABGR
public final static int TYPE_4BYTE_ABGR_
PRE
public final static int TYPE_BYTE_
BINARY
public final static int TYPE_BYTE_GRAY
public final static int TYPE_BYTE_
INDEXED
public final static int TYPE_CUSTOM
public final static int TYPE_INT_ARGB
public final static int TYPE_INT_ARGB_
PRE
public final static int TYPE_INT_BGR
public final static int TYPE_INT_RGB
public final static int TYPE_USHORT_555_
RGB
public final static int TYPE_USHORT_565_
RGB
public final static int TYPE_USHORT_
GRAY
```

**Constructors**
```
public static  BufferedImage(int width,
int height,int imageType)
public  BufferedImage(int width,int
height,int imageType,IndexColorModel cm)
public  BufferedImage(ColorModel cm,
WritableRaster raster,boolean
isRasterPremultiplied,Hashtable
properties)
```

**Methods**
```
public void addTileObserver(TileObserver
to)
public void coerceData(boolean
isAlphaPremultiplied)
public WritableRaster copyData(
WritableRaster outRaster)
public Graphics2D createGraphics()
public void flush()
public WritableRaster getAlphaRaster()
public ColorModel getColorModel()
public Raster getData()
public Raster getData(Rectangle rect)
public Graphics getGraphics()
public int getHeight()
public int getHeight(ImageObserver
observer)
public int getMinTileX()
public int getMinTileY()
public int getMinX()
public int getMinY()
public int getNumXTiles()
public int getNumYTiles()
public Object getProperty(String name,
ImageObserver observer)
public Object getProperty(String name)
public String getPropertyNames()
public WritableRaster getRaster()
```

```
public int getRGB(int x,int y)
public int getRGB(int startX,int startY,
int w,int h,int rgbArray,int offset,int
scansize)
public SampleModel getSampleModel()
public ImageProducer getSource()
public Vector getSources()
public BufferedImage getSubimage(int x,
int y,int w,int h)
public Raster getTile(int tileX,int
tileY)
public int getTileGridXOffset()
public int getTileGridYOffset()
public int getTileHeight()
public int getTileWidth()
public int getType()
public int getWidth()
public int getWidth(ImageObserver
observer)
public WritableRaster getWritableTile(
int tileX,int tileY)
public Point getWritableTileIndices()
public boolean hasTileWriters()
public boolean isAlphaPremultiplied()
public boolean isTileWritable(int tileX,
int tileY)
public void releaseWritableTile(int
tileX,int tileY)
public void removeTileObserver(
TileObserver to)
public void setData(Raster r)
public synchronized void setRGB(int x,
int y,int rgb)
public void setRGB(int startX,int startY,
int w,int h,int rgbArray,int offset,int
scansize)
public String toString()
```

## BufferedImageFilter
```
public class java.awt.image.
BufferedImageFilter
implements java.lang.Cloneable
extends java.awt.image.ImageFilter
extends java.lang.Object
```

**Constructors**
```
public  BufferedImageFilter(
BufferedImageOp op)
```

**Methods**
```
public BufferedImageOp
getBufferedImageOp()
public void imageComplete(int status)
public void setColorModel(ColorModel
model)
public void setDimensions(int width,int
height)
public void setPixels(int x,int y,int w,
int h,ColorModel model,byte pixels,int
off,int scansize)
public void setPixels(int x,int y,int w,
int h,ColorModel model,int pixels,int
off,int scansize)
```

# BufferedInputStream

```
public class java.io.
BufferedInputStream
extends java.io.FilterInputStream
extends java.io.InputStream
extends java.lang.Object
```

### Fields

```
protected byte buf
protected int count
protected int marklimit
protected int markpos
protected int pos
```

### Constructors

```
public  BufferedInputStream(InputStream
in)
public  BufferedInputStream(InputStream
in,int size)
```

### Methods

```
public synchronized int available()
public synchronized void close()
public synchronized void mark(int
readlimit)
public boolean markSupported()
public synchronized int read()
public synchronized int read(byte b,int
off,int len)
public synchronized void reset()
public synchronized long skip(long n)
```

# BufferedOutputStream

```
public class java.io.
BufferedOutputStream
extends java.io.FilterOutputStream
extends java.io.OutputStream
extends java.lang.Object
```

### Fields

```
protected byte buf
protected int count
```

### Constructors

```
public  BufferedOutputStream(
OutputStream out)
public  BufferedOutputStream(
OutputStream out,int size)
```

### Methods

```
public synchronized void flush()
public synchronized void write(int b)
public synchronized void write(byte b,
int off,int len)
```

# BufferedReader

```
public class java.io.BufferedReader
extends java.io.Reader
extends java.lang.Object
```

### Constructors

```
public  BufferedReader(Reader in,int sz)
public  BufferedReader(Reader in)
```

### Methods

```
public void close()
public void mark(int readAheadLimit)
public boolean markSupported()
public int read()
public int read(char cbuf,int off,int
len)
public String readLine()
public boolean ready()
public void reset()
public long skip(long n)
```

# BufferedWriter

```
public class java.io.BufferedWriter
extends java.io.Writer
extends java.lang.Object
```

### Constructors

```
public  BufferedWriter(Writer out)
public  BufferedWriter(Writer out,int sz)
```

### Methods

```
public void close()
public void flush()
public void newLine()
public void write(int c)
public void write(char cbuf,int off,int
len)
public void write(String s,int off,int
len)
```

# Button

```
public class java.awt.Button
extends java.awt.Component
extends java.lang.Object
```

### Constructors

```
public  Button()
public  Button(String label)
```

### Methods

```
public synchronized void
addActionListener(ActionListener l)
public void addNotify()
public String getActionCommand()
public String getLabel()
protected String paramString()
protected void processActionEvent(
ActionEvent e)
protected void processEvent(AWTEvent e)
public synchronized void
removeActionListener(ActionListener l)
public void setActionCommand(String
command)
public void setLabel(String label)
```

# ButtonGroup

```
public class javax.swing.ButtonGroup
implements java.io.Serializable
extends java.lang.Object
```

**Fields**
```
protected java.util.Vector buttons
```

**Constructors**
```
public  ButtonGroup()
```

**Methods**
```
public void add(AbstractButton b)
public Enumeration getElements()
public ButtonModel getSelection()
public boolean isSelected(ButtonModel m)
public void remove(AbstractButton b)
public void setSelected(ButtonModel m,
boolean b)
```

# ButtonUI
```
public abstract class javax.swing.plaf.
ButtonUI
extends javax.swing.plaf.ComponentUI
extends java.lang.Object
```

# Byte
```
public final class java.lang.Byte
implements java.lang.Comparable
extends java.lang.Number
extends java.lang.Object
```

**Fields**
```
public final static byte MAX_VALUE
public final static byte MIN_VALUE
public final static java.lang.Class
TYPE
```

**Constructors**
```
public  Byte(byte value)
public  Byte(String s)
```

**Methods**       ·
```
public byte byteValue()
public int compareTo(Byte anotherByte)
public int compareTo(Object o)
public static Byte decode(String nm)
public double doubleValue()
public boolean equals(Object obj)
public float floatValue()
public int hashCode()
public int intValue()
public long longValue()
public static byte parseByte(String s)
public static byte parseByte(String s,
int radix)
public short shortValue()
public static String toString(byte b)
public String toString()
public static Byte valueOf(String s,int
radix)
public static Byte valueOf(String s)
```

# ByteArrayInputStream
```
public class java.io.
ByteArrayInputStream
extends java.io.InputStream
extends java.lang.Object
```

**Fields**
```
protected byte buf
protected int count
protected int mark
protected int pos
```

**Constructors**
```
public  ByteArrayInputStream(byte buf)
public  ByteArrayInputStream(byte buf,
int offset,int length)
```

**Methods**
```
public synchronized int available()
public synchronized void close()
public void mark(int readAheadLimit)
public boolean markSupported()
public synchronized int read()
public synchronized int read(byte b,int
off,int len)
public synchronized void reset()
public synchronized long skip(long n)
```

# ByteArrayOutputStream
```
public class java.io.
ByteArrayOutputStream
extends java.io.OutputStream
extends java.lang.Object
```

**Fields**
```
protected byte buf
protected int count
```

**Constructors**
```
public  ByteArrayOutputStream()
public  ByteArrayOutputStream(int size)
```

**Methods**
```
public synchronized void close()
public synchronized void reset()
public int size()
public synchronized byte toByteArray()
public String toString()
public String toString(String enc)
public String toString(int hibyte)
public synchronized void write(int b)
public synchronized void write(byte b,
int off,int len)
public synchronized void writeTo(
OutputStream out)
```

# ByteLookupTable
```
public class java.awt.image.
ByteLookupTable
extends java.awt.image.LookupTable
extends java.lang.Object
extends java.lang.Object
```

**Constructors**
```
public  ByteLookupTable(int offset,byte
data)
public  ByteLookupTable(int offset,byte
data)
```

## Methods

```
public final byte getTable()
public int lookupPixel(int src,int dst)
public byte lookupPixel(byte src,byte
dst)
```

# Calendar

```
public abstract class java.util.
Calendar
implements java.lang.Cloneable
implements java.io.Serializable
extends java.lang.Object
```

## Fields

```
public final static int AM
public final static int AM_PM
public final static int APRIL
protected boolean areFieldsSet
public final static int AUGUST
public final static int DATE
public final static int DAY_OF_MONTH
public final static int DAY_OF_WEEK
public final static int DAY_OF_WEEK_IN_
MONTH
public final static int DAY_OF_YEAR
public final static int DECEMBER
public final static int DST_OFFSET
public final static int ERA
public final static int FEBRUARY
protected int fields
public final static int FIELD_COUNT
public final static int FRIDAY
public final static int HOUR
public final static int HOUR_OF_DAY
protected boolean isSet
protected boolean isTimeSet
public final static int JANUARY
public final static int JULY
public final static int JUNE
public final static int MARCH
public final static int MAY
public final static int MILLISECOND
public final static int MINUTE
public final static int MONDAY
public final static int MONTH
public final static int NOVEMBER
public final static int OCTOBER
public final static int PM
public final static int SATURDAY
public final static int SECOND
public final static int SEPTEMBER
public final static int SUNDAY
public final static int THURSDAY
protected long time
public final static int TUESDAY
public final static int UNDECIMBER
public final static int WEDNESDAY
public final static int WEEK_OF_MONTH
public final static int WEEK_OF_YEAR
public final static int YEAR
public final static int ZONE_OFFSET
```

## Constructors

```
protected  Calendar()
protected  Calendar(TimeZone zone,Locale
aLocale)
```

## Methods

```
public abstract void add(int field,int
amount)
public boolean after(Object when)
public boolean before(Object when)
public final void clear()
public final void clear(int field)
public Object clone()
protected void complete()
protected abstract void computeFields()
protected abstract void computeTime()
public boolean equals(Object obj)
public final int get(int field)
public int getActualMaximum(int field)
public int getActualMinimum(int field)
public static synchronized Locale
getAvailableLocales()
public int getFirstDayOfWeek()
public abstract int getGreatestMinimum(
int field)
public static synchronized Calendar
getInstance()
public static synchronized Calendar
getInstance(TimeZone zone)
public static synchronized Calendar
getInstance(Locale aLocale)
public static synchronized Calendar
getInstance(TimeZone zone,Locale aLocale)
public abstract int getLeastMaximum(int
field)
public abstract int getMaximum(int field)
public int getMinimalDaysInFirstWeek()
public abstract int getMinimum(int field)
public final Date getTime()
protected long getTimeInMillis()
public TimeZone getTimeZone()
public int hashCode()
protected final int internalGet(int
field)
public boolean isLenient()
public final boolean isSet(int field)
public abstract void roll(int field,
boolean up)
public void roll(int field,int amount)
public final void set(int field,int
value)
public final void set(int year,int month,
int date)
public final void set(int year,int month,
int date,int hour,int minute)
public final void set(int year,int month,
int date,int hour,int minute,int second)
public void setFirstDayOfWeek(int value)
public void setLenient(boolean lenient)
public void setMinimalDaysInFirstWeek(
int value)
public final void setTime(Date date)
protected void setTimeInMillis(long
millis)
```

```
public void setTimeZone(TimeZone value)
public String toString()
```

# CannotRedoException
```
public class javax.swing.undo.
CannotRedoException
extends java.lang.RuntimeException
extends java.lang.Exception
extends java.lang.Throwable
extends java.lang.Object
```

# CannotUndoException
```
public class javax.swing.undo.
CannotUndoException
extends java.lang.RuntimeException
extends java.lang.Exception
extends java.lang.Throwable
extends java.lang.Object
```

# Canvas
```
public class java.awt.Canvas
extends java.awt.Component
extends java.lang.Object
```

### Constructors
```
public  Canvas()
public  Canvas(GraphicsConfiguration
config)
```

### Methods
```
public void addNotify()
public void paint(Graphics g)
```

# CardLayout
```
public class java.awt.CardLayout
implements java.awt.LayoutManager2
implements java.io.Serializable
extends java.lang.Object
```

### Constructors
```
public  CardLayout()
public  CardLayout(int hgap,int vgap)
```

### Methods
```
public void addLayoutComponent(Component
comp,Object constraints)
public void addLayoutComponent(String
name,Component comp)
public void first(Container parent)
public int getHgap()
public float getLayoutAlignmentX(
Container parent)
public float getLayoutAlignmentY(
Container parent)
public int getVgap()
public void invalidateLayout(Container
target)
public void last(Container parent)
public void layoutContainer(Container
parent)
```

```
public Dimension maximumLayoutSize(
Container target)
public Dimension minimumLayoutSize(
Container parent)
public void next(Container parent)
public Dimension preferredLayoutSize(
Container parent)
public void previous(Container parent)
public void removeLayoutComponent(
Component comp)
public void setHgap(int hgap)
public void setVgap(int vgap)
public void show(Container parent,String
name)
public String toString()
```

# CaretEvent
```
public abstract class javax.swing.event.
CaretEvent
extends java.util.EventObject
extends java.lang.Object
```

### Constructors
```
public  CaretEvent(Object source)
```

### Methods
```
public abstract int getDot()
public abstract int getMark()
```

# CellRendererPane
```
public class javax.swing.
CellRendererPane
implements javax.accessibility.
Accessible
extends java.awt.Container
extends java.awt.Component
extends java.lang.Object
```

### Fields
```
protected javax.accessibility.
AccessibleContext accessibleContext
```

### Constructors
```
public  CellRendererPane()
```

### Methods
```
protected void addImpl(Component x,
Object constraints,int index)
public AccessibleContext
getAccessibleContext()
public void invalidate()
public void paint(Graphics g)
public void paintComponent(Graphics g,
Component c,Container p,int x,int y,int
w,int h,boolean shouldValidate)
public void paintComponent(Graphics g,
Component c,Container p,int x,int y,int
w,int h)
public void paintComponent(Graphics g,
Component c,Container p,Rectangle r)
public void update(Graphics g)
```

# Certificate
public abstract class java.security.cert.
Certificate
extends java.lang.Object

## Constructors
protected  Certificate(String type)

## Methods
public boolean equals(Object other)
public abstract byte getEncoded()
public abstract PublicKey getPublicKey()
public final String getType()
public int hashCode()
public abstract String toString()
public abstract void verify(PublicKey
key)
public abstract void verify(PublicKey
key,String sigProvider)

# CertificateEncodingException
public class java.security.cert.
CertificateEncodingException
extends java.security.cert.
CertificateException
extends java.security.
GeneralSecurityException
extends java.lang.Exception
extends java.lang.Throwable
extends java.lang.Object

## Constructors
public  CertificateEncodingException()
public  CertificateEncodingException(
String message)

# CertificateException
public class java.security.cert.
CertificateException
extends java.security.
GeneralSecurityException
extends java.lang.Exception
extends java.lang.Throwable
extends java.lang.Object

## Constructors
public  CertificateException()
public  CertificateException(String msg)

# CertificateExpiredException
public class java.security.cert.
CertificateExpiredException
extends java.security.cert.
CertificateException
extends java.security.
GeneralSecurityException
extends java.lang.Exception
extends java.lang.Throwable
extends java.lang.Object

## Constructors
public  CertificateExpiredException()
public  CertificateExpiredException(
String message)

# CertificateFactory
public class java.security.cert.
CertificateFactory
extends java.lang.Object

## Constructors
protected  CertificateFactory(
CertificateFactorySpi certFacSpi,
Provider provider,String type)

## Methods
public final Certificate
generateCertificate(InputStream inStream)
public final Collection
generateCertificates(InputStream
inStream)
public final CRL generateCRL(InputStream
inStream)
public final Collection generateCRLs(
InputStream inStream)
public final static CertificateFactory
getInstance(String type)
public final static CertificateFactory
getInstance(String type,String provider)
public final Provider getProvider()
public final String getType()

# CertificateFactorySpi
public abstract class java.security.cert.
CertificateFactorySpi
extends java.lang.Object

## Methods
public abstract Certificate
engineGenerateCertificate(InputStream
inStream)
public abstract Collection
engineGenerateCertificates(InputStream
inStream)
public abstract CRL engineGenerateCRL(
InputStream inStream)
public abstract Collection
engineGenerateCRLs(InputStream inStream)

# CertificateNotYetValidException
public class java.security.cert.
CertificateNotYetValidException
extends java.security.cert.
CertificateException
extends java.security.
GeneralSecurityException
extends java.lang.Exception
extends java.lang.Throwable
extends java.lang.Object

**Constructors**
```
public  CertificateNotYetValidException()
public  CertificateNotYetValidException(
String message)
```

## CertificateParsingException

```
public class java.security.cert.
CertificateParsingException
extends java.security.cert.
CertificateException
extends java.security.
GeneralSecurityException
extends java.lang.Exception
extends java.lang.Throwable
extends java.lang.Object
```

**Constructors**
```
public  CertificateParsingException()
public  CertificateParsingException(
String message)
```

## ChangedCharSetException

```
public class javax.swing.text.
ChangedCharSetException
extends java.io.IOException
extends java.lang.Exception
extends java.lang.Throwable
extends java.lang.Object
```

**Constructors**
```
public  ChangedCharSetException(String
charSetSpec,boolean charSetKey)
```

**Methods**
```
public String getCharSetSpec()
public boolean keyEqualsCharSet()
```

## ChangeEvent

```
public class javax.swing.event.
ChangeEvent
extends java.util.EventObject
extends java.lang.Object
```

**Constructors**
```
public  ChangeEvent(Object source)
```

## Character

```
public final class java.lang.Character
implements java.lang.Comparable
implements java.io.Serializable
extends java.lang.Object
extends java.lang.Object
```

**Fields**
```
public final static int MAX_RADIX
public final static char MAX_VALUE
public final static int MIN_RADIX
public final static char MIN_VALUE
public final static java.lang.Class
TYPE
public final static byte UNASSIGNED
```

**Constructors**
```
public  Character(char value)
```

**Methods**
```
public char charValue()
public int compareTo(Character
anotherCharacter)
public int compareTo(Object o)
public static int digit(char ch,int
radix)
public boolean equals(Object obj)
public static char forDigit(int digit,
int radix)
public static int getNumericValue(char
ch)
public static int getType(char ch)
public int hashCode()
public static boolean isDefined(char ch)
public static boolean isDigit(char ch)
public static boolean
isIdentifierIgnorable(char ch)
public static boolean isISOControl(char
ch)
public static boolean
isJavaIdentifierPart(char ch)
public static boolean
isJavaIdentifierStart(char ch)
public static boolean isJavaLetter(char
ch)
public static boolean
isJavaLetterOrDigit(char ch)
public static boolean isLetter(char ch)
public static boolean isLetterOrDigit(
char ch)
public static boolean isLowerCase(char
ch)
public static boolean isSpace(char ch)
public static boolean isSpaceChar(char
ch)
public static boolean isTitleCase(char
ch)
public static boolean
isUnicodeIdentifierPart(char ch)
public static boolean
isUnicodeIdentifierStart(char ch)
public static boolean isUpperCase(char
ch)
public static boolean isWhitespace(char
ch)
public static char toLowerCase(char ch)
public String toString()
public static char toTitleCase(char ch)
public static char toUpperCase(char ch)
```

## CharArrayReader

```
public class java.io.CharArrayReader
extends java.io.Reader
extends java.lang.Object
```

**Fields**
```
protected char buf
protected int count
protected int markedPos
protected int pos
```

### Constructors
```
public  CharArrayReader(char buf)
public  CharArrayReader(char buf,int
offset,int length)
```

### Methods
```
public void close()
public void mark(int readAheadLimit)
public boolean markSupported()
public int read()
public int read(char b,int off,int len)
public boolean ready()
public void reset()
public long skip(long n)
```

# CharArrayWriter
```
public class java.io.CharArrayWriter
extends java.io.Writer
extends java.lang.Object
```

### Fields
```
protected char buf
protected int count
```

### Constructors
```
public  CharArrayWriter()
public  CharArrayWriter(int initialSize)
```

### Methods
```
public void close()
public void flush()
public void reset()
public int size()
public char toCharArray()
public String toString()
public void write(int c)
public void write(char c,int off,int len)
public void write(String str,int off,int
len)
public void writeTo(Writer out)
```

# CharConversionException
```
public class java.io.
CharConversionException
extends java.io.IOException
extends java.lang.Exception
extends java.lang.Throwable
extends java.lang.Object
```

### Constructors
```
public  CharConversionException()
public  CharConversionException(String s)
```

# Checkbox
```
public class java.awt.Checkbox
implements java.awt.ItemSelectable
extends java.awt.Component
extends java.lang.Object
```

### Constructors
```
public  Checkbox()
public  Checkbox(String label)
```

```
public  Checkbox(String label,boolean
state)
public  Checkbox(String label,boolean
state,CheckboxGroup group)
public  Checkbox(String label,
CheckboxGroup group,boolean state)
```

### Methods
```
public synchronized void addItemListener(
ItemListener l)
public void addNotify()
public CheckboxGroup getCheckboxGroup()
public String getLabel()
public Object getSelectedObjects()
public boolean getState()
protected String paramString()
protected void processEvent(AWTEvent e)
protected void processItemEvent(
ItemEvent e)
public synchronized void
removeItemListener(ItemListener l)
public void setCheckboxGroup(
CheckboxGroup g)
public void setLabel(String label)
public void setState(boolean state)
```

# CheckboxGroup
```
public class java.awt.CheckboxGroup
implements java.io.Serializable
extends java.lang.Object
```

### Constructors
```
public  CheckboxGroup()
```

### Methods
```
public Checkbox getCurrent()
public Checkbox getSelectedCheckbox()
public synchronized void setCurrent(
Checkbox box)
public void setSelectedCheckbox(Checkbox
box)
public String toString()
```

# CheckboxMenuItem
```
public class java.awt.CheckboxMenuItem
implements java.awt.ItemSelectable
extends java.awt.MenuItem
extends java.awt.MenuComponent
extends java.lang.Object
```

### Constructors
```
public  CheckboxMenuItem()
public  CheckboxMenuItem(String label)
public  CheckboxMenuItem(String label,
boolean state)
```

### Methods
```
public synchronized void addItemListener(
ItemListener l)
public void addNotify()
public synchronized Object
getSelectedObjects()
public boolean getState()
```

```
public String paramString()
protected void processEvent(AWTEvent e)
protected void processItemEvent(
ItemEvent e)
public synchronized void
removeItemListener(ItemListener l)
public synchronized void setState(
boolean b)
```

## CheckedInputStream

```
public class java.util.zip.
CheckedInputStream
extends java.io.FilterInputStream
extends java.io.InputStream
extends java.lang.Object
```

### Constructors
```
public  CheckedInputStream(InputStream
in,Checksum cksum)
```

### Methods
```
public Checksum getChecksum()
public int read()
public int read(byte buf,int off,int len)
public long skip(long n)
```

## CheckedOutputStream

```
public class java.util.zip.
CheckedOutputStream
extends java.io.FilterOutputStream
extends java.io.OutputStream
extends java.lang.Object
```

### Constructors
```
public  CheckedOutputStream(OutputStream
out,Checksum cksum)
```

### Methods
```
public Checksum getChecksum()
public void write(int b)
public void write(byte b,int off,int len)
```

## Choice

```
public class java.awt.Choice
implements java.awt.ItemSelectable
extends java.awt.Component
extends java.lang.Object
```

### Constructors
```
public  Choice()
```

### Methods
```
public void add(String item)
public void addItem(String item)
public synchronized void addItemListener(
ItemListener l)
public void addNotify()
public int countItems()
public String getItem(int index)
public int getItemCount()
public int getSelectedIndex()
```

```
public synchronized String
getSelectedItem()
public synchronized Object
getSelectedObjects()
public void insert(String item,int index)
protected String paramString()
protected void processEvent(AWTEvent e)
protected void processItemEvent(
ItemEvent e)
public void remove(String item)
public void remove(int position)
public void removeAll()
public synchronized void
removeItemListener(ItemListener l)
public synchronized void select(int pos)
public synchronized void select(String
str)
```

## ChoiceFormat

```
public class java.text.ChoiceFormat
extends java.text.NumberFormat
extends java.text.Format
extends java.lang.Object
```

### Constructors
```
public  ChoiceFormat(String newPattern)
public  ChoiceFormat(double limits,
String formats)
```

### Methods
```
public void applyPattern(String
newPattern)
public Object clone()
public boolean equals(Object obj)
public StringBuffer format(long number,
StringBuffer toAppendTo,FieldPosition
status)
public StringBuffer format(double number,
StringBuffer toAppendTo,FieldPosition
status)
public Object getFormats()
public double getLimits()
public int hashCode()
public final static double nextDouble(
double d)
public static double nextDouble(double d,
boolean positive)
public Number parse(String text,
ParsePosition status)
public final static double
previousDouble(double d)
public void setChoices(double limits,
String formats)
public String toPattern()
```

## Class

```
public final class java.lang.Class
implements java.io.Serializable
extends java.lang.Object
```

### Constructors
```
private static  Class()
```

## Methods
public static Class forName(String className)
public static Class forName(String name, boolean initialize,ClassLoader loader)
public Class getClasses()
public ClassLoader getClassLoader()
public native Class getComponentType()
public Constructor getConstructor(Class parameterTypes)
public Constructor getConstructors()
public Class getDeclaredClasses()
public Constructor getDeclaredConstructor(Class parameterTypes)
public Constructor getDeclaredConstructors()
public Field getDeclaredField(String name)
public Field getDeclaredFields()
public Method getDeclaredMethod(String name,Class parameterTypes)
public Method getDeclaredMethods()
public native Class getDeclaringClass()
public Field getField(String name)
public Field getFields()
public native Class getInterfaces()
public Method getMethod(String name, Class parameterTypes)
public Method getMethods()
public native int getModifiers()
public native String getName()
public Package getPackage()
public ProtectionDomain getProtectionDomain()
public URL getResource(String name)
public InputStream getResourceAsStream( String name)
public native Object getSigners()
public native Class getSuperclass()
public native boolean isArray()
public native boolean isAssignableFrom( Class cls)
public native boolean isInstance(Object obj)
public native boolean isInterface()
public native boolean isPrimitive()
public Object newInstance()
public String toString()

# ClassCastException
public class java.lang. ClassCastException
extends java.lang.RuntimeException
extends java.lang.Exception
extends java.lang.Throwable
extends java.lang.Object

## Constructors
public  ClassCastException()
public  ClassCastException(String s)

# ClassCircularityError
public class java.lang. ClassCircularityError
extends java.lang.LinkageError
extends java.lang.Error
extends java.lang.Throwable
extends java.lang.Object

## Constructors
public  ClassCircularityError()
public  ClassCircularityError(String s)

# ClassFormatError
public class java.lang.ClassFormatError
extends java.lang.LinkageError
extends java.lang.Error
extends java.lang.Throwable
extends java.lang.Object

## Constructors
public  ClassFormatError()
public  ClassFormatError(String s)

# ClassLoader
public abstract class java.lang. ClassLoader
extends java.lang.Object

## Constructors
protected  ClassLoader(ClassLoader parent)
protected  ClassLoader()

## Methods
protected final Class defineClass(byte b, int off,int len)
protected final Class defineClass(String name,byte b,int off,int len)
protected final Class defineClass(String name,byte b,int off,int len, ProtectionDomain protectionDomain)
protected Package definePackage(String name,String specTitle,String specVersion, String specVendor,String implTitle, String implVersion,String implVendor,URL sealBase)
protected Class findClass(String name)
protected String findLibrary(String libname)
protected final native Class findLoadedClass(String name)
protected URL findResource(String name)
protected Enumeration findResources( String name)
protected final Class findSystemClass( String name)
protected Package getPackage(String name)
protected Package getPackages()
public final ClassLoader getParent()
public URL getResource(String name)
public InputStream getResourceAsStream( String name)

```
public final Enumeration getResources(
String name)
public static ClassLoader
getSystemClassLoader()
public static URL getSystemResource(
String name)
public static InputStream
getSystemResourceAsStream(String name)
public static Enumeration
getSystemResources(String name)
public Class loadClass(String name)
protected synchronized Class loadClass(
String name,boolean resolve)
protected final void resolveClass(Class
c)
protected final void setSigners(Class c,
Object signers)
```

## ClassNotFoundException

```
public class java.lang.
ClassNotFoundException
extends java.lang.Exception
extends java.lang.Throwable
extends java.lang.Object
```

### Constructors
```
public  ClassNotFoundException()
public  ClassNotFoundException(String s)
public  ClassNotFoundException(String s,
Throwable ex)
```

### Methods
```
public Throwable getException()
public void printStackTrace()
public void printStackTrace(PrintStream
ps)
public void printStackTrace(PrintWriter
pw)
```

## Clipboard

```
public class java.awt.datatransfer.
Clipboard
extends java.lang.Object
```

### Fields
```
protected java.awt.datatransfer.
Transferable contents
protected java.awt.datatransfer.
ClipboardOwner owner
```

### Constructors
```
public  Clipboard(String name)
```

### Methods
```
public synchronized Transferable
getContents(Object requestor)
public String getName()
public synchronized void setContents(
Transferable contents,ClipboardOwner
owner)
```

## CloneNotSupportedException

```
public class java.lang.
CloneNotSupportedException
extends java.lang.Exception
extends java.lang.Throwable
extends java.lang.Object
```

### Constructors
```
public  CloneNotSupportedException()
public  CloneNotSupportedException(
String s)
```

## CMMException

```
public class java.awt.color.
CMMException
extends java.lang.RuntimeException
extends java.lang.Exception
extends java.lang.Throwable
extends java.lang.Object
```

### Constructors
```
public  CMMException(String s)
```

## CodeSource

```
public class java.security.CodeSource
implements java.io.Serializable
extends java.lang.Object
```

### Constructors
```
public  CodeSource(URL url,Certificate
certs)
```

### Methods
```
public boolean equals(Object obj)
public final Certificate getCertificates(
)
public final URL getLocation()
public int hashCode()
public boolean implies(CodeSource
codesource)
public String toString()
```

## CollationElementIterator

```
public final class java.text.
CollationElementIterator
extends java.lang.Object
```

### Fields
```
public final static int NULLORDER
```

### Constructors
```
CollationElementIterator()
CollationElementIterator()
```

### Methods
```
public int getMaxExpansion(int order)
public int getOffset()
public int next()
public int previous()
public final static int primaryOrder(int
order)
public void reset()
```

public final static short secondaryOrder(
int order)
public void setOffset(int newOffset)
public void setText(String source)
public void setText(CharacterIterator
source)
public final static short tertiaryOrder(
int order)

## CollationKey

public final class java.text.
CollationKey
implements java.lang.Comparable
extends java.lang.Object

### Constructors

CollationKey()

### Methods

public int compareTo(CollationKey target)
public int compareTo(Object o)
public boolean equals(Object target)
public String getSourceString()
public int hashCode()
public byte toByteArray()

## Collator

public abstract class java.text.
Collator
implements java.lang.Cloneable
implements java.util.Comparator
extends java.lang.Object

### Fields

public final static int CANONICAL_
DECOMPOSITION
public final static int FULL_
DECOMPOSITION
public final static int IDENTICAL
public final static int NO_
DECOMPOSITION
public final static int PRIMARY
public final static int SECONDARY
public final static int TERTIARY

### Constructors

protected  Collator()

### Methods

public Object clone()
public abstract int compare(String
source,String target)
public int compare(Object o1,Object o2)
public boolean equals(String source,
String target)
public boolean equals(Object that)
public static synchronized Locale
getAvailableLocales()
public abstract CollationKey
getCollationKey(String source)
public synchronized int getDecomposition(
)

public static synchronized Collator
getInstance()
public static synchronized Collator
getInstance(Locale desiredLocale)
public synchronized int getStrength()
public abstract int hashCode()
public synchronized void
setDecomposition(int decompositionMode)
public synchronized void setStrength(int
newStrength)

## Collections

public class java.util.Collections
extends java.lang.Object

### Fields

public final static java.util.List EMPTY_
LIST
public final static java.util.Set EMPTY_
SET

### Constructors

private  Collections()

### Methods

public static int binarySearch(List list,
Object key)
public static int binarySearch(List list,
Object key,Comparator c)
public static void copy(List dest,List
src)
public static Enumeration enumeration(
Collection c)
public static void fill(List list,Object
o)
public static Object max(Collection coll)
public static Object max(Collection coll,
Comparator comp)
public static Object min(Collection coll)
public static Object min(Collection coll,
Comparator comp)
public static List nCopies(int n,Object
o)
public static void reverse(List l)
public static Comparator reverseOrder()
public static void shuffle(List list)
public static void shuffle(List list,
Random rnd)
public static Set singleton(Object o)
public static void sort(List list)
public static void sort(List list,
Comparator c)
public static Collection
synchronizedCollection(Collection c)
public static List synchronizedList(List
list)
public static Map synchronizedMap(Map m)
public static Set synchronizedSet(Set s)
public static SortedMap
synchronizedSortedMap(SortedMap m)
public static SortedSet
synchronizedSortedSet(SortedSet s)

```
public static Collection
unmodifiableCollection(Collection c)
public static List unmodifiableList(List
list)
public static Map unmodifiableMap(Map m)
public static Set unmodifiableSet(Set s)
public static SortedMap
unmodifiableSortedMap(SortedMap m)
public static SortedSet
unmodifiableSortedSet(SortedSet s)
```

## Color

```
public class java.awt.Color
implements java.awt.Paint
implements java.io.Serializable
extends java.lang.Object
```

### Fields

```
public final static java.awt.Color
black
public final static java.awt.Color blue
public final static java.awt.Color cyan
public final static java.awt.Color
darkGray
public final static java.awt.Color gray
public final static java.awt.Color
green
public final static java.awt.Color
lightGray
public final static java.awt.Color
magenta
public final static java.awt.Color
orange
public final static java.awt.Color pink
public final static java.awt.Color red
public final static java.awt.Color
white
public final static java.awt.Color
yellow
```

### Constructors

```
public  Color(int r,int g,int b)
public  Color(int r,int g,int b,int a)
public  Color(int rgb)
public  Color(int rgba,boolean hasalpha)
public  Color(float r,float g,float b)
public  Color(float r,float g,float b,
float a)
public  Color(ColorSpace cspace,float
components,float alpha)
```

### Methods

```
public Color brighter()
public synchronized PaintContext
createContext(ColorModel cm,Rectangle r,
Rectangle2D r2d,AffineTransform xform,
RenderingHints hints)
public Color darker()
public static Color decode(String nm)
public boolean equals(Object obj)
public int getAlpha()
public int getBlue()
public static Color getColor(String nm)
```

```
public static Color getColor(String nm,
Color v)
public static Color getColor(String nm,
int v)
public float getColorComponents(float
compArray)
public float getColorComponents(
ColorSpace cspace,float compArray)
public ColorSpace getColorSpace()
public float getComponents(float
compArray)
public float getComponents(ColorSpace
cspace,float compArray)
public int getGreen()
public static Color getHSBColor(float h,
float s,float b)
public int getRed()
public int getRGB()
public float getRGBColorComponents(float
compArray)
public float getRGBComponents(float
compArray)
public int getTransparency()
public int hashCode()
public static int HSBtoRGB(float hue,
float saturation,float brightness)
public static float RGBtoHSB(int r,int g,
int b,float hsbvals)
public String toString()
```

## ColorChooserComponentFactory

```
public class javax.swing.colorchooser.
ColorChooserComponentFactory
extends java.lang.Object
```

### Constructors

```
private  ColorChooserComponentFactory()
```

### Methods

```
public static AbstractColorChooserPanel
getDefaultChooserPanels()
public static JComponent getPreviewPanel(
)
```

## ColorChooserUI

```
public abstract class javax.swing.plaf.
ColorChooserUI
extends javax.swing.plaf.ComponentUI
extends java.lang.Object
```

## ColorConvertOp

```
public class java.awt.image.
ColorConvertOp
implements java.awt.image.
BufferedImageOp
implements java.awt.image.RasterOp
extends java.lang.Object
```

### Constructors

```
public static  ColorConvertOp(
RenderingHints hints)
```

public  ColorConvertOp(ColorSpace cspace,
RenderingHints hints)
public  ColorConvertOp(ColorSpace
srcCspace,ColorSpace dstCspace,
RenderingHints hints)
public  ColorConvertOp(ICC_Profile
profiles,RenderingHints hints)

### Methods
public BufferedImage
createCompatibleDestImage(BufferedImage
src,ColorModel destCM)
public WritableRaster
createCompatibleDestRaster(Raster src)
public final BufferedImage filter(
BufferedImage src,BufferedImage dest)
public final WritableRaster filter(
Raster src,WritableRaster dest)
public final Rectangle2D getBounds2D(
BufferedImage src)
public final Rectangle2D getBounds2D(
Raster src)
public final ICC_Profile getICC_Profiles(
)
public final Point2D getPoint2D(Point2D
srcPt,Point2D dstPt)
public final RenderingHints
getRenderingHints()

## ColorModel
public abstract class java.awt.image.
ColorModel
implements java.awt.Transparency
extends java.lang.Object

### Fields
protected int pixel_bits
protected int transferType

### Constructors
public  ColorModel(int bits)
protected  ColorModel(int pixel_bits,int
bits,ColorSpace cspace,boolean hasAlpha,
boolean isAlphaPremultiplied,int
transparency,int transferType)

### Methods
public ColorModel coerceData(
WritableRaster raster,boolean
isAlphaPremultiplied)
public SampleModel
createCompatibleSampleModel(int w,int h)
public WritableRaster
createCompatibleWritableRaster(int w,int
h)
public boolean equals(Object obj)
public void finalize()
public abstract int getAlpha(int pixel)
public int getAlpha(Object inData)
public WritableRaster getAlphaRaster(
WritableRaster raster)
public abstract int getBlue(int pixel)
public int getBlue(Object inData)

public final ColorSpace getColorSpace()
public int getComponents(int pixel,int
components,int offset)
public int getComponents(Object pixel,
int components,int offset)
public int getComponentSize(int
componentIdx)
public int getComponentSize()
public int getDataElement(int components,
int offset)
public Object getDataElements(int rgb,
Object pixel)
public Object getDataElements(int
components,int offset,Object obj)
public abstract int getGreen(int pixel)
public int getGreen(Object inData)
public float getNormalizedComponents(int
components,int offset,float
normComponents,int normOffset)
public int getNumColorComponents()
public int getNumComponents()
public int getPixelSize()
public abstract int getRed(int pixel)
public int getRed(Object inData)
public int getRGB(int pixel)
public int getRGB(Object inData)
public static ColorModel getRGBdefault()
public int getTransparency()
public int getUnnormalizedComponents(
float normComponents,int normOffset,int
components,int offset)
public final boolean hasAlpha()
public final boolean
isAlphaPremultiplied()
public boolean isCompatibleRaster(Raster
raster)
public boolean isCompatibleSampleModel(
SampleModel sm)
public String toString()

## ColorSpace
public abstract class java.awt.color.
ColorSpace
extends java.lang.Object

### Fields
public final static int CS_CIEXYZ
public final static int CS_GRAY
public final static int CS_LINEAR_RGB
public final static int CS_PYCC
public final static int CS_sRGB
public final static int TYPE_2CLR
public final static int TYPE_3CLR
public final static int TYPE_4CLR
public final static int TYPE_5CLR
public final static int TYPE_6CLR
public final static int TYPE_7CLR
public final static int TYPE_8CLR
public final static int TYPE_9CLR
public final static int TYPE_ACLR
public final static int TYPE_BCLR
public final static int TYPE_CCLR
public final static int TYPE_CMY

```
public final static int TYPE_CMYK
public final static int TYPE_DCLR
public final static int TYPE_ECLR
public final static int TYPE_FCLR
public final static int TYPE_GRAY
public final static int TYPE_HLS
public final static int TYPE_HSV
public final static int TYPE_Lab
public final static int TYPE_Luv
public final static int TYPE_RGB
public final static int TYPE_XYZ
public final static int TYPE_YCbCr
public final static int TYPE_Yxy
```

### Constructors
```
protected  ColorSpace(int type,int
numcomponents)
```

### Methods
```
public abstract float fromCIEXYZ(float
colorvalue)
public abstract float fromRGB(float
rgbvalue)
public static ColorSpace getInstance(int
colorspace)
public String getName(int idx)
public int getNumComponents()
public int getType()
public boolean isCS_sRGB()
public abstract float toCIEXYZ(float
colorvalue)
public abstract float toRGB(float
colorvalue)
```

## ColorUIResource
```
public class javax.swing.plaf.
ColorUIResource
implements javax.swing.plaf.UIResource
extends java.awt.Color
extends java.lang.Object
```

### Constructors
```
public  ColorUIResource(int r,int g,int
b)
public  ColorUIResource(int rgb)
public  ColorUIResource(float r,float g,
float b)
public  ColorUIResource(Color c)
```

## ComboBoxUI
```
public abstract class javax.swing.plaf.
ComboBoxUI
extends javax.swing.plaf.ComponentUI
extends java.lang.Object
```

### Methods
```
public abstract boolean
isFocusTraversable(JComboBox c)
public abstract boolean isPopupVisible(
JComboBox c)
public abstract void setPopupVisible(
JComboBox c,boolean v)
```

## Compiler
```
public final class java.lang.Compiler
extends java.lang.Object
```

### Constructors
```
private  Compiler()
```

### Methods
```
public static native Object command(
Object any)
public static native boolean
compileClass(Class clazz)
public static native boolean
compileClasses(String string)
public static native void disable()
public static native void enable()
```

## Component
```
public abstract class java.awt.
Component
implements java.awt.image.ImageObserver
implements java.awt.MenuContainer
implements java.io.Serializable
extends java.lang.Object
```

### Fields
```
public final static float BOTTOM_
ALIGNMENT
public final static float CENTER_
ALIGNMENT
public final static float LEFT_
ALIGNMENT
public final static float RIGHT_
ALIGNMENT
public final static float TOP_ALIGNMENT
```

### Constructors
```
protected  Component()
```

### Methods
```
public boolean action(Event evt,Object
what)
public synchronized void add(PopupMenu
popup)
public synchronized void
addComponentListener(ComponentListener l)
public synchronized void
addFocusListener(FocusListener l)
public synchronized void
addInputMethodListener(
InputMethodListener l)
public synchronized void addKeyListener(
KeyListener l)
public synchronized void
addMouseListener(MouseListener l)
public synchronized void
addMouseMotionListener(
MouseMotionListener l)
public void addNotify()
public synchronized void
addPropertyChangeListener(
PropertyChangeListener listener)
```

public synchronized void
addPropertyChangeListener(String
propertyName,PropertyChangeListener
listener)
public Rectangle bounds()
public int checkImage(Image image,
ImageObserver observer)
public int checkImage(Image image,int
width,int height,ImageObserver observer)
protected AWTEvent coalesceEvents(
AWTEvent existingEvent,AWTEvent newEvent)
public boolean contains(int x,int y)
public boolean contains(Point p)
public Image createImage(ImageProducer
producer)
public Image createImage(int width,int
height)
public void deliverEvent(Event e)
public void disable()
protected final void disableEvents(long
eventsToDisable)
public final void dispatchEvent(AWTEvent
e)
public void doLayout()
public void enable()
public void enable(boolean b)
protected final void enableEvents(long
eventsToEnable)
public void enableInputMethods(boolean
enable)
protected void firePropertyChange(String
propertyName,Object oldValue,Object
newValue)
public float getAlignmentX()
public float getAlignmentY()
public Color getBackground()
public Rectangle getBounds()
public Rectangle getBounds(Rectangle rv)
public ColorModel getColorModel()
public Component getComponentAt(int x,
int y)
public Component getComponentAt(Point p)
public ComponentOrientation
getComponentOrientation()
public Cursor getCursor()
public synchronized DropTarget
getDropTarget()
public Font getFont()
public FontMetrics getFontMetrics(Font
font)
public Color getForeground()
public Graphics getGraphics()
public int getHeight()
public InputContext getInputContext()
public InputMethodRequests
getInputMethodRequests()
public Locale getLocale()
public Point getLocation()
public Point getLocation(Point rv)
public Point getLocationOnScreen()
public Dimension getMaximumSize()
public Dimension getMinimumSize()
public String getName()
public Container getParent()

public ComponentPeer getPeer()
public Dimension getPreferredSize()
public Dimension getSize()
public Dimension getSize(Dimension rv)
public Toolkit getToolkit()
public final Object getTreeLock()
public int getWidth()
public int getX()
public int getY()
public boolean gotFocus(Event evt,Object
what)
public boolean handleEvent(Event evt)
public boolean hasFocus()
public void hide()
public boolean imageUpdate(Image img,int
flags,int x,int y,int w,int h)
public boolean inside(int x,int y)
public void invalidate()
public boolean isDisplayable()
public boolean isDoubleBuffered()
public boolean isEnabled()
public boolean isFocusTraversable()
public boolean isLightweight()
public boolean isOpaque()
public boolean isShowing()
public boolean isValid()
public boolean isVisible()
public boolean keyDown(Event evt,int key)
public boolean keyUp(Event evt,int key)
public void layout()
public void list()
public void list(PrintStream out)
public void list(PrintStream out,int
indent)
public void list(PrintWriter out)
public void list(PrintWriter out,int
indent)
public Component locate(int x,int y)
public Point location()
public boolean lostFocus(Event evt,
Object what)
public Dimension minimumSize()
public boolean mouseDown(Event evt,int x,
int y)
public boolean mouseDrag(Event evt,int x,
int y)
public boolean mouseEnter(Event evt,int
x,int y)
public boolean mouseExit(Event evt,int x,
int y)
public boolean mouseMove(Event evt,int x,
int y)
public boolean mouseUp(Event evt,int x,
int y)
public void move(int x,int y)
public void nextFocus()
public void paint(Graphics g)
public void paintAll(Graphics g)
protected String paramString()
public boolean postEvent(Event e)
public Dimension preferredSize()
public boolean prepareImage(Image image,
ImageObserver observer)

```
public boolean prepareImage(Image image,
int width,int height,ImageObserver
observer)
public void print(Graphics g)
public void printAll(Graphics g)
protected void processComponentEvent(
ComponentEvent e)
protected void processEvent(AWTEvent e)
protected void processFocusEvent(
FocusEvent e)
protected void processInputMethodEvent(
InputMethodEvent e)
protected void processKeyEvent(KeyEvent
e)
protected void processMouseEvent(
MouseEvent e)
protected void processMouseMotionEvent(
MouseEvent e)
public synchronized void remove(
MenuComponent popup)
public synchronized void
removeComponentListener(
ComponentListener l)
public synchronized void
removeFocusListener(FocusListener l)
public synchronized void
removeInputMethodListener(
InputMethodListener l)
public synchronized void
removeKeyListener(KeyListener l)
public synchronized void
removeMouseListener(MouseListener l)
public synchronized void
removeMouseMotionListener(
MouseMotionListener l)
public void removeNotify()
public synchronized void
removePropertyChangeListener(
PropertyChangeListener listener)
public synchronized void
removePropertyChangeListener(String
propertyName,PropertyChangeListener
listener)
public void repaint()
public void repaint(long tm)
public void repaint(int x,int y,int
width,int height)
public void repaint(long tm,int x,int y,
int width,int height)
public void requestFocus()
public void reshape(int x,int y,int
width,int height)
public void resize(int width,int height)
public void resize(Dimension d)
public void setBackground(Color c)
public void setBounds(int x,int y,int
width,int height)
public void setBounds(Rectangle r)
public void setComponentOrientation(
ComponentOrientation o)
public synchronized void setCursor(
Cursor cursor)
public synchronized void setDropTarget(
DropTarget dt)
```

```
public void setEnabled(boolean b)
public void setFont(Font f)
public void setForeground(Color c)
public void setLocale(Locale l)
public void setLocation(int x,int y)
public void setLocation(Point p)
public void setName(String name)
public void setSize(int width,int height)
public void setSize(Dimension d)
public void setVisible(boolean b)
public void show()
public void show(boolean b)
public Dimension size()
public String toString()
public void transferFocus()
public void update(Graphics g)
public void validate()
```

## ComponentAdapter

```
public abstract class java.awt.event.
ComponentAdapter
implements java.awt.event.
ComponentListener
extends java.lang.Object
```

### Methods

```
public void componentHidden(
ComponentEvent e)
public void componentMoved(
ComponentEvent e)
public void componentResized(
ComponentEvent e)
public void componentShown(
ComponentEvent e)
```

## ComponentColorModel

```
public class java.awt.image.
ComponentColorModel
extends java.awt.image.ColorModel
extends java.lang.Object
```

### Constructors

```
public ComponentColorModel(ColorSpace
colorSpace,int bits,boolean hasAlpha,
boolean isAlphaPremultiplied,int
transparency,int transferType)
```

### Methods

```
public ColorModel coerceData(
WritableRaster raster,boolean
isAlphaPremultiplied)
public SampleModel
createCompatibleSampleModel(int w,int h)
public WritableRaster
createCompatibleWritableRaster(int w,int
h)
public boolean equals(Object obj)
public int getAlpha(int pixel)
public int getAlpha(Object inData)
public WritableRaster getAlphaRaster(
WritableRaster raster)
public int getBlue(int pixel)
public int getBlue(Object inData)
```

public int getComponents(int pixel,int components,int offset)
public int getComponents(Object pixel, int components,int offset)
public int getDataElement(int components, int offset)
public Object getDataElements(int rgb, Object pixel)
public Object getDataElements(int components,int offset,Object obj)
public int getGreen(int pixel)
public int getGreen(Object inData)
public int getRed(int pixel)
public int getRed(Object inData)
public int getRGB(int pixel)
public int getRGB(Object inData)
public boolean isCompatibleRaster(Raster raster)
public boolean isCompatibleSampleModel( SampleModel sm)

## ComponentEvent

public class java.awt.event.
ComponentEvent
extends java.awt.AWTEvent
extends java.util.EventObject
extends java.lang.Object

### Fields

public final static int COMPONENT_FIRST
public final static int COMPONENT_
HIDDEN
public final static int COMPONENT_LAST
public final static int COMPONENT_MOVED
public final static int COMPONENT_
RESIZED
public final static int COMPONENT_SHOWN

### Constructors

public  ComponentEvent(Component source, int id)

### Methods

public Component getComponent()
public String paramString()

## ComponentOrientation

public final class java.awt.
ComponentOrientation
implements java.io.Serializable
extends java.lang.Object

### Fields

public final static java.awt.
ComponentOrientation LEFT_TO_RIGHT
public final static java.awt.
ComponentOrientation RIGHT_TO_LEFT
public final static java.awt.
ComponentOrientation UNKNOWN

### Constructors

private  ComponentOrientation()

### Methods

public static ComponentOrientation
getOrientation(Locale locale)
public static ComponentOrientation
getOrientation(ResourceBundle bdl)
public boolean isHorizontal()
public boolean isLeftToRight()

## ComponentSampleModel

public class java.awt.image.
ComponentSampleModel
extends java.awt.image.SampleModel
extends java.lang.Object

### Fields

protected int bandOffsets
protected int bankIndices
protected int numBands
protected int numBanks
protected int pixelStride
protected int scanlineStride

### Constructors

public static  ComponentSampleModel(int dataType,int w,int h,int pixelStride,int scanlineStride,int bandOffsets)
public  ComponentSampleModel(int dataType,int w,int h,int pixelStride,int scanlineStride,int bankIndices,int bandOffsets)

### Methods

public SampleModel
createCompatibleSampleModel(int w,int h)
public DataBuffer createDataBuffer()
public SampleModel
createSubsetSampleModel(int bands)
public final int getBandOffsets()
public final int getBankIndices()
public Object getDataElements(int x,int y,Object obj,DataBuffer data)
public final int getNumDataElements()
public int getOffset(int x,int y)
public int getOffset(int x,int y,int b)
public int getPixel(int x,int y,int iArray,DataBuffer data)
public int getPixels(int x,int y,int w, int h,int iArray,DataBuffer data)
public final int getPixelStride()
public int getSample(int x,int y,int b, DataBuffer data)
public int getSamples(int x,int y,int w, int h,int b,int iArray,DataBuffer data)
public final int getSampleSize()
public final int getSampleSize(int band)
public final int getScanlineStride()
public void setDataElements(int x,int y, Object obj,DataBuffer data)
public void setPixel(int x,int y, iArray,DataBuffer data)
public void setPixels(int x,int y,int w, int h,int iArray,DataBuffer data)

```
public void setSample(int x,int y,int b,
int s,DataBuffer data)
public void setSamples(int x,int y,int w,
int h,int b,int iArray,DataBuffer data)
```

## ComponentUI

```
public abstract class javax.swing.plaf.
ComponentUI
extends java.lang.Object
```

### Methods

```
public boolean contains(JComponent c,int
x,int y)
public static ComponentUI createUI(
JComponent c)
public Accessible getAccessibleChild(
JComponent c,int i)
public int getAccessibleChildrenCount(
JComponent c)
public Dimension getMaximumSize(
JComponent c)
public Dimension getMinimumSize(
JComponent c)
public Dimension getPreferredSize(
JComponent c)
public void installUI(JComponent c)
public void paint(Graphics g,JComponent
c)
public void uninstallUI(JComponent c)
public void update(Graphics g,JComponent
c)
```

## ComponentView

```
public class javax.swing.text.
ComponentView
extends javax.swing.text.View
extends java.lang.Object
```

### Constructors

```
public  ComponentView(Element elem)
```

### Methods

```
protected Component createComponent()
public float getAlignment(int axis)
public final Component getComponent()
public float getMaximumSpan(int axis)
public float getMinimumSpan(int axis)
public float getPreferredSpan(int axis)
public Shape modelToView(int pos,Shape a,
Bias b)
public void paint(Graphics g,Shape a)
public void setParent(View p)
public void setSize(float width,float
height)
public int viewToModel(float x,float y,
Shape a,Bias bias)
```

## CompositeView

```
public abstract class javax.swing.text.
CompositeView
extends javax.swing.text.View
extends java.lang.Object
```

### Constructors

```
public  CompositeView(Element elem)
```

### Methods

```
public void append(View v)
protected abstract void childAllocation(
int index,Rectangle a)
protected boolean flipEastAndWestAtEnds(
int position,Bias bias)
protected final short getBottomInset()
public Shape getChildAllocation(int
index,Shape a)
protected Rectangle getInsideAllocation(
Shape a)
protected final short getLeftInset()
protected int
getNextEastWestVisualPositionFrom(int
pos,Bias b,Shape a,int direction,Bias
biasRet)
protected int
getNextNorthSouthVisualPositionFrom(int
pos,Bias b,Shape a,int direction,Bias
biasRet)
public int getNextVisualPositionFrom(int
pos,Bias b,Shape a,int direction,Bias
biasRet)
protected final short getRightInset()
protected final short getTopInset()
public View getView(int n)
protected abstract View getViewAtPoint(
int x,int y,Rectangle alloc)
protected View getViewAtPosition(int pos,
Rectangle a)
public int getViewCount()
protected int getViewIndexAtPosition(int
pos)
public void insert(int offs,View v)
protected abstract boolean isAfter(int x,
int y,Rectangle alloc)
protected abstract boolean isBefore(int
x,int y,Rectangle alloc)
protected void loadChildren(ViewFactory
f)
public Shape modelToView(int pos,Shape a,
Bias b)
public Shape modelToView(int p0,Bias b0,
int p1,Bias b1,Shape a)
public void removeAll()
public void replace(int offset,int
length,View views)
protected final void setInsets(short top,
short left,short bottom,short right)
protected final void setParagraphInsets(
AttributeSet attr)
public void setParent(View parent)
public int viewToModel(float x,float y,
Shape a,Bias bias)
```

## CompoundBorder

```
public class javax.swing.border.
CompoundBorder
extends javax.swing.border.
AbstractBorder
extends java.lang.Object
```

### Fields
protected javax.swing.border.Border
insideBorder
protected javax.swing.border.Border
outsideBorder

### Constructors
public  CompoundBorder()
public  CompoundBorder(Border
outsideBorder,Border insideBorder)

### Methods
public Insets getBorderInsets(Component
c,Insets insets)
public Insets getBorderInsets(Component
c)
public Border getInsideBorder()
public Border getOutsideBorder()
public boolean isBorderOpaque()
public void paintBorder(Component c,
Graphics g,int x,int y,int width,int
height)

## CompoundEdit
public class javax.swing.undo.
CompoundEdit
extends javax.swing.undo.
AbstractUndoableEdit
extends java.lang.Object

### Fields
protected java.util.Vector edits

### Constructors
public  CompoundEdit()

### Methods
public boolean addEdit(UndoableEdit
anEdit)
public boolean canRedo()
public boolean canUndo()
public void die()
public void end()
public String getPresentationName()
public String getRedoPresentationName()
public String getUndoPresentationName()
public boolean isInProgress()
public boolean isSignificant()
protected UndoableEdit lastEdit()
public void redo()
public String toString()
public void undo()

## ConcurrentModificationException
public class java.util.
ConcurrentModificationException
extends java.lang.RuntimeException
extends java.lang.Exception
extends java.lang.Throwable
extends java.lang.Object

### Constructors
public  ConcurrentModificationException()
public  ConcurrentModificationException(
String message)

## ConnectException
public class java.net.ConnectException
extends java.net.SocketException
extends java.io.IOException
extends java.lang.Exception
extends java.lang.Throwable
extends java.lang.Object

### Constructors
public  ConnectException(String msg)
public  ConnectException()

## ConnectException
public class java.rmi.ConnectException
extends java.rmi.RemoteException
extends java.io.IOException
extends java.lang.Exception
extends java.lang.Throwable
extends java.lang.Object

### Constructors
public  ConnectException(String s)
public  ConnectException(String s,
Exception ex)

## ConnectIOException
public class java.rmi.
ConnectIOException
extends java.rmi.RemoteException
extends java.io.IOException
extends java.lang.Exception
extends java.lang.Throwable
extends java.lang.Object

### Constructors
public  ConnectIOException(String s)
public  ConnectIOException(String s,
Exception ex)

## Constructor
public final class java.lang.reflect.
Constructor
implements java.lang.reflect.Member
extends java.lang.reflect.
AccessibleObject
extends java.lang.Object

### Constructors
private  Constructor()

### Methods
public boolean equals(Object obj)
public Class getDeclaringClass()
public Class getExceptionTypes()
public int getModifiers()
public String getName()

```
public Class getParameterTypes()
public int hashCode()
public native Object newInstance(Object
initargs)
public String toString()
```

# Container

```
public class java.awt.Container
extends java.awt.Component
extends java.lang.Object
```

## Constructors
```
public  Container()
```

## Methods
```
public Component add(Component comp)
public Component add(String name,
Component comp)
public Component add(Component comp,int
index)
public void add(Component comp,Object
constraints)
public void add(Component comp,Object
constraints,int index)
public synchronized void
addContainerListener(ContainerListener l)
protected void addImpl(Component comp,
Object constraints,int index)
public void addNotify()
public int countComponents()
public void deliverEvent(Event e)
public void doLayout()
public Component findComponentAt(int x,
int y)
public Component findComponentAt(Point p)
public float getAlignmentX()
public float getAlignmentY()
public Component getComponent(int n)
public Component getComponentAt(int x,
int y)
public Component getComponentAt(Point p)
public int getComponentCount()
public Component getComponents()
public Insets getInsets()
public LayoutManager getLayout()
public Dimension getMaximumSize()
public Dimension getMinimumSize()
public Dimension getPreferredSize()
public Insets insets()
public void invalidate()
public boolean isAncestorOf(Component c)
public void layout()
public void list(PrintStream out,int
indent)
public void list(PrintWriter out,int
indent)
public Component locate(int x,int y)
public Dimension minimumSize()
public void paint(Graphics g)
public void paintComponents(Graphics g)
protected String paramString()
public Dimension preferredSize()
public void print(Graphics g)
```

```
public void printComponents(Graphics g)
protected void processContainerEvent(
ContainerEvent e)
protected void processEvent(AWTEvent e)
public void remove(int index)
public void remove(Component comp)
public void removeAll()
public synchronized void
removeContainerListener(
ContainerListener l)
public void removeNotify()
public void setFont(Font f)
public void setLayout(LayoutManager mgr)
public void update(Graphics g)
public void validate()
protected void validateTree()
```

# ContainerAdapter

```
public abstract class java.awt.event.
ContainerAdapter
implements java.awt.event.
ContainerListener
extends java.lang.Object
```

## Methods
```
public void componentAdded(
ContainerEvent e)
public void componentRemoved(
ContainerEvent e)
```

# ContainerEvent

```
public class java.awt.event.
ContainerEvent
extends java.awt.event.ComponentEvent
extends java.awt.AWTEvent
extends java.util.EventObject
extends java.lang.Object
```

## Fields
```
public final static int COMPONENT_ADDED
public final static int COMPONENT_
REMOVED
public final static int CONTAINER_FIRST
public final static int CONTAINER_LAST
```

## Constructors
```
public  ContainerEvent(Component source,
int id,Component child)
```

## Methods
```
public Component getChild()
public Container getContainer()
public String paramString()
```

# ContentHandler

```
public abstract class java.net.
ContentHandler
extends java.lang.Object
```

## Methods
```
public abstract Object getContent(
URLConnection urlc)
```

## ContentModel

public final class javax.swing.text.html.
parser.ContentModel
implements java.io.Serializable
extends java.lang.Object

### Fields

public java.lang.Object content
public javax.swing.text.html.parser.
ContentModel next
public int type

### Constructors

public  ContentModel()
public  ContentModel(Element content)
public  ContentModel(int type,
ContentModel content)
public  ContentModel(int type,Object
content,ContentModel next)

### Methods

public boolean empty()
public boolean first(Object token)
public Element first()
public void getElements(Vector elemVec)
public String toString()

## ConvolveOp

public class java.awt.image.ConvolveOp
implements java.awt.image.
BufferedImageOp
implements java.awt.image.RasterOp
extends java.lang.Object

### Fields

public final static int EDGE_NO_OP
public final static int EDGE_ZERO_FILL

### Constructors

public  ConvolveOp(Kernel kernel,int
edgeCondition,RenderingHints hints)
public  ConvolveOp(Kernel kernel)

### Methods

public BufferedImage
createCompatibleDestImage(BufferedImage
src,ColorModel destCM)
public WritableRaster
createCompatibleDestRaster(Raster src)
public final BufferedImage filter(
BufferedImage src,BufferedImage dst)
public final WritableRaster filter(
Raster src,WritableRaster dst)
public final Rectangle2D getBounds2D(
BufferedImage src)
public final Rectangle2D getBounds2D(
Raster src)
public int getEdgeCondition()
public final Kernel getKernel()
public final Point2D getPoint2D(Point2D
srcPt,Point2D dstPt)
public final RenderingHints
getRenderingHints()

## CRC32

public class java.util.zip.CRC32
implements java.util.zip.Checksum
extends java.lang.Object

### Constructors

public static  CRC32()

### Methods

public long getValue()
public void reset()
public void update(int b)
public void update(byte b,int off,int
len)
public void update(byte b)

## CRL

public abstract class java.security.cert.
CRL
extends java.lang.Object

### Constructors

protected  CRL(String type)

### Methods

public final String getType()
public abstract boolean isRevoked(
Certificate cert)
public abstract String toString()

## CRLException

public class java.security.cert.
CRLException
extends java.security.
GeneralSecurityException
extends java.lang.Exception
extends java.lang.Throwable
extends java.lang.Object

### Constructors

public  CRLException()
public  CRLException(String message)

## CropImageFilter

public class java.awt.image.
CropImageFilter
extends java.awt.image.ImageFilter
extends java.lang.Object

### Constructors

public  CropImageFilter(int x,int y,int
w,int h)

### Methods

public void setDimensions(int w,int h)
public void setPixels(int x,int y,int w,
int h,ColorModel model,byte pixels,int
off,int scansize)
public void setPixels(int x,int y,int w,
int h,ColorModel model,int pixels,int
off,int scansize)
public void setProperties(Hashtable
props)

# CSS

public class javax.swing.text.html.CSS
extends java.lang.Object

### Methods
public static Attribute
getAllAttributeKeys()
public final static Attribute
getAttribute(String name)

# CubicCurve2D

public abstract class java.awt.geom.
CubicCurve2D
implements java.lang.Cloneable
implements java.awt.Shape
extends java.lang.Object

### Constructors
protected  CubicCurve2D()

### Methods
public Object clone()
public boolean contains(double x,double
y)
public boolean contains(Point2D p)
public boolean contains(double x,double
y,double w,double h)
public boolean contains(Rectangle2D r)
public Rectangle getBounds()
public abstract Point2D getCtrlP1()
public abstract Point2D getCtrlP2()
public abstract double getCtrlX1()
public abstract double getCtrlX2()
public abstract double getCtrlY1()
public abstract double getCtrlY2()
public static double getFlatness(double
x1,double y1,double ctrlx1,double ctrly1,
double ctrlx2,double ctrly2,double x2,
double y2)
public static double getFlatness(double
coords,int offset)
public double getFlatness()
public static double getFlatnessSq(
double x1,double y1,double ctrlx1,double
ctrly1,double ctrlx2,double ctrly2,
double x2,double y2)
public static double getFlatnessSq(
double coords,int offset)
public double getFlatnessSq()
public abstract Point2D getP1()
public abstract Point2D getP2()
public PathIterator getPathIterator(
AffineTransform at)
public PathIterator getPathIterator(
AffineTransform at,double flatness)
public abstract double getX1()
public abstract double getX2()
public abstract double getY1()
public abstract double getY2()
public boolean intersects(double x,
double y,double w,double h)
public boolean intersects(Rectangle2D r)
public abstract void setCurve(double x1,
double y1,double ctrlx1,double ctrly1,

double ctrlx2,double ctrly2,double x2,
double y2)
public void setCurve(double coords,int
offset)
public void setCurve(Point2D p1,Point2D
cp1,Point2D cp2,Point2D p2)
public void setCurve(Point2D pts,int
offset)
public void setCurve(CubicCurve2D c)
public static int solveCubic(double eqn)
public void subdivide(CubicCurve2D left,
CubicCurve2D right)
public static void subdivide(
CubicCurve2D src,CubicCurve2D left,
CubicCurve2D right)
public static void subdivide(double src,
int srcoff,double left,int leftoff,
double right,int rightoff)

# Cursor

public class java.awt.Cursor
implements java.io.Serializable
extends java.lang.Object

### Fields
public final static int CROSSHAIR_
CURSOR
public final static int CUSTOM_CURSOR
public final static int DEFAULT_CURSOR
public final static int E_RESIZE_CURSOR
public final static int HAND_CURSOR
public final static int MOVE_CURSOR
protected java.lang.String name
public final static int NE_RESIZE_
CURSOR
public final static int NW_RESIZE_
CURSOR
public final static int N_RESIZE_CURSOR
protected static java.awt.Cursor
predefined
public final static int SE_RESIZE_
CURSOR
public final static int SW_RESIZE_
CURSOR
public final static int S_RESIZE_CURSOR
public final static int TEXT_CURSOR
public final static int WAIT_CURSOR
public final static int W_RESIZE_CURSOR

### Constructors
public  Cursor(int type)
protected  Cursor(String name)

### Methods
public static Cursor getDefaultCursor()
public String getName()
public static Cursor getPredefinedCursor(
int type)
public static Cursor
getSystemCustomCursor(String name)
public int getType()
public String toString()

# DataBuffer

public abstract class java.awt.image.
DataBuffer
extends java.lang.Object

### Fields

protected int banks
protected int dataType
protected int offset
protected int offsets
protected int size
public final static int TYPE_BYTE
public final static int TYPE_DOUBLE
public final static int TYPE_FLOAT
public final static int TYPE_INT
public final static int TYPE_SHORT
public final static int TYPE_UNDEFINED
public final static int TYPE_USHORT

### Constructors

protected  DataBuffer(int dataType,int
size)
protected  DataBuffer(int dataType,int
size,int numBanks)
protected  DataBuffer(int dataType,int
size,int numBanks,int offset)
protected  DataBuffer(int dataType,int
size,int numBanks,int offsets)

### Methods

public int getDataType()
public static int getDataTypeSize(int
type)
public int getElem(int i)
public abstract int getElem(int bank,int
i)
public double getElemDouble(int i)
public double getElemDouble(int bank,int
i)
public float getElemFloat(int i)
public float getElemFloat(int bank,int i)
public int getNumBanks()
public int getOffset()
public int getOffsets()
public int getSize()
public void setElem(int i,int val)
public abstract void setElem(int bank,
int i,int val)
public void setElemDouble(int i,double
val)
public void setElemDouble(int bank,int i,
double val)
public void setElemFloat(int i,float val)
public void setElemFloat(int bank,int i,
float val)

# DataBufferByte

public final class java.awt.image.
DataBufferByte
extends java.awt.image.DataBuffer
extends java.lang.Object

### Constructors

public  DataBufferByte(int size)
public  DataBufferByte(int size,int
numBanks)
public  DataBufferByte(byte dataArray,
int size)
public  DataBufferByte(byte dataArray,
int size,int offset)
public  DataBufferByte(byte dataArray,
int size)
public  DataBufferByte(byte dataArray,
int size,int offsets)

### Methods

public byte getBankData()
public byte getData()
public byte getData(int bank)
public int getElem(int i)
public int getElem(int bank,int i)
public void setElem(int i,int val)
public void setElem(int bank,int i,int
val)

# DataBufferInt

public final class java.awt.image.
DataBufferInt
extends java.awt.image.DataBuffer
extends java.lang.Object

### Constructors

public  DataBufferInt(int size)
public  DataBufferInt(int size,int
numBanks)
public  DataBufferInt(int dataArray,int
size)
public  DataBufferInt(int dataArray,int
size,int offset)
public  DataBufferInt(int dataArray,int
size)
public  DataBufferInt(int dataArray,int
size,int offsets)

### Methods

public int getBankData()
public int getData()
public int getData(int bank)
public int getElem(int i)
public int getElem(int bank,int i)
public void setElem(int i,int val)
public void setElem(int bank,int i,int
val)

# DataBufferShort

public final class java.awt.image.
DataBufferShort
extends java.awt.image.DataBuffer
extends java.lang.Object

### Constructors

public  DataBufferShort(int size)
public  DataBufferShort(int size,int
numBanks)

```
public  DataBufferShort(short dataArray,
int size)
public  DataBufferShort(short dataArray,
int size,int offset)
public  DataBufferShort(short dataArray,
int size)
public  DataBufferShort(short dataArray,
int size,int offsets)
```

### Methods

```
public short getBankData()
public short getData()
public short getData(int bank)
public int getElem(int i)
public int getElem(int bank,int i)
public void setElem(int i,int val)
public void setElem(int bank,int i,int
val)
```

## DataBufferUShort

```
public final class java.awt.image.
DataBufferUShort
extends java.awt.image.DataBuffer
extends java.lang.Object
```

### Constructors

```
public  DataBufferUShort(int size)
public  DataBufferUShort(int size,int
numBanks)
public  DataBufferUShort(short dataArray,
int size)
public  DataBufferUShort(short dataArray,
int size,int offset)
public  DataBufferUShort(short dataArray,
int size)
public  DataBufferUShort(short dataArray,
int size,int offsets)
```

### Methods

```
public short getBankData()
public short getData()
public short getData(int bank)
public int getElem(int i)
public int getElem(int bank,int i)
public void setElem(int i,int val)
public void setElem(int bank,int i,int
val)
```

## DataFlavor

```
public class java.awt.datatransfer.
DataFlavor
implements java.lang.Cloneable
implements java.io.Externalizable
extends java.lang.Object
```

### Fields

```
public final static java.awt.
datatransfer.DataFlavor
javaFileListFlavor
public final static java.lang.String
javaJVMLocalObjectMimeType
public final static java.lang.String
javaRemoteObjectMimeType
```

```
public final static java.lang.String
javaSerializedObjectMimeType
public final static java.awt.
datatransfer.DataFlavor plainTextFlavor
public final static java.awt.
datatransfer.DataFlavor stringFlavor
```

### Constructors

```
private  DataFlavor()
public  DataFlavor(Class
representationClass,String
humanPresentableName)
public  DataFlavor(String mimeType,
String humanPresentableName)
public  DataFlavor(String mimeType,
String humanPresentableName,ClassLoader
classLoader)
public  DataFlavor(String mimeType)
private  DataFlavor()
public  DataFlavor()
```

### Methods

```
public Object clone()
public boolean equals(Object o)
public boolean equals(DataFlavor
dataFlavor)
public boolean equals(String s)
public String getHumanPresentableName()
public String getMimeType()
public String getParameter(String
paramName)
public String getPrimaryType()
public Class getRepresentationClass()
public String getSubType()
public boolean isFlavorJavaFileListType()
public boolean isFlavorRemoteObjectType()
public boolean
isFlavorSerializedObjectType()
public boolean isMimeTypeEqual(String
mimeType)
public final boolean isMimeTypeEqual(
DataFlavor dataFlavor)
public boolean
isMimeTypeSerializedObject()
public boolean
isRepresentationClassInputStream()
public boolean
isRepresentationClassRemote()
public boolean
isRepresentationClassSerializable()
protected String normalizeMimeType(
String mimeType)
protected String
normalizeMimeTypeParameter(String
parameterName,String parameterValue)
public synchronized void readExternal(
ObjectInput is)
public void setHumanPresentableName(
String humanPresentableName)
protected final static Class
tryToLoadClass(String className,
ClassLoader fallback)
public synchronized void writeExternal(
ObjectOutput os)
```

# DataFormatException
public class java.util.zip.
DataFormatException
extends java.lang.Exception
extends java.lang.Throwable
extends java.lang.Object

### Constructors
public  DataFormatException()
public  DataFormatException(String s)

# DatagramPacket
public final class java.net.
DatagramPacket
extends java.lang.Object

### Constructors
public  DatagramPacket(byte buf,int
offset,int length)
public  DatagramPacket(byte buf,int
length)
public  DatagramPacket(byte buf,int
offset,int length,InetAddress address,
int port)
public  DatagramPacket(byte buf,int
length,InetAddress address,int port)

### Methods
public synchronized InetAddress
getAddress()
public synchronized byte getData()
public synchronized int getLength()
public synchronized int getOffset()
public synchronized int getPort()
public synchronized void setAddress(
InetAddress iaddr)
public synchronized void setData(byte
buf,int offset,int length)
public synchronized void setData(byte
buf)
public synchronized void setLength(int
length)
public synchronized void setPort(int
iport)

# DatagramSocket
public class java.net.DatagramSocket
extends java.lang.Object

### Constructors
public static  DatagramSocket()
public  DatagramSocket(int port)
public  DatagramSocket(int port,
InetAddress laddr)

### Methods
public void close()
public void connect(InetAddress address,
int port)
public void disconnect()
public InetAddress getInetAddress()
public InetAddress getLocalAddress()
public int getLocalPort()

public int getPort()
public synchronized int
getReceiveBufferSize()
public synchronized int
getSendBufferSize()
public synchronized int getSoTimeout()
public synchronized void receive(
DatagramPacket p)
public void send(DatagramPacket p)
public synchronized void
setReceiveBufferSize(int size)
public synchronized void
setSendBufferSize(int size)
public synchronized void setSoTimeout(
int timeout)

# DatagramSocketImpl
public abstract class java.net.
DatagramSocketImpl
implements java.net.SocketOptions
extends java.lang.Object

### Fields
protected java.io.FileDescriptor fd
protected int localPort

### Methods
protected abstract void bind(int lport,
InetAddress laddr)
protected abstract void close()
protected abstract void create()
protected FileDescriptor
getFileDescriptor()
protected int getLocalPort()
protected abstract int getTimeToLive()
protected abstract byte getTTL()
protected abstract void join(InetAddress
inetaddr)
protected abstract void leave(
InetAddress inetaddr)
protected abstract int peek(InetAddress
i)
protected abstract void receive(
DatagramPacket p)
protected abstract void send(
DatagramPacket p)
protected abstract void setTimeToLive(
int ttl)
protected abstract void setTTL(byte ttl)

# DataInputStream
public class java.io.DataInputStream
implements java.io.DataInput
extends java.io.FilterInputStream
extends java.io.InputStream
extends java.lang.Object

### Constructors
public  DataInputStream(InputStream in)

### Methods
public final int read(byte b)
public final int read(byte b,int off,int
len)

```
public final boolean readBoolean()
public final byte readByte()
public final char readChar()
public final double readDouble()
public final float readFloat()
public final void readFully(byte b)
public final void readFully(byte b,int
off,int len)
public final int readInt()
public final String readLine()
public final long readLong()
public final short readShort()
public final int readUnsignedByte()
public final int readUnsignedShort()
public final String readUTF()
public final static String readUTF(
DataInput in)
public final int skipBytes(int n)
```

## DataOutputStream

```
public class java.io.DataOutputStream
implements java.io.DataOutput
extends java.io.FilterOutputStream
extends java.io.OutputStream
extends java.lang.Object
```

### Fields

```
protected int written
```

### Constructors

```
public  DataOutputStream(OutputStream
out)
```

### Methods

```
public void flush()
public final int size()
public synchronized void write(int b)
public synchronized void write(byte b,
int off,int len)
public final void writeBoolean(boolean v)
public final void writeByte(int v)
public final void writeBytes(String s)
public final void writeChar(int v)
public final void writeChars(String s)
public final void writeDouble(double v)
public final void writeFloat(float v)
public final void writeInt(int v)
public final void writeLong(long v)
public final void writeShort(int v)
public final void writeUTF(String str)
```

## DataTruncation

```
public class java.sql.DataTruncation
extends java.sql.SQLWarning
extends java.sql.SQLException
extends java.lang.Exception
extends java.lang.Throwable
extends java.lang.Object
```

### Constructors

```
public  DataTruncation(int index,boolean
parameter,boolean read,int dataSize,int
transferSize)
```

### Methods

```
public int getDataSize()
public int getIndex()
public boolean getParameter()
public boolean getRead()
public int getTransferSize()
```

## Date

```
public class java.sql.Date
extends java.util.Date
extends java.lang.Object
```

### Constructors

```
public  Date(int year,int month,int day)
public  Date(long date)
```

### Methods

```
public int getHours()
public int getMinutes()
public int getSeconds()
public void setHours(int i)
public void setMinutes(int i)
public void setSeconds(int i)
public void setTime(long date)
public String toString()
public static Date valueOf(String s)
```

## Date

```
public class java.util.Date
implements java.lang.Cloneable
implements java.lang.Comparable
implements java.io.Serializable
extends java.lang.Object
```

### Constructors

```
public  Date()
public  Date(long date)
public  Date(int year,int month,int date)
public  Date(int year,int month,int date,
int hrs,int min)
public  Date(int year,int month,int date,
int hrs,int min,int sec)
public  Date(String s)
```

### Methods

```
public boolean after(Date when)
public boolean before(Date when)
public Object clone()
public int compareTo(Date anotherDate)
public int compareTo(Object o)
public boolean equals(Object obj)
public int getDate()
public int getDay()
public int getHours()
public int getMinutes()
public int getMonth()
public int getSeconds()
public long getTime()
public int getTimezoneOffset()
public int getYear()
public int hashCode()
public static long parse(String s)
public void setDate(int date)
```

```
public void setHours(int hours)
public void setMinutes(int minutes)
public void setMonth(int month)
public void setSeconds(int seconds)
public void setTime(long time)
public void setYear(int year)
public String toGMTString()
public String toLocaleString()
public String toString()
public static long UTC(int year,int
month,int date,int hrs,int min,int sec)
```

## DateFormat

```
public abstract class java.text.
DateFormat
extends java.text.Format
extends java.lang.Object
```

### Fields

```
public final static int AM_PM_FIELD
protected java.util.Calendar calendar
public final static int DATE_FIELD
public final static int DAY_OF_WEEK_
FIELD
public final static int DAY_OF_WEEK_IN_
MONTH_FIELD
public final static int DAY_OF_YEAR_
FIELD
public final static int DEFAULT
public final static int ERA_FIELD
public final static int FULL
public final static int HOUR0_FIELD
public final static int HOUR1_FIELD
public final static int HOUR_OF_DAY0_
FIELD
public final static int HOUR_OF_DAY1_
FIELD
public final static int LONG
public final static int MEDIUM
public final static int MILLISECOND_
FIELD
public final static int MINUTE_FIELD
public final static int MONTH_FIELD
protected java.text.NumberFormat
numberFormat
public final static int SECOND_FIELD
public final static int SHORT
public final static int TIMEZONE_FIELD
public final static int WEEK_OF_MONTH_
FIELD
public final static int WEEK_OF_YEAR_
FIELD
public final static int YEAR_FIELD
```

### Constructors

```
protected  DateFormat()
```

### Methods

```
public Object clone()
public boolean equals(Object obj)
public final StringBuffer format(Object
obj,StringBuffer toAppendTo,
FieldPosition fieldPosition)
```

```
public abstract StringBuffer format(Date
date,StringBuffer toAppendTo,
FieldPosition fieldPosition)
public final String format(Date date)
public static Locale getAvailableLocales(
)
public Calendar getCalendar()
public final static DateFormat
getDateInstance()
public final static DateFormat
getDateInstance(int style)
public final static DateFormat
getDateInstance(int style,Locale aLocale)
public final static DateFormat
getDateTimeInstance()
public final static DateFormat
getDateTimeInstance(int dateStyle,int
timeStyle)
public final static DateFormat
getDateTimeInstance(int dateStyle,int
timeStyle,Locale aLocale)
public final static DateFormat
getInstance()
public NumberFormat getNumberFormat()
public final static DateFormat
getTimeInstance()
public final static DateFormat
getTimeInstance(int style)
public final static DateFormat
getTimeInstance(int style,Locale aLocale)
public TimeZone getTimeZone()
public int hashCode()
public boolean isLenient()
public Date parse(String text)
public abstract Date parse(String text,
ParsePosition pos)
public Object parseObject(String source,
ParsePosition pos)
public void setCalendar(Calendar
newCalendar)
public void setLenient(boolean lenient)
public void setNumberFormat(NumberFormat
newNumberFormat)
public void setTimeZone(TimeZone zone)
```

## DateFormatSymbols

```
public class java.text.
DateFormatSymbols
implements java.lang.Cloneable
implements java.io.Serializable
extends java.lang.Object
```

### Constructors

```
public  DateFormatSymbols()
public  DateFormatSymbols(Locale locale)
```

### Methods

```
public Object clone()
public boolean equals(Object obj)
public String getAmPmStrings()
public String getEras()
public String getLocalPatternChars()
public String getMonths()
```

```
public String getShortMonths()
public String getShortWeekdays()
public String getWeekdays()
public String getZoneStrings()
public int hashCode()
public void setAmPmStrings(String
newAmpms)
public void setEras(String newEras)
public void setLocalPatternChars(String
newLocalPatternChars)
public void setMonths(String newMonths)
public void setShortMonths(String
newShortMonths)
public void setShortWeekdays(String
newShortWeekdays)
public void setWeekdays(String
newWeekdays)
public void setZoneStrings(String
newZoneStrings)
```

## DateFormatZoneData

```
public final class java.text.resources.
DateFormatZoneData
extends java.util.ListResourceBundle
extends java.util.ResourceBundle
extends java.lang.Object
```

### Methods
```
public Object getContents()
```

## DateFormatZoneData_en

```
public final class java.text.resources.
DateFormatZoneData_en
extends java.util.ListResourceBundle
extends java.util.ResourceBundle
extends java.lang.Object
```

### Methods
```
public Object getContents()
```

## DebugGraphics

```
public class javax.swing.DebugGraphics
extends java.awt.Graphics
extends java.lang.Object
```

### Fields
```
public final static int BUFFERED_OPTION
public final static int FLASH_OPTION
public final static int LOG_OPTION
public final static int NONE_OPTION
```

### Constructors
```
public  DebugGraphics()
public  DebugGraphics(Graphics graphics,
JComponent component)
public  DebugGraphics(Graphics graphics)
```

### Methods
```
public void clearRect(int x,int y,int
width,int height)
public void clipRect(int x,int y,int
width,int height)
```

```
public void copyArea(int x,int y,int
width,int height,int destX,int destY)
public Graphics create()
public Graphics create(int x,int y,int
width,int height)
public void dispose()
public void draw3DRect(int x,int y,int
width,int height,boolean raised)
public void drawArc(int x,int y,int
width,int height,int startAngle,int
arcAngle)
public void drawBytes(byte data,int
offset,int length,int x,int y)
public void drawChars(char data,int
offset,int length,int x,int y)
public boolean drawImage(Image img,int x,
int y,ImageObserver observer)
public boolean drawImage(Image img,int x,
int y,int width,int height,ImageObserver
observer)
public boolean drawImage(Image img,int x,
int y,Color bgcolor,ImageObserver
observer)
public boolean drawImage(Image img,int x,
int y,int width,int height,Color bgcolor,
ImageObserver observer)
public boolean drawImage(Image img,int
dx1,int dy1,int dx2,int dy2,int sx1,int
sy1,int sx2,int sy2,ImageObserver
observer)
public boolean drawImage(Image img,int
dx1,int dy1,int dx2,int dy2,int sx1,int
sy1,int sx2,int sy2,Color bgcolor,
ImageObserver observer)
public void drawLine(int x1,int y1,int
x2,int y2)
public void drawOval(int x,int y,int
width,int height)
public void drawPolygon(int xPoints,int
yPoints,int nPoints)
public void drawPolyline(int xPoints,int
yPoints,int nPoints)
public void drawRect(int x,int y,int
width,int height)
public void drawRoundRect(int x,int y,
int width,int height,int arcWidth,int
arcHeight)
public void drawString(String aString,
int x,int y)
public void drawString(
AttributedCharacterIterator iterator,int
x,int y)
public void fill3DRect(int x,int y,int
width,int height,boolean raised)
public void fillArc(int x,int y,int
width,int height,int startAngle,int
arcAngle)
public void fillOval(int x,int y,int
width,int height)
public void fillPolygon(int xPoints,int
yPoints,int nPoints)
public void fillRect(int x,int y,int
width,int height)
```

```
public void fillRoundRect(int x,int y,
int width,int height,int arcWidth,int
arcHeight)
public static Color flashColor()
public static int flashCount()
public static int flashTime()
public Shape getClip()
public Rectangle getClipBounds()
public Color getColor()
public int getDebugOptions()
public Font getFont()
public FontMetrics getFontMetrics()
public FontMetrics getFontMetrics(Font f)
public boolean isDrawingBuffer()
public static PrintStream logStream()
public void setClip(int x,int y,int
width,int height)
public void setClip(Shape clip)
public void setColor(Color aColor)
public void setDebugOptions(int options)
public static void setFlashColor(Color
flashColor)
public static void setFlashCount(int
flashCount)
public static void setFlashTime(int
flashTime)
public void setFont(Font aFont)
public static void setLogStream(
PrintStream stream)
public void setPaintMode()
public void setXORMode(Color aColor)
public void translate(int x,int y)
```

# DecimalFormat

```
public class java.text.DecimalFormat
extends java.text.NumberFormat
extends java.text.Format
extends java.lang.Object
```

## Constructors

```
public  DecimalFormat()
public  DecimalFormat(String pattern)
public  DecimalFormat(String pattern,
DecimalFormatSymbols symbols)
```

## Methods

```
public void applyLocalizedPattern(String
pattern)
public void applyPattern(String pattern)
public Object clone()
public boolean equals(Object obj)
public StringBuffer format(double number,
StringBuffer result,FieldPosition
fieldPosition)
public StringBuffer format(long number,
StringBuffer result,FieldPosition
fieldPosition)
public DecimalFormatSymbols
getDecimalFormatSymbols()
public int getGroupingSize()
public int getMultiplier()
public String getNegativePrefix()
public String getNegativeSuffix()
```

```
public String getPositivePrefix()
public String getPositiveSuffix()
public int hashCode()
public boolean
isDecimalSeparatorAlwaysShown()
public Number parse(String text,
ParsePosition parsePosition)
public void setDecimalFormatSymbols(
DecimalFormatSymbols newSymbols)
public void
setDecimalSeparatorAlwaysShown(boolean
newValue)
public void setGroupingSize(int newValue)
public void setMaximumFractionDigits(int
newValue)
public void setMaximumIntegerDigits(int
newValue)
public void setMinimumFractionDigits(int
newValue)
public void setMinimumIntegerDigits(int
newValue)
public void setMultiplier(int newValue)
public void setNegativePrefix(String
newValue)
public void setNegativeSuffix(String
newValue)
public void setPositivePrefix(String
newValue)
public void setPositiveSuffix(String
newValue)
public String toLocalizedPattern()
public String toPattern()
```

# DecimalFormatSymbols

```
public final class java.text.
DecimalFormatSymbols
implements java.lang.Cloneable
implements java.io.Serializable
extends java.lang.Object
```

## Constructors

```
public  DecimalFormatSymbols()
public  DecimalFormatSymbols(Locale
locale)
```

## Methods

```
public Object clone()
public boolean equals(Object obj)
public String getCurrencySymbol()
public char getDecimalSeparator()
public char getDigit()
public char getGroupingSeparator()
public String getInfinity()
public String
getInternationalCurrencySymbol()
public char getMinusSign()
public char getMonetaryDecimalSeparator()
public String getNaN()
public char getPatternSeparator()
public char getPercent()
public char getPerMill()
public char getZeroDigit()
public int hashCode()
```

```
public void setCurrencySymbol(String
currency)
public void setDecimalSeparator(char
decimalSeparator)
public void setDigit(char digit)
public void setGroupingSeparator(char
groupingSeparator)
public void setInfinity(String infinity)
public void
setInternationalCurrencySymbol(String
currency)
public void setMinusSign(char minusSign)
public void setMonetaryDecimalSeparator(
char sep)
public void setNaN(String NaN)
public void setPatternSeparator(char
patternSeparator)
public void setPercent(char percent)
public void setPerMill(char perMill)
public void setZeroDigit(char zeroDigit)
```

## DefaultBoundedRangeModel

```
public class javax.swing.
DefaultBoundedRangeModel
implements javax.swing.
BoundedRangeModel
implements java.io.Serializable
extends java.lang.Object
```

### Fields
```
protected transient javax.swing.event.
ChangeEvent changeEvent
protected javax.swing.event.
EventListenerList listenerList
```

### Constructors
```
public DefaultBoundedRangeModel()
public DefaultBoundedRangeModel(int
value,int extent,int min,int max)
```

### Methods
```
public void addChangeListener(
ChangeListener l)
protected void fireStateChanged()
public int getExtent()
public int getMaximum()
public int getMinimum()
public int getValue()
public boolean getValueIsAdjusting()
public void removeChangeListener(
ChangeListener l)
public void setExtent(int n)
public void setMaximum(int n)
public void setMinimum(int n)
public void setRangeProperties(int
newValue,int newExtent,int newMin,int
newMax,boolean adjusting)
public void setValue(int n)
public void setValueIsAdjusting(boolean
b)
public String toString()
```

## DefaultButtonModel

```
public class javax.swing.
DefaultButtonModel
implements javax.swing.ButtonModel
implements java.io.Serializable
extends java.lang.Object
```

### Fields
```
protected java.lang.String
actionCommand
public final static int ARMED
protected transient javax.swing.event.
ChangeEvent changeEvent
public final static int ENABLED
protected javax.swing.ButtonGroup group
protected javax.swing.event.
EventListenerList listenerList
protected int mnemonic
public final static int PRESSED
public final static int ROLLOVER
public final static int SELECTED
protected int stateMask
```

### Constructors
```
public DefaultButtonModel()
```

### Methods
```
public void addActionListener(
ActionListener l)
public void addChangeListener(
ChangeListener l)
public void addItemListener(ItemListener
l)
protected void fireActionPerformed(
ActionEvent e)
protected void fireItemStateChanged(
ItemEvent e)
protected void fireStateChanged()
public String getActionCommand()
public int getMnemonic()
public Object getSelectedObjects()
public boolean isArmed()
public boolean isEnabled()
public boolean isPressed()
public boolean isRollover()
public boolean isSelected()
public void removeActionListener(
ActionListener l)
public void removeChangeListener(
ChangeListener l)
public void removeItemListener(
ItemListener l)
public void setActionCommand(String
actionCommand)
public void setArmed(boolean b)
public void setEnabled(boolean b)
public void setGroup(ButtonGroup group)
public void setMnemonic(int key)
public void setPressed(boolean b)
public void setRollover(boolean b)
public void setSelected(boolean b)
```

# DefaultCaret

```
public class javax.swing.text.
DefaultCaret
implements javax.swing.text.Caret
implements java.awt.event.FocusListener
implements java.awt.event.MouseListener
implements java.awt.event.
MouseMotionListener
extends java.awt.Rectangle
extends java.awt.geom.Rectangle2D
extends java.awt.geom.RectangularShape
extends java.lang.Object
```

## Fields

```
protected transient javax.swing.event.
ChangeEvent changeEvent
protected javax.swing.event.
EventListenerList listenerList
```

## Constructors

```
public  DefaultCaret()
```

## Methods

```
public void addChangeListener(
ChangeListener l)
protected void adjustVisibility(
Rectangle nloc)
protected synchronized void damage(
Rectangle r)
public void deinstall(JTextComponent c)
protected void fireStateChanged()
public void focusGained(FocusEvent e)
public void focusLost(FocusEvent e)
public int getBlinkRate()
protected final JTextComponent
getComponent()
public int getDot()
public Point getMagicCaretPosition()
public int getMark()
protected HighlightPainter
getSelectionPainter()
public void install(JTextComponent c)
public boolean isSelectionVisible()
public boolean isVisible()
public void mouseClicked(MouseEvent e)
public void mouseDragged(MouseEvent e)
public void mouseEntered(MouseEvent e)
public void mouseExited(MouseEvent e)
public void mouseMoved(MouseEvent e)
public void mousePressed(MouseEvent e)
public void mouseReleased(MouseEvent e)
protected void moveCaret(MouseEvent e)
public void moveDot(int dot)
public void paint(Graphics g)
protected void positionCaret(MouseEvent
e)
public void removeChangeListener(
ChangeListener l)
protected final synchronized void
repaint()
public void setBlinkRate(int rate)
public void setDot(int dot)
```

```
public void setMagicCaretPosition(Point
p)
public void setSelectionVisible(boolean
vis)
public void setVisible(boolean e)
public String toString()
```

# DefaultCellEditor

```
public class javax.swing.
DefaultCellEditor
implements java.io.Serializable
implements javax.swing.table.
TableCellEditor
implements javax.swing.tree.
TreeCellEditor
extends java.lang.Object
```

## Fields

```
protected transient javax.swing.event.
ChangeEvent changeEvent
protected int clickCountToStart
protected EditorDelegate delegate
protected javax.swing.JComponent
editorComponent
protected javax.swing.event.
EventListenerList listenerList
```

## Constructors

```
public  DefaultCellEditor(JTextField x)
public  DefaultCellEditor(JCheckBox x)
public  DefaultCellEditor(JComboBox x)
```

## Methods

```
public void addCellEditorListener(
CellEditorListener l)
public void cancelCellEditing()
protected void fireEditingCanceled()
protected void fireEditingStopped()
public Object getCellEditorValue()
public int getClickCountToStart()
public Component getComponent()
public Component
getTableCellEditorComponent(JTable table,
Object value,boolean isSelected,int row,
int column)
public Component
getTreeCellEditorComponent(JTree tree,
Object value,boolean isSelected,boolean
expanded,boolean leaf,int row)
public boolean isCellEditable(
EventObject anEvent)
public void removeCellEditorListener(
CellEditorListener l)
public void setClickCountToStart(int
count)
public boolean shouldSelectCell(
EventObject anEvent)
public boolean stopCellEditing()
```

# DefaultColorSelectionModel

```
public class javax.swing.colorchooser.
DefaultColorSelectionModel
```

implements javax.swing.colorchooser.
ColorSelectionModel
implements java.io.Serializable
extends java.lang.Object

### Fields
protected transient javax.swing.event.
ChangeEvent changeEvent
protected javax.swing.event.
EventListenerList listenerList

### Constructors
public  DefaultColorSelectionModel()
public  DefaultColorSelectionModel(Color
color)

### Methods
public void addChangeListener(
ChangeListener l)
protected void fireStateChanged()
public Color getSelectedColor()
public void removeChangeListener(
ChangeListener l)
public void setSelectedColor(Color color)

## DefaultComboBoxModel
public class javax.swing.
DefaultComboBoxModel
implements javax.swing.
MutableComboBoxModel
implements java.io.Serializable
extends javax.swing.AbstractListModel
extends java.lang.Object

### Constructors
public  DefaultComboBoxModel()
public  DefaultComboBoxModel(Object
items)
public  DefaultComboBoxModel(Vector v)

### Methods
public void addElement(Object anObject)
public Object getElementAt(int index)
public int getIndexOf(Object anObject)
public Object getSelectedItem()
public int getSize()
public void insertElementAt(Object
anObject,int index)
public void removeAllElements()
public void removeElement(Object
anObject)
public void removeElementAt(int index)
public void setSelectedItem(Object
anObject)

## DefaultDesktopManager
public class javax.swing.
DefaultDesktopManager
implements javax.swing.DesktopManager
implements java.io.Serializable
extends java.lang.Object

### Methods
public void activateFrame(JInternalFrame
f)
public void beginDraggingFrame(
JComponent f)
public void beginResizingFrame(
JComponent f,int direction)
public void closeFrame(JInternalFrame f)
public void deactivateFrame(
JInternalFrame f)
public void deiconifyFrame(
JInternalFrame f)
public void dragFrame(JComponent f,int
newX,int newY)
public void endDraggingFrame(JComponent
f)
public void endResizingFrame(JComponent
f)
protected Rectangle getBoundsForIconOf(
JInternalFrame f)
protected Rectangle getPreviousBounds(
JInternalFrame f)
public void iconifyFrame(JInternalFrame
f)
public void maximizeFrame(JInternalFrame
f)
public void minimizeFrame(JInternalFrame
f)
public void openFrame(JInternalFrame f)
protected void removeIconFor(
JInternalFrame f)
public void resizeFrame(JComponent f,int
newX,int newY,int newWidth,int newHeight)
public void setBoundsForFrame(JComponent
f,int newX,int newY,int newWidth,int
newHeight)
protected void setPreviousBounds(
JInternalFrame f,Rectangle r)
protected void setWasIcon(JInternalFrame
f,Boolean value)
protected boolean wasIcon(JInternalFrame
f)

## DefaultEditorKit
public class javax.swing.text.
DefaultEditorKit
extends javax.swing.text.EditorKit
extends java.lang.Object

### Fields
public final static java.lang.String
backwardAction
public final static java.lang.String
beepAction
public final static java.lang.String
beginAction
public final static java.lang.String
beginLineAction
public final static java.lang.String
beginParagraphAction
public final static java.lang.String
beginWordAction

public final static java.lang.String
copyAction
public final static java.lang.String
cutAction
public final static java.lang.String
defaultKeyTypedAction
public final static java.lang.String
deleteNextCharAction
public final static java.lang.String
deletePrevCharAction
public final static java.lang.String
downAction
public final static java.lang.String
endAction
public final static java.lang.String
endLineAction
public final static java.lang.String
EndOfLineStringProperty
public final static java.lang.String
endParagraphAction
public final static java.lang.String
endWordAction
public final static java.lang.String
forwardAction
public final static java.lang.String
insertBreakAction
public final static java.lang.String
insertContentAction
public final static java.lang.String
insertTabAction
public final static java.lang.String
nextWordAction
public final static java.lang.String
pageDownAction
public final static java.lang.String
pageUpAction
public final static java.lang.String
pasteAction
public final static java.lang.String
previousWordAction
public final static java.lang.String
readOnlyAction
public final static java.lang.String
selectAllAction
public final static java.lang.String
selectionBackwardAction
public final static java.lang.String
selectionBeginAction
public final static java.lang.String
selectionBeginLineAction
public final static java.lang.String
selectionBeginParagraphAction
public final static java.lang.String
selectionBeginWordAction
public final static java.lang.String
selectionDownAction
public final static java.lang.String
selectionEndAction
public final static java.lang.String
selectionEndLineAction
public final static java.lang.String
selectionEndParagraphAction
public final static java.lang.String
selectionEndWordAction

public final static java.lang.String
selectionForwardAction
public final static java.lang.String
selectionNextWordAction
public final static java.lang.String
selectionPreviousWordAction
public final static java.lang.String
selectionUpAction
public final static java.lang.String
selectLineAction
public final static java.lang.String
selectParagraphAction
public final static java.lang.String
selectWordAction
public final static java.lang.String
upAction
public final static java.lang.String
writableAction

## Methods
public Object clone()
public Caret createCaret()
public Document createDefaultDocument()
public Action getActions()
public String getContentType()
public ViewFactory getViewFactory()
public void read(InputStream in,Document
doc,int pos)
public void read(Reader in,Document doc,
int pos)
public void write(OutputStream out,
Document doc,int pos,int len)
public void write(Writer out,Document
doc,int pos,int len)

# DefaultFocusManager
public class javax.swing.
DefaultFocusManager
extends javax.swing.FocusManager
extends java.lang.Object

## Methods
public boolean compareTabOrder(Component
a,Component b)
public void focusNextComponent(Component
aComponent)
public void focusPreviousComponent(
Component aComponent)
public Component getComponentAfter(
Container aContainer,Component
aComponent)
public Component getComponentBefore(
Container aContainer,Component
aComponent)
public Component getFirstComponent(
Container aContainer)
public Component getLastComponent(
Container aContainer)
public void processKeyEvent(Component
focusedComponent,KeyEvent anEvent)

## DefaultHighlighter

```
public class javax.swing.text.
DefaultHighlighter
extends javax.swing.text.
LayeredHighlighter
extends java.lang.Object
```

### Fields

```
public static LayeredHighlighter.
LayerPainter DefaultPainter
```

### Constructors

```
public  DefaultHighlighter()
```

### Methods

```
public Object addHighlight(int p0,int p1,
HighlightPainter p)
public void changeHighlight(Object tag,
int p0,int p1)
public void deinstall(JTextComponent c)
public boolean getDrawsLayeredHighlights(
)
public Highlight getHighlights()
public void install(JTextComponent c)
public void paint(Graphics g)
public void paintLayeredHighlights(
Graphics g,int p0,int p1,Shape
viewBounds,JTextComponent editor,View
view)
public void removeAllHighlights()
public void removeHighlight(Object tag)
public void setDrawsLayeredHighlights(
boolean newValue)
```

## DefaultListCellRenderer

```
public class javax.swing.
DefaultListCellRenderer
implements javax.swing.ListCellRenderer
implements java.io.Serializable
extends javax.swing.JLabel
extends javax.swing.JComponent
extends java.awt.Container
extends java.awt.Component
extends java.lang.Object
```

### Fields

```
protected static javax.swing.border.
Border noFocusBorder
```

### Constructors

```
public  DefaultListCellRenderer()
```

### Methods

```
public Component
getListCellRendererComponent(JList list,
Object value,int index,boolean
isSelected,boolean cellHasFocus)
```

## DefaultListModel

```
public class javax.swing.
DefaultListModel
extends javax.swing.AbstractListModel
extends java.lang.Object
```

### Methods

```
public void add(int index,Object element)
public void addElement(Object obj)
public int capacity()
public void clear()
public boolean contains(Object elem)
public void copyInto(Object anArray)
public Object elementAt(int index)
public Enumeration elements()
public void ensureCapacity(int
minCapacity)
public Object firstElement()
public Object get(int index)
public Object getElementAt(int index)
public int getSize()
public int indexOf(Object elem)
public int indexOf(Object elem,int index)
public void insertElementAt(Object obj,
int index)
public boolean isEmpty()
public Object lastElement()
public int lastIndexOf(Object elem)
public int lastIndexOf(Object elem,int
index)
public Object remove(int index)
public void removeAllElements()
public boolean removeElement(Object obj)
public void removeElementAt(int index)
public void removeRange(int fromIndex,
int toIndex)
public Object set(int index,Object
element)
public void setElementAt(Object obj,int
index)
public void setSize(int newSize)
public int size()
public Object toArray()
public String toString()
public void trimToSize()
```

## DefaultListSelectionModel

```
public class javax.swing.
DefaultListSelectionModel
implements java.lang.Cloneable
implements javax.swing.
ListSelectionModel
implements java.io.Serializable
extends java.lang.Object
```

### Fields

```
protected boolean
leadAnchorNotificationEnabled
protected javax.swing.event.
EventListenerList listenerList
```

### Methods

```
public void addListSelectionListener(
ListSelectionListener l)
public void addSelectionInterval(int
index0,int index1)
public void clearSelection()
public Object clone()
```

protected void fireValueChanged(boolean
isAdjusting)
protected void fireValueChanged(int
firstIndex,int lastIndex)
protected void fireValueChanged(int
firstIndex,int lastIndex,boolean
isAdjusting)
public int getAnchorSelectionIndex()
public int getLeadSelectionIndex()
public int getMaxSelectionIndex()
public int getMinSelectionIndex()
public int getSelectionMode()
public boolean getValueIsAdjusting()
public void insertIndexInterval(int
index,int length,boolean before)
public boolean
isLeadAnchorNotificationEnabled()
public boolean isSelectedIndex(int index)
public boolean isSelectionEmpty()
public void removeIndexInterval(int
index0,int index1)
public void removeListSelectionListener(
ListSelectionListener l)
public void removeSelectionInterval(int
index0,int index1)
public void setAnchorSelectionIndex(int
anchorIndex)
public void
setLeadAnchorNotificationEnabled(boolean
flag)
public void setLeadSelectionIndex(int
leadIndex)
public void setSelectionInterval(int
index0,int index1)
public void setSelectionMode(int
selectionMode)
public void setValueIsAdjusting(boolean
isAdjusting)
public String toString()

# DefaultMenuLayout

public class javax.swing.plaf.basic.
DefaultMenuLayout
implements javax.swing.plaf.UIResource
extends javax.swing.BoxLayout
extends java.lang.Object

## Constructors

public DefaultMenuLayout(Container
target,int axis)

# DefaultMetalTheme

public class javax.swing.plaf.metal.
DefaultMetalTheme
extends javax.swing.plaf.metal.
MetalTheme
extends java.lang.Object

## Constructors

public DefaultMetalTheme()

## Methods

public FontUIResource getControlTextFont(
)
public FontUIResource getMenuTextFont()
public String getName()
protected ColorUIResource getPrimary1()
protected ColorUIResource getPrimary2()
protected ColorUIResource getPrimary3()
protected ColorUIResource getSecondary1()
protected ColorUIResource getSecondary2()
protected ColorUIResource getSecondary3()
public FontUIResource getSubTextFont()
public FontUIResource getSystemTextFont()
public FontUIResource getUserTextFont()
public FontUIResource getWindowTitleFont(
)

# DefaultMutableTreeNode

public class javax.swing.tree.
DefaultMutableTreeNode
implements java.lang.Cloneable
implements javax.swing.tree.
MutableTreeNode
implements java.io.Serializable
extends java.lang.Object
extends java.lang.Object

## Fields

protected boolean allowsChildren
protected java.util.Vector children
public final static java.util.
Enumeration EMPTY_ENUMERATION
protected javax.swing.tree.
MutableTreeNode parent
protected transient java.lang.Object
userObject

## Constructors

public DefaultMutableTreeNode()
public DefaultMutableTreeNode(Object
userObject)
public DefaultMutableTreeNode(Object
userObject,boolean allowsChildren)

## Methods

public void add(MutableTreeNode newChild)
public Enumeration
breadthFirstEnumeration()
public Enumeration children()
public Object clone()
public Enumeration depthFirstEnumeration(
)
public boolean getAllowsChildren()
public TreeNode getChildAfter(TreeNode
aChild)
public TreeNode getChildAt(int index)
public TreeNode getChildBefore(TreeNode
aChild)
public int getChildCount()
public int getDepth()
public TreeNode getFirstChild()
public DefaultMutableTreeNode
getFirstLeaf()

```
public int getIndex(TreeNode aChild)
public TreeNode getLastChild()
public DefaultMutableTreeNode
getLastLeaf()
public int getLeafCount()
public int getLevel()
public DefaultMutableTreeNode
getNextLeaf()
public DefaultMutableTreeNode
getNextNode()
public DefaultMutableTreeNode
getNextSibling()
public TreeNode getParent()
public TreeNode getPath()
protected TreeNode getPathToRoot(
TreeNode aNode,int depth)
public DefaultMutableTreeNode
getPreviousLeaf()
public DefaultMutableTreeNode
getPreviousNode()
public DefaultMutableTreeNode
getPreviousSibling()
public TreeNode getRoot()
public TreeNode getSharedAncestor(
DefaultMutableTreeNode aNode)
public int getSiblingCount()
public Object getUserObject()
public Object getUserObjectPath()
public void insert(MutableTreeNode
newChild,int childIndex)
public boolean isLeaf()
public boolean isNodeAncestor(TreeNode
anotherNode)
public boolean isNodeChild(TreeNode
aNode)
public boolean isNodeDescendant(
DefaultMutableTreeNode anotherNode)
public boolean isNodeRelated(
DefaultMutableTreeNode aNode)
public boolean isNodeSibling(TreeNode
anotherNode)
public boolean isRoot()
public Enumeration
pathFromAncestorEnumeration(TreeNode
ancestor)
public Enumeration postorderEnumeration()
public Enumeration preorderEnumeration()
public void remove(int childIndex)
public void remove(MutableTreeNode
aChild)
public void removeAllChildren()
public void removeFromParent()
public void setAllowsChildren(boolean
allows)
public void setParent(MutableTreeNode
newParent)
public void setUserObject(Object
userObject)
public String toString()
```

## DefaultSingleSelectionModel

```
public class javax.swing.
DefaultSingleSelectionModel
```

```
implements java.io.Serializable
implements javax.swing.
SingleSelectionModel
extends java.lang.Object
```

### Fields

```
protected transient javax.swing.event.
ChangeEvent changeEvent
protected javax.swing.event.
EventListenerList listenerList
```

### Methods

```
public void addChangeListener(
ChangeListener l)
public void clearSelection()
protected void fireStateChanged()
public int getSelectedIndex()
public boolean isSelected()
public void removeChangeListener(
ChangeListener l)
public void setSelectedIndex(int index)
```

## DefaultStyledDocument

```
public class javax.swing.text.
DefaultStyledDocument
implements javax.swing.text.
StyledDocument
extends javax.swing.text.
AbstractDocument
extends java.lang.Object
```

### Fields

```
protected ElementBuffer buffer
public final static int BUFFER_SIZE_
DEFAULT
```

### Constructors

```
public DefaultStyledDocument(Content c,
StyleContext styles)
public DefaultStyledDocument(
StyleContext styles)
public DefaultStyledDocument()
```

### Methods

```
public void addDocumentListener(
DocumentListener listener)
public Style addStyle(String nm,Style
parent)
protected void create(ElementSpec data)
protected AbstractElement
createDefaultRoot()
public Color getBackground(AttributeSet
attr)
public Element getCharacterElement(int
pos)
public Element getDefaultRootElement()
public Font getFont(AttributeSet attr)
public Color getForeground(AttributeSet
attr)
public Style getLogicalStyle(int p)
public Element getParagraphElement(int
pos)
public Style getStyle(String nm)
```

public Enumeration getStyleNames()
protected void insert(int offset,
ElementSpec data)
protected void insertUpdate(
DefaultDocumentEvent chng,AttributeSet
attr)
public void removeDocumentListener(
DocumentListener listener)
public void removeStyle(String nm)
protected void removeUpdate(
DefaultDocumentEvent chng)
public void setCharacterAttributes(int
offset,int length,AttributeSet s,boolean
replace)
public void setLogicalStyle(int pos,
Style s)
public void setParagraphAttributes(int
offset,int length,AttributeSet s,boolean
replace)
protected void styleChanged(Style style)

## DefaultTableCellRenderer

public class javax.swing.table.
DefaultTableCellRenderer
implements java.io.Serializable
implements javax.swing.table.
TableCellRenderer
extends javax.swing.JLabel
extends javax.swing.JComponent
extends java.awt.Container
extends java.awt.Component
extends java.lang.Object

### Fields

protected static javax.swing.border.
Border noFocusBorder

### Constructors

public DefaultTableCellRenderer()

### Methods

public Component
getTableCellRendererComponent(JTable
table,Object value,boolean isSelected,
boolean hasFocus,int row,int column)
public void setBackground(Color c)
public void setForeground(Color c)
protected void setValue(Object value)
public void updateUI()

## DefaultTableColumnModel

public class javax.swing.table.
DefaultTableColumnModel
implements javax.swing.event.
ListSelectionListener
implements java.beans.
PropertyChangeListener
implements java.io.Serializable
implements javax.swing.table.
TableColumnModel
extends java.lang.Object

### Fields

protected transient javax.swing.event.
ChangeEvent changeEvent
protected int columnMargin
protected boolean
columnSelectionAllowed
protected javax.swing.event.
EventListenerList listenerList
protected javax.swing.ListSelectionModel
selectionModel
protected java.util.Vector tableColumns
protected int totalColumnWidth

### Constructors

public DefaultTableColumnModel()

### Methods

public void addColumn(TableColumn
aColumn)
public void addColumnModelListener(
TableColumnModelListener x)
protected ListSelectionModel
createSelectionModel()
protected void fireColumnAdded(
TableColumnModelEvent e)
protected void fireColumnMarginChanged()
protected void fireColumnMoved(
TableColumnModelEvent e)
protected void fireColumnRemoved(
TableColumnModelEvent e)
protected void
fireColumnSelectionChanged(
ListSelectionEvent e)
public TableColumn getColumn(int
columnIndex)
public int getColumnCount()
public int getColumnIndex(Object
identifier)
public int getColumnIndexAtX(int
xPosition)
public int getColumnMargin()
public Enumeration getColumns()
public boolean getColumnSelectionAllowed(
)
public int getSelectedColumnCount()
public int getSelectedColumns()
public ListSelectionModel
getSelectionModel()
public int getTotalColumnWidth()
public void moveColumn(int columnIndex,
int newIndex)
public void propertyChange(
PropertyChangeEvent evt)
protected void recalcWidthCache()
public void removeColumn(TableColumn
column)
public void removeColumnModelListener(
TableColumnModelListener x)
public void setColumnMargin(int
newMargin)
public void setColumnSelectionAllowed(
boolean flag)

```
public void setSelectionModel(
ListSelectionModel newModel)
public void valueChanged(
ListSelectionEvent e)
```

## DefaultTableModel

```
public class javax.swing.table.
DefaultTableModel
implements java.io.Serializable
extends javax.swing.table.
AbstractTableModel
extends java.lang.Object
```

### Fields
```
protected java.util.Vector
columnIdentifiers
protected java.util.Vector dataVector
```

### Constructors
```
public  DefaultTableModel()
public  DefaultTableModel(int numRows,
int numColumns)
public  DefaultTableModel(Vector
columnNames,int numRows)
public  DefaultTableModel(Object
columnNames,int numRows)
public  DefaultTableModel(Vector data,
Vector columnNames)
public  DefaultTableModel(Object data,
Object columnNames)
```

### Methods
```
public void addColumn(Object columnName)
public void addColumn(Object columnName,
Vector columnData)
public void addColumn(Object columnName,
Object columnData)
public void addRow(Vector rowData)
public void addRow(Object rowData)
protected static Vector convertToVector(
Object anArray)
protected static Vector convertToVector(
Object anArray)
public int getColumnCount()
public String getColumnName(int column)
public Vector getDataVector()
public int getRowCount()
public Object getValueAt(int row,int
column)
public void insertRow(int row,Vector
rowData)
public void insertRow(int row,Object
rowData)
public boolean isCellEditable(int row,
int column)
public void moveRow(int startIndex,int
endIndex,int toIndex)
public void newDataAvailable(
TableModelEvent event)
public void newRowsAdded(TableModelEvent
event)
public void removeRow(int row)
public void rowsRemoved(TableModelEvent
event)
```

```
public void setColumnIdentifiers(Vector
newIdentifiers)
public void setColumnIdentifiers(Object
newIdentifiers)
public void setDataVector(Vector newData,
Vector columnNames)
public void setDataVector(Object newData,
Object columnNames)
public void setNumRows(int newSize)
public void setValueAt(Object aValue,int
row,int column)
```

## DefaultTextUI

```
public abstract class javax.swing.text.
DefaultTextUI
extends javax.swing.plaf.basic.
BasicTextUI
extends javax.swing.plaf.TextUI
extends javax.swing.plaf.ComponentUI
extends java.lang.Object
```

## DefaultTreeCellEditor

```
public class javax.swing.tree.
DefaultTreeCellEditor
implements java.awt.event.
ActionListener
implements javax.swing.tree.
TreeCellEditor
implements javax.swing.event.
TreeSelectionListener
extends java.lang.Object
```

### Fields
```
protected java.awt.Color
borderSelectionColor
protected boolean canEdit
protected transient java.awt.Component
editingComponent
protected java.awt.Container
editingContainer
protected transient javax.swing.Icon
editingIcon
protected java.awt.Font font
protected transient javax.swing.tree.
TreePath lastPath
protected transient int lastRow
protected transient int offset
protected javax.swing.tree.
TreeCellEditor realEditor
protected javax.swing.tree.
DefaultTreeCellRenderer renderer
protected transient javax.swing.Timer
timer
protected transient javax.swing.JTree
tree
```

### Constructors
```
public  DefaultTreeCellEditor(JTree tree,
DefaultTreeCellRenderer renderer)
public  DefaultTreeCellEditor(JTree tree,
DefaultTreeCellRenderer renderer,
TreeCellEditor editor)
```

## Methods

public void actionPerformed(ActionEvent
e)
public void addCellEditorListener(
CellEditorListener l)
public void cancelCellEditing()
protected boolean canEditImmediately(
EventObject event)
protected Container createContainer()
protected TreeCellEditor
createTreeCellEditor()
protected void determineOffset(JTree
tree,Object value,boolean isSelected,
boolean expanded,boolean leaf,int row)
public Color getBorderSelectionColor()
public Object getCellEditorValue()
public Font getFont()
public Component
getTreeCellEditorComponent(JTree tree,
Object value,boolean isSelected,boolean
expanded,boolean leaf,int row)
protected boolean inHitRegion(int x,int
y)
public boolean isCellEditable(
EventObject event)
protected void prepareForEditing()
public void removeCellEditorListener(
CellEditorListener l)
public void setBorderSelectionColor(
Color newColor)
public void setFont(Font font)
protected void setTree(JTree newTree)
public boolean shouldSelectCell(
EventObject event)
protected boolean
shouldStartEditingTimer(EventObject
event)
protected void startEditingTimer()
public boolean stopCellEditing()
public void valueChanged(
TreeSelectionEvent e)

# DefaultTreeCellRenderer

public class javax.swing.tree.
DefaultTreeCellRenderer
implements javax.swing.tree.
TreeCellRenderer
extends javax.swing.JLabel
extends javax.swing.JComponent
extends java.awt.Container
extends java.awt.Component
extends java.lang.Object

## Fields

protected java.awt.Color
backgroundNonSelectionColor
protected java.awt.Color
backgroundSelectionColor
protected java.awt.Color
borderSelectionColor
protected transient javax.swing.Icon
closedIcon
protected transient javax.swing.Icon
leafIcon

protected transient javax.swing.Icon
openIcon
protected boolean selected
protected java.awt.Color
textNonSelectionColor
protected java.awt.Color
textSelectionColor

## Constructors

public  DefaultTreeCellRenderer()

## Methods

public Color
getBackgroundNonSelectionColor()
public Color getBackgroundSelectionColor(
)
public Color getBorderSelectionColor()
public Icon getClosedIcon()
public Icon getDefaultClosedIcon()
public Icon getDefaultLeafIcon()
public Icon getDefaultOpenIcon()
public Icon getLeafIcon()
public Icon getOpenIcon()
public Dimension getPreferredSize()
public Color getTextNonSelectionColor()
public Color getTextSelectionColor()
public Component
getTreeCellRendererComponent(JTree tree,
Object value,boolean sel,boolean
expanded,boolean leaf,int row,boolean
hasFocus)
public void paint(Graphics g)
public void setBackground(Color color)
public void
setBackgroundNonSelectionColor(Color
newColor)
public void setBackgroundSelectionColor(
Color newColor)
public void setBorderSelectionColor(
Color newColor)
public void setClosedIcon(Icon newIcon)
public void setFont(Font font)
public void setLeafIcon(Icon newIcon)
public void setOpenIcon(Icon newIcon)
public void setTextNonSelectionColor(
Color newColor)
public void setTextSelectionColor(Color
newColor)

# DefaultTreeModel

public class javax.swing.tree.
DefaultTreeModel
implements java.io.Serializable
implements javax.swing.tree.TreeModel
extends java.lang.Object

## Fields

protected boolean asksAllowsChildren
protected javax.swing.event.
EventListenerList listenerList
protected javax.swing.tree.TreeNode
root

### Constructors
```
public  DefaultTreeModel(TreeNode root)
public  DefaultTreeModel(TreeNode root,
boolean asksAllowsChildren)
```

### Methods
```
public void addTreeModelListener(
TreeModelListener l)
public boolean asksAllowsChildren()
protected void fireTreeNodesChanged(
Object source,Object path,int
childIndices,Object children)
protected void fireTreeNodesInserted(
Object source,Object path,int
childIndices,Object children)
protected void fireTreeNodesRemoved(
Object source,Object path,int
childIndices,Object children)
protected void fireTreeStructureChanged(
Object source,Object path,int
childIndices,Object children)
public Object getChild(Object parent,int
index)
public int getChildCount(Object parent)
public int getIndexOfChild(Object parent,
Object child)
public TreeNode getPathToRoot(TreeNode
aNode)
protected TreeNode getPathToRoot(
TreeNode aNode,int depth)
public Object getRoot()
public void insertNodeInto(
MutableTreeNode newChild,MutableTreeNode
parent,int index)
public boolean isLeaf(Object node)
public void nodeChanged(TreeNode node)
public void nodesChanged(TreeNode node,
int childIndices)
public void nodeStructureChanged(
TreeNode node)
public void nodesWereInserted(TreeNode
node,int childIndices)
public void nodesWereRemoved(TreeNode
node,int childIndices,Object
removedChildren)
public void reload()
public void reload(TreeNode node)
public void removeNodeFromParent(
MutableTreeNode node)
public void removeTreeModelListener(
TreeModelListener l)
public void setAsksAllowsChildren(
boolean newValue)
public void setRoot(TreeNode root)
public void valueForPathChanged(TreePath
path,Object newValue)
```

# DefaultTreeSelectionModel
```
public class javax.swing.tree.
DefaultTreeSelectionModel
implements java.lang.Cloneable
implements java.io.Serializable
```

```
implements javax.swing.tree.
TreeSelectionModel
extends java.lang.Object
extends java.lang.Object
```

### Fields
```
protected javax.swing.event.
SwingPropertyChangeSupport
changeSupport
protected int leadIndex
protected javax.swing.tree.TreePath
leadPath
protected int leadRow
protected javax.swing.event.
EventListenerList listenerList
protected javax.swing.
DefaultListSelectionModel
listSelectionModel
protected transient javax.swing.tree.
RowMapper rowMapper
protected javax.swing.tree.TreePath
selection
protected int selectionMode
public final static java.lang.String
SELECTION_MODE_PROPERTY
```

### Constructors
```
public  DefaultTreeSelectionModel()
```

### Methods
```
public synchronized void
addPropertyChangeListener(
PropertyChangeListener listener)
public void addSelectionPath(TreePath
path)
public void addSelectionPaths(TreePath
paths)
public void addTreeSelectionListener(
TreeSelectionListener x)
protected boolean arePathsContiguous(
TreePath paths)
protected boolean canPathsBeAdded(
TreePath paths)
protected boolean canPathsBeRemoved(
TreePath paths)
public void clearSelection()
public Object clone()
protected void fireValueChanged(
TreeSelectionEvent e)
public TreePath getLeadSelectionPath()
public int getLeadSelectionRow()
public int getMaxSelectionRow()
public int getMinSelectionRow()
public RowMapper getRowMapper()
public int getSelectionCount()
public int getSelectionMode()
public TreePath getSelectionPath()
public TreePath getSelectionPaths()
public int getSelectionRows()
protected void insureRowContinuity()
protected void insureUniqueness()
public boolean isPathSelected(TreePath
path)
public boolean isRowSelected(int row)
```

```
public boolean isSelectionEmpty()
protected void notifyPathChange(Vector
changedPaths,TreePath oldLeadSelection)
public synchronized void
removePropertyChangeListener(
PropertyChangeListener listener)
public void removeSelectionPath(TreePath
path)
public void removeSelectionPaths(
TreePath paths)
public void removeTreeSelectionListener(
TreeSelectionListener x)
public void resetRowSelection()
public void setRowMapper(RowMapper
newMapper)
public void setSelectionMode(int mode)
public void setSelectionPath(TreePath
path)
public void setSelectionPaths(TreePath
pPaths)
public String toString()
protected void updateLeadIndex()
```

# Deflater
```
public class java.util.zip.Deflater
extends java.lang.Object
```

### Fields
```
public final static int BEST_
COMPRESSION
public final static int BEST_SPEED
public final static int DEFAULT_
COMPRESSION
public final static int DEFAULT_
STRATEGY
public final static int DEFLATED
public final static int FILTERED
public final static int HUFFMAN_ONLY
public final static int NO_COMPRESSION
```

### Constructors
```
public static  Deflater(int level,
boolean nowrap)
public  Deflater(int level)
public  Deflater()
```

### Methods
```
public synchronized int deflate(byte b,
int off,int len)
public int deflate(byte b)
public synchronized void end()
protected void finalize()
public synchronized void finish()
public synchronized boolean finished()
public synchronized int getAdler()
public synchronized int getTotalIn()
public synchronized int getTotalOut()
public boolean needsInput()
public synchronized void reset()
public synchronized void setDictionary(
byte b,int off,int len)
public void setDictionary(byte b)
public synchronized void setInput(byte b,
int off,int len)
```

```
public void setInput(byte b)
public synchronized void setLevel(int
level)
public synchronized void setStrategy(int
strategy)
```

# DeflaterOutputStream
```
public class java.util.zip.
DeflaterOutputStream
extends java.io.FilterOutputStream
extends java.io.OutputStream
extends java.lang.Object
```

### Fields
```
protected byte buf
protected java.util.zip.Deflater def
```

### Constructors
```
public  DeflaterOutputStream(
OutputStream out,Deflater def,int size)
public  DeflaterOutputStream(
OutputStream out,Deflater def)
public  DeflaterOutputStream(
OutputStream out)
```

### Methods
```
public void close()
protected void deflate()
public void finish()
public void write(int b)
public void write(byte b,int off,int len)
```

# DesktopIconUI
```
public abstract class javax.swing.plaf.
DesktopIconUI
extends javax.swing.plaf.ComponentUI
extends java.lang.Object
```

# DesktopPaneUI
```
public abstract class javax.swing.plaf.
DesktopPaneUI
extends javax.swing.plaf.ComponentUI
extends java.lang.Object
```

# Dialog
```
public class java.awt.Dialog
extends java.awt.Window
extends java.awt.Container
extends java.awt.Component
extends java.lang.Object
```

### Constructors
```
public  Dialog(Frame owner)
public  Dialog(Frame owner,boolean modal)
public  Dialog(Frame owner,String title)
public  Dialog(Frame owner,String title,
boolean modal)
public  Dialog(Dialog owner)
public  Dialog(Dialog owner,String title)
public  Dialog(Dialog owner,String title,
boolean modal)
```

### Methods
```
public void addNotify()
public String getTitle()
public boolean isModal()
public boolean isResizable()
protected String paramString()
public void setModal(boolean b)
public void setResizable(boolean
resizable)
public synchronized void setTitle(String
title)
public void show()
```

## Dictionary
```
public abstract class java.util.
Dictionary
extends java.lang.Object
```

### Constructors
```
public  Dictionary()
```

### Methods
```
public abstract Enumeration elements()
public abstract Object get(Object key)
public abstract boolean isEmpty()
public abstract Enumeration keys()
public abstract Object put(Object key,
Object value)
public abstract Object remove(Object key)
public abstract int size()
```

## DigestException
```
public class java.security.
DigestException
extends java.security.
GeneralSecurityException
extends java.lang.Exception
extends java.lang.Throwable
extends java.lang.Object
```

### Constructors
```
public  DigestException()
public  DigestException(String msg)
```

## DigestInputStream
```
public class java.security.
DigestInputStream
extends java.io.FilterInputStream
extends java.io.InputStream
extends java.lang.Object
```

### Fields
```
protected java.security.MessageDigest
digest
```

### Constructors
```
public  DigestInputStream(InputStream
stream,MessageDigest digest)
```

### Methods
```
public MessageDigest getMessageDigest()
public void on(boolean on)
```

```
public int read()
public int read(byte b,int off,int len)
public void setMessageDigest(
MessageDigest digest)
public String toString()
```

## DigestOutputStream
```
public class java.security.
DigestOutputStream
extends java.io.FilterOutputStream
extends java.io.OutputStream
extends java.lang.Object
```

### Fields
```
protected java.security.MessageDigest
digest
```

### Constructors
```
public  DigestOutputStream(OutputStream
stream,MessageDigest digest)
```

### Methods
```
public MessageDigest getMessageDigest()
public void on(boolean on)
public void setMessageDigest(
MessageDigest digest)
public String toString()
public void write(int b)
public void write(byte b,int off,int len)
```

## Dimension
```
public class java.awt.Dimension
implements java.io.Serializable
extends java.awt.geom.Dimension2D
extends java.lang.Object
```

### Fields
```
public int height
public int width
```

### Constructors
```
public static  Dimension()
public  Dimension(Dimension d)
public  Dimension(int width,int height)
```

### Methods
```
public boolean equals(Object obj)
public double getHeight()
public Dimension getSize()
public double getWidth()
public void setSize(double width,double
height)
public void setSize(Dimension d)
public void setSize(int width,int height)
public String toString()
```

## Dimension2D
```
public abstract class java.awt.geom.
Dimension2D
implements java.lang.Cloneable
extends java.lang.Object
```

### Constructors
```
protected  Dimension2D()
```

### Methods
```
public Object clone()
public abstract double getHeight()
public abstract double getWidth()
public abstract void setSize(double
width,double height)
public void setSize(Dimension2D d)
```

## DimensionUIResource
```
public class javax.swing.plaf.
DimensionUIResource
implements javax.swing.plaf.UIResource
extends java.awt.Dimension
extends java.awt.geom.Dimension2D
extends java.lang.Object
```

### Constructors
```
public  DimensionUIResource(int width,
int height)
```

## DirectColorModel
```
public class java.awt.image.
DirectColorModel
extends java.awt.image.PackedColorModel
extends java.awt.image.ColorModel
extends java.lang.Object
```

### Constructors
```
public  DirectColorModel(int bits,int
rmask,int gmask,int bmask)
public  DirectColorModel(int bits,int
rmask,int gmask,int bmask,int amask)
public  DirectColorModel(ColorSpace
space,int bits,int rmask,int gmask,int
bmask,int amask,boolean
isAlphaPremultiplied,int transferType)
```

### Methods
```
public final ColorModel coerceData(
WritableRaster raster,boolean
isAlphaPremultiplied)
public final WritableRaster
createCompatibleWritableRaster(int w,int
h)
public final int getAlpha(int pixel)
public int getAlpha(Object inData)
public final int getAlphaMask()
public final int getBlue(int pixel)
public int getBlue(Object inData)
public final int getBlueMask()
public final int getComponents(int pixel,
int components,int offset)
public final int getComponents(Object
pixel,int components,int offset)
public int getDataElement(int components,
int offset)
public Object getDataElements(int rgb,
Object pixel)
public Object getDataElements(int
components,int offset,Object obj)
```

```
public final int getGreen(int pixel)
public int getGreen(Object inData)
public final int getGreenMask()
public final int getRed(int pixel)
public int getRed(Object inData)
public final int getRedMask()
public final int getRGB(int pixel)
public int getRGB(Object inData)
public boolean isCompatibleRaster(Raster
raster)
public String toString()
```

## DnDConstants
```
public final class java.awt.dnd.
DnDConstants
extends java.lang.Object
```

### Fields
```
public final static int ACTION_COPY
public final static int ACTION_COPY_OR_
MOVE
public final static int ACTION_LINK
public final static int ACTION_MOVE
public final static int ACTION_NONE
public final static int ACTION_
REFERENCE
```

### Constructors
```
private  DnDConstants()
```

## DocumentParser
```
public class javax.swing.text.html.
parser.DocumentParser
extends javax.swing.text.html.parser.
Parser
extends java.lang.Object
```

### Constructors
```
public  DocumentParser(DTD dtd)
```

### Methods
```
protected void handleComment(char text)
protected void handleEmptyTag(TagElement
tag)
protected void handleEndTag(TagElement
tag)
protected void handleError(int ln,String
errorMsg)
protected void handleStartTag(TagElement
tag)
protected void handleText(char data)
public void parse(Reader in,
ParserCallback callback,boolean
ignoreCharSet)
```

## Double
```
public final class java.lang.Double
implements java.lang.Comparable
extends java.lang.Number
extends java.lang.Object
```

## Fields

```
public final static double MAX_VALUE
public final static double MIN_VALUE
public final static double NaN
public final static double NEGATIVE_
INFINITY
public final static double POSITIVE_
INFINITY
public final static java.lang.Class
TYPE
```

## Constructors

```
public  Double(double value)
public  Double(String s)
```

## Methods

```
public byte byteValue()
public int compareTo(Double
anotherDouble)
public int compareTo(Object o)
public static native long
doubleToLongBits(double value)
public double doubleValue()
public boolean equals(Object obj)
public float floatValue()
public int hashCode()
public int intValue()
public static boolean isInfinite(double
v)
public boolean isInfinite()
public static boolean isNaN(double v)
public boolean isNaN()
public static native double
longBitsToDouble(long bits)
public long longValue()
public static double parseDouble(String
s)
public short shortValue()
public static String toString(double d)
public String toString()
public static Double valueOf(String s)
```

# DragGestureEvent

```
public class java.awt.dnd.
DragGestureEvent
extends java.util.EventObject
extends java.lang.Object
```

## Constructors

```
public  DragGestureEvent(
DragGestureRecognizer dgr,int act,Point
ori,List evs)
```

## Methods

```
public Component getComponent()
public int getDragAction()
public Point getDragOrigin()
public DragSource getDragSource()
public DragGestureRecognizer
getSourceAsDragGestureRecognizer()
public InputEvent getTriggerEvent()
public Iterator iterator()
```

```
public void startDrag(Cursor dragCursor,
Transferable transferable,
DragSourceListener dsl)
public void startDrag(Cursor dragCursor,
Image dragImage,Point imageOffset,
Transferable transferable,
DragSourceListener dsl)
public Object toArray()
public Object toArray(Object array)
```

# DragGestureRecognizer

```
public abstract class java.awt.dnd.
DragGestureRecognizer
extends java.lang.Object
```

## Fields

```
protected java.awt.Component component
protected java.awt.dnd.
DragGestureListener dragGestureListener
protected java.awt.dnd.DragSource
dragSource
protected java.util.ArrayList events
protected int sourceActions
```

## Constructors

```
protected  DragGestureRecognizer(
DragSource ds,Component c,int sa,
DragGestureListener dgl)
protected  DragGestureRecognizer(
DragSource ds,Component c,int sa)
protected  DragGestureRecognizer(
DragSource ds,Component c)
protected  DragGestureRecognizer(
DragSource ds)
```

## Methods

```
public synchronized void
addDragGestureListener(
DragGestureListener dgl)
protected synchronized void appendEvent(
InputEvent awtie)
protected synchronized void
fireDragGestureRecognized(int dragAction,
Point p)
public synchronized Component
getComponent()
public DragSource getDragSource()
public synchronized int getSourceActions(
)
public InputEvent getTriggerEvent()
protected abstract void
registerListeners()
public synchronized void
removeDragGestureListener(
DragGestureListener dgl)
public void resetRecognizer()
public synchronized void setComponent(
Component c)
public synchronized void
setSourceActions(int actions)
protected abstract void
unregisterListeners()
```

# DragSource

public class java.awt.dnd.DragSource
extends java.lang.Object

## Fields

public final static java.awt.Cursor
DefaultCopyDrop
public final static java.awt.Cursor
DefaultCopyNoDrop
public final static java.awt.Cursor
DefaultLinkDrop
public final static java.awt.Cursor
DefaultLinkNoDrop
public final static java.awt.Cursor
DefaultMoveDrop
public final static java.awt.Cursor
DefaultMoveNoDrop

## Constructors

public  DragSource()

## Methods

public DragGestureRecognizer
createDefaultDragGestureRecognizer(
Component c,int actions,
DragGestureListener dgl)
public DragGestureRecognizer
createDragGestureRecognizer(Class
recognizerAbstractClass,Component c,int
actions,DragGestureListener dgl)
protected DragSourceContext
createDragSourceContext(
DragSourceContextPeer dscp,
DragGestureEvent dgl,Cursor dragCursor,
Image dragImage,Point imageOffset,
Transferable t,DragSourceListener dsl)
public static DragSource
getDefaultDragSource()
public FlavorMap getFlavorMap()
public static boolean
isDragImageSupported()
public void startDrag(DragGestureEvent
trigger,Cursor dragCursor,Image
dragImage,Point imageOffset,Transferable
transferable,DragSourceListener dsl,
FlavorMap flavorMap)
public void startDrag(DragGestureEvent
trigger,Cursor dragCursor,Transferable
transferable,DragSourceListener dsl,
FlavorMap flavorMap)
public void startDrag(DragGestureEvent
trigger,Cursor dragCursor,Image
dragImage,Point dragOffset,Transferable
transferable,DragSourceListener dsl)
public void startDrag(DragGestureEvent
trigger,Cursor dragCursor,Transferable
transferable,DragSourceListener dsl)

# DragSourceContext

public class java.awt.dnd.
DragSourceContext

implements java.awt.dnd.
DragSourceListener
extends java.lang.Object

## Fields

protected final static int CHANGED
protected final static int DEFAULT
protected final static int ENTER
protected final static int OVER

## Constructors

public  DragSourceContext(
DragSourceContextPeer dscp,
DragGestureEvent trigger,Cursor
dragCursor,Image dragImage,Point offset,
Transferable t,DragSourceListener dsl)

## Methods

public synchronized void
addDragSourceListener(DragSourceListener
dsl)
public synchronized void dragDropEnd(
DragSourceDropEvent dsde)
public synchronized void dragEnter(
DragSourceDragEvent dsde)
public synchronized void dragExit(
DragSourceEvent dse)
public synchronized void dragOver(
DragSourceDragEvent dsde)
public synchronized void
dropActionChanged(DragSourceDragEvent
dsde)
public Component getComponent()
public Cursor getCursor()
public DragSource getDragSource()
public int getSourceActions()
public Transferable getTransferable()
public DragGestureEvent getTrigger()
public synchronized void
removeDragSourceListener(
DragSourceListener dsl)
public void setCursor(Cursor c)
public void transferablesFlavorsChanged()
protected void updateCurrentCursor(int
dropOp,int targetAct,int status)

# DragSourceDragEvent

public class java.awt.dnd.
DragSourceDragEvent
extends java.awt.dnd.DragSourceEvent
extends java.util.EventObject
extends java.lang.Object

## Constructors

public  DragSourceDragEvent(
DragSourceContext dsc,int dropAction,int
actions,int modifiers)

## Methods

public int getDropAction()
public int getGestureModifiers()
public int getTargetActions()
public int getUserAction()

## DragSourceDropEvent

public class java.awt.dnd.
DragSourceDropEvent
extends java.awt.dnd.DragSourceEvent
extends java.util.EventObject
extends java.lang.Object

### Constructors
public  DragSourceDropEvent(
DragSourceContext dsc,int action,boolean
success)
public  DragSourceDropEvent(
DragSourceContext dsc)

### Methods
public int getDropAction()
public boolean getDropSuccess()

## DragSourceEvent

public class java.awt.dnd.
DragSourceEvent
extends java.util.EventObject
extends java.lang.Object

### Constructors
public  DragSourceEvent(
DragSourceContext dsc)

### Methods
public DragSourceContext
getDragSourceContext()

## DriverManager

public class java.sql.DriverManager
extends java.lang.Object

### Constructors
private  DriverManager()

### Methods
public static synchronized void
deregisterDriver(Driver driver)
public static synchronized Connection
getConnection(String url,Properties info)
public static synchronized Connection
getConnection(String url,String user,
String password)
public static synchronized Connection
getConnection(String url)
public static synchronized Driver
getDriver(String url)
public static synchronized Enumeration
getDrivers()
public static int getLoginTimeout()
public static PrintStream getLogStream()
public static PrintWriter getLogWriter()
public static synchronized void println(
String message)
public static synchronized void
registerDriver(Driver driver)
public static void setLoginTimeout(int
seconds)

public static synchronized void
setLogStream(PrintStream out)
public static synchronized void
setLogWriter(PrintWriter out)

## DriverPropertyInfo

public class java.sql.
DriverPropertyInfo
extends java.lang.Object

### Fields
public java.lang.String choices
public java.lang.String description
public java.lang.String name
public boolean required
public java.lang.String value

### Constructors
public  DriverPropertyInfo(String name,
String value)

## DropTarget

public class java.awt.dnd.DropTarget
implements java.awt.dnd.
DropTargetListener
implements java.io.Serializable
extends java.lang.Object

### Constructors
public  DropTarget(Component c,int ops,
DropTargetListener dtl,boolean act,
FlavorMap fm)
public  DropTarget(Component c,int ops,
DropTargetListener dtl,boolean act)
public  DropTarget()
public  DropTarget(Component c,
DropTargetListener dtl)
public  DropTarget(Component c,int ops,
DropTargetListener dtl)

### Methods
public synchronized void
addDropTargetListener(DropTargetListener
dtl)
public void addNotify(ComponentPeer peer)
protected void clearAutoscroll()
protected DropTargetAutoScroller
createDropTargetAutoScroller(Component c,
Point p)
protected DropTargetContext
createDropTargetContext()
public synchronized void dragEnter(
DropTargetDragEvent dtde)
public synchronized void dragExit(
DropTargetEvent dte)
public synchronized void dragOver(
DropTargetDragEvent dtde)
public synchronized void drop(
DropTargetDropEvent dtde)
public void dropActionChanged(
DropTargetDragEvent dtde)
public synchronized Component
getComponent()

```
public synchronized int
getDefaultActions()
public DropTargetContext
getDropTargetContext()
public FlavorMap getFlavorMap()
protected void initializeAutoscrolling(
Point p)
public synchronized boolean isActive()
public synchronized void
removeDropTargetListener(
DropTargetListener dtl)
public void removeNotify(ComponentPeer
peer)
public synchronized void setActive(
boolean isActive)
public synchronized void setComponent(
Component c)
public synchronized void
setDefaultActions(int ops)
public void setFlavorMap(FlavorMap fm)
protected void updateAutoscroll(Point
dragCursorLocn)
```

## DropTargetContext
```
public class java.awt.dnd.
DropTargetContext
extends java.lang.Object
```

### Constructors
```
DropTargetContext()
```

### Methods
```
protected void acceptDrag(int
dragOperation)
protected void acceptDrop(int
dropOperation)
public synchronized void addNotify(
DropTargetContextPeer dtcp)
protected Transferable
createTransferableProxy(Transferable t,
boolean local)
public void dropComplete(boolean success)
public Component getComponent()
protected DataFlavor
getCurrentDataFlavors()
protected List
getCurrentDataFlavorsAsList()
public DropTarget getDropTarget()
protected int getTargetActions()
protected synchronized Transferable
getTransferable()
protected boolean isDataFlavorSupported(
DataFlavor df)
protected void rejectDrag()
protected void rejectDrop()
public synchronized void removeNotify()
protected void setTargetActions(int
actions)
```

## DropTargetDragEvent
```
public class java.awt.dnd.
DropTargetDragEvent
extends java.awt.dnd.DropTargetEvent
```

```
extends java.util.EventObject
extends java.lang.Object
```

### Constructors
```
public DropTargetDragEvent(
DropTargetContext dtc,Point cursorLocn,
int dropAction,int srcActions)
```

### Methods
```
public void acceptDrag(int dragOperation)
public DataFlavor getCurrentDataFlavors()
public List getCurrentDataFlavorsAsList()
public int getDropAction()
public Point getLocation()
public int getSourceActions()
public boolean isDataFlavorSupported(
DataFlavor df)
public void rejectDrag()
```

## DropTargetDropEvent
```
public class java.awt.dnd.
DropTargetDropEvent
extends java.awt.dnd.DropTargetEvent
extends java.util.EventObject
extends java.lang.Object
```

### Constructors
```
public DropTargetDropEvent(
DropTargetContext dtc,Point cursorLocn,
int dropAction,int srcActions)
public DropTargetDropEvent(
DropTargetContext dtc,Point cursorLocn,
int dropAction,int srcActions,boolean
isLocal)
```

### Methods
```
public void acceptDrop(int dropAction)
public void dropComplete(boolean success)
public DataFlavor getCurrentDataFlavors()
public List getCurrentDataFlavorsAsList()
public int getDropAction()
public Point getLocation()
public int getSourceActions()
public Transferable getTransferable()
public boolean isDataFlavorSupported(
DataFlavor df)
public boolean isLocalTransfer()
public void rejectDrop()
```

## DropTargetEvent
```
public class java.awt.dnd.
DropTargetEvent
extends java.util.EventObject
extends java.lang.Object
```

### Fields
```
protected java.awt.dnd.DropTargetContext
context
```

### Constructors
```
public DropTargetEvent(
DropTargetContext dtc)
```

## Methods

public DropTargetContext
getDropTargetContext()

## DSAParameterSpec

public class java.security.spec.
DSAParameterSpec
implements java.security.spec.
AlgorithmParameterSpec
implements java.security.interfaces.
DSAParams
extends java.lang.Object

### Constructors

public DSAParameterSpec(BigInteger p,
BigInteger q,BigInteger g)

### Methods

public BigInteger getG()
public BigInteger getP()
public BigInteger getQ()

## DSAPrivateKeySpec

public class java.security.spec.
DSAPrivateKeySpec
implements java.security.spec.KeySpec
extends java.lang.Object

### Constructors

public DSAPrivateKeySpec(BigInteger x,
BigInteger p,BigInteger q,BigInteger g)

### Methods

public BigInteger getG()
public BigInteger getP()
public BigInteger getQ()
public BigInteger getX()

## DSAPublicKeySpec

public class java.security.spec.
DSAPublicKeySpec
implements java.security.spec.KeySpec
extends java.lang.Object

### Constructors

public DSAPublicKeySpec(BigInteger y,
BigInteger p,BigInteger q,BigInteger g)

### Methods

public BigInteger getG()
public BigInteger getP()
public BigInteger getQ()
public BigInteger getY()

## DTD

public class javax.swing.text.html.
parser.DTD
implements javax.swing.text.html.parser.
DTDConstants
extends java.lang.Object

## Fields

public final javax.swing.text.html.
parser.Element applet
public final javax.swing.text.html.
parser.Element base
public final javax.swing.text.html.
parser.Element body
public java.util.Hashtable elementHash
public java.util.Vector elements
public java.util.Hashtable entityHash
public static int FILE_VERSION
public final javax.swing.text.html.
parser.Element head
public final javax.swing.text.html.
parser.Element html
public final javax.swing.text.html.
parser.Element isindex
public final javax.swing.text.html.
parser.Element meta
public java.lang.String name
public final javax.swing.text.html.
parser.Element p
public final javax.swing.text.html.
parser.Element param
public final javax.swing.text.html.
parser.Element pcdata
public final javax.swing.text.html.
parser.Element title

## Constructors

protected DTD(String name)

## Methods

protected AttributeList defAttributeList(
String name,int type,int modifier,String
value,String values,AttributeList atts)
protected ContentModel defContentModel(
int type,Object obj,ContentModel next)
protected Element defElement(String name,
int type,boolean omitStart,boolean
omitEnd,ContentModel content,String
exclusions,String inclusions,
AttributeList atts)
public Entity defEntity(String name,int
type,int ch)
protected Entity defEntity(String name,
int type,String str)
public void defineAttributes(String name,
AttributeList atts)
public Element defineElement(String name,
int type,boolean omitStart,boolean
omitEnd,ContentModel content,BitSet
exclusions,BitSet inclusions,
AttributeList atts)
public Entity defineEntity(String name,
int type,char data)
public static DTD getDTD(String name)
public Element getElement(String name)
public Element getElement(int index)
public Entity getEntity(String name)
public Entity getEntity(int ch)
public String getName()

```
public static void putDTDHash(String
name,DTD dtd)
public void read(DataInputStream in)
public String toString()
```

## EditorKit

```
public abstract class javax.swing.text.
EditorKit
implements java.lang.Cloneable
implements java.io.Serializable
extends java.lang.Object
```

### Methods

```
public abstract Object clone()
public abstract Caret createCaret()
public abstract Document
createDefaultDocument()
public void deinstall(JEditorPane c)
public abstract Action getActions()
public abstract String getContentType()
public abstract ViewFactory
getViewFactory()
public void install(JEditorPane c)
public abstract void read(InputStream in,
Document doc,int pos)
public abstract void read(Reader in,
Document doc,int pos)
public abstract void write(OutputStream
out,Document doc,int pos,int len)
public abstract void write(Writer out,
Document doc,int pos,int len)
```

## Element

```
public final class javax.swing.text.html.
parser.Element
implements javax.swing.text.html.parser.
DTDConstants
implements java.io.Serializable
extends java.lang.Object
```

### Fields

```
public javax.swing.text.html.parser.
AttributeList atts
public javax.swing.text.html.parser.
ContentModel content
public java.lang.Object data
public java.util.BitSet exclusions
public java.util.BitSet inclusions
public int index
public java.lang.String name
public boolean oEnd
public boolean oStart
public int type
```

### Constructors

```
Element()
Element()
```

### Methods

```
public AttributeList getAttribute(String
name)
public AttributeList getAttributeByValue(
String name)
public AttributeList getAttributes()
```

```
public ContentModel getContent()
public int getIndex()
public String getName()
public int getType()
public boolean isEmpty()
public static int name2type(String nm)
public boolean omitEnd()
public boolean omitStart()
public String toString()
```

## ElementIterator

```
public class javax.swing.text.
ElementIterator
implements java.lang.Cloneable
extends java.lang.Object
```

### Constructors

```
public  ElementIterator(Document
document)
public  ElementIterator(Element root)
```

### Methods

```
public synchronized Object clone()
public Element current()
public int depth()
public Element first()
public Element next()
public Element previous()
```

## Ellipse2D

```
public abstract class java.awt.geom.
Ellipse2D
extends java.awt.geom.RectangularShape
extends java.lang.Object
```

### Constructors

```
protected  Ellipse2D()
```

### Methods

```
public boolean contains(double x,double
y)
public boolean contains(double x,double
y,double w,double h)
public PathIterator getPathIterator(
AffineTransform at)
public boolean intersects(double x,
double y,double w,double h)
```

## EmptyBorder

```
public class javax.swing.border.
EmptyBorder
implements java.io.Serializable
extends javax.swing.border.
AbstractBorder
extends java.lang.Object
```

### Fields

```
protected int left
```

### Constructors

```
public  EmptyBorder(int top,int left,int
bottom,int right)
public  EmptyBorder(Insets insets)
```

## Methods
```
public Insets getBorderInsets(Component
c)
public Insets getBorderInsets(Component
c,Insets insets)
public boolean isBorderOpaque()
public void paintBorder(Component c,
Graphics g,int x,int y,int width,int
height)
```

# EmptyStackException
```
public class java.util.
EmptyStackException
extends java.lang.RuntimeException
extends java.lang.Exception
extends java.lang.Throwable
extends java.lang.Object
```

## Constructors
```
public EmptyStackException()
```

# EncodedKeySpec
```
public abstract class java.security.spec.
EncodedKeySpec
implements java.security.spec.KeySpec
extends java.lang.Object
```

## Constructors
```
public EncodedKeySpec(byte encodedKey)
```

## Methods
```
public byte getEncoded()
public abstract String getFormat()
```

# Entity
```
public final class javax.swing.text.html.
parser.Entity
implements javax.swing.text.html.parser.
DTDConstants
extends java.lang.Object
```

## Fields
```
public char data
public java.lang.String name
public int type
```

## Constructors
```
public Entity(String name,int type,char
data)
```

## Methods
```
public char getData()
public String getName()
public String getString()
public int getType()
public boolean isGeneral()
public boolean isParameter()
public static int name2type(String nm)
```

# EOFException
```
public class java.io.EOFException
extends java.io.IOException
extends java.lang.Exception
```
```
extends java.lang.Throwable
extends java.lang.Object
```

## Constructors
```
public EOFException()
public EOFException(String s)
```

# Error
```
public class java.lang.Error
extends java.lang.Throwable
extends java.lang.Object
```

## Constructors
```
public Error()
public Error(String s)
```

# EtchedBorder
```
public class javax.swing.border.
EtchedBorder
extends javax.swing.border.
AbstractBorder
extends java.lang.Object
```

## Fields
```
protected int etchType
protected java.awt.Color highlight
public final static int LOWERED
public final static int RAISED
protected java.awt.Color shadow
```

## Constructors
```
public EtchedBorder()
public EtchedBorder(int etchType)
public EtchedBorder(Color highlight,
Color shadow)
public EtchedBorder(int etchType,Color
highlight,Color shadow)
```

## Methods
```
public Insets getBorderInsets(Component
c)
public Insets getBorderInsets(Component
c,Insets insets)
public int getEtchType()
public Color getHighlightColor(Component
c)
public Color getShadowColor(Component c)
public boolean isBorderOpaque()
public void paintBorder(Component c,
Graphics g,int x,int y,int width,int
height)
```

# Event
```
public class java.awt.Event
implements java.io.Serializable
extends java.lang.Object
```

## Fields
```
public final static int ACTION_EVENT
public final static int ALT_MASK
public java.lang.Object arg
public final static int BACK_SPACE
public final static int CAPS_LOCK
```

public int clickCount
public final static int CTRL_MASK
public final static int DELETE
public final static int DOWN
public final static int END
public final static int ENTER
public final static int ESCAPE
public java.awt.Event evt
public final static int F1
public final static int F10
public final static int F11
public final static int F12
public final static int F2
public final static int F3
public final static int F4
public final static int F5
public final static int F6
public final static int F7
public final static int F8
public final static int F9
public final static int GOT_FOCUS
public final static int HOME
public int id
public final static int INSERT
public int key
public final static int KEY_ACTION
public final static int KEY_ACTION_
RELEASE
public final static int KEY_PRESS
public final static int KEY_RELEASE
public final static int LEFT
public final static int LIST_DESELECT
public final static int LIST_SELECT
public final static int LOAD_FILE
public final static int LOST_FOCUS
public final static int META_MASK
public int modifiers
public final static int MOUSE_DOWN
public final static int MOUSE_DRAG
public final static int MOUSE_ENTER
public final static int MOUSE_EXIT
public final static int MOUSE_MOVE
public final static int MOUSE_UP
public final static int NUM_LOCK
public final static int PAUSE
public final static int PGDN
public final static int PGUP
public final static int PRINT_SCREEN
public final static int RIGHT
public final static int SAVE_FILE
public final static int SCROLL_ABSOLUTE
public final static int SCROLL_BEGIN
public final static int SCROLL_END
public final static int SCROLL_LINE_
DOWN
public final static int SCROLL_LINE_UP
public final static int SCROLL_LOCK
public final static int SCROLL_PAGE_
DOWN
public final static int SCROLL_PAGE_UP
public final static int SHIFT_MASK
public final static int TAB
public java.lang.Object target
public final static int UP

public long when
public final static int WINDOW_
DEICONIFY
public final static int WINDOW_DESTROY
public final static int WINDOW_EXPOSE
public final static int WINDOW_ICONIFY
public final static int WINDOW_MOVED
public int x
public int y

### Constructors

public  Event(Object target,long when,
int id,int y,int y,int key,int modifiers,
Object arg)
public  Event(Object target,long when,
int id,int x,int y,int key,int modifiers)
public  Event(Object target,int id,
Object arg)

### Methods

public boolean controlDown()
public boolean metaDown()
protected String paramString()
public boolean shiftDown()
public String toString()
public void translate(int x,int y)

## EventListenerList

public class javax.swing.event.
EventListenerList
implements java.io.Serializable
extends java.lang.Object

### Fields

protected transient java.lang.Object
listenerList

### Methods

public synchronized void add(Class t,
EventListener l)
public int getListenerCount()
public int getListenerCount(Class t)
public Object getListenerList()
public synchronized void remove(Class t,
EventListener l)
public String toString()

## EventObject

public class java.util.EventObject
implements java.io.Serializable
extends java.lang.Object

### Fields

protected transient java.lang.Object
source

### Constructors

public  EventObject(Object source)

### Methods

public Object getSource()
public String toString()

## EventQueue
```
public class java.awt.EventQueue
extends java.lang.Object
```

**Constructors**
```
public  EventQueue()
```

**Methods**
```
protected void dispatchEvent(AWTEvent
event)
public synchronized AWTEvent
getNextEvent()
public static void invokeAndWait(
Runnable runnable)
public static void invokeLater(Runnable
runnable)
public static boolean isDispatchThread()
public synchronized AWTEvent peekEvent()
public synchronized AWTEvent peekEvent(
int id)
protected void pop()
public synchronized void postEvent(
AWTEvent theEvent)
public synchronized void push(EventQueue
newEventQueue)
```

## EventSetDescriptor
```
public class java.beans.
EventSetDescriptor
extends java.beans.FeatureDescriptor
extends java.lang.Object
```

**Constructors**
```
public  EventSetDescriptor(Class
sourceClass,String eventSetName,Class
listenerType,String listenerMethodName)
public  EventSetDescriptor(Class
sourceClass,String eventSetName,Class
listenerType,String listenerMethodNames,
String addListenerMethodName,String
removeListenerMethodName)
public  EventSetDescriptor(String
eventSetName,Class listenerType,Method
listenerMethods,Method addListenerMethod,
Method removeListenerMethod)
public  EventSetDescriptor(String
eventSetName,Class listenerType,
MethodDescriptor
listenerMethodDescriptors,Method
addListenerMethod,Method
removeListenerMethod)
 EventSetDescriptor()
 EventSetDescriptor()
```

**Methods**
```
public Method getAddListenerMethod()
public MethodDescriptor
getListenerMethodDescriptors()
public Method getListenerMethods()
public Class getListenerType()
public Method getRemoveListenerMethod()
public boolean isInDefaultEventSet()
public boolean isUnicast()
```

```
public void setInDefaultEventSet(boolean
inDefaultEventSet)
public void setUnicast(boolean unicast)
```

## Exception
```
public class java.lang.Exception
extends java.lang.Throwable
extends java.lang.Object
```

**Constructors**
```
public  Exception()
public  Exception(String s)
```

## ExceptionInInitializerError
```
public class java.lang.
ExceptionInInitializerError
extends java.lang.LinkageError
extends java.lang.Error
extends java.lang.Throwable
extends java.lang.Object
```

**Constructors**
```
public  ExceptionInInitializerError()
public  ExceptionInInitializerError(
Throwable thrown)
public  ExceptionInInitializerError(
String s)
```

**Methods**
```
public Throwable getException()
public void printStackTrace()
public void printStackTrace(PrintStream
ps)
public void printStackTrace(PrintWriter
pw)
```

## ExpandVetoException
```
public class javax.swing.tree.
ExpandVetoException
extends java.lang.Exception
extends java.lang.Throwable
extends java.lang.Object
```

**Fields**
```
protected javax.swing.event.
TreeExpansionEvent event
```

**Constructors**
```
public  ExpandVetoException(
TreeExpansionEvent event)
public  ExpandVetoException(
TreeExpansionEvent event,String message)
```

## ExportException
```
public class java.rmi.server.
ExportException
extends java.rmi.RemoteException
extends java.io.IOException
extends java.lang.Exception
extends java.lang.Throwable
extends java.lang.Object
```

## Constructors

```
public  ExportException(String s)
public  ExportException(String s,
Exception ex)
```

# FeatureDescriptor

```
public class java.beans.
FeatureDescriptor
extends java.lang.Object
```

## Constructors

```
public  FeatureDescriptor()
 FeatureDescriptor()
 FeatureDescriptor()
```

## Methods

```
public Enumeration attributeNames()
public String getDisplayName()
public String getName()
public String getShortDescription()
public Object getValue(String
attributeName)
public boolean isExpert()
public boolean isHidden()
public boolean isPreferred()
public void setDisplayName(String
displayName)
public void setExpert(boolean expert)
public void setHidden(boolean hidden)
public void setName(String name)
public void setPreferred(boolean
preferred)
public void setShortDescription(String
text)
public void setValue(String
attributeName,Object value)
```

# Field

```
public final class java.lang.reflect.
Field
implements java.lang.reflect.Member
extends java.lang.reflect.
AccessibleObject
extends java.lang.Object
```

## Constructors

```
private  Field()
```

## Methods

```
public boolean equals(Object obj)
public native Object get(Object obj)
public native boolean getBoolean(Object
obj)
public native byte getByte(Object obj)
public native char getChar(Object obj)
public Class getDeclaringClass()
public native double getDouble(Object
obj)
public native float getFloat(Object obj)
public native int getInt(Object obj)
public native long getLong(Object obj)
public int getModifiers()
public String getName()
```

```
public native short getShort(Object obj)
public Class getType()
public int hashCode()
public native void set(Object obj,Object
value)
public native void setBoolean(Object obj,
boolean z)
public native void setByte(Object obj,
byte b)
public native void setChar(Object obj,
char c)
public native void setDouble(Object obj,
double d)
public native void setFloat(Object obj,
float f)
public native void setInt(Object obj,int
i)
public native void setLong(Object obj,
long l)
public native void setShort(Object obj,
short s)
public String toString()
```

# FieldPosition

```
public class java.text.FieldPosition
extends java.lang.Object
```

## Constructors

```
public  FieldPosition(int field)
```

## Methods

```
public boolean equals(Object obj)
public int getBeginIndex()
public int getEndIndex()
public int getField()
public int hashCode()
public void setBeginIndex(int bi)
public void setEndIndex(int ei)
public String toString()
```

# FieldView

```
public class javax.swing.text.FieldView
extends javax.swing.text.PlainView
extends javax.swing.text.View
extends java.lang.Object
```

## Constructors

```
public  FieldView(Element elem)
```

## Methods

```
protected Shape adjustAllocation(Shape a)
protected FontMetrics getFontMetrics()
public float getPreferredSpan(int axis)
public int getResizeWeight(int axis)
public void insertUpdate(DocumentEvent
changes,Shape a,ViewFactory f)
public Shape modelToView(int pos,Shape a,
Bias b)
public void paint(Graphics g,Shape a)
public void removeUpdate(DocumentEvent
changes,Shape a,ViewFactory f)
public int viewToModel(float fx,float fy,
Shape a,Bias bias)
```

# File

```
public class java.io.File
implements java.lang.Comparable
implements java.io.Serializable
extends java.lang.Object
```

## Fields

```
public final static java.lang.String
pathSeparator
public final static char
pathSeparatorChar
public final static java.lang.String
separator
public final static char separatorChar
```

## Constructors

```
private  File()
public  File(String pathname)
public  File(String parent,String child)
public  File(File parent,String child)
```

## Methods

```
public boolean canRead()
public boolean canWrite()
public int compareTo(File pathname)
public int compareTo(Object o)
public boolean createNewFile()
public static File createTempFile(String
prefix,String suffix,File directory)
public static File createTempFile(String
prefix,String suffix)
public boolean delete()
public void deleteOnExit()
public boolean equals(Object obj)
public boolean exists()
public File getAbsoluteFile()
public String getAbsolutePath()
public File getCanonicalFile()
public String getCanonicalPath()
public String getName()
public String getParent()
public File getParentFile()
public String getPath()
public int hashCode()
public boolean isAbsolute()
public boolean isDirectory()
public boolean isFile()
public boolean isHidden()
public long lastModified()
public long length()
public String list()
public String list(FilenameFilter filter)
public File listFiles()
public File listFiles(FilenameFilter
filter)
public File listFiles(FileFilter filter)
public static File listRoots()
public boolean mkdir()
public boolean mkdirs()
public boolean renameTo(File dest)
public boolean setLastModified(long time)
public boolean setReadOnly()
public String toString()
public URL toURL()
```

# FileChooserUI

```
public abstract class javax.swing.plaf.
FileChooserUI
extends javax.swing.plaf.ComponentUI
extends java.lang.Object
```

## Methods

```
public abstract void ensureFileIsVisible(
JFileChooser fc,File f)
public abstract FileFilter
getAcceptAllFileFilter(JFileChooser fc)
public abstract String
getApproveButtonText(JFileChooser fc)
public abstract String getDialogTitle(
JFileChooser fc)
public abstract FileView getFileView(
JFileChooser fc)
public abstract void
rescanCurrentDirectory(JFileChooser fc)
```

# FileDescriptor

```
public final class java.io.
FileDescriptor
extends java.lang.Object
```

## Fields

```
public final static java.io.
FileDescriptor err
public final static java.io.
FileDescriptor in
public final static java.io.
FileDescriptor out
```

## Constructors

```
public  FileDescriptor(int fd)
```

## Methods

```
public native void sync()
public boolean valid()
```

# FileDialog

```
public class java.awt.FileDialog
extends java.awt.Dialog
extends java.awt.Window
extends java.awt.Container
extends java.awt.Component
extends java.lang.Object
```

## Fields

```
public final static int LOAD
public final static int SAVE
```

## Constructors

```
public  FileDialog(Frame parent)
public  FileDialog(Frame parent,String
title)
public  FileDialog(Frame parent,String
title,int mode)
```

## Methods

```
public void addNotify()
public String getDirectory()
public String getFile()
```

```
public FilenameFilter getFilenameFilter()
public int getMode()
protected String paramString()
public void setDirectory(String dir)
public void setFile(String file)
public synchronized void
setFilenameFilter(FilenameFilter filter)
public void setMode(int mode)
```

## FileFilter
```
public abstract class javax.swing.
filechooser.FileFilter
extends java.lang.Object
```

### Methods
```
public abstract boolean accept(File f)
public abstract String getDescription()
```

## FileInputStream
```
public class java.io.FileInputStream
extends java.io.InputStream
extends java.lang.Object
```

### Constructors
```
public  FileInputStream(String name)
public  FileInputStream(File file)
public  FileInputStream(FileDescriptor
fdObj)
```

### Methods
```
public native int available()
public native void close()
protected static void finalize()
public final FileDescriptor getFD()
public native int read()
public int read(byte b)
public int read(byte b,int off,int len)
public native long skip(long n)
```

## FileNotFoundException
```
public class java.io.
FileNotFoundException
extends java.io.IOException
extends java.lang.Exception
extends java.lang.Throwable
extends java.lang.Object
```

### Constructors
```
public  FileNotFoundException()
public  FileNotFoundException(String s)
private  FileNotFoundException()
```

## FileOutputStream
```
public class java.io.FileOutputStream
extends java.io.OutputStream
extends java.lang.Object
```

### Constructors
```
public  FileOutputStream(String name)
public  FileOutputStream(String name,
boolean append)
```

```
public  FileOutputStream(File file)
public  FileOutputStream(FileDescriptor
fdObj)
```

### Methods
```
public native void close()
protected void finalize()
public final FileDescriptor getFD()
public native void write(int b)
public void write(byte b)
public void write(byte b,int off,int len)
```

## FilePermission
```
public final class java.io.
FilePermission
implements java.io.Serializable
extends java.security.Permission
extends java.lang.Object
```

### Constructors
```
public  FilePermission(String path,
String actions)
 FilePermission()
```

### Methods
```
public boolean equals(Object obj)
public String getActions()
public int hashCode()
public boolean implies(Permission p)
public PermissionCollection
newPermissionCollection()
```

## FileReader
```
public class java.io.FileReader
extends java.io.InputStreamReader
extends java.io.Reader
extends java.lang.Object
```

### Constructors
```
public  FileReader(String fileName)
public  FileReader(File file)
public  FileReader(FileDescriptor fd)
```

## FileSystemView
```
public abstract class javax.swing.
filechooser.FileSystemView
extends java.lang.Object
```

### Methods
```
public File createFileObject(File dir,
String filename)
public File createFileObject(String path)
public abstract File createNewFolder(
File containingDir)
public File getFiles(File dir,boolean
useFileHiding)
public static FileSystemView
getFileSystemView()
public File getHomeDirectory()
public File getParentDirectory(File dir)
public abstract File getRoots()
```

```
public abstract boolean isHiddenFile(
File f)
public abstract boolean isRoot(File f)
```

## FileView

```
public abstract class javax.swing.
filechooser.FileView
extends java.lang.Object
```

### Methods

```
public abstract String getDescription(
File f)
public abstract Icon getIcon(File f)
public abstract String getName(File f)
public abstract String
getTypeDescription(File f)
public abstract Boolean isTraversable(
File f)
```

## FileWriter

```
public class java.io.FileWriter
extends java.io.OutputStreamWriter
extends java.io.Writer
extends java.lang.Object
```

### Constructors

```
public  FileWriter(String fileName)
public  FileWriter(String fileName,
boolean append)
public  FileWriter(File file)
public  FileWriter(FileDescriptor fd)
```

## FilteredImageSource

```
public class java.awt.image.
FilteredImageSource
implements java.awt.image.ImageProducer
extends java.lang.Object
```

### Constructors

```
public  FilteredImageSource(
ImageProducer orig,ImageFilter imgf)
```

### Methods

```
public synchronized void addConsumer(
ImageConsumer ic)
public synchronized boolean isConsumer(
ImageConsumer ic)
public synchronized void removeConsumer(
ImageConsumer ic)
public void
requestTopDownLeftRightResend(
ImageConsumer ic)
public void startProduction(
ImageConsumer ic)
```

## FilterInputStream

```
public class java.io.FilterInputStream
extends java.io.InputStream
extends java.lang.Object
```

### Fields

```
protected java.io.InputStream in
```

### Constructors

```
protected  FilterInputStream(InputStream
in)
```

### Methods

```
public int available()
public void close()
public synchronized void mark(int
readlimit)
public boolean markSupported()
public int read()
public int read(byte b)
public int read(byte b,int off,int len)
public synchronized void reset()
public long skip(long n)
```

## FilterOutputStream

```
public class java.io.FilterOutputStream
extends java.io.OutputStream
extends java.lang.Object
```

### Fields

```
protected java.io.OutputStream out
```

### Constructors

```
public  FilterOutputStream(OutputStream
out)
```

### Methods

```
public void close()
public void flush()
public void write(int b)
public void write(byte b)
public void write(byte b,int off,int len)
```

## FilterReader

```
public abstract class java.io.
FilterReader
extends java.io.Reader
extends java.lang.Object
```

### Fields

```
protected java.io.Reader in
```

### Constructors

```
protected  FilterReader(Reader in)
```

### Methods

```
public void close()
public void mark(int readAheadLimit)
public boolean markSupported()
public int read()
public int read(char cbuf,int off,int
len)
public boolean ready()
public void reset()
public long skip(long n)
```

## FilterWriter

```
public abstract class java.io.
FilterWriter
extends java.io.Writer
extends java.lang.Object
```

**Fields**
```
protected java.io.Writer out
```

**Constructors**
```
protected  FilterWriter(Writer out)
```

**Methods**
```
public void close()
public void flush()
public void write(int c)
public void write(char cbuf,int off,int
len)
public void write(String str,int off,int
len)
```

# FixedHeightLayoutCache
```
public class javax.swing.tree.
FixedHeightLayoutCache
extends javax.swing.tree.
AbstractLayoutCache
extends java.lang.Object
```

**Constructors**
```
public  FixedHeightLayoutCache()
```

**Methods**
```
public Rectangle getBounds(TreePath path,
Rectangle placeIn)
public boolean getExpandedState(TreePath
path)
public TreePath getPathClosestTo(int x,
int y)
public TreePath getPathForRow(int row)
public int getRowCount()
public int getRowForPath(TreePath path)
public int getVisibleChildCount(TreePath
path)
public Enumeration getVisiblePathsFrom(
TreePath path)
public void invalidatePathBounds(
TreePath path)
public void invalidateSizes()
public boolean isExpanded(TreePath path)
public void setExpandedState(TreePath
path,boolean isExpanded)
public void setModel(TreeModel newModel)
public void setRootVisible(boolean
rootVisible)
public void setRowHeight(int rowHeight)
public void treeNodesChanged(
TreeModelEvent e)
public void treeNodesInserted(
TreeModelEvent e)
public void treeNodesRemoved(
TreeModelEvent e)
public void treeStructureChanged(
TreeModelEvent e)
```

# FlatteningPathIterator
```
public class java.awt.geom.
FlatteningPathIterator
implements java.awt.geom.PathIterator
extends java.lang.Object
```

**Constructors**
```
public  FlatteningPathIterator(
PathIterator src,double flatness)
public  FlatteningPathIterator(
PathIterator src,double flatness,int
limit)
```

**Methods**
```
public int currentSegment(float coords)
public int currentSegment(double coords)
public double getFlatness()
public int getRecursionLimit()
public int getWindingRule()
public boolean isDone()
public void next()
```

# Float
```
public final class java.lang.Float
implements java.lang.Comparable
extends java.lang.Number
extends java.lang.Object
```

**Fields**
```
public final static float MAX_VALUE
public final static float MIN_VALUE
public final static float NaN
public final static float NEGATIVE_
INFINITY
public final static float POSITIVE_
INFINITY
public final static java.lang.Class
TYPE
```

**Constructors**
```
public  Float(float value)
public  Float(double value)
public  Float(String s)
```

**Methods**
```
public byte byteValue()
public int compareTo(Float anotherFloat)
public int compareTo(Object o)
public double doubleValue()
public boolean equals(Object obj)
public static native int floatToIntBits(
float value)
public float floatValue()
public int hashCode()
public static native float
intBitsToFloat(int bits)
public int intValue()
public static boolean isInfinite(float v)
public boolean isInfinite()
public static boolean isNaN(float v)
public boolean isNaN()
public long longValue()
public static float parseFloat(String s)
public short shortValue()
public static String toString(float f)
public String toString()
public static Float valueOf(String s)
```

## FlowLayout

```
public class java.awt.FlowLayout
implements java.awt.LayoutManager
implements java.io.Serializable
extends java.lang.Object
```

### Fields

```
public final static int CENTER
public final static int LEADING
public final static int LEFT
public final static int RIGHT
public final static int TRAILING
```

### Constructors

```
public  FlowLayout()
public  FlowLayout(int align)
public  FlowLayout(int align,int hgap,
int vgap)
```

### Methods

```
public void addLayoutComponent(String
name,Component comp)
public int getAlignment()
public int getHgap()
public int getVgap()
public void layoutContainer(Container
target)
public Dimension minimumLayoutSize(
Container target)
public Dimension preferredLayoutSize(
Container target)
public void removeLayoutComponent(
Component comp)
public void setAlignment(int align)
public void setHgap(int hgap)
public void setVgap(int vgap)
public String toString()
```

## FocusAdapter

```
public abstract class java.awt.event.
FocusAdapter
implements java.awt.event.FocusListener
extends java.lang.Object
```

### Methods

```
public void focusGained(FocusEvent e)
public void focusLost(FocusEvent e)
```

## FocusEvent

```
public class java.awt.event.FocusEvent
extends java.awt.event.ComponentEvent
extends java.awt.AWTEvent
extends java.util.EventObject
extends java.lang.Object
```

### Fields

```
public final static int FOCUS_FIRST
public final static int FOCUS_GAINED
public final static int FOCUS_LAST
public final static int FOCUS_LOST
```

### Constructors

```
public  FocusEvent(Component source,int
id,boolean temporary)
public  FocusEvent(Component source,int
id)
```

### Methods

```
public boolean isTemporary()
public String paramString()
```

## FocusManager

```
public abstract class javax.swing.
FocusManager
extends java.lang.Object
```

### Fields

```
public final static java.lang.String
FOCUS_MANAGER_CLASS_PROPERTY
```

### Methods

```
public static void
disableSwingFocusManager()
public abstract void focusNextComponent(
Component aComponent)
public abstract void
focusPreviousComponent(Component
aComponent)
public static FocusManager
getCurrentManager()
public static boolean
isFocusManagerEnabled()
public abstract void processKeyEvent(
Component focusedComponent,KeyEvent
anEvent)
public static void setCurrentManager(
FocusManager aFocusManager)
```

## Font

```
public class java.awt.Font
implements java.io.Serializable
extends java.lang.Object
```

### Fields

```
public final static int BOLD
public final static int CENTER_BASELINE
public final static int HANGING_
BASELINE
public final static int ITALIC
protected java.lang.String name
public final static int PLAIN
protected float pointSize
public final static int ROMAN_BASELINE
protected int size
protected int style
```

### Constructors

```
public  Font(String name,int style,int
size)
private  Font()
public  Font(Map attributes)
```

## Methods
```
public boolean canDisplay(char c)
public int canDisplayUpTo(String str)
public int canDisplayUpTo(char text,int
start,int limit)
public int canDisplayUpTo(
CharacterIterator iter,int start,int
limit)
public GlyphVector createGlyphVector(
FontRenderContext frc,String str)
public GlyphVector createGlyphVector(
FontRenderContext frc,char chars)
public GlyphVector createGlyphVector(
FontRenderContext frc,CharacterIterator
ci)
public GlyphVector createGlyphVector(
FontRenderContext frc,int glyphCodes)
public static Font decode(String str)
public Font deriveFont(int style,float
size)
public Font deriveFont(int style,
AffineTransform trans)
public Font deriveFont(float size)
public Font deriveFont(AffineTransform
trans)
public Font deriveFont(int style)
public Font deriveFont(Map attributes)
public boolean equals(Object obj)
protected void finalize()
public Map getAttributes()
public Attribute getAvailableAttributes()
public byte getBaselineFor(char c)
public String getFamily()
public String getFamily(Locale l)
public static Font getFont(Map
attributes)
public static Font getFont(String nm)
public static Font getFont(String nm,
Font font)
public String getFontName()
public String getFontName(Locale l)
public float getItalicAngle()
public LineMetrics getLineMetrics(String
str,FontRenderContext frc)
public LineMetrics getLineMetrics(String
str,int beginIndex,int limit,
FontRenderContext frc)
public LineMetrics getLineMetrics(char
chars,int beginIndex,int limit,
FontRenderContext frc)
public LineMetrics getLineMetrics(
CharacterIterator ci,int beginIndex,int
limit,FontRenderContext frc)
public Rectangle2D getMaxCharBounds(
FontRenderContext frc)
public int getMissingGlyphCode()
public String getName()
public int getNumGlyphs()
public FontPeer getPeer()
public String getPSName()
public int getSize()
public float getSize2D()
public Rectangle2D getStringBounds(
String str,FontRenderContext frc)
```

```
public Rectangle2D getStringBounds(
String str,int beginIndex,int limit,
FontRenderContext frc)
public Rectangle2D getStringBounds(char
chars,int beginIndex,int limit,
FontRenderContext frc)
public Rectangle2D getStringBounds(
CharacterIterator ci,int beginIndex,int
limit,FontRenderContext frc)
public int getStyle()
public AffineTransform getTransform()
public int hashCode()
public boolean hasUniformLineMetrics()
public boolean isBold()
public boolean isItalic()
public boolean isPlain()
public String toString()
```

# FontMetrics
```
public abstract class java.awt.
FontMetrics
implements java.io.Serializable
extends java.lang.Object
```

### Fields
```
protected static java.awt.Font font
```

### Constructors
```
protected  FontMetrics(Font font)
```

### Methods
```
public int bytesWidth(byte data,int off,
int len)
public int charsWidth(char data,int off,
int len)
public int charWidth(int ch)
public int charWidth(char ch)
public int getAscent()
public int getDescent()
public Font getFont()
public int getHeight()
public int getLeading()
public LineMetrics getLineMetrics(String
str,Graphics context)
public LineMetrics getLineMetrics(String
str,int beginIndex,int limit,Graphics
context)
public LineMetrics getLineMetrics(char
chars,int beginIndex,int limit,Graphics
context)
public LineMetrics getLineMetrics(
CharacterIterator ci,int beginIndex,int
limit,Graphics context)
public int getMaxAdvance()
public int getMaxAscent()
public Rectangle2D getMaxCharBounds(
Graphics context)
public int getMaxDecent()
public int getMaxDescent()
public Rectangle2D getStringBounds(
String str,Graphics context)
public Rectangle2D getStringBounds(
String str,int beginIndex,int limit,
Graphics context)
```

public Rectangle2D getStringBounds(char chars,int beginIndex,int limit,Graphics context)
public Rectangle2D getStringBounds( CharacterIterator ci,int beginIndex,int limit,Graphics context)
public int getWidths()
public boolean hasUniformLineMetrics()
public int stringWidth(String str)
public String toString()

## FontRenderContext
public class java.awt.font. FontRenderContext
extends java.lang.Object

### Constructors
protected  FontRenderContext()
public  FontRenderContext( AffineTransform tx,boolean isAntiAliased, boolean usesFractionalMetrics)

### Methods
public AffineTransform getTransform()
public boolean isAntiAliased()
public boolean usesFractionalMetrics()

## FontUIResource
public class javax.swing.plaf. FontUIResource
implements javax.swing.plaf.UIResource
extends java.awt.Font
extends java.lang.Object

### Constructors
public  FontUIResource(String name,int style,int size)
public  FontUIResource(Font font)

## Format
public abstract class java.text.Format
implements java.lang.Cloneable
implements java.io.Serializable
extends java.lang.Object

### Methods
public Object clone()
public final String format(Object obj)
public abstract StringBuffer format( Object obj,StringBuffer toAppendTo, FieldPosition pos)
public abstract Object parseObject( String source,ParsePosition status)
public Object parseObject(String source)

## FormView
public class javax.swing.text.html. FormView
implements java.awt.event. ActionListener
extends javax.swing.text.ComponentView
extends javax.swing.text.View
extends java.lang.Object

### Fields
public final static java.lang.String RESET
public final static java.lang.String SUBMIT

### Constructors
public  FormView(Element elem)

### Methods
public void actionPerformed(ActionEvent evt)
protected Component createComponent()
protected void imageSubmit(String imageData)
protected void submitData(String data)

## Frame
public class java.awt.Frame
implements java.awt.MenuContainer
extends java.awt.Window
extends java.awt.Container
extends java.awt.Component
extends java.lang.Object

### Fields
public final static int CROSSHAIR_ CURSOR
public final static int DEFAULT_CURSOR
public final static int E_RESIZE_CURSOR
public final static int HAND_CURSOR
public final static int ICONIFIED
public final static int MOVE_CURSOR
public final static int NE_RESIZE_ CURSOR
public final static int NORMAL
public final static int NW_RESIZE_ CURSOR
public final static int N_RESIZE_CURSOR
public final static int SE_RESIZE_ CURSOR
public final static int SW_RESIZE_ CURSOR
public final static int S_RESIZE_CURSOR
public final static int TEXT_CURSOR
public final static int WAIT_CURSOR
public final static int W_RESIZE_CURSOR

### Constructors
public static  Frame()
public  Frame(String title)

### Methods
public void addNotify()
protected void finalize()
public int getCursorType()
public static Frame getFrames()
public Image getIconImage()
public MenuBar getMenuBar()
public synchronized int getState()
public String getTitle()
public boolean isResizable()
protected String paramString()
public void remove(MenuComponent m)

public void removeNotify()
public synchronized void setCursor(int cursorType)
public synchronized void setIconImage(Image image)
public void setMenuBar(MenuBar mb)
public void setResizable(boolean resizable)
public synchronized void setState(int state)
public synchronized void setTitle(String title)

## GapContent

public class javax.swing.text.
GapContent
implements AbstractDocument.Content
implements java.io.Serializable
extends java.lang.Object

### Constructors
public  GapContent()
public  GapContent(int initialLength)

### Methods
protected Object allocateArray(int len)
public Position createPosition(int offset)
protected int getArrayLength()
public void getChars(int where,int len, Segment chars)
protected Vector getPositionsInRange( Vector v,int offset,int length)
public String getString(int where,int len)
public UndoableEdit insertString(int where,String str)
public int length()
public UndoableEdit remove(int where,int nitems)
protected void resetMarksAtZero()
protected void shiftEnd(int newSize)
protected void shiftGap(int newGapStart)
protected void shiftGapEndUp(int newGapEnd)
protected void shiftGapStartDown(int newGapStart)
protected void updateUndoPositions( Vector positions,int offset,int length)

## GeneralPath

public final class java.awt.geom.
GeneralPath
implements java.lang.Cloneable
implements java.awt.Shape
extends java.lang.Object

### Fields
public final static int WIND_EVEN_ODD
public final static int WIND_NON_ZERO

### Constructors
public  GeneralPath()
public  GeneralPath(int rule)

public  GeneralPath(int rule,int initialCapacity)
 GeneralPath()
public  GeneralPath(Shape s)

### Methods
public void append(Shape s,boolean connect)
public void append(PathIterator pi, boolean connect)
public Object clone()
public synchronized void closePath()
public boolean contains(double x,double y)
public boolean contains(Point2D p)
public boolean contains(double x,double y,double w,double h)
public boolean contains(Rectangle2D r)
public synchronized Shape createTransformedShape(AffineTransform at)
public synchronized void curveTo(float x1,float y1,float x2,float y2,float x3, float y3)
public Rectangle getBounds()
public synchronized Rectangle2D getBounds2D()
public synchronized Point2D getCurrentPoint()
public PathIterator getPathIterator( AffineTransform at)
public PathIterator getPathIterator( AffineTransform at,double flatness)
public synchronized int getWindingRule()
public boolean intersects(double x, double y,double w,double h)
public boolean intersects(Rectangle2D r)
public synchronized void lineTo(float x, float y)
public synchronized void moveTo(float x, float y)
public synchronized void quadTo(float x1, float y1,float x2,float y2)
public synchronized void reset()
public void setWindingRule(int rule)
public void transform(AffineTransform at)

## GeneralSecurityException

public class java.security.
GeneralSecurityException
extends java.lang.Exception
extends java.lang.Throwable
extends java.lang.Object

### Constructors
public  GeneralSecurityException()
public  GeneralSecurityException(String msg)

## GlyphJustificationInfo

public final class java.awt.font.
GlyphJustificationInfo
extends java.lang.Object

## Fields
```
public final boolean growAbsorb
public final float growLeftLimit
public final int growPriority
public final float growRightLimit
public final static int PRIORITY_
INTERCHAR
public final static int PRIORITY_
KASHIDA
public final static int PRIORITY_NONE
public final static int PRIORITY_
WHITESPACE
public final boolean shrinkAbsorb
public final float shrinkLeftLimit
public final int shrinkPriority
public final float shrinkRightLimit
public final float weight
```

## Constructors
```
public  GlyphJustificationInfo(float
weight,boolean growAbsorb,int
growPriority,float growLeftLimit,float
growRightLimit,boolean shrinkAbsorb,int
shrinkPriority,float shrinkLeftLimit,
float shrinkRightLimit)
```

# GlyphMetrics
```
public final class java.awt.font.
GlyphMetrics
extends java.lang.Object
```

## Fields
```
public final static byte COMBINING
public final static byte COMPONENT
public final static byte LIGATURE
public final static byte STANDARD
public final static byte WHITESPACE
```

## Constructors
```
public  GlyphMetrics(float advance,
Rectangle2D bounds,byte glyphType)
```

## Methods
```
public float getAdvance()
public Rectangle2D getBounds2D()
public float getLSB()
public float getRSB()
public int getType()
public boolean isCombining()
public boolean isComponent()
public boolean isLigature()
public boolean isStandard()
public boolean isWhitespace()
```

# GlyphVector
```
public abstract class java.awt.font.
GlyphVector
implements java.lang.Cloneable
extends java.lang.Object
```

## Methods
```
public abstract boolean equals(
GlyphVector set)
```

```
public abstract Font getFont()
public abstract FontRenderContext
getFontRenderContext()
public abstract int getGlyphCode(int
glyphIndex)
public abstract int getGlyphCodes(int
beginGlyphIndex,int numEntries,int
codeReturn)
public abstract GlyphJustificationInfo
getGlyphJustificationInfo(int glyphIndex)
public abstract Shape
getGlyphLogicalBounds(int glyphIndex)
public abstract GlyphMetrics
getGlyphMetrics(int glyphIndex)
public abstract Shape getGlyphOutline(
int glyphIndex)
public abstract Point2D getGlyphPosition(
int glyphIndex)
public abstract float getGlyphPositions(
int beginGlyphIndex,int numEntries,float
positionReturn)
public abstract AffineTransform
getGlyphTransform(int glyphIndex)
public abstract Shape
getGlyphVisualBounds(int glyphIndex)
public abstract Rectangle2D
getLogicalBounds()
public abstract int getNumGlyphs()
public abstract Shape getOutline()
public abstract Shape getOutline(float x,
float y)
public abstract Rectangle2D
getVisualBounds()
public abstract void
performDefaultLayout()
public abstract void setGlyphPosition(
int glyphIndex,Point2D newPos)
public abstract void setGlyphTransform(
int glyphIndex,AffineTransform newTX)
```

# GradientPaint
```
public class java.awt.GradientPaint
implements java.awt.Paint
extends java.lang.Object
```

## Constructors
```
public  GradientPaint(float x1,float y1,
Color color1,float x2,float y2,Color
color2)
public  GradientPaint(Point2D pt1,Color
color1,Point2D pt2,Color color2)
public  GradientPaint(float x1,float y1,
Color color1,float x2,float y2,Color
color2,boolean cyclic)
public  GradientPaint(Point2D pt1,Color
color1,Point2D pt2,Color color2,boolean
cyclic)
```

## Methods
```
public PaintContext createContext(
ColorModel cm,Rectangle deviceBounds,
Rectangle2D userBounds,AffineTransform
xform,RenderingHints hints)
```

```
public Color getColor1()
public Color getColor2()
public Point2D getPoint1()
public Point2D getPoint2()
public int getTransparency()
public boolean isCyclic()
```

## GraphicAttribute

```
public abstract class java.awt.font.
GraphicAttribute
extends java.lang.Object
```

### Fields

```
public final static int BOTTOM_
ALIGNMENT
public final static int CENTER_BASELINE
public final static int HANGING_
BASELINE
public final static int ROMAN_BASELINE
public final static int TOP_ALIGNMENT
```

### Constructors

```
protected  GraphicAttribute(int
alignment)
```

### Methods

```
public abstract void draw(Graphics2D
graphics,float x,float y)
public abstract float getAdvance()
public final int getAlignment()
public abstract float getAscent()
public Rectangle2D getBounds()
public abstract float getDescent()
public GlyphJustificationInfo
getJustificationInfo()
```

## Graphics

```
public abstract class java.awt.Graphics
extends java.lang.Object
```

### Constructors

```
protected  Graphics()
```

### Methods

```
public abstract void clearRect(int x,int
y,int width,int height)
public abstract void clipRect(int x,int
y,int width,int height)
public abstract void copyArea(int x,int
y,int width,int height,int dx,int dy)
public abstract Graphics create()
public Graphics create(int x,int y,int
width,int height)
public abstract void dispose()
public void draw3DRect(int x,int y,int
width,int height,boolean raised)
public abstract void drawArc(int x,int y,
int width,int height,int startAngle,int
arcAngle)
public void drawBytes(byte data,int
offset,int length,int x,int y)
public void drawChars(char data,int
offset,int length,int x,int y)
```

```
public abstract boolean drawImage(Image
img,int x,int y,ImageObserver observer)
public abstract boolean drawImage(Image
img,int x,int y,int width,int height,
ImageObserver observer)
public abstract boolean drawImage(Image
img,int x,int y,Color bgcolor,
ImageObserver observer)
public abstract boolean drawImage(Image
img,int x,int y,int width,int height,
Color bgcolor,ImageObserver observer)
public abstract boolean drawImage(Image
img,int dx1,int dy1,int dx2,int dy2,int
sx1,int sy1,int sx2,int sy2,
ImageObserver observer)
public abstract boolean drawImage(Image
img,int dx1,int dy1,int dx2,int dy2,int
sx1,int sy1,int sx2,int sy2,Color
bgcolor,ImageObserver observer)
public abstract void drawLine(int x1,int
y1,int x2,int y2)
public abstract void drawOval(int x,int
y,int width,int height)
public abstract void drawPolygon(int
xPoints,int yPoints,int nPoints)
public void drawPolygon(Polygon p)
public abstract void drawPolyline(int
xPoints,int yPoints,int nPoints)
public void drawRect(int x,int y,int
width,int height)
public abstract void drawRoundRect(int x,
int y,int width,int height,int arcWidth,
int arcHeight)
public abstract void drawString(String
str,int x,int y)
public abstract void drawString(
AttributedCharacterIterator iterator,int
x,int y)
public void fill3DRect(int x,int y,int
width,int height,boolean raised)
public abstract void fillArc(int x,int y,
int width,int height,int startAngle,int
arcAngle)
public abstract void fillOval(int x,int
y,int width,int height)
public abstract void fillPolygon(int
xPoints,int yPoints,int nPoints)
public void fillPolygon(Polygon p)
public abstract void fillRect(int x,int
y,int width,int height)
public abstract void fillRoundRect(int x,
int y,int width,int height,int arcWidth,
int arcHeight)
public void finalize()
public abstract Shape getClip()
public abstract Rectangle getClipBounds()
public Rectangle getClipBounds(Rectangle
r)
public Rectangle getClipRect()
public abstract Color getColor()
public abstract Font getFont()
public FontMetrics getFontMetrics()
public abstract FontMetrics
getFontMetrics(Font f)
```

```
public boolean hitClip(int x,int y,int
width,int height)
public abstract void setClip(int x,int y,
int width,int height)
public abstract void setClip(Shape clip)
public abstract void setColor(Color c)
public abstract void setFont(Font font)
public abstract void setPaintMode()
public abstract void setXORMode(Color c1)
public String toString()
public abstract void translate(int x,int
y)
```

## Graphics2D

```
public abstract class java.awt.
Graphics2D
extends java.awt.Graphics
extends java.lang.Object
```

### Constructors

```
protected  Graphics2D()
```

### Methods

```
public abstract void addRenderingHints(
Map hints)
public abstract void clip(Shape s)
public abstract void draw(Shape s)
public void draw3DRect(int x,int y,int
width,int height,boolean raised)
public abstract void drawGlyphVector(
GlyphVector g,float x,float y)
public abstract boolean drawImage(Image
img,AffineTransform xform,ImageObserver
obs)
public abstract void drawImage(
BufferedImage img,BufferedImageOp op,int
x,int y)
public abstract void drawRenderableImage(
RenderableImage img,AffineTransform
xform)
public abstract void drawRenderedImage(
RenderedImage img,AffineTransform xform)
public abstract void drawString(String
str,int x,int y)
public abstract void drawString(String s,
float x,float y)
public abstract void drawString(
AttributedCharacterIterator iterator,int
x,int y)
public abstract void drawString(
AttributedCharacterIterator iterator,
float x,float y)
public abstract void fill(Shape s)
public void fill3DRect(int x,int y,int
width,int height,boolean raised)
public abstract Color getBackground()
public abstract Composite getComposite()
public abstract GraphicsConfiguration
getDeviceConfiguration()
public abstract FontRenderContext
getFontRenderContext()
public abstract Paint getPaint()
```

```
public abstract Object getRenderingHint(
Key hintKey)
public abstract RenderingHints
getRenderingHints()
public abstract Stroke getStroke()
public abstract AffineTransform
getTransform()
public abstract boolean hit(Rectangle
rect,Shape s,boolean onStroke)
public abstract void rotate(double theta)
public abstract void rotate(double theta,
double x,double y)
public abstract void scale(double sx,
double sy)
public abstract void setBackground(Color
color)
public abstract void setComposite(
Composite comp)
public abstract void setPaint(Paint
paint)
public abstract void setRenderingHint(
Key hintKey,Object hintValue)
public abstract void setRenderingHints(
Map hints)
public abstract void setStroke(Stroke s)
public abstract void setTransform(
AffineTransform Tx)
public abstract void shear(double shx,
double shy)
public abstract void transform(
AffineTransform Tx)
public abstract void translate(int x,int
y)
public abstract void translate(double tx,
double ty)
```

## GraphicsConfigTemplate

```
public abstract class java.awt.
GraphicsConfigTemplate
implements java.io.Serializable
extends java.lang.Object
```

### Fields

```
public final static int PREFERRED
public final static int REQUIRED
public final static int UNNECESSARY
```

### Constructors

```
public  GraphicsConfigTemplate()
```

### Methods

```
public abstract GraphicsConfiguration
getBestConfiguration(
GraphicsConfiguration gc)
public abstract boolean
isGraphicsConfigSupported(
GraphicsConfiguration gc)
```

## GraphicsConfiguration

```
public abstract class java.awt.
GraphicsConfiguration
extends java.lang.Object
```

## Constructors
```
protected  GraphicsConfiguration()
```

## Methods
```
public abstract BufferedImage
createCompatibleImage(int width,int
height)
public abstract BufferedImage
createCompatibleImage(int width,int
height,int transparency)
public abstract ColorModel getColorModel(
)
public abstract ColorModel getColorModel(
int transparency)
public abstract AffineTransform
getDefaultTransform()
public abstract GraphicsDevice getDevice(
)
public abstract AffineTransform
getNormalizingTransform()
```

# GraphicsDevice
```
public abstract class java.awt.
GraphicsDevice
extends java.lang.Object
```

## Fields
```
public final static int TYPE_IMAGE_
BUFFER
public final static int TYPE_PRINTER
public final static int TYPE_RASTER_
SCREEN
```

## Constructors
```
protected  GraphicsDevice()
```

## Methods
```
public GraphicsConfiguration
getBestConfiguration(
GraphicsConfigTemplate gct)
public abstract GraphicsConfiguration
getConfigurations()
public abstract GraphicsConfiguration
getDefaultConfiguration()
public abstract String getIDstring()
public abstract int getType()
```

# GraphicsEnvironment
```
public abstract class java.awt.
GraphicsEnvironment
extends java.lang.Object
```

## Constructors
```
protected  GraphicsEnvironment()
```

## Methods
```
public abstract Graphics2D
createGraphics(BufferedImage img)
public abstract Font getAllFonts()
public abstract String
getAvailableFontFamilyNames()
public abstract String
getAvailableFontFamilyNames(Locale l)
```

```
public abstract GraphicsDevice
getDefaultScreenDevice()
public static GraphicsEnvironment
getLocalGraphicsEnvironment()
public abstract GraphicsDevice
getScreenDevices()
```

# GrayFilter
```
public class javax.swing.GrayFilter
extends java.awt.image.RGBImageFilter
extends java.awt.image.ImageFilter
extends java.lang.Object
```

## Constructors
```
public  GrayFilter(boolean b,int p)
```

## Methods
```
public static Image createDisabledImage(
Image i)
public int filterRGB(int x,int y,int rgb)
```

# GregorianCalendar
```
public class java.util.
GregorianCalendar
extends java.util.Calendar
extends java.lang.Object
```

## Fields
```
public final static int AD
public final static int BC
```

## Constructors
```
public  GregorianCalendar()
public  GregorianCalendar(TimeZone zone)
public  GregorianCalendar(Locale aLocale)
public  GregorianCalendar(TimeZone zone,
Locale aLocale)
public  GregorianCalendar(int year,int
month,int date)
public  GregorianCalendar(int year,int
month,int date,int hour,int minute)
public  GregorianCalendar(int year,int
month,int date,int hour,int minute,int
second)
```

## Methods
```
public void add(int field,int amount)
protected void computeFields()
protected void computeTime()
public boolean equals(Object obj)
public int getActualMaximum(int field)
public int getActualMinimum(int field)
public int getGreatestMinimum(int field)
public final Date getGregorianChange()
public int getLeastMaximum(int field)
public int getMaximum(int field)
public int getMinimum(int field)
public int hashCode()
public boolean isLeapYear(int year)
public void roll(int field,boolean up)
public void roll(int field,int amount)
public void setGregorianChange(Date date)
```

# GridBagConstraints

public class java.awt.
GridBagConstraints
implements java.lang.Cloneable
implements java.io.Serializable
extends java.lang.Object

### Fields

public int anchor
public final static int BOTH
public final static int CENTER
public final static int EAST
public int fill
public int gridheight
public int gridwidth
public int gridx
public int gridy
public final static int HORIZONTAL
public java.awt.Insets insets
public int ipadx
public int ipady
public final static int NONE
public final static int NORTH
public final static int NORTHEAST
public final static int NORTHWEST
public final static int RELATIVE
public final static int REMAINDER
public final static int SOUTH
public final static int SOUTHEAST
public final static int SOUTHWEST
public final static int VERTICAL
public double weightx
public double weighty
public final static int WEST

### Constructors

public  GridBagConstraints()
public  GridBagConstraints(int gridx,int
gridy,int gridwidth,int gridheight,
double weightx,double weighty,int anchor,
int fill,Insets insets,int ipadx,int
ipady)

### Methods

public Object clone()

# GridBagLayout

public class java.awt.GridBagLayout
implements java.awt.LayoutManager2
implements java.io.Serializable
extends java.lang.Object

### Fields

public double columnWeights
public int columnWidths
protected java.util.Hashtable comptable
protected java.awt.GridBagConstraints
defaultConstraints
protected GridBagLayoutInfo layoutInfo
protected final static int MAXGRIDSIZE
protected final static int MINSIZE
protected final static int
PREFERREDSIZE

public int rowHeights
public double rowWeights

### Constructors

public  GridBagLayout()

### Methods

public void addLayoutComponent(String
name,Component comp)
public void addLayoutComponent(Component
comp,Object constraints)
protected void AdjustForGravity(
GridBagConstraints constraints,Rectangle
r)
protected void ArrangeGrid(Container
parent)
public GridBagConstraints getConstraints(
Component comp)
public float getLayoutAlignmentX(
Container parent)
public float getLayoutAlignmentY(
Container parent)
public int getLayoutDimensions()
protected GridBagLayoutInfo
GetLayoutInfo(Container parent,int
sizeflag)
public Point getLayoutOrigin()
public double getLayoutWeights()
protected Dimension GetMinSize(Container
parent,GridBagLayoutInfo info)
public void invalidateLayout(Container
target)
public void layoutContainer(Container
parent)
public Point location(int x,int y)
protected GridBagConstraints
lookupConstraints(Component comp)
public Dimension maximumLayoutSize(
Container target)
public Dimension minimumLayoutSize(
Container parent)
public Dimension preferredLayoutSize(
Container parent)
public void removeLayoutComponent(
Component comp)
public void setConstraints(Component
comp,GridBagConstraints constraints)
public String toString()

# GridLayout

public class java.awt.GridLayout
implements java.awt.LayoutManager
implements java.io.Serializable
extends java.lang.Object

### Constructors

public  GridLayout()
public  GridLayout(int rows,int cols)
public  GridLayout(int rows,int cols,int
hgap,int vgap)

## Methods
```
public void addLayoutComponent(String
name,Component comp)
public int getColumns()
public int getHgap()
public int getRows()
public int getVgap()
public void layoutContainer(Container
parent)
public Dimension minimumLayoutSize(
Container parent)
public Dimension preferredLayoutSize(
Container parent)
public void removeLayoutComponent(
Component comp)
public void setColumns(int cols)
public void setHgap(int hgap)
public void setRows(int rows)
public void setVgap(int vgap)
public String toString()
```

# GuardedObject
```
public class java.security.
GuardedObject
implements java.io.Serializable
extends java.lang.Object
```

## Constructors
```
public GuardedObject(Object object,
Guard guard)
```

## Methods
```
public Object getObject()
```

# GZIPInputStream
```
public class java.util.zip.
GZIPInputStream
extends java.util.zip.
InflaterInputStream
extends java.io.FilterInputStream
extends java.io.InputStream
extends java.lang.Object
```

## Fields
```
protected java.util.zip.CRC32 crc
protected boolean eos
public final static int GZIP_MAGIC
```

## Constructors
```
public GZIPInputStream(InputStream in,
int size)
public GZIPInputStream(InputStream in)
```

## Methods
```
public void close()
public int read(byte buf,int off,int len)
```

# GZIPOutputStream
```
public class java.util.zip.
GZIPOutputStream
extends java.util.zip.
DeflaterOutputStream
```
```
extends java.io.FilterOutputStream
extends java.io.OutputStream
extends java.lang.Object
```

## Fields
```
protected java.util.zip.CRC32 crc
```

## Constructors
```
public GZIPOutputStream(OutputStream
out,int size)
public GZIPOutputStream(OutputStream
out)
```

## Methods
```
public void close()
public void finish()
public synchronized void write(byte buf,
int off,int len)
```

# HashMap
```
public class java.util.HashMap
implements java.lang.Cloneable
implements java.util.Map
implements java.io.Serializable
extends java.util.AbstractMap
extends java.lang.Object
```

## Constructors
```
public HashMap(int initialCapacity,
float loadFactor)
public HashMap(int initialCapacity)
public HashMap()
public HashMap(Map t)
```

## Methods
```
public void clear()
public Object clone()
public boolean containsKey(Object key)
public boolean containsValue(Object
value)
public Set entrySet()
public Object get(Object key)
public boolean isEmpty()
public Set keySet()
public Object put(Object key,Object
value)
public void putAll(Map t)
public Object remove(Object key)
public int size()
public Collection values()
```

# HashSet
```
public class java.util.HashSet
implements java.lang.Cloneable
implements java.io.Serializable
implements java.util.Set
extends java.util.AbstractSet
extends java.util.AbstractCollection
extends java.lang.Object
```

## Constructors
```
public HashSet()
public HashSet(Collection c)
```

```
public  HashSet(int initialCapacity,
float loadFactor)
public  HashSet(int initialCapacity)
```

### Methods
```
public boolean add(Object o)
public void clear()
public Object clone()
public boolean contains(Object o)
public boolean isEmpty()
public Iterator iterator()
public boolean remove(Object o)
public int size()
```

## Hashtable
```
public class java.util.Hashtable
implements java.lang.Cloneable
implements java.util.Map
implements java.io.Serializable
extends java.util.Dictionary
extends java.lang.Object
```

### Constructors
```
public  Hashtable(int initialCapacity,
float loadFactor)
public  Hashtable(int initialCapacity)
public  Hashtable()
public  Hashtable(Map t)
```

### Methods
```
public synchronized void clear()
public synchronized Object clone()
public synchronized boolean contains(
Object value)
public synchronized boolean containsKey(
Object key)
public boolean containsValue(Object
value)
public synchronized Enumeration elements(
)
public Set entrySet()
public synchronized boolean equals(
Object o)
public synchronized Object get(Object
key)
public synchronized int hashCode()
public boolean isEmpty()
public synchronized Enumeration keys()
public Set keySet()
public synchronized Object put(Object
key,Object value)
public synchronized void putAll(Map t)
protected void rehash()
public synchronized Object remove(Object
key)
public int size()
public synchronized String toString()
public Collection values()
```

## HTML
```
public class javax.swing.text.html.HTML
extends java.lang.Object
```

### Fields
```
public final static java.lang.String
NULL_ATTRIBUTE_VALUE
```

### Methods
```
public static Attribute
getAllAttributeKeys()
public static Tag getAllTags()
public static Attribute getAttributeKey(
String attName)
public static int
getIntegerAttributeValue(AttributeSet
attr,Attribute key,int def)
public static Tag getTag(String tagName)
```

## HTMLDocument
```
public class javax.swing.text.html.
HTMLDocument
extends javax.swing.text.
DefaultStyledDocument
extends javax.swing.text.
AbstractDocument
extends java.lang.Object
```

### Fields
```
public final static java.lang.String
AdditionalComments
```

### Constructors
```
public  HTMLDocument()
public  HTMLDocument(StyleSheet styles)
public  HTMLDocument(Content c,
StyleSheet styles)
```

### Methods
```
protected void create(ElementSpec data)
protected Element createBranchElement(
Element parent,AttributeSet a)
protected AbstractElement
createDefaultRoot()
protected Element createLeafElement(
Element parent,AttributeSet a,int p0,int
p1)
public URL getBase()
public Iterator getIterator(Tag t)
public boolean getPreservesUnknownTags()
public ParserCallback getReader(int pos)
public ParserCallback getReader(int pos,
int popDepth,int pushDepth,Tag insertTag)
public StyleSheet getStyleSheet()
public int getTokenThreshold()
protected void insert(int offset,
ElementSpec data)
protected void insertUpdate(
DefaultDocumentEvent chng,AttributeSet
attr)
public void
processHTMLFrameHyperlinkEvent(
HTMLFrameHyperlinkEvent e)
public void setBase(URL u)
public void setPreservesUnknownTags(
boolean preservesTags)
public void setTokenThreshold(int n)
```

## HTMLEditorKit

public class javax.swing.text.html.
HTMLEditorKit
extends javax.swing.text.
StyledEditorKit
extends javax.swing.text.
DefaultEditorKit
extends javax.swing.text.EditorKit
extends java.lang.Object

### Fields

public final static java.lang.String
BOLD_ACTION
public final static java.lang.String
COLOR_ACTION
public final static java.lang.String
DEFAULT_CSS
public final static java.lang.String
FONT_CHANGE_BIGGER
public final static java.lang.String
FONT_CHANGE_SMALLER
public final static java.lang.String IMG_
ALIGN_BOTTOM
public final static java.lang.String IMG_
ALIGN_MIDDLE
public final static java.lang.String IMG_
ALIGN_TOP
public final static java.lang.String IMG_
BORDER
public final static java.lang.String
ITALIC_ACTION
public final static java.lang.String
LOGICAL_STYLE_ACTION
public final static java.lang.String
PARA_INDENT_LEFT
public final static java.lang.String
PARA_INDENT_RIGHT

### Constructors

public  HTMLEditorKit()

### Methods

public Object clone()
public Document createDefaultDocument()
protected void createInputAttributes(
Element element,MutableAttributeSet set)
public void deinstall(JEditorPane c)
public Action getActions()
public String getContentType()
protected Parser getParser()
public StyleSheet getStyleSheet()
public ViewFactory getViewFactory()
public void insertHTML(HTMLDocument doc,
int offset,String html,int popDepth,int
pushDepth,Tag insertTag)
public void install(JEditorPane c)
public void read(Reader in,Document doc,
int pos)
public void setStyleSheet(StyleSheet s)
public void write(Writer out,Document
doc,int pos,int len)

## HTMLFrameHyperlinkEvent

public class javax.swing.text.html.
HTMLFrameHyperlinkEvent
extends javax.swing.event.
HyperlinkEvent
extends java.util.EventObject
extends java.lang.Object

### Constructors

public  HTMLFrameHyperlinkEvent(Object
source,EventType type,URL targetURL,
String targetFrame)
public  HTMLFrameHyperlinkEvent(Object
source,EventType type,URL targetURL,
String desc,String targetFrame)
public  HTMLFrameHyperlinkEvent(Object
source,EventType type,URL targetURL,
Element sourceElement,String targetFrame)
public  HTMLFrameHyperlinkEvent(Object
source,EventType type,URL targetURL,
String desc,Element sourceElement,String
targetFrame)

### Methods

public Element getSourceElement()
public String getTarget()

## HTMLWriter

public class javax.swing.text.html.
HTMLWriter
extends javax.swing.text.AbstractWriter
extends java.lang.Object

### Constructors

public  HTMLWriter(Writer w,HTMLDocument
doc)
public  HTMLWriter(Writer w,HTMLDocument
doc,int pos,int len)

### Methods

protected void
closeOutUnwantedEmbeddedTags(
AttributeSet attr)
protected void comment(Element elem)
protected void emptyTag(Element elem)
protected void endTag(Element elem)
protected boolean isBlockTag(
AttributeSet attr)
protected boolean matchNameAttribute(
AttributeSet attr,Tag tag)
protected void selectContent(
AttributeSet attr)
protected void startTag(Element elem)
protected boolean synthesizedElement(
Element elem)
protected void text(Element elem)
protected void textAreaContent(
AttributeSet attr)
public void write()
protected void write(String content)
protected void writeAttributes(
AttributeSet attr)

```
protected void writeEmbeddedTags(
AttributeSet attr)
protected void writeOption(Option option)
```

## HttpURLConnection

```
public abstract class java.net.
HttpURLConnection
extends java.net.URLConnection
extends java.lang.Object
```

### Fields

```
public final static int HTTP_ACCEPTED
public final static int HTTP_BAD_
GATEWAY
public final static int HTTP_BAD_METHOD
public final static int HTTP_BAD_
REQUEST
public final static int HTTP_CLIENT_
TIMEOUT
public final static int HTTP_CONFLICT
public final static int HTTP_CREATED
public final static int HTTP_ENTITY_TOO_
LARGE
public final static int HTTP_FORBIDDEN
public final static int HTTP_GATEWAY_
TIMEOUT
public final static int HTTP_GONE
public final static int HTTP_INTERNAL_
ERROR
public final static int HTTP_LENGTH_
REQUIRED
public final static int HTTP_MOVED_PERM
public final static int HTTP_MOVED_TEMP
public final static int HTTP_MULT_
CHOICE
public final static int HTTP_NOT_
ACCEPTABLE
public final static int HTTP_NOT_
AUTHORITATIVE
public final static int HTTP_NOT_FOUND
public final static int HTTP_NOT_
MODIFIED
public final static int HTTP_NO_CONTENT
public final static int HTTP_OK
public final static int HTTP_PARTIAL
public final static int HTTP_PAYMENT_
REQUIRED
public final static int HTTP_PRECON_
FAILED
public final static int HTTP_PROXY_AUTH
public final static int HTTP_REQ_TOO_
LONG
public final static int HTTP_RESET
public final static int HTTP_SEE_OTHER
public final static int HTTP_SERVER_
ERROR
public final static int HTTP_
UNAUTHORIZED
public final static int HTTP_
UNAVAILABLE
public final static int HTTP_UNSUPPORTED_
TYPE
public final static int HTTP_USE_PROXY
```

```
public final static int HTTP_VERSION
protected java.lang.String method
protected int responseCode
protected java.lang.String
responseMessage
```

### Constructors

```
protected  HttpURLConnection(URL u)
```

### Methods

```
public abstract void disconnect()
public InputStream getErrorStream()
public static boolean getFollowRedirects(
)
public Permission getPermission()
public String getRequestMethod()
public int getResponseCode()
public String getResponseMessage()
public static void setFollowRedirects(
boolean set)
public void setRequestMethod(String
method)
public abstract boolean usingProxy()
```

## HyperlinkEvent

```
public class javax.swing.event.
HyperlinkEvent
extends java.util.EventObject
extends java.lang.Object
```

### Constructors

```
public  HyperlinkEvent(Object source,
EventType type,URL u)
public  HyperlinkEvent(Object source,
EventType type,URL u,String desc)
```

### Methods

```
public String getDescription()
public EventType getEventType()
public URL getURL()
```

## ICC_ColorSpace

```
public class java.awt.color.ICC_
ColorSpace
extends java.awt.color.ColorSpace
extends java.lang.Object
```

### Constructors

```
public  ICC_ColorSpace(ICC_Profile
profile)
```

### Methods

```
public float fromCIEXYZ(float colorvalue)
public float fromRGB(float rgbvalue)
public ICC_Profile getProfile()
public float toCIEXYZ(float colorvalue)
public float toRGB(float colorvalue)
```

## ICC_Profile

```
public class java.awt.color.ICC_Profile
extends java.lang.Object
extends java.lang.Object
```

## Fields

public final static int CLASS_ABSTRACT
public final static int CLASS_
COLORSPACECONVERSION
public final static int CLASS_
DEVICELINK
public final static int CLASS_DISPLAY
public final static int CLASS_INPUT
public final static int CLASS_
NAMEDCOLOR
public final static int CLASS_OUTPUT
public final static int
icAbsoluteColorimetric
public final static int icCurveCount
public final static int icCurveData
public final static int icHdrAttributes
public final static int icHdrCmmId
public final static int icHdrColorSpace
public final static int icHdrCreator
public final static int icHdrDate
public final static int
icHdrDeviceClass
public final static int icHdrFlags
public final static int icHdrIlluminant
public final static int icHdrMagic
public final static int
icHdrManufacturer
public final static int icHdrModel
public final static int icHdrPcs
public final static int icHdrPlatform
public final static int
icHdrRenderingIntent
public final static int icHdrSize
public final static int icHdrVersion
public final static int icPerceptual
public final static int
icRelativeColorimetric
public final static int icSaturation
public final static int
icSigAbstractClass
public final static int icSigAToB0Tag
public final static int icSigAToB1Tag
public final static int icSigAToB2Tag
public final static int
icSigBlueColorantTag
public final static int icSigBlueTRCTag
public final static int icSigBToA0Tag
public final static int icSigBToA1Tag
public final static int icSigBToA2Tag
public final static int
icSigCalibrationDateTimeTag
public final static int
icSigCharTargetTag
public final static int icSigCmyData
public final static int icSigCmykData
public final static int
icSigColorSpaceClass
public final static int
icSigCopyrightTag
public final static int
icSigDeviceMfgDescTag
public final static int
icSigDeviceModelDescTag

public final static int
icSigDisplayClass
public final static int icSigGamutTag
public final static int icSigGrayData
public final static int icSigGrayTRCTag
public final static int
icSigGreenColorantTag
public final static int
icSigGreenTRCTag
public final static int icSigHead
public final static int icSigHlsData
public final static int icSigHsvData
public final static int icSigInputClass
public final static int icSigLabData
public final static int icSigLinkClass
public final static int
icSigLuminanceTag
public final static int icSigLuvData
public final static int
icSigMeasurementTag
public final static int
icSigMediaBlackPointTag
public final static int
icSigMediaWhitePointTag
public final static int
icSigNamedColor2Tag
public final static int
icSigNamedColorClass
public final static int
icSigOutputClass
public final static int
icSigPreview0Tag
public final static int
icSigPreview1Tag
public final static int
icSigPreview2Tag
public final static int
icSigProfileDescriptionTag
public final static int
icSigProfileSequenceDescTag
public final static int icSigPs2CRD0Tag
public final static int icSigPs2CRD1Tag
public final static int icSigPs2CRD2Tag
public final static int icSigPs2CRD3Tag
public final static int icSigPs2CSATag
public final static int
icSigPs2RenderingIntentTag
public final static int
icSigRedColorantTag
public final static int icSigRedTRCTag
public final static int icSigRgbData
public final static int
icSigScreeningDescTag
public final static int
icSigScreeningTag
public final static int icSigSpace2CLR
public final static int icSigSpace3CLR
public final static int icSigSpace4CLR
public final static int icSigSpace5CLR
public final static int icSigSpace6CLR
public final static int icSigSpace7CLR
public final static int icSigSpace8CLR
public final static int icSigSpace9CLR
public final static int icSigSpaceACLR

```
public final static int icSigSpaceBCLR
public final static int icSigSpaceCCLR
public final static int icSigSpaceDCLR
public final static int icSigSpaceECLR
public final static int icSigSpaceFCLR
public final static int
icSigTechnologyTag
public final static int icSigUcrBgTag
public final static int
icSigViewingCondDescTag
public final static int
icSigViewingConditionsTag
public final static int icSigXYZData
public final static int icSigYCbCrData
public final static int icSigYxyData
public final static int icTagReserved
public final static int icTagType
public final static int icXYZNumberX
```

### Constructors
```
 ICC_Profile()
 ICC_Profile()
```

### Methods
```
protected void finalize()
public int getColorSpaceType()
public byte getData()
public byte getData(int tagSignature)
public static ICC_Profile getInstance(
byte data)
public static ICC_Profile getInstance(
int cspace)
public static ICC_Profile getInstance(
String fileName)
public static ICC_Profile getInstance(
InputStream s)
public int getMajorVersion()
public int getMinorVersion()
public int getNumComponents()
public int getPCSType()
public int getProfileClass()
public void setData(int tagSignature,
byte tagData)
public void write(String fileName)
public void write(OutputStream s)
```

## ICC_ProfileGray
```
public class java.awt.color.ICC_
ProfileGray
extends java.awt.color.ICC_Profile
extends java.lang.Object
extends java.lang.Object
```

### Constructors
```
 ICC_ProfileGray()
 ICC_ProfileGray()
```

### Methods
```
public float getGamma()
public float getMediaWhitePoint()
public short getTRC()
```

## ICC_ProfileRGB
```
public class java.awt.color.ICC_
ProfileRGB
extends java.awt.color.ICC_Profile
extends java.lang.Object
extends java.lang.Object
```

### Fields
```
public final static int BLUECOMPONENT
public final static int GREENCOMPONENT
public final static int REDCOMPONENT
```

### Constructors
```
 ICC_ProfileRGB()
 ICC_ProfileRGB()
```

### Methods
```
public float getGamma(int component)
public float getMatrix()
public float getMediaWhitePoint()
public short getTRC(int component)
```

## IconUIResource
```
public class javax.swing.plaf.
IconUIResource
implements javax.swing.Icon
implements java.io.Serializable
implements javax.swing.plaf.UIResource
extends java.lang.Object
```

### Constructors
```
public  IconUIResource(Icon delegate)
```

### Methods
```
public int getIconHeight()
public int getIconWidth()
public void paintIcon(Component c,
Graphics g,int x,int y)
```

## IconView
```
public class javax.swing.text.IconView
extends javax.swing.text.View
extends java.lang.Object
```

### Constructors
```
public  IconView(Element elem)
```

### Methods
```
public float getAlignment(int axis)
public float getPreferredSpan(int axis)
public Shape modelToView(int pos,Shape a,
Bias b)
public void paint(Graphics g,Shape a)
public void setSize(float width,float
height)
public int viewToModel(float x,float y,
Shape a,Bias bias)
Identity
public abstract class java.security.
Identity
implements java.security.Principal
implements java.io.Serializable
extends java.lang.Object
```

### Constructors
```
protected  Identity()
public  Identity(String name,
IdentityScope scope)
public  Identity(String name)
```

### Methods
```
public void addCertificate(Certificate
certificate)
public Certificate certificates()
public final boolean equals(Object
identity)
public String getInfo()
public final String getName()
public PublicKey getPublicKey()
public final IdentityScope getScope()
public int hashCode()
protected boolean identityEquals(
Identity identity)
public void removeCertificate(
Certificate certificate)
public void setInfo(String info)
public void setPublicKey(PublicKey key)
public String toString()
public String toString(boolean detailed)
```

## IdentityScope
```
public abstract class java.security.
IdentityScope
extends java.security.Identity
extends java.lang.Object
```

### Constructors
```
protected  IdentityScope()
public  IdentityScope(String name)
public  IdentityScope(String name,
IdentityScope scope)
```

### Methods
```
public abstract void addIdentity(
Identity identity)
public abstract Identity getIdentity(
String name)
public Identity getIdentity(Principal
principal)
public abstract Identity getIdentity(
PublicKey key)
public static IdentityScope
getSystemScope()
public abstract Enumeration identities()
public abstract void removeIdentity(
Identity identity)
protected static void setSystemScope(
IdentityScope scope)
public abstract int size()
public String toString()
```

## IllegalAccessError
```
public class java.lang.
IllegalAccessError
extends java.lang.
IncompatibleClassChangeError
extends java.lang.LinkageError
```

```
extends java.lang.Error
extends java.lang.Throwable
extends java.lang.Object
```

### Constructors
```
public  IllegalAccessError()
public  IllegalAccessError(String s)
```

## IllegalAccessException
```
public class java.lang.
IllegalAccessException
extends java.lang.Exception
extends java.lang.Throwable
extends java.lang.Object
```

### Constructors
```
public  IllegalAccessException()
public  IllegalAccessException(String s)
```

## IllegalArgumentException
```
public class java.lang.
IllegalArgumentException
extends java.lang.RuntimeException
extends java.lang.Exception
extends java.lang.Throwable
extends java.lang.Object
```

### Constructors
```
public  IllegalArgumentException()
public  IllegalArgumentException(String
s)
```

## IllegalComponentStateException
```
public class java.awt.
IllegalComponentStateException
extends java.lang.IllegalStateException
extends java.lang.RuntimeException
extends java.lang.Exception
extends java.lang.Throwable
extends java.lang.Object
```

### Constructors
```
public  IllegalComponentStateException()
public  IllegalComponentStateException(
String s)
```

## IllegalMonitorStateException
```
public class java.lang.
IllegalMonitorStateException
extends java.lang.RuntimeException
extends java.lang.Exception
extends java.lang.Throwable
extends java.lang.Object
```

### Constructors
```
public  IllegalMonitorStateException()
public  IllegalMonitorStateException(
String s)
```

## IllegalPathStateException
```
public class java.awt.geom.
IllegalPathStateException
```

extends java.lang.RuntimeException
extends java.lang.Exception
extends java.lang.Throwable
extends java.lang.Object

### Constructors
public IllegalPathStateException()
public IllegalPathStateException(String s)

## IllegalStateException
public class java.lang.
IllegalStateException
extends java.lang.RuntimeException
extends java.lang.Exception
extends java.lang.Throwable
extends java.lang.Object

### Constructors
public IllegalStateException()
public IllegalStateException(String s)

## IllegalThreadStateException
public class java.lang.
IllegalThreadStateException
extends java.lang.
IllegalArgumentException
extends java.lang.RuntimeException
extends java.lang.Exception
extends java.lang.Throwable
extends java.lang.Object

### Constructors
public IllegalThreadStateException()
public IllegalThreadStateException(
String s)

## Image
public abstract class java.awt.Image
extends java.lang.Object

### Fields
public final static int SCALE_AREA_
AVERAGING
public final static int SCALE_DEFAULT
public final static int SCALE_FAST
public final static int SCALE_REPLICATE
public final static int SCALE_SMOOTH
public final static java.lang.Object
UndefinedProperty

### Methods
public abstract void flush()
public abstract Graphics getGraphics()
public abstract int getHeight(
ImageObserver observer)
public abstract Object getProperty(
String name,ImageObserver observer)
public Image getScaledInstance(int width,
int height,int hints)
public abstract ImageProducer getSource()
public abstract int getWidth(
ImageObserver observer)

## ImageFilter
public class java.awt.image.ImageFilter
implements java.lang.Cloneable
implements java.awt.image.ImageConsumer
extends java.lang.Object

### Fields
protected java.awt.image.ImageConsumer
consumer

### Methods
public Object clone()
public ImageFilter getFilterInstance(
ImageConsumer ic)
public void imageComplete(int status)
public void resendTopDownLeftRight(
ImageProducer ip)
public void setColorModel(ColorModel
model)
public void setDimensions(int width,int
height)
public void setHints(int hints)
public void setPixels(int x,int y,int w,
int h,ColorModel model,byte pixels,int
off,int scansize)
public void setPixels(int x,int y,int w,
int h,ColorModel model,int pixels,int
off,int scansize)
public void setProperties(Hashtable
props)

## ImageGraphicAttribute
public final class java.awt.font.
ImageGraphicAttribute
extends java.awt.font.GraphicAttribute
extends java.lang.Object

### Constructors
public ImageGraphicAttribute(Image
image,int alignment)
public ImageGraphicAttribute(Image
image,int alignment,float originX,float
originY)

### Methods
public void draw(Graphics2D graphics,
float x,float y)
public boolean equals(Object rhs)
public boolean equals(
ImageGraphicAttribute rhs)
public float getAdvance()
public float getAscent()
public Rectangle2D getBounds()
public float getDescent()
public int hashCode()

## ImageIcon
public class javax.swing.ImageIcon
implements javax.swing.Icon
implements java.io.Serializable
extends java.lang.Object

### Fields
```
protected final static java.awt.
Component component
protected final static java.awt.
MediaTracker tracker
```

### Constructors
```
public  ImageIcon(String filename,String
description)
public  ImageIcon(String filename)
public  ImageIcon(URL location,String
description)
public  ImageIcon(URL location)
public  ImageIcon(Image image,String
description)
public  ImageIcon(Image image)
public  ImageIcon(byte imageData,String
description)
public  ImageIcon(byte imageData)
public  ImageIcon()
```

### Methods
```
public String getDescription()
public int getIconHeight()
public int getIconWidth()
public Image getImage()
public int getImageLoadStatus()
public ImageObserver getImageObserver()
protected void loadImage(Image image)
public synchronized void paintIcon(
Component c,Graphics g,int x,int y)
public void setDescription(String
description)
public void setImage(Image image)
public void setImageObserver(
ImageObserver observer)
```

# ImagingOpException
```
public class java.awt.image.
ImagingOpException
extends java.lang.RuntimeException
extends java.lang.Exception
extends java.lang.Throwable
extends java.lang.Object
```

### Constructors
```
public  ImagingOpException(String s)
```

# IncompatibleClassChangeError
```
public class java.lang.
IncompatibleClassChangeError
extends java.lang.LinkageError
extends java.lang.Error
extends java.lang.Throwable
extends java.lang.Object
```

### Constructors
```
public  IncompatibleClassChangeError()
public  IncompatibleClassChangeError(
String s)
```

# IndexColorModel
```
public class java.awt.image.
IndexColorModel
extends java.awt.image.ColorModel
extends java.lang.Object
```

### Constructors
```
public static  IndexColorModel(int bits,
int size,byte r,byte g,byte b)
public  IndexColorModel(int bits,int
size,byte r,byte g,byte b,int trans)
public  IndexColorModel(int bits,int
size,byte r,byte g,byte b,byte a)
public  IndexColorModel(int bits,int
size,byte cmap,int start,boolean
hasalpha)
public  IndexColorModel(int bits,int
size,byte cmap,int start,boolean
hasalpha,int trans)
public  IndexColorModel(int bits,int
size,int cmap,int start,boolean hasalpha,
int trans,int transferType)
```

### Methods
```
public BufferedImage
convertToIntDiscrete(Raster raster,
boolean forceARGB)
public SampleModel
createCompatibleSampleModel(int w,int h)
public WritableRaster
createCompatibleWritableRaster(int w,int
h)
public void finalize()
public final int getAlpha(int pixel)
public final void getAlphas(byte a)
public final int getBlue(int pixel)
public final void getBlues(byte b)
public int getComponents(int pixel,int
components,int offset)
public int getComponents(Object pixel,
int components,int offset)
public int getComponentSize()
public int getDataElement(int components,
int offset)
public Object getDataElements(int rgb,
Object pixel)
public Object getDataElements(int
components,int offset,Object pixel)
public final int getGreen(int pixel)
public final void getGreens(byte g)
public final int getMapSize()
public final int getRed(int pixel)
public final void getReds(byte r)
public final int getRGB(int pixel)
public final void getRGBs(int rgb)
public int getTransparency()
public final int getTransparentPixel()
public boolean isCompatibleRaster(Raster
raster)
public boolean isCompatibleSampleModel(
SampleModel sm)
public String toString()
```

## IndexedPropertyDescriptor

```
public class java.beans.
IndexedPropertyDescriptor
extends java.beans.PropertyDescriptor
extends java.beans.FeatureDescriptor
extends java.lang.Object
```

### Constructors

```
public  IndexedPropertyDescriptor(String
propertyName,Class beanClass)
public  IndexedPropertyDescriptor(String
propertyName,Class beanClass,String
getterName,String setterName,String
indexedGetterName,String
indexedSetterName)
public  IndexedPropertyDescriptor(String
propertyName,Method getter,Method setter,
Method indexedGetter,Method
indexedSetter)
 IndexedPropertyDescriptor()
 IndexedPropertyDescriptor()
```

### Methods

```
public Class getIndexedPropertyType()
public Method getIndexedReadMethod()
public Method getIndexedWriteMethod()
public void setIndexedReadMethod(Method
getter)
public void setIndexedWriteMethod(Method
setter)
```

## IndexOutOfBoundsException

```
public class java.lang.
IndexOutOfBoundsException
extends java.lang.RuntimeException
extends java.lang.Exception
extends java.lang.Throwable
extends java.lang.Object
```

### Constructors

```
public  IndexOutOfBoundsException()
public  IndexOutOfBoundsException(String
s)
```

## InetAddress

```
public final class java.net.InetAddress
implements java.io.Serializable
extends java.lang.Object
```

### Constructors

```
static  InetAddress()
 InetAddress()
```

### Methods

```
public boolean equals(Object obj)
public byte getAddress()
public static InetAddress getAllByName(
String host)
public static InetAddress getByName(
String host)
public String getHostAddress()
public String getHostName()
```

```
public static synchronized InetAddress
getLocalHost()
public int hashCode()
public boolean isMulticastAddress()
public String toString()
```

## Inflater

```
public class java.util.zip.Inflater
extends java.lang.Object
```

### Constructors

```
public static  Inflater(boolean nowrap)
public  Inflater()
```

### Methods

```
public synchronized void end()
protected void finalize()
public synchronized boolean finished()
public synchronized int getAdler()
public synchronized int getRemaining()
public synchronized int getTotalIn()
public synchronized int getTotalOut()
public synchronized int inflate(byte b,
int off,int len)
public int inflate(byte b)
public synchronized boolean
needsDictionary()
public synchronized boolean needsInput()
public synchronized void reset()
public synchronized void setDictionary(
byte b,int off,int len)
public void setDictionary(byte b)
public synchronized void setInput(byte b,
int off,int len)
public void setInput(byte b)
```

## InflaterInputStream

```
public class java.util.zip.
InflaterInputStream
extends java.io.FilterInputStream
extends java.io.InputStream
extends java.lang.Object
```

### Fields

```
protected byte buf
protected java.util.zip.Inflater inf
protected int len
```

### Constructors

```
public  InflaterInputStream(InputStream
in,Inflater inf,int size)
public  InflaterInputStream(InputStream
in,Inflater inf)
public  InflaterInputStream(InputStream
in)
```

### Methods

```
public int available()
public void close()
protected void fill()
public int read()
public int read(byte b,int off,int len)
public long skip(long n)
```

# InheritableThreadLocal
public class java.lang.
InheritableThreadLocal
extends java.lang.ThreadLocal
extends java.lang.Object

**Constructors**
public  InheritableThreadLocal()

**Methods**
protected Object childValue(Object
parentValue)

# InlineView
public class javax.swing.text.html.
InlineView
extends javax.swing.text.LabelView
extends javax.swing.text.View
extends java.lang.Object

**Constructors**
public  InlineView(Element elem)

**Methods**
public AttributeSet getAttributes()
protected StyleSheet getStyleSheet()
public boolean isVisible()
protected void
setPropertiesFromAttributes()

# InputContext
public class java.awt.im.InputContext
extends java.lang.Object

**Constructors**
protected  InputContext()

**Methods**
public synchronized void dispatchEvent(
AWTEvent event)
public void dispose()
public synchronized void endComposition()
public Object
getInputMethodControlObject()
public static InputContext getInstance()
public void removeNotify(Component
client)
public boolean selectInputMethod(Locale
locale)
public void setCharacterSubsets(Subset
subsets)

# InputEvent
public abstract class java.awt.event.
InputEvent
extends java.awt.event.ComponentEvent
extends java.awt.AWTEvent
extends java.util.EventObject
extends java.lang.Object

**Fields**
public final static int ALT_GRAPH_MASK
public final static int ALT_MASK

public final static int BUTTON1_MASK
public final static int BUTTON2_MASK
public final static int BUTTON3_MASK
public final static int CTRL_MASK
public final static int META_MASK
public final static int SHIFT_MASK

**Constructors**
 InputEvent()

**Methods**
public void consume()
public int getModifiers()
public long getWhen()
public boolean isAltDown()
public boolean isAltGraphDown()
public boolean isConsumed()
public boolean isControlDown()
public boolean isMetaDown()
public boolean isShiftDown()

# InputMethodEvent
public class java.awt.event.
InputMethodEvent
extends java.awt.AWTEvent
extends java.util.EventObject
extends java.lang.Object

**Fields**
public final static int CARET_POSITION_
CHANGED
public final static int INPUT_METHOD_
FIRST
public final static int INPUT_METHOD_
LAST
public final static int INPUT_METHOD_
TEXT_CHANGED

**Constructors**
public  InputMethodEvent(Component
source,int id,
AttributedCharacterIterator text,int
committedCharacterCount,TextHitInfo
caret,TextHitInfo visiblePosition)
public  InputMethodEvent(Component
source,int id,TextHitInfo caret,
TextHitInfo visiblePosition)

**Methods**
public void consume()
public TextHitInfo getCaret()
public int getCommittedCharacterCount()
public AttributedCharacterIterator
getText()
public TextHitInfo getVisiblePosition()
public boolean isConsumed()
public String paramString()

# InputMethodHighlight
public class java.awt.im.
InputMethodHighlight
extends java.lang.Object

### Fields

```
public final static int CONVERTED_TEXT
public final static int RAW_TEXT
public final static java.awt.im.
InputMethodHighlight SELECTED_CONVERTED_
TEXT_HIGHLIGHT
public final static java.awt.im.
InputMethodHighlight SELECTED_RAW_TEXT_
HIGHLIGHT
public final static java.awt.im.
InputMethodHighlight UNSELECTED_
CONVERTED_TEXT_HIGHLIGHT
public final static java.awt.im.
InputMethodHighlight UNSELECTED_RAW_TEXT_
HIGHLIGHT
```

### Constructors

```
public  InputMethodHighlight(boolean
selected,int state)
public  InputMethodHighlight(boolean
selected,int state,int variation)
```

### Methods

```
public int getState()
public int getVariation()
public boolean isSelected()
```

## InputStream

```
public abstract class java.io.
InputStream
extends java.lang.Object
```

### Methods

```
public int available()
public void close()
public synchronized void mark(int
readlimit)
public boolean markSupported()
public abstract int read()
public int read(byte b)
public int read(byte b,int off,int len)
public synchronized void reset()
public long skip(long n)
```

## InputStreamReader

```
public class java.io.InputStreamReader
extends java.io.Reader
extends java.lang.Object
```

### Constructors

```
public  InputStreamReader(InputStream in)
public  InputStreamReader(InputStream in,
String enc)
private  InputStreamReader()
```

### Methods

```
public void close()
public String getEncoding()
public int read()
public int read(char cbuf,int off,int
len)
public boolean ready()
```

## InputSubset

```
public final class java.awt.im.
InputSubset
extends java.lang.Object
```

### Fields

```
public final static java.awt.im.
InputSubset HALFWIDTH_KATAKANA
public final static java.awt.im.
InputSubset HANJA
public final static java.awt.im.
InputSubset KANJI
public final static java.awt.im.
InputSubset LATIN
public final static java.awt.im.
InputSubset LATIN_DIGITS
public final static java.awt.im.
InputSubset SIMPLIFIED_HANZI
public final static java.awt.im.
InputSubset TRADITIONAL_HANZI
```

### Constructors

```
private  InputSubset()
```

## Insets

```
public class java.awt.Insets
implements java.lang.Cloneable
implements java.io.Serializable
extends java.lang.Object
```

### Fields

```
public int bottom
public int left
public int right
public int top
```

### Constructors

```
public static  Insets(int top,int left,
int bottom,int right)
```

### Methods

```
public Object clone()
public boolean equals(Object obj)
public String toString()
```

## InsetsUIResource

```
public class javax.swing.plaf.
InsetsUIResource
implements javax.swing.plaf.UIResource
extends java.awt.Insets
extends java.lang.Object
```

### Constructors

```
public  InsetsUIResource(int top,int
left,int bottom,int right)
```

## InstantiationError

```
public class java.lang.
InstantiationError
extends java.lang.
IncompatibleClassChangeError
extends java.lang.LinkageError
```

extends java.lang.Error
extends java.lang.Throwable
extends java.lang.Object

### Constructors
public  InstantiationError()
public  InstantiationError(String s)

## InstantiationException
public class java.lang.
InstantiationException
extends java.lang.Exception
extends java.lang.Throwable
extends java.lang.Object

### Constructors
public  InstantiationException()
public  InstantiationException(String s)

## Integer
public final class java.lang.Integer
implements java.lang.Comparable
extends java.lang.Number
extends java.lang.Object

### Fields
public final static int MAX_VALUE
public final static int MIN_VALUE
public final static java.lang.Class
TYPE

### Constructors
public  Integer(int value)
public  Integer(String s)

### Methods
public byte byteValue()
public int compareTo(Integer
anotherInteger)
public int compareTo(Object o)
public static Integer decode(String nm)
public double doubleValue()
public boolean equals(Object obj)
public float floatValue()
public static Integer getInteger(String
nm)
public static Integer getInteger(String
nm,int val)
public static Integer getInteger(String
nm,Integer val)
public int hashCode()
public int intValue()
public long longValue()
public static int parseInt(String s,int
radix)
public static int parseInt(String s)
public short shortValue()
public static String toBinaryString(int
i)
public static String toHexString(int i)
public static String toOctalString(int i)

public static String toString(int i,int
radix)
public static String toString(int i)
public String toString()
public static Integer valueOf(String s,
int radix)
public static Integer valueOf(String s)

## InternalError
public class java.lang.InternalError
extends java.lang.VirtualMachineError
extends java.lang.Error
extends java.lang.Throwable
extends java.lang.Object

### Constructors
public  InternalError()
public  InternalError(String s)

## InternalFrameAdapter
public abstract class javax.swing.event.
InternalFrameAdapter
implements javax.swing.event.
InternalFrameListener
extends java.lang.Object

### Methods
public void internalFrameActivated(
InternalFrameEvent e)
public void internalFrameClosed(
InternalFrameEvent e)
public void internalFrameClosing(
InternalFrameEvent e)
public void internalFrameDeactivated(
InternalFrameEvent e)
public void internalFrameDeiconified(
InternalFrameEvent e)
public void internalFrameIconified(
InternalFrameEvent e)
public void internalFrameOpened(
InternalFrameEvent e)

## InternalFrameEvent
public class javax.swing.event.
InternalFrameEvent
extends java.awt.AWTEvent
extends java.util.EventObject
extends java.lang.Object

### Fields
public final static int INTERNAL_FRAME_
ACTIVATED
public final static int INTERNAL_FRAME_
CLOSED
public final static int INTERNAL_FRAME_
CLOSING
public final static int INTERNAL_FRAME_
DEACTIVATED
public final static int INTERNAL_FRAME_
DEICONIFIED
public final static int INTERNAL_FRAME_
FIRST

```
public final static int INTERNAL_FRAME_
ICONIFIED
public final static int INTERNAL_FRAME_
LAST
public final static int INTERNAL_FRAME_
OPENED
```

**Constructors**
```
public  InternalFrameEvent(
JInternalFrame source,int id)
```

**Methods**
```
public String paramString()
```

## InternalFrameUI
```
public abstract class javax.swing.plaf.
InternalFrameUI
extends javax.swing.plaf.ComponentUI
extends java.lang.Object
```

## InterruptedException
```
public class java.lang.
InterruptedException
extends java.lang.Exception
extends java.lang.Throwable
extends java.lang.Object
```

**Constructors**
```
public  InterruptedException()
public  InterruptedException(String s)
```

## InterruptedIOException
```
public class java.io.
InterruptedIOException
extends java.io.IOException
extends java.lang.Exception
extends java.lang.Throwable
extends java.lang.Object
```

**Fields**
```
public int bytesTransferred
```

**Constructors**
```
public  InterruptedIOException()
public  InterruptedIOException(String s)
```

## IntrospectionException
```
public class java.beans.
IntrospectionException
extends java.lang.Exception
extends java.lang.Throwable
extends java.lang.Object
```

**Constructors**
```
public  IntrospectionException(String
mess)
```

## Introspector
```
public class java.beans.Introspector
extends java.lang.Object
```

**Fields**
```
public final static int IGNORE_ALL_
BEANINFO
public final static int IGNORE_IMMEDIATE_
BEANINFO
public final static int USE_ALL_
BEANINFO
```

**Constructors**
```
private  Introspector()
```

**Methods**
```
public static String decapitalize(String
name)
public static void flushCaches()
public static void flushFromCaches(Class
clz)
public static BeanInfo getBeanInfo(Class
beanClass)
public static BeanInfo getBeanInfo(Class
beanClass,int flags)
public static BeanInfo getBeanInfo(Class
beanClass,Class stopClass)
public static synchronized String
getBeanInfoSearchPath()
public static synchronized void
setBeanInfoSearchPath(String path)
```

## InvalidAlgorithmParameterException
```
public class java.security.
InvalidAlgorithmParameterException
extends java.security.
GeneralSecurityException
extends java.lang.Exception
extends java.lang.Throwable
extends java.lang.Object
```

**Constructors**
```
public
InvalidAlgorithmParameterException()
public
InvalidAlgorithmParameterException(
String msg)
```

## InvalidClassException
```
public class java.io.
InvalidClassException
extends java.io.ObjectStreamException
extends java.io.IOException
extends java.lang.Exception
extends java.lang.Throwable
extends java.lang.Object
```

**Fields**
```
public java.lang.String classname
```

**Constructors**
```
public  InvalidClassException(String
reason)
public  InvalidClassException(String
cname,String reason)
```

### Methods
```
public String getMessage()
```

# InvalidDnDOperationException
```
public class java.awt.dnd.
InvalidDnDOperationException
extends java.lang.IllegalStateException
extends java.lang.RuntimeException
extends java.lang.Exception
extends java.lang.Throwable
extends java.lang.Object
```

### Constructors
```
public  InvalidDnDOperationException()
public  InvalidDnDOperationException(
String msg)
```

# InvalidKeyException
```
public class java.security.
InvalidKeyException
extends java.security.KeyException
extends java.security.
GeneralSecurityException
extends java.lang.Exception
extends java.lang.Throwable
extends java.lang.Object
```

### Constructors
```
public  InvalidKeyException()
public  InvalidKeyException(String msg)
```

# InvalidKeySpecException
```
public class java.security.spec.
InvalidKeySpecException
extends java.security.
GeneralSecurityException
extends java.lang.Exception
extends java.lang.Throwable
extends java.lang.Object
```

### Constructors
```
public  InvalidKeySpecException()
public  InvalidKeySpecException(String
msg)
```

# InvalidObjectException
```
public class java.io.
InvalidObjectException
extends java.io.ObjectStreamException
extends java.io.IOException
extends java.lang.Exception
extends java.lang.Throwable
extends java.lang.Object
```

### Constructors
```
public  InvalidObjectException(String
reason)
```

# InvalidParameterException
```
public class java.security.
InvalidParameterException
```
```
extends java.lang.
IllegalArgumentException
extends java.lang.RuntimeException
extends java.lang.Exception
extends java.lang.Throwable
extends java.lang.Object
```

### Constructors
```
public  InvalidParameterException()
public  InvalidParameterException(String
msg)
```

# InvalidParameterSpecException
```
public class java.security.spec.
InvalidParameterSpecException
extends java.security.
GeneralSecurityException
extends java.lang.Exception
extends java.lang.Throwable
extends java.lang.Object
```

### Constructors
```
public  InvalidParameterSpecException()
public  InvalidParameterSpecException(
String msg)
```

# InvocationEvent
```
public class java.awt.event.
InvocationEvent
implements java.awt.ActiveEvent
extends java.awt.AWTEvent
extends java.util.EventObject
extends java.lang.Object
```

### Fields
```
protected boolean catchExceptions
public final static int INVOCATION_
DEFAULT
public final static int INVOCATION_
FIRST
public final static int INVOCATION_LAST
protected java.lang.Object notifier
protected java.lang.Runnable runnable
```

### Constructors
```
public  InvocationEvent(Object source,
Runnable runnable)
public  InvocationEvent(Object source,
Runnable runnable,Object notifier,
boolean catchExceptions)
protected  InvocationEvent(Object source,
int id,Runnable runnable,Object notifier,
boolean catchExceptions)
```

### Methods
```
public void dispatch()
public Exception getException()
public String paramString()
```

# InvocationTargetException
```
public class java.lang.reflect.
InvocationTargetException
```

```
extends java.lang.Exception
extends java.lang.Throwable
extends java.lang.Object
```

**Constructors**
```
protected  InvocationTargetException()
public  InvocationTargetException(
Throwable target)
public  InvocationTargetException(
Throwable target,String s)
```

**Methods**
```
public Throwable getTargetException()
public void printStackTrace()
public void printStackTrace(PrintStream
ps)
public void printStackTrace(PrintWriter
pw)
```

## IOException

```
public class java.io.IOException
extends java.lang.Exception
extends java.lang.Throwable
extends java.lang.Object
```

**Constructors**
```
public  IOException()
public  IOException(String s)
```

## ItemEvent

```
public class java.awt.event.ItemEvent
extends java.awt.AWTEvent
extends java.util.EventObject
extends java.lang.Object
```

**Fields**
```
public final static int DESELECTED
public final static int ITEM_FIRST
public final static int ITEM_LAST
public final static int ITEM_STATE_
CHANGED
public final static int SELECTED
```

**Constructors**
```
public  ItemEvent(ItemSelectable source,
int id,Object item,int stateChange)
```

**Methods**
```
public Object getItem()
public ItemSelectable getItemSelectable()
public int getStateChange()
public String paramString()
```

## JApplet

```
public class javax.swing.JApplet
implements javax.accessibility.
Accessible
implements javax.swing.
RootPaneContainer
extends java.applet.Applet
extends java.awt.Panel
extends java.awt.Container
```

```
extends java.awt.Component
extends java.lang.Object
```

**Fields**
```
protected javax.accessibility.
AccessibleContext accessibleContext
protected javax.swing.JRootPane
rootPane
protected boolean
rootPaneCheckingEnabled
```

**Constructors**
```
public  JApplet()
```

**Methods**
```
protected void addImpl(Component comp,
Object constraints,int index)
protected JRootPane createRootPane()
public AccessibleContext
getAccessibleContext()
public Container getContentPane()
public Component getGlassPane()
public JMenuBar getJMenuBar()
public JLayeredPane getLayeredPane()
public JRootPane getRootPane()
protected boolean
isRootPaneCheckingEnabled()
protected String paramString()
protected void processKeyEvent(KeyEvent
e)
public void setContentPane(Container
contentPane)
public void setGlassPane(Component
glassPane)
public void setJMenuBar(JMenuBar menuBar)
public void setLayeredPane(JLayeredPane
layeredPane)
public void setLayout(LayoutManager
manager)
protected void setRootPane(JRootPane
root)
protected void
setRootPaneCheckingEnabled(boolean
enabled)
public void update(Graphics g)
```

## JarEntry

```
public class java.util.jar.JarEntry
extends java.util.zip.ZipEntry
extends java.lang.Object
```

**Constructors**
```
public  JarEntry(String name)
public  JarEntry(ZipEntry ze)
public  JarEntry(JarEntry je)
```

**Methods**
```
public Attributes getAttributes()
public Certificate getCertificates()
```

## JarException

```
public class java.util.jar.JarException
extends java.util.zip.ZipException
```

```
extends java.io.IOException
extends java.lang.Exception
extends java.lang.Throwable
extends java.lang.Object
```

**Constructors**
```
public  JarException()
public  JarException(String s)
```

## JarFile
```
public class java.util.jar.JarFile
extends java.util.zip.ZipFile
extends java.lang.Object
```

**Fields**
```
public final static java.lang.String
MANIFEST_NAME
```

**Constructors**
```
public  JarFile(String name)
public  JarFile(String name,boolean
verify)
public  JarFile(File file)
public  JarFile(File file,boolean verify)
```

**Methods**
```
public Enumeration entries()
public ZipEntry getEntry(String name)
public synchronized InputStream
getInputStream(ZipEntry ze)
public JarEntry getJarEntry(String name)
public Manifest getManifest()
```

## JarInputStream
```
public class java.util.jar.
JarInputStream
extends java.util.zip.ZipInputStream
extends java.util.zip.
InflaterInputStream
extends java.io.FilterInputStream
extends java.io.InputStream
extends java.lang.Object
```

**Constructors**
```
public  JarInputStream(InputStream in)
public  JarInputStream(InputStream in,
boolean verify)
```

**Methods**
```
protected ZipEntry createZipEntry(String
name)
public Manifest getManifest()
public ZipEntry getNextEntry()
public JarEntry getNextJarEntry()
public int read(byte b,int off,int len)
```

## JarOutputStream
```
public class java.util.jar.
JarOutputStream
extends java.util.zip.ZipOutputStream
extends java.util.zip.
DeflaterOutputStream
```

```
extends java.io.FilterOutputStream
extends java.io.OutputStream
extends java.lang.Object
```

**Constructors**
```
public  JarOutputStream(OutputStream out,
Manifest man)
public  JarOutputStream(OutputStream out)
```

**Methods**
```
public void putNextEntry(ZipEntry ze)
```

## JarURLConnection
```
public abstract class java.net.
JarURLConnection
extends java.net.URLConnection
extends java.lang.Object
```

**Fields**
```
protected java.net.URLConnection
jarFileURLConnection
```

**Constructors**
```
protected  JarURLConnection(URL url)
```

**Methods**
```
public Attributes getAttributes()
public Certificate getCertificates()
public String getEntryName()
public JarEntry getJarEntry()
public abstract JarFile getJarFile()
public URL getJarFileURL()
public Attributes getMainAttributes()
public Manifest getManifest()
```

## JButton
```
public class javax.swing.JButton
implements javax.accessibility.
Accessible
extends javax.swing.AbstractButton
extends javax.swing.JComponent
extends java.awt.Container
extends java.awt.Component
extends java.lang.Object
```

**Constructors**
```
public  JButton()
public  JButton(Icon icon)
public  JButton(String text)
public  JButton(String text,Icon icon)
```

**Methods**
```
public AccessibleContext
getAccessibleContext()
public String getUIClassID()
public boolean isDefaultButton()
public boolean isDefaultCapable()
protected String paramString()
public void setDefaultCapable(boolean
defaultCapable)
public void updateUI()
```

## JCheckBox

```
public class javax.swing.JCheckBox
implements javax.accessibility.
Accessible
extends javax.swing.JToggleButton
extends javax.swing.AbstractButton
extends javax.swing.JComponent
extends java.awt.Container
extends java.awt.Component
extends java.lang.Object
```

### Constructors

```
public  JCheckBox()
public  JCheckBox(Icon icon)
public  JCheckBox(Icon icon,boolean
selected)
public  JCheckBox(String text)
public  JCheckBox(String text,boolean
selected)
public  JCheckBox(String text,Icon icon)
public  JCheckBox(String text,Icon icon,
boolean selected)
```

### Methods

```
public AccessibleContext
getAccessibleContext()
public String getUIClassID()
protected String paramString()
public void updateUI()
```

## JCheckBoxMenuItem

```
public class javax.swing.
JCheckBoxMenuItem
implements javax.accessibility.
Accessible
implements javax.swing.SwingConstants
extends javax.swing.JMenuItem
extends javax.swing.AbstractButton
extends javax.swing.JComponent
extends java.awt.Container
extends java.awt.Component
extends java.lang.Object
```

### Constructors

```
public  JCheckBoxMenuItem()
public  JCheckBoxMenuItem(Icon icon)
public  JCheckBoxMenuItem(String text)
public  JCheckBoxMenuItem(String text,
Icon icon)
public  JCheckBoxMenuItem(String text,
boolean b)
public  JCheckBoxMenuItem(String text,
Icon icon,boolean b)
```

### Methods

```
public AccessibleContext
getAccessibleContext()
public synchronized Object
getSelectedObjects()
public boolean getState()
public String getUIClassID()
protected void init(String text,Icon
icon)
```

```
protected String paramString()
public void requestFocus()
public synchronized void setState(
boolean b)
public void updateUI()
```

## JColorChooser

```
public class javax.swing.JColorChooser
implements javax.accessibility.
Accessible
extends javax.swing.JComponent
extends java.awt.Container
extends java.awt.Component
extends java.lang.Object
```

### Fields

```
protected javax.accessibility.
AccessibleContext accessibleContext
public final static java.lang.String
CHOOSER_PANELS_PROPERTY
public final static java.lang.String
PREVIEW_PANEL_PROPERTY
public final static java.lang.String
SELECTION_MODEL_PROPERTY
```

### Constructors

```
public  JColorChooser()
public  JColorChooser(Color initialColor)
public  JColorChooser(
ColorSelectionModel model)
```

### Methods

```
public void addChooserPanel(
AbstractColorChooserPanel panel)
public static JDialog createDialog(
Component c,String title,boolean modal,
JColorChooser chooserPane,ActionListener
okListener,ActionListener cancelListener)
public AccessibleContext
getAccessibleContext()
public AbstractColorChooserPanel
getChooserPanels()
public Color getColor()
public JComponent getPreviewPanel()
public ColorSelectionModel
getSelectionModel()
public ColorChooserUI getUI()
public String getUIClassID()
protected String paramString()
public AbstractColorChooserPanel
removeChooserPanel(
AbstractColorChooserPanel panel)
public void setChooserPanels(
AbstractColorChooserPanel panels)
public void setColor(Color color)
public void setColor(int r,int g,int b)
public void setColor(int c)
public void setPreviewPanel(JComponent
preview)
public void setSelectionModel(
ColorSelectionModel newModel)
public void setUI(ColorChooserUI ui)
```

public static Color showDialog(Component
component,String title,Color
initialColor)
public void updateUI()

## JComboBox

public class javax.swing.JComboBox
implements javax.accessibility.
Accessible
implements java.awt.event.
ActionListener
implements java.awt.ItemSelectable
implements javax.swing.event.
ListDataListener
extends javax.swing.JComponent
extends java.awt.Container
extends java.awt.Component
extends java.lang.Object

### Fields

protected java.lang.String
actionCommand
protected javax.swing.ComboBoxModel
dataModel
protected javax.swing.ComboBoxEditor
editor
protected boolean isEditable
protected KeySelectionManager
keySelectionManager
protected boolean
lightWeightPopupEnabled
protected int maximumRowCount
protected javax.swing.ListCellRenderer
renderer
protected java.lang.Object
selectedItemReminder

### Constructors

public  JComboBox(ComboBoxModel aModel)
public  JComboBox(Object items)
public  JComboBox(Vector items)
public  JComboBox()

### Methods

public void actionPerformed(ActionEvent
e)
public void addActionListener(
ActionListener l)
public void addItem(Object anObject)
public void addItemListener(ItemListener
aListener)
public void configureEditor(
ComboBoxEditor anEditor,Object anItem)
public void contentsChanged(
ListDataEvent e)
protected KeySelectionManager
createDefaultKeySelectionManager()
protected void fireActionEvent()
protected void fireItemStateChanged(
ItemEvent e)
public AccessibleContext
getAccessibleContext()
public String getActionCommand()
public ComboBoxEditor getEditor()

public Object getItemAt(int index)
public int getItemCount()
public KeySelectionManager
getKeySelectionManager()
public int getMaximumRowCount()
public ComboBoxModel getModel()
public ListCellRenderer getRenderer()
public int getSelectedIndex()
public Object getSelectedItem()
public Object getSelectedObjects()
public ComboBoxUI getUI()
public String getUIClassID()
public void hidePopup()
public void insertItemAt(Object anObject,
int index)
protected void installAncestorListener()
public void intervalAdded(ListDataEvent
e)
public void intervalRemoved(
ListDataEvent e)
public boolean isEditable()
public boolean isFocusTraversable()
public boolean isLightWeightPopupEnabled(
)
public boolean isPopupVisible()
protected String paramString()
public void processKeyEvent(KeyEvent e)
public void removeActionListener(
ActionListener l)
public void removeAllItems()
public void removeItem(Object anObject)
public void removeItemAt(int anIndex)
public void removeItemListener(
ItemListener aListener)
protected void selectedItemChanged()
public boolean selectWithKeyChar(char
keyChar)
public void setActionCommand(String
aCommand)
public void setEditable(boolean aFlag)
public void setEditor(ComboBoxEditor
anEditor)
public void setEnabled(boolean b)
public void setKeySelectionManager(
KeySelectionManager aManager)
public void setLightWeightPopupEnabled(
boolean aFlag)
public void setMaximumRowCount(int count)
public void setModel(ComboBoxModel
aModel)
public void setPopupVisible(boolean v)
public void setRenderer(ListCellRenderer
aRenderer)
public void setSelectedIndex(int anIndex)
public void setSelectedItem(Object
anObject)
public void setUI(ComboBoxUI ui)
public void showPopup()
public void updateUI()

## JComponent

public abstract class javax.swing.
JComponent
implements java.io.Serializable

```
extends java.awt.Container
extends java.awt.Component
extends java.lang.Object
```

## Fields
```
protected javax.accessibility.
AccessibleContext accessibleContext
protected javax.swing.event.
EventListenerList listenerList
public final static java.lang.String
TOOL_TIP_TEXT_KEY
protected transient javax.swing.plaf.
ComponentUI ui
public final static int UNDEFINED_
CONDITION
public final static int WHEN_ANCESTOR_OF_
FOCUSED_COMPONENT
public final static int WHEN_FOCUSED
public final static int WHEN_IN_FOCUSED_
WINDOW
```

## Constructors
```
public  JComponent()
```

## Methods
```
public void addAncestorListener(
AncestorListener listener)
public void addNotify()
public synchronized void
addPropertyChangeListener(
PropertyChangeListener listener)
public synchronized void
addVetoableChangeListener(
VetoableChangeListener listener)
public void computeVisibleRect(Rectangle
visibleRect)
public boolean contains(int x,int y)
public JToolTip createToolTip()
protected void firePropertyChange(String
propertyName,Object oldValue,Object
newValue)
public void firePropertyChange(String
propertyName,byte oldValue,byte newValue)
public void firePropertyChange(String
propertyName,char oldValue,char newValue)
public void firePropertyChange(String
propertyName,short oldValue,short
newValue)
public void firePropertyChange(String
propertyName,int oldValue,int newValue)
public void firePropertyChange(String
propertyName,long oldValue,long newValue)
public void firePropertyChange(String
propertyName,float oldValue,float
newValue)
public void firePropertyChange(String
propertyName,double oldValue,double
newValue)
public void firePropertyChange(String
propertyName,boolean oldValue,boolean
newValue)
protected void fireVetoableChange(String
propertyName,Object oldValue,Object
newValue)
```

```
public AccessibleContext
getAccessibleContext()
public ActionListener
getActionForKeyStroke(KeyStroke
aKeyStroke)
public float getAlignmentX()
public float getAlignmentY()
public boolean getAutoscrolls()
public Border getBorder()
public Rectangle getBounds(Rectangle rv)
public final Object getClientProperty(
Object key)
protected Graphics getComponentGraphics(
Graphics g)
public int getConditionForKeyStroke(
KeyStroke aKeyStroke)
public int getDebugGraphicsOptions()
public Graphics getGraphics()
public int getHeight()
public Insets getInsets()
public Insets getInsets(Insets insets)
public Point getLocation(Point rv)
public Dimension getMaximumSize()
public Dimension getMinimumSize()
public Component
getNextFocusableComponent()
public Dimension getPreferredSize()
public KeyStroke getRegisteredKeyStrokes(
)
public JRootPane getRootPane()
public Dimension getSize(Dimension rv)
public Point getToolTipLocation(
MouseEvent event)
public String getToolTipText()
public String getToolTipText(MouseEvent
event)
public Container getTopLevelAncestor()
public String getUIClassID()
public Rectangle getVisibleRect()
public int getWidth()
public int getX()
public int getY()
public void grabFocus()
public boolean hasFocus()
public boolean isDoubleBuffered()
public boolean isFocusCycleRoot()
public boolean isFocusTraversable()
public static boolean
isLightweightComponent(Component c)
public boolean isManagingFocus()
public boolean isOpaque()
public boolean isOptimizedDrawingEnabled(
)
public boolean isPaintingTile()
public boolean isRequestFocusEnabled()
public boolean isValidateRoot()
public void paint(Graphics g)
protected void paintBorder(Graphics g)
protected void paintChildren(Graphics g)
protected void paintComponent(Graphics g)
public void paintImmediately(int x,int y,
int w,int h)
public void paintImmediately(Rectangle r)
protected String paramString()
```

```
protected void processComponentKeyEvent(
KeyEvent e)
protected void processFocusEvent(
FocusEvent e)
protected void processKeyEvent(KeyEvent
e)
protected void processMouseMotionEvent(
MouseEvent e)
public final void putClientProperty(
Object key,Object value)
public void registerKeyboardAction(
ActionListener anAction,String aCommand,
KeyStroke aKeyStroke,int aCondition)
public void registerKeyboardAction(
ActionListener anAction,KeyStroke
aKeyStroke,int aCondition)
public void removeAncestorListener(
AncestorListener listener)
public void removeNotify()
public synchronized void
removePropertyChangeListener(
PropertyChangeListener listener)
public synchronized void
removeVetoableChangeListener(
VetoableChangeListener listener)
public void repaint(long tm,int x,int y,
int width,int height)
public void repaint(Rectangle r)
public boolean requestDefaultFocus()
public void requestFocus()
public void resetKeyboardActions()
public void reshape(int x,int y,int w,
int h)
public void revalidate()
public void scrollRectToVisible(
Rectangle aRect)
public void setAlignmentX(float
alignmentX)
public void setAlignmentY(float
alignmentY)
public void setAutoscrolls(boolean
autoscrolls)
public void setBackground(Color bg)
public void setBorder(Border border)
public void setDebugGraphicsOptions(int
debugOptions)
public void setDoubleBuffered(boolean
aFlag)
public void setEnabled(boolean enabled)
public void setFont(Font font)
public void setForeground(Color fg)
public void setMaximumSize(Dimension
maximumSize)
public void setMinimumSize(Dimension
minimumSize)
public void setNextFocusableComponent(
Component aComponent)
public void setOpaque(boolean isOpaque)
public void setPreferredSize(Dimension
preferredSize)
public void setRequestFocusEnabled(
boolean aFlag)
public void setToolTipText(String text)
protected void setUI(ComponentUI newUI)
```

```
public void setVisible(boolean aFlag)
public void unregisterKeyboardAction(
KeyStroke aKeyStroke)
public void update(Graphics g)
public void updateUI()
```

## JDesktopPane

```
public class javax.swing.JDesktopPane
implements javax.accessibility.
Accessible
extends javax.swing.JLayeredPane
extends javax.swing.JComponent
extends java.awt.Container
extends java.awt.Component
extends java.lang.Object
```

### Constructors
```
public  JDesktopPane()
```

### Methods
```
public AccessibleContext
getAccessibleContext()
public JInternalFrame getAllFrames()
public JInternalFrame
getAllFramesInLayer(int layer)
public DesktopManager getDesktopManager()
public DesktopPaneUI getUI()
public String getUIClassID()
public boolean isOpaque()
protected String paramString()
public void setDesktopManager(
DesktopManager d)
public void setUI(DesktopPaneUI ui)
public void updateUI()
```

## JDialog

```
public class javax.swing.JDialog
implements javax.accessibility.
Accessible
implements javax.swing.
RootPaneContainer
implements javax.swing.WindowConstants
extends java.awt.Dialog
extends java.awt.Window
extends java.awt.Container
extends java.awt.Component
extends java.lang.Object
```

### Fields
```
protected javax.accessibility.
AccessibleContext accessibleContext
protected javax.swing.JRootPane
rootPane
protected boolean
rootPaneCheckingEnabled
```

### Constructors
```
public  JDialog()
public  JDialog(Frame owner)
public  JDialog(Frame owner,boolean
modal)
public  JDialog(Frame owner,String title)
```

```
public   JDialog(Frame owner,String title,
boolean modal)
public   JDialog(Dialog owner)
public   JDialog(Dialog owner,boolean
modal)
public   JDialog(Dialog owner,String
title)
public   JDialog(Dialog owner,String
title,boolean modal)
```

### Methods

```
protected void addImpl(Component comp,
Object constraints,int index)
protected JRootPane createRootPane()
protected void dialogInit()
public AccessibleContext
getAccessibleContext()
public Container getContentPane()
public int getDefaultCloseOperation()
public Component getGlassPane()
public JMenuBar getJMenuBar()
public JLayeredPane getLayeredPane()
public JRootPane getRootPane()
protected boolean
isRootPaneCheckingEnabled()
protected String paramString()
protected void processWindowEvent(
WindowEvent e)
public void setContentPane(Container
contentPane)
public void setDefaultCloseOperation(int
operation)
public void setGlassPane(Component
glassPane)
public void setJMenuBar(JMenuBar menu)
public void setLayeredPane(JLayeredPane
layeredPane)
public void setLayout(LayoutManager
manager)
public void setLocationRelativeTo(
Component c)
protected void setRootPane(JRootPane
root)
protected void
setRootPaneCheckingEnabled(boolean
enabled)
public void update(Graphics g)
```

## JEditorPane

```
public class javax.swing.JEditorPane
extends javax.swing.text.JTextComponent
extends javax.swing.JComponent
extends java.awt.Container
extends java.awt.Component
extends java.lang.Object
```

### Constructors

```
public   JEditorPane()
public   JEditorPane(URL initialPage)
public   JEditorPane(String url)
public   JEditorPane(String type,String
text)
```

### Methods

```
public synchronized void
addHyperlinkListener(HyperlinkListener
listener)
protected EditorKit
createDefaultEditorKit()
public static EditorKit
createEditorKitForContentType(String
type)
public void fireHyperlinkUpdate(
HyperlinkEvent e)
public AccessibleContext
getAccessibleContext()
public final String getContentType()
public final EditorKit getEditorKit()
public EditorKit
getEditorKitForContentType(String type)
public URL getPage()
public Dimension getPreferredSize()
public boolean
getScrollableTracksViewportHeight()
public boolean
getScrollableTracksViewportWidth()
protected InputStream getStream(URL page)
public String getText()
public String getUIClassID()
public boolean isManagingFocus()
protected static String paramString()
protected void processComponentKeyEvent(
KeyEvent e)
public void read(InputStream in,Object
desc)
public static void
registerEditorKitForContentType(String
type,String classname)
public static void
registerEditorKitForContentType(String
type,String classname,ClassLoader loader)
public synchronized void
removeHyperlinkListener(
HyperlinkListener listener)
public void replaceSelection(String
content)
protected void scrollToReference(String
reference)
public final void setContentType(String
type)
public void setEditorKit(EditorKit kit)
public void setEditorKitForContentType(
String type,EditorKit k)
public void setPage(URL page)
public void setPage(String url)
public void setText(String t)
```

## JFileChooser

```
public class javax.swing.JFileChooser
implements javax.accessibility.
Accessible
extends javax.swing.JComponent
extends java.awt.Container
extends java.awt.Component
extends java.lang.Object
```

## Fields

protected javax.accessibility.
AccessibleContext accessibleContext
public final static java.lang.String
ACCESSORY_CHANGED_PROPERTY
public final static java.lang.String
APPROVE_BUTTON_MNEMONIC_CHANGED_
PROPERTY
public final static java.lang.String
APPROVE_BUTTON_TEXT_CHANGED_PROPERTY
public final static java.lang.String
APPROVE_BUTTON_TOOL_TIP_TEXT_CHANGED_
PROPERTY
public final static int APPROVE_OPTION
public final static java.lang.String
APPROVE_SELECTION
public final static int CANCEL_OPTION
public final static java.lang.String
CANCEL_SELECTION
public final static java.lang.String
CHOOSABLE_FILE_FILTER_CHANGED_PROPERTY
public final static int CUSTOM_DIALOG
public final static java.lang.String
DIALOG_TITLE_CHANGED_PROPERTY
public final static java.lang.String
DIALOG_TYPE_CHANGED_PROPERTY
public final static int DIRECTORIES_
ONLY
public final static java.lang.String
DIRECTORY_CHANGED_PROPERTY
public final static int ERROR_OPTION
public final static int FILES_AND_
DIRECTORIES
public final static int FILES_ONLY
public final static java.lang.String
FILE_FILTER_CHANGED_PROPERTY
public final static java.lang.String
FILE_HIDING_CHANGED_PROPERTY
public final static java.lang.String
FILE_SELECTION_MODE_CHANGED_PROPERTY
public final static java.lang.String
FILE_SYSTEM_VIEW_CHANGED_PROPERTY
public final static java.lang.String
FILE_VIEW_CHANGED_PROPERTY
public final static java.lang.String
MULTI_SELECTION_ENABLED_CHANGED_
PROPERTY
public final static int OPEN_DIALOG
public final static int SAVE_DIALOG
public final static java.lang.String
SELECTED_FILES_CHANGED_PROPERTY
public final static java.lang.String
SELECTED_FILE_CHANGED_PROPERTY

## Constructors

public JFileChooser()
public JFileChooser(String
currentDirectoryPath)
public JFileChooser(File
currentDirectory)
public JFileChooser(FileSystemView fsv)
public JFileChooser(File
currentDirectory,FileSystemView fsv)

public JFileChooser(String
currentDirectoryPath,FileSystemView fsv)

## Methods

public boolean accept(File f)
public void addActionListener(
ActionListener l)
public void addChoosableFileFilter(
FileFilter filter)
public void approveSelection()
public void cancelSelection()
public void changeToParentDirectory()
public void ensureFileIsVisible(File f)
protected void fireActionPerformed(
String command)
public FileFilter getAcceptAllFileFilter(
)
public AccessibleContext
getAccessibleContext()
public JComponent getAccessory()
public int getApproveButtonMnemonic()
public String getApproveButtonText()
public String
getApproveButtonToolTipText()
public FileFilter
getChoosableFileFilters()
public File getCurrentDirectory()
public String getDescription(File f)
public String getDialogTitle()
public int getDialogType()
public FileFilter getFileFilter()
public int getFileSelectionMode()
public FileSystemView getFileSystemView()
public FileView getFileView()
public Icon getIcon(File f)
public String getName(File f)
public File getSelectedFile()
public File getSelectedFiles()
public String getTypeDescription(File f)
public FileChooserUI getUI()
public String getUIClassID()
public boolean
isDirectorySelectionEnabled()
public boolean isFileHidingEnabled()
public boolean isFileSelectionEnabled()
public boolean isMultiSelectionEnabled()
public boolean isTraversable(File f)
protected String paramString()
public void removeActionListener(
ActionListener l)
public boolean removeChoosableFileFilter(
FileFilter f)
public void rescanCurrentDirectory()
public void resetChoosableFileFilters()
public void setAccessory(JComponent
newAccessory)
public void setApproveButtonMnemonic(int
mnemonic)
public void setApproveButtonMnemonic(
char mnemonic)
public void setApproveButtonText(String
approveButtonText)

```
public void setApproveButtonToolTipText(
String toolTipText)
public void setCurrentDirectory(File dir)
public void setDialogTitle(String
dialogTitle)
public void setDialogType(int dialogType)
public void setFileFilter(FileFilter
filter)
public void setFileHidingEnabled(boolean
b)
public void setFileSelectionMode(int
mode)
public void setFileSystemView(
FileSystemView fsv)
public void setFileView(FileView
fileView)
public void setMultiSelectionEnabled(
boolean b)
public void setSelectedFile(File
selectedFile)
public void setSelectedFiles(File
selectedFiles)
protected void setup(FileSystemView view)
public int showDialog(Component parent,
String approveButtonText)
public int showOpenDialog(Component
parent)
public int showSaveDialog(Component
parent)
public void updateUI()
```

## JFrame

```
public class javax.swing.JFrame
implements javax.accessibility.
Accessible
implements javax.swing.
RootPaneContainer
implements javax.swing.WindowConstants
extends java.awt.Frame
extends java.awt.Window
extends java.awt.Container
extends java.awt.Component
extends java.lang.Object
```

### Fields

```
protected javax.accessibility.
AccessibleContext accessibleContext
protected javax.swing.JRootPane
rootPane
protected boolean
rootPaneCheckingEnabled
```

### Constructors

```
public  JFrame()
public  JFrame(String title)
```

### Methods

```
protected void addImpl(Component comp,
Object constraints,int index)
protected JRootPane createRootPane()
protected void frameInit()
public AccessibleContext
getAccessibleContext()
```

```
public Container getContentPane()
public int getDefaultCloseOperation()
public Component getGlassPane()
public JMenuBar getJMenuBar()
public JLayeredPane getLayeredPane()
public JRootPane getRootPane()
protected boolean
isRootPaneCheckingEnabled()
protected String paramString()
protected void processKeyEvent(KeyEvent
e)
protected void processWindowEvent(
WindowEvent e)
public void setContentPane(Container
contentPane)
public void setDefaultCloseOperation(int
operation)
public void setGlassPane(Component
glassPane)
public void setJMenuBar(JMenuBar menubar)
public void setLayeredPane(JLayeredPane
layeredPane)
public void setLayout(LayoutManager
manager)
protected void setRootPane(JRootPane
root)
protected void
setRootPaneCheckingEnabled(boolean
enabled)
public void update(Graphics g)
```

## JInternalFrame

```
public class javax.swing.JInternalFrame
implements javax.accessibility.
Accessible
implements javax.swing.
RootPaneContainer
implements javax.swing.WindowConstants
extends javax.swing.JComponent
extends java.awt.Container
extends java.awt.Component
extends java.lang.Object
```

### Fields

```
protected boolean closable
public final static java.lang.String
CONTENT_PANE_PROPERTY
protected JDesktopIcon desktopIcon
protected javax.swing.Icon frameIcon
public final static java.lang.String
FRAME_ICON_PROPERTY
public final static java.lang.String
GLASS_PANE_PROPERTY
protected boolean iconable
protected boolean isClosed
protected boolean isIcon
protected boolean isMaximum
protected boolean isSelected
public final static java.lang.String IS_
CLOSED_PROPERTY
public final static java.lang.String IS_
ICON_PROPERTY
```

public final static java.lang.String IS_
MAXIMUM_PROPERTY
public final static java.lang.String IS_
SELECTED_PROPERTY
public final static java.lang.String
LAYERED_PANE_PROPERTY
protected boolean maximizable
public final static java.lang.String
MENU_BAR_PROPERTY
protected boolean resizable
protected javax.swing.JRootPane
rootPane
protected boolean
rootPaneCheckingEnabled
public final static java.lang.String
ROOT_PANE_PROPERTY
protected java.lang.String title
public final static java.lang.String
TITLE_PROPERTY

### Constructors
public  JInternalFrame()
public  JInternalFrame(String title)
public  JInternalFrame(String title,
boolean resizable)
public  JInternalFrame(String title,
boolean resizable,boolean closable)
public  JInternalFrame(String title,
boolean resizable,boolean closable,
boolean maximizable)
public  JInternalFrame(String title,
boolean resizable,boolean closable,
boolean maximizable,boolean iconifiable)

### Methods
protected void addImpl(Component comp,
Object constraints,int index)
public void addInternalFrameListener(
InternalFrameListener l)
protected JRootPane createRootPane()
public void dispose()
protected void fireInternalFrameEvent(
int id)
public AccessibleContext
getAccessibleContext()
public Color getBackground()
public Container getContentPane()
public int getDefaultCloseOperation()
public JDesktopIcon getDesktopIcon()
public JDesktopPane getDesktopPane()
public Color getForeground()
public Icon getFrameIcon()
public Component getGlassPane()
public JMenuBar getJMenuBar()
public int getLayer()
public JLayeredPane getLayeredPane()
public JMenuBar getMenuBar()
public JRootPane getRootPane()
public String getTitle()
public InternalFrameUI getUI()
public String getUIClassID()
public final String getWarningString()
public boolean isClosable()
public boolean isClosed()

public boolean isIcon()
public boolean isIconifiable()
public boolean isMaximizable()
public boolean isMaximum()
public boolean isResizable()
protected boolean
isRootPaneCheckingEnabled()
public boolean isSelected()
public void moveToBack()
public void moveToFront()
public void pack()
protected String paramString()
public void removeInternalFrameListener(
InternalFrameListener l)
public void reshape(int x,int y,int
width,int height)
public void setBackground(Color c)
public void setClosable(boolean b)
public void setClosed(boolean b)
public void setContentPane(Container c)
public void setDefaultCloseOperation(int
operation)
public void setDesktopIcon(JDesktopIcon
d)
public void setForeground(Color c)
public void setFrameIcon(Icon icon)
public void setGlassPane(Component glass)
public void setIcon(boolean b)
public void setIconifiable(boolean b)
public void setJMenuBar(JMenuBar m)
public void setLayer(Integer layer)
public void setLayeredPane(JLayeredPane
layered)
public void setLayout(LayoutManager
manager)
public void setMaximizable(boolean b)
public void setMaximum(boolean b)
public void setMenuBar(JMenuBar m)
public void setResizable(boolean b)
protected void setRootPane(JRootPane
root)
protected void
setRootPaneCheckingEnabled(boolean
enabled)
public void setSelected(boolean selected)
public void setTitle(String title)
public void setUI(InternalFrameUI ui)
public void setVisible(boolean b)
public void show()
public void toBack()
public void toFront()
public void updateUI()

## JLabel
public class javax.swing.JLabel
implements javax.accessibility.
Accessible
implements javax.swing.SwingConstants
extends javax.swing.JComponent
extends java.awt.Container
extends java.awt.Component
extends java.lang.Object

## Fields
```
protected java.awt.Component labelFor
```

## Constructors
```
public  JLabel(String text,Icon icon,int
horizontalAlignment)
public  JLabel(String text,int
horizontalAlignment)
public  JLabel(String text)
public  JLabel(Icon image,int
horizontalAlignment)
public  JLabel(Icon image)
public  JLabel()
```

## Methods
```
protected int checkHorizontalKey(int key,
String message)
protected int checkVerticalKey(int key,
String message)
public AccessibleContext
getAccessibleContext()
public Icon getDisabledIcon()
public int getDisplayedMnemonic()
public int getHorizontalAlignment()
public int getHorizontalTextPosition()
public Icon getIcon()
public int getIconTextGap()
public Component getLabelFor()
public String getText()
public LabelUI getUI()
public String getUIClassID()
public int getVerticalAlignment()
public int getVerticalTextPosition()
protected String paramString()
public void setDisabledIcon(Icon
disabledIcon)
public void setDisplayedMnemonic(int key)
public void setDisplayedMnemonic(char
aChar)
public void setHorizontalAlignment(int
alignment)
public void setHorizontalTextPosition(
int textPosition)
public void setIcon(Icon icon)
public void setIconTextGap(int
iconTextGap)
public void setLabelFor(Component c)
public void setText(String text)
public void setUI(LabelUI ui)
public void setVerticalAlignment(int
alignment)
public void setVerticalTextPosition(int
textPosition)
public void updateUI()
```

## JLayeredPane
```
public class javax.swing.JLayeredPane
implements javax.accessibility.
Accessible
extends javax.swing.JComponent
extends java.awt.Container
extends java.awt.Component
extends java.lang.Object
```

## Fields
```
public final static java.lang.Integer
DEFAULT_LAYER
public final static java.lang.Integer
DRAG_LAYER
public final static java.lang.Integer
FRAME_CONTENT_LAYER
public final static java.lang.String
LAYER_PROPERTY
public final static java.lang.Integer
MODAL_LAYER
public final static java.lang.Integer
PALETTE_LAYER
public final static java.lang.Integer
POPUP_LAYER
```

## Constructors
```
public  JLayeredPane()
```

## Methods
```
protected void addImpl(Component comp,
Object constraints,int index)
public AccessibleContext
getAccessibleContext()
public int getComponentCountInLayer(int
layer)
public Component getComponentsInLayer(
int layer)
protected Hashtable getComponentToLayer()
public int getIndexOf(Component c)
public static int getLayer(JComponent c)
public int getLayer(Component c)
public static JLayeredPane
getLayeredPaneAbove(Component c)
protected Integer getObjectForLayer(int
layer)
public int getPosition(Component c)
public int highestLayer()
protected int insertIndexForLayer(int
layer,int position)
public boolean isOptimizedDrawingEnabled(
)
public int lowestLayer()
public void moveToBack(Component c)
public void moveToFront(Component c)
public void paint(Graphics g)
protected String paramString()
public static void putLayer(JComponent c,
int layer)
public void remove(int index)
public void setLayer(Component c,int
layer)
public void setLayer(Component c,int
layer,int position)
public void setPosition(Component c,int
position)
```

## JList
```
public class javax.swing.JList
implements javax.accessibility.
Accessible
implements javax.swing.Scrollable
extends javax.swing.JComponent
```

extends java.awt.Container
extends java.awt.Component
extends java.lang.Object

## Constructors
public  JList(ListModel dataModel)
public  JList(Object listData)
public  JList(Vector listData)
public  JList()

## Methods
public void addListSelectionListener(
ListSelectionListener listener)
public void addSelectionInterval(int
anchor,int lead)
public void clearSelection()
protected ListSelectionModel
createSelectionModel()
public void ensureIndexIsVisible(int
index)
protected void fireSelectionValueChanged(
int firstIndex,int lastIndex,boolean
isAdjusting)
public AccessibleContext
getAccessibleContext()
public int getAnchorSelectionIndex()
public Rectangle getCellBounds(int
index1,int index2)
public ListCellRenderer getCellRenderer()
public int getFirstVisibleIndex()
public int getFixedCellHeight()
public int getFixedCellWidth()
public int getLastVisibleIndex()
public int getLeadSelectionIndex()
public int getMaxSelectionIndex()
public int getMinSelectionIndex()
public ListModel getModel()
public Dimension
getPreferredScrollableViewportSize()
public Object getPrototypeCellValue()
public int getScrollableBlockIncrement(
Rectangle visibleRect,int orientation,
int direction)
public boolean
getScrollableTracksViewportHeight()
public boolean
getScrollableTracksViewportWidth()
public int getScrollableUnitIncrement(
Rectangle visibleRect,int orientation,
int direction)
public int getSelectedIndex()
public int getSelectedIndices()
public Object getSelectedValue()
public Object getSelectedValues()
public Color getSelectionBackground()
public Color getSelectionForeground()
public int getSelectionMode()
public ListSelectionModel
getSelectionModel()
public ListUI getUI()
public String getUIClassID()
public boolean getValueIsAdjusting()
public int getVisibleRowCount()
public Point indexToLocation(int index)
public boolean isSelectedIndex(int index)

public boolean isSelectionEmpty()
public int locationToIndex(Point
location)
protected String paramString()
public void removeListSelectionListener(
ListSelectionListener listener)
public void removeSelectionInterval(int
index0,int index1)
public void setCellRenderer(
ListCellRenderer cellRenderer)
public void setFixedCellHeight(int
height)
public void setFixedCellWidth(int width)
public void setListData(Object listData)
public void setListData(Vector listData)
public void setModel(ListModel model)
public void setPrototypeCellValue(Object
prototypeCellValue)
public void setSelectedIndex(int index)
public void setSelectedIndices(int
indices)
public void setSelectedValue(Object
anObject,boolean shouldScroll)
public void setSelectionBackground(Color
selectionBackground)
public void setSelectionForeground(Color
selectionForeground)
public void setSelectionInterval(int
anchor,int lead)
public void setSelectionMode(int
selectionMode)
public void setSelectionModel(
ListSelectionModel selectionModel)
public void setUI(ListUI ui)
public void setValueIsAdjusting(boolean
b)
public void setVisibleRowCount(int
visibleRowCount)
public void updateUI()

## JMenu
public class javax.swing.JMenu
implements javax.accessibility.
Accessible
implements javax.swing.MenuElement
extends javax.swing.JMenuItem
extends javax.swing.AbstractButton
extends javax.swing.JComponent
extends java.awt.Container
extends java.awt.Component
extends java.lang.Object

### Fields
protected WinListener popupListener

### Constructors
public  JMenu()
public  JMenu(String s)
public  JMenu(String s,boolean b)

### Methods
public JMenuItem add(JMenuItem menuItem)
public Component add(Component c)
public JMenuItem add(String s)

```
public JMenuItem add(Action a)
public void addMenuListener(MenuListener
l)
public void addSeparator()
protected PropertyChangeListener
createActionChangeListener(JMenuItem b)
protected WinListener createWinListener(
JPopupMenu p)
public void doClick(int pressTime)
protected void fireMenuCanceled()
protected void fireMenuDeselected()
protected void fireMenuSelected()
public AccessibleContext
getAccessibleContext()
public Component getComponent()
public int getDelay()
public JMenuItem getItem(int pos)
public int getItemCount()
public Component getMenuComponent(int n)
public int getMenuComponentCount()
public Component getMenuComponents()
public JPopupMenu getPopupMenu()
public MenuElement getSubElements()
public String getUIClassID()
public void insert(String s,int pos)
public JMenuItem insert(JMenuItem mi,int
pos)
public JMenuItem insert(Action a,int pos)
public void insertSeparator(int index)
public boolean isMenuComponent(Component
c)
public boolean isPopupMenuVisible()
public boolean isSelected()
public boolean isTearOff()
public boolean isTopLevelMenu()
public void menuSelectionChanged(boolean
isIncluded)
protected String paramString()
protected void processKeyEvent(KeyEvent
e)
public void remove(JMenuItem item)
public void remove(int pos)
public void remove(Component c)
public void removeAll()
public void removeMenuListener(
MenuListener l)
public void setAccelerator(KeyStroke
keyStroke)
public void setDelay(int d)
public void setMenuLocation(int x,int y)
public void setModel(ButtonModel
newModel)
public void setPopupMenuVisible(boolean
b)
public void setSelected(boolean b)
public void updateUI()
```

## JMenuBar

```
public class javax.swing.JMenuBar
implements javax.accessibility.
Accessible
implements javax.swing.MenuElement
extends javax.swing.JComponent
```

```
extends java.awt.Container
extends java.awt.Component
extends java.lang.Object
```

### Constructors
```
public  JMenuBar()
```

### Methods
```
public JMenu add(JMenu c)
public void addNotify()
public AccessibleContext
getAccessibleContext()
public Component getComponent()
public Component getComponentAtIndex(int
i)
public int getComponentIndex(Component c)
public JMenu getHelpMenu()
public Insets getMargin()
public JMenu getMenu(int index)
public int getMenuCount()
public SingleSelectionModel
getSelectionModel()
public MenuElement getSubElements()
public MenuBarUI getUI()
public String getUIClassID()
public boolean isBorderPainted()
public boolean isManagingFocus()
public boolean isSelected()
public void menuSelectionChanged(boolean
isIncluded)
protected void paintBorder(Graphics g)
protected String paramString()
public void processKeyEvent(KeyEvent e,
MenuElement path,MenuSelectionManager
manager)
public void processMouseEvent(MouseEvent
event,MenuElement path,
MenuSelectionManager manager)
public void removeNotify()
public void setBorderPainted(boolean s)
public void setHelpMenu(JMenu menu)
public void setMargin(Insets margin)
public void setSelected(Component sel)
public void setSelectionModel(
SingleSelectionModel model)
public void setUI(MenuBarUI ui)
public void updateUI()
```

## JMenuItem

```
public class javax.swing.JMenuItem
implements javax.accessibility.
Accessible
implements javax.swing.MenuElement
extends javax.swing.AbstractButton
extends javax.swing.JComponent
extends java.awt.Container
extends java.awt.Component
extends java.lang.Object
```

### Constructors
```
public  JMenuItem()
public  JMenuItem(Icon icon)
public  JMenuItem(String text)
```

```
public  JMenuItem(String text,Icon icon)
public  JMenuItem(String text,int
mnemonic)
```

## Methods

```
public void addMenuDragMouseListener(
MenuDragMouseListener l)
public void addMenuKeyListener(
MenuKeyListener l)
protected void fireMenuDragMouseDragged(
MenuDragMouseEvent event)
protected void fireMenuDragMouseEntered(
MenuDragMouseEvent event)
protected void fireMenuDragMouseExited(
MenuDragMouseEvent event)
protected void fireMenuDragMouseReleased(
MenuDragMouseEvent event)
protected void fireMenuKeyPressed(
MenuKeyEvent event)
protected void fireMenuKeyReleased(
MenuKeyEvent event)
protected void fireMenuKeyTyped(
MenuKeyEvent event)
public KeyStroke getAccelerator()
public AccessibleContext
getAccessibleContext()
public Component getComponent()
public MenuElement getSubElements()
public String getUIClassID()
protected void init(String text,Icon
icon)
public boolean isArmed()
public void menuSelectionChanged(boolean
isIncluded)
protected String paramString()
public void processKeyEvent(KeyEvent e,
MenuElement path,MenuSelectionManager
manager)
public void processMenuDragMouseEvent(
MenuDragMouseEvent e)
public void processMenuKeyEvent(
MenuKeyEvent e)
public void processMouseEvent(MouseEvent
e,MenuElement path,MenuSelectionManager
manager)
public void removeMenuDragMouseListener(
MenuDragMouseListener l)
public void removeMenuKeyListener(
MenuKeyListener l)
public void setAccelerator(KeyStroke
keyStroke)
public void setArmed(boolean b)
public void setEnabled(boolean b)
public void setUI(MenuItemUI ui)
public void updateUI()
```

# JOptionPane

```
public class javax.swing.JOptionPane
implements javax.accessibility.
Accessible
extends javax.swing.JComponent
extends java.awt.Container
extends java.awt.Component
extends java.lang.Object
```

## Fields

```
public final static int CANCEL_OPTION
public final static int CLOSED_OPTION
public final static int DEFAULT_OPTION
public final static int ERROR_MESSAGE
protected transient javax.swing.Icon
icon
public final static java.lang.String
ICON_PROPERTY
public final static int INFORMATION_
MESSAGE
protected transient java.lang.Object
initialSelectionValue
protected transient java.lang.Object
initialValue
public final static java.lang.String
INITIAL_SELECTION_VALUE_PROPERTY
public final static java.lang.String
INITIAL_VALUE_PROPERTY
protected transient java.lang.Object
inputValue
public final static java.lang.String
INPUT_VALUE_PROPERTY
protected transient java.lang.Object
message
protected int messageType
public final static java.lang.String
MESSAGE_PROPERTY
public final static java.lang.String
MESSAGE_TYPE_PROPERTY
public final static int NO_OPTION
public final static int OK_CANCEL_
OPTION
public final static int OK_OPTION
protected transient java.lang.Object
options
public final static java.lang.String
OPTIONS_PROPERTY
protected int optionType
public final static java.lang.String
OPTION_TYPE_PROPERTY
public final static int PLAIN_MESSAGE
public final static int QUESTION_
MESSAGE
protected transient java.lang.Object
selectionValues
public final static java.lang.String
SELECTION_VALUES_PROPERTY
public final static java.lang.Object
UNINITIALIZED_VALUE
protected transient java.lang.Object
value
public final static java.lang.String
VALUE_PROPERTY
protected boolean wantsInput
public final static java.lang.String
WANTS_INPUT_PROPERTY
public final static int WARNING_MESSAGE
public final static int YES_NO_CANCEL_
OPTION
public final static int YES_NO_OPTION
public final static int YES_OPTION
```

## Constructors

```
public JOptionPane()
public JOptionPane(Object message)
public JOptionPane(Object message,int
messageType)
public JOptionPane(Object message,int
messageType,int optionType)
public JOptionPane(Object message,int
messageType,int optionType,Icon icon)
public JOptionPane(Object message,int
messageType,int optionType,Icon icon,
Object options)
public JOptionPane(Object message,int
messageType,int optionType,Icon icon,
Object options,Object initialValue)
```

## Methods

```
public JDialog createDialog(Component
parentComponent,String title)
public JInternalFrame
createInternalFrame(Component
parentComponent,String title)
public AccessibleContext
getAccessibleContext()
public static JDesktopPane
getDesktopPaneForComponent(Component
parentComponent)
public static Frame getFrameForComponent(
Component parentComponent)
public Icon getIcon()
public Object getInitialSelectionValue()
public Object getInitialValue()
public Object getInputValue()
public int getMaxCharactersPerLineCount()
public Object getMessage()
public int getMessageType()
public Object getOptions()
public int getOptionType()
public static Frame getRootFrame()
public Object getSelectionValues()
public OptionPaneUI getUI()
public String getUIClassID()
public Object getValue()
public boolean getWantsInput()
protected String paramString()
public void selectInitialValue()
public void setIcon(Icon newIcon)
public void setInitialSelectionValue(
Object newValue)
public void setInitialValue(Object
newInitialValue)
public void setInputValue(Object
newValue)
public void setMessage(Object newMessage)
public void setMessageType(int newType)
public void setOptions(Object newOptions)
public void setOptionType(int newType)
public static void setRootFrame(Frame
newRootFrame)
public void setSelectionValues(Object
newValues)
public void setUI(OptionPaneUI ui)
public void setValue(Object newValue)
```

```
public void setWantsInput(boolean
newValue)
public static int showConfirmDialog(
Component parentComponent,Object message)
public static int showConfirmDialog(
Component parentComponent,Object message,
String title,int optionType)
public static int showConfirmDialog(
Component parentComponent,Object message,
String title,int optionType,int
messageType)
public static int showConfirmDialog(
Component parentComponent,Object message,
String title,int optionType,int
messageType,Icon icon)
public static String showInputDialog(
Object message)
public static String showInputDialog(
Component parentComponent,Object message)
public static String showInputDialog(
Component parentComponent,Object message,
String title,int messageType)
public static Object showInputDialog(
Component parentComponent,Object message,
String title,int messageType,Icon icon,
Object selectionValues,Object
initialSelectionValue)
public static int
showInternalConfirmDialog(Component
parentComponent,Object message)
public static int
showInternalConfirmDialog(Component
parentComponent,Object message,String
title,int optionType)
public static int
showInternalConfirmDialog(Component
parentComponent,Object message,String
title,int optionType,int messageType)
public static int
showInternalConfirmDialog(Component
parentComponent,Object message,String
title,int optionType,int messageType,
Icon icon)
public static String
showInternalInputDialog(Component
parentComponent,Object message)
public static String
showInternalInputDialog(Component
parentComponent,Object message,String
title,int messageType)
public static Object
showInternalInputDialog(Component
parentComponent,Object message,String
title,int messageType,Icon icon,Object
selectionValues,Object
initialSelectionValue)
public static void
showInternalMessageDialog(Component
parentComponent,Object message)
public static void
showInternalMessageDialog(Component
parentComponent,Object message,String
title,int messageType)
```

```
public static void
showInternalMessageDialog(Component
parentComponent,Object message,String
title,int messageType,Icon icon)
public static int
showInternalOptionDialog(Component
parentComponent,Object message,String
title,int optionType,int messageType,
Icon icon,Object options,Object
initialValue)
public static void showMessageDialog(
Component parentComponent,Object message)
public static void showMessageDialog(
Component parentComponent,Object message,
String title,int messageType)
public static void showMessageDialog(
Component parentComponent,Object message,
String title,int messageType,Icon icon)
public static int showOptionDialog(
Component parentComponent,Object message,
String title,int optionType,int
messageType,Icon icon,Object options,
Object initialValue)
public void updateUI()
```

## JPanel

```
public class javax.swing.JPanel
implements javax.accessibility.
Accessible
extends javax.swing.JComponent
extends java.awt.Container
extends java.awt.Component
extends java.lang.Object
```

### Constructors

```
public  JPanel(LayoutManager layout,
boolean isDoubleBuffered)
public  JPanel(LayoutManager layout)
public  JPanel(boolean isDoubleBuffered)
public  JPanel()
```

### Methods

```
public AccessibleContext
getAccessibleContext()
public String getUIClassID()
protected String paramString()
public void updateUI()
```

## JPasswordField

```
public class javax.swing.JPasswordField
extends javax.swing.JTextField
extends javax.swing.text.JTextComponent
extends javax.swing.JComponent
extends java.awt.Container
extends java.awt.Component
extends java.lang.Object
```

### Constructors

```
public  JPasswordField()
public  JPasswordField(String text)
public  JPasswordField(int columns)
public  JPasswordField(String text,int
columns)
```

```
public  JPasswordField(Document doc,
String txt,int columns)
```

### Methods

```
public void copy()
public void cut()
public boolean echoCharIsSet()
public AccessibleContext
getAccessibleContext()
public char getEchoChar()
public char getPassword()
public String getText()
public String getText(int offs,int len)
public String getUIClassID()
protected String paramString()
public void setEchoChar(char c)
```

## JPopupMenu

```
public class javax.swing.JPopupMenu
implements javax.accessibility.
Accessible
implements javax.swing.MenuElement
extends javax.swing.JComponent
extends java.awt.Container
extends java.awt.Component
extends java.lang.Object
```

### Constructors

```
public  JPopupMenu()
public  JPopupMenu(String label)
```

### Methods

```
public JMenuItem add(JMenuItem menuItem)
public JMenuItem add(String s)
public JMenuItem add(Action a)
public void addPopupMenuListener(
PopupMenuListener l)
public void addSeparator()
protected PropertyChangeListener
createActionChangeListener(JMenuItem b)
protected void firePopupMenuCanceled()
protected void
firePopupMenuWillBecomeInvisible()
protected void
firePopupMenuWillBecomeVisible()
public AccessibleContext
getAccessibleContext()
public Component getComponent()
public Component getComponentAtIndex(int
i)
public int getComponentIndex(Component c)
public static boolean
getDefaultLightWeightPopupEnabled()
public Component getInvoker()
public String getLabel()
public Insets getMargin()
public SingleSelectionModel
getSelectionModel()
public MenuElement getSubElements()
public PopupMenuUI getUI()
public String getUIClassID()
public void insert(Action a,int index)
```

```
public void insert(Component component,
int index)
public boolean isBorderPainted()
public boolean isLightWeightPopupEnabled(
)
public boolean isVisible()
public void menuSelectionChanged(boolean
isIncluded)
public void pack()
protected void paintBorder(Graphics g)
protected String paramString()
public void processKeyEvent(KeyEvent e,
MenuElement path,MenuSelectionManager
manager)
public void processMouseEvent(MouseEvent
event,MenuElement path,
MenuSelectionManager manager)
public void remove(Component comp)
public void removePopupMenuListener(
PopupMenuListener l)
public void setBorderPainted(boolean b)
public static void
setDefaultLightWeightPopupEnabled(
boolean aFlag)
public void setInvoker(Component invoker)
public void setLabel(String label)
public void setLightWeightPopupEnabled(
boolean aFlag)
public void setLocation(int x,int y)
public void setPopupSize(Dimension d)
public void setPopupSize(int width,int
height)
public void setSelected(Component sel)
public void setSelectionModel(
SingleSelectionModel model)
public void setUI(PopupMenuUI ui)
public void setVisible(boolean b)
public void show(Component invoker,int x,
int y)
public void updateUI()
```

## JProgressBar

```
public class javax.swing.JProgressBar
implements javax.accessibility.
Accessible
implements javax.swing.SwingConstants
extends javax.swing.JComponent
extends java.awt.Container
extends java.awt.Component
extends java.lang.Object
```

### Fields

```
protected transient javax.swing.event.
ChangeEvent changeEvent
protected javax.swing.event.
ChangeListener changeListener
protected javax.swing.BoundedRangeModel
model
protected int orientation
protected boolean paintBorder
protected boolean paintString
protected java.lang.String
progressString
```

### Constructors

```
public JProgressBar()
public JProgressBar(int orient)
public JProgressBar(int min,int max)
public JProgressBar(int orient,int min,
int max)
public JProgressBar(BoundedRangeModel
newModel)
```

### Methods

```
public void addChangeListener(
ChangeListener l)
protected ChangeListener
createChangeListener()
protected void fireStateChanged()
public AccessibleContext
getAccessibleContext()
public int getMaximum()
public int getMinimum()
public BoundedRangeModel getModel()
public int getOrientation()
public double getPercentComplete()
public String getString()
public ProgressBarUI getUI()
public String getUIClassID()
public int getValue()
public boolean isBorderPainted()
public boolean isStringPainted()
protected void paintBorder(Graphics g)
protected String paramString()
public void removeChangeListener(
ChangeListener l)
public void setBorderPainted(boolean b)
public void setMaximum(int n)
public void setMinimum(int n)
public void setModel(BoundedRangeModel
newModel)
public void setOrientation(int
newOrientation)
public void setString(String s)
public void setStringPainted(boolean b)
public void setUI(ProgressBarUI ui)
public void setValue(int n)
public void updateUI()
```

## JRadioButton

```
public class javax.swing.JRadioButton
implements javax.accessibility.
Accessible
extends javax.swing.JToggleButton
extends javax.swing.AbstractButton
extends javax.swing.JComponent
extends java.awt.Container
extends java.awt.Component
extends java.lang.Object
```

### Constructors

```
public JRadioButton()
public JRadioButton(Icon icon)
public JRadioButton(Icon icon,boolean
selected)
public JRadioButton(String text)
public JRadioButton(String text,boolean
selected)
```

```
public  JRadioButton(String text,Icon
icon)
public  JRadioButton(String text,Icon
icon,boolean selected)
```

### Methods
```
public AccessibleContext
getAccessibleContext()
public String getUIClassID()
protected String paramString()
public void updateUI()
```

## JRadioButtonMenuItem
```
public class javax.swing.
JRadioButtonMenuItem
implements javax.accessibility.
Accessible
extends javax.swing.JMenuItem
extends javax.swing.AbstractButton
extends javax.swing.JComponent
extends java.awt.Container
extends java.awt.Component
extends java.lang.Object
```

### Constructors
```
public  JRadioButtonMenuItem()
public  JRadioButtonMenuItem(Icon icon)
public  JRadioButtonMenuItem(String text)
public  JRadioButtonMenuItem(String text,
Icon icon)
public  JRadioButtonMenuItem(String text,
boolean b)
public  JRadioButtonMenuItem(Icon icon,
boolean selected)
public  JRadioButtonMenuItem(String text,
Icon icon,boolean selected)
```

### Methods
```
public AccessibleContext
getAccessibleContext()
public String getUIClassID()
protected void init(String text,Icon
icon)
protected String paramString()
public void requestFocus()
public void updateUI()
```

## JRootPane
```
public class javax.swing.JRootPane
implements javax.accessibility.
Accessible
extends javax.swing.JComponent
extends java.awt.Container
extends java.awt.Component
extends java.lang.Object
```

### Fields
```
protected java.awt.Container
contentPane
protected javax.swing.JButton
defaultButton
protected DefaultAction
defaultPressAction
```

```
protected DefaultAction
defaultReleaseAction
protected java.awt.Component glassPane
protected javax.swing.JLayeredPane
layeredPane
protected javax.swing.JMenuBar menuBar
```

### Constructors
```
public  JRootPane()
```

### Methods
```
protected void addImpl(Component comp,
Object constraints,int index)
public void addNotify()
protected Container createContentPane()
protected Component createGlassPane()
protected JLayeredPane createLayeredPane(
)
protected LayoutManager createRootLayout(
)
public AccessibleContext
getAccessibleContext()
public Container getContentPane()
public JButton getDefaultButton()
public Component getGlassPane()
public JMenuBar getJMenuBar()
public JLayeredPane getLayeredPane()
public JMenuBar getMenuBar()
public boolean isFocusCycleRoot()
public boolean isValidateRoot()
protected String paramString()
public void removeNotify()
public void setContentPane(Container
content)
public void setDefaultButton(JButton
defaultButton)
public void setGlassPane(Component glass)
public void setJMenuBar(JMenuBar menu)
public void setLayeredPane(JLayeredPane
layered)
public void setMenuBar(JMenuBar menu)
```

## JScrollBar
```
public class javax.swing.JScrollBar
implements javax.accessibility.
Accessible
implements java.awt.Adjustable
extends javax.swing.JComponent
extends java.awt.Container
extends java.awt.Component
extends java.lang.Object
```

### Fields
```
protected int blockIncrement
protected javax.swing.BoundedRangeModel
model
protected int orientation
protected int unitIncrement
```

### Constructors
```
public  JScrollBar(int orientation,int
value,int extent,int min,int max)
public  JScrollBar(int orientation)
public  JScrollBar()
```

## Methods
```
public void addAdjustmentListener(
AdjustmentListener l)
protected void
fireAdjustmentValueChanged(int id,int
type,int value)
public AccessibleContext
getAccessibleContext()
public int getBlockIncrement(int
direction)
public int getBlockIncrement()
public int getMaximum()
public Dimension getMaximumSize()
public int getMinimum()
public Dimension getMinimumSize()
public BoundedRangeModel getModel()
public int getOrientation()
public ScrollBarUI getUI()
public String getUIClassID()
public int getUnitIncrement(int
direction)
public int getUnitIncrement()
public int getValue()
public boolean getValueIsAdjusting()
public int getVisibleAmount()
protected String paramString()
public void removeAdjustmentListener(
AdjustmentListener l)
public void setBlockIncrement(int
blockIncrement)
public void setEnabled(boolean x)
public void setMaximum(int maximum)
public void setMinimum(int minimum)
public void setModel(BoundedRangeModel
newModel)
public void setOrientation(int
orientation)
public void setUnitIncrement(int
unitIncrement)
public void setValue(int value)
public void setValueIsAdjusting(boolean
b)
public void setValues(int newValue,int
newExtent,int newMin,int newMax)
public void setVisibleAmount(int extent)
public void updateUI()
```

# JScrollPane
```
public class javax.swing.JScrollPane
implements javax.accessibility.
Accessible
implements javax.swing.
ScrollPaneConstants
extends javax.swing.JComponent
extends java.awt.Container
extends java.awt.Component
extends java.lang.Object
```

## Fields
```
protected javax.swing.JViewport
columnHeader
protected javax.swing.JScrollBar
horizontalScrollBar
```

```
protected int horizontalScrollBarPolicy
protected java.awt.Component lowerLeft
protected java.awt.Component lowerRight
protected javax.swing.JViewport
rowHeader
protected java.awt.Component upperLeft
protected java.awt.Component upperRight
protected javax.swing.JScrollBar
verticalScrollBar
protected int verticalScrollBarPolicy
protected javax.swing.JViewport
viewport
```

## Constructors
```
public JScrollPane(Component view,int
vsbPolicy,int hsbPolicy)
public JScrollPane(Component view)
public JScrollPane(int vsbPolicy,int
hsbPolicy)
public JScrollPane()
```

## Methods
```
public JScrollBar
createHorizontalScrollBar()
public JScrollBar
createVerticalScrollBar()
protected JViewport createViewport()
public AccessibleContext
getAccessibleContext()
public JViewport getColumnHeader()
public Component getCorner(String key)
public JScrollBar getHorizontalScrollBar(
)
public int getHorizontalScrollBarPolicy()
public JViewport getRowHeader()
public ScrollPaneUI getUI()
public String getUIClassID()
public JScrollBar getVerticalScrollBar()
public int getVerticalScrollBarPolicy()
public JViewport getViewport()
public Border getViewportBorder()
public Rectangle getViewportBorderBounds(
)
public boolean isOpaque()
public boolean isValidateRoot()
protected String paramString()
public void setColumnHeader(JViewport
columnHeader)
public void setColumnHeaderView(
Component view)
public void setCorner(String key,
Component corner)
public void setHorizontalScrollBar(
JScrollBar horizontalScrollBar)
public void setHorizontalScrollBarPolicy(
int policy)
public void setLayout(LayoutManager
layout)
public void setRowHeader(JViewport
rowHeader)
public void setRowHeaderView(Component
view)
public void setUI(ScrollPaneUI ui)
```

```
public void setVerticalScrollBar(
JScrollBar verticalScrollBar)
public void setVerticalScrollBarPolicy(
int policy)
public void setViewport(JViewport
viewport)
public void setViewportBorder(Border
viewportBorder)
public void setViewportView(Component
view)
public void updateUI()
```

## JSeparator

```
public class javax.swing.JSeparator
implements javax.accessibility.
Accessible
implements javax.swing.SwingConstants
extends javax.swing.JComponent
extends java.awt.Container
extends java.awt.Component
extends java.lang.Object
```

### Constructors

```
public  JSeparator()
public  JSeparator(int orientation)
```

### Methods

```
public AccessibleContext
getAccessibleContext()
public int getOrientation()
public SeparatorUI getUI()
public String getUIClassID()
public boolean isFocusTraversable()
protected String paramString()
public void setOrientation(int
orientation)
public void setUI(SeparatorUI ui)
public void updateUI()
```

## JSlider

```
public class javax.swing.JSlider
implements javax.accessibility.
Accessible
implements javax.swing.SwingConstants
extends javax.swing.JComponent
extends java.awt.Container
extends java.awt.Component
extends java.lang.Object
```

### Fields

```
protected transient javax.swing.event.
ChangeEvent changeEvent
protected javax.swing.event.
ChangeListener changeListener
protected int majorTickSpacing
protected int minorTickSpacing
protected int orientation
protected javax.swing.BoundedRangeModel
sliderModel
protected boolean snapToTicks
```

### Constructors

```
public  JSlider()
```

```
public  JSlider(int orientation)
public  JSlider(int min,int max)
public  JSlider(int min,int max,int
value)
public  JSlider(int orientation,int min,
int max,int value)
public  JSlider(BoundedRangeModel brm)
```

### Methods

```
public void addChangeListener(
ChangeListener l)
protected ChangeListener
createChangeListener()
public Hashtable createStandardLabels(
int increment)
public Hashtable createStandardLabels(
int increment,int start)
protected void fireStateChanged()
public AccessibleContext
getAccessibleContext()
public int getExtent()
public boolean getInverted()
public Dictionary getLabelTable()
public int getMajorTickSpacing()
public int getMaximum()
public int getMinimum()
public int getMinorTickSpacing()
public BoundedRangeModel getModel()
public int getOrientation()
public boolean getPaintLabels()
public boolean getPaintTicks()
public boolean getPaintTrack()
public boolean getSnapToTicks()
public SliderUI getUI()
public String getUIClassID()
public int getValue()
public boolean getValueIsAdjusting()
protected String paramString()
public void removeChangeListener(
ChangeListener l)
public void setExtent(int extent)
public void setInverted(boolean b)
public void setLabelTable(Dictionary
labels)
public void setMajorTickSpacing(int n)
public void setMaximum(int maximum)
public void setMinimum(int minimum)
public void setMinorTickSpacing(int n)
public void setModel(BoundedRangeModel
newModel)
public void setOrientation(int
orientation)
public void setPaintLabels(boolean b)
public void setPaintTicks(boolean b)
public void setPaintTrack(boolean b)
public void setSnapToTicks(boolean b)
public void setUI(SliderUI ui)
public void setValue(int n)
public void setValueIsAdjusting(boolean
b)
protected void updateLabelUIs()
public void updateUI()
```

# JSplitPane

```
public class javax.swing.JSplitPane
implements javax.accessibility.
Accessible
extends javax.swing.JComponent
extends java.awt.Container
extends java.awt.Component
extends java.lang.Object
```

## Fields

```
public final static java.lang.String
BOTTOM
protected boolean continuousLayout
public final static java.lang.String
CONTINUOUS_LAYOUT_PROPERTY
public final static java.lang.String
DIVIDER
protected int dividerSize
public final static java.lang.String
DIVIDER_SIZE_PROPERTY
public final static int HORIZONTAL_
SPLIT
protected int lastDividerLocation
public final static java.lang.String
LAST_DIVIDER_LOCATION_PROPERTY
public final static java.lang.String
LEFT
protected java.awt.Component
leftComponent
protected boolean oneTouchExpandable
public final static java.lang.String ONE_
TOUCH_EXPANDABLE_PROPERTY
protected int orientation
public final static java.lang.String
ORIENTATION_PROPERTY
public final static java.lang.String
RIGHT
protected java.awt.Component
rightComponent
public final static java.lang.String
TOP
public final static int VERTICAL_SPLIT
```

## Constructors

```
public  JSplitPane()
public  JSplitPane(int newOrientation)
public  JSplitPane(int newOrientation,
boolean newContinuousLayout)
public  JSplitPane(int newOrientation,
Component newLeftComponent,Component
newRightComponent)
public  JSplitPane(int newOrientation,
boolean newContinuousLayout,Component
newLeftComponent,Component
newRightComponent)
```

## Methods

```
protected void addImpl(Component comp,
Object constraints,int index)
public AccessibleContext
getAccessibleContext()
public Component getBottomComponent()
public int getDividerLocation()
```

```
public int getDividerSize()
public int getLastDividerLocation()
public Component getLeftComponent()
public int getMaximumDividerLocation()
public int getMinimumDividerLocation()
public int getOrientation()
public Component getRightComponent()
public Component getTopComponent()
public SplitPaneUI getUI()
public String getUIClassID()
public boolean isContinuousLayout()
public boolean isOneTouchExpandable()
protected void paintChildren(Graphics g)
protected String paramString()
public void remove(Component component)
public void remove(int index)
public void removeAll()
public void resetToPreferredSizes()
public void setBottomComponent(Component
comp)
public void setContinuousLayout(boolean
newContinuousLayout)
public void setDividerLocation(double
proportionalLocation)
public void setDividerLocation(int
location)
public void setDividerSize(int newSize)
public void setLastDividerLocation(int
newLastLocation)
public void setLeftComponent(Component
comp)
public void setOneTouchExpandable(
boolean newValue)
public void setOrientation(int
orientation)
public void setRightComponent(Component
comp)
public void setTopComponent(Component
comp)
public void setUI(SplitPaneUI ui)
public void updateUI()
```

# JTabbedPane

```
public class javax.swing.JTabbedPane
implements javax.accessibility.
Accessible
implements java.io.Serializable
implements javax.swing.SwingConstants
extends javax.swing.JComponent
extends java.awt.Container
extends java.awt.Component
extends java.lang.Object
```

## Fields

```
protected transient javax.swing.event.
ChangeEvent changeEvent
protected javax.swing.event.
ChangeListener changeListener
protected javax.swing.
SingleSelectionModel model
protected int tabPlacement
```

## Constructors
```
public  JTabbedPane()
public  JTabbedPane(int tabPlacement)
```

## Methods
```
public Component add(Component component)
public Component add(String title,
Component component)
public Component add(Component component,
int index)
public void add(Component component,
Object constraints)
public void add(Component component,
Object constraints,int index)
public void addChangeListener(
ChangeListener l)
public void addTab(String title,Icon
icon,Component component,String tip)
public void addTab(String title,Icon
icon,Component component)
public void addTab(String title,
Component component)
protected ChangeListener
createChangeListener()
protected void fireStateChanged()
public AccessibleContext
getAccessibleContext()
public Color getBackgroundAt(int index)
public Rectangle getBoundsAt(int index)
public Component getComponentAt(int
index)
public Icon getDisabledIconAt(int index)
public Color getForegroundAt(int index)
public Icon getIconAt(int index)
public SingleSelectionModel getModel()
public Component getSelectedComponent()
public int getSelectedIndex()
public int getTabCount()
public int getTabPlacement()
public int getTabRunCount()
public String getTitleAt(int index)
public String getToolTipText(MouseEvent
event)
public TabbedPaneUI getUI()
public String getUIClassID()
public int indexOfComponent(Component
component)
public int indexOfTab(String title)
public int indexOfTab(Icon icon)
public void insertTab(String title,Icon
icon,Component component,String tip,int
index)
public boolean isEnabledAt(int index)
protected String paramString()
public void remove(Component component)
public void removeAll()
public void removeChangeListener(
ChangeListener l)
public void removeTabAt(int index)
public void setBackgroundAt(int index,
Color background)
public void setComponentAt(int index,
Component component)
```

```
public void setDisabledIconAt(int index,
Icon disabledIcon)
public void setEnabledAt(int index,
boolean enabled)
public void setForegroundAt(int index,
Color foreground)
public void setIconAt(int index,Icon
icon)
public void setModel(
SingleSelectionModel model)
public void setSelectedComponent(
Component c)
public void setSelectedIndex(int index)
public void setTabPlacement(int
tabPlacement)
public void setTitleAt(int index,String
title)
public void setUI(TabbedPaneUI ui)
public void updateUI()
```

# JTable
```
public class javax.swing.JTable
implements javax.accessibility.
Accessible
implements javax.swing.event.
CellEditorListener
implements javax.swing.event.
ListSelectionListener
implements javax.swing.Scrollable
implements javax.swing.event.
TableColumnModelListener
implements javax.swing.event.
TableModelListener
extends javax.swing.JComponent
extends java.awt.Container
extends java.awt.Component
extends java.lang.Object
```

## Fields
```
protected boolean
autoCreateColumnsFromModel
protected int autoResizeMode
public final static int AUTO_RESIZE_ALL_
COLUMNS
public final static int AUTO_RESIZE_LAST_
COLUMN
public final static int AUTO_RESIZE_NEXT_
COLUMN
public final static int AUTO_RESIZE_OFF
public final static int AUTO_RESIZE_
SUBSEQUENT_COLUMNS
protected transient javax.swing.table.
TableCellEditor cellEditor
protected boolean cellSelectionEnabled
protected javax.swing.table.
TableColumnModel columnModel
protected javax.swing.table.TableModel
dataModel
protected transient java.util.Hashtable
defaultEditorsByColumnClass
protected transient java.util.Hashtable
defaultRenderersByColumnClass
protected transient int editingColumn
```

```
protected transient int editingRow
protected transient java.awt.Component
editorComp
protected java.awt.Color gridColor
protected java.awt.Dimension
preferredViewportSize
protected int rowHeight
protected int rowMargin
protected boolean rowSelectionAllowed
protected java.awt.Color
selectionBackground
protected java.awt.Color
selectionForeground
protected javax.swing.ListSelectionModel
selectionModel
protected boolean showHorizontalLines
protected boolean showVerticalLines
protected javax.swing.table.JTableHeader
tableHeader
```

## Constructors

```
public  JTable()
public  JTable(TableModel dm)
public  JTable(TableModel dm,
TableColumnModel cm)
public  JTable(TableModel dm,
TableColumnModel cm,ListSelectionModel
sm)
public  JTable(int numRows,int
numColumns)
public  JTable(Vector rowData,Vector
columnNames)
public  JTable(Object rowData,Object
columnNames)
```

## Methods

```
public void addColumn(TableColumn
aColumn)
public void addColumnSelectionInterval(
int index0,int index1)
public void addNotify()
public void addRowSelectionInterval(int
index0,int index1)
public void clearSelection()
public void columnAdded(
TableColumnModelEvent e)
public int columnAtPoint(Point point)
public void columnMarginChanged(
ChangeEvent e)
public void columnMoved(
TableColumnModelEvent e)
public void columnRemoved(
TableColumnModelEvent e)
public void columnSelectionChanged(
ListSelectionEvent e)
protected void
configureEnclosingScrollPane()
public int convertColumnIndexToModel(int
viewColumnIndex)
public int convertColumnIndexToView(int
modelColumnIndex)
protected TableColumnModel
createDefaultColumnModel()
```

```
public void
createDefaultColumnsFromModel()
protected TableModel
createDefaultDataModel()
protected void createDefaultEditors()
protected void createDefaultRenderers()
protected ListSelectionModel
createDefaultSelectionModel()
protected JTableHeader
createDefaultTableHeader()
public static JScrollPane
createScrollPaneForTable(JTable aTable)
public boolean editCellAt(int row,int
column)
public boolean editCellAt(int row,int
column,EventObject e)
public void editingCanceled(ChangeEvent
e)
public void editingStopped(ChangeEvent e)
public AccessibleContext
getAccessibleContext()
public boolean
getAutoCreateColumnsFromModel()
public int getAutoResizeMode()
public TableCellEditor getCellEditor()
public TableCellEditor getCellEditor(int
row,int column)
public Rectangle getCellRect(int row,int
column,boolean includeSpacing)
public TableCellRenderer getCellRenderer(
int row,int column)
public boolean getCellSelectionEnabled()
public TableColumn getColumn(Object
identifier)
public Class getColumnClass(int column)
public int getColumnCount()
public TableColumnModel getColumnModel()
public String getColumnName(int column)
public boolean getColumnSelectionAllowed(
)
public TableCellEditor getDefaultEditor(
Class columnClass)
public TableCellRenderer
getDefaultRenderer(Class columnClass)
public int getEditingColumn()
public int getEditingRow()
public Component getEditorComponent()
public Color getGridColor()
public Dimension getIntercellSpacing()
public TableModel getModel()
public Dimension
getPreferredScrollableViewportSize()
public int getRowCount()
public int getRowHeight()
public int getRowMargin()
public boolean getRowSelectionAllowed()
public int getScrollableBlockIncrement(
Rectangle visibleRect,int orientation,
int direction)
public boolean
getScrollableTracksViewportHeight()
public boolean
getScrollableTracksViewportWidth()
```

public int getScrollableUnitIncrement(
Rectangle visibleRect,int orientation,
int direction)
public int getSelectedColumn()
public int getSelectedColumnCount()
public int getSelectedColumns()
public int getSelectedRow()
public int getSelectedRowCount()
public int getSelectedRows()
public Color getSelectionBackground()
public Color getSelectionForeground()
public ListSelectionModel
getSelectionModel()
public boolean getShowHorizontalLines()
public boolean getShowVerticalLines()
public JTableHeader getTableHeader()
public String getToolTipText(MouseEvent
event)
public TableUI getUI()
public String getUIClassID()
public Object getValueAt(int row,int
column)
protected void initializeLocalVars()
public boolean isCellEditable(int row,
int column)
public boolean isCellSelected(int row,
int column)
public boolean isColumnSelected(int
column)
public boolean isEditing()
public boolean isManagingFocus()
public boolean isRowSelected(int row)
public void moveColumn(int column,int
targetColumn)
protected String paramString()
public Component prepareEditor(
TableCellEditor editor,int row,int
column)
public Component prepareRenderer(
TableCellRenderer renderer,int row,int
column)
public void removeColumn(TableColumn
aColumn)
public void
removeColumnSelectionInterval(int index0,
int index1)
public void removeEditor()
public void removeRowSelectionInterval(
int index0,int index1)
public void reshape(int x,int y,int
width,int height)
protected void resizeAndRepaint()
public int rowAtPoint(Point point)
public void selectAll()
public void
setAutoCreateColumnsFromModel(boolean
createColumns)
public void setAutoResizeMode(int mode)
public void setCellEditor(
TableCellEditor anEditor)
public void setCellSelectionEnabled(
boolean flag)
public void setColumnModel(
TableColumnModel newModel)

public void setColumnSelectionAllowed(
boolean flag)
public void setColumnSelectionInterval(
int index0,int index1)
public void setDefaultEditor(Class
columnClass,TableCellEditor editor)
public void setDefaultRenderer(Class
columnClass,TableCellRenderer renderer)
public void setEditingColumn(int aColumn)
public void setEditingRow(int aRow)
public void setGridColor(Color newColor)
public void setIntercellSpacing(
Dimension newSpacing)
public void setModel(TableModel newModel)
public void
setPreferredScrollableViewportSize(
Dimension size)
public void setRowHeight(int newHeight)
public void setRowMargin(int rowMargin)
public void setRowSelectionAllowed(
boolean flag)
public void setRowSelectionInterval(int
index0,int index1)
public void setSelectionBackground(Color
selectionBackground)
public void setSelectionForeground(Color
selectionForeground)
public void setSelectionMode(int
selectionMode)
public void setSelectionModel(
ListSelectionModel newModel)
public void setShowGrid(boolean b)
public void setShowHorizontalLines(
boolean b)
public void setShowVerticalLines(boolean
b)
public void setTableHeader(JTableHeader
newHeader)
public void setUI(TableUI ui)
public void setValueAt(Object aValue,int
row,int column)
public void sizeColumnsToFit(boolean
lastColumnOnly)
public void sizeColumnsToFit(int
resizingColumn)
public void tableChanged(TableModelEvent
e)
public void updateUI()
public void valueChanged(
ListSelectionEvent e)

## JTableHeader

public class javax.swing.table.
JTableHeader
implements javax.accessibility.
Accessible
implements javax.swing.event.
TableColumnModelListener
extends javax.swing.JComponent
extends java.awt.Container
extends java.awt.Component
extends java.lang.Object

## Fields

```
protected javax.swing.table.
TableColumnModel columnModel
protected transient javax.swing.table.
TableColumn draggedColumn
protected transient int draggedDistance
protected boolean reorderingAllowed
protected boolean resizingAllowed
protected transient javax.swing.table.
TableColumn resizingColumn
protected javax.swing.JTable table
protected boolean updateTableInRealTime
```

## Constructors

```
public  JTableHeader()
public  JTableHeader(TableColumnModel cm)
```

## Methods

```
public void columnAdded(
TableColumnModelEvent e)
public int columnAtPoint(Point point)
public void columnMarginChanged(
ChangeEvent e)
public void columnMoved(
TableColumnModelEvent e)
public void columnRemoved(
TableColumnModelEvent e)
public void columnSelectionChanged(
ListSelectionEvent e)
protected TableColumnModel
createDefaultColumnModel()
public AccessibleContext
getAccessibleContext()
public TableColumnModel getColumnModel()
public TableColumn getDraggedColumn()
public int getDraggedDistance()
public Rectangle getHeaderRect(int
columnIndex)
public boolean getReorderingAllowed()
public boolean getResizingAllowed()
public TableColumn getResizingColumn()
public JTable getTable()
public String getToolTipText(MouseEvent
event)
public TableHeaderUI getUI()
public String getUIClassID()
public boolean getUpdateTableInRealTime()
protected void initializeLocalVars()
protected String paramString()
public void resizeAndRepaint()
public void setColumnModel(
TableColumnModel newModel)
public void setDraggedColumn(TableColumn
aColumn)
public void setDraggedDistance(int
distance)
public void setReorderingAllowed(boolean
b)
public void setResizingAllowed(boolean b)
public void setResizingColumn(
TableColumn aColumn)
public void setTable(JTable aTable)
public void setUI(TableHeaderUI ui)
```

```
public void setUpdateTableInRealTime(
boolean flag)
public void updateUI()
```

## JTextArea

```
public class javax.swing.JTextArea
extends javax.swing.text.JTextComponent
extends javax.swing.JComponent
extends java.awt.Container
extends java.awt.Component
extends java.lang.Object
```

## Constructors

```
public  JTextArea()
public  JTextArea(String text)
public  JTextArea(int rows,int columns)
public  JTextArea(String text,int rows,
int columns)
public  JTextArea(Document doc)
public  JTextArea(Document doc,String
text,int rows,int columns)
```

## Methods

```
public void append(String str)
protected Document createDefaultModel()
public AccessibleContext
getAccessibleContext()
public int getColumns()
protected int getColumnWidth()
public int getLineCount()
public int getLineEndOffset(int line)
public int getLineOfOffset(int offset)
public int getLineStartOffset(int line)
public boolean getLineWrap()
public Dimension
getPreferredScrollableViewportSize()
public Dimension getPreferredSize()
protected int getRowHeight()
public int getRows()
public boolean
getScrollableTracksViewportWidth()
public int getScrollableUnitIncrement(
Rectangle visibleRect,int orientation,
int direction)
public int getTabSize()
public String getUIClassID()
public boolean getWrapStyleWord()
public void insert(String str,int pos)
public boolean isManagingFocus()
protected String paramString()
protected void processComponentKeyEvent(
KeyEvent e)
public void replaceRange(String str,int
start,int end)
public void setColumns(int columns)
public void setFont(Font f)
public void setLineWrap(boolean wrap)
public void setRows(int rows)
public void setTabSize(int size)
public void setWrapStyleWord(boolean
word)
```

# JTextComponent

public abstract class javax.swing.text.
JTextComponent
implements javax.accessibility.
Accessible
implements javax.swing.Scrollable
extends javax.swing.JComponent
extends java.awt.Container
extends java.awt.Component
extends java.lang.Object

## Fields

public final static java.lang.String
DEFAULT_KEYMAP
public final static java.lang.String
FOCUS_ACCELERATOR_KEY

## Constructors

public  JTextComponent()

## Methods

public void addCaretListener(
CaretListener listener)
public static Keymap addKeymap(String nm,
Keymap parent)
public void copy()
public void cut()
protected void fireCaretUpdate(
CaretEvent e)
public AccessibleContext
getAccessibleContext()
public Action getActions()
public Caret getCaret()
public Color getCaretColor()
public int getCaretPosition()
public Color getDisabledTextColor()
public Document getDocument()
public char getFocusAccelerator()
public Highlighter getHighlighter()
public InputMethodRequests
getInputMethodRequests()
public Keymap getKeymap()
public static Keymap getKeymap(String nm)
public Insets getMargin()
public Dimension
getPreferredScrollableViewportSize()
public int getScrollableBlockIncrement(
Rectangle visibleRect,int orientation,
int direction)
public boolean
getScrollableTracksViewportHeight()
public boolean
getScrollableTracksViewportWidth()
public int getScrollableUnitIncrement(
Rectangle visibleRect,int orientation,
int direction)
public String getSelectedText()
public Color getSelectedTextColor()
public Color getSelectionColor()
public int getSelectionEnd()
public int getSelectionStart()
public String getText(int offs,int len)
public String getText()

public TextUI getUI()
public boolean isEditable()
public boolean isFocusTraversable()
public boolean isOpaque()
public static void loadKeymap(Keymap map,
KeyBinding bindings,Action actions)
public Rectangle modelToView(int pos)
public void moveCaretPosition(int pos)
protected String paramString()
public void paste()
protected void processComponentKeyEvent(
KeyEvent e)
protected void processInputMethodEvent(
InputMethodEvent e)
public void read(Reader in,Object desc)
public void removeCaretListener(
CaretListener listener)
public static Keymap removeKeymap(String
nm)
public void removeNotify()
public void replaceSelection(String
content)
public void select(int selectionStart,
int selectionEnd)
public void selectAll()
public void setCaret(Caret c)
public void setCaretColor(Color c)
public void setCaretPosition(int
position)
public void setDisabledTextColor(Color c)
public void setDocument(Document doc)
public void setEditable(boolean b)
public void setEnabled(boolean b)
public void setFocusAccelerator(char
aKey)
public void setHighlighter(Highlighter h)
public void setKeymap(Keymap map)
public void setMargin(Insets m)
public void setOpaque(boolean o)
public void setSelectedTextColor(Color c)
public void setSelectionColor(Color c)
public void setSelectionEnd(int
selectionEnd)
public void setSelectionStart(int
selectionStart)
public void setText(String t)
public void setUI(TextUI ui)
public void updateUI()
public int viewToModel(Point pt)
public void write(Writer out)

# JTextField

public class javax.swing.JTextField
implements javax.swing.SwingConstants
extends javax.swing.text.JTextComponent
extends javax.swing.JComponent
extends java.awt.Container
extends java.awt.Component
extends java.lang.Object

## Fields

public final static java.lang.String
notifyAction

### Constructors

```
public JTextField()
public JTextField(String text)
public JTextField(int columns)
public JTextField(String text,int
columns)
public JTextField(Document doc,String
text,int columns)
```

### Methods

```
public synchronized void
addActionListener(ActionListener l)
protected Document createDefaultModel()
protected void fireActionPerformed()
public AccessibleContext
getAccessibleContext()
public Action getActions()
public int getColumns()
protected int getColumnWidth()
public int getHorizontalAlignment()
public BoundedRangeModel
getHorizontalVisibility()
public Dimension getPreferredSize()
public int getScrollOffset()
public String getUIClassID()
public boolean isValidateRoot()
protected String paramString()
public void postActionEvent()
public synchronized void
removeActionListener(ActionListener l)
public void scrollRectToVisible(
Rectangle r)
public void setActionCommand(String
command)
public void setColumns(int columns)
public void setFont(Font f)
public void setHorizontalAlignment(int
alignment)
public void setScrollOffset(int
scrollOffset)
```

## JTextPane

```
public class javax.swing.JTextPane
extends javax.swing.JEditorPane
extends javax.swing.text.JTextComponent
extends javax.swing.JComponent
extends java.awt.Container
extends java.awt.Component
extends java.lang.Object
```

### Constructors

```
public JTextPane()
public JTextPane(StyledDocument doc)
```

### Methods

```
public Style addStyle(String nm,Style
parent)
protected EditorKit
createDefaultEditorKit()
public AttributeSet
getCharacterAttributes()
public MutableAttributeSet
getInputAttributes()
```

```
public Style getLogicalStyle()
public AttributeSet
getParagraphAttributes()
public boolean
getScrollableTracksViewportWidth()
public Style getStyle(String nm)
public StyledDocument getStyledDocument()
protected final StyledEditorKit
getStyledEditorKit()
public String getUIClassID()
public void insertComponent(Component c)
public void insertIcon(Icon g)
protected String paramString()
public void removeStyle(String nm)
public void replaceSelection(String
content)
public void setCharacterAttributes(
AttributeSet attr,boolean replace)
public void setDocument(Document doc)
public final void setEditorKit(EditorKit
kit)
public void setLogicalStyle(Style s)
public void setParagraphAttributes(
AttributeSet attr,boolean replace)
public void setStyledDocument(
StyledDocument doc)
```

## JToggleButton

```
public class javax.swing.JToggleButton
implements javax.accessibility.
Accessible
extends javax.swing.AbstractButton
extends javax.swing.JComponent
extends java.awt.Container
extends java.awt.Component
extends java.lang.Object
```

### Constructors

```
public JToggleButton()
public JToggleButton(Icon icon)
public JToggleButton(Icon icon,boolean
selected)
public JToggleButton(String text)
public JToggleButton(String text,
boolean selected)
public JToggleButton(String text,Icon
icon)
public JToggleButton(String text,Icon
icon,boolean selected)
```

### Methods

```
public AccessibleContext
getAccessibleContext()
public String getUIClassID()
protected String paramString()
public void updateUI()
```

## JToolBar

```
public class javax.swing.JToolBar
implements javax.accessibility.
Accessible
implements javax.swing.SwingConstants
extends javax.swing.JComponent
```

extends java.awt.Container
extends java.awt.Component
extends java.lang.Object

## Constructors
public JToolBar()
public JToolBar(int orientation)

## Methods
public JButton add(Action a)
protected void addImpl(Component comp,
Object constraints,int index)
public void addSeparator()
public void addSeparator(Dimension size)
protected PropertyChangeListener
createActionChangeListener(JButton b)
public AccessibleContext
getAccessibleContext()
public Component getComponentAtIndex(int
i)
public int getComponentIndex(Component c)
public Insets getMargin()
public int getOrientation()
public ToolBarUI getUI()
public String getUIClassID()
public boolean isBorderPainted()
public boolean isFloatable()
protected void paintBorder(Graphics g)
protected String paramString()
public void remove(Component comp)
public void setBorderPainted(boolean b)
public void setFloatable(boolean b)
public void setMargin(Insets m)
public void setOrientation(int o)
public void setUI(ToolBarUI ui)
public void updateUI()

# JToolTip
public class javax.swing.JToolTip
implements javax.accessibility.
Accessible
extends javax.swing.JComponent
extends java.awt.Container
extends java.awt.Component
extends java.lang.Object

## Constructors
public JToolTip()

## Methods
public AccessibleContext
getAccessibleContext()
public JComponent getComponent()
public String getTipText()
public ToolTipUI getUI()
public String getUIClassID()
protected String paramString()
public void setComponent(JComponent c)
public void setTipText(String tipText)
public void updateUI()

# JTree
public class javax.swing.JTree
implements javax.accessibility.
Accessible
implements javax.swing.Scrollable
extends javax.swing.JComponent
extends java.awt.Container
extends java.awt.Component
extends java.lang.Object

## Fields
protected transient javax.swing.tree.
TreeCellEditor cellEditor
protected transient javax.swing.tree.
TreeCellRenderer cellRenderer
public final static java.lang.String
CELL_EDITOR_PROPERTY
public final static java.lang.String
CELL_RENDERER_PROPERTY
protected boolean editable
public final static java.lang.String
EDITABLE_PROPERTY
protected boolean
invokesStopCellEditing
public final static java.lang.String
INVOKES_STOP_CELL_EDITING_PROPERTY
protected boolean largeModel
public final static java.lang.String
LARGE_MODEL_PROPERTY
protected boolean rootVisible
public final static java.lang.String
ROOT_VISIBLE_PROPERTY
protected int rowHeight
public final static java.lang.String ROW_
HEIGHT_PROPERTY
protected boolean scrollsOnExpand
public final static java.lang.String
SCROLLS_ON_EXPAND_PROPERTY
protected transient javax.swing.tree.
TreeSelectionModel selectionModel
protected transient
TreeSelectionRedirector
selectionRedirector
public final static java.lang.String
SELECTION_MODEL_PROPERTY
protected boolean showsRootHandles
public final static java.lang.String
SHOWS_ROOT_HANDLES_PROPERTY
protected int toggleClickCount
protected transient javax.swing.tree.
TreeModel treeModel
protected transient javax.swing.event.
TreeModelListener treeModelListener
public final static java.lang.String
TREE_MODEL_PROPERTY
protected int visibleRowCount
public final static java.lang.String
VISIBLE_ROW_COUNT_PROPERTY

## Constructors
public JTree()
public JTree(Object value)
public JTree(Vector value)

public  JTree(Hashtable value)
public  JTree(TreeNode root)
public  JTree(TreeNode root,boolean
asksAllowsChildren)
public  JTree(TreeModel newModel)

## Methods
public void addSelectionInterval(int
index0,int index1)
public void addSelectionPath(TreePath
path)
public void addSelectionPaths(TreePath
paths)
public void addSelectionRow(int row)
public void addSelectionRows(int rows)
public void addTreeExpansionListener(
TreeExpansionListener tel)
public void addTreeSelectionListener(
TreeSelectionListener tsl)
public void addTreeWillExpandListener(
TreeWillExpandListener tel)
public void cancelEditing()
public void clearSelection()
protected void clearToggledPaths()
public void collapsePath(TreePath path)
public void collapseRow(int row)
public String convertValueToText(Object
value,boolean selected,boolean expanded,
boolean leaf,int row,boolean hasFocus)
protected static TreeModel
createTreeModel(Object value)
protected TreeModelListener
createTreeModelListener()
public void expandPath(TreePath path)
public void expandRow(int row)
public void fireTreeCollapsed(TreePath
path)
public void fireTreeExpanded(TreePath
path)
public void fireTreeWillCollapse(
TreePath path)
public void fireTreeWillExpand(TreePath
path)
protected void fireValueChanged(
TreeSelectionEvent e)
public AccessibleContext
getAccessibleContext()
public TreeCellEditor getCellEditor()
public TreeCellRenderer getCellRenderer()
public TreePath
getClosestPathForLocation(int x,int y)
public int getClosestRowForLocation(int
x,int y)
protected static TreeModel
getDefaultTreeModel()
protected Enumeration
getDescendantToggledPaths(TreePath
parent)
public TreePath getEditingPath()
public Enumeration
getExpandedDescendants(TreePath parent)
public boolean getInvokesStopCellEditing(
)

public Object
getLastSelectedPathComponent()
public TreePath getLeadSelectionPath()
public int getLeadSelectionRow()
public int getMaxSelectionRow()
public int getMinSelectionRow()
public TreeModel getModel()
protected TreePath getPathBetweenRows(
int index0,int index1)
public Rectangle getPathBounds(TreePath
path)
public TreePath getPathForLocation(int x,
int y)
public TreePath getPathForRow(int row)
public Dimension
getPreferredScrollableViewportSize()
public Rectangle getRowBounds(int row)
public int getRowCount()
public int getRowForLocation(int x,int y)
public int getRowForPath(TreePath path)
public int getRowHeight()
public int getScrollableBlockIncrement(
Rectangle visibleRect,int orientation,
int direction)
public boolean
getScrollableTracksViewportHeight()
public boolean
getScrollableTracksViewportWidth()
public int getScrollableUnitIncrement(
Rectangle visibleRect,int orientation,
int direction)
public boolean getScrollsOnExpand()
public int getSelectionCount()
public TreeSelectionModel
getSelectionModel()
public TreePath getSelectionPath()
public TreePath getSelectionPaths()
public int getSelectionRows()
public boolean getShowsRootHandles()
public String getToolTipText(MouseEvent
event)
public TreeUI getUI()
public String getUIClassID()
public int getVisibleRowCount()
public boolean hasBeenExpanded(TreePath
path)
public boolean isCollapsed(TreePath path)
public boolean isCollapsed(int row)
public boolean isEditable()
public boolean isEditing()
public boolean isExpanded(TreePath path)
public boolean isExpanded(int row)
public boolean isFixedRowHeight()
public boolean isLargeModel()
public boolean isPathEditable(TreePath
path)
public boolean isPathSelected(TreePath
path)
public boolean isRootVisible()
public boolean isRowSelected(int row)
public boolean isSelectionEmpty()
public boolean isVisible(TreePath path)
public void makeVisible(TreePath path)
protected String paramString()

protected void
removeDescendantToggledPaths(Enumeration
toRemove)
public void removeSelectionInterval(int
index0,int index1)
public void removeSelectionPath(TreePath
path)
public void removeSelectionPaths(
TreePath paths)
public void removeSelectionRow(int row)
public void removeSelectionRows(int rows)
public void removeTreeExpansionListener(
TreeExpansionListener tel)
public void removeTreeSelectionListener(
TreeSelectionListener tsl)
public void removeTreeWillExpandListener(
TreeWillExpandListener tel)
public void scrollPathToVisible(TreePath
path)
public void scrollRowToVisible(int row)
public void setCellEditor(TreeCellEditor
cellEditor)
public void setCellRenderer(
TreeCellRenderer x)
public void setEditable(boolean flag)
protected void setExpandedState(TreePath
path,boolean state)
public void setInvokesStopCellEditing(
boolean newValue)
public void setLargeModel(boolean
newValue)
public void setModel(TreeModel newModel)
public void setRootVisible(boolean
rootVisible)
public void setRowHeight(int rowHeight)
public void setScrollsOnExpand(boolean
newValue)
public void setSelectionInterval(int
index0,int index1)
public void setSelectionModel(
TreeSelectionModel selectionModel)
public void setSelectionPath(TreePath
path)
public void setSelectionPaths(TreePath
paths)
public void setSelectionRow(int row)
public void setSelectionRows(int rows)
public void setShowsRootHandles(boolean
newValue)
public void setUI(TreeUI ui)
public void setVisibleRowCount(int
newCount)
public void startEditingAtPath(TreePath
path)
public boolean stopEditing()
public void treeDidChange()
public void updateUI()

## JViewport

public class javax.swing.JViewport
implements javax.accessibility.
Accessible
extends javax.swing.JComponent
extends java.awt.Container

extends java.awt.Component
extends java.lang.Object

### Fields
protected boolean backingStore
protected transient java.awt.Image
backingStoreImage
protected boolean isViewSizeSet
protected java.awt.Point
lastPaintPosition
protected boolean scrollUnderway

### Constructors
public JViewport()

### Methods
public void addChangeListener(
ChangeListener l)
protected void addImpl(Component child,
Object constraints,int index)
protected boolean computeBlit(int dx,int
dy,Point blitFrom,Point blitTo,Dimension
blitSize,Rectangle blitPaint)
protected LayoutManager
createLayoutManager()
protected ViewListener
createViewListener()
protected void fireStateChanged()
public AccessibleContext
getAccessibleContext()
public Dimension getExtentSize()
public final Insets getInsets()
public final Insets getInsets(Insets
insets)
public Component getView()
public Point getViewPosition()
public Rectangle getViewRect()
public Dimension getViewSize()
public boolean isBackingStoreEnabled()
public boolean isOptimizedDrawingEnabled(
)
public void paint(Graphics g)
protected String paramString()
public void remove(Component child)
public void removeChangeListener(
ChangeListener l)
public void repaint(long tm,int x,int y,
int w,int h)
public void reshape(int x,int y,int w,
int h)
public void scrollRectToVisible(
Rectangle contentRect)
public void setBackingStoreEnabled(
boolean x)
public final void setBorder(Border
border)
public void setExtentSize(Dimension
newExtent)
public void setView(Component view)
public void setViewPosition(Point p)
public void setViewSize(Dimension
newSize)
public Dimension toViewCoordinates(
Dimension size)
public Point toViewCoordinates(Point p)

## JWindow

```
public class javax.swing.JWindow
implements javax.accessibility.
Accessible
implements javax.swing.
RootPaneContainer
extends java.awt.Window
extends java.awt.Container
extends java.awt.Component
extends java.lang.Object
```

### Fields

```
protected javax.accessibility.
AccessibleContext accessibleContext
protected javax.swing.JRootPane
rootPane
protected boolean
rootPaneCheckingEnabled
```

### Constructors

```
public  JWindow()
public  JWindow(Frame owner)
public  JWindow(Window owner)
```

### Methods

```
protected void addImpl(Component comp,
Object constraints,int index)
protected JRootPane createRootPane()
public AccessibleContext
getAccessibleContext()
public Container getContentPane()
public Component getGlassPane()
public JLayeredPane getLayeredPane()
public JRootPane getRootPane()
protected boolean
isRootPaneCheckingEnabled()
protected String paramString()
public void setContentPane(Container
contentPane)
public void setGlassPane(Component
glassPane)
public void setLayeredPane(JLayeredPane
layeredPane)
public void setLayout(LayoutManager
manager)
protected void setRootPane(JRootPane
root)
protected void
setRootPaneCheckingEnabled(boolean
enabled)
protected void windowInit()
```

## Kernel

```
public class java.awt.image.Kernel
implements java.lang.Cloneable
extends java.lang.Object
```

### Constructors

```
public static  Kernel(int width,int
height,float data)
```

### Methods

```
public Object clone()
public final int getHeight()
```

```
public final float getKernelData(float
data)
public final int getWidth()
public final int getXOrigin()
public final int getYOrigin()
```

## KeyAdapter

```
public abstract class java.awt.event.
KeyAdapter
implements java.awt.event.KeyListener
extends java.lang.Object
```

### Methods

```
public void keyPressed(KeyEvent e)
public void keyReleased(KeyEvent e)
public void keyTyped(KeyEvent e)
```

## KeyEvent

```
public class java.awt.event.KeyEvent
extends java.awt.event.InputEvent
extends java.awt.event.ComponentEvent
extends java.awt.AWTEvent
extends java.util.EventObject
extends java.lang.Object
```

### Fields

```
public final static char CHAR_UNDEFINED
public final static int KEY_FIRST
public final static int KEY_LAST
public final static int KEY_PRESSED
public final static int KEY_RELEASED
public final static int KEY_TYPED
public final static int VK_0
public final static int VK_1
public final static int VK_2
public final static int VK_3
public final static int VK_4
public final static int VK_5
public final static int VK_6
public final static int VK_7
public final static int VK_8
public final static int VK_9
public final static int VK_A
public final static int VK_ACCEPT
public final static int VK_ADD
public final static int VK_AGAIN
public final static int VK_ALL_
CANDIDATES
public final static int VK_ALPHANUMERIC
public final static int VK_ALT
public final static int VK_ALT_GRAPH
public final static int VK_AMPERSAND
public final static int VK_ASTERISK
public final static int VK_AT
public final static int VK_B
public final static int VK_BACK_QUOTE
public final static int VK_BACK_SLASH
public final static int VK_BACK_SPACE
public final static int VK_BRACELEFT
public final static int VK_BRACERIGHT
public final static int VK_C
public final static int VK_CANCEL
public final static int VK_CAPS_LOCK
public final static int VK_CIRCUMFLEX
```

```
public final static int VK_CLEAR
public final static int VK_CLOSE_
BRACKET
public final static int VK_CODE_INPUT
public final static int VK_COLON
public final static int VK_COMMA
public final static int VK_COMPOSE
public final static int VK_CONTROL
public final static int VK_CONVERT
public final static int VK_COPY
public final static int VK_CUT
public final static int VK_D
public final static int VK_DEAD_
ABOVEDOT
public final static int VK_DEAD_
ABOVERING
public final static int VK_DEAD_ACUTE
public final static int VK_DEAD_BREVE
public final static int VK_DEAD_CARON
public final static int VK_DEAD_CEDILLA
public final static int VK_DEAD_
CIRCUMFLEX
public final static int VK_DEAD_
DIAERESIS
public final static int VK_DEAD_
DOUBLEACUTE
public final static int VK_DEAD_GRAVE
public final static int VK_DEAD_IOTA
public final static int VK_DEAD_MACRON
public final static int VK_DEAD_OGONEK
public final static int VK_DEAD_
SEMIVOICED_SOUND
public final static int VK_DEAD_TILDE
public final static int VK_DEAD_VOICED_
SOUND
public final static int VK_DECIMAL
public final static int VK_DELETE
public final static int VK_DIVIDE
public final static int VK_DOLLAR
public final static int VK_DOWN
public final static int VK_E
public final static int VK_END
public final static int VK_ENTER
public final static int VK_EQUALS
public final static int VK_ESCAPE
public final static int VK_EURO_SIGN
public final static int VK_EXCLAMATION_
MARK
public final static int VK_F
public final static int VK_F1
public final static int VK_F10
public final static int VK_F11
public final static int VK_F12
public final static int VK_F13
public final static int VK_F14
public final static int VK_F15
public final static int VK_F16
public final static int VK_F17
public final static int VK_F18
public final static int VK_F19
public final static int VK_F2
public final static int VK_F20
public final static int VK_F21
public final static int VK_F22

public final static int VK_F23
public final static int VK_F24
public final static int VK_F3
public final static int VK_F4
public final static int VK_F5
public final static int VK_F6
public final static int VK_F7
public final static int VK_F8
public final static int VK_F9
public final static int VK_FINAL
public final static int VK_FIND
public final static int VK_FULL_WIDTH
public final static int VK_G
public final static int VK_GREATER
public final static int VK_H
public final static int VK_HALF_WIDTH
public final static int VK_HELP
public final static int VK_HIRAGANA
public final static int VK_HOME
public final static int VK_I
public final static int VK_INSERT
public final static int VK_INVERTED_
EXCLAMATION_MARK
public final static int VK_J
public final static int VK_JAPANESE_
HIRAGANA
public final static int VK_JAPANESE_
KATAKANA
public final static int VK_JAPANESE_
ROMAN
public final static int VK_K
public final static int VK_KANA
public final static int VK_KANJI
public final static int VK_KATAKANA
public final static int VK_KP_DOWN
public final static int VK_KP_LEFT
public final static int VK_KP_RIGHT
public final static int VK_KP_UP
public final static int VK_L
public final static int VK_LEFT
public final static int VK_LEFT_
PARENTHESIS
public final static int VK_LESS
public final static int VK_M
public final static int VK_META
public final static int VK_MINUS
public final static int VK_MODECHANGE
public final static int VK_MULTIPLY
public final static int VK_N
public final static int VK_NONCONVERT
public final static int VK_NUMBER_SIGN
public final static int VK_NUMPAD0
public final static int VK_NUMPAD1
public final static int VK_NUMPAD2
public final static int VK_NUMPAD3
public final static int VK_NUMPAD4
public final static int VK_NUMPAD5
public final static int VK_NUMPAD6
public final static int VK_NUMPAD7
public final static int VK_NUMPAD8
public final static int VK_NUMPAD9
public final static int VK_NUM_LOCK
public final static int VK_O
public final static int VK_OPEN_BRACKET
```

```
public final static int VK_P
public final static int VK_PAGE_DOWN
public final static int VK_PAGE_UP
public final static int VK_PASTE
public final static int VK_PAUSE
public final static int VK_PERIOD
public final static int VK_PLUS
public final static int VK_PREVIOUS_
CANDIDATE
public final static int VK_PRINTSCREEN
public final static int VK_PROPS
public final static int VK_Q
public final static int VK_QUOTE
public final static int VK_QUOTEDBL
public final static int VK_R
public final static int VK_RIGHT
public final static int VK_RIGHT_
PARENTHESIS
public final static int VK_ROMAN_
CHARACTERS
public final static int VK_S
public final static int VK_SCROLL_LOCK
public final static int VK_SEMICOLON
public final static int VK_SEPARATER
public final static int VK_SHIFT
public final static int VK_SLASH
public final static int VK_SPACE
public final static int VK_STOP
public final static int VK_SUBTRACT
public final static int VK_T
public final static int VK_TAB
public final static int VK_U
public final static int VK_UNDEFINED
public final static int VK_UNDERSCORE
public final static int VK_UNDO
public final static int VK_UP
public final static int VK_V
public final static int VK_W
public final static int VK_X
public final static int VK_Y
public final static int VK_Z
```

### Constructors

```
public  KeyEvent(Component source,int id,
long when,int modifiers,int keyCode,char
keyChar)
public  KeyEvent(Component source,int id,
long when,int modifiers,int keyCode)
```

### Methods

```
public char getKeyChar()
public int getKeyCode()
public static String getKeyModifiersText(
int modifiers)
public static String getKeyText(int
keyCode)
public boolean isActionKey()
public String paramString()
public void setKeyChar(char keyChar)
public void setKeyCode(int keyCode)
public void setModifiers(int modifiers)
```

## KeyException

```
public class java.security.KeyException
extends java.security.
GeneralSecurityException
extends java.lang.Exception
extends java.lang.Throwable
extends java.lang.Object
```

### Constructors

```
public  KeyException()
public  KeyException(String msg)
```

## KeyFactory

```
public class java.security.KeyFactory
extends java.lang.Object
```

### Constructors

```
protected  KeyFactory(KeyFactorySpi
keyFacSpi,Provider provider,String
algorithm)
```

### Methods

```
public final PrivateKey generatePrivate(
KeySpec keySpec)
public final PublicKey generatePublic(
KeySpec keySpec)
public final String getAlgorithm()
public static KeyFactory getInstance(
String algorithm)
public static KeyFactory getInstance(
String algorithm,String provider)
public final KeySpec getKeySpec(Key key,
Class keySpec)
public final Provider getProvider()
public final Key translateKey(Key key)
```

## KeyFactorySpi

```
public abstract class java.security.
KeyFactorySpi
extends java.lang.Object
```

### Methods

```
protected abstract PrivateKey
engineGeneratePrivate(KeySpec keySpec)
protected abstract PublicKey
engineGeneratePublic(KeySpec keySpec)
protected abstract KeySpec
engineGetKeySpec(Key key,Class keySpec)
protected abstract Key
engineTranslateKey(Key key)
```

## KeyManagementException

```
public class java.security.
KeyManagementException
extends java.security.KeyException
extends java.security.
GeneralSecurityException
extends java.lang.Exception
extends java.lang.Throwable
extends java.lang.Object
```

## Constructors

```
public  KeyManagementException()
public  KeyManagementException(String
msg)
```

# KeyPair

```
public final class java.security.
KeyPair
implements java.io.Serializable
extends java.lang.Object
```

## Constructors

```
public  KeyPair(PublicKey publicKey,
PrivateKey privateKey)
```

## Methods

```
public PrivateKey getPrivate()
public PublicKey getPublic()
```

# KeyPairGenerator

```
public abstract class java.security.
KeyPairGenerator
extends java.security.
KeyPairGeneratorSpi
extends java.lang.Object
```

## Constructors

```
protected  KeyPairGenerator(String
algorithm)
```

## Methods

```
public final KeyPair genKeyPair()
public String getAlgorithm()
public static KeyPairGenerator
getInstance(String algorithm)
public static KeyPairGenerator
getInstance(String algorithm,String
provider)
public final Provider getProvider()
public void initialize(int keysize)
public void initialize(int keysize,
SecureRandom random)
public void initialize(
AlgorithmParameterSpec params)
public void initialize(
AlgorithmParameterSpec params,
SecureRandom random)
```

# KeyPairGeneratorSpi

```
public abstract class java.security.
KeyPairGeneratorSpi
extends java.lang.Object
```

## Methods

```
public abstract KeyPair generateKeyPair()
public abstract void initialize(int
keysize,SecureRandom random)
public void initialize(
AlgorithmParameterSpec params,
SecureRandom random)
```

# KeyStore

```
public class java.security.KeyStore
extends java.lang.Object
```

## Constructors

```
protected  KeyStore(KeyStoreSpi
keyStoreSpi,Provider provider,String
type)
```

## Methods

```
public final Enumeration aliases()
public final boolean containsAlias(
String alias)
public final void deleteEntry(String
alias)
public final Certificate getCertificate(
String alias)
public final String getCertificateAlias(
Certificate cert)
public final Certificate
getCertificateChain(String alias)
public final Date getCreationDate(String
alias)
public final static String
getDefaultType()
public static KeyStore getInstance(
String type)
public static KeyStore getInstance(
String type,String provider)
public final Key getKey(String alias,
char password)
public final Provider getProvider()
public final String getType()
public final boolean isCertificateEntry(
String alias)
public final boolean isKeyEntry(String
alias)
public final void load(InputStream
stream,char password)
public final void setCertificateEntry(
String alias,Certificate cert)
public final void setKeyEntry(String
alias,Key key,char password,Certificate
chain)
public final void setKeyEntry(String
alias,byte key,Certificate chain)
public final int size()
public final void store(OutputStream
stream,char password)
```

# KeyStoreException

```
public class java.security.
KeyStoreException
extends java.security.
GeneralSecurityException
extends java.lang.Exception
extends java.lang.Throwable
extends java.lang.Object
```

## Constructors

```
public  KeyStoreException()
public  KeyStoreException(String msg)
```

## KeyStoreSpi

public abstract class java.security.
KeyStoreSpi
extends java.lang.Object

### Methods

public abstract Enumeration
engineAliases()
public abstract boolean
engineContainsAlias(String alias)
public abstract void engineDeleteEntry(
String alias)
public abstract Certificate
engineGetCertificate(String alias)
public abstract String
engineGetCertificateAlias(Certificate
cert)
public abstract Certificate
engineGetCertificateChain(String alias)
public abstract Date
engineGetCreationDate(String alias)
public abstract Key engineGetKey(String
alias,char password)
public abstract boolean
engineIsCertificateEntry(String alias)
public abstract boolean engineIsKeyEntry(
String alias)
public abstract void engineLoad(
InputStream stream,char password)
public abstract void
engineSetCertificateEntry(String alias,
Certificate cert)
public abstract void engineSetKeyEntry(
String alias,Key key,char password,
Certificate chain)
public abstract void engineSetKeyEntry(
String alias,byte key,Certificate chain)
public abstract int engineSize()
public abstract void engineStore(
OutputStream stream,char password)

## KeyStroke

public class javax.swing.KeyStroke
implements java.io.Serializable
extends java.lang.Object

### Constructors

private  KeyStroke()

### Methods

public boolean equals(Object anObject)
public char getKeyChar()
public int getKeyCode()
public static KeyStroke getKeyStroke(
char keyChar)
public static KeyStroke getKeyStroke(
char keyChar,boolean onKeyRelease)
public static KeyStroke getKeyStroke(int
keyCode,int modifiers,boolean
onKeyRelease)
public static KeyStroke getKeyStroke(int
keyCode,int modifiers)

public static KeyStroke getKeyStroke(
String representation)
public static KeyStroke
getKeyStrokeForEvent(KeyEvent anEvent)
public int getModifiers()
public int hashCode()
public boolean isOnKeyRelease()
public String toString()

## Label

public class java.awt.Label
extends java.awt.Component
extends java.lang.Object

### Fields

public final static int CENTER
public final static int LEFT
public final static int RIGHT

### Constructors

public  Label()
public  Label(String text)
public  Label(String text,int alignment)

### Methods

public void addNotify()
public int getAlignment()
public String getText()
protected String paramString()
public synchronized void setAlignment(
int alignment)
public void setText(String text)

## LabelUI

public abstract class javax.swing.plaf.
LabelUI
extends javax.swing.plaf.ComponentUI
extends java.lang.Object

## LabelView

public class javax.swing.text.LabelView
extends javax.swing.text.View
extends java.lang.Object

### Constructors

public  LabelView(Element elem)

### Methods

public View breakView(int axis,int p0,
float pos,float len)
public void changedUpdate(DocumentEvent
e,Shape a,ViewFactory f)
public View createFragment(int p0,int p1)
public float getAlignment(int axis)
public int getBreakWeight(int axis,float
pos,float len)
protected Font getFont()
protected FontMetrics getFontMetrics()
public int getNextVisualPositionFrom(int
pos,Bias b,Shape a,int direction,Bias
biasRet)
public float getPreferredSpan(int axis)

public void insertUpdate(DocumentEvent e,
Shape a,ViewFactory f)
public Shape modelToView(int pos,Shape a,
Bias b)
public void paint(Graphics g,Shape a)
public void removeUpdate(DocumentEvent
changes,Shape a,ViewFactory f)
protected void
setPropertiesFromAttributes()
protected void setStrikeThrough(boolean
s)
protected void setSubscript(boolean s)
protected void setSuperscript(boolean s)
protected void setUnderline(boolean u)
public String toString()
public int viewToModel(float x,float y,
Shape a,Bias biasReturn)

# LastOwnerException

public class java.security.acl.
LastOwnerException
extends java.lang.Exception
extends java.lang.Throwable
extends java.lang.Object

## Constructors
public  LastOwnerException()

# LayeredHighlighter

public abstract class javax.swing.text.
LayeredHighlighter
implements javax.swing.text.Highlighter
extends java.lang.Object

## Methods
public abstract void
paintLayeredHighlights(Graphics g,int p0,
int p1,Shape viewBounds,JTextComponent
editor,View view)

# Lease

public final class java.rmi.dgc.Lease
implements java.io.Serializable
extends java.lang.Object

## Constructors
public  Lease(VMID id,long duration)

## Methods
public long getValue()
public VMID getVMID()

# Line2D

public abstract class java.awt.geom.
Line2D
implements java.lang.Cloneable
implements java.awt.Shape
extends java.lang.Object

## Constructors
protected  Line2D()

## Methods
public Object clone()
public boolean contains(double x,double
y)
public boolean contains(Point2D p)
public boolean contains(double x,double
y,double w,double h)
public boolean contains(Rectangle2D r)
public Rectangle getBounds()
public abstract Point2D getP1()
public abstract Point2D getP2()
public PathIterator getPathIterator(
AffineTransform at)
public PathIterator getPathIterator(
AffineTransform at,double flatness)
public abstract double getX1()
public abstract double getX2()
public abstract double getY1()
public abstract double getY2()
public boolean intersects(double x,
double y,double w,double h)
public boolean intersects(Rectangle2D r)
public boolean intersectsLine(double X1,
double Y1,double X2,double Y2)
public boolean intersectsLine(Line2D l)
public static boolean linesIntersect(
double X1,double Y1,double X2,double Y2,
double X3,double Y3,double X4,double Y4)
public static double ptLineDist(double
X1,double Y1,double X2,double Y2,double
PX,double PY)
public double ptLineDist(double PX,
double PY)
public double ptLineDist(Point2D pt)
public static double ptLineDistSq(double
X1,double Y1,double X2,double Y2,double
PX,double PY)
public double ptLineDistSq(double PX,
double PY)
public double ptLineDistSq(Point2D pt)
public static double ptSegDist(double X1,
double Y1,double X2,double Y2,double PX,
double PY)
public double ptSegDist(double PX,double
PY)
public double ptSegDist(Point2D pt)
public static double ptSegDistSq(double
X1,double Y1,double X2,double Y2,double
PX,double PY)
public double ptSegDistSq(double PX,
double PY)
public double ptSegDistSq(Point2D pt)
public static int relativeCCW(double X1,
double Y1,double X2,double Y2,double PX,
double PY)
public int relativeCCW(double PX,double
PY)
public int relativeCCW(Point2D p)
public abstract void setLine(double X1,
double Y1,double X2,double Y2)
public void setLine(Point2D p1,Point2D
p2)
public void setLine(Line2D l)

## LineBorder

public class javax.swing.border.
LineBorder
extends javax.swing.border.
AbstractBorder
extends java.lang.Object

### Fields

protected java.awt.Color lineColor
protected boolean roundedCorners
protected int thickness

### Constructors

public  LineBorder(Color color)
public  LineBorder(Color color,int
thickness)
 LineBorder()

### Methods

public static Border
createBlackLineBorder()
public static Border
createGrayLineBorder()
public Insets getBorderInsets(Component
c)
public Insets getBorderInsets(Component
c,Insets insets)
public Color getLineColor()
public int getThickness()
public boolean isBorderOpaque()
public void paintBorder(Component c,
Graphics g,int x,int y,int width,int
height)

## LineBreakMeasurer

public final class java.awt.font.
LineBreakMeasurer
extends java.lang.Object

### Constructors

public  LineBreakMeasurer(
AttributedCharacterIterator text,
FontRenderContext frc)
public  LineBreakMeasurer(
AttributedCharacterIterator text,
BreakIterator breakIter,
FontRenderContext frc)

### Methods

public void deleteChar(
AttributedCharacterIterator newParagraph,
int deletePos)
public int getPosition()
public void insertChar(
AttributedCharacterIterator newParagraph,
int insertPos)
public TextLayout nextLayout(float
maxAdvance)
public TextLayout nextLayout(float
wrappingWidth,int offsetLimit,boolean
requireNextWord)
public int nextOffset(float maxAdvance)

public int nextOffset(float
wrappingWidth,int offsetLimit,boolean
requireNextWord)
public void setPosition(int newPosition)

## LineMetrics

public abstract class java.awt.font.
LineMetrics
extends java.lang.Object

### Methods

public abstract float getAscent()
public abstract int getBaselineIndex()
public abstract float getBaselineOffsets(
)
public abstract float getDescent()
public abstract float getHeight()
public abstract float getLeading()
public abstract int getNumChars()
public abstract float
getStrikethroughOffset()
public abstract float
getStrikethroughThickness()
public abstract float getUnderlineOffset(
)
public abstract float
getUnderlineThickness()

## LineNumberInputStream

public class java.io.
LineNumberInputStream
extends java.io.FilterInputStream
extends java.io.InputStream
extends java.lang.Object

### Constructors

public  LineNumberInputStream(
InputStream in)

### Methods

public int available()
public int getLineNumber()
public void mark(int readlimit)
public int read()
public int read(byte b,int off,int len)
public void reset()
public void setLineNumber(int lineNumber)
public long skip(long n)

## LineNumberReader

public class java.io.LineNumberReader
extends java.io.BufferedReader
extends java.io.Reader
extends java.lang.Object

### Constructors

public  LineNumberReader(Reader in)
public  LineNumberReader(Reader in,int
sz)

### Methods

public int getLineNumber()
public void mark(int readAheadLimit)

```
public int read()
public int read(char cbuf,int off,int
len)
public String readLine()
public void reset()
public void setLineNumber(int lineNumber)
public long skip(long n)
```

# LinkageError

```
public class java.lang.LinkageError
extends java.lang.Error
extends java.lang.Throwable
extends java.lang.Object
```

## Constructors
```
public  LinkageError()
public  LinkageError(String s)
```

# LinkedList

```
public class java.util.LinkedList
implements java.lang.Cloneable
implements java.util.List
implements java.io.Serializable
extends java.util.
AbstractSequentialList
extends java.util.AbstractList
extends java.util.AbstractCollection
extends java.lang.Object
```

## Constructors
```
public  LinkedList()
public  LinkedList(Collection c)
```

## Methods
```
public boolean add(Object o)
public void add(int index,Object element)
public boolean addAll(Collection c)
public boolean addAll(int index,
Collection c)
public void addFirst(Object o)
public void addLast(Object o)
public void clear()
public Object clone()
public boolean contains(Object o)
public Object get(int index)
public Object getFirst()
public Object getLast()
public int indexOf(Object o)
public int lastIndexOf(Object o)
public ListIterator listIterator(int
index)
public boolean remove(Object o)
public Object remove(int index)
public Object removeFirst()
public Object removeLast()
public Object set(int index,Object
element)
public int size()
public Object toArray()
public Object toArray(Object a)
```

# List

```
public class java.awt.List
implements java.awt.ItemSelectable
extends java.awt.Component
extends java.lang.Object
```

## Constructors
```
public  List()
public  List(int rows)
public  List(int rows,boolean
multipleMode)
```

## Methods
```
public void add(String item)
public void add(String item,int index)
public synchronized void
addActionListener(ActionListener l)
public void addItem(String item)
public synchronized void addItem(String
item,int index)
public synchronized void addItemListener(
ItemListener l)
public void addNotify()
public boolean allowsMultipleSelections()
public synchronized void clear()
public int countItems()
public void delItem(int position)
public synchronized void delItems(int
start,int end)
public synchronized void deselect(int
index)
public String getItem(int index)
public int getItemCount()
public synchronized String getItems()
public Dimension getMinimumSize(int rows)
public Dimension getMinimumSize()
public Dimension getPreferredSize(int
rows)
public Dimension getPreferredSize()
public int getRows()
public synchronized int getSelectedIndex(
)
public synchronized int
getSelectedIndexes()
public synchronized String
getSelectedItem()
public synchronized String
getSelectedItems()
public Object getSelectedObjects()
public int getVisibleIndex()
public boolean isIndexSelected(int index)
public boolean isMultipleMode()
public boolean isSelected(int index)
public synchronized void makeVisible(int
index)
public Dimension minimumSize(int rows)
public Dimension minimumSize()
protected String paramString()
public Dimension preferredSize(int rows)
public Dimension preferredSize()
protected void processActionEvent(
ActionEvent e)
protected void processEvent(AWTEvent e)
```

protected void processItemEvent(
ItemEvent e)
public synchronized void remove(String
item)
public void remove(int position)
public synchronized void
removeActionListener(ActionListener l)
public void removeAll()
public synchronized void
removeItemListener(ItemListener l)
public void removeNotify()
public synchronized void replaceItem(
String newValue,int index)
public void select(int index)
public void setMultipleMode(boolean b)
public synchronized void
setMultipleSelections(boolean b)

## ListDataEvent

public class javax.swing.event.
ListDataEvent
extends java.util.EventObject
extends java.lang.Object

### Fields

public final static int CONTENTS_
CHANGED
public final static int INTERVAL_ADDED
public final static int INTERVAL_
REMOVED

### Constructors

public ListDataEvent(Object source,int
type,int index0,int index1)

### Methods

public int getIndex0()
public int getIndex1()
public int getType()

## ListResourceBundle

public abstract class java.util.
ListResourceBundle
extends java.util.ResourceBundle
extends java.lang.Object

### Constructors

public ListResourceBundle()

### Methods

protected abstract Object getContents()
public Enumeration getKeys()
public final Object handleGetObject(
String key)

## ListSelectionEvent

public class javax.swing.event.
ListSelectionEvent
extends java.util.EventObject
extends java.lang.Object

### Constructors

public ListSelectionEvent(Object source,
int firstIndex,int lastIndex,boolean
isAdjusting)

### Methods

public int getFirstIndex()
public int getLastIndex()
public boolean getValueIsAdjusting()
public String toString()

## ListUI

public abstract class javax.swing.plaf.
ListUI
extends javax.swing.plaf.ComponentUI
extends java.lang.Object

### Methods

public abstract Rectangle getCellBounds(
JList list,int index1,int index2)
public abstract Point indexToLocation(
JList list,int index)
public abstract int locationToIndex(
JList list,Point location)

## ListView

public class javax.swing.text.html.
ListView
extends javax.swing.text.html.BlockView
extends javax.swing.text.BoxView
extends javax.swing.text.CompositeView
extends javax.swing.text.View
extends java.lang.Object

### Constructors

public ListView(Element elem)

### Methods

public float getAlignment(int axis)
public void paint(Graphics g,Shape
allocation)
protected void paintChild(Graphics g,
Rectangle alloc,int index)

## Locale

public final class java.util.Locale
implements java.lang.Cloneable
implements java.io.Serializable
extends java.lang.Object

### Fields

public final static java.util.Locale
CANADA
public final static java.util.Locale
CANADA_FRENCH
public final static java.util.Locale
CHINA
public final static java.util.Locale
CHINESE
public final static java.util.Locale
ENGLISH

```
public final static java.util.Locale
FRANCE
public final static java.util.Locale
FRENCH
public final static java.util.Locale
GERMAN
public final static java.util.Locale
GERMANY
public final static java.util.Locale
ITALIAN
public final static java.util.Locale
ITALY
public final static java.util.Locale
JAPAN
public final static java.util.Locale
JAPANESE
public final static java.util.Locale
KOREA
public final static java.util.Locale
KOREAN
public final static java.util.Locale
PRC
public final static java.util.Locale
SIMPLIFIED_CHINESE
public final static java.util.Locale
TAIWAN
public final static java.util.Locale
TRADITIONAL_CHINESE
public final static java.util.Locale UK
public final static java.util.Locale US
```

### Constructors
```
public  Locale(String language,String
country,String variant)
public  Locale(String language,String
country)
```

### Methods
```
public Object clone()
public boolean equals(Object obj)
public static Locale getAvailableLocales(
)
public String getCountry()
public static Locale getDefault()
public final String getDisplayCountry()
public String getDisplayCountry(Locale
inLocale)
public final String getDisplayLanguage()
public String getDisplayLanguage(Locale
inLocale)
public final String getDisplayName()
public String getDisplayName(Locale
inLocale)
public final String getDisplayVariant()
public String getDisplayVariant(Locale
inLocale)
public String getISO3Country()
public String getISO3Language()
public static String getISOCountries()
public static String getISOLanguages()
public String getLanguage()
public String getVariant()
public synchronized int hashCode()
```

```
public static synchronized void
setDefault(Locale newLocale)
public final String toString()
```

## LocaleData
```
public class java.text.resources.
LocaleData
extends java.lang.Object
```

### Methods
```
public static Locale getAvailableLocales(
String key)
```

## LocaleElements
```
public class java.text.resources.
LocaleElements
extends java.util.ListResourceBundle
extends java.util.ResourceBundle
extends java.lang.Object
```

### Methods
```
public Object getContents()
```

## LocaleElements_en
```
public class java.text.resources.
LocaleElements_en
extends java.util.ListResourceBundle
extends java.util.ResourceBundle
extends java.lang.Object
```

### Methods
```
public Object getContents()
```

## LocaleElements_en_US
```
public class java.text.resources.
LocaleElements_en_US
extends java.util.ListResourceBundle
extends java.util.ResourceBundle
extends java.lang.Object
```

### Methods
```
public Object getContents()
```

## LocateRegistry
```
public final class java.rmi.registry.
LocateRegistry
extends java.lang.Object
```

### Constructors
```
private  LocateRegistry()
```

### Methods
```
public static Registry createRegistry(
int port)
public static Registry createRegistry(
int port,RMIClientSocketFactory csf,
RMIServerSocketFactory ssf)
public static Registry getRegistry()
public static Registry getRegistry(int
port)
public static Registry getRegistry(
String host)
```

```
public static Registry getRegistry(
String host,int port)
public static Registry getRegistry(
String host,int port,
RMIClientSocketFactory csf)
```

## LogStream

```
public class java.rmi.server.LogStream
extends java.io.PrintStream
extends java.io.FilterOutputStream
extends java.io.OutputStream
extends java.lang.Object
```

### Fields

```
public final static int BRIEF
public final static int SILENT
public final static int VERBOSE
```

### Constructors

```
private  LogStream()
```

### Methods

```
public static synchronized PrintStream
getDefaultStream()
public synchronized OutputStream
getOutputStream()
public static LogStream log(String name)
public static int parseLevel(String s)
public static synchronized void
setDefaultStream(PrintStream newDefault)
public synchronized void setOutputStream(
OutputStream out)
public String toString()
public void write(int b)
public void write(byte b,int off,int len)
```

## Long

```
public final class java.lang.Long
implements java.lang.Comparable
extends java.lang.Number
extends java.lang.Object
```

### Fields

```
public final static long MAX_VALUE
public final static long MIN_VALUE
public final static java.lang.Class
TYPE
```

### Constructors

```
public  Long(long value)
public  Long(String s)
```

### Methods

```
public byte byteValue()
public int compareTo(Long anotherLong)
public int compareTo(Object o)
public static Long decode(String nm)
public double doubleValue()
public boolean equals(Object obj)
public float floatValue()
public static Long getLong(String nm)
public static Long getLong(String nm,
long val)
```

```
public static Long getLong(String nm,
Long val)
public int hashCode()
public int intValue()
public long longValue()
public static long parseLong(String s,
int radix)
public static long parseLong(String s)
public short shortValue()
public static String toBinaryString(long
i)
public static String toHexString(long i)
public static String toOctalString(long
i)
public static String toString(long i,int
radix)
public static String toString(long i)
public String toString()
public static Long valueOf(String s,int
radix)
public static Long valueOf(String s)
```

## LookAndFeel

```
public abstract class javax.swing.
LookAndFeel
extends java.lang.Object
```

### Methods

```
public UIDefaults getDefaults()
public abstract String getDescription()
public abstract String getID()
public abstract String getName()
public void initialize()
public static void installBorder(
JComponent c,String defaultBorderName)
public static void installColors(
JComponent c,String defaultBgName,String
defaultFgName)
public static void installColorsAndFont(
JComponent c,String defaultBgName,String
defaultFgName,String defaultFontName)
public abstract boolean
isNativeLookAndFeel()
public abstract boolean
isSupportedLookAndFeel()
public static Object makeIcon(Class
baseClass,String gifFile)
public static KeyBinding makeKeyBindings(
Object keyBindingList)
public String toString()
public void uninitialize()
public static void uninstallBorder(
JComponent c)
```

## LookupOp

```
public class java.awt.image.LookupOp
implements java.awt.image.
BufferedImageOp
implements java.awt.image.RasterOp
extends java.lang.Object
```

### Constructors

```
public  LookupOp(LookupTable lookup,
RenderingHints hints)
```

## Methods

```
public BufferedImage
createCompatibleDestImage(BufferedImage
src,ColorModel destCM)
public WritableRaster
createCompatibleDestRaster(Raster src)
public final BufferedImage filter(
BufferedImage src,BufferedImage dst)
public final WritableRaster filter(
Raster src,WritableRaster dst)
public final Rectangle2D getBounds2D(
BufferedImage src)
public final Rectangle2D getBounds2D(
Raster src)
public final Point2D getPoint2D(Point2D
srcPt,Point2D dstPt)
public final RenderingHints
getRenderingHints()
public final LookupTable getTable()
```

# LookupTable

```
public abstract class java.awt.image.
LookupTable
extends java.lang.Object
extends java.lang.Object
```

## Constructors

```
protected LookupTable(int offset,int
numComponents)
```

## Methods

```
public int getNumComponents()
public int getOffset()
public abstract int lookupPixel(int src,
int dest)
```

# MalformedURLException

```
public class java.net.
MalformedURLException
extends java.io.IOException
extends java.lang.Exception
extends java.lang.Throwable
extends java.lang.Object
```

## Constructors

```
public MalformedURLException()
public MalformedURLException(String msg)
```

# Manifest

```
public class java.util.jar.Manifest
implements java.lang.Cloneable
extends java.lang.Object
```

## Constructors

```
public Manifest()
public Manifest(InputStream is)
public Manifest(Manifest man)
```

## Methods

```
public void clear()
public Object clone()
public boolean equals(Object o)
```

```
public Attributes getAttributes(String
name)
public Map getEntries()
public Attributes getMainAttributes()
public int hashCode()
public void read(InputStream is)
public void write(OutputStream out)
```

# MarshalException

```
public class java.rmi.MarshalException
extends java.rmi.RemoteException
extends java.io.IOException
extends java.lang.Exception
extends java.lang.Throwable
extends java.lang.Object
```

## Constructors

```
public MarshalException(String s)
public MarshalException(String s,
Exception ex)
```

# MarshalledObject

```
public final class java.rmi.
MarshalledObject
implements java.io.Serializable
extends java.lang.Object
```

## Constructors

```
public MarshalledObject(Object obj)
```

## Methods

```
public boolean equals(Object obj)
public Object get()
public int hashCode()
```

# Math

```
public final class java.lang.Math
extends java.lang.Object
```

## Fields

```
public final static double E
public final static double PI
```

## Constructors

```
private Math()
```

## Methods

```
public static int abs(int a)
public static long abs(long a)
public static float abs(float a)
public static double abs(double a)
public static native double acos(double
a)
public static native double asin(double
a)
public static native double atan(double
a)
public static native double atan2(double
a,double b)
public static native double ceil(double
a)
public static native double cos(double a)
```

```
public static native double exp(double a)
public static native double floor(double
a)
public static native double
IEEEremainder(double f1,double f2)
public static native double log(double a)
public static int max(int a,int b)
public static long max(long a,long b)
public static float max(float a,float b)
public static double max(double a,double
b)
public static int min(int a,int b)
public static long min(long a,long b)
public static float min(float a,float b)
public static double min(double a,double
b)
public static native double pow(double a,
double b)
public static synchronized double random(
)
public static native double rint(double
a)
public static int round(float a)
public static long round(double a)
public static native double sin(double a)
public static native double sqrt(double
a)
public static native double tan(double a)
public static double toDegrees(double
angrad)
public static double toRadians(double
angdeg)
```

## MatteBorder

```
public class javax.swing.border.
MatteBorder
extends javax.swing.border.EmptyBorder
extends javax.swing.border.
AbstractBorder
extends java.lang.Object
```

### Fields

```
protected java.awt.Color color
protected javax.swing.Icon tileIcon
```

### Constructors

```
public  MatteBorder(int top,int left,int
bottom,int right,Color color)
public  MatteBorder(int top,int left,int
bottom,int right,Icon tileIcon)
public  MatteBorder(Icon tileIcon)
```

### Methods

```
public Insets getBorderInsets(Component
c)
public boolean isBorderOpaque()
public void paintBorder(Component c,
Graphics g,int x,int y,int width,int
height)
```

## MediaTracker

```
public class java.awt.MediaTracker
implements java.io.Serializable
extends java.lang.Object
```

### Fields

```
public final static int ABORTED
public final static int COMPLETE
public final static int ERRORED
public final static int LOADING
```

### Constructors

```
public  MediaTracker(Component comp)
```

### Methods

```
public void addImage(Image image,int id)
public synchronized void addImage(Image
image,int id,int w,int h)
public boolean checkAll()
public boolean checkAll(boolean load)
public boolean checkID(int id)
public boolean checkID(int id,boolean
load)
public synchronized Object getErrorsAny()
public synchronized Object getErrorsID(
int id)
public synchronized boolean isErrorAny()
public synchronized boolean isErrorID(
int id)
public synchronized void removeImage(
Image image)
public synchronized void removeImage(
Image image,int id)
public synchronized void removeImage(
Image image,int id,int width,int height)
public int statusAll(boolean load)
public int statusID(int id,boolean load)
public void waitForAll()
public synchronized boolean waitForAll(
long ms)
public void waitForID(int id)
public synchronized boolean waitForID(
int id,long ms)
```

## MemoryImageSource

```
public class java.awt.image.
MemoryImageSource
implements java.awt.image.ImageProducer
extends java.lang.Object
```

### Constructors

```
public  MemoryImageSource(int w,int h,
ColorModel cm,byte pix,int off,int scan)
public  MemoryImageSource(int w,int h,
ColorModel cm,byte pix,int off,int scan,
Hashtable props)
public  MemoryImageSource(int w,int h,
ColorModel cm,int pix,int off,int scan)
public  MemoryImageSource(int w,int h,
ColorModel cm,int pix,int off,int scan,
Hashtable props)
public  MemoryImageSource(int w,int h,
int pix,int off,int scan)
public  MemoryImageSource(int w,int h,
int pix,int off,int scan,Hashtable props)
```

### Methods

```
public synchronized void addConsumer(
ImageConsumer ic)
```

public synchronized boolean isConsumer(
ImageConsumer ic)
public void newPixels()
public synchronized void newPixels(int x,
int y,int w,int h)
public synchronized void newPixels(int x,
int y,int w,int h,boolean framenotify)
public synchronized void newPixels(byte
newpix,ColorModel newmodel,int offset,
int scansize)
public synchronized void newPixels(int
newpix,ColorModel newmodel,int offset,
int scansize)
public synchronized void removeConsumer(
ImageConsumer ic)
public void
requestTopDownLeftRightResend(
ImageConsumer ic)
public synchronized void setAnimated(
boolean animated)
public synchronized void
setFullBufferUpdates(boolean fullbuffers)
public void startProduction(
ImageConsumer ic)

# Menu

public class java.awt.Menu
implements java.awt.MenuContainer
extends java.awt.MenuItem
extends java.awt.MenuComponent
extends java.lang.Object

## Constructors
public  Menu()
public  Menu(String label)
public  Menu(String label,boolean
tearOff)

## Methods
public MenuItem add(MenuItem mi)
public void add(String label)
public void addNotify()
public void addSeparator()
public int countItems()
public MenuItem getItem(int index)
public int getItemCount()
public void insert(MenuItem menuitem,int
index)
public void insert(String label,int
index)
public void insertSeparator(int index)
public boolean isTearOff()
public String paramString()
public void remove(int index)
public void remove(MenuComponent item)
public void removeAll()
public void removeNotify()

# MenuBar

public class java.awt.MenuBar
implements java.awt.MenuContainer
extends java.awt.MenuComponent
extends java.lang.Object

## Constructors
public  MenuBar()

## Methods
public Menu add(Menu m)
public void addNotify()
public int countMenus()
public void deleteShortcut(MenuShortcut
s)
public Menu getHelpMenu()
public Menu getMenu(int i)
public int getMenuCount()
public MenuItem getShortcutMenuItem(
MenuShortcut s)
public void remove(int index)
public void remove(MenuComponent m)
public void removeNotify()
public void setHelpMenu(Menu m)
public synchronized Enumeration
shortcuts()

# MenuBarUI

public abstract class javax.swing.plaf.
MenuBarUI
extends javax.swing.plaf.ComponentUI
extends java.lang.Object

# MenuComponent

public abstract class java.awt.
MenuComponent
implements java.io.Serializable
extends java.lang.Object

## Constructors
public  MenuComponent()

## Methods
public final void dispatchEvent(AWTEvent
e)
public Font getFont()
public String getName()
public MenuContainer getParent()
public MenuComponentPeer getPeer()
protected final Object getTreeLock()
protected String paramString()
public boolean postEvent(Event evt)
protected void processEvent(AWTEvent e)
public void removeNotify()
public void setFont(Font f)
public void setName(String name)
public String toString()

# MenuDragMouseEvent

public class javax.swing.event.
MenuDragMouseEvent
extends java.awt.event.MouseEvent
extends java.awt.event.InputEvent
extends java.awt.event.ComponentEvent
extends java.awt.AWTEvent
extends java.util.EventObject
extends java.lang.Object

### Constructors
```
public  MenuDragMouseEvent(Component
source,int id,long when,int modifiers,
int x,int y,int clickCount,boolean
popupTrigger,MenuElement p,
MenuSelectionManager m)
```

### Methods
```
public MenuSelectionManager
getMenuSelectionManager()
public MenuElement getPath()
```

## MenuEvent
```
public class javax.swing.event.
MenuEvent
extends java.util.EventObject
extends java.lang.Object
```

### Constructors
```
public  MenuEvent(Object source)
```

## MenuItem
```
public class java.awt.MenuItem
extends java.awt.MenuComponent
extends java.lang.Object
```

### Constructors
```
public  MenuItem()
public  MenuItem(String label)
public  MenuItem(String label,
MenuShortcut s)
```

### Methods
```
public synchronized void
addActionListener(ActionListener l)
public void addNotify()
public void deleteShortcut()
public synchronized void disable()
protected final void disableEvents(long
eventsToDisable)
public synchronized void enable()
public void enable(boolean b)
protected final void enableEvents(long
eventsToEnable)
public String getActionCommand()
public String getLabel()
public MenuShortcut getShortcut()
public boolean isEnabled()
public String paramString()
protected void processActionEvent(
ActionEvent e)
protected void processEvent(AWTEvent e)
public synchronized void
removeActionListener(ActionListener l)
public void setActionCommand(String
command)
public synchronized void setEnabled(
boolean b)
public synchronized void setLabel(String
label)
public void setShortcut(MenuShortcut s)
```

## MenuItemUI
```
public abstract class javax.swing.plaf.
MenuItemUI
extends javax.swing.plaf.ButtonUI
extends javax.swing.plaf.ComponentUI
extends java.lang.Object
```

## MenuKeyEvent
```
public class javax.swing.event.
MenuKeyEvent
extends java.awt.event.KeyEvent
extends java.awt.event.InputEvent
extends java.awt.event.ComponentEvent
extends java.awt.AWTEvent
extends java.util.EventObject
extends java.lang.Object
```

### Constructors
```
public  MenuKeyEvent(Component source,
int id,long when,int modifiers,int
keyCode,char keyChar,MenuElement p,
MenuSelectionManager m)
```

### Methods
```
public MenuSelectionManager
getMenuSelectionManager()
public MenuElement getPath()
```

## MenuSelectionManager
```
public class javax.swing.
MenuSelectionManager
extends java.lang.Object
```

### Fields
```
protected transient javax.swing.event.
ChangeEvent changeEvent
protected javax.swing.event.
EventListenerList listenerList
```

### Methods
```
public void addChangeListener(
ChangeListener l)
public void clearSelectedPath()
public Component componentForPoint(
Component source,Point sourcePoint)
public static MenuSelectionManager
defaultManager()
protected void fireStateChanged()
public MenuElement getSelectedPath()
public boolean
isComponentPartOfCurrentMenu(Component c)
public void processKeyEvent(KeyEvent e)
public void processMouseEvent(MouseEvent
event)
public void removeChangeListener(
ChangeListener l)
public void setSelectedPath(MenuElement
path)
```

## MenuShortcut
```
public class java.awt.MenuShortcut
implements java.io.Serializable
extends java.lang.Object
```

## Constructors

```
public  MenuShortcut(int key)
public  MenuShortcut(int key,boolean
useShiftModifier)
```

## Methods

```
public boolean equals(MenuShortcut s)
public boolean equals(Object obj)
public int getKey()
public int hashCode()
protected String paramString()
public String toString()
public boolean usesShiftModifier()
```

# MessageDigest

```
public abstract class java.security.
MessageDigest
extends java.security.MessageDigestSpi
extends java.lang.Object
```

## Constructors

```
protected  MessageDigest(String
algorithm)
```

## Methods

```
public Object clone()
public byte digest()
public int digest(byte buf,int offset,
int len)
public byte digest(byte input)
public final String getAlgorithm()
public final int getDigestLength()
public static MessageDigest getInstance(
String algorithm)
public static MessageDigest getInstance(
String algorithm,String provider)
public final Provider getProvider()
public static boolean isEqual(byte
digesta,byte digestb)
public void reset()
public String toString()
public void update(byte input)
public void update(byte input,int offset,
int len)
public void update(byte input)
```

# MessageDigestSpi

```
public abstract class java.security.
MessageDigestSpi
extends java.lang.Object
```

## Methods

```
public Object clone()
protected abstract byte engineDigest()
protected int engineDigest(byte buf,int
offset,int len)
protected int engineGetDigestLength()
protected abstract void engineReset()
protected abstract void engineUpdate(
byte input)
protected abstract void engineUpdate(
byte input,int offset,int len)
```

# MessageFormat

```
public class java.text.MessageFormat
extends java.text.Format
extends java.lang.Object
```

## Constructors

```
public  MessageFormat(String pattern)
private  MessageFormat()
```

## Methods

```
public void applyPattern(String
newPattern)
public Object clone()
public boolean equals(Object obj)
public final StringBuffer format(Object
source,StringBuffer result,FieldPosition
ignore)
public static String format(String
pattern,Object arguments)
public final StringBuffer format(Object
source,StringBuffer result,FieldPosition
ignore)
public Format getFormats()
public Locale getLocale()
public int hashCode()
public Object parse(String source,
ParsePosition status)
public Object parse(String source)
public Object parseObject(String text,
ParsePosition status)
public void setFormat(int variable,
Format newFormat)
public void setFormats(Format newFormats)
public void setLocale(Locale theLocale)
public String toPattern()
```

# MetalBorders

```
public class javax.swing.plaf.metal.
MetalBorders
extends java.lang.Object
```

# MetalButtonUI

```
public class javax.swing.plaf.metal.
MetalButtonUI
extends javax.swing.plaf.basic.
BasicButtonUI
extends javax.swing.plaf.ButtonUI
extends javax.swing.plaf.ComponentUI
extends java.lang.Object
```

## Fields

```
protected java.awt.Color
disabledTextColor
protected java.awt.Color focusColor
protected java.awt.Color selectColor
```

## Methods

```
protected BasicButtonListener
createButtonListener(AbstractButton b)
public static ComponentUI createUI(
JComponent c)
protected Color getDisabledTextColor()
protected Color getFocusColor()
```

```
protected Color getSelectColor()
public void installDefaults(
AbstractButton b)
protected void paintButtonPressed(
Graphics g,AbstractButton b)
protected void paintFocus(Graphics g,
AbstractButton b,Rectangle viewRect,
Rectangle textRect,Rectangle iconRect)
protected void paintText(Graphics g,
JComponent c,Rectangle textRect,String
text)
public void uninstallDefaults(
AbstractButton b)
```

## MetalCheckBoxIcon

```
public class javax.swing.plaf.metal.
MetalCheckBoxIcon
implements javax.swing.Icon
implements java.io.Serializable
implements javax.swing.plaf.UIResource
extends java.lang.Object
```

### Methods

```
protected void drawCheck(Component c,
Graphics g,int x,int y)
protected int getControlSize()
public int getIconHeight()
public int getIconWidth()
public void paintIcon(Component c,
Graphics g,int x,int y)
```

## MetalCheckBoxUI

```
public class javax.swing.plaf.metal.
MetalCheckBoxUI
extends javax.swing.plaf.metal.
MetalRadioButtonUI
extends javax.swing.plaf.basic.
BasicRadioButtonUI
extends javax.swing.plaf.basic.
BasicToggleButtonUI
extends javax.swing.plaf.basic.
BasicButtonUI
extends javax.swing.plaf.ButtonUI
extends javax.swing.plaf.ComponentUI
extends java.lang.Object
```

### Methods

```
public static ComponentUI createUI(
JComponent b)
public String getPropertyPrefix()
public void installDefaults(
AbstractButton b)
protected void uninstallDefaults(
AbstractButton b)
```

## MetalComboBoxButton

```
public class javax.swing.plaf.metal.
MetalComboBoxButton
extends javax.swing.JButton
extends javax.swing.AbstractButton
extends javax.swing.JComponent
extends java.awt.Container
```

```
extends java.awt.Component
extends java.lang.Object
```

### Fields

```
protected javax.swing.JComboBox
comboBox
protected javax.swing.Icon comboIcon
protected boolean iconOnly
protected javax.swing.JList listBox
protected javax.swing.CellRendererPane
rendererPane
```

### Constructors

```
MetalComboBoxButton()
public  MetalComboBoxButton(JComboBox cb,
Icon i,CellRendererPane pane,JList list)
public  MetalComboBoxButton(JComboBox cb,
Icon i,boolean onlyIcon,CellRendererPane
pane,JList list)
```

### Methods

```
public final JComboBox getComboBox()
public final Icon getComboIcon()
public boolean isFocusTraversable()
public final boolean isIconOnly()
public void paintComponent(Graphics g)
public final void setComboBox(JComboBox
cb)
public final void setComboIcon(Icon i)
public final void setIconOnly(boolean
isIconOnly)
```

## MetalComboBoxEditor

```
public class javax.swing.plaf.metal.
MetalComboBoxEditor
extends javax.swing.plaf.basic.
BasicComboBoxEditor
extends java.lang.Object
```

### Fields

```
protected static java.awt.Insets
editorBorderInsets
```

### Constructors

```
public  MetalComboBoxEditor()
```

## MetalComboBoxIcon

```
public class javax.swing.plaf.metal.
MetalComboBoxIcon
implements javax.swing.Icon
implements java.io.Serializable
extends java.lang.Object
```

### Methods

```
public int getIconHeight()
public int getIconWidth()
public void paintIcon(Component c,
Graphics g,int x,int y)
```

## MetalComboBoxUI

```
public class javax.swing.plaf.metal.
MetalComboBoxUI
```

extends javax.swing.plaf.basic.
BasicComboBoxUI
extends javax.swing.plaf.ComboBoxUI
extends javax.swing.plaf.ComponentUI
extends java.lang.Object

## Methods
public void configureArrowButton()
public void configureEditor()
protected JButton createArrowButton()
protected ComboBoxEditor createEditor()
protected LayoutManager
createLayoutManager()
protected ComboPopup createPopup()
public PropertyChangeListener
createPropertyChangeListener()
public static ComponentUI createUI(
JComponent c)
protected void editablePropertyChanged(
PropertyChangeEvent e)
public Dimension getMinimumSize(
JComponent c)
protected void installKeyboardActions()
protected void installListeners()
public void installUI(JComponent c)
public boolean isFocusTraversable(
JComboBox c)
public void layoutComboBox(Container
parent,MetalComboBoxLayoutManager
manager)
public void paint(Graphics g,JComponent
c)
protected void removeListeners()
protected void selectNextPossibleValue()
protected void
selectPreviousPossibleValue()
public void unconfigureArrowButton()
public void unconfigureEditor()
protected void uninstallKeyboardActions()
protected void uninstallListeners()
public void uninstallUI(JComponent c)

## MetalDesktopIconUI
public class javax.swing.plaf.metal.
MetalDesktopIconUI
extends javax.swing.plaf.basic.
BasicDesktopIconUI
extends javax.swing.plaf.DesktopIconUI
extends javax.swing.plaf.ComponentUI
extends java.lang.Object

### Constructors
public  MetalDesktopIconUI()

### Methods
public static ComponentUI createUI(
JComponent c)
public Dimension getPreferredSize(
JComponent c)
protected void installComponents()
protected void installDefaults()
protected void uninstallComponents()

## MetalFileChooserUI
public class javax.swing.plaf.metal.
MetalFileChooserUI
extends javax.swing.plaf.basic.
BasicFileChooserUI
extends javax.swing.plaf.FileChooserUI
extends javax.swing.plaf.ComponentUI
extends java.lang.Object

### Constructors
public  MetalFileChooserUI(JFileChooser
filechooser)

### Methods
protected DirectoryComboBoxModel
createDirectoryComboBoxModel(
JFileChooser fc)
protected DirectoryComboBoxRenderer
createDirectoryComboBoxRenderer(
JFileChooser fc)
protected FilterComboBoxModel
createFilterComboBoxModel()
protected FilterComboBoxRenderer
createFilterComboBoxRenderer()
protected JPanel createList(JFileChooser
fc)
public PropertyChangeListener
createPropertyChangeListener(
JFileChooser fc)
public static ComponentUI createUI(
JComponent c)
public void ensureFileIsVisible(
JFileChooser fc,File f)
protected JButton getApproveButton(
JFileChooser fc)
public String getDirectoryName()
public String getFileName()
public Dimension getMaximumSize(
JComponent c)
public Dimension getMinimumSize(
JComponent c)
public Dimension getPreferredSize(
JComponent c)
public void installComponents(
JFileChooser fc)
protected void installStrings(
JFileChooser fc)
public void rescanCurrentDirectory(
JFileChooser fc)
public void setDirectoryName(String
dirname)
public void setFileName(String filename)
public void uninstallUI(JComponent c)
public void valueChanged(
ListSelectionEvent e)

## MetalIconFactory
public class javax.swing.plaf.metal.
MetalIconFactory
implements java.io.Serializable
extends java.lang.Object

### Fields
```
public final static boolean DARK
public final static boolean LIGHT
```

### Methods
```
public static Icon
getCheckBoxMenuItemIcon()
public static Icon
getFileChooserDetailViewIcon()
public static Icon
getFileChooserHomeFolderIcon()
public static Icon
getFileChooserListViewIcon()
public static Icon
getFileChooserNewFolderIcon()
public static Icon
getFileChooserUpFolderIcon()
public static Icon
getHorizontalSliderThumbIcon()
public static Icon
getInternalFrameAltMaximizeIcon(int size)
public static Icon
getInternalFrameCloseIcon(int size)
public static Icon
getInternalFrameDefaultMenuIcon()
public static Icon
getInternalFrameMaximizeIcon(int size)
public static Icon
getInternalFrameMinimizeIcon(int size)
public static Icon getMenuArrowIcon()
public static Icon getMenuItemArrowIcon()
public static Icon getMenuItemCheckIcon()
public static Icon getRadioButtonIcon()
public static Icon
getRadioButtonMenuItemIcon()
public static Icon getTreeComputerIcon()
public static Icon getTreeControlIcon(
boolean isCollapsed)
public static Icon
getTreeFloppyDriveIcon()
public static Icon getTreeFolderIcon()
public static Icon getTreeHardDriveIcon()
public static Icon getTreeLeafIcon()
public static Icon
getVerticalSliderThumbIcon()
```

## MetalInternalFrameUI
```
public class javax.swing.plaf.metal.
MetalInternalFrameUI
extends javax.swing.plaf.basic.
BasicInternalFrameUI
extends javax.swing.plaf.
InternalFrameUI
extends javax.swing.plaf.ComponentUI
extends java.lang.Object
```

### Fields
```
protected static java.lang.String IS_
PALETTE
```

### Constructors
```
public  MetalInternalFrameUI(
JInternalFrame b)
```

### Methods
```
protected JComponent createNorthPane(
JInternalFrame w)
public static ComponentUI createUI(
JComponent c)
protected void installKeyboardActions()
public void installUI(JComponent c)
protected void replacePane(JComponent
currentPane,JComponent newPane)
public void setPalette(boolean isPalette)
protected void uninstallKeyboardActions()
public void uninstallUI(JComponent c)
```

## MetalLabelUI
```
public class javax.swing.plaf.metal.
MetalLabelUI
extends javax.swing.plaf.basic.
BasicLabelUI
extends javax.swing.plaf.LabelUI
extends javax.swing.plaf.ComponentUI
extends java.lang.Object
```

### Fields
```
protected static javax.swing.plaf.metal.
MetalLabelUI metalLabelUI
```

### Methods
```
public static ComponentUI createUI(
JComponent c)
protected void paintDisabledText(JLabel
l,Graphics g,String s,int textX,int
textY)
```

## MetalLookAndFeel
```
public class javax.swing.plaf.metal.
MetalLookAndFeel
extends javax.swing.plaf.basic.
BasicLookAndFeel
extends javax.swing.LookAndFeel
extends java.lang.Object
```

### Methods
```
protected void createDefaultTheme()
public static ColorUIResource
getAcceleratorForeground()
public static ColorUIResource
getAcceleratorSelectedForeground()
public static ColorUIResource getBlack()
public static ColorUIResource getControl(
)
public static ColorUIResource
getControlDarkShadow()
public static ColorUIResource
getControlDisabled()
public static ColorUIResource
getControlHighlight()
public static ColorUIResource
getControlInfo()
public static ColorUIResource
getControlShadow()
public static ColorUIResource
getControlTextColor()
```

```
public static FontUIResource
getControlTextFont()
public UIDefaults getDefaults()
public String getDescription()
public static ColorUIResource
getDesktopColor()
public static ColorUIResource
getFocusColor()
public static ColorUIResource
getHighlightedTextColor()
public String getID()
public static ColorUIResource
getInactiveControlTextColor()
public static ColorUIResource
getInactiveSystemTextColor()
public static ColorUIResource
getMenuBackground()
public static ColorUIResource
getMenuDisabledForeground()
public static ColorUIResource
getMenuForeground()
public static ColorUIResource
getMenuSelectedBackground()
public static ColorUIResource
getMenuSelectedForeground()
public static FontUIResource
getMenuTextFont()
public String getName()
public static ColorUIResource
getPrimaryControl()
public static ColorUIResource
getPrimaryControlDarkShadow()
public static ColorUIResource
getPrimaryControlHighlight()
public static ColorUIResource
getPrimaryControlInfo()
public static ColorUIResource
getPrimaryControlShadow()
public static ColorUIResource
getSeparatorBackground()
public static ColorUIResource
getSeparatorForeground()
public static FontUIResource
getSubTextFont()
public static ColorUIResource
getSystemTextColor()
public static FontUIResource
getSystemTextFont()
public static ColorUIResource
getTextHighlightColor()
public static ColorUIResource
getUserTextColor()
public static FontUIResource
getUserTextFont()
public static ColorUIResource getWhite()
public static ColorUIResource
getWindowBackground()
public static ColorUIResource
getWindowTitleBackground()
public static FontUIResource
getWindowTitleFont()
public static ColorUIResource
getWindowTitleForeground()
```

```
public static ColorUIResource
getWindowTitleInactiveBackground()
public static ColorUIResource
getWindowTitleInactiveForeground()
protected void initClassDefaults(
UIDefaults table)
protected void initComponentDefaults(
UIDefaults table)
protected void initSystemColorDefaults(
UIDefaults table)
public boolean isNativeLookAndFeel()
public boolean isSupportedLookAndFeel()
public static void setCurrentTheme(
MetalTheme theme)
```

## MetalPopupMenuSeparatorUI

```
public class javax.swing.plaf.metal.
MetalPopupMenuSeparatorUI
extends javax.swing.plaf.metal.
MetalSeparatorUI
extends javax.swing.plaf.basic.
BasicSeparatorUI
extends javax.swing.plaf.SeparatorUI
extends javax.swing.plaf.ComponentUI
extends java.lang.Object
```

### Methods

```
public static ComponentUI createUI(
JComponent c)
public Dimension getPreferredSize(
JComponent c)
public void paint(Graphics g,JComponent
c)
```

## MetalProgressBarUI

```
public class javax.swing.plaf.metal.
MetalProgressBarUI
extends javax.swing.plaf.basic.
BasicProgressBarUI
extends javax.swing.plaf.ProgressBarUI
extends javax.swing.plaf.ComponentUI
extends java.lang.Object
```

### Methods

```
public static ComponentUI createUI(
JComponent c)
public void paint(Graphics g,JComponent
c)
```

## MetalRadioButtonUI

```
public class javax.swing.plaf.metal.
MetalRadioButtonUI
extends javax.swing.plaf.basic.
BasicRadioButtonUI
extends javax.swing.plaf.basic.
BasicToggleButtonUI
extends javax.swing.plaf.basic.
BasicButtonUI
extends javax.swing.plaf.ButtonUI
extends javax.swing.plaf.ComponentUI
extends java.lang.Object
```

### Fields
```
protected java.awt.Color
disabledTextColor
protected java.awt.Color focusColor
protected java.awt.Color selectColor
```

### Methods
```
public static ComponentUI createUI(
JComponent c)
protected Color getDisabledTextColor()
protected Color getFocusColor()
protected Color getSelectColor()
public void installDefaults(
AbstractButton b)
public synchronized void paint(Graphics
g,JComponent c)
protected void paintFocus(Graphics g,
Rectangle t,Dimension d)
protected void uninstallDefaults(
AbstractButton b)
```

## MetalScrollBarUI
```
public class javax.swing.plaf.metal.
MetalScrollBarUI
extends javax.swing.plaf.basic.
BasicScrollBarUI
extends javax.swing.plaf.ScrollBarUI
extends javax.swing.plaf.ComponentUI
extends java.lang.Object
```

### Fields
```
protected javax.swing.plaf.metal.
MetalBumps bumps
protected javax.swing.plaf.metal.
MetalScrollButton decreaseButton
public final static java.lang.String
FREE_STANDING_PROP
protected javax.swing.plaf.metal.
MetalScrollButton increaseButton
protected boolean isFreeStanding
protected int scrollBarWidth
```

### Methods
```
protected void configureScrollBarColors()
protected JButton createDecreaseButton(
int orientation)
protected JButton createIncreaseButton(
int orientation)
protected PropertyChangeListener
createPropertyChangeListener()
public static ComponentUI createUI(
JComponent c)
protected Dimension getMinimumThumbSize()
public Dimension getPreferredSize(
JComponent c)
protected void installDefaults()
protected void installListeners()
protected void paintThumb(Graphics g,
JComponent c,Rectangle thumbBounds)
protected void paintTrack(Graphics g,
JComponent c,Rectangle trackBounds)
protected void setThumbBounds(int x,int
y,int width,int height)
```

## MetalScrollButton
```
public class javax.swing.plaf.metal.
MetalScrollButton
extends javax.swing.plaf.basic.
BasicArrowButton
extends javax.swing.JButton
extends javax.swing.AbstractButton
extends javax.swing.JComponent
extends java.awt.Container
extends java.awt.Component
extends java.lang.Object
```

### Constructors
```
public MetalScrollButton(int direction,
int width,boolean freeStanding)
```

### Methods
```
public int getButtonWidth()
public Dimension getMaximumSize()
public Dimension getMinimumSize()
public Dimension getPreferredSize()
public void paint(Graphics g)
public void setFreeStanding(boolean
freeStanding)
```

## MetalScrollPaneUI
```
public class javax.swing.plaf.metal.
MetalScrollPaneUI
extends javax.swing.plaf.basic.
BasicScrollPaneUI
extends javax.swing.plaf.ScrollPaneUI
extends javax.swing.plaf.ComponentUI
extends java.lang.Object
```

### Methods
```
protected PropertyChangeListener
createScrollBarSwapListener()
public static ComponentUI createUI(
JComponent x)
public void installListeners(JScrollPane
scrollPane)
public void installUI(JComponent c)
public void uninstallListeners(
JScrollPane scrollPane)
public void uninstallUI(JComponent c)
```

## MetalSeparatorUI
```
public class javax.swing.plaf.metal.
MetalSeparatorUI
extends javax.swing.plaf.basic.
BasicSeparatorUI
extends javax.swing.plaf.SeparatorUI
extends javax.swing.plaf.ComponentUI
extends java.lang.Object
```

### Methods
```
public static ComponentUI createUI(
JComponent c)
public Dimension getPreferredSize(
JComponent c)
protected void installDefaults(
JSeparator s)
```

```
public void paint(Graphics g,JComponent
c)
```

# MetalSliderUI

```
public class javax.swing.plaf.metal.
MetalSliderUI
extends javax.swing.plaf.basic.
BasicSliderUI
extends javax.swing.plaf.SliderUI
extends javax.swing.plaf.ComponentUI
extends java.lang.Object
```

## Fields

```
protected static java.awt.Color
darkShadowColor
protected boolean filledSlider
protected static java.awt.Color
highlightColor
protected static javax.swing.Icon
horizThumbIcon
protected final java.lang.String SLIDER_
FILL
protected static java.awt.Color
thumbColor
protected static int tickLength
protected final int TICK_BUFFER
protected static int trackWidth
protected static javax.swing.Icon
vertThumbIcon
```

## Constructors

```
public  MetalSliderUI()
```

## Methods

```
protected PropertyChangeListener
createPropertyChangeListener(JSlider
slider)
public static ComponentUI createUI(
JComponent c)
protected int getThumbOverhang()
protected Dimension getThumbSize()
public int getTickLength()
protected int getTrackLength()
protected int getTrackWidth()
public void installUI(JComponent c)
public void paintFocus(Graphics g)
protected void
paintMajorTickForHorizSlider(Graphics g,
Rectangle tickBounds,int x)
protected void
paintMajorTickForVertSlider(Graphics g,
Rectangle tickBounds,int y)
protected void
paintMinorTickForHorizSlider(Graphics g,
Rectangle tickBounds,int x)
protected void
paintMinorTickForVertSlider(Graphics g,
Rectangle tickBounds,int y)
public void paintThumb(Graphics g)
public void paintTrack(Graphics g)
protected void scrollDueToClickInTrack(
int dir)
```

# MetalSplitPaneUI

```
public class javax.swing.plaf.metal.
MetalSplitPaneUI
extends javax.swing.plaf.basic.
BasicSplitPaneUI
extends javax.swing.plaf.SplitPaneUI
extends javax.swing.plaf.ComponentUI
extends java.lang.Object
```

## Methods

```
public BasicSplitPaneDivider
createDefaultDivider()
public static ComponentUI createUI(
JComponent x)
```

# MetalTabbedPaneUI

```
public class javax.swing.plaf.metal.
MetalTabbedPaneUI
extends javax.swing.plaf.basic.
BasicTabbedPaneUI
extends javax.swing.plaf.TabbedPaneUI
extends javax.swing.plaf.ComponentUI
extends java.lang.Object
```

## Fields

```
protected int minTabWidth
protected java.awt.Color selectColor
protected java.awt.Color
selectHighlight
protected java.awt.Color
tabAreaBackground
```

## Methods

```
protected int calculateMaxTabHeight(int
tabPlacement)
protected LayoutManager
createLayoutManager()
public static ComponentUI createUI(
JComponent x)
protected Color getColorForGap(int
currentRun,int x,int y)
protected int getTabLabelShiftX(int
tabPlacement,int tabIndex,boolean
isSelected)
protected int getTabLabelShiftY(int
tabPlacement,int tabIndex,boolean
isSelected)
protected int getTabRunOverlay(int
tabPlacement)
protected void installDefaults()
public void paint(Graphics g,JComponent
c)
protected void paintBottomTabBorder(int
tabIndex,Graphics g,int x,int y,int w,
int h,int btm,int rght,boolean
isSelected)
protected void
paintContentBorderBottomEdge(Graphics g,
int tabPlacement,int selectedIndex,int x,
int y,int w,int h)
protected void
paintContentBorderLeftEdge(Graphics g,
```

```
int tabPlacement,int selectedIndex,int x,
int y,int w,int h)
protected void
paintContentBorderRightEdge(Graphics g,
int tabPlacement,int selectedIndex,int x,
int y,int w,int h)
protected void paintContentBorderTopEdge(
Graphics g,int tabPlacement,int
selectedIndex,int x,int y,int w,int h)
protected void paintFocusIndicator(
Graphics g,int tabPlacement,Rectangle
rects,int tabIndex,Rectangle iconRect,
Rectangle textRect,boolean isSelected)
protected void paintHighlightBelowTab()
protected void paintLeftTabBorder(int
tabIndex,Graphics g,int x,int y,int w,
int h,int btm,int rght,boolean
isSelected)
protected void paintRightTabBorder(int
tabIndex,Graphics g,int x,int y,int w,
int h,int btm,int rght,boolean
isSelected)
protected void paintTabBackground(
Graphics g,int tabPlacement,int tabIndex,
int x,int y,int w,int h,boolean
isSelected)
protected void paintTabBorder(Graphics g,
int tabPlacement,int tabIndex,int x,int
y,int w,int h,boolean isSelected)
protected void paintTopTabBorder(int
tabIndex,Graphics g,int x,int y,int w,
int h,int btm,int rght,boolean
isSelected)
protected boolean shouldFillGap(int
currentRun,int tabIndex,int x,int y)
protected boolean shouldPadTabRun(int
tabPlacement,int run)
protected boolean shouldRotateTabRuns(
int tabPlacement,int selectedRun)
public void update(Graphics g,JComponent
c)
```

## MetalTextFieldUI

```
public class javax.swing.plaf.metal.
MetalTextFieldUI
extends javax.swing.plaf.basic.
BasicTextFieldUI
extends javax.swing.plaf.basic.
BasicTextUI
extends javax.swing.plaf.TextUI
extends javax.swing.plaf.ComponentUI
extends java.lang.Object
```

### Methods

```
public static ComponentUI createUI(
JComponent c)
public void installUI(JComponent c)
public void propertyChange(
PropertyChangeEvent e)
```

## MetalTheme

```
public abstract class javax.swing.plaf.
metal.MetalTheme
extends java.lang.Object
```

### Methods

```
public void addCustomEntriesToTable(
UIDefaults table)
public ColorUIResource
getAcceleratorForeground()
public ColorUIResource
getAcceleratorSelectedForeground()
protected ColorUIResource getBlack()
public ColorUIResource getControl()
public ColorUIResource
getControlDarkShadow()
public ColorUIResource
getControlDisabled()
public ColorUIResource
getControlHighlight()
public ColorUIResource getControlInfo()
public ColorUIResource getControlShadow()
public ColorUIResource
getControlTextColor()
public abstract FontUIResource
getControlTextFont()
public ColorUIResource getDesktopColor()
public ColorUIResource getFocusColor()
public ColorUIResource
getHighlightedTextColor()
public ColorUIResource
getInactiveControlTextColor()
public ColorUIResource
getInactiveSystemTextColor()
public ColorUIResource getMenuBackground(
)
public ColorUIResource
getMenuDisabledForeground()
public ColorUIResource getMenuForeground(
)
public ColorUIResource
getMenuSelectedBackground()
public ColorUIResource
getMenuSelectedForeground()
public abstract FontUIResource
getMenuTextFont()
public abstract String getName()
protected abstract ColorUIResource
getPrimary1()
protected abstract ColorUIResource
getPrimary2()
protected abstract ColorUIResource
getPrimary3()
public ColorUIResource getPrimaryControl(
)
public ColorUIResource
getPrimaryControlDarkShadow()
public ColorUIResource
getPrimaryControlHighlight()
public ColorUIResource
getPrimaryControlInfo()
public ColorUIResource
getPrimaryControlShadow()
protected abstract ColorUIResource
getSecondary1()
protected abstract ColorUIResource
getSecondary2()
protected abstract ColorUIResource
getSecondary3()
```

public ColorUIResource
getSeparatorBackground()
public ColorUIResource
getSeparatorForeground()
public abstract FontUIResource
getSubTextFont()
public ColorUIResource
getSystemTextColor()
public abstract FontUIResource
getSystemTextFont()
public ColorUIResource
getTextHighlightColor()
public ColorUIResource getUserTextColor()
public abstract FontUIResource
getUserTextFont()
protected ColorUIResource getWhite()
public ColorUIResource
getWindowBackground()
public ColorUIResource
getWindowTitleBackground()
public abstract FontUIResource
getWindowTitleFont()
public ColorUIResource
getWindowTitleForeground()
public ColorUIResource
getWindowTitleInactiveBackground()
public ColorUIResource
getWindowTitleInactiveForeground()

# MetalToggleButtonUI

public class javax.swing.plaf.metal.
MetalToggleButtonUI
extends javax.swing.plaf.basic.
BasicToggleButtonUI
extends javax.swing.plaf.basic.
BasicButtonUI
extends javax.swing.plaf.ButtonUI
extends javax.swing.plaf.ComponentUI
extends java.lang.Object

## Fields

protected java.awt.Color
disabledTextColor
protected java.awt.Color focusColor
protected java.awt.Color selectColor

## Methods

public static ComponentUI createUI(
JComponent b)
protected Color getDisabledTextColor()
protected Color getFocusColor()
protected Color getSelectColor()
public void installDefaults(
AbstractButton b)
protected void paintButtonPressed(
Graphics g,AbstractButton b)
protected void paintFocus(Graphics g,
AbstractButton b,Rectangle viewRect,
Rectangle textRect,Rectangle iconRect)
protected void paintText(Graphics g,
JComponent c,Rectangle textRect,String
text)
protected void uninstallDefaults(
AbstractButton b)

# MetalToolBarUI

public class javax.swing.plaf.metal.
MetalToolBarUI
extends javax.swing.plaf.basic.
BasicToolBarUI
extends javax.swing.plaf.ToolBarUI
extends javax.swing.plaf.ComponentUI
extends java.lang.Object

## Fields

protected java.awt.event.
ContainerListener contListener
protected java.beans.
PropertyChangeListener rolloverListener

## Methods

protected ContainerListener
createContainerListener()
protected MouseInputListener
createDockingListener()
protected PropertyChangeListener
createRolloverListener()
public static ComponentUI createUI(
JComponent c)
protected void installListeners()
protected void installNonRolloverBorders(
JComponent c)
protected void installNormalBorders(
JComponent c)
protected void installRolloverBorders(
JComponent c)
public void installUI(JComponent c)
public boolean isRolloverBorders()
protected void setBorderToNonRollover(
Component c)
protected void setBorderToNormal(
Component c)
protected void setBorderToRollover(
Component c)
protected void setDragOffset(Point p)
public void setRolloverBorders(boolean
rollover)
protected void uninstallListeners()
public void uninstallUI(JComponent c)

# MetalToolTipUI

public class javax.swing.plaf.metal.
MetalToolTipUI
extends javax.swing.plaf.basic.
BasicToolTipUI
extends javax.swing.plaf.ToolTipUI
extends javax.swing.plaf.ComponentUI
extends java.lang.Object

## Fields

public final static int
padSpaceBetweenStrings

## Constructors

public  MetalToolTipUI()

## Methods

public static ComponentUI createUI(
JComponent c)

```
public String getAcceleratorString()
public Dimension getPreferredSize(
JComponent c)
public void installUI(JComponent c)
public void paint(Graphics g,JComponent
c)
```

## MetalTreeUI

```
public class javax.swing.plaf.metal.
MetalTreeUI
extends javax.swing.plaf.basic.
BasicTreeUI
extends javax.swing.plaf.TreeUI
extends javax.swing.plaf.ComponentUI
extends java.lang.Object
```

### Constructors
```
public  MetalTreeUI()
```

### Methods
```
public static ComponentUI createUI(
JComponent x)
protected void decodeLineStyle(Object
lineStyleFlag)
protected int getHorizontalLegBuffer()
public void installUI(JComponent c)
protected boolean
isLocationInExpandControl(int row,int
rowLevel,int mouseX,int mouseY)
public void paint(Graphics g,JComponent
c)
protected void paintHorizontalPartOfLeg(
Graphics g,Rectangle clipBounds,Insets
insets,Rectangle bounds,TreePath path,
int row,boolean isExpanded,boolean
hasBeenExpanded,boolean isLeaf)
protected void paintHorizontalSeparators(
Graphics g,JComponent c)
protected void paintVerticalPartOfLeg(
Graphics g,Rectangle clipBounds,Insets
insets,TreePath path)
public void uninstallUI(JComponent c)
```

## Method

```
public final class java.lang.reflect.
Method
implements java.lang.reflect.Member
extends java.lang.reflect.
AccessibleObject
extends java.lang.Object
```

### Constructors
```
private  Method()
```

### Methods
```
public boolean equals(Object obj)
public Class getDeclaringClass()
public Class getExceptionTypes()
public int getModifiers()
public String getName()
public Class getParameterTypes()
public Class getReturnType()
public int hashCode()
```

```
public native Object invoke(Object obj,
Object args)
public String toString()
```

## MethodDescriptor

```
public class java.beans.
MethodDescriptor
extends java.beans.FeatureDescriptor
extends java.lang.Object
```

### Constructors
```
public  MethodDescriptor(Method method)
public  MethodDescriptor(Method method,
ParameterDescriptor parameterDescriptors)
 MethodDescriptor()
 MethodDescriptor()
```

### Methods
```
public Method getMethod()
public ParameterDescriptor
getParameterDescriptors()
```

## MinimalHTMLWriter

```
public class javax.swing.text.html.
MinimalHTMLWriter
extends javax.swing.text.AbstractWriter
extends java.lang.Object
```

### Constructors
```
public  MinimalHTMLWriter(Writer w,
StyledDocument doc)
public  MinimalHTMLWriter(Writer w,
StyledDocument doc,int pos,int len)
```

### Methods
```
protected void endFontTag()
protected boolean inFontTag()
protected boolean isText(Element elem)
protected void startFontTag(String style)
protected void text(Element elem)
public void write()
protected void writeAttributes(
AttributeSet attr)
protected void writeBody()
protected void writeComponent(Element
elem)
protected void writeContent(Element elem,
boolean needsIndenting)
protected void writeEndParagraph()
protected void writeEndTag(String endTag)
protected void writeHeader()
protected void writeHTMLTags(
AttributeSet attr)
protected void writeImage(Element elem)
protected void writeLeaf(Element elem)
protected void writeNonHTMLAttributes(
AttributeSet attr)
protected void writeStartParagraph(
Element elem)
protected void writeStartTag(String tag)
protected void writeStyles()
```

# MissingResourceException

public class java.util.
MissingResourceException
extends java.lang.RuntimeException
extends java.lang.Exception
extends java.lang.Throwable
extends java.lang.Object

## Constructors

public MissingResourceException(String
s,String className,String key)

## Methods

public String getClassName()
public String getKey()

# Modifier

public class java.lang.reflect.Modifier
extends java.lang.Object

## Fields

public final static int ABSTRACT
public final static int FINAL
public final static int INTERFACE
public final static int NATIVE
public final static int PRIVATE
public final static int PROTECTED
public final static int PUBLIC
public final static int STATIC
public final static int STRICT
public final static int SYNCHRONIZED
public final static int TRANSIENT
public final static int VOLATILE

## Methods

public static boolean isAbstract(int mod)
public static boolean isFinal(int mod)
public static boolean isInterface(int
mod)
public static boolean isNative(int mod)
public static boolean isPrivate(int mod)
public static boolean isProtected(int
mod)
public static boolean isPublic(int mod)
public static boolean isStatic(int mod)
public static boolean isStrict(int mod)
public static boolean isSynchronized(int
mod)
public static boolean isTransient(int
mod)
public static boolean isVolatile(int mod)
public static String toString(int mod)

# MouseAdapter

public abstract class java.awt.event.
MouseAdapter
implements java.awt.event.MouseListener
extends java.lang.Object

## Methods

public void mouseClicked(MouseEvent e)
public void mouseEntered(MouseEvent e)
public void mouseExited(MouseEvent e)

public void mousePressed(MouseEvent e)
public void mouseReleased(MouseEvent e)

# MouseDragGestureRecognizer

public abstract class java.awt.dnd.
MouseDragGestureRecognizer
implements java.awt.event.MouseListener
implements java.awt.event.
MouseMotionListener
extends java.awt.dnd.
DragGestureRecognizer
extends java.lang.Object

## Constructors

protected MouseDragGestureRecognizer(
DragSource ds,Component c,int act,
DragGestureListener dgl)
protected MouseDragGestureRecognizer(
DragSource ds,Component c,int act)
protected MouseDragGestureRecognizer(
DragSource ds,Component c)
protected MouseDragGestureRecognizer(
DragSource ds)

## Methods

public void mouseClicked(MouseEvent e)
public void mouseDragged(MouseEvent e)
public void mouseEntered(MouseEvent e)
public void mouseExited(MouseEvent e)
public void mouseMoved(MouseEvent e)
public void mousePressed(MouseEvent e)
public void mouseReleased(MouseEvent e)
protected void registerListeners()
protected void unregisterListeners()

# MouseEvent

public class java.awt.event.MouseEvent
extends java.awt.event.InputEvent
extends java.awt.event.ComponentEvent
extends java.awt.AWTEvent
extends java.util.EventObject
extends java.lang.Object

## Fields

public final static int MOUSE_CLICKED
public final static int MOUSE_DRAGGED
public final static int MOUSE_ENTERED
public final static int MOUSE_EXITED
public final static int MOUSE_FIRST
public final static int MOUSE_LAST
public final static int MOUSE_MOVED
public final static int MOUSE_PRESSED
public final static int MOUSE_RELEASED

## Constructors

public MouseEvent(Component source,int
id,long when,int modifiers,int x,int y,
int clickCount,boolean popupTrigger)

## Methods

public int getClickCount()
public Point getPoint()
public int getX()

```
public int getY()
public boolean isPopupTrigger()
public String paramString()
public synchronized void translatePoint(
int x,int y)
```

# MouseInputAdapter

```
public abstract class javax.swing.event.
MouseInputAdapter
implements javax.swing.event.
MouseInputListener
extends java.lang.Object
```

## Methods

```
public void mouseClicked(MouseEvent e)
public void mouseDragged(MouseEvent e)
public void mouseEntered(MouseEvent e)
public void mouseExited(MouseEvent e)
public void mouseMoved(MouseEvent e)
public void mousePressed(MouseEvent e)
public void mouseReleased(MouseEvent e)
```

# MouseMotionAdapter

```
public abstract class java.awt.event.
MouseMotionAdapter
implements java.awt.event.
MouseMotionListener
extends java.lang.Object
```

## Methods

```
public void mouseDragged(MouseEvent e)
public void mouseMoved(MouseEvent e)
```

# MultiButtonUI

```
public class javax.swing.plaf.multi.
MultiButtonUI
extends javax.swing.plaf.ButtonUI
extends javax.swing.plaf.ComponentUI
extends java.lang.Object
```

## Fields

```
protected java.util.Vector uis
```

## Methods

```
public boolean contains(JComponent a,int
b,int c)
public static ComponentUI createUI(
JComponent a)
public Accessible getAccessibleChild(
JComponent a,int b)
public int getAccessibleChildrenCount(
JComponent a)
public Dimension getMaximumSize(
JComponent a)
public Dimension getMinimumSize(
JComponent a)
public Dimension getPreferredSize(
JComponent a)
public ComponentUI getUIs()
public void installUI(JComponent a)
public void paint(Graphics a,JComponent
b)
```

```
public void uninstallUI(JComponent a)
public void update(Graphics a,JComponent
b)
```

# MulticastSocket

```
public class java.net.MulticastSocket
extends java.net.DatagramSocket
extends java.lang.Object
```

## Constructors

```
public  MulticastSocket()
public  MulticastSocket(int port)
```

## Methods

```
public InetAddress getInterface()
public int getTimeToLive()
public byte getTTL()
public void joinGroup(InetAddress
mcastaddr)
public void leaveGroup(InetAddress
mcastaddr)
public void send(DatagramPacket p,byte
ttl)
public void setInterface(InetAddress inf)
public void setTimeToLive(int ttl)
public void setTTL(byte ttl)
```

# MultiColorChooserUI

```
public class javax.swing.plaf.multi.
MultiColorChooserUI
extends javax.swing.plaf.ColorChooserUI
extends javax.swing.plaf.ComponentUI
extends java.lang.Object
```

## Fields

```
protected java.util.Vector uis
```

## Methods

```
public boolean contains(JComponent a,int
b,int c)
public static ComponentUI createUI(
JComponent a)
public Accessible getAccessibleChild(
JComponent a,int b)
public int getAccessibleChildrenCount(
JComponent a)
public Dimension getMaximumSize(
JComponent a)
public Dimension getMinimumSize(
JComponent a)
public Dimension getPreferredSize(
JComponent a)
public ComponentUI getUIs()
public void installUI(JComponent a)
public void paint(Graphics a,JComponent
b)
public void uninstallUI(JComponent a)
public void update(Graphics a,JComponent
b)
```

# MultiComboBoxUI

public class javax.swing.plaf.multi.
MultiComboBoxUI
extends javax.swing.plaf.ComboBoxUI
extends javax.swing.plaf.ComponentUI
extends java.lang.Object

## Fields
protected java.util.Vector uis

## Methods
public boolean contains(JComponent a,int
b,int c)
public static ComponentUI createUI(
JComponent a)
public Accessible getAccessibleChild(
JComponent a,int b)
public int getAccessibleChildrenCount(
JComponent a)
public Dimension getMaximumSize(
JComponent a)
public Dimension getMinimumSize(
JComponent a)
public Dimension getPreferredSize(
JComponent a)
public ComponentUI getUIs()
public void installUI(JComponent a)
public boolean isFocusTraversable(
JComboBox a)
public boolean isPopupVisible(JComboBox
a)
public void paint(Graphics a,JComponent
b)
public void setPopupVisible(JComboBox a,
boolean b)
public void uninstallUI(JComponent a)
public void update(Graphics a,JComponent
b)

# MultiDesktopIconUI

public class javax.swing.plaf.multi.
MultiDesktopIconUI
extends javax.swing.plaf.DesktopIconUI
extends javax.swing.plaf.ComponentUI
extends java.lang.Object

## Fields
protected java.util.Vector uis

## Methods
public boolean contains(JComponent a,int
b,int c)
public static ComponentUI createUI(
JComponent a)
public Accessible getAccessibleChild(
JComponent a,int b)
public int getAccessibleChildrenCount(
JComponent a)
public Dimension getMaximumSize(
JComponent a)
public Dimension getMinimumSize(
JComponent a)

public Dimension getPreferredSize(
JComponent a)
public ComponentUI getUIs()
public void installUI(JComponent a)
public void paint(Graphics a,JComponent
b)
public void uninstallUI(JComponent a)
public void update(Graphics a,JComponent
b)

# MultiDesktopPaneUI

public class javax.swing.plaf.multi.
MultiDesktopPaneUI
extends javax.swing.plaf.DesktopPaneUI
extends javax.swing.plaf.ComponentUI
extends java.lang.Object

## Fields
protected java.util.Vector uis

## Methods
public boolean contains(JComponent a,int
b,int c)
public static ComponentUI createUI(
JComponent a)
public Accessible getAccessibleChild(
JComponent a,int b)
public int getAccessibleChildrenCount(
JComponent a)
public Dimension getMaximumSize(
JComponent a)
public Dimension getMinimumSize(
JComponent a)
public Dimension getPreferredSize(
JComponent a)
public ComponentUI getUIs()
public void installUI(JComponent a)
public void paint(Graphics a,JComponent
b)
public void uninstallUI(JComponent a)
public void update(Graphics a,JComponent
b)

# MultiFileChooserUI

public class javax.swing.plaf.multi.
MultiFileChooserUI
extends javax.swing.plaf.FileChooserUI
extends javax.swing.plaf.ComponentUI
extends java.lang.Object

## Fields
protected java.util.Vector uis

## Methods
public boolean contains(JComponent a,int
b,int c)
public static ComponentUI createUI(
JComponent a)
public void ensureFileIsVisible(
JFileChooser a,File b)
public FileFilter getAcceptAllFileFilter(
JFileChooser a)

```
public Accessible getAccessibleChild(
JComponent a,int b)
public int getAccessibleChildrenCount(
JComponent a)
public String getApproveButtonText(
JFileChooser a)
public String getDialogTitle(
JFileChooser a)
public FileView getFileView(JFileChooser
a)
public Dimension getMaximumSize(
JComponent a)
public Dimension getMinimumSize(
JComponent a)
public Dimension getPreferredSize(
JComponent a)
public ComponentUI getUIs()
public void installUI(JComponent a)
public void paint(Graphics a,JComponent
b)
public void rescanCurrentDirectory(
JFileChooser a)
public void uninstallUI(JComponent a)
public void update(Graphics a,JComponent
b)
```

## MultiInternalFrameUI

```
public class javax.swing.plaf.multi.
MultiInternalFrameUI
extends javax.swing.plaf.
InternalFrameUI
extends javax.swing.plaf.ComponentUI
extends java.lang.Object
```

### Fields
```
protected java.util.Vector uis
```

### Methods
```
public boolean contains(JComponent a,int
b,int c)
public static ComponentUI createUI(
JComponent a)
public Accessible getAccessibleChild(
JComponent a,int b)
public int getAccessibleChildrenCount(
JComponent a)
public Dimension getMaximumSize(
JComponent a)
public Dimension getMinimumSize(
JComponent a)
public Dimension getPreferredSize(
JComponent a)
public ComponentUI getUIs()
public void installUI(JComponent a)
public void paint(Graphics a,JComponent
b)
public void uninstallUI(JComponent a)
public void update(Graphics a,JComponent
b)
```

## MultiLabelUI

```
public class javax.swing.plaf.multi.
MultiLabelUI
```

```
extends javax.swing.plaf.LabelUI
extends javax.swing.plaf.ComponentUI
extends java.lang.Object
```

### Fields
```
protected java.util.Vector uis
```

### Methods
```
public boolean contains(JComponent a,int
b,int c)
public static ComponentUI createUI(
JComponent a)
public Accessible getAccessibleChild(
JComponent a,int b)
public int getAccessibleChildrenCount(
JComponent a)
public Dimension getMaximumSize(
JComponent a)
public Dimension getMinimumSize(
JComponent a)
public Dimension getPreferredSize(
JComponent a)
public ComponentUI getUIs()
public void installUI(JComponent a)
public void paint(Graphics a,JComponent
b)
public void uninstallUI(JComponent a)
public void update(Graphics a,JComponent
b)
```

## MultiListUI

```
public class javax.swing.plaf.multi.
MultiListUI
extends javax.swing.plaf.ListUI
extends javax.swing.plaf.ComponentUI
extends java.lang.Object
```

### Fields
```
protected java.util.Vector uis
```

### Methods
```
public boolean contains(JComponent a,int
b,int c)
public static ComponentUI createUI(
JComponent a)
public Accessible getAccessibleChild(
JComponent a,int b)
public int getAccessibleChildrenCount(
JComponent a)
public Rectangle getCellBounds(JList a,
int b,int c)
public Dimension getMaximumSize(
JComponent a)
public Dimension getMinimumSize(
JComponent a)
public Dimension getPreferredSize(
JComponent a)
public ComponentUI getUIs()
public Point indexToLocation(JList a,int
b)
public void installUI(JComponent a)
public int locationToIndex(JList a,Point
b)
```

```
public void paint(Graphics a,JComponent
b)
public void uninstallUI(JComponent a)
public void update(Graphics a,JComponent
b)
```

# MultiLookAndFeel

```
public class javax.swing.plaf.multi.
MultiLookAndFeel
extends javax.swing.LookAndFeel
extends java.lang.Object
```

### Methods

```
public static ComponentUI createUIs(
ComponentUI mui,Vector uis,JComponent
target)
public UIDefaults getDefaults()
public String getDescription()
public String getID()
public String getName()
public boolean isNativeLookAndFeel()
public boolean isSupportedLookAndFeel()
protected static ComponentUI uisToArray(
Vector uis)
```

# MultiMenuBarUI

```
public class javax.swing.plaf.multi.
MultiMenuBarUI
extends javax.swing.plaf.MenuBarUI
extends javax.swing.plaf.ComponentUI
extends java.lang.Object
```

### Fields

```
protected java.util.Vector uis
```

### Methods

```
public boolean contains(JComponent a,int
b,int c)
public static ComponentUI createUI(
JComponent a)
public Accessible getAccessibleChild(
JComponent a,int b)
public int getAccessibleChildrenCount(
JComponent a)
public Dimension getMaximumSize(
JComponent a)
public Dimension getMinimumSize(
JComponent a)
public Dimension getPreferredSize(
JComponent a)
public ComponentUI getUIs()
public void installUI(JComponent a)
public void paint(Graphics a,JComponent
b)
public void uninstallUI(JComponent a)
public void update(Graphics a,JComponent
b)
```

# MultiMenuItemUI

```
public class javax.swing.plaf.multi.
MultiMenuItemUI
extends javax.swing.plaf.MenuItemUI
```

```
extends javax.swing.plaf.ButtonUI
extends javax.swing.plaf.ComponentUI
extends java.lang.Object
```

### Fields

```
protected java.util.Vector uis
```

### Methods

```
public boolean contains(JComponent a,int
b,int c)
public static ComponentUI createUI(
JComponent a)
public Accessible getAccessibleChild(
JComponent a,int b)
public int getAccessibleChildrenCount(
JComponent a)
public Dimension getMaximumSize(
JComponent a)
public Dimension getMinimumSize(
JComponent a)
public Dimension getPreferredSize(
JComponent a)
public ComponentUI getUIs()
public void installUI(JComponent a)
public void paint(Graphics a,JComponent
b)
public void uninstallUI(JComponent a)
public void update(Graphics a,JComponent
b)
```

# MultiOptionPaneUI

```
public class javax.swing.plaf.multi.
MultiOptionPaneUI
extends javax.swing.plaf.OptionPaneUI
extends javax.swing.plaf.ComponentUI
extends java.lang.Object
```

### Fields

```
protected java.util.Vector uis
```

### Methods

```
public boolean contains(JComponent a,int
b,int c)
public boolean containsCustomComponents(
JOptionPane a)
public static ComponentUI createUI(
JComponent a)
public Accessible getAccessibleChild(
JComponent a,int b)
public int getAccessibleChildrenCount(
JComponent a)
public Dimension getMaximumSize(
JComponent a)
public Dimension getMinimumSize(
JComponent a)
public Dimension getPreferredSize(
JComponent a)
public ComponentUI getUIs()
public void installUI(JComponent a)
public void paint(Graphics a,JComponent
b)
public void selectInitialValue(
JOptionPane a)
```

```
public void uninstallUI(JComponent a)
public void update(Graphics a,JComponent
b)
```

## MultiPanelUI

```
public class javax.swing.plaf.multi.
MultiPanelUI
extends javax.swing.plaf.PanelUI
extends javax.swing.plaf.ComponentUI
extends java.lang.Object
```

### Fields
```
protected java.util.Vector uis
```

### Methods
```
public boolean contains(JComponent a,int
b,int c)
public static ComponentUI createUI(
JComponent a)
public Accessible getAccessibleChild(
JComponent a,int b)
public int getAccessibleChildrenCount(
JComponent a)
public Dimension getMaximumSize(
JComponent a)
public Dimension getMinimumSize(
JComponent a)
public Dimension getPreferredSize(
JComponent a)
public ComponentUI getUIs()
public void installUI(JComponent a)
public void paint(Graphics a,JComponent
b)
public void uninstallUI(JComponent a)
public void update(Graphics a,JComponent
b)
```

## MultiPixelPackedSampleModel

```
public class java.awt.image.
MultiPixelPackedSampleModel
extends java.awt.image.SampleModel
extends java.lang.Object
```

### Constructors
```
public MultiPixelPackedSampleModel(int
dataType,int w,int h,int numberOfBits)
public MultiPixelPackedSampleModel(int
dataType,int w,int h,int numberOfBits,
int scanlineStride,int dataBitOffset)
```

### Methods
```
public SampleModel
createCompatibleSampleModel(int w,int h)
public DataBuffer createDataBuffer()
public SampleModel
createSubsetSampleModel(int bands)
public int getBitOffset(int x)
public int getDataBitOffset()
public Object getDataElements(int x,int
y,Object obj,DataBuffer data)
public int getNumDataElements()
public int getOffset(int x,int y)
```

```
public int getPixel(int x,int y,int
iArray,DataBuffer data)
public int getPixelBitStride()
public int getSample(int x,int y,int b,
DataBuffer data)
public int getSampleSize()
public int getSampleSize(int band)
public int getScanlineStride()
public int getTransferType()
public void setDataElements(int x,int y,
Object obj,DataBuffer data)
public void setPixel(int x,int y,int
iArray,DataBuffer data)
public void setSample(int x,int y,int b,
int s,DataBuffer data)
```

## MultiPopupMenuUI

```
public class javax.swing.plaf.multi.
MultiPopupMenuUI
extends javax.swing.plaf.PopupMenuUI
extends javax.swing.plaf.ComponentUI
extends java.lang.Object
```

### Fields
```
protected java.util.Vector uis
```

### Methods
```
public boolean contains(JComponent a,int
b,int c)
public static ComponentUI createUI(
JComponent a)
public Accessible getAccessibleChild(
JComponent a,int b)
public int getAccessibleChildrenCount(
JComponent a)
public Dimension getMaximumSize(
JComponent a)
public Dimension getMinimumSize(
JComponent a)
public Dimension getPreferredSize(
JComponent a)
public ComponentUI getUIs()
public void installUI(JComponent a)
public void paint(Graphics a,JComponent
b)
public void uninstallUI(JComponent a)
public void update(Graphics a,JComponent
b)
```

## MultiProgressBarUI

```
public class javax.swing.plaf.multi.
MultiProgressBarUI
extends javax.swing.plaf.ProgressBarUI
extends javax.swing.plaf.ComponentUI
extends java.lang.Object
```

### Fields
```
protected java.util.Vector uis
```

### Methods
```
public boolean contains(JComponent a,int
b,int c)
```

```
public static ComponentUI createUI(
JComponent a)
public Accessible getAccessibleChild(
JComponent a,int b)
public int getAccessibleChildrenCount(
JComponent a)
public Dimension getMaximumSize(
JComponent a)
public Dimension getMinimumSize(
JComponent a)
public Dimension getPreferredSize(
JComponent a)
public ComponentUI getUIs()
public void installUI(JComponent a)
public void paint(Graphics a,JComponent
b)
public void uninstallUI(JComponent a)
public void update(Graphics a,JComponent
b)
```

## MultiScrollBarUI

```
public class javax.swing.plaf.multi.
MultiScrollBarUI
extends javax.swing.plaf.ScrollBarUI
extends javax.swing.plaf.ComponentUI
extends java.lang.Object
```

### Fields
```
protected java.util.Vector uis
```

### Methods
```
public boolean contains(JComponent a,int
b,int c)
public static ComponentUI createUI(
JComponent a)
public Accessible getAccessibleChild(
JComponent a,int b)
public int getAccessibleChildrenCount(
JComponent a)
public Dimension getMaximumSize(
JComponent a)
public Dimension getMinimumSize(
JComponent a)
public Dimension getPreferredSize(
JComponent a)
public ComponentUI getUIs()
public void installUI(JComponent a)
public void paint(Graphics a,JComponent
b)
public void uninstallUI(JComponent a)
public void update(Graphics a,JComponent
b)
```

## MultiScrollPaneUI

```
public class javax.swing.plaf.multi.
MultiScrollPaneUI
extends javax.swing.plaf.ScrollPaneUI
extends javax.swing.plaf.ComponentUI
extends java.lang.Object
```

### Fields
```
protected java.util.Vector uis
```

### Methods
```
public boolean contains(JComponent a,int
b,int c)
public static ComponentUI createUI(
JComponent a)
public Accessible getAccessibleChild(
JComponent a,int b)
public int getAccessibleChildrenCount(
JComponent a)
public Dimension getMaximumSize(
JComponent a)
public Dimension getMinimumSize(
JComponent a)
public Dimension getPreferredSize(
JComponent a)
public ComponentUI getUIs()
public void installUI(JComponent a)
public void paint(Graphics a,JComponent
b)
public void uninstallUI(JComponent a)
public void update(Graphics a,JComponent
b)
```

## MultiSeparatorUI

```
public class javax.swing.plaf.multi.
MultiSeparatorUI
extends javax.swing.plaf.SeparatorUI
extends javax.swing.plaf.ComponentUI
extends java.lang.Object
```

### Fields
```
protected java.util.Vector uis
```

### Methods
```
public boolean contains(JComponent a,int
b,int c)
public static ComponentUI createUI(
JComponent a)
public Accessible getAccessibleChild(
JComponent a,int b)
public int getAccessibleChildrenCount(
JComponent a)
public Dimension getMaximumSize(
JComponent a)
public Dimension getMinimumSize(
JComponent a)
public Dimension getPreferredSize(
JComponent a)
public ComponentUI getUIs()
public void installUI(JComponent a)
public void paint(Graphics a,JComponent
b)
public void uninstallUI(JComponent a)
public void update(Graphics a,JComponent
b)
```

## MultiSliderUI

```
public class javax.swing.plaf.multi.
MultiSliderUI
extends javax.swing.plaf.SliderUI
extends javax.swing.plaf.ComponentUI
extends java.lang.Object
```

## Fields

```
protected java.util.Vector uis
```

## Methods

```
public boolean contains(JComponent a,int
b,int c)
public static ComponentUI createUI(
JComponent a)
public Accessible getAccessibleChild(
JComponent a,int b)
public int getAccessibleChildrenCount(
JComponent a)
public Dimension getMaximumSize(
JComponent a)
public Dimension getMinimumSize(
JComponent a)
public Dimension getPreferredSize(
JComponent a)
public ComponentUI getUIs()
public void installUI(JComponent a)
public void paint(Graphics a,JComponent
b)
public void uninstallUI(JComponent a)
public void update(Graphics a,JComponent
b)
```

# MultiSplitPaneUI

```
public class javax.swing.plaf.multi.
MultiSplitPaneUI
extends javax.swing.plaf.SplitPaneUI
extends javax.swing.plaf.ComponentUI
extends java.lang.Object
```

## Fields

```
protected java.util.Vector uis
```

## Methods

```
public boolean contains(JComponent a,int
b,int c)
public static ComponentUI createUI(
JComponent a)
public void finishedPaintingChildren(
JSplitPane a,Graphics b)
public Accessible getAccessibleChild(
JComponent a,int b)
public int getAccessibleChildrenCount(
JComponent a)
public int getDividerLocation(JSplitPane
a)
public int getMaximumDividerLocation(
JSplitPane a)
public Dimension getMaximumSize(
JComponent a)
public int getMinimumDividerLocation(
JSplitPane a)
public Dimension getMinimumSize(
JComponent a)
public Dimension getPreferredSize(
JComponent a)
public ComponentUI getUIs()
public void installUI(JComponent a)
public void paint(Graphics a,JComponent
b)
```

```
public void resetToPreferredSizes(
JSplitPane a)
public void setDividerLocation(
JSplitPane a,int b)
public void uninstallUI(JComponent a)
public void update(Graphics a,JComponent
b)
```

# MultiTabbedPaneUI

```
public class javax.swing.plaf.multi.
MultiTabbedPaneUI
extends javax.swing.plaf.TabbedPaneUI
extends javax.swing.plaf.ComponentUI
extends java.lang.Object
```

## Fields

```
protected java.util.Vector uis
```

## Methods

```
public boolean contains(JComponent a,int
b,int c)
public static ComponentUI createUI(
JComponent a)
public Accessible getAccessibleChild(
JComponent a,int b)
public int getAccessibleChildrenCount(
JComponent a)
public Dimension getMaximumSize(
JComponent a)
public Dimension getMinimumSize(
JComponent a)
public Dimension getPreferredSize(
JComponent a)
public Rectangle getTabBounds(
JTabbedPane a,int b)
public int getTabRunCount(JTabbedPane a)
public ComponentUI getUIs()
public void installUI(JComponent a)
public void paint(Graphics a,JComponent
b)
public int tabForCoordinate(JTabbedPane
a,int b,int c)
public void uninstallUI(JComponent a)
public void update(Graphics a,JComponent
b)
```

# MultiTableHeaderUI

```
public class javax.swing.plaf.multi.
MultiTableHeaderUI
extends javax.swing.plaf.TableHeaderUI
extends javax.swing.plaf.ComponentUI
extends java.lang.Object
```

## Fields

```
protected java.util.Vector uis
```

## Methods

```
public boolean contains(JComponent a,int
b,int c)
public static ComponentUI createUI(
JComponent a)
public Accessible getAccessibleChild(
JComponent a,int b)
```

```
public int getAccessibleChildrenCount(
JComponent a)
public Dimension getMaximumSize(
JComponent a)
public Dimension getMinimumSize(
JComponent a)
public Dimension getPreferredSize(
JComponent a)
public ComponentUI getUIs()
public void installUI(JComponent a)
public void paint(Graphics a,JComponent
a)
public void uninstallUI(JComponent a)
public void update(Graphics a,JComponent
b)
```

# MultiTableUI

```
public class javax.swing.plaf.multi.
MultiTableUI
extends javax.swing.plaf.TableUI
extends javax.swing.plaf.ComponentUI
extends java.lang.Object
```

### Fields

```
protected java.util.Vector uis
```

### Methods

```
public boolean contains(JComponent a,int
b,int c)
public static ComponentUI createUI(
JComponent a)
public Accessible getAccessibleChild(
JComponent a,int b)
public int getAccessibleChildrenCount(
JComponent a)
public Dimension getMaximumSize(
JComponent a)
public Dimension getMinimumSize(
JComponent a)
public Dimension getPreferredSize(
JComponent a)
public ComponentUI getUIs()
public void installUI(JComponent a)
public void paint(Graphics a,JComponent
b)
public void uninstallUI(JComponent a)
public void update(Graphics a,JComponent
b)
```

# MultiTextUI

```
public class javax.swing.plaf.multi.
MultiTextUI
extends javax.swing.plaf.TextUI
extends javax.swing.plaf.ComponentUI
extends java.lang.Object
```

### Fields

```
protected java.util.Vector uis
```

### Methods

```
public boolean contains(JComponent a,int
b,int c)
```

```
public static ComponentUI createUI(
JComponent a)
public void damageRange(JTextComponent a,
int b,int c)
public void damageRange(JTextComponent t,
int p0,int p1,Bias firstBias,Bias
secondBias)
public Accessible getAccessibleChild(
JComponent a,int b)
public int getAccessibleChildrenCount(
JComponent a)
public EditorKit getEditorKit(
JTextComponent a)
public Dimension getMaximumSize(
JComponent a)
public Dimension getMinimumSize(
JComponent a)
public int getNextVisualPositionFrom(
JTextComponent t,int pos,Bias b,int
direction,Bias biasRet)
public Dimension getPreferredSize(
JComponent a)
public View getRootView(JTextComponent a)
public ComponentUI getUIs()
public void installUI(JComponent a)
public Rectangle modelToView(
JTextComponent a,int b)
public Rectangle modelToView(
JTextComponent t,int pos,Bias bias)
public void paint(Graphics a,JComponent
b)
public void uninstallUI(JComponent a)
public void update(Graphics a,JComponent
b)
public int viewToModel(JTextComponent a,
Point b)
public int viewToModel(JTextComponent t,
Point pt,Bias biasReturn)
```

# MultiToolBarUI

```
public class javax.swing.plaf.multi.
MultiToolBarUI
extends javax.swing.plaf.ToolBarUI
extends javax.swing.plaf.ComponentUI
extends java.lang.Object
```

### Fields

```
protected java.util.Vector uis
```

### Methods

```
public boolean contains(JComponent a,int
b,int c)
public static ComponentUI createUI(
JComponent a)
public Accessible getAccessibleChild(
JComponent a,int b)
public int getAccessibleChildrenCount(
JComponent a)
public Dimension getMaximumSize(
JComponent a)
public Dimension getMinimumSize(
JComponent a)
```

```
public Dimension getPreferredSize(
JComponent a)
public ComponentUI getUIs()
public void installUI(JComponent a)
public void paint(Graphics a,JComponent
b)
public void uninstallUI(JComponent a)
public void update(Graphics a,JComponent
b)
```

## MultiToolTipUI

```
public class javax.swing.plaf.multi.
MultiToolTipUI
extends javax.swing.plaf.ToolTipUI
extends javax.swing.plaf.ComponentUI
extends java.lang.Object
```

### Fields
```
protected java.util.Vector uis
```

### Methods
```
public boolean contains(JComponent a,int
b,int c)
public static ComponentUI createUI(
JComponent a)
public Accessible getAccessibleChild(
JComponent a,int b)
public int getAccessibleChildrenCount(
JComponent a)
public Dimension getMaximumSize(
JComponent a)
public Dimension getMinimumSize(
JComponent a)
public Dimension getPreferredSize(
JComponent a)
public ComponentUI getUIs()
public void installUI(JComponent a)
public void paint(Graphics a,JComponent
b)
public void uninstallUI(JComponent a)
public void update(Graphics a,JComponent
b)
```

## MultiTreeUI

```
public class javax.swing.plaf.multi.
MultiTreeUI
extends javax.swing.plaf.TreeUI
extends javax.swing.plaf.ComponentUI
extends java.lang.Object
```

### Fields
```
protected java.util.Vector uis
```

### Methods
```
public void cancelEditing(JTree a)
public boolean contains(JComponent a,int
b,int c)
public static ComponentUI createUI(
JComponent a)
public Accessible getAccessibleChild(
JComponent a,int b)
public int getAccessibleChildrenCount(
JComponent a)
```

```
public TreePath
getClosestPathForLocation(JTree a,int b,
int c)
public TreePath getEditingPath(JTree a)
public Dimension getMaximumSize(
JComponent a)
public Dimension getMinimumSize(
JComponent a)
public Rectangle getPathBounds(JTree a,
TreePath b)
public TreePath getPathForRow(JTree a,
int b)
public Dimension getPreferredSize(
JComponent a)
public int getRowCount(JTree a)
public int getRowForPath(JTree a,
TreePath b)
public ComponentUI getUIs()
public void installUI(JComponent a)
public boolean isEditing(JTree a)
public void paint(Graphics a,JComponent
b)
public void startEditingAtPath(JTree a,
TreePath b)
public boolean stopEditing(JTree a)
public void uninstallUI(JComponent a)
public void update(Graphics a,JComponent
b)
```

## MultiViewportUI

```
public class javax.swing.plaf.multi.
MultiViewportUI
extends javax.swing.plaf.ViewportUI
extends javax.swing.plaf.ComponentUI
extends java.lang.Object
```

### Fields
```
protected java.util.Vector uis
```

### Methods
```
public boolean contains(JComponent a,int
b,int c)
public static ComponentUI createUI(
JComponent a)
public Accessible getAccessibleChild(
JComponent a,int b)
public int getAccessibleChildrenCount(
JComponent a)
public Dimension getMaximumSize(
JComponent a)
public Dimension getMinimumSize(
JComponent a)
public Dimension getPreferredSize(
JComponent a)
public ComponentUI getUIs()
public void installUI(JComponent a)
public void paint(Graphics a,JComponent
b)
public void uninstallUI(JComponent a)
public void update(Graphics a,JComponent
b)
```

## Naming
```
public final class java.rmi.Naming
extends java.lang.Object
```

### Constructors
```
private  Naming()
```

### Methods
```
public static void bind(String name,
Remote obj)
public static String list(String name)
public static Remote lookup(String name)
public static void rebind(String name,
Remote obj)
public static void unbind(String name)
```

## NegativeArraySizeException
```
public class java.lang.
NegativeArraySizeException
extends java.lang.RuntimeException
extends java.lang.Exception
extends java.lang.Throwable
extends java.lang.Object
```

### Constructors
```
public  NegativeArraySizeException()
public  NegativeArraySizeException(
String s)
```

## NetPermission
```
public final class java.net.
NetPermission
extends java.security.BasicPermission
extends java.security.Permission
extends java.lang.Object
```

### Constructors
```
public  NetPermission(String name)
public  NetPermission(String name,String
actions)
```

## NoClassDefFoundError
```
public class java.lang.
NoClassDefFoundError
extends java.lang.LinkageError
extends java.lang.Error
extends java.lang.Throwable
extends java.lang.Object
```

### Constructors
```
public  NoClassDefFoundError()
public  NoClassDefFoundError(String s)
```

## NoninvertibleTransformException
```
public class java.awt.geom.
NoninvertibleTransformException
extends java.lang.Exception
extends java.lang.Throwable
extends java.lang.Object
```

### Constructors
```
public  NoninvertibleTransformException(
String s)
```

## NoRouteToHostException
```
public class java.net.
NoRouteToHostException
extends java.net.SocketException
extends java.io.IOException
extends java.lang.Exception
extends java.lang.Throwable
extends java.lang.Object
```

### Constructors
```
public  NoRouteToHostException(String
msg)
public  NoRouteToHostException()
```

## NoSuchAlgorithmException
```
public class java.security.
NoSuchAlgorithmException
extends java.security.
GeneralSecurityException
extends java.lang.Exception
extends java.lang.Throwable
extends java.lang.Object
```

### Constructors
```
public  NoSuchAlgorithmException()
public  NoSuchAlgorithmException(String
msg)
```

## NoSuchElementException
```
public class java.util.
NoSuchElementException
extends java.lang.RuntimeException
extends java.lang.Exception
extends java.lang.Throwable
extends java.lang.Object
```

### Constructors
```
public  NoSuchElementException()
public  NoSuchElementException(String s)
```

## NoSuchFieldError
```
public class java.lang.NoSuchFieldError
extends java.lang.
IncompatibleClassChangeError
extends java.lang.LinkageError
extends java.lang.Error
extends java.lang.Throwable
extends java.lang.Object
```

### Constructors
```
public  NoSuchFieldError()
public  NoSuchFieldError(String s)
```

## NoSuchFieldException
```
public class java.lang.
NoSuchFieldException
extends java.lang.Exception
```

extends java.lang.Throwable
extends java.lang.Object

**Constructors**
public  NoSuchFieldException()
public  NoSuchFieldException(String s)

## NoSuchMethodError
public class java.lang.
NoSuchMethodError
extends java.lang.
IncompatibleClassChangeError
extends java.lang.LinkageError
extends java.lang.Error
extends java.lang.Throwable
extends java.lang.Object

**Constructors**
public  NoSuchMethodError()
public  NoSuchMethodError(String s)

## NoSuchMethodException
public class java.lang.
NoSuchMethodException
extends java.lang.Exception
extends java.lang.Throwable
extends java.lang.Object

**Constructors**
public  NoSuchMethodException()
public  NoSuchMethodException(String s)

## NoSuchObjectException
public class java.rmi.
NoSuchObjectException
extends java.rmi.RemoteException
extends java.io.IOException
extends java.lang.Exception
extends java.lang.Throwable
extends java.lang.Object

**Constructors**
public  NoSuchObjectException(String s)

## NoSuchProviderException
public class java.security.
NoSuchProviderException
extends java.security.
GeneralSecurityException
extends java.lang.Exception
extends java.lang.Throwable
extends java.lang.Object

**Constructors**
public  NoSuchProviderException()
public  NoSuchProviderException(String
msg)

## NotActiveException
public class java.io.NotActiveException
extends java.io.ObjectStreamException
extends java.io.IOException

extends java.lang.Exception
extends java.lang.Throwable
extends java.lang.Object

**Constructors**
public  NotActiveException(String reason)
public  NotActiveException()

## NotBoundException
public class java.rmi.NotBoundException
extends java.lang.Exception
extends java.lang.Throwable
extends java.lang.Object

**Constructors**
public  NotBoundException()
public  NotBoundException(String s)

## NotOwnerException
public class java.security.acl.
NotOwnerException
extends java.lang.Exception
extends java.lang.Throwable
extends java.lang.Object

**Constructors**
public  NotOwnerException()

## NotSerializableException
public class java.io.
NotSerializableException
extends java.io.ObjectStreamException
extends java.io.IOException
extends java.lang.Exception
extends java.lang.Throwable
extends java.lang.Object

**Constructors**
public  NotSerializableException(String
classname)
public  NotSerializableException()

## NullPointerException
public class java.lang.
NullPointerException
extends java.lang.RuntimeException
extends java.lang.Exception
extends java.lang.Throwable
extends java.lang.Object

**Constructors**
public  NullPointerException()
public  NullPointerException(String s)

## Number
public abstract class java.lang.Number
implements java.io.Serializable
extends java.lang.Object

**Methods**
public byte byteValue()
public abstract double doubleValue()

```
public abstract float floatValue()
public abstract int intValue()
public abstract long longValue()
public short shortValue()
```

# NumberFormat

```
public abstract class java.text.
NumberFormat
extends java.text.Format
extends java.lang.Object
```

### Fields

```
public final static int FRACTION_FIELD
public final static int INTEGER_FIELD
```

### Methods

```
public Object clone()
public boolean equals(Object obj)
public final StringBuffer format(Object
number,StringBuffer toAppendTo,
FieldPosition pos)
public final String format(double number)
public final String format(long number)
public abstract StringBuffer format(
double number,StringBuffer toAppendTo,
FieldPosition pos)
public abstract StringBuffer format(long
number,StringBuffer toAppendTo,
FieldPosition pos)
public static Locale getAvailableLocales(
)
public final static NumberFormat
getCurrencyInstance()
public static NumberFormat
getCurrencyInstance(Locale inLocale)
public final static NumberFormat
getInstance()
public static NumberFormat getInstance(
Locale inLocale)
public int getMaximumFractionDigits()
public int getMaximumIntegerDigits()
public int getMinimumFractionDigits()
public int getMinimumIntegerDigits()
public final static NumberFormat
getNumberInstance()
public static NumberFormat
getNumberInstance(Locale inLocale)
public final static NumberFormat
getPercentInstance()
public static NumberFormat
getPercentInstance(Locale inLocale)
public int hashCode()
public boolean isGroupingUsed()
public boolean isParseIntegerOnly()
public abstract Number parse(String text,
ParsePosition parsePosition)
public Number parse(String text)
public final Object parseObject(String
source,ParsePosition parsePosition)
public void setGroupingUsed(boolean
newValue)
public void setMaximumFractionDigits(int
newValue)
```

```
public void setMaximumIntegerDigits(int
newValue)
public void setMinimumFractionDigits(int
newValue)
public void setMinimumIntegerDigits(int
newValue)
public void setParseIntegerOnly(boolean
value)
```

# NumberFormatException

```
public class java.lang.
NumberFormatException
extends java.lang.
IllegalArgumentException
extends java.lang.RuntimeException
extends java.lang.Exception
extends java.lang.Throwable
extends java.lang.Object
```

### Constructors

```
public  NumberFormatException()
public  NumberFormatException(String s)
```

# Object

```
public class java.lang.Object
extends java.lang.Object
```

### Methods

```
protected native Object clone()
public boolean equals(Object obj)
protected void finalize()
public final static native Class
getClass()
public native int hashCode()
public final native void notify()
public final native void notifyAll()
public String toString()
public final native void wait(long
timeout)
public final void wait(long timeout,int
nanos)
public final void wait()
```

# ObjectInputStream

```
public class java.io.ObjectInputStream
implements java.io.ObjectInput
implements java.io.
ObjectStreamConstants
extends java.io.InputStream
extends java.lang.Object
```

### Constructors

```
public  ObjectInputStream(InputStream in)
protected  ObjectInputStream()
```

### Methods

```
public int available()
public void close()
public void defaultReadObject()
protected boolean enableResolveObject(
boolean enable)
public int read()
```

```
public int read(byte b,int off,int len)
public boolean readBoolean()
public byte readByte()
public char readChar()
public double readDouble()
public GetField readFields()
public float readFloat()
public void readFully(byte data)
public void readFully(byte data,int
offset,int size)
public int readInt()
public String readLine()
public long readLong()
public final Object readObject()
protected Object readObjectOverride()
public short readShort()
protected void readStreamHeader()
public int readUnsignedByte()
public int readUnsignedShort()
public String readUTF()
public synchronized void
registerValidation(ObjectInputValidation
obj,int prio)
protected Class resolveClass(
ObjectStreamClass v)
protected Object resolveObject(Object
obj)
public int skipBytes(int len)
```

## ObjectOutputStream

```
public class java.io.ObjectOutputStream
implements java.io.ObjectOutput
implements java.io.
ObjectStreamConstants
extends java.io.OutputStream
extends java.lang.Object
```

### Constructors
```
public  ObjectOutputStream(OutputStream
out)
protected  ObjectOutputStream()
```

### Methods
```
protected void annotateClass(Class cl)
public void close()
public void defaultWriteObject()
protected void drain()
protected boolean enableReplaceObject(
boolean enable)
public void flush()
public PutField putFields()
protected Object replaceObject(Object
obj)
public void reset()
public void useProtocolVersion(int
version)
public void write(int data)
public void write(byte b)
public void write(byte b,int off,int len)
public void writeBoolean(boolean data)
public void writeByte(int data)
public void writeBytes(String data)
public void writeChar(int data)
```

```
public void writeChars(String data)
public void writeDouble(double data)
public void writeFields()
public void writeFloat(float data)
public void writeInt(int data)
public void writeLong(long data)
public final void writeObject(Object obj)
protected void writeObjectOverride(
Object obj)
public void writeShort(int data)
protected void writeStreamHeader()
public void writeUTF(String data)
```

## ObjectStreamClass

```
public class java.io.ObjectStreamClass
implements java.io.Serializable
extends java.lang.Object
```

### Fields
```
public final static java.io.
ObjectStreamField NO_FIELDS
```

### Constructors
```
private  ObjectStreamClass()
 ObjectStreamClass()
```

### Methods
```
public Class forClass()
public ObjectStreamField getField(String
name)
public ObjectStreamField getFields()
public String getName()
public long getSerialVersionUID()
public static ObjectStreamClass lookup(
Class cl)
public String toString()
```

## ObjectStreamException

```
public abstract class java.io.
ObjectStreamException
extends java.io.IOException
extends java.lang.Exception
extends java.lang.Throwable
extends java.lang.Object
```

### Constructors
```
protected  ObjectStreamException(String
classname)
protected  ObjectStreamException()
```

## ObjectStreamField

```
public class java.io.ObjectStreamField
implements java.lang.Comparable
extends java.lang.Object
```

### Constructors
```
public  ObjectStreamField(String n,Class
clazz)
 ObjectStreamField()
 ObjectStreamField()
private  ObjectStreamField()
 ObjectStreamField()
```

### Methods
```
public int compareTo(Object o)
public String getName()
public int getOffset()
public Class getType()
public char getTypeCode()
public String getTypeString()
public boolean isPrimitive()
protected void setOffset(int offset)
public String toString()
```

## ObjectView
```
public class javax.swing.text.html.
ObjectView
extends javax.swing.text.ComponentView
extends javax.swing.text.View
extends java.lang.Object
```

### Constructors
```
public  ObjectView(Element elem)
```

### Methods
```
protected Component createComponent()
```

## ObjID
```
public final class java.rmi.server.
ObjID
implements java.io.Serializable
extends java.lang.Object
```

### Fields
```
public final static int ACTIVATOR_ID
public final static int DGC_ID
public final static int REGISTRY_ID
```

### Constructors
```
public  ObjID()
public  ObjID(int num)
private  ObjID()
```

### Methods
```
public boolean equals(Object obj)
public int hashCode()
public static ObjID read(ObjectInput in)
public String toString()
public void write(ObjectOutput out)
```

## Observable
```
public class java.util.Observable
extends java.lang.Object
```

### Constructors
```
public  Observable()
```

### Methods
```
public synchronized void addObserver(
Observer o)
protected synchronized void clearChanged(
)
public synchronized int countObservers()
```

```
public synchronized void deleteObserver(
Observer o)
public synchronized void deleteObservers(
)
public synchronized boolean hasChanged()
public void notifyObservers()
public void notifyObservers(Object arg)
protected synchronized void setChanged()
```

## Operation
```
public class java.rmi.server.Operation
extends java.lang.Object
```

### Constructors
```
public  Operation(String op)
```

### Methods
```
public String getOperation()
public String toString()
```

## Option
```
public class javax.swing.text.html.
Option
extends java.lang.Object
```

### Constructors
```
public  Option(AttributeSet attr)
```

### Methods
```
public AttributeSet getAttributes()
public String getLabel()
public String getValue()
public boolean isSelected()
public void setLabel(String label)
protected void setSelection(boolean
state)
public String toString()
```

## OptionalDataException
```
public class java.io.
OptionalDataException
extends java.io.ObjectStreamException
extends java.io.IOException
extends java.lang.Exception
extends java.lang.Throwable
extends java.lang.Object
```

### Fields
```
public boolean eof
public int length
```

### Constructors
```
 OptionalDataException()
 OptionalDataException()
```

## OptionPaneUI
```
public abstract class javax.swing.plaf.
OptionPaneUI
extends javax.swing.plaf.ComponentUI
extends java.lang.Object
```

### Methods

public abstract boolean
containsCustomComponents(JOptionPane op)
public abstract void selectInitialValue(
JOptionPane op)

## OutOfMemoryError

public class java.lang.OutOfMemoryError
extends java.lang.VirtualMachineError
extends java.lang.Error
extends java.lang.Throwable
extends java.lang.Object

### Constructors

public  OutOfMemoryError()
public  OutOfMemoryError(String s)

## OutputStream

public abstract class java.io.
OutputStream
extends java.lang.Object

### Methods

public void close()
public void flush()
public abstract void write(int b)
public void write(byte b)
public void write(byte b,int off,int len)

## OutputStreamWriter

public class java.io.OutputStreamWriter
extends java.io.Writer
extends java.lang.Object

### Constructors

public  OutputStreamWriter(OutputStream
out,String enc)
public  OutputStreamWriter(OutputStream
out)
private  OutputStreamWriter()

### Methods

public void close()
public void flush()
public String getEncoding()
public void write(int c)
public void write(char cbuf,int off,int
len)
public void write(String str,int off,int
len)

## OverlayLayout

public class javax.swing.OverlayLayout
implements java.awt.LayoutManager2
implements java.io.Serializable
extends java.lang.Object

### Constructors

public  OverlayLayout(Container target)

### Methods

public void addLayoutComponent(String
name,Component comp)

public void addLayoutComponent(Component
comp,Object constraints)
public float getLayoutAlignmentX(
Container target)
public float getLayoutAlignmentY(
Container target)
public void invalidateLayout(Container
target)
public void layoutContainer(Container
target)
public Dimension maximumLayoutSize(
Container target)
public Dimension minimumLayoutSize(
Container target)
public Dimension preferredLayoutSize(
Container target)
public void removeLayoutComponent(
Component comp)

## Package

public class java.lang.Package
extends java.lang.Object

### Constructors

 Package()
private  Package()

### Methods

public String getImplementationTitle()
public String getImplementationVendor()
public String getImplementationVersion()
public String getName()
public static Package getPackage(String
name)
public static Package getPackages()
public String getSpecificationTitle()
public String getSpecificationVendor()
public String getSpecificationVersion()
public int hashCode()
public boolean isCompatibleWith(String
desired)
public boolean isSealed()
public boolean isSealed(URL url)
public String toString()

## PackedColorModel

public abstract class java.awt.image.
PackedColorModel
extends java.awt.image.ColorModel
extends java.lang.Object

### Constructors

public  PackedColorModel(ColorSpace
space,int bits,int colorMaskArray,int
alphaMask,boolean isAlphaPremultiplied,
int trans,int transferType)
public  PackedColorModel(ColorSpace
space,int bits,int rmask,int gmask,int
bmask,int amask,boolean
isAlphaPremultiplied,int trans,int
transferType)

## Methods
public SampleModel
createCompatibleSampleModel(int w,int h)
public boolean equals(Object obj)
public WritableRaster getAlphaRaster(
WritableRaster raster)
public final int getMask(int index)
public final int getMasks()
public boolean isCompatibleSampleModel(
SampleModel sm)

# PageFormat
public class java.awt.print.PageFormat
implements java.lang.Cloneable
extends java.lang.Object

## Fields
public final static int LANDSCAPE
public final static int PORTRAIT
public final static int REVERSE_
LANDSCAPE

## Constructors
public  PageFormat()

## Methods
public Object clone()
public double getHeight()
public double getImageableHeight()
public double getImageableWidth()
public double getImageableX()
public double getImageableY()
public double getMatrix()
public int getOrientation()
public Paper getPaper()
public double getWidth()
public void setOrientation(int
orientation)
public void setPaper(Paper paper)

# PaintEvent
public class java.awt.event.PaintEvent
extends java.awt.event.ComponentEvent
extends java.awt.AWTEvent
extends java.util.EventObject
extends java.lang.Object

## Fields
public final static int PAINT
public final static int PAINT_FIRST
public final static int PAINT_LAST
public final static int UPDATE

## Constructors
public  PaintEvent(Component source,int
id,Rectangle updateRect)

## Methods
public Rectangle getUpdateRect()
public String paramString()
public void setUpdateRect(Rectangle
updateRect)

# Panel
public class java.awt.Panel
extends java.awt.Container
extends java.awt.Component
extends java.lang.Object

## Constructors
public  Panel()
public  Panel(LayoutManager layout)

## Methods
public void addNotify()

# PanelUI
public abstract class javax.swing.plaf.
PanelUI
extends javax.swing.plaf.ComponentUI
extends java.lang.Object

# Paper
public class java.awt.print.Paper
implements java.lang.Cloneable
extends java.lang.Object

## Constructors
public  Paper()

## Methods
public Object clone()
public double getHeight()
public double getImageableHeight()
public double getImageableWidth()
public double getImageableX()
public double getImageableY()
public double getWidth()
public void setImageableArea(double x,
double y,double width,double height)
public void setSize(double width,double
height)

# ParagraphView
public class javax.swing.text.html.
ParagraphView
extends javax.swing.text.ParagraphView
extends javax.swing.text.BoxView
extends javax.swing.text.CompositeView
extends javax.swing.text.View
extends java.lang.Object

## Constructors
public  ParagraphView(Element elem)

## Methods
protected SizeRequirements
calculateMinorAxisRequirements(int axis,
SizeRequirements r)
public void changedUpdate(DocumentEvent
e,Shape a,ViewFactory f)
public AttributeSet getAttributes()
public float getMaximumSpan(int axis)
public float getMinimumSpan(int axis)
public float getPreferredSpan(int axis)

protected StyleSheet getStyleSheet()
public boolean isVisible()
public void setParent(View parent)
protected void
setPropertiesFromAttributes()

## ParagraphView

public class javax.swing.text.
ParagraphView
implements javax.swing.text.TabExpander
extends javax.swing.text.BoxView
extends javax.swing.text.CompositeView
extends javax.swing.text.View
extends java.lang.Object

### Fields

protected int firstLineIndent

### Constructors

public  ParagraphView(Element elem)

### Methods

protected void adjustRow(Row r,int
desiredSpan,int x)
public View breakView(int axis,float len,
Shape a)
protected SizeRequirements
calculateMinorAxisRequirements(int axis,
SizeRequirements r)
public void changedUpdate(DocumentEvent
changes,Shape a,ViewFactory f)
protected int
findOffsetToCharactersInString(char
string,int start)
protected boolean flipEastAndWestAtEnds(
int position,Bias bias)
public float getAlignment(int axis)
public int getBreakWeight(int axis,float
len)
protected int getClosestPositionTo(int
pos,Bias b,Shape a,int direction,Bias
biasRet,int rowIndex,int x)
protected View getLayoutView(int index)
protected int getLayoutViewCount()
protected int
getNextNorthSouthVisualPositionFrom(int
pos,Bias b,Shape a,int direction,Bias
biasRet)
protected float getPartialSize(int
startOffset,int endOffset)
protected float getTabBase()
protected TabSet getTabSet()
protected View getViewAtPosition(int pos,
Rectangle a)
protected int getViewIndexAtPosition(int
pos)
public void insertUpdate(DocumentEvent
changes,Shape a,ViewFactory f)
protected void layout(int width,int
height)
protected void loadChildren(ViewFactory
f)

public float nextTabStop(float x,int
tabOffset)
public void paint(Graphics g,Shape a)
public void removeUpdate(DocumentEvent
changes,Shape a,ViewFactory f)
protected void setFirstLineIndent(float
fi)
protected void setJustification(int j)
protected void setLineSpacing(float ls)
protected void
setPropertiesFromAttributes()

## ParameterBlock

public class java.awt.image.renderable.
ParameterBlock
implements java.lang.Cloneable
implements java.io.Serializable
extends java.lang.Object

### Fields

protected java.util.Vector parameters
protected java.util.Vector sources

### Constructors

public  ParameterBlock()
public  ParameterBlock(Vector sources)
public  ParameterBlock(Vector sources,
Vector parameters)

### Methods

public ParameterBlock add(Object obj)
public ParameterBlock add(byte b)
public ParameterBlock add(char c)
public ParameterBlock add(short s)
public ParameterBlock add(int i)
public ParameterBlock add(long l)
public ParameterBlock add(float f)
public ParameterBlock add(double d)
public ParameterBlock addSource(Object
source)
public Object clone()
public byte getByteParameter(int index)
public char getCharParameter(int index)
public double getDoubleParameter(int
index)
public float getFloatParameter(int index)
public int getIntParameter(int index)
public long getLongParameter(int index)
public int getNumParameters()
public int getNumSources()
public Object getObjectParameter(int
index)
public Class getParamClasses()
public Vector getParameters()
public RenderableImage
getRenderableSource(int index)
public RenderedImage getRenderedSource(
int index)
public short getShortParameter(int index)
public Object getSource(int index)
public Vector getSources()
public void removeParameters()
public void removeSources()

```
public ParameterBlock set(Object obj,int
index)
public ParameterBlock set(byte b,int
index)
public ParameterBlock set(char c,int
index)
public ParameterBlock set(short s,int
index)
public ParameterBlock set(int i,int
index)
public ParameterBlock set(long l,int
index)
public ParameterBlock set(float f,int
index)
public ParameterBlock set(double d,int
index)
public void setParameters(Vector
parameters)
public ParameterBlock setSource(Object
source,int index)
public void setSources(Vector sources)
public Object shallowClone()
```

## ParameterDescriptor

```
public class java.beans.
ParameterDescriptor
extends java.beans.FeatureDescriptor
extends java.lang.Object
```

### Constructors

```
public  ParameterDescriptor()
 ParameterDescriptor()
```

## ParseException

```
public class java.text.ParseException
extends java.lang.Exception
extends java.lang.Throwable
extends java.lang.Object
```

### Constructors

```
public  ParseException(String s,int
errorOffset)
```

### Methods

```
public int getErrorOffset()
```

## ParsePosition

```
public class java.text.ParsePosition
extends java.lang.Object
```

### Constructors

```
public  ParsePosition(int index)
```

### Methods

```
public boolean equals(Object obj)
public int getErrorIndex()
public int getIndex()
public int hashCode()
public void setErrorIndex(int ei)
public void setIndex(int index)
public String toString()
```

## Parser

```
public class javax.swing.text.html.
parser.Parser
implements javax.swing.text.html.parser.
DTDConstants
extends java.lang.Object
```

### Fields

```
protected javax.swing.text.html.parser.
DTD dtd
protected boolean strict
```

### Constructors

```
public  Parser(DTD dtd)
```

### Methods

```
protected void endTag(boolean omitted)
protected void error(String err,String
arg1,String arg2,String arg3)
protected void error(String err,String
arg1,String arg2)
protected void error(String err,String
arg1)
protected void error(String err)
protected void flushAttributes()
protected SimpleAttributeSet
getAttributes()
protected int getCurrentLine()
protected int getCurrentPos()
protected void handleComment(char text)
protected void handleEmptyTag(TagElement
tag)
protected void handleEndTag(TagElement
tag)
protected void handleEOFInComment()
protected void handleError(int ln,String
msg)
protected void handleStartTag(TagElement
tag)
protected void handleText(char text)
protected void handleTitle(char text)
protected TagElement makeTag(Element
elem,boolean fictional)
protected TagElement makeTag(Element
elem)
protected void markFirstTime(Element
elem)
public synchronized void parse(Reader in)
public String parseDTDMarkup()
protected boolean
parseMarkupDeclarations(StringBuffer
strBuff)
protected void startTag(TagElement tag)
```

## ParserDelegator

```
public class javax.swing.text.html.
parser.ParserDelegator
extends java.lang.Object
```

### Constructors

```
public  ParserDelegator()
```

## Methods

```
protected static DTD createDTD(DTD dtd,
String name)
public void parse(Reader r,
ParserCallback cb,boolean ignoreCharSet)
protected static void setDefaultDTD()
```

# PasswordAuthentication

```
public final class java.net.
PasswordAuthentication
extends java.lang.Object
```

## Constructors

```
public  PasswordAuthentication(String
userName,char password)
```

## Methods

```
public char getPassword()
public String getUserName()
```

# PasswordView

```
public class javax.swing.text.
PasswordView
extends javax.swing.text.FieldView
extends javax.swing.text.PlainView
extends javax.swing.text.View
extends java.lang.Object
```

## Constructors

```
public  PasswordView(Element elem)
```

## Methods

```
protected int drawEchoCharacter(Graphics
g,int x,int y,char c)
protected int drawSelectedText(Graphics
g,int x,int y,int p0,int p1)
protected int drawUnselectedText(
Graphics g,int x,int y,int p0,int p1)
public Shape modelToView(int pos,Shape a,
Bias b)
public int viewToModel(float fx,float fy,
Shape a,Bias bias)
```

# Permission

```
public abstract class java.security.
Permission
implements java.security.Guard
implements java.io.Serializable
extends java.lang.Object
```

## Constructors

```
public  Permission(String name)
```

## Methods

```
public void checkGuard(Object object)
public abstract boolean equals(Object
obj)
public abstract String getActions()
public final String getName()
public abstract int hashCode()
public abstract boolean implies(
Permission permission)
```

```
public PermissionCollection
newPermissionCollection()
public String toString()
```

# PermissionCollection

```
public abstract class java.security.
PermissionCollection
implements java.io.Serializable
extends java.lang.Object
```

## Methods

```
public abstract void add(Permission
permission)
public abstract Enumeration elements()
public abstract boolean implies(
Permission permission)
public boolean isReadOnly()
public void setReadOnly()
public String toString()
```

# Permissions

```
public final class java.security.
Permissions
implements java.io.Serializable
extends java.security.
PermissionCollection
extends java.lang.Object
```

## Constructors

```
public  Permissions()
```

## Methods

```
public void add(Permission permission)
public Enumeration elements()
public boolean implies(Permission
permission)
```

# PhantomReference

```
public class java.lang.ref.
PhantomReference
extends java.lang.ref.Reference
extends java.lang.Object
```

## Constructors

```
public  PhantomReference(Object referent,
ReferenceQueue q)
```

## Methods

```
public Object get()
```

# PipedInputStream

```
public class java.io.PipedInputStream
extends java.io.InputStream
extends java.lang.Object
```

## Fields

```
protected byte buffer
protected int in
protected int out
protected final static int PIPE_SIZE
```

## Constructors
```
public  PipedInputStream(
PipedOutputStream src)
public  PipedInputStream()
```

## Methods
```
public synchronized int available()
public void close()
public void connect(PipedOutputStream
src)
public synchronized int read()
public synchronized int read(byte b,int
off,int len)
protected synchronized void receive(int
b)
```

# PipedOutputStream
```
public class java.io.PipedOutputStream
extends java.io.OutputStream
extends java.lang.Object
```

## Constructors
```
public  PipedOutputStream(
PipedInputStream snk)
public  PipedOutputStream()
```

## Methods
```
public void close()
public synchronized void connect(
PipedInputStream snk)
public synchronized void flush()
public void write(int b)
public void write(byte b,int off,int len)
```

# PipedReader
```
public class java.io.PipedReader
extends java.io.Reader
extends java.lang.Object
```

## Constructors
```
public  PipedReader(PipedWriter src)
public  PipedReader()
```

## Methods
```
public void close()
public void connect(PipedWriter src)
public synchronized int read()
public synchronized int read(char cbuf,
int off,int len)
public synchronized boolean ready()
```

# PipedWriter
```
public class java.io.PipedWriter
extends java.io.Writer
extends java.lang.Object
```

## Constructors
```
public  PipedWriter(PipedReader snk)
public  PipedWriter()
```

## Methods
```
public void close()
```

```
public synchronized void connect(
PipedReader snk)
public synchronized void flush()
public void write(int c)
public void write(char cbuf,int off,int
len)
```

# PixelGrabber
```
public class java.awt.image.
PixelGrabber
implements java.awt.image.ImageConsumer
extends java.lang.Object
```

## Constructors
```
public  PixelGrabber(Image img,int x,int
y,int w,int h,int pix,int off,int
scansize)
public  PixelGrabber(ImageProducer ip,
int x,int y,int w,int h,int pix,int off,
int scansize)
public  PixelGrabber(Image img,int x,int
y,int w,int h,boolean forceRGB)
```

## Methods
```
public synchronized void abortGrabbing()
public synchronized ColorModel
getColorModel()
public synchronized int getHeight()
public synchronized Object getPixels()
public synchronized int getStatus()
public synchronized int getWidth()
public boolean grabPixels()
public synchronized boolean grabPixels(
long ms)
public synchronized void imageComplete(
int status)
public void setColorModel(ColorModel
model)
public void setDimensions(int width,int
height)
public void setHints(int hints)
public void setPixels(int srcX,int srcY,
int srcW,int srcH,ColorModel model,byte
pixels,int srcOff,int srcScan)
public void setPixels(int srcX,int srcY,
int srcW,int srcH,ColorModel model,int
pixels,int srcOff,int srcScan)
public void setProperties(Hashtable
props)
public synchronized void startGrabbing()
public synchronized int status()
```

# PixelInterleavedSampleModel
```
public class java.awt.image.
PixelInterleavedSampleModel
extends java.awt.image.
ComponentSampleModel
extends java.awt.image.SampleModel
extends java.lang.Object
```

## Constructors
```
public  PixelInterleavedSampleModel(int
dataType,int w,int h,int pixelStride,int
scanlineStride,int bandOffsets)
```

### Methods
public SampleModel
createCompatibleSampleModel(int w,int h)
public SampleModel
createSubsetSampleModel(int bands)

## PKCS8EncodedKeySpec
public class java.security.spec.
PKCS8EncodedKeySpec
extends java.security.spec.
EncodedKeySpec
extends java.lang.Object

### Constructors
public PKCS8EncodedKeySpec(byte
encodedKey)

### Methods
public byte getEncoded()
public final String getFormat()

## PlainDocument
public class javax.swing.text.
PlainDocument
extends javax.swing.text.
AbstractDocument
extends java.lang.Object

### Fields
public final static java.lang.String
lineLimitAttribute
public final static java.lang.String
tabSizeAttribute

### Constructors
public PlainDocument()
protected PlainDocument(Content c)

### Methods
protected AbstractElement
createDefaultRoot()
public Element getDefaultRootElement()
public Element getParagraphElement(int
pos)
protected void insertUpdate(
DefaultDocumentEvent chng,AttributeSet
attr)
protected void removeUpdate(
DefaultDocumentEvent chng)

## PlainView
public class javax.swing.text.PlainView
implements javax.swing.text.TabExpander
extends javax.swing.text.View
extends java.lang.Object

### Fields
protected java.awt.FontMetrics metrics

### Constructors
public PlainView(Element elem)

### Methods
public void changedUpdate(DocumentEvent
changes,Shape a,ViewFactory f)
protected void drawLine(int lineIndex,
Graphics g,int x,int y)
protected int drawSelectedText(Graphics
g,int x,int y,int p0,int p1)
protected int drawUnselectedText(
Graphics g,int x,int y,int p0,int p1)
protected final Segment getLineBuffer()
public float getPreferredSpan(int axis)
protected int getTabSize()
public void insertUpdate(DocumentEvent
changes,Shape a,ViewFactory f)
public Shape modelToView(int pos,Shape a,
Bias b)
public float nextTabStop(float x,int
tabOffset)
public void paint(Graphics g,Shape a)
public void preferenceChanged(View child,
boolean width,boolean height)
public void removeUpdate(DocumentEvent
changes,Shape a,ViewFactory f)
public int viewToModel(float fx,float fy,
Shape a,Bias bias)

## Point
public class java.awt.Point
implements java.io.Serializable
extends java.awt.geom.Point2D
extends java.lang.Object

### Fields
public int x
public int y

### Constructors
public Point()
public Point(Point p)
public Point(int x,int y)

### Methods
public boolean equals(Object obj)
public Point getLocation()
public double getX()
public double getY()
public void move(int x,int y)
public void setLocation(Point p)
public void setLocation(int x,int y)
public void setLocation(double x,double
y)
public String toString()
public void translate(int x,int y)

## Point2D
public abstract class java.awt.geom.
Point2D
implements java.lang.Cloneable
extends java.lang.Object

### Constructors
protected Point2D()

## Methods

```
public Object clone()
public static double distance(double X1,
double Y1,double X2,double Y2)
public double distance(double PX,double
PY)
public double distance(Point2D pt)
public static double distanceSq(double
X1,double Y1,double X2,double Y2)
public double distanceSq(double PX,
double PY)
public double distanceSq(Point2D pt)
public boolean equals(Object obj)
public abstract double getX()
public abstract double getY()
public int hashCode()
public abstract void setLocation(double
x,double y)
public void setLocation(Point2D p)
```

# Policy

```
public abstract class java.security.
Policy
extends java.lang.Object
```

### Methods

```
public abstract PermissionCollection
getPermissions(CodeSource codesource)
public static Policy getPolicy()
public abstract void refresh()
public static void setPolicy(Policy
policy)
```

# Polygon

```
public class java.awt.Polygon
implements java.io.Serializable
implements java.awt.Shape
extends java.lang.Object
```

### Fields

```
protected java.awt.Rectangle bounds
public int npoints
public int xpoints
public int ypoints
```

### Constructors

```
public  Polygon()
public  Polygon(int xpoints,int ypoints,
int npoints)
```

### Methods

```
public void addPoint(int x,int y)
public boolean contains(Point p)
public boolean contains(int x,int y)
public boolean contains(double x,double
y)
public boolean contains(Point2D p)
public boolean contains(double x,double
y,double w,double h)
public boolean contains(Rectangle2D r)
public Rectangle getBoundingBox()
public Rectangle getBounds()
public Rectangle2D getBounds2D()
```

```
public PathIterator getPathIterator(
AffineTransform at)
public PathIterator getPathIterator(
AffineTransform at,double flatness)
public boolean inside(int x,int y)
public boolean intersects(double x,
double y,double w,double h)
public boolean intersects(Rectangle2D r)
public void translate(int deltaX,int
deltaY)
```

# PopupMenu

```
public class java.awt.PopupMenu
extends java.awt.Menu
extends java.awt.MenuItem
extends java.awt.MenuComponent
extends java.lang.Object
```

### Constructors

```
public  PopupMenu()
public  PopupMenu(String label)
```

### Methods

```
public void addNotify()
public void show(Component origin,int x,
int y)
```

# PopupMenuEvent

```
public class javax.swing.event.
PopupMenuEvent
extends java.util.EventObject
extends java.lang.Object
```

### Constructors

```
public  PopupMenuEvent(Object source)
```

# PopupMenuUI

```
public abstract class javax.swing.plaf.
PopupMenuUI
extends javax.swing.plaf.ComponentUI
extends java.lang.Object
```

# PrinterAbortException

```
public class java.awt.print.
PrinterAbortException
extends java.awt.print.PrinterException
extends java.lang.Exception
extends java.lang.Throwable
extends java.lang.Object
```

### Constructors

```
public  PrinterAbortException()
public  PrinterAbortException(String msg)
```

# PrinterException

```
public class java.awt.print.
PrinterException
extends java.lang.Exception
extends java.lang.Throwable
extends java.lang.Object
```

### Constructors

```
public  PrinterException()
public  PrinterException(String msg)
```

## PrinterIOException

```
public class java.awt.print.
PrinterIOException
extends java.awt.print.PrinterException
extends java.lang.Exception
extends java.lang.Throwable
extends java.lang.Object
```

### Constructors

```
public  PrinterIOException(IOException
exception)
```

### Methods

```
public IOException getIOException()
```

## PrinterJob

```
public abstract class java.awt.print.
PrinterJob
extends java.lang.Object
```

### Constructors

```
public  PrinterJob()
```

### Methods

```
public abstract void cancel()
public abstract PageFormat defaultPage(
PageFormat page)
public PageFormat defaultPage()
public abstract int getCopies()
public abstract String getJobName()
public static PrinterJob getPrinterJob()
public abstract String getUserName()
public abstract boolean isCancelled()
public abstract PageFormat pageDialog(
PageFormat page)
public abstract void print()
public abstract boolean printDialog()
public abstract void setCopies(int
copies)
public abstract void setJobName(String
jobName)
public abstract void setPageable(
Pageable document)
public abstract void setPrintable(
Printable painter)
public abstract void setPrintable(
Printable painter,PageFormat format)
public abstract PageFormat validatePage(
PageFormat page)
```

## PrintJob

```
public abstract class java.awt.PrintJob
extends java.lang.Object
```

### Methods

```
public abstract void end()
public void finalize()
public abstract Graphics getGraphics()
```

```
public abstract Dimension
getPageDimension()
public abstract int getPageResolution()
public abstract boolean lastPageFirst()
```

## PrintStream

```
public class java.io.PrintStream
extends java.io.FilterOutputStream
extends java.io.OutputStream
extends java.lang.Object
```

### Constructors

```
public  PrintStream(OutputStream out)
public  PrintStream(OutputStream out,
boolean autoFlush)
```

### Methods

```
public boolean checkError()
public void close()
public void flush()
public void print(boolean b)
public void print(char c)
public void print(int i)
public void print(long l)
public void print(float f)
public void print(double d)
public void print(char s)
public void print(String s)
public void print(Object obj)
public void println()
public void println(boolean x)
public void println(char x)
public void println(int x)
public void println(long x)
public void println(float x)
public void println(double x)
public void println(char x)
public void println(String x)
public void println(Object x)
protected void setError()
public void write(int b)
public void write(byte buf,int off,int
len)
```

## PrintWriter

```
public class java.io.PrintWriter
extends java.io.Writer
extends java.lang.Object
```

### Fields

```
protected java.io.Writer out
```

### Constructors

```
public  PrintWriter(Writer out)
public  PrintWriter(Writer out,boolean
autoFlush)
public  PrintWriter(OutputStream out)
public  PrintWriter(OutputStream out,
boolean autoFlush)
```

### Methods

```
public boolean checkError()
public void close()
```

```
public void flush()
public void print(boolean b)
public void print(char c)
public void print(int i)
public void print(long l)
public void print(float f)
public void print(double d)
public void print(char s)
public void print(String s)
public void print(Object obj)
public void println()
public void println(boolean x)
public void println(char x)
public void println(int x)
public void println(long x)
public void println(float x)
public void println(double x)
public void println(char x)
public void println(String x)
public void println(Object x)
protected void setError()
public void write(int c)
public void write(char buf,int off,int
len)
public void write(char buf)
public void write(String s,int off,int
len)
public void write(String s)
```

## PrivilegedActionException

```
public class java.security.
PrivilegedActionException
extends java.lang.Exception
extends java.lang.Throwable
extends java.lang.Object
```

### Constructors

```
public  PrivilegedActionException(
Exception exception)
```

### Methods

```
public Exception getException()
public void printStackTrace()
public void printStackTrace(PrintStream
ps)
public void printStackTrace(PrintWriter
pw)
```

## Process

```
public abstract class java.lang.Process
extends java.lang.Object
```

### Methods

```
public abstract void destroy()
public abstract int exitValue()
public abstract InputStream
getErrorStream()
public abstract InputStream
getInputStream()
public abstract OutputStream
getOutputStream()
public abstract int waitFor()
```

## ProfileDataException

```
public class java.awt.color.
ProfileDataException
extends java.lang.RuntimeException
extends java.lang.Exception
extends java.lang.Throwable
extends java.lang.Object
```

### Constructors

```
public  ProfileDataException(String s)
```

## ProgressBarUI

```
public abstract class javax.swing.plaf.
ProgressBarUI
extends javax.swing.plaf.ComponentUI
extends java.lang.Object
```

## ProgressMonitor

```
public class javax.swing.
ProgressMonitor
extends java.lang.Object
```

### Constructors

```
public  ProgressMonitor(Component
parentComponent,Object message,String
note,int min,int max)
private  ProgressMonitor()
```

### Methods

```
public void close()
public int getMaximum()
public int getMillisToDecideToPopup()
public int getMillisToPopup()
public int getMinimum()
public String getNote()
public boolean isCanceled()
public void setMaximum(int m)
public void setMillisToDecideToPopup(int
millisToDecideToPopup)
public void setMillisToPopup(int
millisToPopup)
public void setMinimum(int m)
public void setNote(String note)
public void setProgress(int nv)
```

## ProgressMonitorInputStream

```
public class javax.swing.
ProgressMonitorInputStream
extends java.io.FilterInputStream
extends java.io.InputStream
extends java.lang.Object
```

### Constructors

```
public  ProgressMonitorInputStream(
Component parentComponent,Object message,
InputStream in)
```

### Methods

```
public void close()
public ProgressMonitor
getProgressMonitor()
public int read()
public int read(byte b)
```

```
public int read(byte b,int off,int len)
public synchronized void reset()
public long skip(long n)
```

# Properties

```
public class java.util.Properties
extends java.util.Hashtable
extends java.util.Dictionary
extends java.lang.Object
```

## Fields

```
protected java.util.Properties defaults
```

## Constructors

```
public  Properties()
public  Properties(Properties defaults)
```

## Methods

```
public String getProperty(String key)
public String getProperty(String key,
String defaultValue)
public void list(PrintStream out)
public void list(PrintWriter out)
public synchronized void load(
InputStream inStream)
public Enumeration propertyNames()
public synchronized void save(
OutputStream out,String header)
public synchronized Object setProperty(
String key,String value)
public synchronized void store(
OutputStream out,String header)
```

# PropertyChangeEvent

```
public class java.beans.
PropertyChangeEvent
extends java.util.EventObject
extends java.lang.Object
```

## Constructors

```
public  PropertyChangeEvent(Object
source,String propertyName,Object
oldValue,Object newValue)
```

## Methods

```
public Object getNewValue()
public Object getOldValue()
public Object getPropagationId()
public String getPropertyName()
public void setPropagationId(Object
propagationId)
```

# PropertyChangeSupport

```
public class java.beans.
PropertyChangeSupport
implements java.io.Serializable
extends java.lang.Object
```

## Constructors

```
public  PropertyChangeSupport(Object
sourceBean)
```

## Methods

```
public synchronized void
addPropertyChangeListener(
PropertyChangeListener listener)
public synchronized void
addPropertyChangeListener(String
propertyName,PropertyChangeListener
listener)
public void firePropertyChange(String
propertyName,Object oldValue,Object
newValue)
public void firePropertyChange(String
propertyName,int oldValue,int newValue)
public void firePropertyChange(String
propertyName,boolean oldValue,boolean
newValue)
public void firePropertyChange(
PropertyChangeEvent evt)
public synchronized boolean hasListeners(
String propertyName)
public synchronized void
removePropertyChangeListener(
PropertyChangeListener listener)
public synchronized void
removePropertyChangeListener(String
propertyName,PropertyChangeListener listener)
```

# PropertyDescriptor

```
public class java.beans.
PropertyDescriptor
extends java.beans.FeatureDescriptor
extends java.lang.Object
```

## Constructors

```
public  PropertyDescriptor(String
propertyName,Class beanClass)
public  PropertyDescriptor(String
propertyName,Class beanClass,String
getterName,String setterName)
public  PropertyDescriptor(String
propertyName,Method getter,Method setter)
 PropertyDescriptor()
 PropertyDescriptor()
```

## Methods

```
public Class getPropertyEditorClass()
public Class getPropertyType()
public Method getReadMethod()
public Method getWriteMethod()
public boolean isBound()
public boolean isConstrained()
public void setBound(boolean bound)
public void setConstrained(boolean
constrained)
public void setPropertyEditorClass(Class
propertyEditorClass)
public void setReadMethod(Method getter)
public void setWriteMethod(Method setter)
```

# PropertyEditorManager

```
public class java.beans.
PropertyEditorManager
extends java.lang.Object
```

### Methods

```
public static synchronized
PropertyEditor findEditor(Class
targetType)
public static synchronized String
getEditorSearchPath()
public static void registerEditor(Class
targetType,Class editorClass)
public static synchronized void
setEditorSearchPath(String path)
```

## PropertyEditorSupport

```
public class java.beans.
PropertyEditorSupport
implements java.beans.PropertyEditor
extends java.lang.Object
```

### Constructors

```
protected  PropertyEditorSupport()
protected  PropertyEditorSupport(Object
source)
```

### Methods

```
public synchronized void
addPropertyChangeListener(
PropertyChangeListener listener)
public void firePropertyChange()
public String getAsText()
public Component getCustomEditor()
public String
getJavaInitializationString()
public String getTags()
public Object getValue()
public boolean isPaintable()
public void paintValue(Graphics gfx,
Rectangle box)
public synchronized void
removePropertyChangeListener(
PropertyChangeListener listener)
public void setAsText(String text)
public void setValue(Object value)
public boolean supportsCustomEditor()
```

## PropertyPermission

```
public final class java.util.
PropertyPermission
extends java.security.BasicPermission
extends java.security.Permission
extends java.lang.Object
```

### Constructors

```
public  PropertyPermission(String name,
String actions)
```

### Methods

```
public boolean equals(Object obj)
public String getActions()
public int hashCode()
public boolean implies(Permission p)
public PermissionCollection
newPermissionCollection()
```

## PropertyResourceBundle

```
public class java.util.
PropertyResourceBundle
extends java.util.ResourceBundle
extends java.lang.Object
```

### Constructors

```
public  PropertyResourceBundle(
InputStream stream)
```

### Methods

```
public Enumeration getKeys()
public Object handleGetObject(String key)
```

## PropertyVetoException

```
public class java.beans.
PropertyVetoException
extends java.lang.Exception
extends java.lang.Throwable
extends java.lang.Object
```

### Constructors

```
public  PropertyVetoException(String
mess,PropertyChangeEvent evt)
```

### Methods

```
public PropertyChangeEvent
getPropertyChangeEvent()
```

## ProtectionDomain

```
public class java.security.
ProtectionDomain
extends java.lang.Object
```

### Constructors

```
public  ProtectionDomain(CodeSource
codesource,PermissionCollection
permissions)
```

### Methods

```
public final CodeSource getCodeSource()
public final PermissionCollection
getPermissions()
public boolean implies(Permission
permission)
public String toString()
```

## ProtocolException

```
public class java.net.ProtocolException
extends java.io.IOException
extends java.lang.Exception
extends java.lang.Throwable
extends java.lang.Object
```

### Constructors

```
public  ProtocolException(String host)
public  ProtocolException()
```

## Provider

```
public abstract class java.security.
Provider
extends java.util.Properties
```

```
extends java.util.Hashtable
extends java.util.Dictionary
extends java.lang.Object
```

**Constructors**
```
protected  Provider(String name,double
version,String info)
 Provider()
```

**Methods**
```
public synchronized void clear()
public Set entrySet()
public String getInfo()
public String getName()
public double getVersion()
public Set keySet()
public synchronized void load(
InputStream inStream)
public synchronized Object put(Object
key,Object value)
public synchronized void putAll(Map t)
public synchronized Object remove(Object
key)
public String toString()
public Collection values()
```

## ProviderException
```
public class java.security.
ProviderException
extends java.lang.RuntimeException
extends java.lang.Exception
extends java.lang.Throwable
extends java.lang.Object
```

**Constructors**
```
public  ProviderException()
public  ProviderException(String s)
```

## PushbackInputStream
```
public class java.io.
PushbackInputStream
extends java.io.FilterInputStream
extends java.io.InputStream
extends java.lang.Object
```

**Fields**
```
protected byte buf
protected int pos
```

**Constructors**
```
public  PushbackInputStream(InputStream
in,int size)
public  PushbackInputStream(InputStream
in)
```

**Methods**
```
public int available()
public synchronized void close()
public boolean markSupported()
public int read()
public int read(byte b,int off,int len)
public long skip(long n)
public void unread(int b)
```

```
public void unread(byte b,int off,int
len)
public void unread(byte b)
```

## PushbackReader
```
public class java.io.PushbackReader
extends java.io.FilterReader
extends java.io.Reader
extends java.lang.Object
```

**Constructors**
```
public  PushbackReader(Reader in,int
size)
public  PushbackReader(Reader in)
```

**Methods**
```
public void close()
public void mark(int readAheadLimit)
public boolean markSupported()
public int read()
public int read(char cbuf,int off,int
len)
public boolean ready()
public void reset()
public void unread(int c)
public void unread(char cbuf,int off,int
len)
public void unread(char cbuf)
```

## QuadCurve2D
```
public abstract class java.awt.geom.
QuadCurve2D
implements java.lang.Cloneable
implements java.awt.Shape
extends java.lang.Object
```

**Constructors**
```
protected  QuadCurve2D()
```

**Methods**
```
public Object clone()
public boolean contains(double x,double
y)
public boolean contains(Point2D p)
public boolean contains(double x,double
y,double w,double h)
public boolean contains(Rectangle2D r)
public Rectangle getBounds()
public abstract Point2D getCtrlPt()
public abstract double getCtrlX()
public abstract double getCtrlY()
public static double getFlatness(double
x1,double y1,double ctrlx,double ctrly,
double x2,double y2)
public static double getFlatness(double
coords,int offset)
public double getFlatness()
public static double getFlatnessSq(
double x1,double y1,double ctrlx,double
ctrly,double x2,double y2)
public static double getFlatnessSq(
double coords,int offset)
public double getFlatnessSq()
```

public abstract Point2D getP1()
public abstract Point2D getP2()
public PathIterator getPathIterator(
AffineTransform at)
public PathIterator getPathIterator(
AffineTransform at,double flatness)
public abstract double getX1()
public abstract double getX2()
public abstract double getY1()
public abstract double getY2()
public boolean intersects(double x,
double y,double w,double h)
public boolean intersects(Rectangle2D r)
public abstract void setCurve(double x1,
double y1,double ctrlx,double ctrly,
double x2,double y2)
public void setCurve(double coords,int
offset)
public void setCurve(Point2D p1,Point2D
cp,Point2D p2)
public void setCurve(Point2D pts,int
offset)
public void setCurve(QuadCurve2D c)
public static int solveQuadratic(double
eqn)
public void subdivide(QuadCurve2D left,
QuadCurve2D right)
public static void subdivide(QuadCurve2D
src,QuadCurve2D left,QuadCurve2D right)
public static void subdivide(double src,
int srcoff,double left,int leftoff,
double right,int rightoff)

# Random

public class java.util.Random
implements java.io.Serializable
extends java.lang.Object

## Constructors

public  Random()
public  Random(long seed)

## Methods

protected synchronized int next(int bits)
public boolean nextBoolean()
public void nextBytes(byte bytes)
public double nextDouble()
public float nextFloat()
public synchronized double nextGaussian()
public int nextInt()
public int nextInt(int n)
public long nextLong()
public synchronized void setSeed(long
seed)

# RandomAccessFile

public class java.io.RandomAccessFile
implements java.io.DataInput
implements java.io.DataOutput
extends java.lang.Object

## Constructors

public  RandomAccessFile(String name,
String mode)

public  RandomAccessFile(File file,
String mode)

## Methods

public native void close()
public final FileDescriptor getFD()
public native long getFilePointer()
public native long length()
public native int read()
public int read(byte b,int off,int len)
public int read(byte b)
public final boolean readBoolean()
public final byte readByte()
public final char readChar()
public final double readDouble()
public final float readFloat()
public final void readFully(byte b)
public final void readFully(byte b,int
off,int len)
public final int readInt()
public final String readLine()
public final long readLong()
public final short readShort()
public final int readUnsignedByte()
public final int readUnsignedShort()
public final String readUTF()
public native void seek(long pos)
public native void setLength(long
newLength)
public int skipBytes(int n)
public native void write(int b)
public void write(byte b)
public void write(byte b,int off,int len)
public final void writeBoolean(boolean v)
public final void writeByte(int v)
public final void writeBytes(String s)
public final void writeChar(int v)
public final void writeChars(String s)
public final void writeDouble(double v)
public final void writeFloat(float v)
public final void writeInt(int v)
public final void writeLong(long v)
public final void writeShort(int v)
public final void writeUTF(String str)

# Raster

public class java.awt.image.Raster
extends java.lang.Object

## Fields

protected java.awt.image.DataBuffer
dataBuffer
protected int height
protected int minX
protected int minY
protected int numBands
protected int numDataElements
protected java.awt.image.Raster parent
protected java.awt.image.SampleModel
sampleModel
protected int sampleModelTranslateX
protected int sampleModelTranslateY
protected int width

## Constructors

```
protected  Raster(SampleModel
sampleModel,Point origin)
protected  Raster(SampleModel
sampleModel,DataBuffer dataBuffer,Point
origin)
protected  Raster(SampleModel
sampleModel,DataBuffer dataBuffer,
Rectangle aRegion,Point
sampleModelTranslate,Raster parent)
```

## Methods

```
public static WritableRaster
createBandedRaster(int dataType,int w,
int h,int bands,Point location)
public static WritableRaster
createBandedRaster(int dataType,int w,
int h,int scanlineStride,int bankIndices,
int bandOffsets,Point location)
public static WritableRaster
createBandedRaster(DataBuffer dataBuffer,
int w,int h,int scanlineStride,int
bankIndices,int bandOffsets,Point
location)
public Raster createChild(int parentX,
int parentY,int width,int height,int
childMinX,int childMinY,int bandList)
public WritableRaster
createCompatibleWritableRaster()
public WritableRaster
createCompatibleWritableRaster(int w,int
h)
public WritableRaster
createCompatibleWritableRaster(Rectangle
rect)
public WritableRaster
createCompatibleWritableRaster(int x,int
y,int w,int h)
public static WritableRaster
createInterleavedRaster(int dataType,int
w,int h,int bands,Point location)
public static WritableRaster
createInterleavedRaster(int dataType,int
w,int h,int scanlineStride,int
pixelStride,int bandOffsets,Point
location)
public static WritableRaster
createInterleavedRaster(DataBuffer
dataBuffer,int w,int h,int
scanlineStride,int pixelStride,int
bandOffsets,Point location)
public static WritableRaster
createPackedRaster(int dataType,int w,
int h,int bandMasks,Point location)
public static WritableRaster
createPackedRaster(int dataType,int w,
int h,int bands,int bitsPerBand,Point
location)
public static WritableRaster
createPackedRaster(DataBuffer dataBuffer,
int w,int h,int scanlineStride,int
bandMasks,Point location)
public static WritableRaster
createPackedRaster(DataBuffer dataBuffer,
```

```
int w,int h,int bitsPerPixel,Point
location)
public static Raster createRaster(
SampleModel sm,DataBuffer db,Point
location)
public Raster createTranslatedChild(int
childMinX,int childMinY)
public static WritableRaster
createWritableRaster(SampleModel sm,
Point location)
public static WritableRaster
createWritableRaster(SampleModel sm,
DataBuffer db,Point location)
public Rectangle getBounds()
public DataBuffer getDataBuffer()
public Object getDataElements(int x,int
y,Object outData)
public Object getDataElements(int x,int
y,int w,int h,Object outData)
public final int getHeight()
public final int getMinX()
public final int getMinY()
public final int getNumBands()
public final int getNumDataElements()
public Raster getParent()
public int getPixel(int x,int y,int
iArray)
public float getPixel(int x,int y,float
fArray)
public double getPixel(int x,int y,
double dArray)
public int getPixels(int x,int y,int w,
int h,int iArray)
public float getPixels(int x,int y,int w,
int h,float fArray)
public double getPixels(int x,int y,int
w,int h,double dArray)
public int getSample(int x,int y,int b)
public double getSampleDouble(int x,int
y,int b)
public float getSampleFloat(int x,int y,
int b)
public SampleModel getSampleModel()
public final int
getSampleModelTranslateX()
public final int
getSampleModelTranslateY()
public int getSamples(int x,int y,int w,
int h,int b,int iArray)
public float getSamples(int x,int y,int
w,int h,int b,float fArray)
public double getSamples(int x,int y,int
w,int h,int b,double dArray)
public final int getTransferType()
public final int getWidth()
```

## RasterFormatException

```
public class java.awt.image.
RasterFormatException
extends java.lang.RuntimeException
extends java.lang.Exception
extends java.lang.Throwable
extends java.lang.Object
```

### Constructors
```
public  RasterFormatException(String s)
```

# Reader
```
public abstract class java.io.Reader
extends java.lang.Object
```

### Fields
```
protected java.lang.Object lock
```

### Constructors
```
protected  Reader()
protected  Reader(Object lock)
```

### Methods
```
public abstract void close()
public void mark(int readAheadLimit)
public boolean markSupported()
public int read()
public int read(char cbuf)
public abstract int read(char cbuf,int
off,int len)
public boolean ready()
public void reset()
public long skip(long n)
```

# Rectangle
```
public class java.awt.Rectangle
implements java.io.Serializable
implements java.awt.Shape
extends java.awt.geom.Rectangle2D
extends java.awt.geom.RectangularShape
extends java.lang.Object
```

### Fields
```
public int height
public int width
public int x
public int y
```

### Constructors
```
public static  Rectangle()
public  Rectangle(Rectangle r)
public  Rectangle(int x,int y,int width,
int height)
public  Rectangle(int width,int height)
public  Rectangle(Point p,Dimension d)
public  Rectangle(Point p)
public  Rectangle(Dimension d)
```

### Methods
```
public void add(int newx,int newy)
public void add(Point pt)
public void add(Rectangle r)
public boolean contains(Point p)
public boolean contains(int x,int y)
public boolean contains(Rectangle r)
public boolean contains(int X,int Y,int
W,int H)
public Rectangle2D createIntersection(
Rectangle2D r)
public Rectangle2D createUnion(
Rectangle2D r)
```

```
public boolean equals(Object obj)
public Rectangle getBounds()
public Rectangle2D getBounds2D()
public double getHeight()
public Point getLocation()
public Dimension getSize()
public double getWidth()
public double getX()
public double getY()
public void grow(int h,int v)
public boolean inside(int x,int y)
public Rectangle intersection(Rectangle
r)
public boolean intersects(Rectangle r)
public boolean isEmpty()
public void move(int x,int y)
public int outcode(double x,double y)
public void reshape(int x,int y,int
width,int height)
public void resize(int width,int height)
public void setBounds(Rectangle r)
public void setBounds(int x,int y,int
width,int height)
public void setLocation(Point p)
public void setLocation(int x,int y)
public void setRect(double x,double y,
double width,double height)
public void setSize(Dimension d)
public void setSize(int width,int height)
public String toString()
public void translate(int x,int y)
public Rectangle union(Rectangle r)
```

# Rectangle2D
```
public abstract class java.awt.geom.
Rectangle2D
extends java.awt.geom.RectangularShape
extends java.lang.Object
```

### Fields
```
public final static int OUT_BOTTOM
public final static int OUT_LEFT
public final static int OUT_RIGHT
public final static int OUT_TOP
```

### Constructors
```
protected  Rectangle2D()
```

### Methods
```
public void add(double newx,double newy)
public void add(Point2D pt)
public void add(Rectangle2D r)
public boolean contains(double x,double
y)
public boolean contains(double x,double
y,double w,double h)
public abstract Rectangle2D
createIntersection(Rectangle2D r)
public abstract Rectangle2D createUnion(
Rectangle2D r)
public boolean equals(Object obj)
public Rectangle2D getBounds2D()
```

```
public PathIterator getPathIterator(
AffineTransform at)
public PathIterator getPathIterator(
AffineTransform at,double flatness)
public int hashCode()
public static void intersect(Rectangle2D
src1,Rectangle2D src2,Rectangle2D dest)
public boolean intersects(double x,
double y,double w,double h)
public boolean intersectsLine(double x1,
double y1,double x2,double y2)
public boolean intersectsLine(Line2D l)
public abstract int outcode(double x,
double y)
public int outcode(Point2D p)
public void setFrame(double x,double y,
double w,double h)
public abstract void setRect(double x,
double y,double w,double h)
public void setRect(Rectangle2D r)
public static void union(Rectangle2D
src1,Rectangle2D src2,Rectangle2D dest)
```

## RectangularShape

```
public abstract class java.awt.geom.
RectangularShape
implements java.lang.Cloneable
implements java.awt.Shape
extends java.lang.Object
```

### Constructors
```
protected  RectangularShape()
```

### Methods
```
public Object clone()
public boolean contains(Point2D p)
public boolean contains(Rectangle2D r)
public Rectangle getBounds()
public double getCenterX()
public double getCenterY()
public Rectangle2D getFrame()
public abstract double getHeight()
public double getMaxX()
public double getMaxY()
public double getMinX()
public double getMinY()
public PathIterator getPathIterator(
AffineTransform at,double flatness)
public abstract double getWidth()
public abstract double getX()
public abstract double getY()
public boolean intersects(Rectangle2D r)
public abstract boolean isEmpty()
public abstract void setFrame(double x,
double y,double w,double h)
public void setFrame(Point2D loc,
Dimension2D size)
public void setFrame(Rectangle2D r)
public void setFrameFromCenter(double
centerX,double centerY,double cornerX,
double cornerY)
public void setFrameFromCenter(Point2D
center,Point2D corner)
```

```
public void setFrameFromDiagonal(double
x1,double y1,double x2,double y2)
public void setFrameFromDiagonal(Point2D
p1,Point2D p2)
```

## Reference

```
public abstract class java.lang.ref.
Reference
extends java.lang.Object
```

### Constructors
```
 Reference()
 Reference()
```

### Methods
```
public void clear()
public boolean enqueue()
public static Object get()
public boolean isEnqueued()
```

## ReferenceQueue

```
public class java.lang.ref.
ReferenceQueue
extends java.lang.Object
```

### Constructors
```
public  ReferenceQueue()
```

### Methods
```
public Reference poll()
public Reference remove(long timeout)
public Reference remove()
```

## ReflectPermission

```
public final class java.lang.reflect.
ReflectPermission
extends java.security.BasicPermission
extends java.security.Permission
extends java.lang.Object
```

### Constructors
```
public  ReflectPermission(String name)
public  ReflectPermission(String name,
String actions)
```

## RemoteException

```
public class java.rmi.RemoteException
extends java.io.IOException
extends java.lang.Exception
extends java.lang.Throwable
extends java.lang.Object
```

### Fields
```
public java.lang.Throwable detail
```

### Constructors
```
public  RemoteException()
public  RemoteException(String s)
public  RemoteException(String s,
Throwable ex)
```

## Methods
```
public String getMessage()
public void printStackTrace(PrintStream
ps)
public void printStackTrace()
public void printStackTrace(PrintWriter
pw)
```

# RemoteObject
```
public abstract class java.rmi.server.
RemoteObject
implements java.rmi.Remote
implements java.io.Serializable
extends java.lang.Object
```

### Fields
```
protected transient java.rmi.server.
RemoteRef ref
```

### Constructors
```
protected   RemoteObject()
protected   RemoteObject(RemoteRef newref)
```

### Methods
```
public boolean equals(Object obj)
public RemoteRef getRef()
public int hashCode()
public String toString()
public static Remote toStub(Remote obj)
```

# RemoteServer
```
public abstract class java.rmi.server.
RemoteServer
extends java.rmi.server.RemoteObject
extends java.lang.Object
```

### Constructors
```
protected   RemoteServer()
protected   RemoteServer(RemoteRef ref)
```

### Methods
```
public static String getClientHost()
public static PrintStream getLog()
public static void setLog(OutputStream
out)
```

# RemoteStub
```
public abstract class java.rmi.server.
RemoteStub
extends java.rmi.server.RemoteObject
extends java.lang.Object
```

### Constructors
```
protected   RemoteStub()
protected   RemoteStub(RemoteRef ref)
```

### Methods
```
protected static void setRef(RemoteStub
stub,RemoteRef ref)
```

# RenderableImageOp
```
public class java.awt.image.renderable.
RenderableImageOp
```
```
implements java.awt.image.renderable.
RenderableImage
extends java.lang.Object
```

### Constructors
```
public  RenderableImageOp(
ContextualRenderedImageFactory CRIF,
ParameterBlock paramBlock)
```

### Methods
```
public RenderedImage
createDefaultRendering()
public RenderedImage createRendering(
RenderContext renderContext)
public RenderedImage
createScaledRendering(int w,int h,
RenderingHints hints)
public float getHeight()
public float getMinX()
public float getMinY()
public ParameterBlock getParameterBlock()
public Object getProperty(String name)
public String getPropertyNames()
public Vector getSources()
public float getWidth()
public boolean isDynamic()
public ParameterBlock setParameterBlock(
ParameterBlock paramBlock)
```

# RenderableImageProducer
```
public class java.awt.image.renderable.
RenderableImageProducer
implements java.awt.image.ImageProducer
implements java.lang.Runnable
extends java.lang.Object
```

### Constructors
```
public  RenderableImageProducer(
RenderableImage rdblImage,RenderContext
rc)
```

### Methods
```
public synchronized void addConsumer(
ImageConsumer ic)
public synchronized boolean isConsumer(
ImageConsumer ic)
public synchronized void removeConsumer(
ImageConsumer ic)
public void
requestTopDownLeftRightResend(
ImageConsumer ic)
public void run()
public synchronized void
setRenderContext(RenderContext rc)
public synchronized void startProduction(
ImageConsumer ic)
```

# RenderContext
```
public class java.awt.image.renderable.
RenderContext
implements java.lang.Cloneable
extends java.lang.Object
```

### Constructors

```
public  RenderContext(AffineTransform
usr2dev,Shape aoi,RenderingHints hints)
public  RenderContext(AffineTransform
usr2dev)
public  RenderContext(AffineTransform
usr2dev,RenderingHints hints)
public  RenderContext(AffineTransform
usr2dev,Shape aoi)
```

### Methods

```
public Object clone()
public void concetenateTransform(
AffineTransform modTransform)
public Shape getAreaOfInterest()
public RenderingHints getRenderingHints()
public AffineTransform getTransform()
public void preConcetenateTransform(
AffineTransform modTransform)
public void setAreaOfInterest(Shape
newAoi)
public void setRenderingHints(
RenderingHints hints)
public void setTransform(AffineTransform
newTransform)
```

## RenderingHints

```
public class java.awt.RenderingHints
implements java.lang.Cloneable
implements java.util.Map
extends java.lang.Object
```

### Fields

```
public final static Key KEY_ALPHA_
INTERPOLATION
public final static Key KEY_
ANTIALIASING
public final static Key KEY_COLOR_
RENDERING
public final static Key KEY_DITHERING
public final static Key KEY_
FRACTIONALMETRICS
public final static Key KEY_
INTERPOLATION
public final static Key KEY_RENDERING
public final static Key KEY_TEXT_
ANTIALIASING
public final static java.lang.Object
VALUE_ALPHA_INTERPOLATION_DEFAULT
public final static java.lang.Object
VALUE_ALPHA_INTERPOLATION_QUALITY
public final static java.lang.Object
VALUE_ALPHA_INTERPOLATION_SPEED
public final static java.lang.Object
VALUE_ANTIALIAS_DEFAULT
public final static java.lang.Object
VALUE_ANTIALIAS_OFF
public final static java.lang.Object
VALUE_ANTIALIAS_ON
public final static java.lang.Object
VALUE_COLOR_RENDER_DEFAULT
public final static java.lang.Object
VALUE_COLOR_RENDER_QUALITY
```

```
public final static java.lang.Object
VALUE_COLOR_RENDER_SPEED
public final static java.lang.Object
VALUE_DITHER_DEFAULT
public final static java.lang.Object
VALUE_DITHER_DISABLE
public final static java.lang.Object
VALUE_DITHER_ENABLE
public final static java.lang.Object
VALUE_FRACTIONALMETRICS_DEFAULT
public final static java.lang.Object
VALUE_FRACTIONALMETRICS_OFF
public final static java.lang.Object
VALUE_FRACTIONALMETRICS_ON
public final static java.lang.Object
VALUE_INTERPOLATION_BICUBIC
public final static java.lang.Object
VALUE_INTERPOLATION_BILINEAR
public final static java.lang.Object
VALUE_INTERPOLATION_NEAREST_NEIGHBOR
public final static java.lang.Object
VALUE_RENDER_DEFAULT
public final static java.lang.Object
VALUE_RENDER_QUALITY
public final static java.lang.Object
VALUE_RENDER_SPEED
public final static java.lang.Object
VALUE_TEXT_ANTIALIAS_DEFAULT
public final static java.lang.Object
VALUE_TEXT_ANTIALIAS_OFF
public final static java.lang.Object
VALUE_TEXT_ANTIALIAS_ON
```

### Constructors

```
public  RenderingHints(Map init)
public  RenderingHints(Key key,Object
value)
```

### Methods

```
public void add(RenderingHints hints)
public void clear()
public Object clone()
public boolean containsKey(Object key)
public boolean containsValue(Object
value)
public Set entrySet()
public boolean equals(Object o)
public Object get(Object key)
public int hashCode()
public boolean isEmpty()
public Set keySet()
public Object put(Object key,Object
value)
public void putAll(Map m)
public Object remove(Object key)
public int size()
public String toString()
public Collection values()
```

## RepaintManager

```
public class javax.swing.RepaintManager
extends java.lang.Object
```

## Constructors
public  RepaintManager()

## Methods
public synchronized void addDirtyRegion(
JComponent c,int x,int y,int w,int h)
public synchronized void
addInvalidComponent(JComponent
invalidComponent)
public static RepaintManager
currentManager(Component c)
public static RepaintManager
currentManager(JComponent c)
public Rectangle getDirtyRegion(
JComponent aComponent)
public Dimension
getDoubleBufferMaximumSize()
public Image getOffscreenBuffer(
Component c,int proposedWidth,int
proposedHeight)
public boolean isCompletelyDirty(
JComponent aComponent)
public boolean isDoubleBufferingEnabled()
public void markCompletelyClean(
JComponent aComponent)
public void markCompletelyDirty(
JComponent aComponent)
public void paintDirtyRegions()
public synchronized void
removeInvalidComponent(JComponent
component)
public static void setCurrentManager(
RepaintManager aRepaintManager)
public void setDoubleBufferingEnabled(
boolean aFlag)
public void setDoubleBufferMaximumSize(
Dimension d)
public synchronized String toString()
public void validateInvalidComponents()

# ReplicateScaleFilter
public class java.awt.image.
ReplicateScaleFilter
extends java.awt.image.ImageFilter
extends java.lang.Object

## Fields
protected int destHeight
protected int destWidth
protected java.lang.Object outpixbuf
protected int srccols
protected int srcHeight
protected int srcrows
protected int srcWidth

## Constructors
public  ReplicateScaleFilter(int width,
int height)

## Methods
public void setDimensions(int w,int h)
public void setPixels(int x,int y,int w,
int h,ColorModel model,byte pixels,int
off,int scansize)

public void setPixels(int x,int y,int w,
int h,ColorModel model,int pixels,int
off,int scansize)
public void setProperties(Hashtable
props)

# RescaleOp
public class java.awt.image.RescaleOp
implements java.awt.image.
BufferedImageOp
implements java.awt.image.RasterOp
extends java.lang.Object

## Constructors
public  RescaleOp(float scaleFactors,
float offsets,RenderingHints hints)
public  RescaleOp(float scaleFactor,
float offset,RenderingHints hints)

## Methods
public BufferedImage
createCompatibleDestImage(BufferedImage
src,ColorModel destCM)
public WritableRaster
createCompatibleDestRaster(Raster src)
public final BufferedImage filter(
BufferedImage src,BufferedImage dst)
public final WritableRaster filter(
Raster src,WritableRaster dst)
public final Rectangle2D getBounds2D(
BufferedImage src)
public final Rectangle2D getBounds2D(
Raster src)
public final int getNumFactors()
public final float getOffsets(float
offsets)
public final Point2D getPoint2D(Point2D
srcPt,Point2D dstPt)
public final RenderingHints
getRenderingHints()
public final float getScaleFactors(float
scaleFactors)

# ResourceBundle
public abstract class java.util.
ResourceBundle
extends java.lang.Object

## Fields
protected java.util.ResourceBundle
parent

## Constructors
public  ResourceBundle()

## Methods
public final static ResourceBundle
getBundle(String baseName)
public final static ResourceBundle
getBundle(String baseName,Locale locale)
public static ResourceBundle getBundle(
String baseName,Locale locale,
ClassLoader loader)
public abstract Enumeration getKeys()

```
public Locale getLocale()
public final Object getObject(String key)
public final String getString(String key)
public final String getStringArray(
String key)
protected abstract Object
handleGetObject(String key)
protected void setParent(ResourceBundle
parent)
```

## RGBImageFilter

```
public abstract class java.awt.image.
RGBImageFilter
extends java.awt.image.ImageFilter
extends java.lang.Object
```

### Fields

```
protected boolean
canFilterIndexColorModel
protected java.awt.image.ColorModel
newmodel
protected java.awt.image.ColorModel
origmodel
```

### Methods

```
public IndexColorModel
filterIndexColorModel(IndexColorModel
icm)
public abstract int filterRGB(int x,int
y,int rgb)
public void filterRGBPixels(int x,int y,
int w,int h,int pixels,int off,int
scansize)
public void setColorModel(ColorModel
model)
public void setPixels(int x,int y,int w,
int h,ColorModel model,byte pixels,int
off,int scansize)
public void setPixels(int x,int y,int w,
int h,ColorModel model,int pixels,int
off,int scansize)
public void substituteColorModel(
ColorModel oldcm,ColorModel newcm)
```

## RMIClassLoader

```
public class java.rmi.server.
RMIClassLoader
extends java.lang.Object
```

### Constructors

```
private  RMIClassLoader()
```

### Methods

```
public static String getClassAnnotation(
Class cl)
public static Object getSecurityContext(
ClassLoader loader)
public static Class loadClass(String
name)
public static Class loadClass(URL
codebase,String name)
public static Class loadClass(String
codebase,String name)
```

## RMISecurityException

```
public class java.rmi.
RMISecurityException
extends java.lang.SecurityException
extends java.lang.RuntimeException
extends java.lang.Exception
extends java.lang.Throwable
extends java.lang.Object
```

### Constructors

```
public  RMISecurityException(String name)
public  RMISecurityException(String name,
String arg)
```

## RMISecurityManager

```
public class java.rmi.
RMISecurityManager
extends java.lang.SecurityManager
extends java.lang.Object
```

### Constructors

```
public  RMISecurityManager()
```

### Methods

```
public void checkPackageAccess(String
pkgname)
```

## RMISocketFactory

```
public abstract class java.rmi.server.
RMISocketFactory
implements java.rmi.server.
RMIClientSocketFactory
implements java.rmi.server.
RMIServerSocketFactory
extends java.lang.Object
```

### Constructors

```
public  RMISocketFactory()
```

### Methods

```
public abstract ServerSocket
createServerSocket(int port)
public abstract Socket createSocket(
String host,int port)
public static synchronized
RMISocketFactory getDefaultSocketFactory(
)
public static synchronized
RMIFailureHandler getFailureHandler()
public static synchronized
RMISocketFactory getSocketFactory()
public static synchronized void
setFailureHandler(RMIFailureHandler fh)
public static synchronized void
setSocketFactory(RMISocketFactory fac)
```

## RoundRectangle2D

```
public abstract class java.awt.geom.
RoundRectangle2D
extends java.awt.geom.RectangularShape
extends java.lang.Object
```

## Constructors

```
protected  RoundRectangle2D()
```

## Methods

```
public boolean contains(double x,double
y)
public boolean contains(double x,double
y,double w,double h)
public abstract double getArcHeight()
public abstract double getArcWidth()
public PathIterator getPathIterator(
AffineTransform at)
public boolean intersects(double x,
double y,double w,double h)
public void setFrame(double x,double y,
double w,double h)
public abstract void setRoundRect(double
x,double y,double w,double h,double
arcWidth,double arcHeight)
public void setRoundRect(
RoundRectangle2D rr)
```

# RSAPrivateCrtKeySpec

```
public class java.security.spec.
RSAPrivateCrtKeySpec
extends java.security.spec.
RSAPrivateKeySpec
extends java.lang.Object
```

## Constructors

```
public  RSAPrivateCrtKeySpec(BigInteger
modulus,BigInteger publicExponent,
BigInteger privateExponent,BigInteger
primeP,BigInteger primeQ,BigInteger
primeExponentP,BigInteger primeExponentQ,
BigInteger crtCoefficient)
```

## Methods

```
public BigInteger getCrtCoefficient()
public BigInteger getPrimeExponentP()
public BigInteger getPrimeExponentQ()
public BigInteger getPrimeP()
public BigInteger getPrimeQ()
public BigInteger getPublicExponent()
```

# RSAPrivateKeySpec

```
public class java.security.spec.
RSAPrivateKeySpec
implements java.security.spec.KeySpec
extends java.lang.Object
```

## Constructors

```
public  RSAPrivateKeySpec(BigInteger
modulus,BigInteger privateExponent)
```

## Methods

```
public BigInteger getModulus()
public BigInteger getPrivateExponent()
```

# RSAPublicKeySpec

```
public class java.security.spec.
RSAPublicKeySpec
implements java.security.spec.KeySpec
extends java.lang.Object
```

## Constructors

```
public  RSAPublicKeySpec(BigInteger
modulus,BigInteger publicExponent)
```

## Methods

```
public BigInteger getModulus()
public BigInteger getPublicExponent()
```

# RTFEditorKit

```
public class javax.swing.text.rtf.
RTFEditorKit
extends javax.swing.text.
StyledEditorKit
extends javax.swing.text.
DefaultEditorKit
extends javax.swing.text.EditorKit
extends java.lang.Object
```

## Constructors

```
public  RTFEditorKit()
```

## Methods

```
public Object clone()
public String getContentType()
public void read(InputStream in,Document
doc,int pos)
public void read(Reader in,Document doc,
int pos)
public void write(OutputStream out,
Document doc,int pos,int len)
public void write(Writer out,Document
doc,int pos,int len)
```

# RuleBasedCollator

```
public class java.text.
RuleBasedCollator
extends java.text.Collator
extends java.lang.Object
```

## Constructors

```
public  RuleBasedCollator(String rules)
 RuleBasedCollator()
```

## Methods

```
public Object clone()
public int compare(String source,String
target)
public boolean equals(Object obj)
public CollationElementIterator
getCollationElementIterator(String
source)
public CollationElementIterator
getCollationElementIterator(
CharacterIterator source)
public CollationKey getCollationKey(
String source)
public String getRules()
public int hashCode()
```

## Runtime

```
public class java.lang.Runtime
extends java.lang.Object
```

### Constructors
```
private  Runtime()
```

### Methods
```
public Process exec(String command)
public Process exec(String command,
String envp)
public Process exec(String cmdarray)
public Process exec(String cmdarray,
String envp)
public void exit(int status)
public native long freeMemory()
public native void gc()
public InputStream
getLocalizedInputStream(InputStream in)
public OutputStream
getLocalizedOutputStream(OutputStream
out)
public static Runtime getRuntime()
public void load(String filename)
public void loadLibrary(String libname)
public void runFinalization()
public static void runFinalizersOnExit(
boolean value)
public native long totalMemory()
public native void traceInstructions(
boolean on)
public native void traceMethodCalls(
boolean on)
```

## RuntimeException

```
public class java.lang.RuntimeException
extends java.lang.Exception
extends java.lang.Throwable
extends java.lang.Object
```

### Constructors
```
public  RuntimeException()
public  RuntimeException(String s)
```

## RuntimePermission

```
public final class java.lang.
RuntimePermission
extends java.security.BasicPermission
extends java.security.Permission
extends java.lang.Object
```

### Constructors
```
public  RuntimePermission(String name)
public  RuntimePermission(String name,
String actions)
```

## SampleModel

```
public abstract class java.awt.image.
SampleModel
extends java.lang.Object
```

### Fields
```
protected int dataType
protected int height
protected int numBands
protected int width
```

### Constructors
```
public static  SampleModel(int dataType,
int w,int h,int numBands)
```

### Methods
```
public abstract SampleModel
createCompatibleSampleModel(int w,int h)
public abstract DataBuffer
createDataBuffer()
public abstract SampleModel
createSubsetSampleModel(int bands)
public abstract Object getDataElements(
int x,int y,Object obj,DataBuffer data)
public Object getDataElements(int x,int
y,int w,int h,Object obj,DataBuffer data)
public final int getDataType()
public final int getHeight()
public final int getNumBands()
public abstract int getNumDataElements()
public int getPixel(int x,int y,int
iArray,DataBuffer data)
public float getPixel(int x,int y,float
fArray,DataBuffer data)
public double getPixel(int x,int y,
double dArray,DataBuffer data)
public int getPixels(int x,int y,int w,
int h,int iArray,DataBuffer data)
public float getPixels(int x,int y,int w,
int h,float fArray,DataBuffer data)
public double getPixels(int x,int y,int
w,int h,double dArray,DataBuffer data)
public abstract int getSample(int x,int
y,int b,DataBuffer data)
public double getSampleDouble(int x,int
y,int b,DataBuffer data)
public float getSampleFloat(int x,int y,
int b,DataBuffer data)
public int getSamples(int x,int y,int w,
int h,int b,int iArray,DataBuffer data)
public float getSamples(int x,int y,int
w,int h,int b,float fArray,DataBuffer
data)
public double getSamples(int x,int y,int
w,int h,int b,double dArray,DataBuffer
data)
public abstract int getSampleSize()
public abstract int getSampleSize(int
band)
public int getTransferType()
public final int getWidth()
public abstract void setDataElements(int
x,int y,Object obj,DataBuffer data)
public void setDataElements(int x,int y,
int w,int h,Object obj,DataBuffer data)
public void setPixel(int x,int y,int
iArray,DataBuffer data)
public void setPixel(int x,int y,float
fArray,DataBuffer data)
```

public void setPixel(int x,int y,double dArray,DataBuffer data)
public void setPixels(int x,int y,int w, int h,int iArray,DataBuffer data)
public void setPixels(int x,int y,int w, int h,float fArray,DataBuffer data)
public void setPixels(int x,int y,int w, int h,double dArray,DataBuffer data)
public abstract void setSample(int x,int y,int b,int s,DataBuffer data)
public void setSample(int x,int y,int b, float s,DataBuffer data)
public void setSample(int x,int y,int b, double s,DataBuffer data)
public void setSamples(int x,int y,int w, int h,int b,int iArray,DataBuffer data)
public void setSamples(int x,int y,int w, int h,int b,float fArray,DataBuffer data)
public void setSamples(int x,int y,int w, int h,int b,double dArray,DataBuffer data)

# Scrollbar

public class java.awt.Scrollbar
implements java.awt.Adjustable
extends java.awt.Component
extends java.lang.Object

## Fields

public final static int HORIZONTAL
public final static int VERTICAL

## Constructors

public static  Scrollbar()
public  Scrollbar(int orientation)
public  Scrollbar(int orientation,int value,int visible,int minimum,int maximum)

## Methods

public synchronized void addAdjustmentListener(AdjustmentListener l)
public void addNotify()
public int getBlockIncrement()
public int getLineIncrement()
public int getMaximum()
public int getMinimum()
public int getOrientation()
public int getPageIncrement()
public int getUnitIncrement()
public int getValue()
public int getVisible()
public int getVisibleAmount()
protected String paramString()
protected void processAdjustmentEvent(AdjustmentEvent e)
protected void processEvent(AWTEvent e)
public synchronized void removeAdjustmentListener(AdjustmentListener l)
public void setBlockIncrement(int v)

public synchronized void setLineIncrement(int v)
public void setMaximum(int newMaximum)
public void setMinimum(int newMinimum)
public void setOrientation(int orientation)
public synchronized void setPageIncrement(int v)
public void setUnitIncrement(int v)
public void setValue(int newValue)
public synchronized void setValues(int value,int visible,int minimum,int maximum)
public void setVisibleAmount(int newAmount)

# ScrollBarUI

public abstract class javax.swing.plaf.ScrollBarUI
extends javax.swing.plaf.ComponentUI
extends java.lang.Object

# ScrollPane

public class java.awt.ScrollPane
extends java.awt.Container
extends java.awt.Component
extends java.lang.Object

## Fields

public final static int SCROLLBARS_ALWAYS
public final static int SCROLLBARS_AS_NEEDED
public final static int SCROLLBARS_NEVER

## Constructors

public  ScrollPane()
public  ScrollPane(int scrollbarDisplayPolicy)

## Methods

protected final void addImpl(Component comp,Object constraints,int index)
public void addNotify()
public void doLayout()
public Adjustable getHAdjustable()
public int getHScrollbarHeight()
public int getScrollbarDisplayPolicy()
public Point getScrollPosition()
public Adjustable getVAdjustable()
public Dimension getViewportSize()
public int getVScrollbarWidth()
public void layout()
public String paramString()
public void printComponents(Graphics g)
public final void setLayout(LayoutManager mgr)
public void setScrollPosition(int x,int y)
public void setScrollPosition(Point p)

## ScrollPaneLayout

```
public class javax.swing.
ScrollPaneLayout
implements java.awt.LayoutManager
implements javax.swing.
ScrollPaneConstants
implements java.io.Serializable
extends java.lang.Object
```

### Fields

```
protected javax.swing.JViewport colHead
protected javax.swing.JScrollBar hsb
protected int hsbPolicy
protected java.awt.Component lowerLeft
protected java.awt.Component lowerRight
protected javax.swing.JViewport rowHead
protected java.awt.Component upperLeft
protected java.awt.Component upperRight
protected javax.swing.JViewport
viewport
protected javax.swing.JScrollBar vsb
protected int vsbPolicy
```

### Methods

```
public void addLayoutComponent(String s,
Component c)
protected Component
addSingletonComponent(Component oldC,
Component newC)
public JViewport getColumnHeader()
public Component getCorner(String key)
public JScrollBar getHorizontalScrollBar(
)
public int getHorizontalScrollBarPolicy()
public JViewport getRowHeader()
public JScrollBar getVerticalScrollBar()
public int getVerticalScrollBarPolicy()
public JViewport getViewport()
public Rectangle getViewportBorderBounds(
JScrollPane scrollpane)
public void layoutContainer(Container
parent)
public Dimension minimumLayoutSize(
Container parent)
public Dimension preferredLayoutSize(
Container parent)
public void removeLayoutComponent(
Component c)
public void setHorizontalScrollBarPolicy(
int x)
public void setVerticalScrollBarPolicy(
int x)
public void syncWithScrollPane(
JScrollPane sp)
```

## ScrollPaneUI

```
public abstract class javax.swing.plaf.
ScrollPaneUI
extends javax.swing.plaf.ComponentUI
extends java.lang.Object
```

## SecureClassLoader

```
public class java.security.
SecureClassLoader
extends java.lang.ClassLoader
extends java.lang.Object
```

### Constructors

```
protected  SecureClassLoader(ClassLoader
parent)
protected  SecureClassLoader()
```

### Methods

```
protected final Class defineClass(String
name,byte b,int off,int len,CodeSource
cs)
protected PermissionCollection
getPermissions(CodeSource codesource)
```

## SecureRandom

```
public class java.security.SecureRandom
extends java.util.Random
extends java.lang.Object
```

### Constructors

```
public  SecureRandom()
public  SecureRandom(byte seed)
protected  SecureRandom(SecureRandomSpi
secureRandomSpi,Provider provider)
```

### Methods

```
public byte generateSeed(int numBytes)
public static SecureRandom getInstance(
String algorithm)
public static SecureRandom getInstance(
String algorithm,String provider)
public final Provider getProvider()
public static byte getSeed(int numBytes)
protected final int next(int numBits)
public synchronized void nextBytes(byte
bytes)
public synchronized void setSeed(byte
seed)
public void setSeed(long seed)
```

## SecureRandomSpi

```
public abstract class java.security.
SecureRandomSpi
implements java.io.Serializable
extends java.lang.Object
```

### Methods

```
protected abstract byte
engineGenerateSeed(int numBytes)
protected abstract void engineNextBytes(
byte bytes)
protected abstract void engineSetSeed(
byte seed)
```

## Security

```
public final class java.security.
Security
extends java.lang.Object
```

## Constructors
private  Security()

## Methods
public static int addProvider(Provider provider)
public static String getAlgorithmProperty(String algName, String propName)
public static String getProperty(String key)
public static Provider getProvider( String name)
public static Provider getProviders()
public static int insertProviderAt( Provider provider,int position)
public static void removeProvider(String name)
public static void setProperty(String key,String datum)

# SecurityException
public class java.lang. SecurityException
extends java.lang.RuntimeException
extends java.lang.Exception
extends java.lang.Throwable
extends java.lang.Object

## Constructors
public  SecurityException()
public  SecurityException(String s)

# SecurityManager
public class java.lang.SecurityManager
extends java.lang.Object

## Fields
protected boolean inCheck

## Constructors
public  SecurityManager()

## Methods
public void checkAccept(String host,int port)
public void checkAccess(Thread t)
public void checkAccess(ThreadGroup g)
public void checkAwtEventQueueAccess()
public void checkConnect(String host,int port)
public void checkConnect(String host,int port,Object context)
public void checkCreateClassLoader()
public void checkDelete(String file)
public void checkExec(String cmd)
public void checkExit(int status)
public void checkLink(String lib)
public void checkListen(int port)
public void checkMemberAccess(Class clazz,int which)
public void checkMulticast(InetAddress maddr)
public void checkMulticast(InetAddress maddr,byte ttl)
public void checkPackageAccess(String pkg)
public void checkPackageDefinition( String pkg)
public void checkPermission(Permission perm)
public void checkPermission(Permission perm,Object context)
public void checkPrintJobAccess()
public void checkPropertiesAccess()
public void checkPropertyAccess(String key)
public void checkRead(FileDescriptor fd)
public void checkRead(String file)
public void checkRead(String file,Object context)
public void checkSecurityAccess(String target)
public void checkSetFactory()
public void checkSystemClipboardAccess()
public boolean checkTopLevelWindow( Object window)
public void checkWrite(FileDescriptor fd)
public void checkWrite(String file)
protected native int classDepth(String name)
protected int classLoaderDepth()
protected ClassLoader currentClassLoader( )
protected Class currentLoadedClass()
protected native Class getClassContext()
public boolean getInCheck()
public Object getSecurityContext()
public ThreadGroup getThreadGroup()
protected boolean inClass(String name)
protected boolean inClassLoader()

# SecurityPermission
public final class java.security. SecurityPermission
extends java.security.BasicPermission
extends java.security.Permission
extends java.lang.Object

## Constructors
public  SecurityPermission(String name)
public  SecurityPermission(String name, String actions)

# Segment
public class javax.swing.text.Segment
extends java.lang.Object

## Fields
public char array
public int count
public int offset

## Constructors
public  Segment()
public  Segment(char array,int offset, int count)

**Methods**
public String toString()

# SeparatorUI
public abstract class javax.swing.plaf.
SeparatorUI
extends javax.swing.plaf.ComponentUI
extends java.lang.Object

# SequenceInputStream
public class java.io.
SequenceInputStream
extends java.io.InputStream
extends java.lang.Object

**Constructors**
public  SequenceInputStream(Enumeration
e)
public  SequenceInputStream(InputStream
s1,InputStream s2)

**Methods**
public int available()
public void close()
public int read()
public int read(byte b,int off,int len)

# SerializablePermission
public final class java.io.
SerializablePermission
extends java.security.BasicPermission
extends java.security.Permission
extends java.lang.Object

**Constructors**
public  SerializablePermission(String
name)
public  SerializablePermission(String
name,String actions)

# ServerCloneException
public class java.rmi.server.
ServerCloneException
extends java.lang.
CloneNotSupportedException
extends java.lang.Exception
extends java.lang.Throwable
extends java.lang.Object

**Fields**
public java.lang.Exception detail

**Constructors**
public  ServerCloneException(String s)
public  ServerCloneException(String s,
Exception ex)

**Methods**
public String getMessage()
public void printStackTrace(PrintStream ps)
public void printStackTrace()
public void printStackTrace(PrintWriter pw)

# ServerError
public class java.rmi.ServerError
extends java.rmi.RemoteException
extends java.io.IOException
extends java.lang.Exception
extends java.lang.Throwable
extends java.lang.Object

**Constructors**
public  ServerError(String s,Error err)

# ServerException
public class java.rmi.ServerException
extends java.rmi.RemoteException
extends java.io.IOException
extends java.lang.Exception
extends java.lang.Throwable
extends java.lang.Object

**Constructors**
public  ServerException(String s)
public  ServerException(String s,
Exception ex)

# ServerNotActiveException
public class java.rmi.server.
ServerNotActiveException
extends java.lang.Exception
extends java.lang.Throwable
extends java.lang.Object

**Constructors**
public  ServerNotActiveException()
public  ServerNotActiveException(String
s)

# ServerRuntimeException
public class java.rmi.
ServerRuntimeException
extends java.rmi.RemoteException
extends java.io.IOException
extends java.lang.Exception
extends java.lang.Throwable
extends java.lang.Object

**Constructors**
public  ServerRuntimeException(String s,
Exception ex)

# ServerSocket
public class java.net.ServerSocket
extends java.lang.Object

**Constructors**
private  ServerSocket()
public  ServerSocket(int port)
public  ServerSocket(int port,int
backlog)
public  ServerSocket(int port,int
backlog,InetAddress bindAddr)

### Methods
```
public Socket accept()
public void close()
public InetAddress getInetAddress()
public int getLocalPort()
public synchronized int getSoTimeout()
protected final void implAccept(Socket s)
public static synchronized void
setSocketFactory(SocketImplFactory fac)
public synchronized void setSoTimeout(
int timeout)
public String toString()
```

## ShapeGraphicAttribute
```
public final class java.awt.font.
ShapeGraphicAttribute
extends java.awt.font.GraphicAttribute
extends java.lang.Object
```

### Fields
```
public final static boolean FILL
public final static boolean STROKE
```

### Constructors
```
public  ShapeGraphicAttribute(Shape
shape,int alignment,boolean stroke)
```

### Methods
```
public void draw(Graphics2D graphics,
float x,float y)
public boolean equals(Object rhs)
public boolean equals(
ShapeGraphicAttribute rhs)
public float getAdvance()
public float getAscent()
public Rectangle2D getBounds()
public float getDescent()
public int hashCode()
```

## Short
```
public final class java.lang.Short
implements java.lang.Comparable
extends java.lang.Number
extends java.lang.Object
```

### Fields
```
public final static short MAX_VALUE
public final static short MIN_VALUE
public final static java.lang.Class
TYPE
```

### Constructors
```
public  Short(short value)
public  Short(String s)
```

### Methods
```
public byte byteValue()
public int compareTo(Short anotherShort)
public int compareTo(Object o)
public static Short decode(String nm)
public double doubleValue()
public boolean equals(Object obj)
public float floatValue()
```

```
public int hashCode()
public int intValue()
public long longValue()
public static short parseShort(String s)
public static short parseShort(String s,
int radix)
public short shortValue()
public static String toString(short s)
public String toString()
public static Short valueOf(String s,int
radix)
public static Short valueOf(String s)
```

## ShortLookupTable
```
public class java.awt.image.
ShortLookupTable
extends java.awt.image.LookupTable
extends java.lang.Object
```

### Constructors
```
public  ShortLookupTable(int offset,
short data)
public  ShortLookupTable(int offset,
short data)
```

### Methods
```
public final short getTable()
public int lookupPixel(int src,int dst)
public short lookupPixel(short src,short
dst)
```

## Signature
```
public abstract class java.security.
Signature
extends java.security.SignatureSpi
extends java.lang.Object
```

### Fields
```
protected final static int SIGN
protected int state
protected final static int
UNINITIALIZED
protected final static int VERIFY
```

### Constructors
```
protected  Signature(String algorithm)
```

### Methods
```
public Object clone()
public final String getAlgorithm()
public static Signature getInstance(
String algorithm)
public static Signature getInstance(
String algorithm,String provider)
public final Object getParameter(String
param)
public final Provider getProvider()
public final void initSign(PrivateKey
privateKey)
public final void initSign(PrivateKey
privateKey,SecureRandom random)
```

```
public final void initVerify(PublicKey
publicKey)
public final void setParameter(String
param,Object value)
public final void setParameter(
AlgorithmParameterSpec params)
public final byte sign()
public final int sign(byte outbuf,int
offset,int len)
public String toString()
public final void update(byte b)
public final void update(byte data)
public final void update(byte data,int
off,int len)
public final boolean verify(byte
signature)
```

## SignatureException

```
public class java.security.
SignatureException
extends java.security.
GeneralSecurityException
extends java.lang.Exception
extends java.lang.Throwable
extends java.lang.Object
```

### Constructors

```
public  SignatureException()
public  SignatureException(String msg)
```

## SignatureSpi

```
public abstract class java.security.
SignatureSpi
extends java.lang.Object
```

### Fields

```
protected java.security.SecureRandom
appRandom
```

### Methods

```
public Object clone()
protected abstract Object
engineGetParameter(String param)
protected abstract void engineInitSign(
PrivateKey privateKey)
protected void engineInitSign(PrivateKey
privateKey,SecureRandom random)
protected abstract void engineInitVerify(
PublicKey publicKey)
protected abstract void
engineSetParameter(String param,Object
value)
protected void engineSetParameter(
AlgorithmParameterSpec params)
protected abstract byte engineSign()
protected int engineSign(byte outbuf,int
offset,int len)
protected abstract void engineUpdate(
byte b)
protected abstract void engineUpdate(
byte b,int off,int len)
protected abstract boolean engineVerify(
byte sigBytes)
```

## SignedObject

```
public final class java.security.
SignedObject
implements java.io.Serializable
extends java.lang.Object
```

### Constructors

```
public  SignedObject(Serializable object,
PrivateKey signingKey,Signature
signingEngine)
```

### Methods

```
public String getAlgorithm()
public Object getObject()
public byte getSignature()
public boolean verify(PublicKey
verificationKey,Signature
verificationEngine)
```

## Signer

```
public abstract class java.security.
Signer
extends java.security.Identity
extends java.lang.Object
```

### Constructors

```
protected  Signer()
public  Signer(String name)
public  Signer(String name,IdentityScope
scope)
```

### Methods

```
public PrivateKey getPrivateKey()
public final void setKeyPair(KeyPair
pair)
public String toString()
```

## SimpleAttributeSet

```
public class javax.swing.text.
SimpleAttributeSet
implements java.lang.Cloneable
implements javax.swing.text.
MutableAttributeSet
implements java.io.Serializable
extends java.lang.Object
```

### Fields

```
public final static javax.swing.text.
AttributeSet EMPTY
```

### Constructors

```
public  SimpleAttributeSet()
public  SimpleAttributeSet(AttributeSet
source)
private  SimpleAttributeSet()
```

### Methods

```
public void addAttribute(Object name,
Object value)
public void addAttributes(AttributeSet
attributes)
public Object clone()
```

```
public boolean containsAttribute(Object
name,Object value)
public boolean containsAttributes(
AttributeSet attributes)
public AttributeSet copyAttributes()
public boolean equals(Object obj)
public Object getAttribute(Object name)
public int getAttributeCount()
public Enumeration getAttributeNames()
public AttributeSet getResolveParent()
public int hashCode()
public boolean isDefined(Object attrName)
public boolean isEmpty()
public boolean isEqual(AttributeSet attr)
public void removeAttribute(Object name)
public void removeAttributes(Enumeration
names)
public void removeAttributes(
AttributeSet attributes)
public void setResolveParent(
AttributeSet parent)
public String toString()
```

## SimpleBeanInfo

```
public class java.beans.SimpleBeanInfo
implements java.beans.BeanInfo
extends java.lang.Object
```

### Methods

```
public BeanInfo getAdditionalBeanInfo()
public BeanDescriptor getBeanDescriptor()
public int getDefaultEventIndex()
public int getDefaultPropertyIndex()
public EventSetDescriptor
getEventSetDescriptors()
public Image getIcon(int iconKind)
public MethodDescriptor
getMethodDescriptors()
public PropertyDescriptor
getPropertyDescriptors()
public Image loadImage(String
resourceName)
```

## SimpleDateFormat

```
public class java.text.SimpleDateFormat
extends java.text.DateFormat
extends java.text.Format
extends java.lang.Object
```

### Constructors

```
public  SimpleDateFormat()
public  SimpleDateFormat(String pattern)
public  SimpleDateFormat(String pattern,
Locale loc)
public  SimpleDateFormat(String pattern,
DateFormatSymbols formatData)
 SimpleDateFormat()
```

### Methods

```
public void applyLocalizedPattern(String
pattern)
public void applyPattern(String pattern)
public Object clone()
```

```
public boolean equals(Object obj)
public StringBuffer format(Date date,
StringBuffer toAppendTo,FieldPosition
pos)
public Date get2DigitYearStart()
public DateFormatSymbols
getDateFormatSymbols()
public int hashCode()
public Date parse(String text,
ParsePosition pos)
public void set2DigitYearStart(Date
startDate)
public void setDateFormatSymbols(
DateFormatSymbols newFormatSymbols)
public String toLocalizedPattern()
public String toPattern()
```

## SimpleTimeZone

```
public class java.util.SimpleTimeZone
extends java.util.TimeZone
extends java.lang.Object
```

### Constructors

```
public  SimpleTimeZone(int rawOffset,
String ID)
public  SimpleTimeZone(int rawOffset,
String ID,int startMonth,int startDay,
int startDayOfWeek,int startTime,int
endMonth,int endDay,int endDayOfWeek,int
endTime)
public  SimpleTimeZone(int rawOffset,
String ID,int startMonth,int startDay,
int startDayOfWeek,int startTime,int
endMonth,int endDay,int endDayOfWeek,int
endTime,int dstSavings)
```

### Methods

```
public Object clone()
public boolean equals(Object obj)
public int getDSTSavings()
public int getOffset(int era,int year,
int month,int day,int dayOfWeek,int
millis)
public int getRawOffset()
public synchronized int hashCode()
public boolean hasSameRules(TimeZone
other)
public boolean inDaylightTime(Date date)
public void setDSTSavings(int
millisSavedDuringDST)
public void setEndRule(int month,int
dayOfWeekInMonth,int dayOfWeek,int time)
public void setEndRule(int month,int
dayOfMonth,int time)
public void setEndRule(int month,int
dayOfMonth,int dayOfWeek,int time,
boolean after)
public void setRawOffset(int
offsetMillis)
public void setStartRule(int month,int
dayOfWeekInMonth,int dayOfWeek,int time)
public void setStartRule(int month,int
dayOfMonth,int time)
```

```
public void setStartRule(int month,int
dayOfMonth,int dayOfWeek,int time,
boolean after)
public void setStartYear(int year)
public String toString()
public boolean useDaylightTime()
```

## SinglePixelPackedSampleModel

```
public class java.awt.image.
SinglePixelPackedSampleModel
extends java.awt.image.SampleModel
extends java.lang.Object
```

### Constructors

```
public static
SinglePixelPackedSampleModel(int
dataType,int w,int h,int bitMasks)
public  SinglePixelPackedSampleModel(int
dataType,int w,int h,int scanlineStride,
int bitMasks)
```

### Methods

```
public SampleModel
createCompatibleSampleModel(int w,int h)
public DataBuffer createDataBuffer()
public SampleModel
createSubsetSampleModel(int bands)
public int getBitMasks()
public int getBitOffsets()
public Object getDataElements(int x,int
y,Object obj,DataBuffer data)
public int getNumDataElements()
public int getOffset(int x,int y)
public int getPixel(int x,int y,int
iArray,DataBuffer data)
public int getPixels(int x,int y,int w,
int h,int iArray,DataBuffer data)
public int getSample(int x,int y,int b,
DataBuffer data)
public int getSamples(int x,int y,int w,
int h,int b,int iArray,DataBuffer data)
public int getSampleSize()
public int getSampleSize(int band)
public int getScanlineStride()
public void setDataElements(int x,int y,
Object obj,DataBuffer data)
public void setPixel(int x,int y,int
iArray,DataBuffer data)
public void setPixels(int x,int y,int w,
int h,int iArray,DataBuffer data)
public void setSample(int x,int y,int b,
int s,DataBuffer data)
public void setSamples(int x,int y,int w,
int h,int b,int iArray,DataBuffer data)
```

## SizeRequirements

```
public class javax.swing.
SizeRequirements
implements java.io.Serializable
extends java.lang.Object
```

### Fields

```
public float alignment
```

```
public int maximum
public int minimum
public int preferred
```

### Constructors

```
public  SizeRequirements()
public  SizeRequirements(int min,int
pref,int max,float a)
```

### Methods

```
public static int adjustSizes(int delta,
SizeRequirements children)
public static void
calculateAlignedPositions(int allocated,
SizeRequirements total,SizeRequirements
children,int offsets,int spans)
public static void
calculateTiledPositions(int allocated,
SizeRequirements total,SizeRequirements
children,int offsets,int spans)
public static SizeRequirements
getAlignedSizeRequirements(
SizeRequirements children)
public static SizeRequirements
getTiledSizeRequirements(
SizeRequirements children)
public String toString()
```

## SkeletonMismatchException

```
public class java.rmi.server.
SkeletonMismatchException
extends java.rmi.RemoteException
extends java.io.IOException
extends java.lang.Exception
extends java.lang.Throwable
extends java.lang.Object
```

### Constructors

```
public  SkeletonMismatchException(String
s)
```

## SkeletonNotFoundException

```
public class java.rmi.server.
SkeletonNotFoundException
extends java.rmi.RemoteException
extends java.io.IOException
extends java.lang.Exception
extends java.lang.Throwable
extends java.lang.Object
```

### Constructors

```
public  SkeletonNotFoundException(String
s)
public  SkeletonNotFoundException(String
s,Exception ex)
```

## SliderUI

```
public abstract class javax.swing.plaf.
SliderUI
extends javax.swing.plaf.ComponentUI
extends java.lang.Object
```

# Socket

    public class java.net.Socket
    extends java.lang.Object

## Constructors

    protected  Socket()
    protected  Socket(SocketImpl impl)
    public  Socket(String host,int port)
    public  Socket(InetAddress address,int
    port)
    public  Socket(String host,int port,
    InetAddress localAddr,int localPort)
    public  Socket(InetAddress address,int
    port,InetAddress localAddr,int localPort)
    public  Socket(String host,int port,
    boolean stream)
    public  Socket(InetAddress host,int port,
    boolean stream)
    private  Socket()

## Methods

    public synchronized void close()
    public InetAddress getInetAddress()
    public InputStream getInputStream()
    public InetAddress getLocalAddress()
    public int getLocalPort()
    public OutputStream getOutputStream()
    public int getPort()
    public synchronized int
    getReceiveBufferSize()
    public synchronized int
    getSendBufferSize()
    public int getSoLinger()
    public synchronized int getSoTimeout()
    public boolean getTcpNoDelay()
    public synchronized void
    setReceiveBufferSize(int size)
    public synchronized void
    setSendBufferSize(int size)
    public static synchronized void
    setSocketImplFactory(SocketImplFactory
    fac)
    public void setSoLinger(boolean on,int
    linger)
    public synchronized void setSoTimeout(
    int timeout)
    public void setTcpNoDelay(boolean on)
    public String toString()

# SocketException

    public class java.net.SocketException
    extends java.io.IOException
    extends java.lang.Exception
    extends java.lang.Throwable
    extends java.lang.Object

## Constructors

    public  SocketException(String msg)
    public  SocketException()

# SocketImpl

    public abstract class java.net.
    SocketImpl

    implements java.net.SocketOptions
    extends java.lang.Object

## Fields

    protected java.net.InetAddress address
    protected java.io.FileDescriptor fd
    protected int localport
    protected int port

## Methods

    protected abstract void accept(
    SocketImpl s)
    protected abstract int available()
    protected abstract void bind(InetAddress
    host,int port)
    protected abstract void close()
    protected abstract void connect(String
    host,int port)
    protected abstract void connect(
    InetAddress address,int port)
    protected abstract void create(boolean
    stream)
    protected FileDescriptor
    getFileDescriptor()
    protected InetAddress getInetAddress()
    protected abstract InputStream
    getInputStream()
    protected int getLocalPort()
    protected abstract OutputStream
    getOutputStream()
    protected int getPort()
    protected abstract void listen(int
    backlog)
    public String toString()

# SocketPermission

    public final class java.net.
    SocketPermission
    implements java.io.Serializable
    extends java.security.Permission
    extends java.lang.Object

## Constructors

    public static  SocketPermission(String
    host,String action)
     SocketPermission()

## Methods

    public boolean equals(Object obj)
    public String getActions()
    public int hashCode()
    public boolean implies(Permission p)
    public PermissionCollection
    newPermissionCollection()

# SocketSecurityException

    public class java.rmi.server.
    SocketSecurityException
    extends java.rmi.server.ExportException
    extends java.rmi.RemoteException
    extends java.io.IOException
    extends java.lang.Exception
    extends java.lang.Throwable

extends java.lang.Object

### Constructors
```
public  SocketSecurityException(String s)
public  SocketSecurityException(String s,
Exception ex)
```

## SoftBevelBorder
```
public class javax.swing.border.
SoftBevelBorder
extends javax.swing.border.BevelBorder
extends javax.swing.border.
AbstractBorder
extends java.lang.Object
```

### Constructors
```
public  SoftBevelBorder(int bevelType)
public  SoftBevelBorder(int bevelType,
Color highlight,Color shadow)
public  SoftBevelBorder(int bevelType,
Color highlightOuter,Color
highlightInner,Color shadowOuter,Color
shadowInner)
```

### Methods
```
public Insets getBorderInsets(Component
c)
public boolean isBorderOpaque()
public void paintBorder(Component c,
Graphics g,int x,int y,int width,int
height)
```

## SoftReference
```
public class java.lang.ref.
SoftReference
extends java.lang.ref.Reference
extends java.lang.Object
```

### Constructors
```
public  SoftReference(Object referent)
public  SoftReference(Object referent,
ReferenceQueue q)
```

### Methods
```
public Object get()
```

## SplitPaneUI
```
public abstract class javax.swing.plaf.
SplitPaneUI
extends javax.swing.plaf.ComponentUI
extends java.lang.Object
```

### Methods
```
public abstract void
finishedPaintingChildren(JSplitPane jc,
Graphics g)
public abstract int getDividerLocation(
JSplitPane jc)
public abstract int
getMaximumDividerLocation(JSplitPane jc)
public abstract int
getMinimumDividerLocation(JSplitPane jc)
```

```
public abstract void
resetToPreferredSizes(JSplitPane jc)
public abstract void setDividerLocation(
JSplitPane jc,int location)
```

## SQLException
```
public class java.sql.SQLException
extends java.lang.Exception
extends java.lang.Throwable
extends java.lang.Object
```

### Constructors
```
public  SQLException(String reason,
String SQLState,int vendorCode)
public  SQLException(String reason,
String SQLState)
public  SQLException(String reason)
public  SQLException()
```

### Methods
```
public int getErrorCode()
public SQLException getNextException()
public String getSQLState()
public synchronized void
setNextException(SQLException ex)
```

## SQLWarning
```
public class java.sql.SQLWarning
extends java.sql.SQLException
extends java.lang.Exception
extends java.lang.Throwable
extends java.lang.Object
```

### Constructors
```
public  SQLWarning(String reason,String
SQLstate,int vendorCode)
public  SQLWarning(String reason,String
SQLstate)
public  SQLWarning(String reason)
public  SQLWarning()
```

### Methods
```
public SQLWarning getNextWarning()
public void setNextWarning(SQLWarning w)
```

## Stack
```
public class java.util.Stack
extends java.util.Vector
extends java.util.AbstractList
extends java.util.AbstractCollection
extends java.lang.Object
```

### Constructors
```
public  Stack()
```

### Methods
```
public boolean empty()
public synchronized Object peek()
public synchronized Object pop()
public Object push(Object item)
public synchronized int search(Object o)
```

# StackOverflowError

public class java.lang.
StackOverflowError
extends java.lang.VirtualMachineError
extends java.lang.Error
extends java.lang.Throwable
extends java.lang.Object

## Constructors

public StackOverflowError()
public StackOverflowError(String s)

# StateEdit

public class javax.swing.undo.StateEdit
extends javax.swing.undo.
AbstractUndoableEdit
extends java.lang.Object

## Fields

protected javax.swing.undo.StateEditable
object
protected java.util.Hashtable postState
protected java.util.Hashtable preState
protected final static java.lang.String
RCSID
protected java.lang.String undoRedoName

## Constructors

public StateEdit(StateEditable anObject)
public StateEdit(StateEditable anObject,
String name)

## Methods

public void end()
public String getPresentationName()
protected void init(StateEditable
anObject,String name)
public void redo()
protected void removeRedundantState()
public void undo()

# StreamCorruptedException

public class java.io.
StreamCorruptedException
extends java.io.ObjectStreamException
extends java.io.IOException
extends java.lang.Exception
extends java.lang.Throwable
extends java.lang.Object

## Constructors

public StreamCorruptedException(String
reason)
public StreamCorruptedException()

# StreamTokenizer

public class java.io.StreamTokenizer
extends java.lang.Object

## Fields

public double nval
public java.lang.String sval

public int ttype
public final static int TT_EOF
public final static int TT_EOL
public final static int TT_NUMBER
public final static int TT_WORD

## Constructors

private StreamTokenizer()
public StreamTokenizer(InputStream is)
public StreamTokenizer(Reader r)

## Methods

public void commentChar(int ch)
public void eolIsSignificant(boolean
flag)
public int lineno()
public void lowerCaseMode(boolean fl)
public int nextToken()
public void ordinaryChar(int ch)
public void ordinaryChars(int low,int hi)
public void parseNumbers()
public void pushBack()
public void quoteChar(int ch)
public void resetSyntax()
public void slashSlashComments(boolean
flag)
public void slashStarComments(boolean
flag)
public String toString()
public void whitespaceChars(int low,int
hi)
public void wordChars(int low,int hi)

# String

public final class java.lang.String
implements java.lang.Comparable
implements java.io.Serializable
extends java.lang.Object

## Fields

public final static java.util.Comparator
CASE_INSENSITIVE_ORDER

## Constructors

public String()
public String(String value)
public String(char value)
public String(char value,int offset,int
count)
public String(byte ascii,int hibyte,int
offset,int count)
public String(byte ascii,int hibyte)
private String()
public String(byte bytes,int offset,int
length,String enc)
public String(byte bytes,String enc)
public String(byte bytes,int offset,int
length)
public String(byte bytes)
public String(StringBuffer buffer)
private String()

## Methods

```
public char charAt(int index)
public int compareTo(String
anotherString)
public int compareTo(Object o)
public int compareToIgnoreCase(String
str)
public String concat(String str)
public static String copyValueOf(char
data,int offset,int count)
public static String copyValueOf(char
data)
public boolean endsWith(String suffix)
public boolean equals(Object anObject)
public boolean equalsIgnoreCase(String
anotherString)
public void getBytes(int srcBegin,int
srcEnd,byte dst,int dstBegin)
public byte getBytes(String enc)
public byte getBytes()
public void getChars(int srcBegin,int
srcEnd,char dst,int dstBegin)
public int hashCode()
public int indexOf(int ch)
public int indexOf(int ch,int fromIndex)
public int indexOf(String str)
public int indexOf(String str,int
fromIndex)
public native String intern()
public int lastIndexOf(int ch)
public int lastIndexOf(int ch,int
fromIndex)
public int lastIndexOf(String str)
public int lastIndexOf(String str,int
fromIndex)
public int length()
public boolean regionMatches(int toffset,
String other,int ooffset,int len)
public boolean regionMatches(boolean
ignoreCase,int toffset,String other,int
ooffset,int len)
public String replace(char oldChar,char
newChar)
public boolean startsWith(String prefix,
int toffset)
public boolean startsWith(String prefix)
public String substring(int beginIndex)
public String substring(int beginIndex,
int endIndex)
public char toCharArray()
public String toLowerCase(Locale locale)
public String toLowerCase()
public String toString()
public String toUpperCase(Locale locale)
public String toUpperCase()
public String trim()
public static String valueOf(Object obj)
public static String valueOf(char data)
public static String valueOf(char data,
int offset,int count)
public static String valueOf(boolean b)
public static String valueOf(char c)
public static String valueOf(int i)
public static String valueOf(long l)
```

```
public static String valueOf(float f)
public static String valueOf(double d)
```

## StringBuffer

```
public final class java.lang.
StringBuffer
implements java.io.Serializable
extends java.lang.Object
```

### Constructors

```
public  StringBuffer()
public  StringBuffer(int length)
public  StringBuffer(String str)
```

### Methods

```
public synchronized StringBuffer append(
Object obj)
public synchronized StringBuffer append(
String str)
public synchronized StringBuffer append(
char str)
public synchronized StringBuffer append(
char str,int offset,int len)
public StringBuffer append(boolean b)
public synchronized StringBuffer append(
char c)
public StringBuffer append(int i)
public StringBuffer append(long l)
public StringBuffer append(float f)
public StringBuffer append(double d)
public int capacity()
public synchronized char charAt(int
index)
public synchronized StringBuffer delete(
int start,int end)
public synchronized StringBuffer
deleteCharAt(int index)
public synchronized void ensureCapacity(
int minimumCapacity)
public synchronized void getChars(int
srcBegin,int srcEnd,char dst,int
dstBegin)
public synchronized StringBuffer insert(
int index,char str,int offset,int len)
public synchronized StringBuffer insert(
int offset,Object obj)
public synchronized StringBuffer insert(
int offset,String str)
public synchronized StringBuffer insert(
int offset,char str)
public StringBuffer insert(int offset,
boolean b)
public synchronized StringBuffer insert(
int offset,char c)
public StringBuffer insert(int offset,
int i)
public StringBuffer insert(int offset,
long l)
public StringBuffer insert(int offset,
float f)
public StringBuffer insert(int offset,
double d)
public int length()
```

```
public synchronized StringBuffer replace(
int start,int end,String str)
public synchronized StringBuffer reverse(
)
public synchronized void setCharAt(int
index,char ch)
public synchronized void setLength(int
newLength)
public String substring(int start)
public synchronized String substring(int
start,int end)
public String toString()
```

# StringBufferInputStream

```
public class java.io.
StringBufferInputStream
extends java.io.InputStream
extends java.lang.Object
```

### Fields

```
protected java.lang.String buffer
protected int count
protected int pos
```

### Constructors

```
public  StringBufferInputStream(String s)
```

### Methods

```
public synchronized int available()
public synchronized int read()
public synchronized int read(byte b,int
off,int len)
public synchronized void reset()
public synchronized long skip(long n)
```

# StringCharacterIterator

```
public final class java.text.
StringCharacterIterator
implements java.text.CharacterIterator
extends java.lang.Object
```

### Constructors

```
public  StringCharacterIterator(String
text)
public  StringCharacterIterator(String
text,int pos)
public  StringCharacterIterator(String
text,int begin,int end,int pos)
```

### Methods

```
public Object clone()
public char current()
public boolean equals(Object obj)
public char first()
public int getBeginIndex()
public int getEndIndex()
public int getIndex()
public int hashCode()
public char last()
public char next()
public char previous()
public char setIndex(int p)
public void setText(String text)
```

# StringContent

```
public final class javax.swing.text.
StringContent
implements AbstractDocument.Content
implements java.io.Serializable
extends java.lang.Object
```

### Constructors

```
public  StringContent()
public  StringContent(int initialLength)
```

### Methods

```
public Position createPosition(int
offset)
public void getChars(int where,int len,
Segment chars)
protected Vector getPositionsInRange(
Vector v,int offset,int length)
public String getString(int where,int
len)
public UndoableEdit insertString(int
where,String str)
public int length()
public UndoableEdit remove(int where,int
nitems)
protected void updateUndoPositions(
Vector positions)
```

# StringIndexOutOfBoundsException

```
public class java.lang.
StringIndexOutOfBoundsException
extends java.lang.
IndexOutOfBoundsException
extends java.lang.RuntimeException
extends java.lang.Exception
extends java.lang.Throwable
extends java.lang.Object
```

### Constructors

```
public  StringIndexOutOfBoundsException()
public  StringIndexOutOfBoundsException(
String s)
public  StringIndexOutOfBoundsException(
int index)
```

# StringReader

```
public class java.io.StringReader
extends java.io.Reader
extends java.lang.Object
```

### Constructors

```
public  StringReader(String s)
```

### Methods

```
public void close()
public void mark(int readAheadLimit)
public boolean markSupported()
public int read()
public int read(char cbuf,int off,int
len)
public boolean ready()
public void reset()
public long skip(long ns)
```

## StringSelection

```
public class java.awt.datatransfer.
StringSelection
implements java.awt.datatransfer.
ClipboardOwner
implements java.awt.datatransfer.
Transferable
extends java.lang.Object
```

### Constructors
```
public  StringSelection(String data)
```

### Methods
```
public synchronized Object
getTransferData(DataFlavor flavor)
public synchronized DataFlavor
getTransferDataFlavors()
public boolean isDataFlavorSupported(
DataFlavor flavor)
public void lostOwnership(Clipboard
clipboard,Transferable contents)
```

## StringTokenizer

```
public class java.util.StringTokenizer
implements java.util.Enumeration
extends java.lang.Object
```

### Constructors
```
public  StringTokenizer(String str,
String delim,boolean returnTokens)
public  StringTokenizer(String str,
String delim)
public  StringTokenizer(String str)
```

### Methods
```
public int countTokens()
public boolean hasMoreElements()
public boolean hasMoreTokens()
public Object nextElement()
public String nextToken()
public String nextToken(String delim)
```

## StringWriter

```
public class java.io.StringWriter
extends java.io.Writer
extends java.lang.Object
```

### Constructors
```
public  StringWriter()
public  StringWriter(int initialSize)
```

### Methods
```
public void close()
public void flush()
public StringBuffer getBuffer()
public String toString()
public void write(int c)
public void write(char cbuf,int off,int
len)
public void write(String str)
public void write(String str,int off,int
len)
```

## StubNotFoundException

```
public class java.rmi.
StubNotFoundException
extends java.rmi.RemoteException
extends java.io.IOException
extends java.lang.Exception
extends java.lang.Throwable
extends java.lang.Object
```

### Constructors
```
public  StubNotFoundException(String s)
public  StubNotFoundException(String s,
Exception ex)
```

## StyleConstants

```
public class javax.swing.text.
StyleConstants
extends java.lang.Object
```

### Fields
```
public final static java.lang.Object
Alignment
public final static int ALIGN_CENTER
public final static int ALIGN_JUSTIFIED
public final static int ALIGN_LEFT
public final static int ALIGN_RIGHT
public final static java.lang.Object
Background
public final static java.lang.Object
BidiLevel
public final static java.lang.Object
Bold
public final static java.lang.Object
ComponentAttribute
public final static java.lang.String
ComponentElementName
public final static java.lang.Object
ComposedTextAttribute
public final static java.lang.Object
FirstLineIndent
public final static java.lang.Object
FontFamily
public final static java.lang.Object
FontSize
public final static java.lang.Object
Foreground
public final static java.lang.Object
IconAttribute
public final static java.lang.String
IconElementName
public final static java.lang.Object
Italic
public final static java.lang.Object
LeftIndent
public final static java.lang.Object
LineSpacing
public final static java.lang.Object
ModelAttribute
public final static java.lang.Object
NameAttribute
public final static java.lang.Object
Orientation
```

public final static java.lang.Object
ResolveAttribute
public final static java.lang.Object
RightIndent
public final static java.lang.Object
SpaceAbove
public final static java.lang.Object
SpaceBelow
public final static java.lang.Object
StrikeThrough
public final static java.lang.Object
Subscript
public final static java.lang.Object
Superscript
public final static java.lang.Object
TabSet
public final static java.lang.Object
Underline

### Constructors
static  StyleConstants()

### Methods
public static int getAlignment(
AttributeSet a)
public static Color getBackground(
AttributeSet a)
public static int getBidiLevel(
AttributeSet a)
public static Component getComponent(
AttributeSet a)
public static float getFirstLineIndent(
AttributeSet a)
public static String getFontFamily(
AttributeSet a)
public static int getFontSize(
AttributeSet a)
public static Color getForeground(
AttributeSet a)
public static Icon getIcon(AttributeSet
a)
public static float getLeftIndent(
AttributeSet a)
public static float getLineSpacing(
AttributeSet a)
public static float getRightIndent(
AttributeSet a)
public static float getSpaceAbove(
AttributeSet a)
public static float getSpaceBelow(
AttributeSet a)
public static TabSet getTabSet(
AttributeSet a)
public static boolean isBold(
AttributeSet a)
public static boolean isItalic(
AttributeSet a)
public static boolean isStrikeThrough(
AttributeSet a)
public static boolean isSubscript(
AttributeSet a)
public static boolean isSuperscript(
AttributeSet a)

public static boolean isUnderline(
AttributeSet a)
public static void setAlignment(
MutableAttributeSet a,int align)
public static void setBackground(
MutableAttributeSet a,Color fg)
public static void setBidiLevel(
MutableAttributeSet a,int o)
public static void setBold(
MutableAttributeSet a,boolean b)
public static void setComponent(
MutableAttributeSet a,Component c)
public static void setFirstLineIndent(
MutableAttributeSet a,float i)
public static void setFontFamily(
MutableAttributeSet a,String fam)
public static void setFontSize(
MutableAttributeSet a,int s)
public static void setForeground(
MutableAttributeSet a,Color fg)
public static void setIcon(
MutableAttributeSet a,Icon c)
public static void setItalic(
MutableAttributeSet a,boolean b)
public static void setLeftIndent(
MutableAttributeSet a,float i)
public static void setLineSpacing(
MutableAttributeSet a,float i)
public static void setRightIndent(
MutableAttributeSet a,float i)
public static void setSpaceAbove(
MutableAttributeSet a,float i)
public static void setSpaceBelow(
MutableAttributeSet a,float i)
public static void setStrikeThrough(
MutableAttributeSet a,boolean b)
public static void setSubscript(
MutableAttributeSet a,boolean b)
public static void setSuperscript(
MutableAttributeSet a,boolean b)
public static void setTabSet(
MutableAttributeSet a,TabSet tabs)
public static void setUnderline(
MutableAttributeSet a,boolean b)
public String toString()

## StyleContext
public class javax.swing.text.
StyleContext
implements AbstractDocument.
AttributeContext
implements java.io.Serializable
extends java.lang.Object

### Fields
public final static java.lang.String
DEFAULT_STYLE

### Constructors
public  StyleContext()

## Methods

public synchronized AttributeSet
addAttribute(AttributeSet old,Object
name,Object value)
public synchronized AttributeSet
addAttributes(AttributeSet old,
AttributeSet attr)
public void addChangeListener(
ChangeListener l)
public Style addStyle(String nm,Style
parent)
protected MutableAttributeSet
createLargeAttributeSet(AttributeSet a)
protected SmallAttributeSet
createSmallAttributeSet(AttributeSet a)
public Color getBackground(AttributeSet
attr)
protected int getCompressionThreshold()
public final static StyleContext
getDefaultStyleContext()
public AttributeSet getEmptySet()
public Font getFont(AttributeSet attr)
public Font getFont(String family,int
style,int size)
public FontMetrics getFontMetrics(Font f)
public Color getForeground(AttributeSet
attr)
public static Object getStaticAttribute(
Object key)
public static Object
getStaticAttributeKey(Object key)
public Style getStyle(String nm)
public Enumeration getStyleNames()
public void readAttributes(
ObjectInputStream in,MutableAttributeSet
a)
public static void readAttributeSet(
ObjectInputStream in,MutableAttributeSet
a)
public void reclaim(AttributeSet a)
public static void
registerStaticAttributeKey(Object key)
public synchronized AttributeSet
removeAttribute(AttributeSet old,Object
name)
public synchronized AttributeSet
removeAttributes(AttributeSet old,
Enumeration names)
public synchronized AttributeSet
removeAttributes(AttributeSet old,
AttributeSet attrs)
public void removeChangeListener(
ChangeListener l)
public void removeStyle(String nm)
public String toString()
public void writeAttributes(
ObjectOutputStream out,AttributeSet a)
public static void writeAttributeSet(
ObjectOutputStream out,AttributeSet a)

## StyledEditorKit

public class javax.swing.text.
StyledEditorKit

extends javax.swing.text.
DefaultEditorKit
extends javax.swing.text.EditorKit
extends java.lang.Object

### Methods

public Object clone()
public Document createDefaultDocument()
protected void createInputAttributes(
Element element,MutableAttributeSet set)
public void deinstall(JEditorPane c)
public Action getActions()
public Element getCharacterAttributeRun()
public MutableAttributeSet
getInputAttributes()
public ViewFactory getViewFactory()
public void install(JEditorPane c)

## StyleSheet

public class javax.swing.text.html.
StyleSheet
extends javax.swing.text.StyleContext
extends java.lang.Object

### Constructors

public StyleSheet()

### Methods

public void addRule(String rule)
public Color getBackground(AttributeSet
a)
public BoxPainter getBoxPainter(
AttributeSet a)
public AttributeSet getDeclaration(
String decl)
public Font getFont(AttributeSet a)
public Color getForeground(AttributeSet
a)
public static int getIndexOfSize(float
pt)
public ListPainter getListPainter(
AttributeSet a)
public float getPointSize(int index)
public float getPointSize(String size)
public Style getRule(Tag t,Element e)
public Style getRule(String selector)
public AttributeSet getViewAttributes(
View v)
public void loadRules(Reader in,URL ref)
public void setBaseFontSize(int sz)
public void setBaseFontSize(String size)
public Color stringToColor(String str)
public static AttributeSet
translateHTMLToCSS(AttributeSet
htmlAttrSet)

## SwingPropertyChangeSupport

public final class javax.swing.event.
SwingPropertyChangeSupport
extends java.beans.
PropertyChangeSupport
extends java.lang.Object

## Constructors

```
public  SwingPropertyChangeSupport(
Object sourceBean)
```

## Methods

```
public synchronized void
addPropertyChangeListener(
PropertyChangeListener listener)
public synchronized void
addPropertyChangeListener(String
propertyName,PropertyChangeListener
listener)
public void firePropertyChange(String
propertyName,Object oldValue,Object
newValue)
public void firePropertyChange(
PropertyChangeEvent evt)
public synchronized boolean hasListeners(
String propertyName)
public synchronized void
removePropertyChangeListener(
PropertyChangeListener listener)
public synchronized void
removePropertyChangeListener(String
propertyName,PropertyChangeListener
listener)
```

# SwingUtilities

```
public class javax.swing.SwingUtilities
implements javax.swing.SwingConstants
extends java.lang.Object
```

## Constructors

```
private  SwingUtilities()
```

## Methods

```
public static Rectangle
computeDifference(Rectangle rectA,
Rectangle rectB)
public static Rectangle
computeIntersection(int x,int y,int
width,int height,Rectangle dest)
public static int computeStringWidth(
FontMetrics fm,String str)
public static Rectangle computeUnion(int
x,int y,int width,int height,Rectangle
dest)
public static MouseEvent
convertMouseEvent(Component source,
MouseEvent sourceEvent,Component
destination)
public static Point convertPoint(
Component source,Point aPoint,Component
destination)
public static Point convertPoint(
Component source,int x,int y,Component
destination)
public static void
convertPointFromScreen(Point p,Component
c)
public static void convertPointToScreen(
Point p,Component c)
```

```
public static Rectangle convertRectangle(
Component source,Rectangle aRectangle,
Component destination)
public static Component findFocusOwner(
Component c)
public static Accessible getAccessibleAt(
Component c,Point p)
public static Accessible
getAccessibleChild(Component c,int i)
public static int
getAccessibleChildrenCount(Component c)
public static int
getAccessibleIndexInParent(Component c)
public static AccessibleStateSet
getAccessibleStateSet(Component c)
public static Container getAncestorNamed(
String name,Component comp)
public static Container
getAncestorOfClass(Class c,Component
comp)
public static Component
getDeepestComponentAt(Component parent,
int x,int y)
public static Rectangle getLocalBounds(
Component aComponent)
public static Component getRoot(
Component c)
public static JRootPane getRootPane(
Component c)
public static void invokeAndWait(
Runnable doRun)
public static void invokeLater(Runnable
doRun)
public static boolean isDescendingFrom(
Component a,Component b)
public static boolean
isEventDispatchThread()
public static boolean isLeftMouseButton(
MouseEvent anEvent)
public static boolean
isMiddleMouseButton(MouseEvent anEvent)
public final static boolean
isRectangleContainingRectangle(Rectangle
a,Rectangle b)
public static boolean isRightMouseButton(
MouseEvent anEvent)
public static String layoutCompoundLabel(
JComponent c,FontMetrics fm,String text,
Icon icon,int verticalAlignment,int
horizontalAlignment,int
verticalTextPosition,int
horizontalTextPosition,Rectangle viewR,
Rectangle iconR,Rectangle textR,int
textIconGap)
public static String layoutCompoundLabel(
FontMetrics fm,String text,Icon icon,int
verticalAlignment,int
horizontalAlignment,int
verticalTextPosition,int
horizontalTextPosition,Rectangle viewR,
Rectangle iconR,Rectangle textR,int
textIconGap)
```

```
public static void paintComponent(
Graphics g,Component c,Container p,int x,
int y,int w,int h)
public static void paintComponent(
Graphics g,Component c,Container p,
Rectangle r)
public static void updateComponentTreeUI(
Component c)
public static Window windowForComponent(
Component aComponent)
```

## SyncFailedException

```
public class java.io.
SyncFailedException
extends java.io.IOException
extends java.lang.Exception
extends java.lang.Throwable
extends java.lang.Object
```

### Constructors
```
public  SyncFailedException(String desc)
```

## System

```
public final class java.lang.System
extends java.lang.Object
```

### Fields
```
public final static java.io.PrintStream
err
public final static java.io.InputStream
in
public final static java.io.PrintStream
out
```

### Constructors
```
private static  System()
```

### Methods
```
public static native void arraycopy(
Object src,int src_position,Object dst,
int dst_position,int length)
public static native long
currentTimeMillis()
public static void exit(int status)
public static void gc()
public static String getenv(String name)
public static Properties getProperties()
public static String getProperty(String
key)
public static String getProperty(String
key,String def)
public static SecurityManager
getSecurityManager()
public static native int
identityHashCode(Object x)
public static void load(String filename)
public static void loadLibrary(String
libname)
public static native String
mapLibraryName(String libname)
public static void runFinalization()
public static void runFinalizersOnExit(
boolean value)
```

```
public static void setErr(PrintStream
err)
public static void setIn(InputStream in)
public static void setOut(PrintStream
out)
public static void setProperties(
Properties props)
public static String setProperty(String
key,String value)
public static synchronized void
setSecurityManager(SecurityManager s)
```

## SystemColor

```
public final class java.awt.SystemColor
implements java.io.Serializable
extends java.awt.Color
extends java.lang.Object
```

### Fields
```
public final static java.awt.SystemColor
activeCaption
public final static java.awt.SystemColor
activeCaptionBorder
public final static java.awt.SystemColor
activeCaptionText
public final static int ACTIVE_CAPTION
public final static int ACTIVE_CAPTION_
BORDER
public final static int ACTIVE_CAPTION_
TEXT
public final static int CONTROL
public final static java.awt.SystemColor
control
public final static java.awt.SystemColor
controlDkShadow
public final static java.awt.SystemColor
controlHighlight
public final static java.awt.SystemColor
controlLtHighlight
public final static java.awt.SystemColor
controlShadow
public final static java.awt.SystemColor
controlText
public final static int CONTROL_DK_
SHADOW
public final static int CONTROL_
HIGHLIGHT
public final static int CONTROL_LT_
HIGHLIGHT
public final static int CONTROL_SHADOW
public final static int CONTROL_TEXT
public final static int DESKTOP
public final static java.awt.SystemColor
desktop
public final static java.awt.SystemColor
inactiveCaption
public final static java.awt.SystemColor
inactiveCaptionBorder
public final static java.awt.SystemColor
inactiveCaptionText
public final static int INACTIVE_
CAPTION
```

public final static int INACTIVE_CAPTION_
BORDER
public final static int INACTIVE_CAPTION_
TEXT
public final static int INFO
public final static java.awt.SystemColor
info
public final static java.awt.SystemColor
infoText
public final static int INFO_TEXT
public final static int MENU
public final static java.awt.SystemColor
menu
public final static java.awt.SystemColor
menuText
public final static int MENU_TEXT
public final static int NUM_COLORS
public final static int SCROLLBAR
public final static java.awt.SystemColor
scrollbar
public final static int TEXT
public final static java.awt.SystemColor
text
public final static java.awt.SystemColor
textHighlight
public final static java.awt.SystemColor
textHighlightText
public final static java.awt.SystemColor
textInactiveText
public final static java.awt.SystemColor
textText
public final static int TEXT_HIGHLIGHT
public final static int TEXT_HIGHLIGHT_
TEXT
public final static int TEXT_INACTIVE_
TEXT
public final static int TEXT_TEXT
public final static int WINDOW
public final static java.awt.SystemColor
window
public final static java.awt.SystemColor
windowBorder
public final static java.awt.SystemColor
windowText
public final static int WINDOW_BORDER
public final static int WINDOW_TEXT

### Constructors
private  SystemColor()

### Methods
public PaintContext createContext(
ColorModel cm,Rectangle r,Rectangle2D
r2d,AffineTransform xform,RenderingHints
hints)
public int getRGB()
public String toString()

## SystemFlavorMap
public final class java.awt.datatransfer.
SystemFlavorMap
implements java.awt.datatransfer.
FlavorMap

extends java.lang.Object

### Constructors
private  SystemFlavorMap()

### Methods
public static DataFlavor
decodeDataFlavor(String atom)
public static String decodeJavaMIMEType(
String atom)
public static String encodeDataFlavor(
DataFlavor df)
public static String encodeJavaMIMEType(
String mimeType)
public static FlavorMap
getDefaultFlavorMap()
public synchronized Map
getFlavorsForNatives(String natives)
public synchronized Map
getNativesForFlavors(DataFlavor flavors)
public static boolean isJavaMIMEType(
String atom)

## TabbedPaneUI
public abstract class javax.swing.plaf.
TabbedPaneUI
extends javax.swing.plaf.ComponentUI
extends java.lang.Object

### Methods
public abstract Rectangle getTabBounds(
JTabbedPane pane,int index)
public abstract int getTabRunCount(
JTabbedPane pane)
public abstract int tabForCoordinate(
JTabbedPane pane,int x,int y)

## TableColumn
public class javax.swing.table.
TableColumn
implements java.io.Serializable
extends java.lang.Object
extends java.lang.Object

### Fields
protected javax.swing.table.
TableCellEditor cellEditor
protected javax.swing.table.
TableCellRenderer cellRenderer
public final static java.lang.String
CELL_RENDERER_PROPERTY
public final static java.lang.String
COLUMN_WIDTH_PROPERTY
protected javax.swing.table.
TableCellRenderer headerRenderer
protected java.lang.Object headerValue
public final static java.lang.String
HEADER_RENDERER_PROPERTY
public final static java.lang.String
HEADER_VALUE_PROPERTY
protected java.lang.Object identifier
protected boolean isResizable
protected int maxWidth

```
protected int minWidth
protected int modelIndex
protected transient int
resizedPostingDisableCount
protected int width
```

### Constructors
```
public  TableColumn()
public  TableColumn(int modelIndex)
public  TableColumn(int modelIndex,int
width)
public  TableColumn(int modelIndex,int
width,TableCellRenderer cellRenderer,
TableCellEditor cellEditor)
```

### Methods
```
public synchronized void
addPropertyChangeListener(
PropertyChangeListener listener)
protected TableCellRenderer
createDefaultHeaderRenderer()
public void disableResizedPosting()
public void enableResizedPosting()
public TableCellEditor getCellEditor()
public TableCellRenderer getCellRenderer(
)
public TableCellRenderer
getHeaderRenderer()
public Object getHeaderValue()
public Object getIdentifier()
public int getMaxWidth()
public int getMinWidth()
public int getModelIndex()
public int getPreferredWidth()
public boolean getResizable()
public int getWidth()
public synchronized void
removePropertyChangeListener(
PropertyChangeListener listener)
public void setCellEditor(
TableCellEditor anEditor)
public void setCellRenderer(
TableCellRenderer aRenderer)
public void setHeaderRenderer(
TableCellRenderer aRenderer)
public void setHeaderValue(Object aValue)
public void setIdentifier(Object
anIdentifier)
public void setMaxWidth(int maxWidth)
public void setMinWidth(int minWidth)
public void setModelIndex(int anIndex)
public void setPreferredWidth(int
preferredWidth)
public void setResizable(boolean flag)
public void setWidth(int width)
public void sizeWidthToFit()
```

## TableColumnModelEvent
```
public class javax.swing.event.
TableColumnModelEvent
extends java.util.EventObject
extends java.lang.Object
```

### Fields
```
protected int fromIndex
protected int toIndex
```

### Constructors
```
public  TableColumnModelEvent(
TableColumnModel source,int from,int to)
```

### Methods
```
public int getFromIndex()
public int getToIndex()
```

## TableHeaderUI
```
public abstract class javax.swing.plaf.
TableHeaderUI
extends javax.swing.plaf.ComponentUI
extends java.lang.Object
```

## TableModelEvent
```
public class javax.swing.event.
TableModelEvent
extends java.util.EventObject
extends java.lang.Object
```

### Fields
```
public final static int ALL_COLUMNS
protected int column
public final static int DELETE
protected int firstRow
public final static int HEADER_ROW
public final static int INSERT
protected int lastRow
protected int type
public final static int UPDATE
```

### Constructors
```
public  TableModelEvent(TableModel
source)
public  TableModelEvent(TableModel
source,int row)
public  TableModelEvent(TableModel
source,int firstRow,int lastRow)
public  TableModelEvent(TableModel
source,int firstRow,int lastRow,int
column)
public  TableModelEvent(TableModel
source,int firstRow,int lastRow,int
column,int type)
```

### Methods
```
public int getColumn()
public int getFirstRow()
public int getLastRow()
public int getType()
```

## TableUI
```
public abstract class javax.swing.plaf.
TableUI
extends javax.swing.plaf.ComponentUI
extends java.lang.Object
```

## TableView

public abstract class javax.swing.text.
TableView
extends javax.swing.text.BoxView
extends javax.swing.text.CompositeView
extends javax.swing.text.View
extends java.lang.Object

### Constructors

public  TableView(Element elem)

### Methods

protected SizeRequirements
calculateMinorAxisRequirements(int axis,
SizeRequirements r)
protected TableCell createTableCell(
Element elem)
protected TableRow createTableRow(
Element elem)
protected View getViewAtPosition(int pos,
Rectangle a)
protected void layoutColumns(int
targetSpan,int offsets,int spans,
SizeRequirements reqs)
protected void layoutMinorAxis(int
targetSpan,int axis,int offsets,int
spans)
protected void loadChildren(ViewFactory
f)

## TabSet

public class javax.swing.text.TabSet
implements java.io.Serializable
extends java.lang.Object

### Constructors

public  TabSet(TabStop tabs)

### Methods

public TabStop getTab(int index)
public TabStop getTabAfter(float
location)
public int getTabCount()
public int getTabIndex(TabStop tab)
public int getTabIndexAfter(float
location)
public String toString()

## TabStop

public class javax.swing.text.TabStop
implements java.io.Serializable
extends java.lang.Object

### Fields

public final static int ALIGN_BAR
public final static int ALIGN_CENTER
public final static int ALIGN_DECIMAL
public final static int ALIGN_LEFT
public final static int ALIGN_RIGHT
public final static int LEAD_DOTS
public final static int LEAD_EQUALS
public final static int LEAD_HYPHENS
public final static int LEAD_NONE

public final static int LEAD_THICKLINE
public final static int LEAD_UNDERLINE

### Constructors

public  TabStop(float pos)
public  TabStop(float pos,int align,int
leader)

### Methods

public boolean equals(Object other)
public int getAlignment()
public int getLeader()
public float getPosition()
public int hashCode()
public String toString()

## TagElement

public class javax.swing.text.html.
parser.TagElement
extends java.lang.Object

### Constructors

public  TagElement(Element elem)
public  TagElement(Element elem,boolean
fictional)

### Methods

public boolean breaksFlow()
public boolean fictional()
public Element getElement()
public Tag getHTMLTag()
public boolean isPreformatted()

## TextAction

public abstract class javax.swing.text.
TextAction
extends javax.swing.AbstractAction
extends java.lang.Object

### Constructors

public  TextAction(String name)

### Methods

public final static Action augmentList(
Action list1,Action list2)
protected final JTextComponent
getFocusedComponent()
protected final JTextComponent
getTextComponent(ActionEvent e)

## TextArea

public class java.awt.TextArea
extends java.awt.TextComponent
extends java.awt.Component
extends java.lang.Object

### Fields

public final static int SCROLLBARS_BOTH
public final static int SCROLLBARS_
HORIZONTAL_ONLY
public final static int SCROLLBARS_NONE
public final static int SCROLLBARS_
VERTICAL_ONLY

## Constructors

```
public static  TextArea()
public  TextArea(String text)
public  TextArea(int rows,int columns)
public  TextArea(String text,int rows,
int columns)
public  TextArea(String text,int rows,
int columns,int scrollbars)
```

## Methods

```
public void addNotify()
public void append(String str)
public synchronized void appendText(
String str)
public int getColumns()
public Dimension getMinimumSize(int rows,
int columns)
public Dimension getMinimumSize()
public Dimension getPreferredSize(int
rows,int columns)
public Dimension getPreferredSize()
public int getRows()
public int getScrollbarVisibility()
public void insert(String str,int pos)
public synchronized void insertText(
String str,int pos)
public Dimension minimumSize(int rows,
int columns)
public Dimension minimumSize()
protected String paramString()
public Dimension preferredSize(int rows,
int columns)
public Dimension preferredSize()
public void replaceRange(String str,int
start,int end)
public synchronized void replaceText(
String str,int start,int end)
public void setColumns(int columns)
public void setRows(int rows)
```

# TextAttribute

```
public final class java.awt.font.
TextAttribute
extends java.lang.Object
```

## Fields

```
public final static java.awt.font.
TextAttribute BACKGROUND
public final static java.awt.font.
TextAttribute BIDI_EMBEDDING
public final static java.awt.font.
TextAttribute CHAR_REPLACEMENT
public final static java.awt.font.
TextAttribute FAMILY
public final static java.awt.font.
TextAttribute FONT
public final static java.awt.font.
TextAttribute FOREGROUND
public final static java.awt.font.
TextAttribute INPUT_METHOD_HIGHLIGHT
public final static java.awt.font.
TextAttribute JUSTIFICATION
```

```
public final static java.lang.Float
JUSTIFICATION_FULL
public final static java.lang.Float
JUSTIFICATION_NONE
public final static java.awt.font.
TextAttribute POSTURE
public final static java.lang.Float
POSTURE_OBLIQUE
public final static java.lang.Float
POSTURE_REGULAR
public final static java.awt.font.
TextAttribute RUN_DIRECTION
public final static java.lang.Boolean
RUN_DIRECTION_LTR
public final static java.lang.Boolean
RUN_DIRECTION_RTL
public final static java.awt.font.
TextAttribute SIZE
public final static java.awt.font.
TextAttribute STRIKETHROUGH
public final static java.lang.Boolean
STRIKETHROUGH_ON
public final static java.awt.font.
TextAttribute SUPERSCRIPT
public final static java.lang.Integer
SUPERSCRIPT_SUB
public final static java.lang.Integer
SUPERSCRIPT_SUPER
public final static java.awt.font.
TextAttribute SWAP_COLORS
public final static java.lang.Boolean
SWAP_COLORS_ON
public final static java.awt.font.
TextAttribute TRANSFORM
public final static java.awt.font.
TextAttribute UNDERLINE
public final static java.lang.Integer
UNDERLINE_ON
public final static java.awt.font.
TextAttribute WEIGHT
public final static java.lang.Float
WEIGHT_BOLD
public final static java.lang.Float
WEIGHT_DEMIBOLD
public final static java.lang.Float
WEIGHT_DEMILIGHT
public final static java.lang.Float
WEIGHT_EXTRABOLD
public final static java.lang.Float
WEIGHT_EXTRA_LIGHT
public final static java.lang.Float
WEIGHT_HEAVY
public final static java.lang.Float
WEIGHT_LIGHT
public final static java.lang.Float
WEIGHT_MEDIUM
public final static java.lang.Float
WEIGHT_REGULAR
public final static java.lang.Float
WEIGHT_SEMIBOLD
public final static java.lang.Float
WEIGHT_ULTRABOLD
public final static java.awt.font.
TextAttribute WIDTH
```

```
public final static java.lang.Float
WIDTH_CONDENSED
public final static java.lang.Float
WIDTH_EXTENDED
public final static java.lang.Float
WIDTH_REGULAR
public final static java.lang.Float
WIDTH_SEMI_CONDENSED
public final static java.lang.Float
WIDTH_SEMI_EXTENDED
```

### Constructors
```
protected  TextAttribute(String name)
```

### Methods
```
protected Object readResolve()
```

# TextComponent
```
public class java.awt.TextComponent
extends java.awt.Component
extends java.lang.Object
```

### Fields
```
protected transient java.awt.event.
TextListener textListener
```

### Constructors
```
 TextComponent()
```

### Methods
```
public synchronized void addTextListener(
TextListener l)
public synchronized int getCaretPosition(
)
public synchronized String
getSelectedText()
public synchronized int getSelectionEnd()
public synchronized int
getSelectionStart()
public synchronized String getText()
public boolean isEditable()
protected String paramString()
protected void processEvent(AWTEvent e)
protected void processTextEvent(
TextEvent e)
public void removeNotify()
public synchronized void
removeTextListener(TextListener l)
public synchronized void select(int
selectionStart,int selectionEnd)
public synchronized void selectAll()
public synchronized void
setCaretPosition(int position)
public synchronized void setEditable(
boolean b)
public synchronized void setSelectionEnd(
int selectionEnd)
public synchronized void
setSelectionStart(int selectionStart)
public synchronized void setText(String
t)
```

# TextEvent
```
public class java.awt.event.TextEvent
extends java.awt.AWTEvent
extends java.util.EventObject
extends java.lang.Object
```

### Fields
```
public final static int TEXT_FIRST
public final static int TEXT_LAST
public final static int TEXT_VALUE_
CHANGED
```

### Constructors
```
public  TextEvent(Object source,int id)
```

### Methods
```
public String paramString()
```

# TextField
```
public class java.awt.TextField
extends java.awt.TextComponent
extends java.awt.Component
extends java.lang.Object
```

### Constructors
```
public static  TextField()
public  TextField(String text)
public  TextField(int columns)
public  TextField(String text,int
columns)
```

### Methods
```
public synchronized void
addActionListener(ActionListener l)
public void addNotify()
public boolean echoCharIsSet()
public int getColumns()
public char getEchoChar()
public Dimension getMinimumSize(int
columns)
public Dimension getMinimumSize()
public Dimension getPreferredSize(int
columns)
public Dimension getPreferredSize()
public Dimension minimumSize(int columns)
public Dimension minimumSize()
protected String paramString()
public Dimension preferredSize(int
columns)
public Dimension preferredSize()
protected void processActionEvent(
ActionEvent e)
protected void processEvent(AWTEvent e)
public synchronized void
removeActionListener(ActionListener l)
public synchronized void setColumns(int
columns)
public void setEchoChar(char c)
public synchronized void
setEchoCharacter(char c)
public void setText(String t)
```

## TextHitInfo

public final class java.awt.font.
TextHitInfo
extends java.lang.Object

### Constructors

private TextHitInfo()

### Methods

public static TextHitInfo afterOffset(
int offset)
public static TextHitInfo beforeOffset(
int offset)
public boolean equals(Object obj)
public boolean equals(TextHitInfo
hitInfo)
public int getCharIndex()
public int getInsertionIndex()
public TextHitInfo getOffsetHit(int
delta)
public TextHitInfo getOtherHit()
public int hashCode()
public boolean isLeadingEdge()
public static TextHitInfo leading(int
charIndex)
public String toString()
public static TextHitInfo trailing(int
charIndex)

## TextLayout

public final class java.awt.font.
TextLayout
implements java.lang.Cloneable
extends java.lang.Object

### Fields

public final static CaretPolicy DEFAULT_
CARET_POLICY

### Constructors

public TextLayout(String string,Font
font,FontRenderContext frc)
public TextLayout(String string,Map
attributes,FontRenderContext frc)
public TextLayout(
AttributedCharacterIterator text,
FontRenderContext frc)
TextLayout()

### Methods

protected Object clone()
public void draw(Graphics2D g2,float x,
float y)
public boolean equals(Object obj)
public boolean equals(TextLayout rhs)
public float getAdvance()
public float getAscent()
public byte getBaseline()
public float getBaselineOffsets()
public Shape getBlackBoxBounds(int
firstEndpoint,int secondEndpoint)
public Rectangle2D getBounds()

public float getCaretInfo(TextHitInfo
hit,Rectangle2D bounds)
public float getCaretInfo(TextHitInfo
hit)
public Shape getCaretShape(TextHitInfo
hit,Rectangle2D bounds)
public Shape getCaretShape(TextHitInfo
hit)
public Shape getCaretShapes(int offset,
Rectangle2D bounds,CaretPolicy policy)
public Shape getCaretShapes(int offset,
Rectangle2D bounds)
public Shape getCaretShapes(int offset)
public int getCharacterCount()
public byte getCharacterLevel(int index)
public float getDescent()
public TextLayout getJustifiedLayout(
float justificationWidth)
public float getLeading()
public Shape getLogicalHighlightShape(
int firstEndpoint,int secondEndpoint,
Rectangle2D bounds)
public Shape getLogicalHighlightShape(
int firstEndpoint,int secondEndpoint)
public int
getLogicalRangesForVisualSelection(
TextHitInfo firstEndpoint,TextHitInfo
secondEndpoint)
public TextHitInfo getNextLeftHit(
TextHitInfo hit)
public TextHitInfo getNextLeftHit(int
offset,CaretPolicy policy)
public TextHitInfo getNextLeftHit(int
offset)
public TextHitInfo getNextRightHit(
TextHitInfo hit)
public TextHitInfo getNextRightHit(int
offset,CaretPolicy policy)
public TextHitInfo getNextRightHit(int
offset)
public Shape getOutline(AffineTransform
tx)
public float getVisibleAdvance()
public Shape getVisualHighlightShape(
TextHitInfo firstEndpoint,TextHitInfo
secondEndpoint,Rectangle2D bounds)
public Shape getVisualHighlightShape(
TextHitInfo firstEndpoint,TextHitInfo
secondEndpoint)
public TextHitInfo getVisualOtherHit(
TextHitInfo hit)
protected void handleJustify(float
justificationWidth)
public int hashCode()
public TextHitInfo hitTestChar(float x,
float y,Rectangle2D bounds)
public TextHitInfo hitTestChar(float x,
float y)
public boolean isLeftToRight()
public boolean isVertical()
public String toString()

# TextUI

public abstract class javax.swing.plaf.
TextUI
extends javax.swing.plaf.ComponentUI
extends java.lang.Object

### Methods

public abstract void damageRange(
JTextComponent t,int p0,int p1)
public abstract void damageRange(
JTextComponent t,int p0,int p1,Bias
firstBias,Bias secondBias)
public abstract EditorKit getEditorKit(
JTextComponent t)
public abstract int
getNextVisualPositionFrom(JTextComponent
t,int pos,Bias b,int direction,Bias
biasRet)
public abstract View getRootView(
JTextComponent t)
public abstract Rectangle modelToView(
JTextComponent t,int pos)
public abstract Rectangle modelToView(
JTextComponent t,int pos,Bias bias)
public abstract int viewToModel(
JTextComponent t,Point pt)
public abstract int viewToModel(
JTextComponent t,Point pt,Bias
biasReturn)

# TexturePaint

public class java.awt.TexturePaint
implements java.awt.Paint
extends java.lang.Object

### Constructors

public TexturePaint(BufferedImage txtr,
Rectangle2D anchor)

### Methods

public PaintContext createContext(
ColorModel cm,Rectangle deviceBounds,
Rectangle2D userBounds,AffineTransform
xform,RenderingHints hints)
public Rectangle2D getAnchorRect()
public BufferedImage getImage()
public int getTransparency()

# Thread

public class java.lang.Thread
implements java.lang.Runnable
extends java.lang.Object

### Fields

public final static int MAX_PRIORITY
public final static int MIN_PRIORITY
public final static int NORM_PRIORITY

### Constructors

public Thread()
public Thread(Runnable target)
public Thread(ThreadGroup group,
Runnable target)

public Thread(String name)
public Thread(ThreadGroup group,String
name)
public Thread(Runnable target,String
name)
public Thread(ThreadGroup group,
Runnable target,String name)

### Methods

public static int activeCount()
public final void checkAccess()
public native int countStackFrames()
public static native Thread
currentThread()
public void destroy()
public static void dumpStack()
public static int enumerate(Thread
tarray)
public ClassLoader getContextClassLoader(
)
public final String getName()
public final int getPriority()
public final ThreadGroup getThreadGroup()
public void interrupt()
public static boolean interrupted()
public final native boolean isAlive()
public final boolean isDaemon()
public boolean isInterrupted()
public final synchronized void join(long
millis)
public final synchronized void join(long
millis,int nanos)
public final void join()
public final void resume()
public void run()
public void setContextClassLoader(
ClassLoader cl)
public final void setDaemon(boolean on)
public final void setName(String name)
public final void setPriority(int
newPriority)
public static native void sleep(long
millis)
public static void sleep(long millis,int
nanos)
public synchronized native void start()
public final void stop()
public final synchronized void stop(
Throwable obj)
public final void suspend()
public String toString()
public static native void yield()

# ThreadDeath

public class java.lang.ThreadDeath
extends java.lang.Error
extends java.lang.Throwable
extends java.lang.Object

# ThreadGroup

public class java.lang.ThreadGroup
extends java.lang.Object

## Constructors

```
private  ThreadGroup()
public  ThreadGroup(String name)
public  ThreadGroup(ThreadGroup parent,
String name)
```

## Methods

```
public int activeCount()
public int activeGroupCount()
public boolean allowThreadSuspension(
boolean b)
public final void checkAccess()
public final void destroy()
public int enumerate(Thread list)
public int enumerate(Thread list,boolean
recurse)
public int enumerate(ThreadGroup list)
public int enumerate(ThreadGroup list,
boolean recurse)
public final int getMaxPriority()
public final String getName()
public final ThreadGroup getParent()
public final void interrupt()
public final boolean isDaemon()
public synchronized boolean isDestroyed()
public void list()
public final boolean parentOf(
ThreadGroup g)
public final void resume()
public final void setDaemon(boolean
daemon)
public final void setMaxPriority(int pri)
public final void stop()
public final void suspend()
public String toString()
public void uncaughtException(Thread t,
Throwable e)
```

## ThreadLocal

```
public class java.lang.ThreadLocal
extends java.lang.Object
```

### Constructors

```
public  ThreadLocal()
```

### Methods

```
public Object get()
protected Object initialValue()
public void set(Object value)
```

## Throwable

```
public class java.lang.Throwable
implements java.io.Serializable
extends java.lang.Object
```

### Constructors

```
public  Throwable()
public  Throwable(String message)
```

### Methods

```
public native Throwable fillInStackTrace(
)
public String getLocalizedMessage()
```

```
public String getMessage()
public void printStackTrace()
public void printStackTrace(PrintStream
s)
public void printStackTrace(PrintWriter
s)
public String toString()
```

## Time

```
public class java.sql.Time
extends java.util.Date
extends java.lang.Object
```

### Constructors

```
public  Time(int hour,int minute,int
second)
public  Time(long time)
```

### Methods

```
public int getDate()
public int getDay()
public int getMonth()
public int getYear()
public void setDate(int i)
public void setMonth(int i)
public void setTime(long time)
public void setYear(int i)
public String toString()
public static Time valueOf(String s)
```

## Timer

```
public class javax.swing.Timer
implements java.io.Serializable
extends java.lang.Object
```

### Fields

```
protected javax.swing.event.
EventListenerList listenerList
```

### Constructors

```
public  Timer(int delay,ActionListener
listener)
```

### Methods

```
public void addActionListener(
ActionListener listener)
protected void fireActionPerformed(
ActionEvent e)
public int getDelay()
public int getInitialDelay()
public static boolean getLogTimers()
public boolean isCoalesce()
public boolean isRepeats()
public boolean isRunning()
public void removeActionListener(
ActionListener listener)
public void restart()
public void setCoalesce(boolean flag)
public void setDelay(int delay)
public void setInitialDelay(int
initialDelay)
public static void setLogTimers(boolean
flag)
```

```
public void setRepeats(boolean flag)
public void start()
public void stop()
```

# Timestamp

```
public class java.sql.Timestamp
extends java.util.Date
extends java.lang.Object
```

### Constructors
```
public  Timestamp(int year,int month,int
date,int hour,int minute,int second,int
nano)
public  Timestamp(long time)
```

### Methods
```
public boolean after(Timestamp ts)
public boolean before(Timestamp ts)
public boolean equals(Timestamp ts)
public boolean equals(Object ts)
public int getNanos()
public void setNanos(int n)
public String toString()
public static Timestamp valueOf(String s)
```

# TimeZone

```
public abstract class java.util.
TimeZone
implements java.lang.Cloneable
implements java.io.Serializable
extends java.lang.Object
```

### Fields
```
public final static int LONG
public final static int SHORT
```

### Constructors
```
public  TimeZone()
```

### Methods
```
public Object clone()
public static synchronized String
getAvailableIDs(int rawOffset)
public static synchronized String
getAvailableIDs()
public static synchronized TimeZone
getDefault()
public final String getDisplayName()
public final String getDisplayName(
Locale locale)
public final String getDisplayName(
boolean daylight,int style)
public String getDisplayName(boolean
daylight,int style,Locale locale)
public String getID()
public abstract int getOffset(int era,
int year,int month,int day,int dayOfWeek,
int milliseconds)
public abstract int getRawOffset()
public static synchronized TimeZone
getTimeZone(String ID)
public boolean hasSameRules(TimeZone
other)
```

```
public abstract boolean inDaylightTime(
Date date)
public static synchronized void
setDefault(TimeZone zone)
public void setID(String ID)
public abstract void setRawOffset(int
offsetMillis)
public abstract boolean useDaylightTime()
```

# TitledBorder

```
public class javax.swing.border.
TitledBorder
extends javax.swing.border.
AbstractBorder
extends java.lang.Object
```

### Fields
```
public final static int ABOVE_BOTTOM
public final static int ABOVE_TOP
public final static int BELOW_BOTTOM
public final static int BELOW_TOP
protected javax.swing.border.Border
border
public final static int BOTTOM
public final static int CENTER
public final static int DEFAULT_
JUSTIFICATION
public final static int DEFAULT_
POSITION
protected final static int EDGE_SPACING
public final static int LEFT
public final static int RIGHT
protected final static int TEXT_INSET_H
protected final static int TEXT_SPACING
protected java.lang.String title
protected java.awt.Color titleColor
protected java.awt.Font titleFont
protected int titleJustification
protected int titlePosition
public final static int TOP
```

### Constructors
```
public  TitledBorder(String title)
public  TitledBorder(Border border)
public  TitledBorder(Border border,
String title)
public  TitledBorder(Border border,
String title,int titleJustification,int
titlePosition)
public  TitledBorder(Border border,
String title,int titleJustification,int
titlePosition,Font titleFont)
public  TitledBorder(Border border,
String title,int titleJustification,int
titlePosition,Font titleFont,Color
titleColor)
```

### Methods
```
public Border getBorder()
public Insets getBorderInsets(Component
c)
public Insets getBorderInsets(Component
c,Insets insets)
```

```
protected Font getFont(Component c)
public Dimension getMinimumSize(
Component c)
public String getTitle()
public Color getTitleColor()
public Font getTitleFont()
public int getTitleJustification()
public int getTitlePosition()
public boolean isBorderOpaque()
public void paintBorder(Component c,
Graphics g,int x,int y,int width,int
height)
public void setBorder(Border border)
public void setTitle(String title)
public void setTitleColor(Color
titleColor)
public void setTitleFont(Font titleFont)
public void setTitleJustification(int
titleJustification)
public void setTitlePosition(int
titlePosition)
```

## ToolBarUI

```
public abstract class javax.swing.plaf.
ToolBarUI
extends javax.swing.plaf.ComponentUI
extends java.lang.Object
```

## Toolkit

```
public abstract class java.awt.Toolkit
extends java.lang.Object
```

### Fields

```
protected final java.util.Map
desktopProperties
protected final java.beans.
PropertyChangeSupport
desktopPropsSupport
```

### Methods

```
public void addAWTEventListener(
AWTEventListener listener,long eventMask)
public synchronized void
addPropertyChangeListener(String name,
PropertyChangeListener pcl)
public abstract void beep()
public abstract int checkImage(Image
image,int width,int height,ImageObserver
observer)
protected abstract ButtonPeer
createButton(Button target)
protected abstract CanvasPeer
createCanvas(Canvas target)
protected abstract CheckboxPeer
createCheckbox(Checkbox target)
protected abstract CheckboxMenuItemPeer
createCheckboxMenuItem(CheckboxMenuItem
target)
protected abstract ChoicePeer
createChoice(Choice target)
protected LightweightPeer
createComponent(Component target)
```

```
public Cursor createCustomCursor(Image
cursor,Point hotSpot,String name)
protected abstract DialogPeer
createDialog(Dialog target)
public DragGestureRecognizer
createDragGestureRecognizer(Class
abstractRecognizerClass,DragSource ds,
Component c,int srcActions,
DragGestureListener dgl)
public abstract DragSourceContextPeer
createDragSourceContextPeer(
DragGestureEvent dge)
protected abstract FileDialogPeer
createFileDialog(FileDialog target)
protected abstract FramePeer createFrame(
Frame target)
public abstract Image createImage(String
filename)
public abstract Image createImage(URL
url)
public abstract Image createImage(
ImageProducer producer)
public Image createImage(byte imagedata)
public abstract Image createImage(byte
imagedata,int imageoffset,int
imagelength)
protected abstract LabelPeer createLabel(
Label target)
protected abstract ListPeer createList(
List target)
protected abstract MenuPeer createMenu(
Menu target)
protected abstract MenuBarPeer
createMenuBar(MenuBar target)
protected abstract MenuItemPeer
createMenuItem(MenuItem target)
protected abstract PanelPeer createPanel(
Panel target)
protected abstract PopupMenuPeer
createPopupMenu(PopupMenu target)
protected abstract ScrollbarPeer
createScrollbar(Scrollbar target)
protected abstract ScrollPanePeer
createScrollPane(ScrollPane target)
protected abstract TextAreaPeer
createTextArea(TextArea target)
protected abstract TextFieldPeer
createTextField(TextField target)
protected abstract WindowPeer
createWindow(Window target)
public Dimension getBestCursorSize(int
preferredWidth,int preferredHeight)
public abstract ColorModel getColorModel(
)
public static synchronized Toolkit
getDefaultToolkit()
public final synchronized Object
getDesktopProperty(String propertyName)
public abstract String getFontList()
public abstract FontMetrics
getFontMetrics(Font font)
protected abstract FontPeer getFontPeer(
String name,int style)
```

```
public abstract Image getImage(String
filename)
public abstract Image getImage(URL url)
public int getMaximumCursorColors()
public int getMenuShortcutKeyMask()
protected static Container
getNativeContainer(Component c)
public abstract PrintJob getPrintJob(
Frame frame,String jobtitle,Properties
props)
public static String getProperty(String
key,String defaultValue)
public abstract int getScreenResolution()
public abstract Dimension getScreenSize()
public abstract Clipboard
getSystemClipboard()
public final EventQueue
getSystemEventQueue()
protected abstract EventQueue
getSystemEventQueueImpl()
protected void
initializeDesktopProperties()
protected Object
lazilyLoadDesktopProperty(String name)
protected void loadSystemColors(int
systemColors)
public abstract boolean prepareImage(
Image image,int width,int height,
ImageObserver observer)
public void removeAWTEventListener(
AWTEventListener listener)
public synchronized void
removePropertyChangeListener(String name,
PropertyChangeListener pcl)
protected final synchronized void
setDesktopProperty(String name,Object
newValue)
public abstract void sync()
```

## ToolTipManager

```
public class javax.swing.ToolTipManager
implements java.awt.event.
MouseMotionListener
extends java.awt.event.MouseAdapter
extends java.lang.Object
```

### Fields
```
protected boolean
heavyWeightPopupEnabled
protected boolean
lightWeightPopupEnabled
```

### Constructors
```
 ToolTipManager()
```

### Methods
```
public int getDismissDelay()
public int getInitialDelay()
public int getReshowDelay()
public boolean isEnabled()
public boolean isLightWeightPopupEnabled(
)
public void mouseDragged(MouseEvent
event)
```

```
public void mouseEntered(MouseEvent
event)
public void mouseExited(MouseEvent event)
public void mouseMoved(MouseEvent event)
public void mousePressed(MouseEvent
event)
public void registerComponent(JComponent
component)
public void setDismissDelay(int
microSeconds)
public void setEnabled(boolean flag)
public void setInitialDelay(int
microSeconds)
public void setLightWeightPopupEnabled(
boolean aFlag)
public void setReshowDelay(int
microSeconds)
public static ToolTipManager
sharedInstance()
public void unregisterComponent(
JComponent component)
```

## ToolTipUI

```
public abstract class javax.swing.plaf.
ToolTipUI
extends javax.swing.plaf.ComponentUI
extends java.lang.Object
```

## TooManyListenersException

```
public class java.util.
TooManyListenersException
extends java.lang.Exception
extends java.lang.Throwable
extends java.lang.Object
```

### Constructors
```
public  TooManyListenersException()
public  TooManyListenersException(String
s)
```

## TransformAttribute

```
public final class java.awt.font.
TransformAttribute
implements java.io.Serializable
extends java.lang.Object
```

### Constructors
```
public  TransformAttribute(
AffineTransform transform)
```

### Methods
```
public AffineTransform getTransform()
```

## TreeExpansionEvent

```
public class javax.swing.event.
TreeExpansionEvent
extends java.util.EventObject
extends java.lang.Object
```

### Fields
```
protected javax.swing.tree.TreePath
path
```

## Constructors
```
public  TreeExpansionEvent(Object source,
TreePath path)
```

## Methods
```
public TreePath getPath()
```

# TreeMap
```
public class java.util.TreeMap
implements java.lang.Cloneable
implements java.io.Serializable
implements java.util.SortedMap
extends java.util.AbstractMap
extends java.lang.Object
```

## Constructors
```
public  TreeMap()
public  TreeMap(Comparator c)
public  TreeMap(Map m)
public  TreeMap(SortedMap m)
```

## Methods
```
public void clear()
public Object clone()
public Comparator comparator()
public boolean containsKey(Object key)
public boolean containsValue(Object
value)
public Set entrySet()
public Object firstKey()
public Object get(Object key)
public SortedMap headMap(Object toKey)
public Set keySet()
public Object lastKey()
public Object put(Object key,Object
value)
public void putAll(Map map)
public Object remove(Object key)
public int size()
public SortedMap subMap(Object fromKey,
Object toKey)
public SortedMap tailMap(Object fromKey)
public Collection values()
```

# TreeModelEvent
```
public class javax.swing.event.
TreeModelEvent
extends java.util.EventObject
extends java.lang.Object
```

## Fields
```
protected int childIndices
protected java.lang.Object children
protected javax.swing.tree.TreePath
path
```

## Constructors
```
public  TreeModelEvent(Object source,
Object path,int childIndices,Object
children)
public  TreeModelEvent(Object source,
TreePath path,int childIndices,Object
children)
```

```
public  TreeModelEvent(Object source,
Object path)
public  TreeModelEvent(Object source,
TreePath path)
```

## Methods
```
public int getChildIndices()
public Object getChildren()
public Object getPath()
public TreePath getTreePath()
public String toString()
```

# TreePath
```
public class javax.swing.tree.TreePath
implements java.io.Serializable
extends java.lang.Object
extends java.lang.Object
```

## Constructors
```
public  TreePath(Object path)
public  TreePath(Object singlePath)
protected  TreePath(TreePath parent,
Object lastElement)
protected  TreePath(Object path,int
length)
protected  TreePath()
```

## Methods
```
public boolean equals(Object o)
public Object getLastPathComponent()
public TreePath getParentPath()
public Object getPath()
public Object getPathComponent(int
element)
public int getPathCount()
public int hashCode()
public boolean isDescendant(TreePath
aTreePath)
public TreePath pathByAddingChild(Object
child)
public String toString()
```

# TreeSelectionEvent
```
public class javax.swing.event.
TreeSelectionEvent
extends java.util.EventObject
extends java.lang.Object
```

## Fields
```
protected boolean areNew
protected javax.swing.tree.TreePath
newLeadSelectionPath
protected javax.swing.tree.TreePath
oldLeadSelectionPath
protected javax.swing.tree.TreePath
paths
```

## Constructors
```
public  TreeSelectionEvent(Object source,
TreePath paths,boolean areNew,TreePath
oldLeadSelectionPath,TreePath
newLeadSelectionPath)
```

```
public  TreeSelectionEvent(Object source,
TreePath path,boolean isNew,TreePath
oldLeadSelectionPath,TreePath
newLeadSelectionPath)
```

### Methods
```
public Object cloneWithSource(Object
newSource)
public TreePath getNewLeadSelectionPath()
public TreePath getOldLeadSelectionPath()
public TreePath getPath()
public TreePath getPaths()
public boolean isAddedPath()
public boolean isAddedPath(TreePath path)
```

## TreeSet
```
public class java.util.TreeSet
implements java.lang.Cloneable
implements java.io.Serializable
implements java.util.SortedSet
extends java.util.AbstractSet
extends java.util.AbstractCollection
extends java.lang.Object
```

### Constructors
```
private  TreeSet()
public  TreeSet()
public  TreeSet(Comparator c)
public  TreeSet(Collection c)
public  TreeSet(SortedSet s)
```

### Methods
```
public boolean add(Object o)
public boolean addAll(Collection c)
public void clear()
public Object clone()
public Comparator comparator()
public boolean contains(Object o)
public Object first()
public SortedSet headSet(Object
toElement)
public boolean isEmpty()
public Iterator iterator()
public Object last()
public boolean remove(Object o)
public int size()
public SortedSet subSet(Object
fromElement,Object toElement)
public SortedSet tailSet(Object
fromElement)
```

## TreeUI
```
public abstract class javax.swing.plaf.
TreeUI
extends javax.swing.plaf.ComponentUI
extends java.lang.Object
```

### Methods
```
public abstract void cancelEditing(JTree
tree)
public abstract TreePath
getClosestPathForLocation(JTree tree,int
x,int y)
```

```
public abstract TreePath getEditingPath(
JTree tree)
public abstract Rectangle getPathBounds(
JTree tree,TreePath path)
public abstract TreePath getPathForRow(
JTree tree,int row)
public abstract int getRowCount(JTree
tree)
public abstract int getRowForPath(JTree
tree,TreePath path)
public abstract boolean isEditing(JTree
tree)
public abstract void startEditingAtPath(
JTree tree,TreePath path)
public abstract boolean stopEditing(
JTree tree)
```

## Types
```
public class java.sql.Types
extends java.lang.Object
```

### Fields
```
public final static int ARRAY
public final static int BIGINT
public final static int BINARY
public final static int BIT
public final static int BLOB
public final static int CHAR
public final static int CLOB
public final static int DATE
public final static int DECIMAL
public final static int DISTINCT
public final static int DOUBLE
public final static int FLOAT
public final static int INTEGER
public final static int JAVA_OBJECT
public final static int LONGVARBINARY
public final static int LONGVARCHAR
public final static int NULL
public final static int NUMERIC
public final static int OTHER
public final static int REAL
public final static int REF
public final static int SMALLINT
public final static int STRUCT
public final static int TIME
public final static int TIMESTAMP
public final static int TINYINT
public final static int VARBINARY
public final static int VARCHAR
```

### Constructors
```
private  Types()
```

## UID
```
public final class java.rmi.server.UID
implements java.io.Serializable
extends java.lang.Object
```

### Constructors
```
public  UID()
public  UID(short num)
private  UID()
```

### Methods
```
public boolean equals(Object obj)
public int hashCode()
public static UID read(DataInput in)
public String toString()
public void write(DataOutput out)
```

## UIDefaults
```
public class javax.swing.UIDefaults
extends java.util.Hashtable
extends java.util.Dictionary
extends java.lang.Object
```

### Constructors
```
public  UIDefaults()
public  UIDefaults(Object keyValueList)
```

### Methods
```
public synchronized void
addPropertyChangeListener(
PropertyChangeListener listener)
protected void firePropertyChange(String
propertyName,Object oldValue,Object
newValue)
public Object get(Object key)
public Border getBorder(Object key)
public Color getColor(Object key)
public Dimension getDimension(Object key)
public Font getFont(Object key)
public Icon getIcon(Object key)
public Insets getInsets(Object key)
public int getInt(Object key)
public String getString(Object key)
public ComponentUI getUI(JComponent
target)
public Class getUIClass(String uiClassID,
ClassLoader uiClassLoader)
public Class getUIClass(String uiClassID)
protected void getUIError(String msg)
public Object put(Object key,Object
value)
public void putDefaults(Object
keyValueList)
public synchronized void
removePropertyChangeListener(
PropertyChangeListener listener)
```

## UIManager
```
public class javax.swing.UIManager
implements java.io.Serializable
extends java.lang.Object
```

### Methods
```
public static void
addAuxiliaryLookAndFeel(LookAndFeel laf)
public static synchronized void
addPropertyChangeListener(
PropertyChangeListener listener)
public static Object get(Object key)
public static LookAndFeel
getAuxiliaryLookAndFeels()
public static Border getBorder(Object
key)
```

```
public static Color getColor(Object key)
public static String
getCrossPlatformLookAndFeelClassName()
public static UIDefaults getDefaults()
public static Dimension getDimension(
Object key)
public static Font getFont(Object key)
public static Icon getIcon(Object key)
public static Insets getInsets(Object
key)
public static LookAndFeelInfo
getInstalledLookAndFeels()
public static int getInt(Object key)
public static LookAndFeel getLookAndFeel(
)
public static UIDefaults
getLookAndFeelDefaults()
public static String getString(Object
key)
public static String
getSystemLookAndFeelClassName()
public static ComponentUI getUI(
JComponent target)
public static void installLookAndFeel(
LookAndFeelInfo info)
public static void installLookAndFeel(
String name,String className)
public static Object put(Object key,
Object value)
public static boolean
removeAuxiliaryLookAndFeel(LookAndFeel
laf)
public static synchronized void
removePropertyChangeListener(
PropertyChangeListener listener)
public static void
setInstalledLookAndFeels(LookAndFeelInfo
infos)
public static void setLookAndFeel(
LookAndFeel newLookAndFeel)
public static void setLookAndFeel(String
className)
```

## UndoableEditEvent
```
public class javax.swing.event.
UndoableEditEvent
extends java.util.EventObject
extends java.lang.Object
```

### Constructors
```
public  UndoableEditEvent(Object source,
UndoableEdit edit)
```

### Methods
```
public UndoableEdit getEdit()
```

## UndoableEditSupport
```
public class javax.swing.undo.
UndoableEditSupport
extends java.lang.Object
```

### Fields
```
protected javax.swing.undo.CompoundEdit
compoundEdit
```

protected java.util.Vector listeners
protected java.lang.Object realSource
protected int updateLevel

### Constructors
public  UndoableEditSupport()
public  UndoableEditSupport(Object r)

### Methods
public synchronized void
addUndoableEditListener(
UndoableEditListener l)
public synchronized void beginUpdate()
protected CompoundEdit
createCompoundEdit()
public synchronized void endUpdate()
public int getUpdateLevel()
public synchronized void postEdit(
UndoableEdit e)
public synchronized void
removeUndoableEditListener(
UndoableEditListener l)
public String toString()
protected void _postEdit(UndoableEdit e)

## UndoManager
public class javax.swing.undo.
UndoManager
implements javax.swing.event.
UndoableEditListener
extends javax.swing.undo.CompoundEdit
extends javax.swing.undo.
AbstractUndoableEdit
extends java.lang.Object

### Constructors
public  UndoManager()

### Methods
public synchronized boolean addEdit(
UndoableEdit anEdit)
public synchronized boolean canRedo()
public synchronized boolean canUndo()
public synchronized boolean
canUndoOrRedo()
public synchronized void discardAllEdits(
)
protected UndoableEdit editToBeRedone()
protected UndoableEdit editToBeUndone()
public synchronized void end()
public synchronized int getLimit()
public synchronized String
getRedoPresentationName()
public synchronized String
getUndoOrRedoPresentationName()
public synchronized String
getUndoPresentationName()
public synchronized void redo()
protected void redoTo(UndoableEdit edit)
public synchronized void setLimit(int l)
public String toString()
protected void trimEdits(int from,int to)
protected void trimForLimit()

public synchronized void undo()
public void undoableEditHappened(
UndoableEditEvent e)
public synchronized void undoOrRedo()
protected void undoTo(UndoableEdit edit)

## UnexpectedException
public class java.rmi.
UnexpectedException
extends java.rmi.RemoteException
extends java.io.IOException
extends java.lang.Exception
extends java.lang.Throwable
extends java.lang.Object

### Constructors
public  UnexpectedException(String s)
public  UnexpectedException(String s,
Exception ex)

## UnicastRemoteObject
public class java.rmi.server.
UnicastRemoteObject
extends java.rmi.server.RemoteServer
extends java.rmi.server.RemoteObject
extends java.lang.Object

### Constructors
protected  UnicastRemoteObject()
protected  UnicastRemoteObject(int port)
protected  UnicastRemoteObject(int port,
RMIClientSocketFactory csf,
RMIServerSocketFactory ssf)

### Methods
public Object clone()
public static RemoteStub exportObject(
Remote obj)
public static Remote exportObject(Remote
obj,int port)
public static Remote exportObject(Remote
obj,int port,RMIClientSocketFactory csf,
RMIServerSocketFactory ssf)
public static boolean unexportObject(
Remote obj,boolean force)

## UnknownError
public class java.lang.UnknownError
extends java.lang.VirtualMachineError
extends java.lang.Error
extends java.lang.Throwable
extends java.lang.Object

### Constructors
public  UnknownError()
public  UnknownError(String s)

## UnknownGroupException
public class java.rmi.activation.
UnknownGroupException
extends java.rmi.activation.
ActivationException

```
extends java.lang.Exception
extends java.lang.Throwable
extends java.lang.Object
```

**Constructors**
```
public  UnknownGroupException(String s)
```

## UnknownHostException
```
public class java.net.
UnknownHostException
extends java.io.IOException
extends java.lang.Exception
extends java.lang.Throwable
extends java.lang.Object
```

**Constructors**
```
public  UnknownHostException(String host)
public  UnknownHostException()
```

## UnknownHostException
```
public class java.rmi.
UnknownHostException
extends java.rmi.RemoteException
extends java.io.IOException
extends java.lang.Exception
extends java.lang.Throwable
extends java.lang.Object
```

**Constructors**
```
public  UnknownHostException(String s)
public  UnknownHostException(String s,
Exception ex)
```

## UnknownObjectException
```
public class java.rmi.activation.
UnknownObjectException
extends java.rmi.activation.
ActivationException
extends java.lang.Exception
extends java.lang.Throwable
extends java.lang.Object
```

**Constructors**
```
public  UnknownObjectException(String s)
```

## UnknownServiceException
```
public class java.net.
UnknownServiceException
extends java.io.IOException
extends java.lang.Exception
extends java.lang.Throwable
extends java.lang.Object
```

**Constructors**
```
public  UnknownServiceException()
public  UnknownServiceException(String
msg)
```

## UnmarshalException
```
public class java.rmi.
UnmarshalException
extends java.rmi.RemoteException
```

```
extends java.io.IOException
extends java.lang.Exception
extends java.lang.Throwable
extends java.lang.Object
```

**Constructors**
```
public  UnmarshalException(String s)
public  UnmarshalException(String s,
Exception ex)
```

## UnrecoverableKeyException
```
public class java.security.
UnrecoverableKeyException
extends java.security.
GeneralSecurityException
extends java.lang.Exception
extends java.lang.Throwable
extends java.lang.Object
```

**Constructors**
```
public  UnrecoverableKeyException()
public  UnrecoverableKeyException(String
msg)
```

## UnresolvedPermission
```
public final class java.security.
UnresolvedPermission
implements java.io.Serializable
extends java.security.Permission
extends java.lang.Object
```

**Constructors**
```
public  UnresolvedPermission(String type,
String name,String actions,Certificate
certs)
```

**Methods**
```
public boolean equals(Object obj)
public String getActions()
public int hashCode()
public boolean implies(Permission p)
public PermissionCollection
newPermissionCollection()
public String toString()
```

## UnsatisfiedLinkError
```
public class java.lang.
UnsatisfiedLinkError
extends java.lang.LinkageError
extends java.lang.Error
extends java.lang.Throwable
extends java.lang.Object
```

**Constructors**
```
public  UnsatisfiedLinkError()
public  UnsatisfiedLinkError(String s)
```

## UnsupportedClassVersionError
```
public class java.lang.
UnsupportedClassVersionError
extends java.lang.ClassFormatError
extends java.lang.LinkageError
```

extends java.lang.Error
extends java.lang.Throwable
extends java.lang.Object

### Constructors
public  UnsupportedClassVersionError()
public  UnsupportedClassVersionError(
String s)

## UnsupportedEncodingException
public class java.io.
UnsupportedEncodingException
extends java.io.IOException
extends java.lang.Exception
extends java.lang.Throwable
extends java.lang.Object

### Constructors
public  UnsupportedEncodingException()
public  UnsupportedEncodingException(
String s)

## UnsupportedFlavorException
public class java.awt.datatransfer.
UnsupportedFlavorException
extends java.lang.Exception
extends java.lang.Throwable
extends java.lang.Object

### Constructors
public  UnsupportedFlavorException(
DataFlavor flavor)

## UnsupportedLookAndFeelException
public class javax.swing.
UnsupportedLookAndFeelException
extends java.lang.Exception
extends java.lang.Throwable
extends java.lang.Object

### Constructors
public  UnsupportedLookAndFeelException(
String s)

## UnsupportedOperationException
public class java.lang.
UnsupportedOperationException
extends java.lang.RuntimeException
extends java.lang.Exception
extends java.lang.Throwable
extends java.lang.Object

### Constructors
public  UnsupportedOperationException()
public  UnsupportedOperationException(
String message)

## URL
public final class java.net.URL
implements java.io.Serializable
extends java.lang.Object

### Constructors
public  URL(String protocol,String host,
int port,String file)
public  URL(String protocol,String host,
String file)
public  URL(String protocol,String host,
int port,String file,URLStreamHandler
handler)
public  URL(String spec)
public  URL(URL context,String spec)
public  URL(URL context,String spec,
URLStreamHandler handler)

### Methods
public boolean equals(Object obj)
public final Object getContent()
public String getFile()
public String getHost()
public int getPort()
public String getProtocol()
public String getRef()
public synchronized int hashCode()
public URLConnection openConnection()
public final InputStream openStream()
public boolean sameFile(URL other)
protected void set(String protocol,
String host,int port,String file,String
ref)
public static synchronized void
setURLStreamHandlerFactory(
URLStreamHandlerFactory fac)
public String toExternalForm()
public String toString()

## URLClassLoader
public class java.net.URLClassLoader
extends java.security.SecureClassLoader
extends java.lang.ClassLoader
extends java.lang.Object

### Constructors
public  URLClassLoader(URL urls,
ClassLoader parent)
public  URLClassLoader(URL urls)
public  URLClassLoader(URL urls,
ClassLoader parent,
URLStreamHandlerFactory factory)

### Methods
protected void addURL(URL url)
protected Package definePackage(String
name,Manifest man,URL url)
protected Class findClass(String name)
public URL findResource(String name)
public Enumeration findResources(String
name)
protected PermissionCollection
getPermissions(CodeSource codesource)
public URL getURLs()
public static URLClassLoader newInstance(
URL urls,ClassLoader parent)
public static URLClassLoader newInstance(
URL urls)

## URLConnection

public abstract class java.net.
URLConnection
extends java.lang.Object

### Fields

protected boolean allowUserInteraction
protected boolean connected
protected boolean doInput
protected boolean doOutput
protected long ifModifiedSince
protected java.net.URL url
protected boolean useCaches

### Constructors

protected  URLConnection(URL url)

### Methods

public abstract void connect()
public boolean getAllowUserInteraction()
public Object getContent()
public String getContentEncoding()
public int getContentLength()
public String getContentType()
public long getDate()
public static boolean
getDefaultAllowUserInteraction()
public static String
getDefaultRequestProperty(String key)
public boolean getDefaultUseCaches()
public boolean getDoInput()
public boolean getDoOutput()
public long getExpiration()
public static FileNameMap getFileNameMap(
)
public String getHeaderField(String name)
public String getHeaderField(int n)
public long getHeaderFieldDate(String
name,long Default)
public int getHeaderFieldInt(String name,
int Default)
public String getHeaderFieldKey(int n)
public long getIfModifiedSince()
public InputStream getInputStream()
public long getLastModified()
public OutputStream getOutputStream()
public Permission getPermission()
public String getRequestProperty(String
key)
public URL getURL()
public boolean getUseCaches()
protected static String
guessContentTypeFromName(String fname)
public static String
guessContentTypeFromStream(InputStream
is)
public void setAllowUserInteraction(
boolean allowuserinteraction)
public static synchronized void
setContentHandlerFactory(
ContentHandlerFactory fac)
public static void
setDefaultAllowUserInteraction(boolean
defaultallowuserinteraction)

public static void
setDefaultRequestProperty(String key,
String value)
public void setDefaultUseCaches(boolean
defaultusecaches)
public void setDoInput(boolean doinput)
public void setDoOutput(boolean dooutput)
public static void setFileNameMap(
FileNameMap map)
public void setIfModifiedSince(long
ifmodifiedsince)
public void setRequestProperty(String
key,String value)
public void setUseCaches(boolean
usecaches)
public String toString()

## URLDecoder

public class java.net.URLDecoder
extends java.lang.Object

### Methods

public static String decode(String s)

## URLEncoder

public class java.net.URLEncoder
extends java.lang.Object

### Constructors

private static  URLEncoder()

### Methods

public static String encode(String s)

## URLStreamHandler

public abstract class java.net.
URLStreamHandler
extends java.lang.Object

### Methods

protected abstract URLConnection
openConnection(URL u)
protected void parseURL(URL u,String
spec,int start,int limit)
protected void setURL(URL u,String
protocol,String host,int port,String
file,String ref)
protected String toExternalForm(URL u)

## UTFDataFormatException

public class java.io.
UTFDataFormatException
extends java.io.IOException
extends java.lang.Exception
extends java.lang.Throwable
extends java.lang.Object

### Constructors

public  UTFDataFormatException()
public  UTFDataFormatException(String s)

# Utilities

public class javax.swing.text.Utilities
extends java.lang.Object

## Methods

public final static int drawTabbedText(
Segment s,int x,int y,Graphics g,
TabExpander e,int startOffset)
public final static int getBreakLocation(
Segment s,FontMetrics metrics,int x0,int
x,TabExpander e,int startOffset)
public final static int getNextWord(
JTextComponent c,int offs)
public final static Element
getParagraphElement(JTextComponent c,int
offs)
public final static int getPositionAbove(
JTextComponent c,int offs,int x)
public final static int getPositionBelow(
JTextComponent c,int offs,int x)
public final static int getPreviousWord(
JTextComponent c,int offs)
public final static int getRowEnd(
JTextComponent c,int offs)
public final static int getRowStart(
JTextComponent c,int offs)
public final static int
getTabbedTextOffset(Segment s,
FontMetrics metrics,int x0,int x,
TabExpander e,int startOffset)
public final static int
getTabbedTextOffset(Segment s,
FontMetrics metrics,int x0,int x,
TabExpander e,int startOffset,boolean
round)
public final static int
getTabbedTextWidth(Segment s,FontMetrics
metrics,int x,TabExpander e,int
startOffset)
public final static int getWordEnd(
JTextComponent c,int offs)
public final static int getWordStart(
JTextComponent c,int offs)

# VariableHeightLayoutCache

public class javax.swing.tree.
VariableHeightLayoutCache
extends javax.swing.tree.
AbstractLayoutCache
extends java.lang.Object

## Constructors

public  VariableHeightLayoutCache()

## Methods

public Rectangle getBounds(TreePath path,
Rectangle placeIn)
public boolean getExpandedState(TreePath
path)
public TreePath getPathClosestTo(int x,
int y)
public TreePath getPathForRow(int row)

public int getPreferredWidth(Rectangle
bounds)
public int getRowCount()
public int getRowForPath(TreePath path)
public int getVisibleChildCount(TreePath
path)
public Enumeration getVisiblePathsFrom(
TreePath path)
public void invalidatePathBounds(
TreePath path)
public void invalidateSizes()
public boolean isExpanded(TreePath path)
public void setExpandedState(TreePath
path,boolean isExpanded)
public void setModel(TreeModel newModel)
public void setNodeDimensions(
NodeDimensions nd)
public void setRootVisible(boolean
rootVisible)
public void setRowHeight(int rowHeight)
public void treeNodesChanged(
TreeModelEvent e)
public void treeNodesInserted(
TreeModelEvent e)
public void treeNodesRemoved(
TreeModelEvent e)
public void treeStructureChanged(
TreeModelEvent e)

# Vector

public class java.util.Vector
implements java.lang.Cloneable
implements java.util.List
implements java.io.Serializable
extends java.util.AbstractList
extends java.util.AbstractCollection
extends java.lang.Object

## Fields

protected int capacityIncrement
protected int elementCount
protected java.lang.Object elementData

## Constructors

public  Vector(int initialCapacity,int
capacityIncrement)
public  Vector(int initialCapacity)
public  Vector()
public  Vector(Collection c)

## Methods

public synchronized boolean add(Object o)
public void add(int index,Object element)
public synchronized boolean addAll(
Collection c)
public synchronized boolean addAll(int
index,Collection c)
public synchronized void addElement(
Object obj)
public int capacity()
public void clear()
public synchronized Object clone()
public boolean contains(Object elem)

```
public synchronized boolean containsAll(
Collection c)
public synchronized void copyInto(Object
anArray)
public synchronized Object elementAt(int
index)
public Enumeration elements()
public synchronized void ensureCapacity(
int minCapacity)
public synchronized boolean equals(
Object o)
public synchronized Object firstElement()
public synchronized Object get(int index)
public synchronized int hashCode()
public int indexOf(Object elem)
public synchronized int indexOf(Object
elem,int index)
public synchronized void insertElementAt(
Object obj,int index)
public boolean isEmpty()
public synchronized Object lastElement()
public int lastIndexOf(Object elem)
public synchronized int lastIndexOf(
Object elem,int index)
public boolean remove(Object o)
public synchronized Object remove(int
index)
public synchronized boolean removeAll(
Collection c)
public synchronized void
removeAllElements()
public synchronized boolean
removeElement(Object obj)
public synchronized void removeElementAt(
int index)
protected void removeRange(int fromIndex,
int toIndex)
public synchronized boolean retainAll(
Collection c)
public synchronized Object set(int index,
Object element)
public synchronized void setElementAt(
Object obj,int index)
public synchronized void setSize(int
newSize)
public int size()
public List subList(int fromIndex,int
toIndex)
public synchronized Object toArray()
public synchronized Object toArray(
Object a)
public synchronized String toString()
public synchronized void trimToSize()
```

## VerifyError

```
public class java.lang.VerifyError
extends java.lang.LinkageError
extends java.lang.Error
extends java.lang.Throwable
extends java.lang.Object
```

### Constructors

```
public  VerifyError()
public  VerifyError(String s)
```

## VetoableChangeSupport

```
public class java.beans.
VetoableChangeSupport
implements java.io.Serializable
extends java.lang.Object
```

### Constructors

```
public  VetoableChangeSupport(Object
sourceBean)
```

### Methods

```
public synchronized void
addVetoableChangeListener(
VetoableChangeListener listener)
public synchronized void
addVetoableChangeListener(String
propertyName,VetoableChangeListener
listener)
public void fireVetoableChange(String
propertyName,Object oldValue,Object
newValue)
public void fireVetoableChange(String
propertyName,int oldValue,int newValue)
public void fireVetoableChange(String
propertyName,boolean oldValue,boolean
newValue)
public void fireVetoableChange(
PropertyChangeEvent evt)
public synchronized boolean hasListeners(
String propertyName)
public synchronized void
removeVetoableChangeListener(
VetoableChangeListener listener)
public synchronized void
removeVetoableChangeListener(String
propertyName,VetoableChangeListener
listener)
```

## View

```
public abstract class javax.swing.text.
View
implements javax.swing.SwingConstants
extends java.lang.Object
```

### Fields

```
public final static int BadBreakWeight
public final static int
ExcellentBreakWeight
public final static int
ForcedBreakWeight
public final static int GoodBreakWeight
public final static int X_AXIS
public final static int Y_AXIS
```

### Constructors

```
public  View(Element elem)
```

### Methods

```
public View breakView(int axis,int
offset,float pos,float len)
public void changedUpdate(DocumentEvent
e,Shape a,ViewFactory f)
public View createFragment(int p0,int p1)
public float getAlignment(int axis)
```

public AttributeSet getAttributes()
public int getBreakWeight(int axis,float
pos,float len)
public Shape getChildAllocation(int
index,Shape a)
public Container getContainer()
public Document getDocument()
public Element getElement()
public int getEndOffset()
public float getMaximumSpan(int axis)
public float getMinimumSpan(int axis)
public int getNextVisualPositionFrom(int
pos,Bias b,Shape a,int direction,Bias
biasRet)
public View getParent()
public abstract float getPreferredSpan(
int axis)
public int getResizeWeight(int axis)
public int getStartOffset()
public View getView(int n)
public int getViewCount()
public ViewFactory getViewFactory()
public void insertUpdate(DocumentEvent e,
Shape a,ViewFactory f)
public boolean isVisible()
public abstract Shape modelToView(int
pos,Shape a,Bias b)
public Shape modelToView(int p0,Bias b0,
int p1,Bias b1,Shape a)
public Shape modelToView(int pos,Shape a)
public abstract void paint(Graphics g,
Shape allocation)
public void preferenceChanged(View child,
boolean width,boolean height)
public void removeUpdate(DocumentEvent e,
Shape a,ViewFactory f)
public void setParent(View parent)
public void setSize(float width,float
height)
public abstract int viewToModel(float x,
float y,Shape a,Bias biasReturn)
public int viewToModel(float x,float y,
Shape a)

## ViewportLayout

public class javax.swing.ViewportLayout
implements java.awt.LayoutManager
implements java.io.Serializable
extends java.lang.Object

### Methods

public void addLayoutComponent(String
name,Component c)
public void layoutContainer(Container
parent)
public Dimension minimumLayoutSize(
Container parent)
public Dimension preferredLayoutSize(
Container parent)
public void removeLayoutComponent(
Component c)

## ViewportUI

public abstract class javax.swing.plaf.
ViewportUI
extends javax.swing.plaf.ComponentUI
extends java.lang.Object

## VirtualMachineError

public abstract class java.lang.
VirtualMachineError
extends java.lang.Error
extends java.lang.Throwable
extends java.lang.Object

### Constructors

public  VirtualMachineError()
public  VirtualMachineError(String s)

## VMID

public final class java.rmi.dgc.VMID
implements java.io.Serializable
extends java.lang.Object

### Constructors

public  VMID()

### Methods

public boolean equals(Object obj)
public int hashCode()
public static boolean isUnique()
public String toString()

## Void

public final class java.lang.Void
extends java.lang.Object

### Fields

public final static java.lang.Class
TYPE

### Constructors

private  Void()

## WeakHashMap

public class java.util.WeakHashMap
implements java.util.Map
extends java.util.AbstractMap
extends java.lang.Object

### Constructors

public  WeakHashMap(int initialCapacity,
float loadFactor)
public  WeakHashMap(int initialCapacity)
public  WeakHashMap()

### Methods

public void clear()
public boolean containsKey(Object key)
public Set entrySet()
public Object get(Object key)
public boolean isEmpty()

```
public Object put(Object key,Object
value)
public Object remove(Object key)
public int size()
```

## WeakReference

```
public class java.lang.ref.
WeakReference
extends java.lang.ref.Reference
extends java.lang.Object
```

### Constructors

```
public  WeakReference(Object referent)
public  WeakReference(Object referent,
ReferenceQueue q)
```

## Window

```
public class java.awt.Window
extends java.awt.Container
extends java.awt.Component
extends java.lang.Object
```

### Constructors

```
 Window()
public  Window(Frame owner)
public  Window(Window owner)
```

### Methods

```
public void addNotify()
public synchronized void
addWindowListener(WindowListener l)
public void applyResourceBundle(
ResourceBundle rb)
public void applyResourceBundle(String
rbName)
public void dispose()
protected void finalize()
public Component getFocusOwner()
public InputContext getInputContext()
public Locale getLocale()
public Window getOwnedWindows()
public Window getOwner()
public Toolkit getToolkit()
public final String getWarningString()
public boolean isShowing()
public void pack()
public boolean postEvent(Event e)
protected void processEvent(AWTEvent e)
protected void processWindowEvent(
WindowEvent e)
public synchronized void
removeWindowListener(WindowListener l)
public void show()
public void toBack()
public void toFront()
```

## WindowAdapter

```
public abstract class java.awt.event.
WindowAdapter
implements java.awt.event.
WindowListener
extends java.lang.Object
```

### Methods

```
public void windowActivated(WindowEvent
e)
public void windowClosed(WindowEvent e)
public void windowClosing(WindowEvent e)
public void windowDeactivated(
WindowEvent e)
public void windowDeiconified(
WindowEvent e)
public void windowIconified(WindowEvent
e)
public void windowOpened(WindowEvent e)
```

## WindowEvent

```
public class java.awt.event.WindowEvent
extends java.awt.event.ComponentEvent
extends java.awt.AWTEvent
extends java.util.EventObject
extends java.lang.Object
```

### Fields

```
public final static int WINDOW_
ACTIVATED
public final static int WINDOW_CLOSED
public final static int WINDOW_CLOSING
public final static int WINDOW_
DEACTIVATED
public final static int WINDOW_
DEICONIFIED
public final static int WINDOW_FIRST
public final static int WINDOW_
ICONIFIED
public final static int WINDOW_LAST
public final static int WINDOW_OPENED
```

### Constructors

```
public  WindowEvent(Window source,int id)
```

### Methods

```
public Window getWindow()
public String paramString()
```

## WrappedPlainView

```
public class javax.swing.text.
WrappedPlainView
implements javax.swing.text.TabExpander
extends javax.swing.text.BoxView
extends javax.swing.text.CompositeView
extends javax.swing.text.View
extends java.lang.Object
```

### Constructors

```
public  WrappedPlainView(Element elem)
public  WrappedPlainView(Element elem,
boolean wordWrap)
```

### Methods

```
protected int calculateBreakPosition(int
p0,int p1)
public void changedUpdate(DocumentEvent
e,Shape a,ViewFactory f)
protected void drawLine(int p0,int p1,
Graphics g,int x,int y)
```

protected int drawSelectedText(Graphics
g,int x,int y,int p0,int p1)
protected int drawUnselectedText(
Graphics g,int x,int y,int p0,int p1)
protected final Segment getLineBuffer()
public float getMaximumSpan(int axis)
public float getMinimumSpan(int axis)
public float getPreferredSpan(int axis)
protected int getTabSize()
public void insertUpdate(DocumentEvent e,
Shape a,ViewFactory f)
protected void loadChildren(ViewFactory
f)
public float nextTabStop(float x,int
tabOffset)
public void paint(Graphics g,Shape a)
public void removeUpdate(DocumentEvent e,
Shape a,ViewFactory f)
public void setSize(float width,float
height)

# WritableRaster

public class java.awt.image.
WritableRaster
extends java.awt.image.Raster
extends java.lang.Object

### Constructors

protected  WritableRaster(SampleModel
sampleModel,Point origin)
protected  WritableRaster(SampleModel
sampleModel,DataBuffer dataBuffer,Point
origin)
protected  WritableRaster(SampleModel
sampleModel,DataBuffer dataBuffer,
Rectangle aRegion,Point
sampleModelTranslate,WritableRaster
parent)

### Methods

public WritableRaster
createWritableChild(int parentX,int
parentY,int w,int h,int childMinX,int
childMinY,int bandList)
public WritableRaster
createWritableTranslatedChild(int
childMinX,int childMinY)
public WritableRaster getWritableParent()
public void setDataElements(int x,int y,
Object inData)
public void setDataElements(int x,int y,
Raster inRaster)
public void setDataElements(int x,int y,
int w,int h,Object inData)
public void setPixel(int x,int y,int
iArray)
public void setPixel(int x,int y,float
fArray)
public void setPixel(int x,int y,double
dArray)
public void setPixels(int x,int y,int w,
int h,int iArray)
public void setPixels(int x,int y,int w,
int h,float fArray)

public void setPixels(int x,int y,int w,
int h,double dArray)
public void setRect(Raster srcRaster)
public void setRect(int dx,int dy,Raster
srcRaster)
public void setSample(int x,int y,int b,
int s)
public void setSample(int x,int y,int b,
float s)
public void setSample(int x,int y,int b,
double s)
public void setSamples(int x,int y,int w,
int h,int b,int iArray)
public void setSamples(int x,int y,int w,
int h,int b,float fArray)
public void setSamples(int x,int y,int w,
int h,int b,double dArray)

# WriteAbortedException

public class java.io.
WriteAbortedException
extends java.io.ObjectStreamException
extends java.io.IOException
extends java.lang.Exception
extends java.lang.Throwable
extends java.lang.Object

### Fields

public java.lang.Exception detail

### Constructors

public  WriteAbortedException(String s,
Exception ex)

### Methods

public String getMessage()

# Writer

public abstract class java.io.Writer
extends java.lang.Object

### Fields

protected java.lang.Object lock

### Constructors

protected  Writer()
protected  Writer(Object lock)

### Methods

public abstract void close()
public abstract void flush()
public void write(int c)
public void write(char cbuf)
public abstract void write(char cbuf,int
off,int len)
public void write(String str)
public void write(String str,int off,int
len)

# X509Certificate

public abstract class java.security.cert.
X509Certificate

```
implements java.security.cert.
X509Extension
extends java.security.cert.Certificate
extends java.lang.Object
```

### Constructors

```
protected  X509Certificate()
```

### Methods

```
public abstract void checkValidity()
public abstract void checkValidity(Date
date)
public abstract int getBasicConstraints()
public abstract Principal getIssuerDN()
public abstract boolean
getIssuerUniqueID()
public abstract boolean getKeyUsage()
public abstract Date getNotAfter()
public abstract Date getNotBefore()
public abstract BigInteger
getSerialNumber()
public abstract String getSigAlgName()
public abstract String getSigAlgOID()
public abstract byte getSigAlgParams()
public abstract byte getSignature()
public abstract Principal getSubjectDN()
public abstract boolean
getSubjectUniqueID()
public abstract byte getTBSCertificate()
public abstract int getVersion()
```

## X509CRL

```
public abstract class java.security.cert.
X509CRL
implements java.security.cert.
X509Extension
extends java.security.cert.CRL
extends java.lang.Object
```

### Constructors

```
protected  X509CRL()
```

### Methods

```
public boolean equals(Object other)
public abstract byte getEncoded()
public abstract Principal getIssuerDN()
public abstract Date getNextUpdate()
public abstract X509CRLEntry
getRevokedCertificate(BigInteger
serialNumber)
public abstract Set
getRevokedCertificates()
public abstract String getSigAlgName()
public abstract String getSigAlgOID()
public abstract byte getSigAlgParams()
public abstract byte getSignature()
public abstract byte getTBSCertList()
public abstract Date getThisUpdate()
public abstract int getVersion()
public int hashCode()
public abstract void verify(PublicKey
key)
public abstract void verify(PublicKey
key,String sigProvider)
```

## X509CRLEntry

```
public abstract class java.security.cert.
X509CRLEntry
implements java.security.cert.
X509Extension
extends java.lang.Object
```

### Methods

```
public boolean equals(Object other)
public abstract byte getEncoded()
public abstract Date getRevocationDate()
public abstract BigInteger
getSerialNumber()
public abstract boolean hasExtensions()
public int hashCode()
public abstract String toString()
```

## X509EncodedKeySpec

```
public class java.security.spec.
X509EncodedKeySpec
extends java.security.spec.
EncodedKeySpec
extends java.lang.Object
```

### Constructors

```
public  X509EncodedKeySpec(byte
encodedKey)
```

### Methods

```
public byte getEncoded()
public final String getFormat()
```

## ZipEntry

```
public class java.util.zip.ZipEntry
implements java.lang.Cloneable
implements java.util.zip.ZipConstants
extends java.lang.Object
```

### Fields

```
public final static int DEFLATED
public final static int STORED
```

### Constructors

```
public  ZipEntry(String name)
public  ZipEntry(ZipEntry e)
 ZipEntry()
 ZipEntry()
```

### Methods

```
public Object clone()
public String getComment()
public long getCompressedSize()
public long getCrc()
public byte getExtra()
public int getMethod()
public String getName()
public long getSize()
public long getTime()
public int hashCode()
public boolean isDirectory()
public void setComment(String comment)
public void setCompressedSize(long csize)
public void setCrc(long crc)
```

```
public void setExtra(byte extra)
public void setMethod(int method)
public void setSize(long size)
public void setTime(long time)
public String toString()
```

# ZipException

```
public class java.util.zip.ZipException
extends java.io.IOException
extends java.lang.Exception
extends java.lang.Throwable
extends java.lang.Object
```

### Constructors

```
public  ZipException()
public  ZipException(String s)
```

# ZipFile

```
public class java.util.zip.ZipFile
implements java.util.zip.ZipConstants
extends java.lang.Object
```

### Constructors

```
public  ZipFile(String name)
public  ZipFile(File file)
```

### Methods

```
public void close()
public Enumeration entries()
public ZipEntry getEntry(String name)
public InputStream getInputStream(
ZipEntry entry)
public String getName()
public int size()
```

# ZipInputStream

```
public class java.util.zip.
ZipInputStream
implements java.util.zip.ZipConstants
extends java.util.zip.
InflaterInputStream
extends java.io.FilterInputStream
extends java.io.InputStream
extends java.lang.Object
```

### Constructors

```
public  ZipInputStream(InputStream in)
```

### Methods

```
public int available()
public void close()
public void closeEntry()
protected ZipEntry createZipEntry(String
name)
public ZipEntry getNextEntry()
public int read(byte b,int off,int len)
public long skip(long n)
```

# ZipOutputStream

```
public class java.util.zip.
ZipOutputStream
implements java.util.zip.ZipConstants
extends java.util.zip.
DeflaterOutputStream
extends java.io.FilterOutputStream
extends java.io.OutputStream
extends java.lang.Object
```

### Fields

```
public final static int DEFLATED
public final static int STORED
```

### Constructors

```
public  ZipOutputStream(OutputStream out)
```

### Methods

```
public void close()
public void closeEntry()
public void finish()
public void putNextEntry(ZipEntry e)
public void setComment(String comment)
public void setLevel(int level)
public void setMethod(int method)
public synchronized void write(byte b,
int off,int len)
```

Glossary

**Abstract**   An abstract class may not be directly instantiated. Abstract classes are intended to be subclassed, with non-abstract methods overriding abstract methods.

**Arithmetic Promotion**   Conversion of data to a wider type, in the course of an arithmetic operation.

**Assignment Conversion**   Conversion of data from one type to another, in the course of assigning a value of one type to a variable of a different type.

**AWT**   Java's Abstract Windowing Toolkit.

**Bytecode**   The code format of Java class files.

**Casting**   Explicit conversion from one data type to another.

**Character Encoding**   A mapping from characters to bit sequences.

**Clipping**   Restriction of the set of pixels that are affected by the `drawXXX()` methods of the `java.awt.Graphics` class.

**Clip Region**   The region within a component that is affected by the `drawXXX()` methods of the `java.awt.Graphics` class.

**Container**   A GUI component that can contain other components.

**Deep Comparison**   Comparison of some or all of the instance variables of two objects.

**Event Listener**   An object that is delegated to handle events of a certain type originating from a source object.

**Feature**   An element of a class that can be modified by a modifier such as `private` or `static`. A class' features are its data, its methods, and the class itself.

**Final**   A final member variable may not be modified. A final method may not be overridden. A final class may not be extended.

**Friendly**   A friendly feature may be accessed from the class itself, or from any member of the class' package. Unlike `private`, `protected`, and `public`, "friendly" is not a Java keyword.

**Garbage Collection**   Automatic de-allocation of unused memory.

**GUI**   Graphical User Interface.

**GUI Thread**   A thread that handles GUI input and responds to `repaint()` calls.

**Inner Class**   A class that is defined within, and can only be used by another class.

**Instance**   A single example or occurrence of a class.

**JAR**   Acronym for Java ARchive file.

**JDK**   Java Developer's Kit.

**JVM**   Java Virtual Machine.

**Layout Manager**   A class that dictates the size and location of components within a container.

**Method**   A function associated with a class.

**Method-Call Conversion**   Conversion of data from one type to another, in the course of passing a value of one type into a method call that expects a variable of a different type.

**Modal**   A modal dialog consumes all input directed at its parent component. Normal input dispatching resumes once a modal dialog is dismissed.

**Monitor**   An object that can block and revive threads. In Java, monitors have synchronized code.

**Narrowing Conversion**   Conversion to a new data type that encompasses a narrower range than the original data type.

**Native**   A native method calls code that resides in a library that is loaded on the local computer.

**Overload**   Overloaded methods of a class have the same method name but different argument lists and possibly different return types.

**Override**   A class overrides an inherited method by providing a method with the same name, argument list, and return type.

**Package**   A collection of classes.

**Polygon**   A closed, connected sequence of line segments.

**Polyline**   An open, connected sequence of line segments.

**Preemptive Scheduling** A thread-scheduling algorithm in which a thread may be kicked out of the CPU at any moment.

**Primitive** A primitive data type is a basic data type (as contrasted to an object reference or an array). Java's primitive types are `boolean`, `char`, `byte`, `short`, `int`, `long`, `float`, and `double`.

**Private** A private feature of a class may only be accessed by an instance of that class.

**Protected** A protected feature of a class may be accessed from the class itself, from any subclass of the class, or from any member of the class' package.

**Public** A public feature of a class may be accessed from any class whatsoever.

**Repair** Re-drawing of pixels in response to exposure.

**Scope** The scope of a variable is the portion of code within which the variable is defined.

**Shallow Comparison** Comparison of two object references.

**Static** A static feature is associated with a class rather than with an individual instance of the class. A static method may not access non-static variables.

**Synchronized** Synchronized code requires the executing thread to obtain the lock of the executing object.

**Thread Scheduler** Portion of a Java Virtual Machine that is responsible for determining which thread gets to execute.

**Time-Sliced Scheduling** A thread-scheduling algorithm in which threads take turns to use the CPU.

**Transient** A transient variable is never serialized.

**Unicode** A 16-bit encoding for representing characters. Java's `char` and `String` classes use Unicode encoding.

**Widening Conversion** Conversion to a new data type that encompasses a wider range than the original data type.

**Wrapper** A class that encapsulates a single primitive value. Java's wrapper classes reside in the `java.lang` package.

# Index

**Note to the Reader:** Throughout this index **boldfaced** page numbers indicate primary discussions of a topic. *Italicized* page numbers indicate illustrations.

## T